D1923018

ATLAS
OF
AMSTERDAM

ATLAS
OF
AMSTERDAM

NOORDHOFF ATLAS PRODUCTIONS GRONINGEN

Atlas of Amsterdam

The *Atlas of Amsterdam* uses hundreds of maps, graphs, photos and drawings to provide a fascinating insight into the Dutch capital, painting a picture that goes far beyond the usual stereotypes. Of course, this atlas also portrays Amsterdam as a city of culture and history, with its monuments, museums and theatres, but when you look closer, Amsterdam is so much more. It is a true working city, for example, that continues to flourish thanks to its seaport and airport, its services sector, its creative industry and tourism. It is also a city where churchgoers are very much in the minority, but where at the same time the most diverse religions have taken root. The atlas presents all of this and much more, with care and attention to detail.

The *Atlas of Amsterdam* consists of several themed chapters on the evolution of the city, its inhabitants, the city authorities, economics, infrastructure, religion, entertainment and culture. In addition to the valuable information and advice provided by OIS, Research, Information and Statistics, City of Amsterdam, countless other experts have also assisted with this publication. As a result, the *Atlas of Amsterdam* offers a wealth of interesting information on key topics such as demographics, social differences, economics, sport, health, crime and politics. But it also features intriguing and little-known facts such as the neighbourhood with the greatest imbalance in the male/female ratio, the places where criminals settle their scores, the sites where many bicycle accidents occur and much more.

All this information is presented in maps and graphs in the typically informative style of Noordhoff Uitgevers' atlas series (*De Bosatlas*). In the best atlas tradition, the emphasis lies on painting an overall picture. This is a necessary virtue for an atlas about Amsterdam, as it would be simply impossible to create an exhaustive reference work on such a multifaceted and colourful city. Even so, the *Atlas of Amsterdam* provides a surprisingly detailed overview of today's Amsterdam. We hope that you will enjoy using this atlas for reference purposes and return to it frequently.

Groningen, April 2016
The publisher

Photo: Schinkelsluis, © Peter Elenbaas

Contents

1 Evolution of the city

2 Amsterdammers

3

Public services

4

Economy

5

Traffic and transport

6

World view

7

Leisure

8

Culture

9

Districts

10

City map

Index

DE BIJENKORF
Sligro

1

Evolution of the city

◁
The Dam
Photo Karel Tomeï

1 Introduction

Concentric city

On a map, Amsterdam looks like an onion sliced in half. Comprising the Dam and the streets up to the Singel, its mediaeval centre is encircled by the 17th-century Canal Ring and the 19th-century ring of urban development. The concentric pattern was only abandoned in the 20th century.

Looking for alternatives

20th-century construction reflects new ideas of city life. For a long time, the natural response to a lack of housing was to build new compact districts around the old city. This is even true of Berlage's Plan Zuid development (1915), though its architects did at least try to create a more tasteful design than in De Pijp. However, aversion to the city was growing. People needed parks, gardens and a more human scale, which explains the emergence of intimate 'garden villages' on the edge of the city in the 1930s (especially in Amsterdam Noord). The architects who adhered to the 'Het Nieuwe Bouwen' movement had a different solution. In post-war districts like Nieuw-West and Buitenveldert, their designs let in 'light and air' and strictly separated residential and commercial areas.

Overspill towns

In the 1960s and 1970s, town planners ventured even further afield and built new districts far outside the city boundaries. Old towns like Purmerend, Hoorn and Diemen were expanded significantly and completely new towns like Lelystad and Almere were even created. Meanwhile, the intention was to transform Amsterdam's centre into a modern city, with offices and wide access roads leading to the heart of the city centre, and renovate the dilapidated 19th-century working-class districts.

Exodus

Many Amsterdammers moved to the new 'commuter towns', but the promised refurbishment was delayed. Many houses earmarked for demolition stood empty, despite the severe housing shortage. Dissatisfied young people started to squat in these

The Dam
Few visible signs remain of the dam that was built in the Amstel river around 1260 on the spot where Amsterdam first emerged as a town. The water has gone and the only mediaeval building left is the 15th-century Nieuwe Kerk (bottom left). The 17th-century town hall (today's Royal Palace) and the National Monument, which was erected in 1956 in commemoration of the victims of World War Two, are far more striking structures.

buildings. The residents' aversion to the modernisation of the city centre grew.

Concentration

This swing in public opinion also affected the local authority's views – life in the city seemed not so bad after all. So 'concentration' replaced expansion as the new motto, with vacant city areas filled and new residential districts like KNSM-eiland and IJburg built near the city centre. This concentration will continue over the next decades. Amsterdam is growing increasingly crowded and compact. Even so, this situation does not seem to act as a deterrent, as house prices in Amsterdam are rising faster than average.

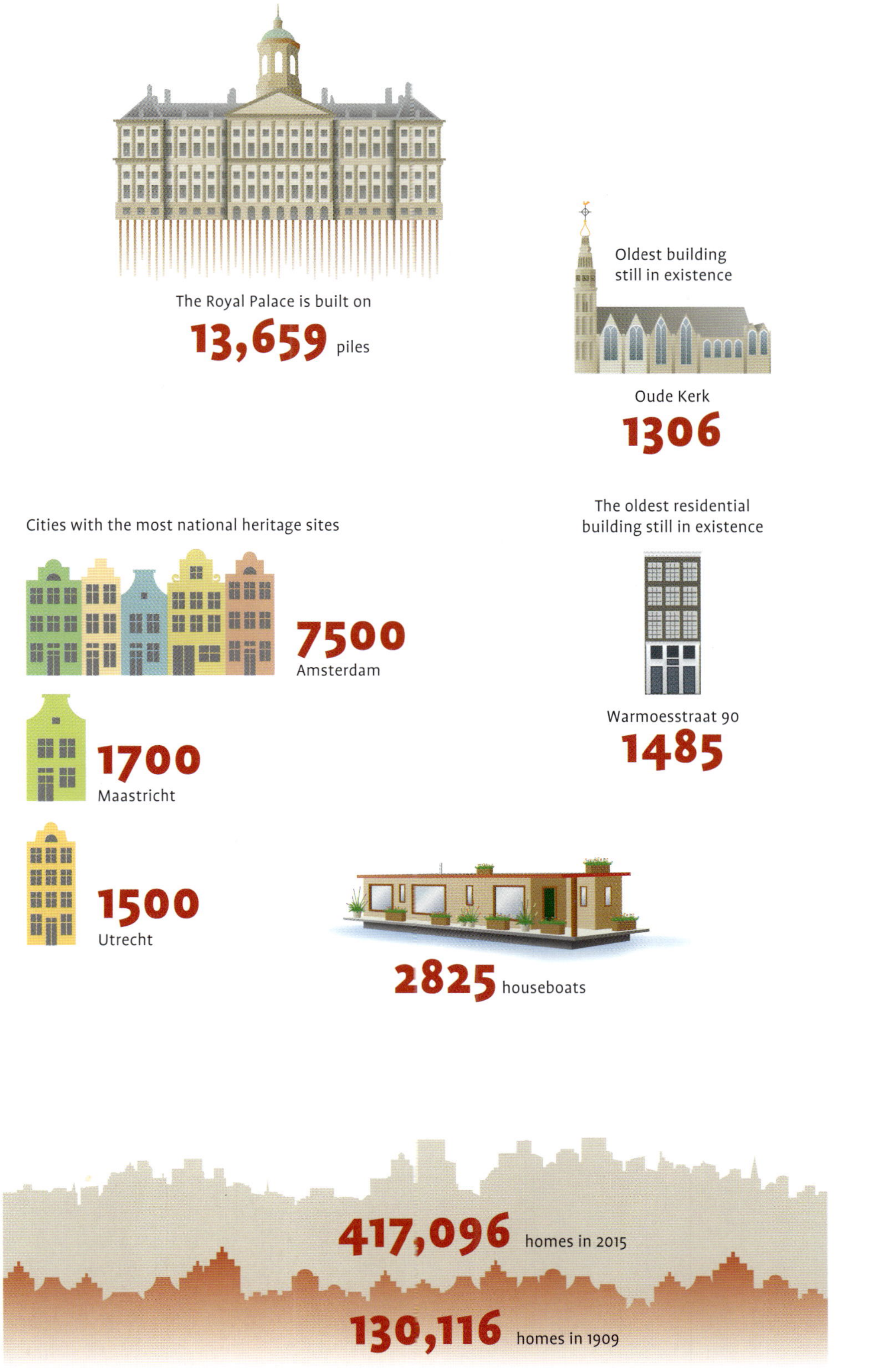

Sources: City of Amsterdam / OIS, Research, Information and Statistics, City of Amsterdam / Rijksmonumenten

© Noordhoff Uitgevers

Mediaeval Amsterdam

Other than a few buildings, very little of mediaeval Amsterdam remains today. However, archaeologists are still making surprising discoveries, like when they uncovered the foundations of Van Amstel Castle in 1994. The mediaeval pattern of streets and canals has also remained virtually intact.
In 1275, the people living near the dam in the Amstel river were granted exemption from tolls. This privilege and the convenient location at the mouth of the Amstel made Amsterdam attractive to traders and craftsmen. In the late 15th century, Amsterdam had all the characteristics of a mediaeval city – defensive walls with imposing gates, churches and chapels, monasteries, public buildings and a varied population with an elite class of merchants and entrepreneurs. But Amsterdam did not stand out in any way. At that time, there were dozens of Dutch cities similar to Amsterdam.

❶ Growth of the city up to 1578

❷ Amsterdam around 1300

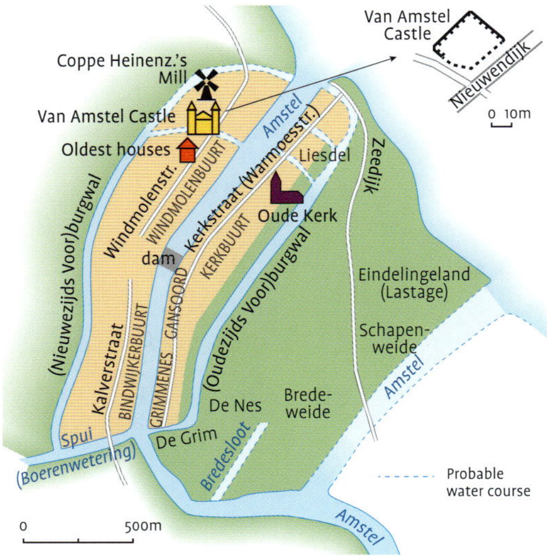

❶ - ❷ Living around the dam

Sometime between 1200 and 1260, residents constructed a dam in the Amstel river due to problems with the water levels there. In the 11th century, they had started to clear the peat bogs around their settlements, but this caused the soil to subside and disrupted natural drainage. Agricultural areas became increasingly waterlogged and were ultimately only suitable for raising livestock. The salty water of the IJ and the Zuiderzee, which linked directly to the North Sea, was an even greater threat. Residents of the five neighbourhoods on the banks of the Amstel built dams and dikes to protect themselves against floods. The dam in the Amstel included a drainage sluice. Amsterdam gradually extended out from the nucleus formed by this dam. Interestingly enough, Amsterdam was protected by defensive walls much later than other towns. The first city wall, some 6 metres high, with several dozen towers and five access gates, was not built until 1482.

Sources: B. M. J. Speet (1); Geschiedenis van Amsterdam, part 1 (2)

© Noordhoff Uitgevers

❸ Monks and nuns

The nineteen male and female monasteries within the city walls and the Begijnhof occupied a large part of the city's land area. As well as the monastic buildings themselves, most monasteries also had their own bakery, brewery, weaving mill, bleachfield and herb garden. There were also barns with winter stables for the livestock that grazed in the meadows outside the city during the summer. When the protestants took control of Amsterdam in 1578, the city council seized all of the monasteries. Most were demolished to make way for residential buildings.

❹ A fashionable street

In 1557, Warmoesstraat was by far the most expensive street in Amsterdam. Most of its residents were involved in trade in one form or another. This was an attractive street for them because the warehouses situated at the back of the residences had direct access to the Damrak waterfront. This is still clearly apparent in the area between Oudebrugsteeg and Nieuwebrugsteeg. In view of their elevated economic and social position, the residents of this street played a prominent role in city politics.

❺ One of many

Mediaeval cities had a fair amount of autonomy from the territorial lord. Their city rights were recorded in official documents. Amsterdam was granted city rights of this nature in 1300 and 1342, long after Dordrecht, Leiden, Haarlem and other Dutch cities, so in that respect, Amsterdam is a young city.

❸ Monasteries

❹ Warmoesstraat

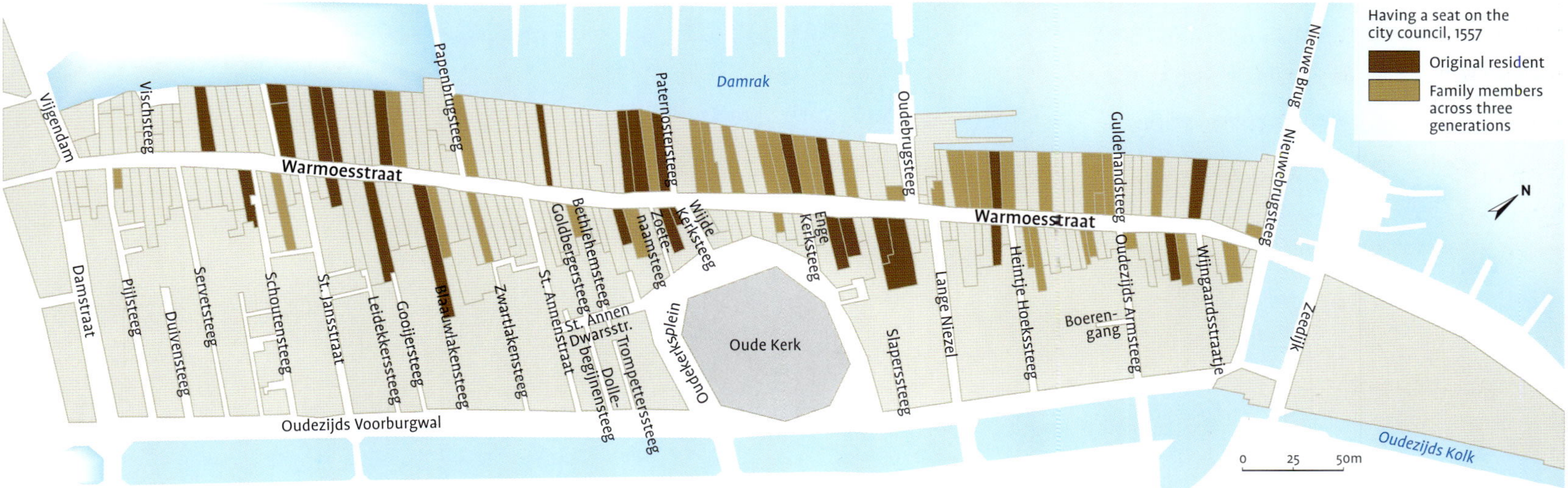

❺ Cities around 1550

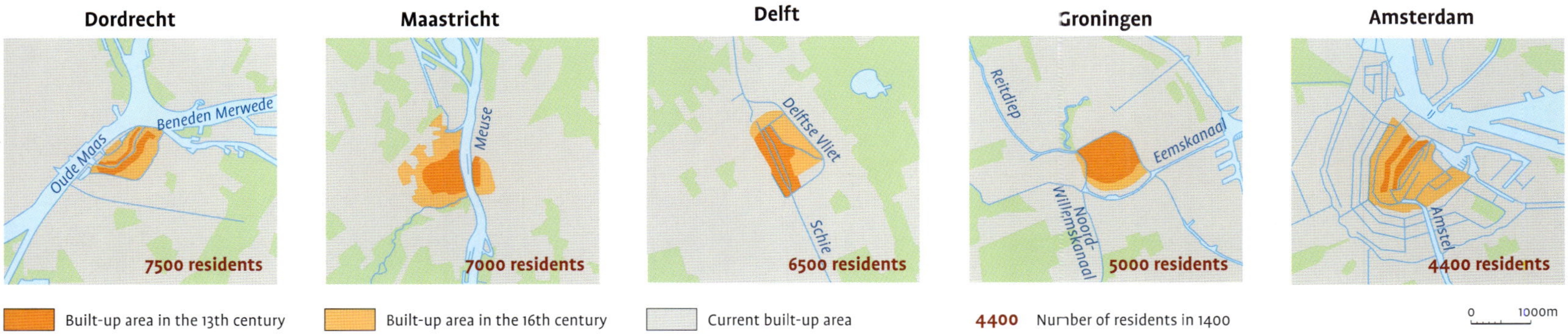

Sources: T. Bakker, De middeleeuwse kloosters van Amsterdam (3); R. Van der Leeuw-Kistemaker, Wonen en werken in de Warmoesstraat van de 14de tot het midden van de 16de eeuw (4); R. Rutte & J. E. Abrahamse, Atlas van de Verstedelijking in Nederland (5)

© Noordhoff Uitgevers

The Dam

Amsterdam gets its name from the dam in the Amstel river, which has turned into a large square over the centuries. The Dam is the historic heart of the city and a major tourist attraction.

From water barrier to town square

Around 1260: construction of a dam in the Amstel river connecting the two riverbanks and preventing the inflow of saltwater; small ships could pass through a lock.

Around 1300
The dam was widened and part of it became a fish market.

The market expanded to include all kinds of goods and a **weighing house** was built in **1341**.

1368
After being granted city rights shortly after 1300, the city built its first town hall.

Around 1400
Construction of the **Nieuwe Kerk** started.

1452
Reconstruction of the town hall after a major fire in the city.

1563
New **weighing house**.

1599
Construction of *Huis onder 't zeil*.

1607
Trade was booming and part of the Rokin canal was filled in to allow construction of the **Koopmansbeurs** merchant hall.

1655
Festive inauguration of the new town hall.

1808
King Louis Napoléon Bonaparte had the town hall converted into a **palace**. He had the weighing house torn down to improve the view.

1841
New **Beurs van Zocher** stock exchange.
Replaced in 1903 by the Beurs van Berlage.

1856
Unveiling of statue *Naatje op de Dam*.
Removed in 1912.

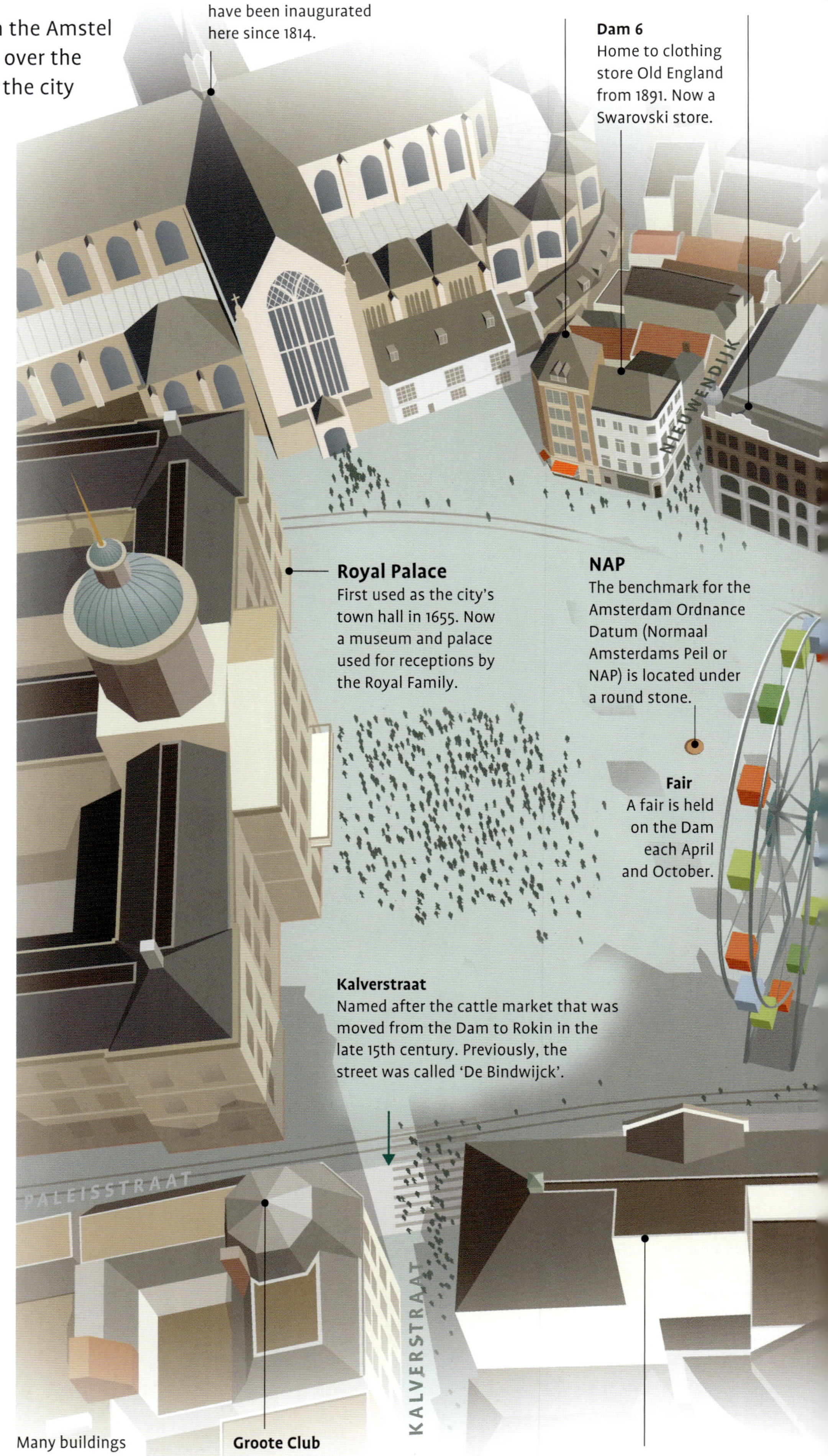

Nieuwe Kerk
Built around 1400, after 'Nieuwe Zijde' became an autonomous parish. All new Dutch monarchs have been inaugurated here since 1814.

Dam 10
Built in 1913 as the national railways travel office. Now Dam Good Coffee.

Dam 4
Built in 1886 for freight company Van Gend & Loos. Now an H&M fashion store.

Dam 6
Home to clothing store Old England from 1891. Now a Swarovski store.

Royal Palace
First used as the city's town hall in 1655. Now a museum and palace used for receptions by the Royal Family.

NAP
The benchmark for the Amsterdam Ordnance Datum (Normaal Amsterdams Peil or NAP) is located under a round stone.

Fair
A fair is held on the Dam each April and October.

Kalverstraat
Named after the cattle market that was moved from the Dam to Rokin in the late 15th century. Previously, the street was called 'De Bindwijck'.

Many buildings around the Dam were replaced in the early 20th century, resulting in the situation as it is today.

Groote Club
Built in 1912 for the gentleman's club of the same name. Merged with the Industrieele Club in 1975. On 7 May 1945, Germans soldiers stationed in this building opened fire on Amsterdammers who were celebrating the liberation of the Netherlands, killing several dozen.

Peek & Cloppenburg
Built between 1914 and 191[illegible] as a clothing emporium. A section has been rented Madame Tussauds Wax Museum since 1991.

Sources: Royal Palace Amsterdam / Amsterdam City Archives / City of Amsterdam / T. Bakker, Van 'die Plaetse' tot de Dam / M. G. Emeis, Het paleis op de Dam / Wikipedia; Photo: © Hollandse Hoogte

Dam 2
Built in 1934. The stone plaque depicting St. Nicholas originates from an older building, café De Bisschop, which previously stood on this spot. Now an ABN AMRO bank.

Pigeons
The Dam is known for its many pigeons. Their numbers have declined significantly in comparison to former times. The city council has put up nets and pigeon spikes and enforced a ban on feeding. The Dam is also much cleaner these days, so it attracts fewer birds.

De Bijenkorf
A department store dating back to 1915 and originally started by the Goudsmit family. This store was the successor to their first haberdashery shop on Nieuwendijk.

Dam 7
The Royal Dam Center, an office complex built in 1991. This is the Dam's newest building.

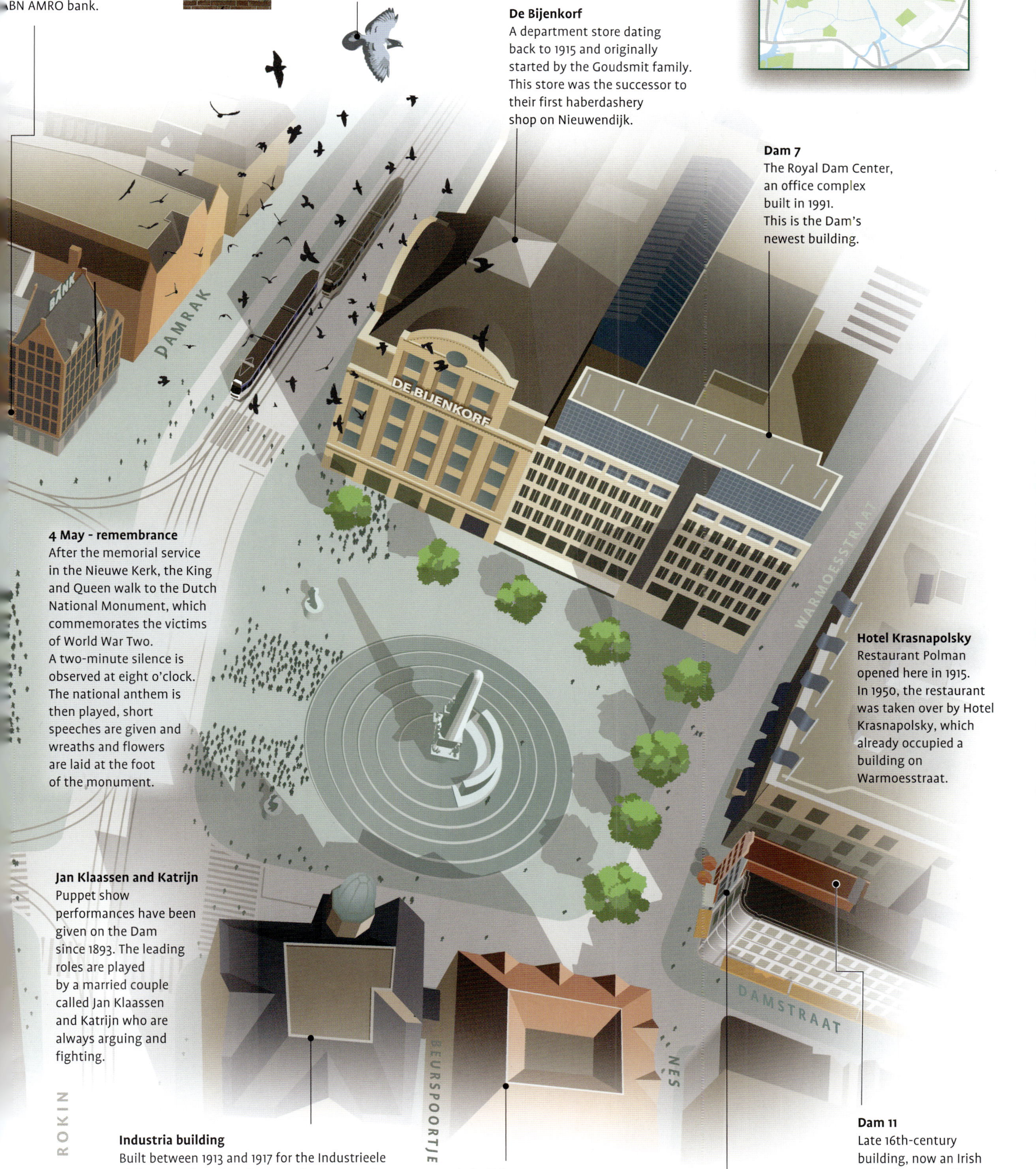

4 May - remembrance
After the memorial service in the Nieuwe Kerk, the King and Queen walk to the Dutch National Monument, which commemorates the victims of World War Two. A two-minute silence is observed at eight o'clock. The national anthem is then played, short speeches are given and wreaths and flowers are laid at the foot of the monument.

Hotel Krasnapolsky
Restaurant Polman opened here in 1915. In 1950, the restaurant was taken over by Hotel Krasnapolsky, which already occupied a building on Warmoesstraat.

Jan Klaassen and Katrijn
Puppet show performances have been given on the Dam since 1893. The leading roles are played by a married couple called Jan Klaassen and Katrijn who are always arguing and fighting.

Industria building
Built between 1913 and 1917 for the Industrieele Club: a meeting place for manufacturers and entrepreneurs who did not feel welcome at the Groote Club on the corner of Kalverstraat, which was more of a meeting place for traders.

Instantia building
Commissioned in 1913 by a company called Amsterdamse Naaimachinehandel. It now houses a souvenir shop on the ground floor.

Dam 13-15
Bars and restaurants dating from around 1880.

Dam 11
Late 16th-century building, now an Irish Pub called Yip Fellows. The second oldest building on the Dam, after the Nieuwe Kerk.

© Noordhoff Uitgevers

Canal Ring

Around 1550, the Southern Netherlands was a very prosperous area and Antwerp was Europe's most powerful mercantile city. However, after the Spanish conquest, this dominance soon evaporated. Of the approximately 150,000 Walloons and Flemings who emigrated to the North, around 40,000 went to Amsterdam. Their arrival was a godsend for the city, as they brought with them business acumen, new trade contacts and markets and above all new financial techniques. The boom that this created in Amsterdam acted as a magnet for other immigrants, resulting in a severe lack of living accommodation, which could only be solved by expanding the city. A further consequence was that the divide between rich and poor grew ever greater.

❶ Expansion phases 1587-1672

❷ Population development in the 17th century

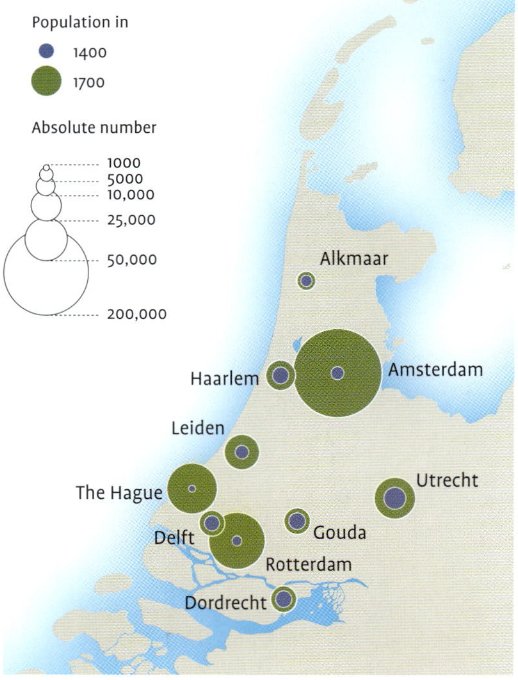

❸ Migration in the 17th century

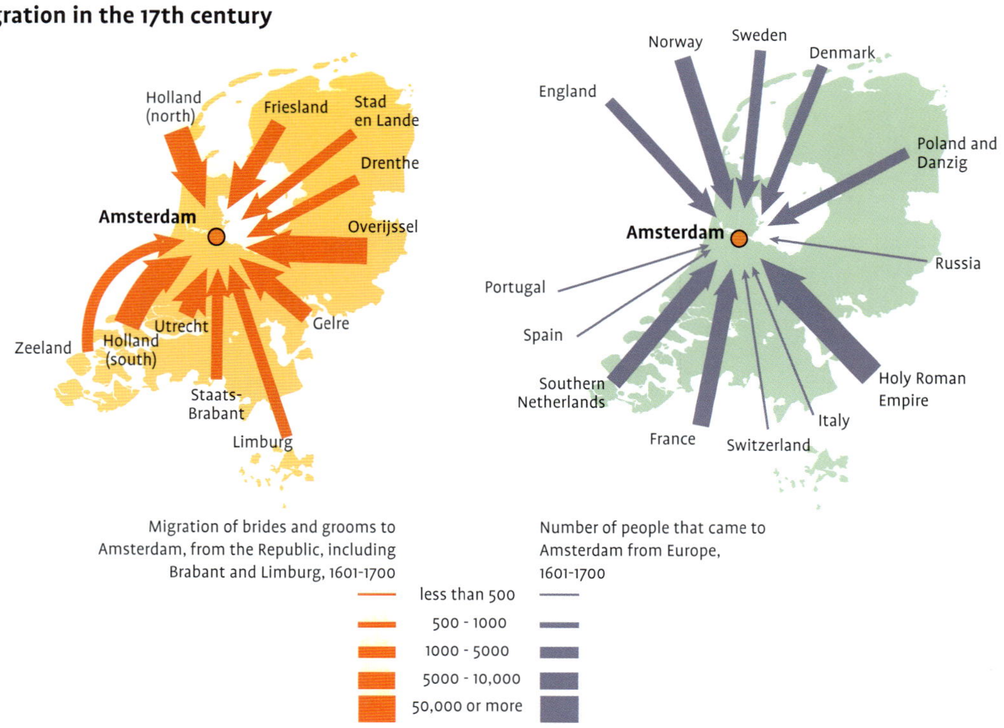

Sources: M. Frijhoff & M. Prak (red.), Geschiedenis van Amsterdam, part II-1 (1, 3); R. Rutte & J. E. Abrahamse, Atlas van de Verstedelijking in Nederland (2)

© Noordhoff Uitgevers

❹ Impoverished: Jordaan

In the year 1742

There are **41,561** family households in Amsterdam

Annual incomes exceeding 600 guilders are taxed:

32%, 13,249 family households in total

68%, 28,312 families with an annual income below 600 guilders

On Goudsbloemstraat district 51, only **33** family households are taxed

10-20%

80-90% = 130-300 families with a non-taxable annual income

6 bakers	2 barbers	1 midwife
6 pub landlords	2 dairy traders	1 funeral director
6 grocers	2 carpenters	1 brush trader
	2 porters	1 depositor
	2 barge skippers	1 rentier

❺ Rich: the twenty richest Amsterdammers

❻ Care institutions up to 1800

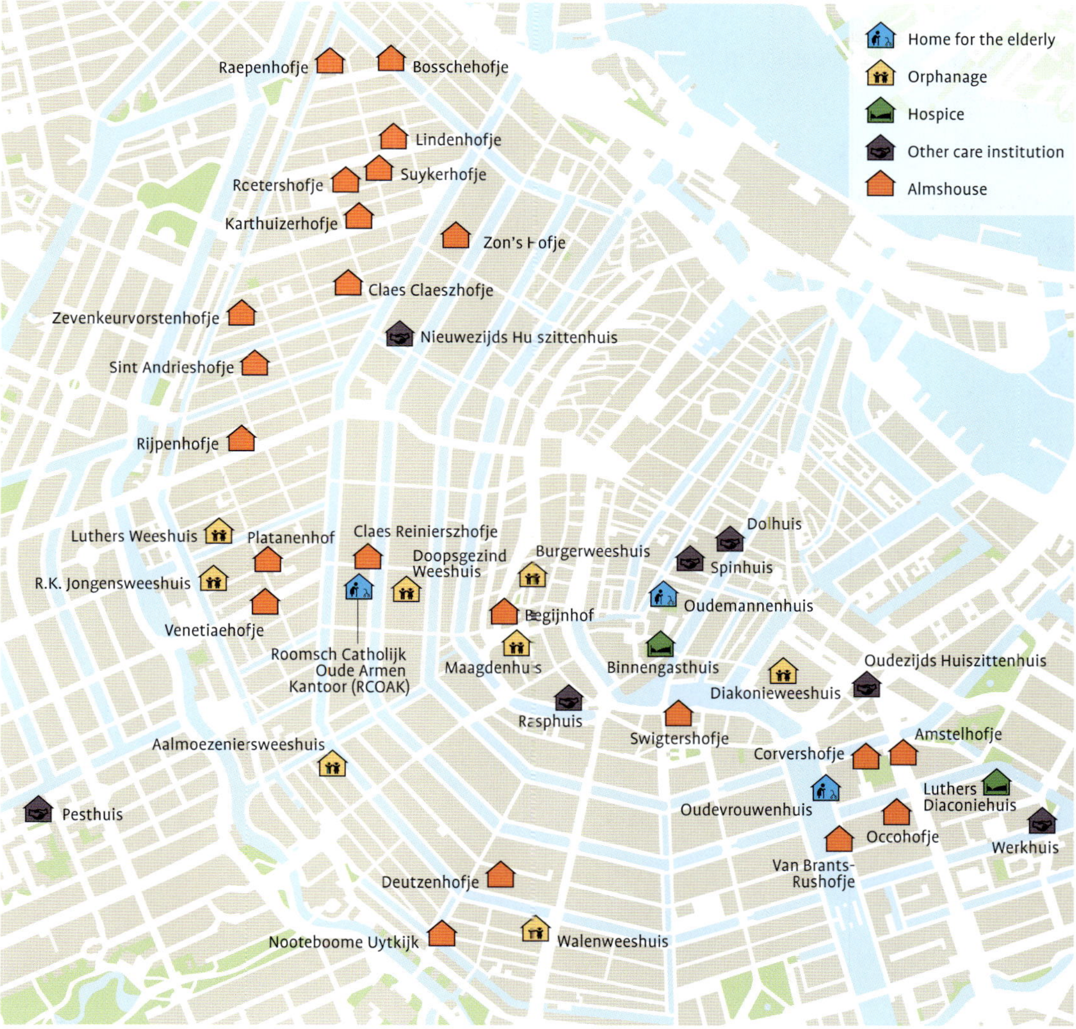

❶ Semicircular wall

Between 1580 and 1680, the city's population rose from 30,000 to 205,000. Expansion was inevitable, so a start was made between 1578 and 1596. Two plans for further expansion were submitted in 1613. Hendrick Staets wanted to surround the city with a semicircular defensive wall. The city council deemed this plan too ambitious and instead chose Derde Uitleg, the more modest plan put forward by Lucas Sinck. Fifty years later, Staets' plan was belatedly implemented as part of the Vierde Uitleg expansion plan.

❷ - ❸ A cultural melting pot

In the Golden Age, Holland became one of Europe's most densely populated areas. Amsterdam attracted the most migrants – so many that they eventually outnumbered the city's native population. The different cultures mixed quickly. This is apparent in the Amsterdam accent, which is strongly influenced by the Brabant dialect and other immigrant languages.

❹ Exiled to the outskirts

During the Derde Uitleg, the edge of the new city area was reserved for craft industries and activities like tanning leather and dying textiles. 130 years later, the area's residents were still relatively poor.

❺ Living in style

From the outset, the Canal Ring was the area where wealthy Amsterdammers lived and worked. The twenty richest Amsterdammers had fortunes that were more than one thousand times greater than the annual income of a simple craftsman from the Jordaan.

❻ Caring for the less fortunate

In the past, the differences between the rich and the poor were much more pronounced than today. The city council mainly concerned itself with the needs of the native citizens, while the numerous needy migrants relied on the charity of the Christian denominations they had joined and of private individuals. The latter mainly founded almshouses for old men and women.

Sources: W. F. H. Oldewelt, Kohier van de Personele Quotisatie te Amsterdam over het jaar 1742 (4); K. Zandvliet, De 250 rijksten van de Gouden Eeuw (5); B. M. J. Speet (6)

© Noordhoff Uitgevers

Blossoming Amsterdam

Amsterdam found itself in a serious crisis during the first half of the 19th century. Large parts of the city were in a dilapidated, dirty and downtrodden state. From 1870, the tide turned and the Industrial Revolution led to new opportunities for the city. More and more jobs were created and Amsterdam once again became an attractive place to settle. However, as in the Golden Age, the city's wealth was not fairly distributed. The factory workers, who mostly came from poor areas in the country, were crammed into segregated residential areas in the Oost, Oud-Zuid and West districts. The new wealthy elite occupied spacious homes and beautiful villas on the outskirts of the Vondelpark.

❶ Expansion phases 1860-1900

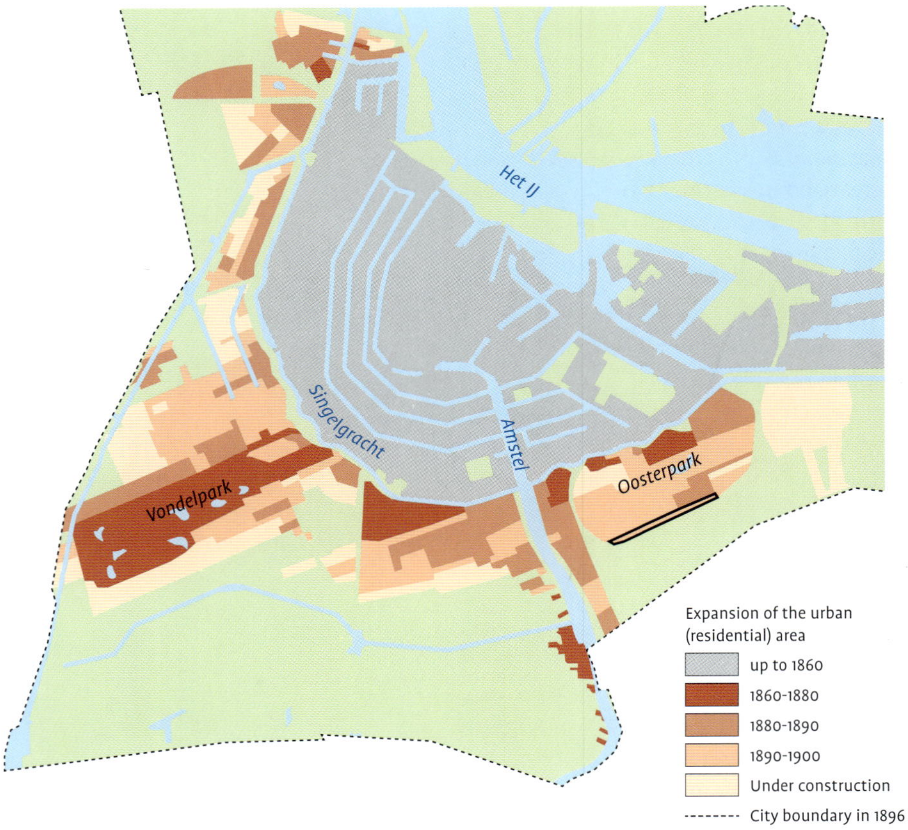

❷ Cities around 1900

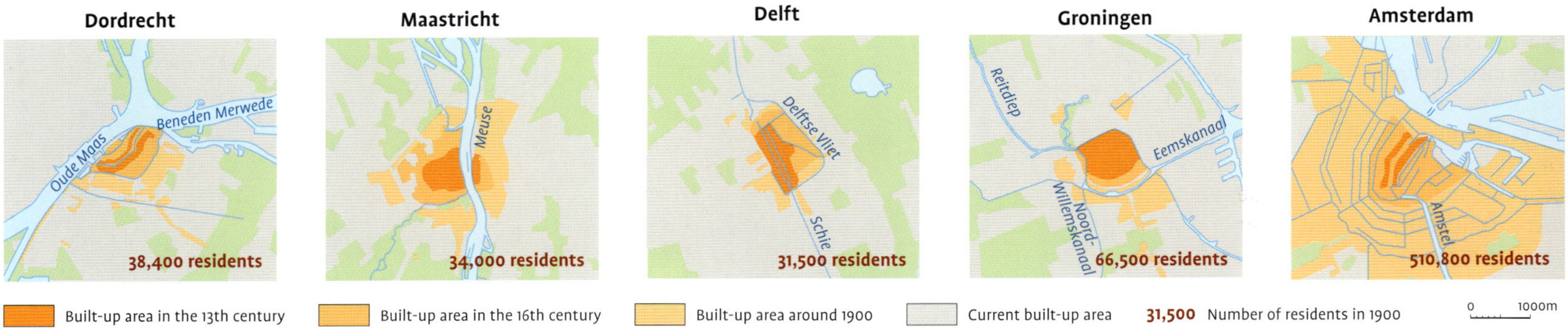

❸ Population development 1700-1900

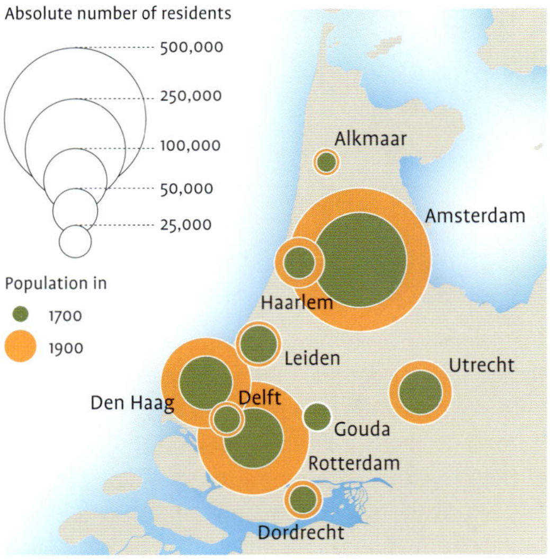

❹ Basic Amsterdam: apartments on Jacob van Campenstraat

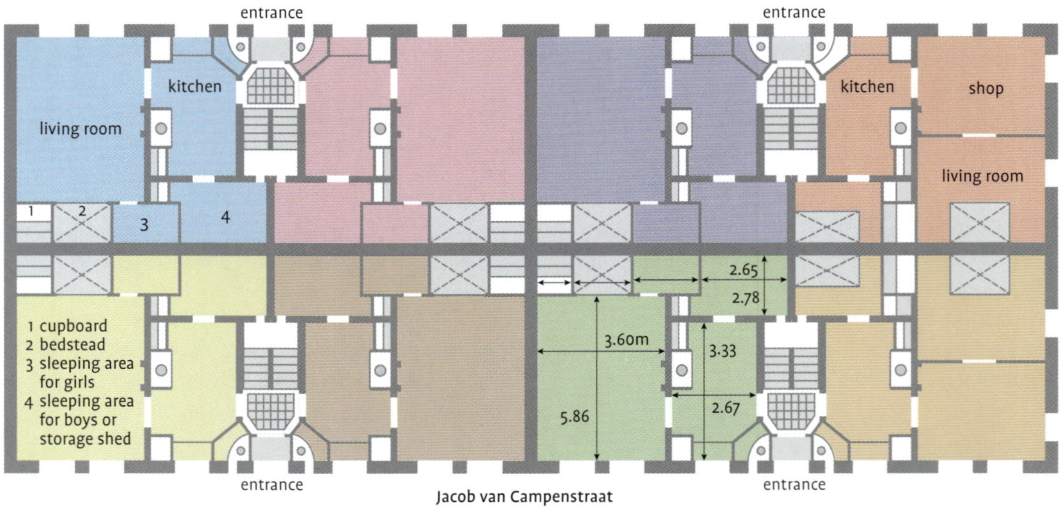

Sources: *Geschiedenis van Amsterdam, part III (1); R. Rutte & J. E. Abrahamse, Atlas van de Verstedelijking in Nederland (2-3); C. Schade, Woningbouw voor arbeiders in het 19de-eeuwse Amsterdam (4)*

© Noordhoff Uitgevers

❶ - ❸ Emerging from a deep valley

As a result of the Industrial Revolution, the population of Amsterdam increased from 228,000 residents in 1850 to 510,800 in 1900. For the first time in two hundred years, plans for expanding the city were once again drawn up.

❹ and ❽ Back-to-back

Before 1900, Amsterdam's city council had shown little interest in residential construction. Speculators had free rein and built cheap, rectangular, multi-storey complexes outside the natural boundary formed by the main city canal. The storeys of some, like those on Jacob van Campenstraat, were even partitioned through the middle to create homes at the front and back, so the occupants only had windows on one side. This cheap, mass-production construction method was called 'Revolutiebouw', or jerry-building. Even so, many occupants saw their homes as an improvement. For the first time in their lives, they had running water, gas and sanitation facilities. Other initiatives were developed for the elite. The 'Vereeniging tot Aanleg van een Rij- en Wandelpark' association was founded in 1864 to create today's Vondelpark. Expensive homes with a semi-basement, an elevated ground floor and another two or three storeys were built in this attractive area, resulting in fashionable streets like P. C. Hooftstraat and Vondelstraat.

❺ - ❻ Toxic vapours

A cholera epidemic broke out in the city in 1866, claiming the lives of 1151 residents. People suspected that the disease was caused by toxic vapours rising up from contaminated water and rubbish dumps. In order to prevent further epidemics, the city council decided to fill in numerous canals and prioritise construction of a water distribution and sewer system.

❼ 19th-century legacy

The City of Amsterdam owns about 80% of the city's land. Most of it is made available on a leasehold basis, with home owners paying annual ground rent. This system was introduced in 1896 to benefit from the land's increasing value and prevent speculation. Revenue for the City amounts to around 80 million euros each year.

❺ Cholera epidemic of 1866

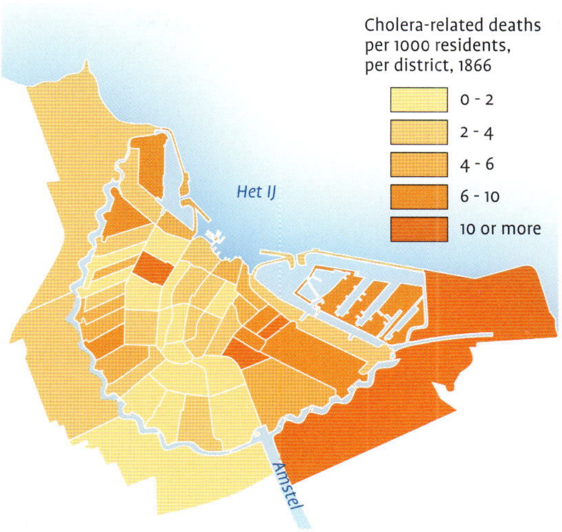

❻ Canals filled in between 1834 and 1899

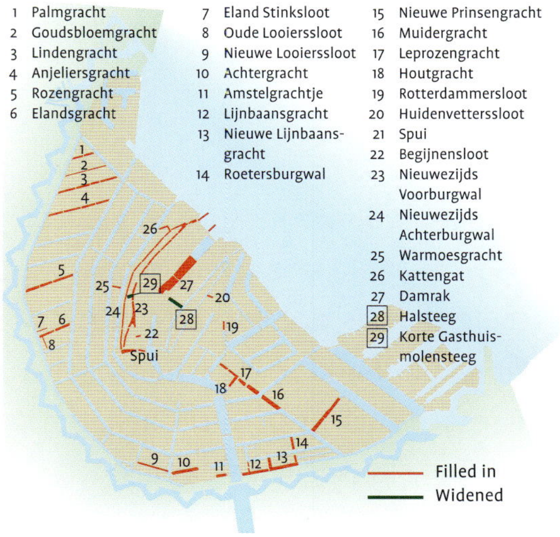

❼ Land ownership and leasehold

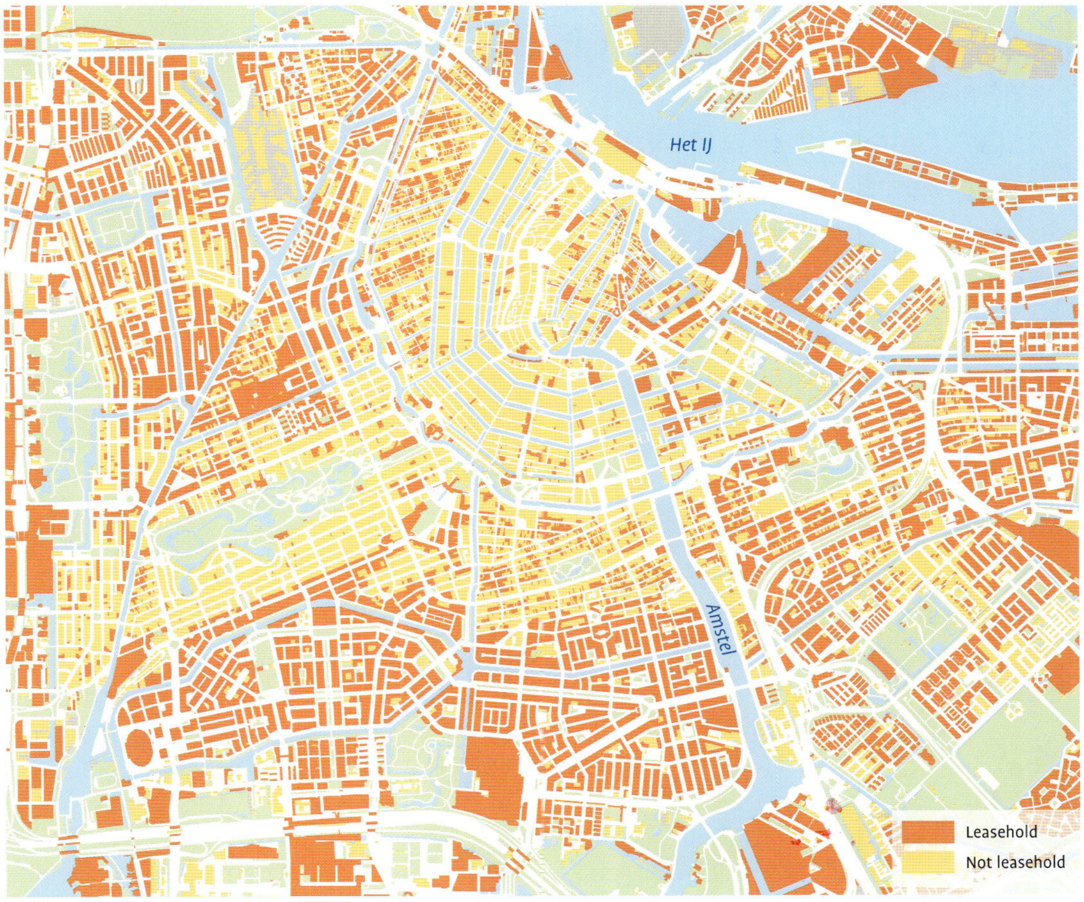

❽ Fashionable Amsterdam: Van Eeghenstraat

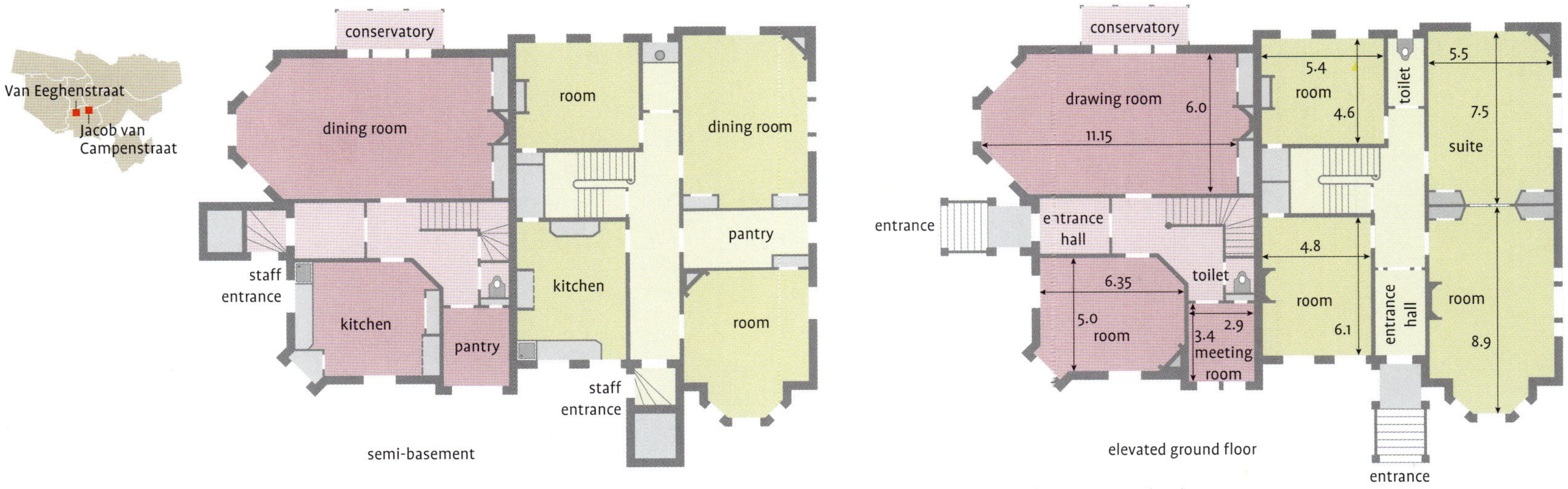

architectural plans of a double villa at Van Eeghenstraat 80-82 (1899)

Sources: Amsterdam City Archives (5); Geschiedenis van Amsterdam, part III (6); OIS, Research, Information and Statistics, City of Amsterdam (7); Amsterdam City Archives (8)

© Noordhoff Uitgevers

Public housing

The population continued to grow at the same rapid rate after 1900. As a result, the demand for suitable but affordable working-class homes also increased each year. Until then, the city council had allowed social forces to regulate the housing market. The 1901 'Woningwet', or Housing Act, changed that approach, as it required the council to draw up expansion and zoning plans and set requirements and specifications for new construction. The council had the power to expropriate existing homes that did not satisfy these requirements. Housing associations also became eligible for government grants, so public housing figured highly on the council's political agenda from that time on. In 1915, the council even set up a housing department to construct and manage homes.

❶ Expansion phases 1900-1945

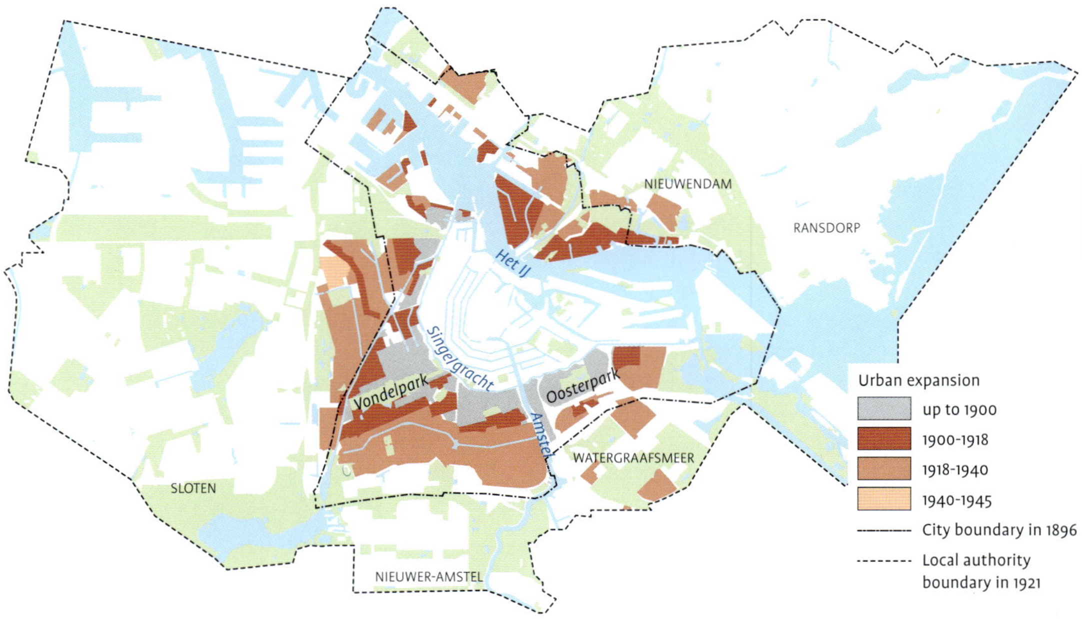

❶ Annexations

The local authority boundary had to be changed to enable expansion. On 1 May 1896, Nieuwer-Amstel local council (today's Amstelveen) had to relinquish 1145 hectares and 25,136 residents. Nieuwer-Amstel's brand-new town hall on the banks of the Amstel (close to Ceintuurbaan) also transferred to the City of Amsterdam. The boundary was adjusted again later in 1921. The local councils of Sloten, Watergraafsmeer, Nieuwendam and Ransdorp were dissolved and the boundary between Amsterdam and Nieuwer-Amstel was moved to Kalfjeslaan. This created space for new construction.

❷ Tackling slum formation

In 1889, there were around 117,000 homes in the city, nearly half of which had only one or two rooms. Conditions were most distressing on the islands of Uilenburg, Marken (Valkenburg) and Rapenburg, part of the poverty-stricken Jodenhoek area. 82% of the homes on and around the islands had a surface area below 15m² per adult. The 1901 'Woningwet', or Housing Act, forced the city council to intervene. Renovation of the islands began in 1916, starting with the totally run-down Uilenburg. Alongside the construction of new homes, the street layout was altered to create a much more spacious environment.

❷ Uilenburg renovation

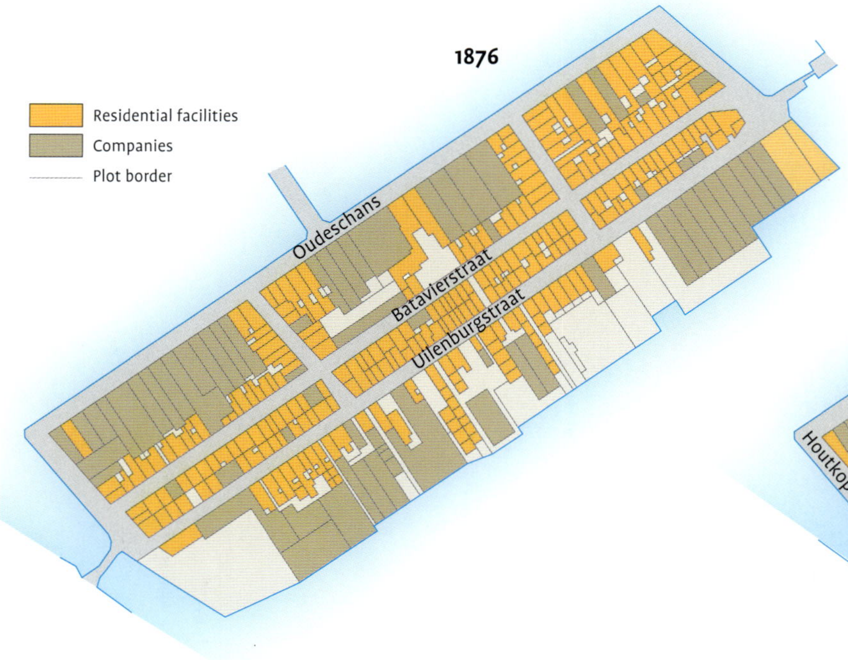

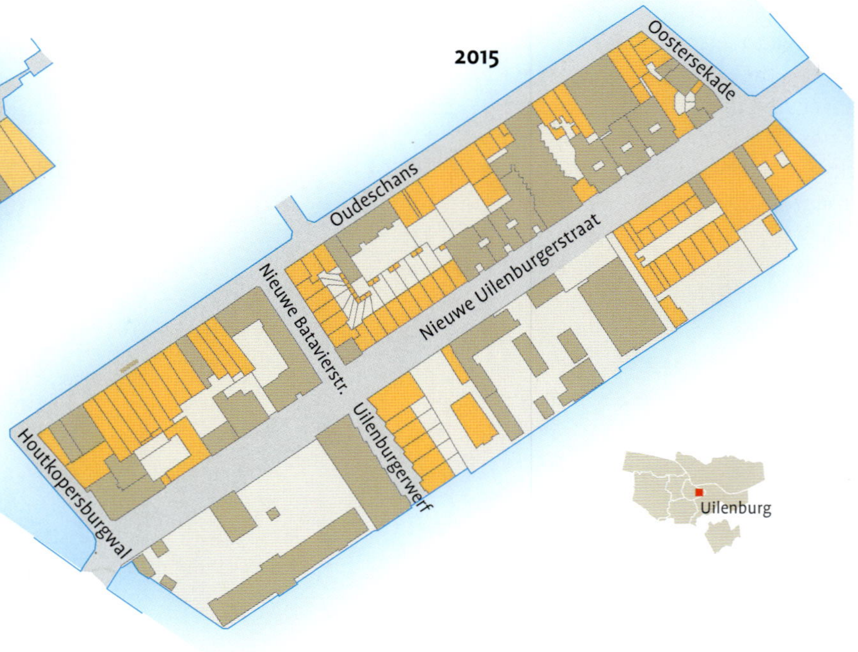

Sources: *M. Carasso-Kok (red.), Geschiedenis van Amsterdam, part IV: Tweestrijd om de hoofdstad 1900-2000 (1); Amsterdam City Archives / OIS, Research, Information and Statistics, City of Amsterdam (2)*

© Noordhoff Uitgevers

❸ Housing associations in the 'Indische Buurt'

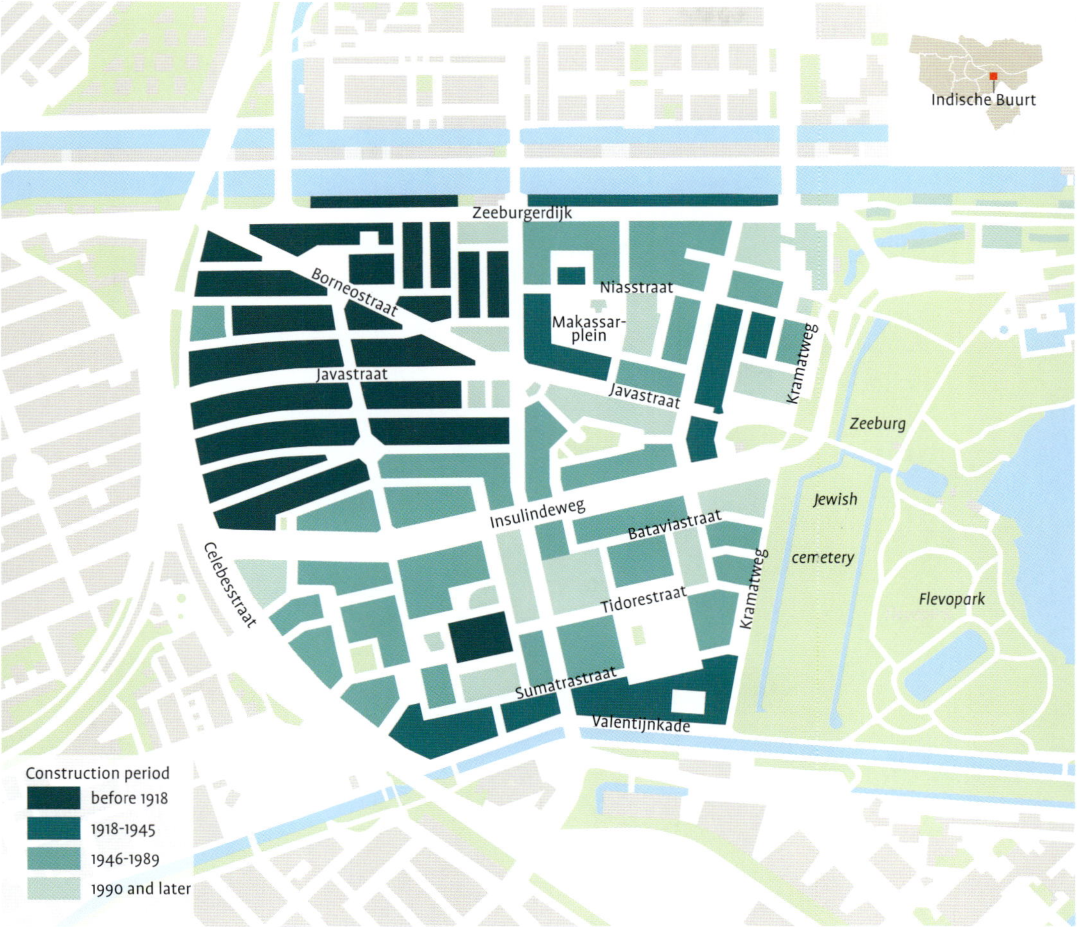

Number of homes owned by housing associations in 1970

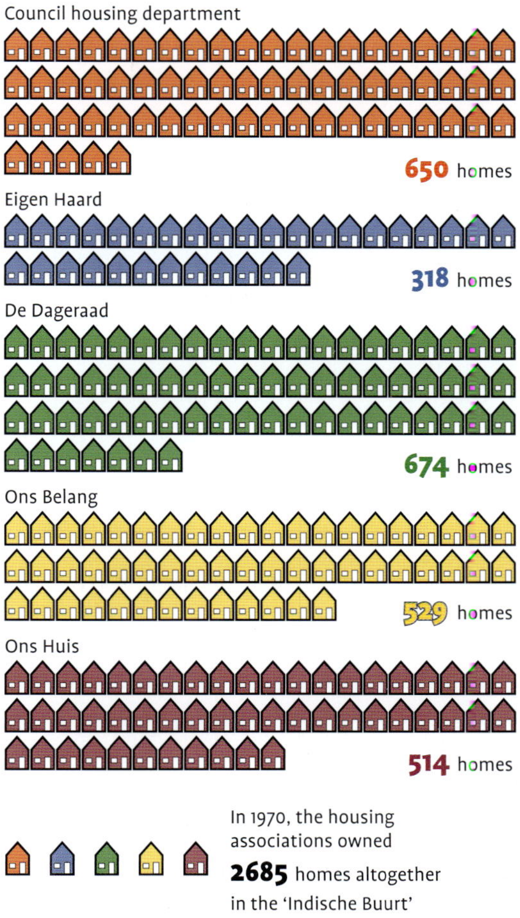

❸ Building homes for ordinary Amsterdammers

Founded in 1903 by employees of the city's tram service, Rochdale was the first housing association in the city to be accredited and subsidised by the government. By 1925, there were nearly 60 associations, each with its own grass-roots supporters. Schaepman and Het Oosten built homes for the Catholics, Patrimonium for the Protestants and Rochdale and De Dageraad for the socialists. In some districts, like the 'Indische Buurt', housing associations owned nearly all residential properties. Today, rented social housing provided by associations is still significant, though it is declining – around 45% of Amsterdam's 417,096 homes fall in this category.

❹ Back to nature

In 1898, the Englishman Ebenezer Howard advocated the creation of residential communities with extensive green space, far from the city. He felt that people could only be protected from the misery of overcrowded working class districts and retain their community spirit and love of nature in 'garden cities' of this sort. Arie Keppler, manager of the city council's housing department, embraced Howard's ideas. With the support of Floor Wibaut, alderman for public housing, he chose Amsterdam-Noord as a test site. Six garden villages were built from 1916 to 1929, each with welcoming low-level architecture, small gates, squares, curved streets, extensive green areas and, where possible, front and back gardens. To entice workers away from the pub, the authorities built public reading rooms and community centres, like the Zonnehuis (1932) in the garden village of Oostzaan.

❹ Garden villages in Amsterdam-Noord

Source: *City of Amsterdam, Sociale woningbouw Amsterdam 1968-1986 (3, 4)*

© Noordhoff Uitgevers

Berlage's city

Berlage's name is associated with the Beurs van Berlage, the Plan Zuid development and the 'Berlagebrug' bridge over the Amstel. However, not many people realise that architect and urban planner Hendrik Petrus Berlage (1856-1934) also left his mark on Amsterdam in many other places. Berlage mainly drew his inspiration from Renaissance Italian town houses and city palaces with their stark lines, rectangular shapes and sparse decorative elements. He is often said to adhere to the Amsterdam School, but this is incorrect. In fact, he was very critical of this style. He also rejected De Stijl and Het Nieuwe Bouwen, new architectural movements that became popular in the 1920s. Where one movement erred by excess in its exclusive focus on beauty and decoration, the other sacrificed everything to functionality. He sought to create a link between structure and decorative elements by striking a balance between efficiency and visual beauty.

❶ Berlage's Plan Zuid development, 1915

❷ Plan Zuid, today

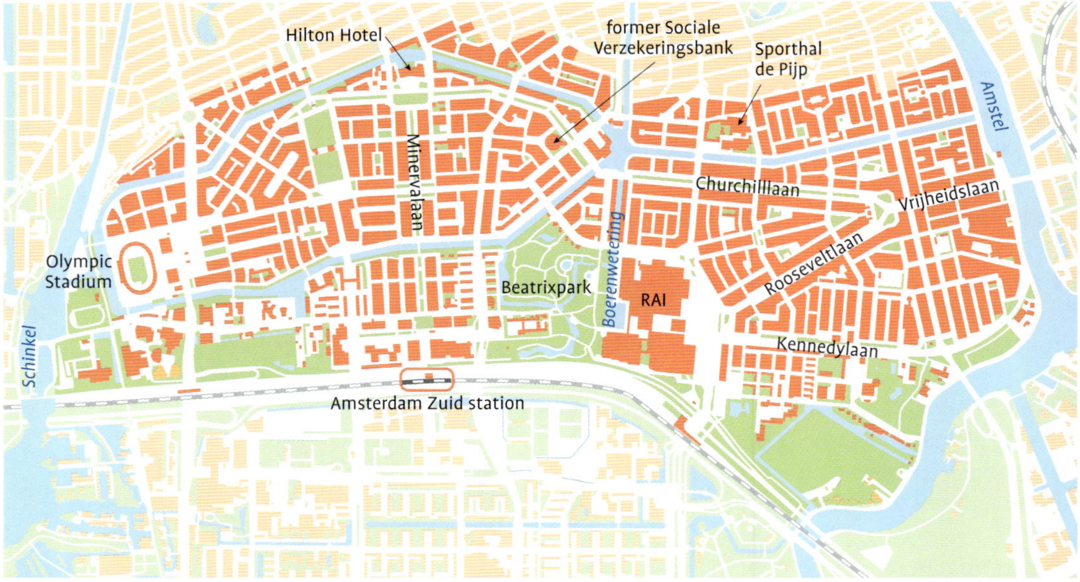

❶ - ❷ Perfect collaboration

In 1917, the city council approved Berlage's expansion plan for developing the new Zuid city area, which he had submitted two years earlier. The plan called for two different areas, which would be separated from each other by the Boerenwetering canal. The eastern area comprised a street plan running from east to west, while the structure of the western area featured a north-to-south orientation.

The actual implementation of this plan took nearly 30 years, during which the plan was continuously amended. The western area in particular, with Minervalaan as its central axis, was changed significantly and the garden village that Berlage had planned to build south of Vrijheidslaan and Rooseveltlaan never materialised. By the time construction was due to start in this area (today's 'Rivierenbuurt'), the Great Depression had already started and spending cuts were being made across the board.

Berlage put up little opposition to these amendments to his plan. On the contrary, in 1927, he called the new Zuid area a textbook example of harmonious collaboration between urban planners, architects and the government.

❸ - ❹ Party hall

Berlage's business-like style is evident in many of his designs and Mercatorplein is perhaps the best example. In 1922, the city council launched the Plan West development, also known as the '6000 homes plan'. Berlage was asked to design a square and the associated buildings for the new development in Amsterdam-West. Once again inspired by Italian architecture, he designed a square with towers, arcades and gates to accentuate the enclosed space. In his words, the square was to become a 'party hall' for the working people, so he planned a large public building in the middle where residents could meet each other. However, due to budget cuts this building was never constructed. The balconies looking out onto the square were revolutionary, since the prevailing opinion of the time was that workers should seek happiness within their family environments and stay away from the vulgarities of street life. After falling into disrepair and having to be demolished in 1961, the north tower was rebuilt in 1995.

Source: Amsterdam City Archives (1)

© Noordhoff Uitgevers

❸ **Berlage's architectural heritage**

❹ **Mercatorplein**

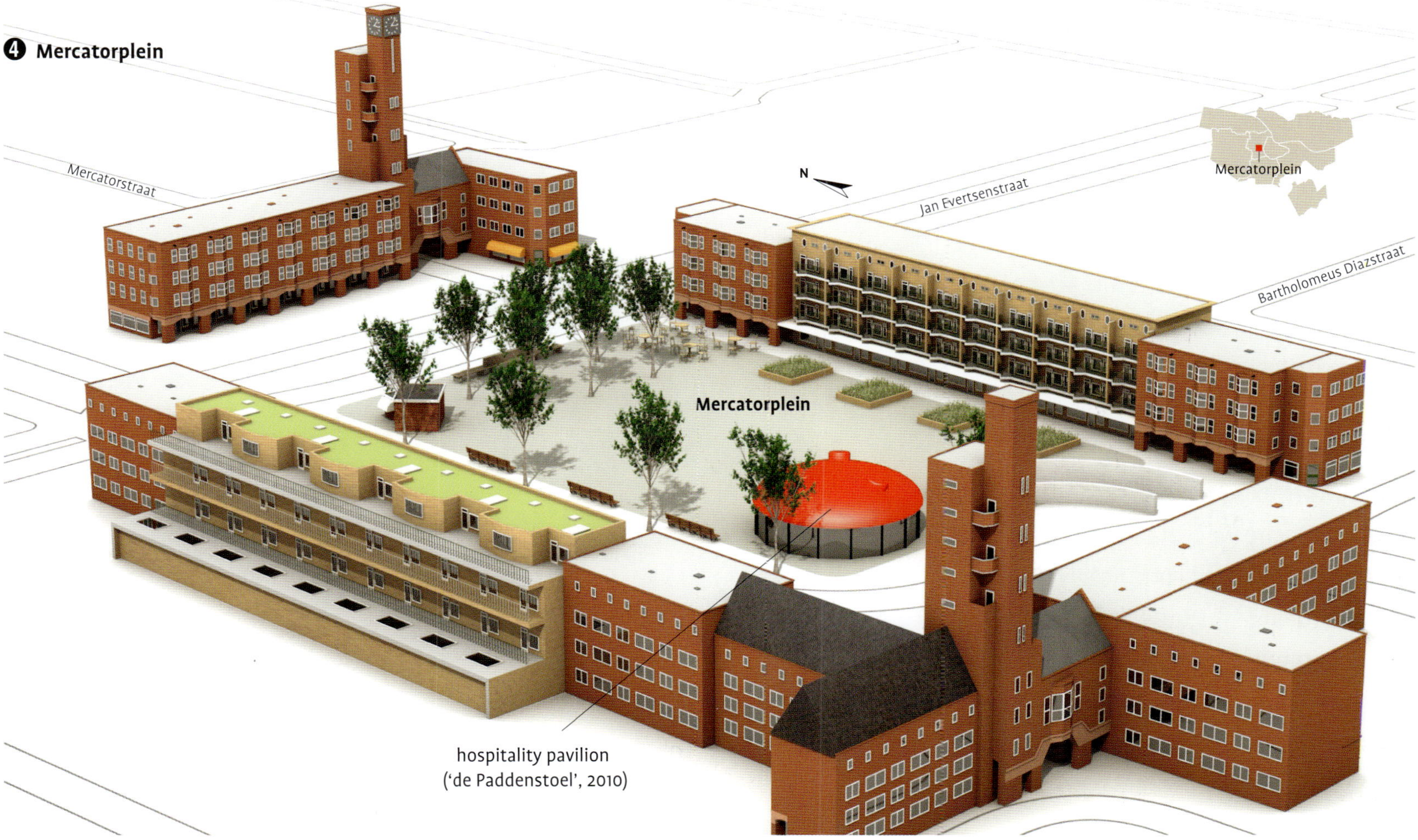

Source: *City of Amsterdam (3)*

© Noordhoff Uitgevers

The Amsterdam School

The construction of around 2000 homes in Amsterdam-Zuid commenced in 1921. These residential complexes were the first buildings in the 'Rivierenbuurt', a district that was largely designed by architects of the Amsterdam School.

The style of the Amsterdam School is closely related to art movements like Expressionism, Art Nouveau, Art Deco and Jugendstil. The movement is named after Amsterdam as this is where its three main architects (Michiel de Klerk, Jo van der Meij and Piet Kramer) mainly worked. All three were trained by architect Eduard Cuypers. Around 1910, they started to design buildings that largely relied on their external appearance to catch the eye. For them, architecture was not engineering, but rather an art form that should evoke emotions and feelings. Being actually able to enjoy living in a home was of secondary importance. Homes had to look nice above all else.
In the 1930s, the Amsterdam School adopted a more sober style, partly due to criticism of the high construction and maintenance costs. Some homes had turned out to be three times more expensive than normal ones. After the war, the Amsterdam School disappeared completely. Due to the housing shortage, fast, efficient and cheap building methods had become the norm. This corresponded to the principles of a new architectural style called Het Nieuwe Bouwen.

❶ Design of the 'IJselbuurt'

❷ Vrijheidslaan residential complex

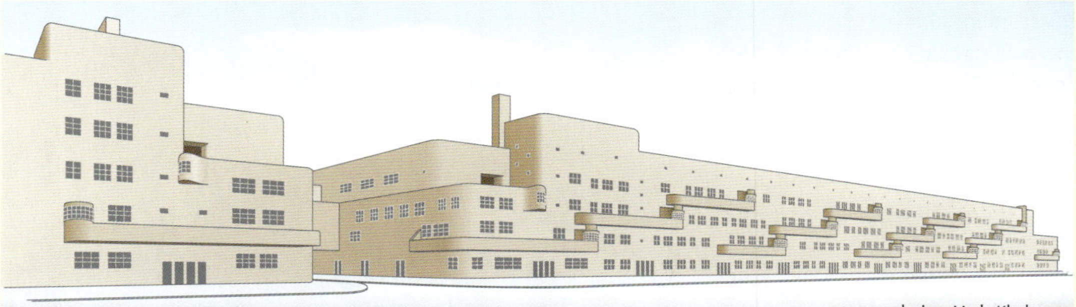

design: M. de Klerk, 1921

❸ Meerhuizenplein

design: A. J. Westerman, 1922

© Noordhoff Uitgevers

❹ Selection of buildings in the Amsterdam School style

❶ - ❸ Decorative facades

As you can see in several places in Amsterdam, the residential complex's front facade is the most characteristic aspect of the Amsterdam School. It had to be presented as a visually stunning and sculptured whole. This was achieved by alternating masonry with copious use of ornamental bands, curved roof lines, projections and set-back areas in the exterior facades and steeply inclined tiled roofs. Intensive use was also made of various types of different coloured brick, ornamental wrought ironwork, sculptures and stained-glass windows.

❹ - ❺ Homes, schools and bridges

Many of the residential complexes in Berlage's Plan Zuid development were designed by architects of the Amsterdam School. This is striking, because the more business-like Berlage did not really care for this movement. Piet Kramer (1881-1961) played a prominent role in Berlage's team of fellow architects. He specialised in bridges and designed around 200 in total. Most of them are located in Zuid, West and the Amsterdam Forest, but some are in the city centre. His first bridges have all the characteristics of the Amsterdam School, but as time passed, they became more sober and therefore more cost-effective in terms of construction and maintenance.

❺ Selection of bridges designed by Piet Kramer

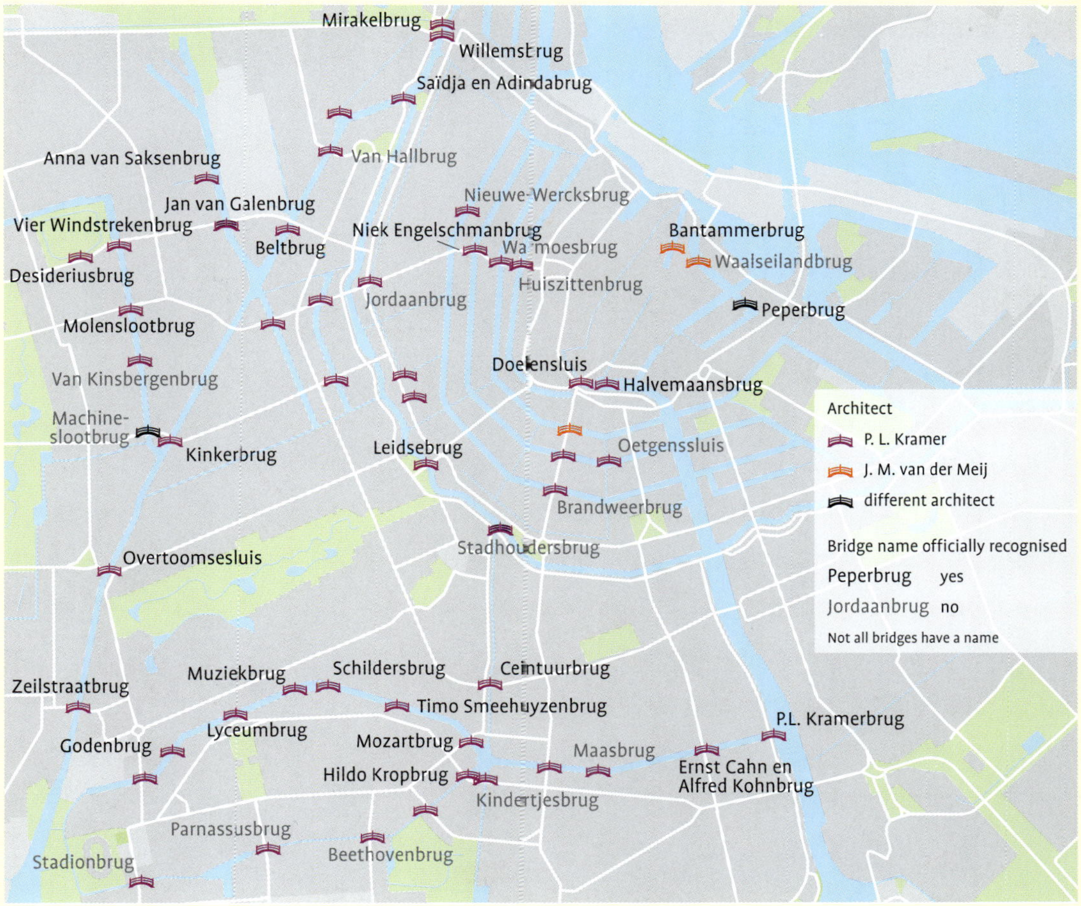

Sources: W. De Wit, The Amsterdam School. Dutch Expressionist Architecture, 1915-1930 (4); T. Bakker, De Amsterdamse School (bridges) / www.bruggenvanamsterdam.nl (names) (5)

© Noordhoff Uitgevers

Het Nieuwe Bouwen

Supporters of the De Stijl, Het Nieuwe Bouwen and Nieuwe Zakelijkheid movements felt that houses were for living in, not for looking at with amazement and wonder. These new architectural movements became increasingly important from the 1930s onwards and the City of Amsterdam's 'Algemeen Uitbreidingsplan', or General Expansion Plan (1935), gave their adherents the opportunity to put their ideas into practice. When the war broke out a few years later, the plan had to be put on hold until after 1945. In Nieuw-West and Zuidoost, new districts were constructed that were totally different from the pre-war city districts in terms of urban planning and architectural design. Parts of the latter districts were so run-down and dilapidated by that time that demolition or renovation had become unavoidable.

❶ Implementation of the 1935 'Algemeen Uitbreidingsplan'

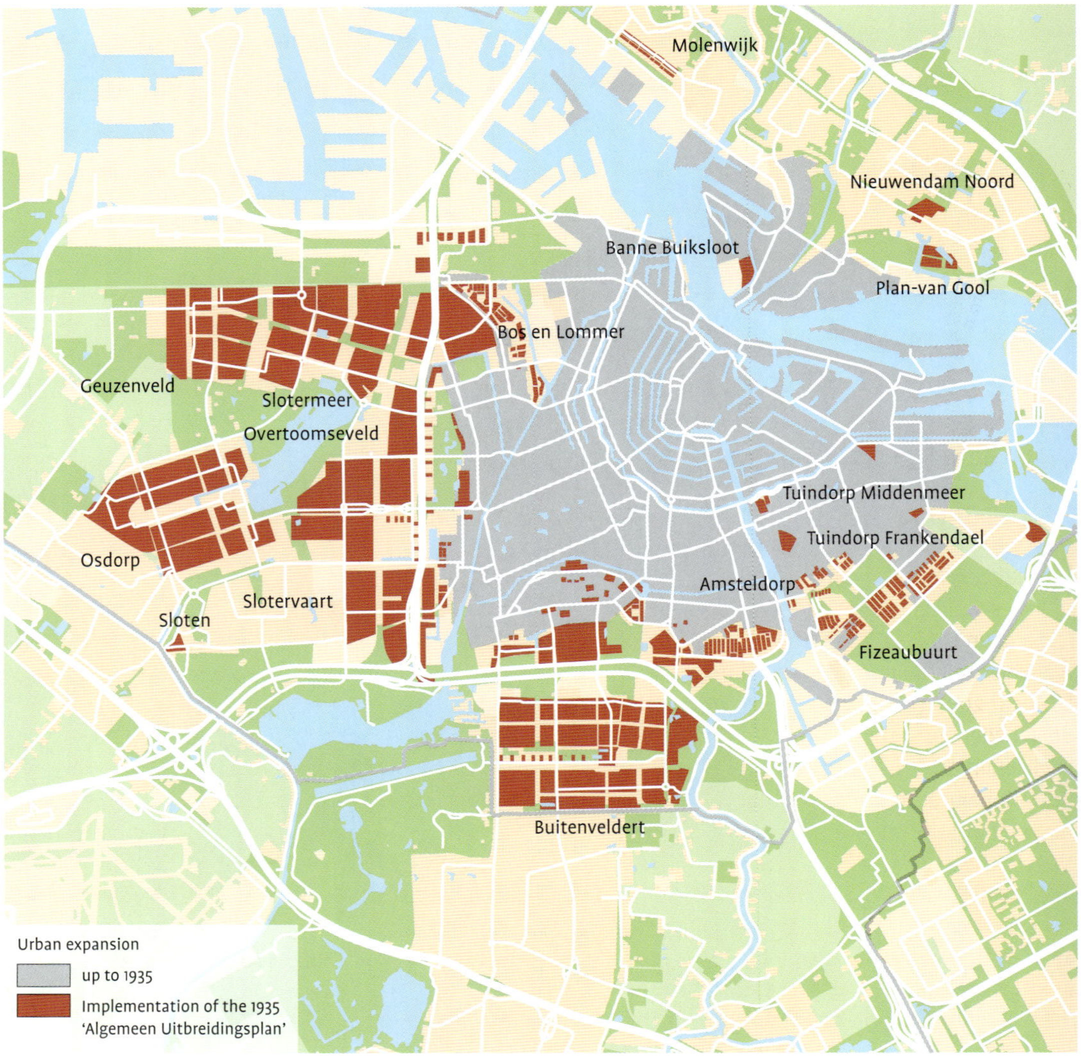

❷ Bijlmermeer

1992

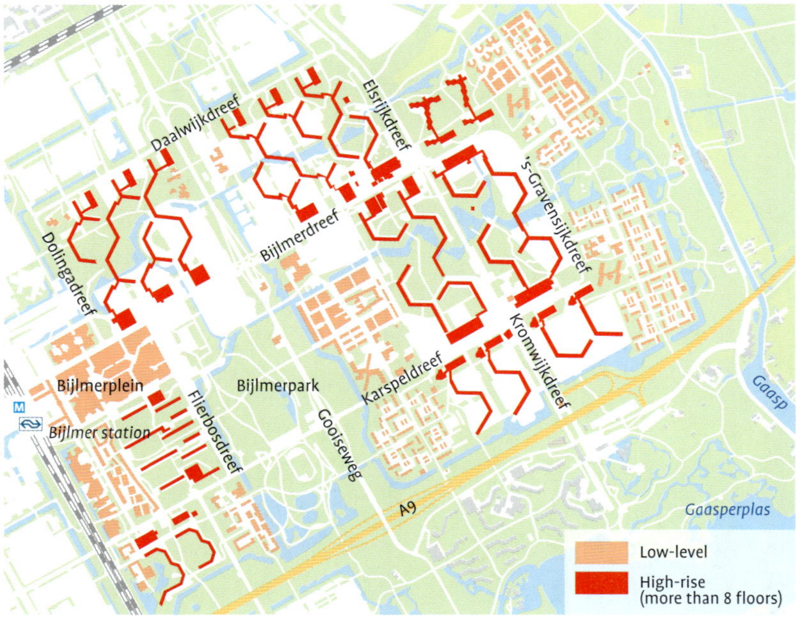

2014

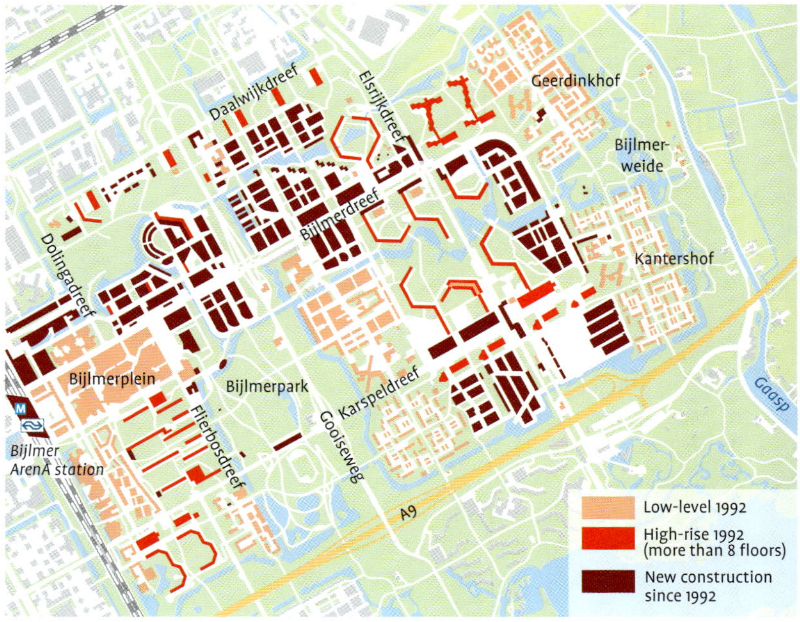

Sources: City of Amsterdam, Zuidoost District/Projectbureau Vernieuwing Bijlmermeer (2)

© Noordhoff Uitgevers

❸ Dapperbuurt

❶ Light, space and gardens

Cornelis van Eesteren's and Jacoba Mulder's 'Algemeen Uitbreidingsplan' assumed that Amsterdam would have one million residents by the year 2000. The two architects were adherents of Het Nieuwe Bouwen, and functionality was their main priority. Living and working areas had to be separated by gardens, and traffic nuisance in residential areas had to be minimised. The homes themselves also had to be as functional as possible. Rather than closed oblong complexes, they had to be long or L-shaped blocks of flats with plenty of windows, allowing the residents to enjoy the sun, spaciousness and gardens.

❷ A failed experiment

After completion of the garden cities of Slotermeer, Geuzenveld, Osdorp and Buitenveldert, work started on constructing the Bijlmermeer development in 1966. What should have been a success story turned into a nightmare. In 1985, a quarter of the flats were empty because 'De Bijlmer' was associated with an impersonal scale, drugs problems, crime and other city issues. As a result, 'De Bijlmer' increasingly became a last refuge for disadvantaged residents of Amsterdam. Total restructuring was the only remaining option for saving the district. This started in the 1990s.

❸ Urban renewal

There were two faces to Amsterdam in the 1960s and 1970s. While future-oriented construction was taking place on the west and south periphery, the old city districts were falling into decay, so many Amsterdammers moved away. The city council adopted a radical approach in order to reverse this trend. The old working-class districts had to be replaced with new developments similar to the garden cities, which led to vehement protests, particularly in the 'Dapperbuurt'. This neighbourhood was partially demolished but then reconstructed, taking into account the existing structure and the residents' desire for a more personal scale.

❹ - ❺ Steel, glass and concrete

Before the war, Weesperstraat was a lively shopping street in the 'Jodenbuurt', but by 1945, it was deserted and the shops had been looted. The post-war reconstruction plan involved demolishing all buildings and constructing a wide thoroughfare. Steel, glass and concrete buildings were constructed on the east side, while the west side was temporarily left alone, since a metro line was planned for this area. Once the metro was complete, the west side was also developed.

❹ Weesperstraat 1876-2015

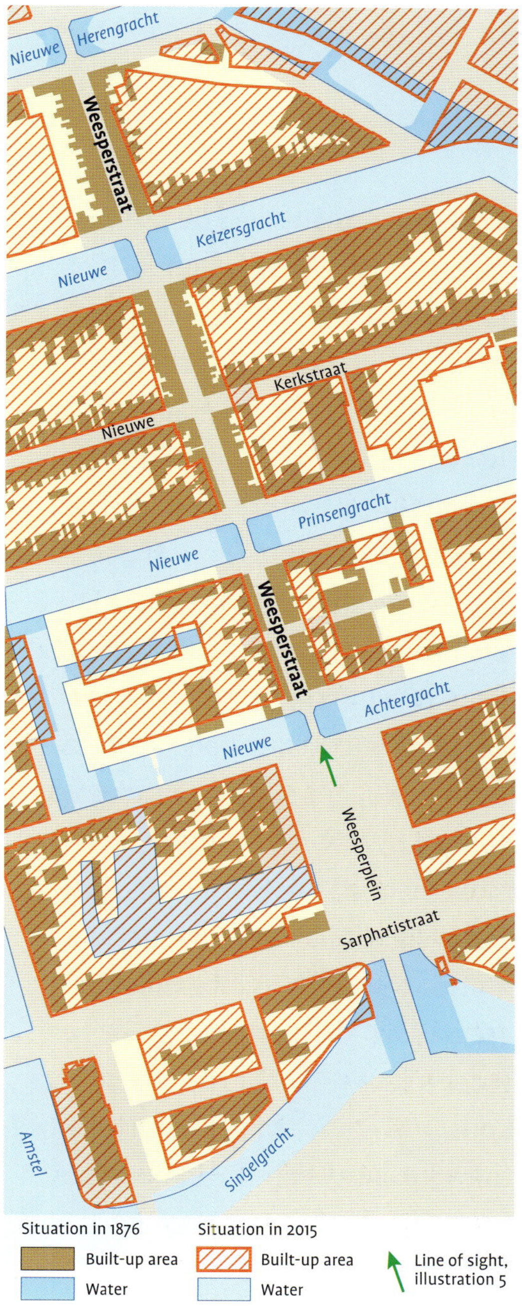

❺ Weesperstraat today

Sources: Sociale woningbouw Amsterdam: 68-86. Gemeentelijke Dienst Volkshuisvesting Amsterdam (3); www.theobakker.net (4)

© Noordhoff Uitgevers

Alternative living

Most Amsterdammers by far live in a house or a flat. A small minority has adopted an alternative way of living, mostly by choice, but sometimes out of sheer necessity. Itinerant caravan dwellers often form close-knit groups that prefer to live as inconspicuously as possible, whereas houseboats are part of the city's rich tapestry and even constitute a tourist attraction. Around 1980, Amsterdam was the country's most notorious squatters' stronghold, but since squatting was banned by law in 2010, the squatters' movement has become marginalised. Some squatters have joined the motley crew of homeless people, drug addicts, illegal immigrants and eccentrics who roam the city streets. Constantly pursued by the city council, they are always on the lookout for new alternative spaces for their tents, shacks and caravans.

❶ Caravans

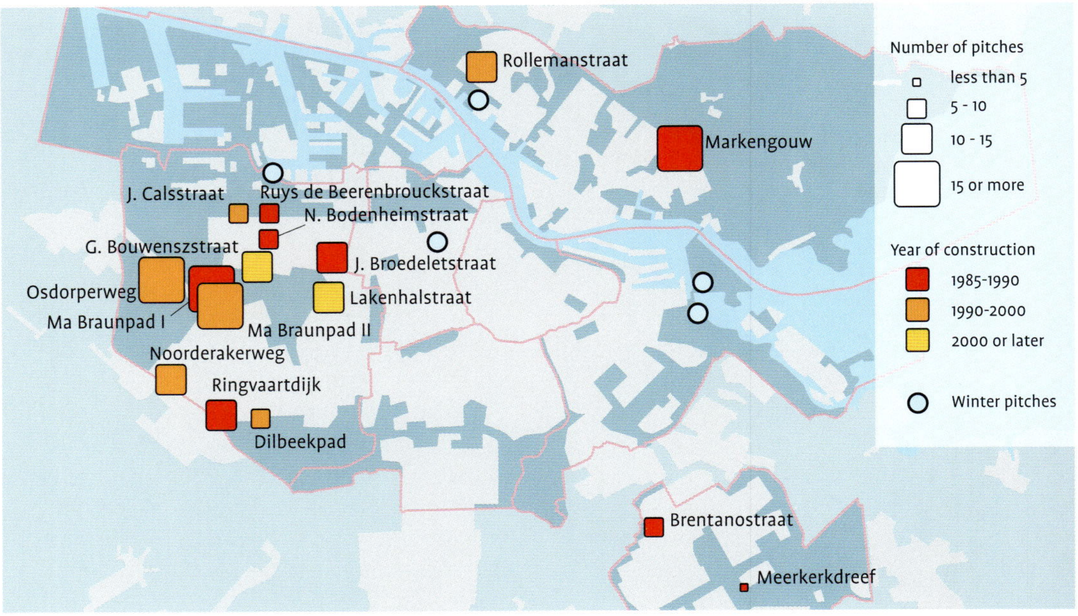

❷ Houseboats

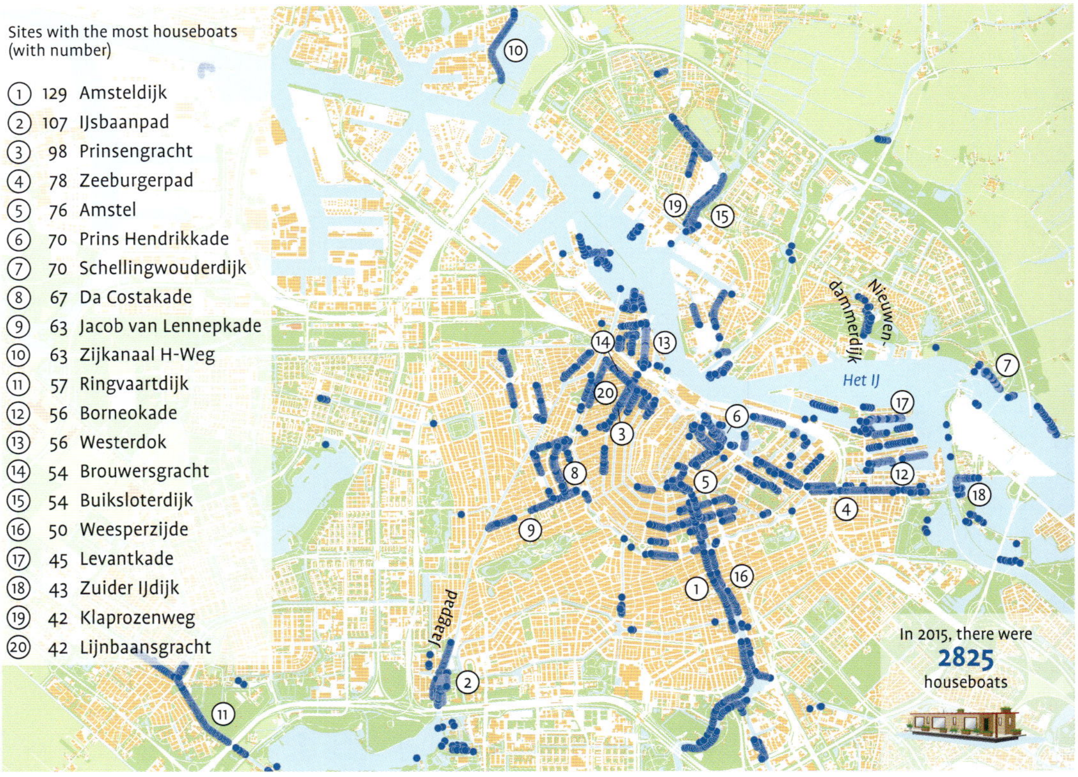

❶ Caravans

Amsterdam has 167 pitches for caravans, distributed over 16 sites. On top of that, there are also five sites with 130 winter pitches for fairground and circus travellers. Since the abolition of the 'Woonwagenwet', or Caravans Act, in 1999, caravan owners are subject to the same rules of residence as 'normal' inhabitants of Amsterdam.

❸ Reuse of barges as houseboats in the city centre

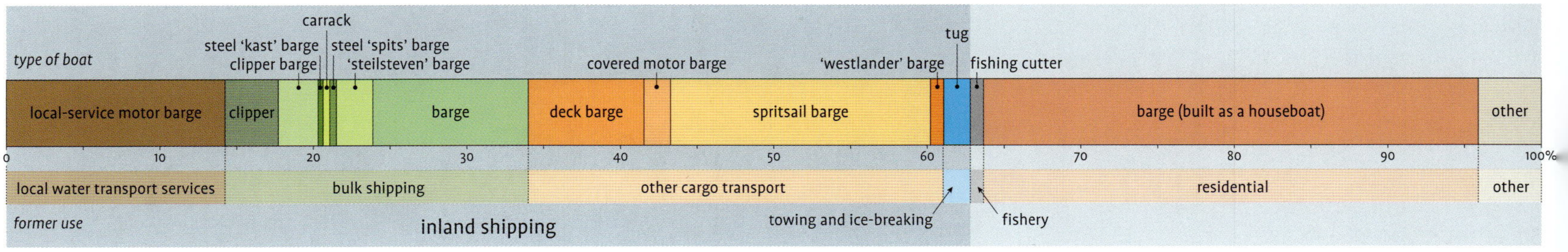

© Noordhoff Uitgevers

❹ Notorious squats

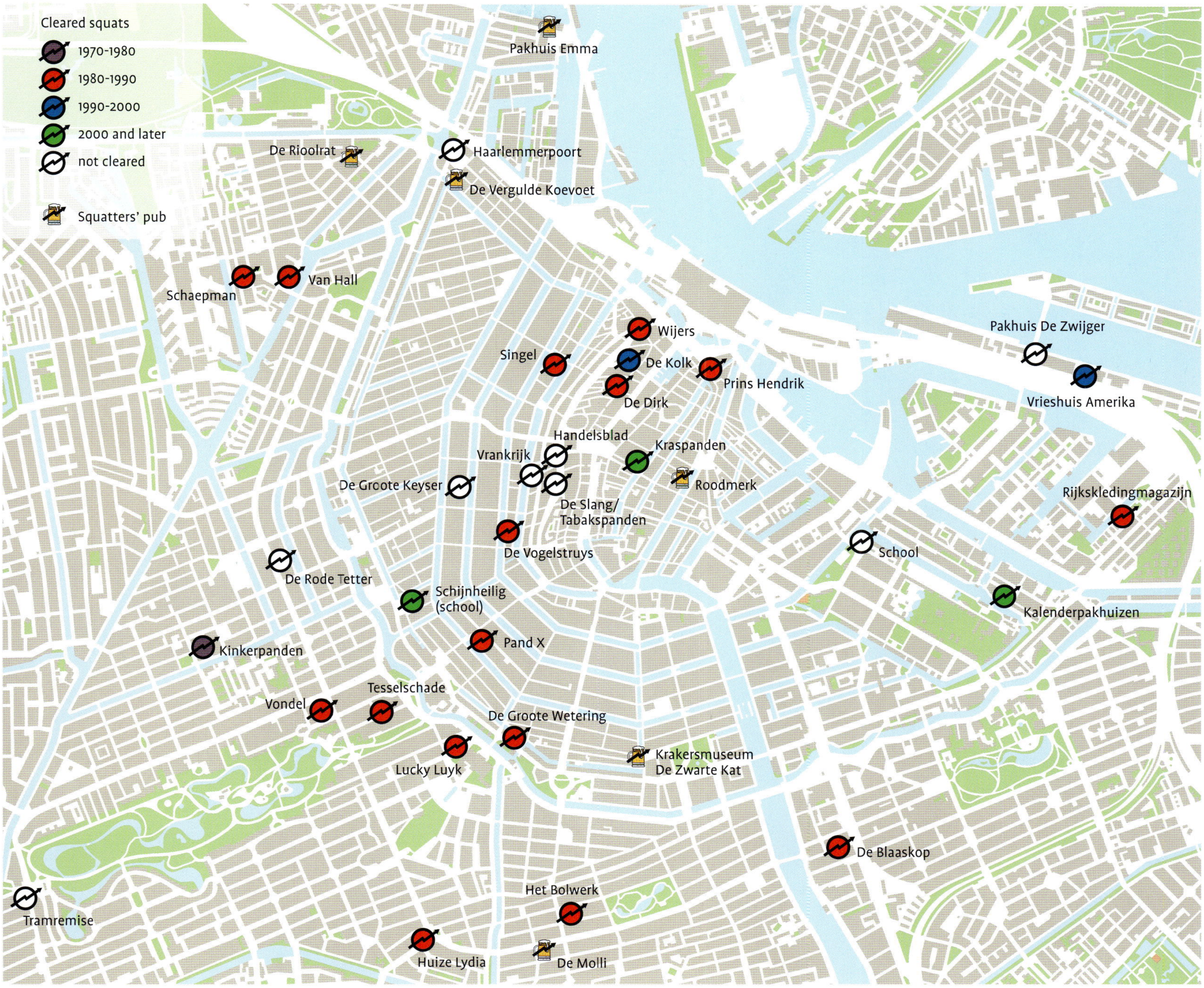

❷ - ❸ Houseboats

Amsterdam has almost 3000 berths for houseboats. In 1918, there were only 85, but this number has increased enormously since the 1950s due to the housing shortage. The city council has now stopped allocating new berths. Since many people want to live on a houseboat, the prices for boats and berths are increasing rapidly.

❹ - ❺ 'No home, no coronation'

The squatters' movement started in the 1960s. Buildings in Amsterdam-Oost had been condemned and the occupants had to vacate their homes, but demolition was delayed and homeseekers reoccupied the vacant buildings. Initially, the public was rather sympathetic to the squatters, as the empty buildings annoyed many people, but the tide turned in 1980. The squatters caused a commotion with their slogan of 'No home, no coronation' during Queen Beatrix's inauguration and their use of violence when resisting eviction did the movement no good. Squatting has been prohibited by law since 2010.

❺ Squatting

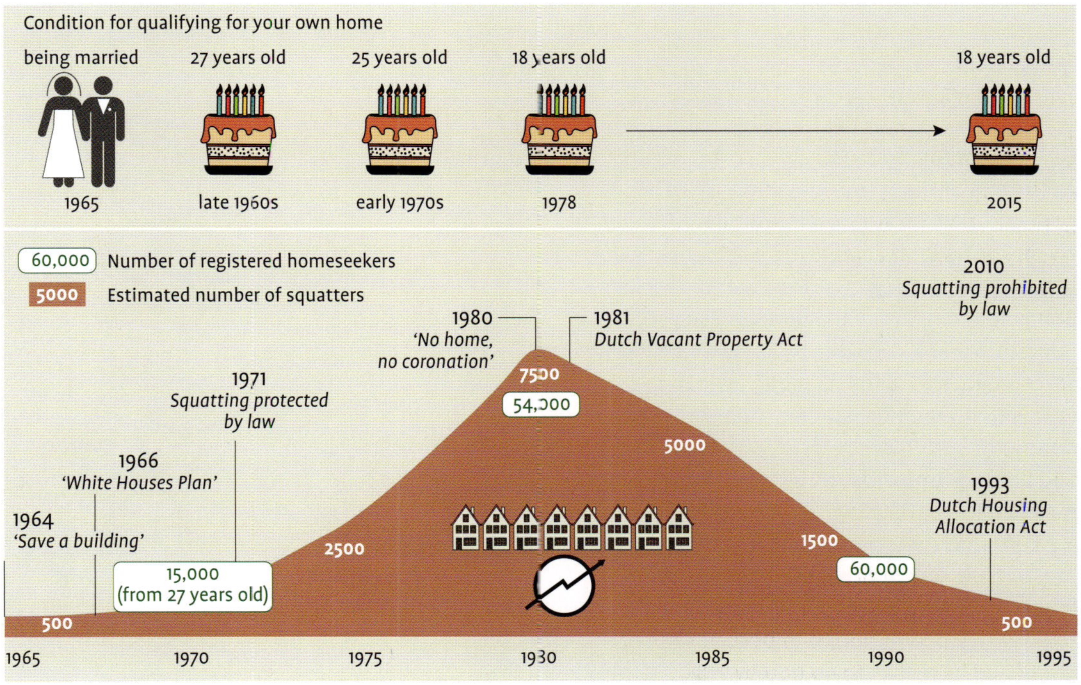

© Noordhoff Uitgevers

Amsterdam relocates

Amsterdam was not a pleasant place to live for many citizens in the seventies. In 1970, 44,000 of the 260,000 rental homes had been earmarked for demolition, while a further 100,000 homes required drastic renovation. Many Amsterdammers had had enough of neglect in their neighbourhoods, increasing unemployment levels due to the decline in industry and shipbuilding, housing shortages and the increase in petty crimes committed by drug addicts. They 'defected' to towns on the edge of Amsterdam. Families with children in particular turned their backs on the city. The local council welcomed this exodus in the hope that the housing problem would automatically resolve itself, but this did not happen.

❶ Today's Amsterdam Metropolitan Area in 1950

Built-up area | Port, industrial area, business area | Motorway | Main road | Railway | Amsterdam Metropolitan Area border

❷ Amsterdam Metropolitan Area in 2015

❶ - ❷ Exodus

At the end of the 1950s, Amsterdam had a population of 872,000, an absolute record. Twenty years later, a mere 675,000 people were listed in the civil registry. That number included many newcomers such as Surinamese people, migrant workers from North Africa and Turkey, and students. At a conservative estimate, it seems that around 425,000 people left their city during those two decades, despite being 'born and bred' in Amsterdam. The majority opted to build a new life in the virgin reclaimed polder area of Almere. Purmerend, also not far from Amsterdam, was another popular destination. In 1960, it was still a predominantly agricultural town with a population of 10,000, but the population had increased to 50,000 by 1985.

© Noordhoff Uitgevers

❸ Development of Almere

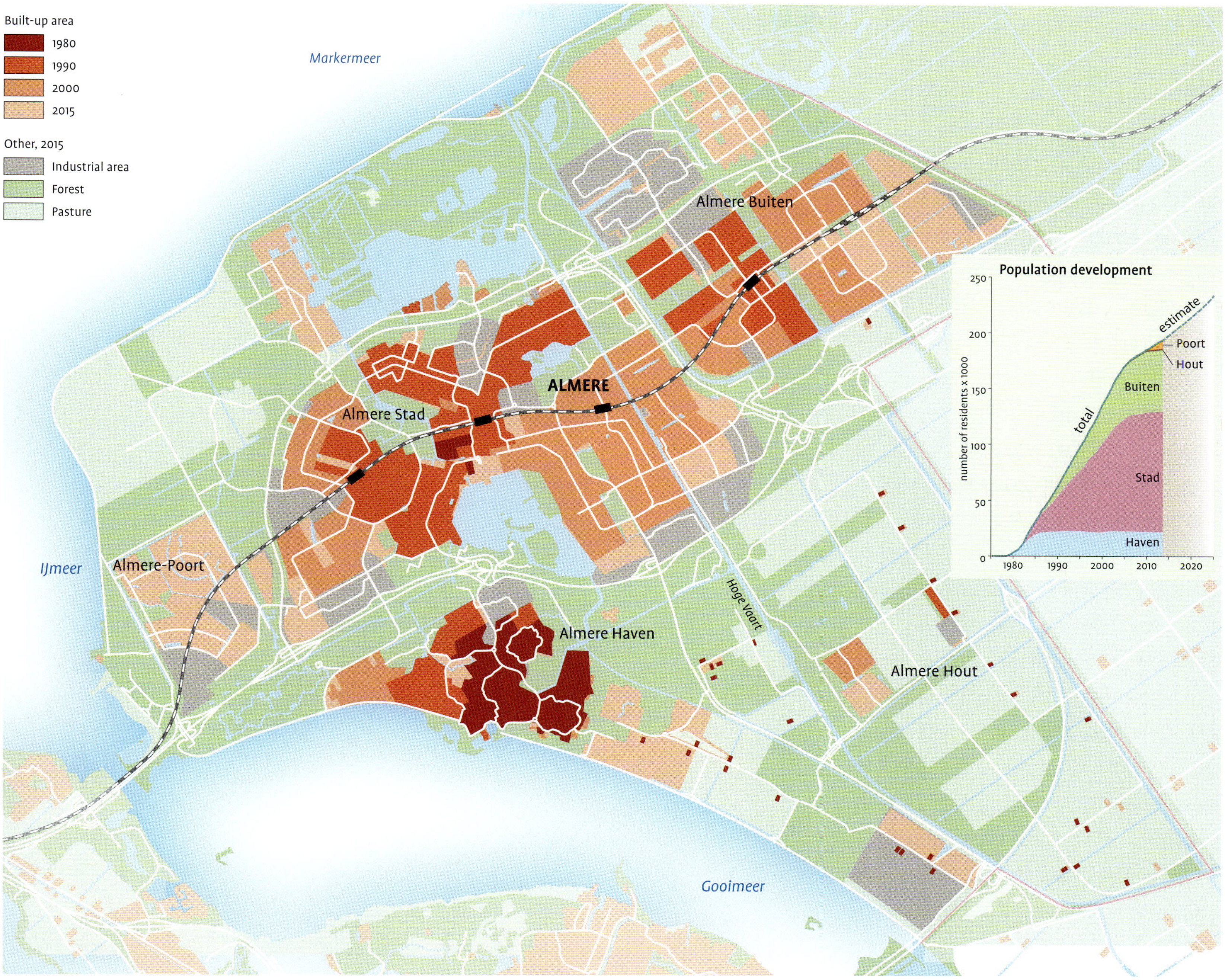

❸ A city appears out of nowhere

On 30 November 1976, 25 families were given the keys to the first houses in Almere Haven under the watchful eye of the Dutch Minister of Transport, Public Works and Water Management. Amsterdam hoped that Almere, as an overspill town, would help to resolve the city's housing problem. Today, Almere has matured into a city with nearly 200,000 residents, nearly one third of which comes from the Amsterdam area. The latter figure is not expected to increase significantly in future years as Amsterdam has now become more attractive for families.

❹ Stuck in traffic

Since Almere's population has grown so much, the A1 and A6 motorways have difficulty accommodating rush-hour traffic to and from Amsterdam. In 2011, work started on widening the A1 between Amsterdam and Muiderberg and the A6 up to Almere Haven. A new bridge will be built next to the existing 'Hollandse Brug' and the railway bridge near Muiderberg will be moved. The work is scheduled for completion in 2020.

❹ Commuter traffic to and from the Almere/Lelystad region

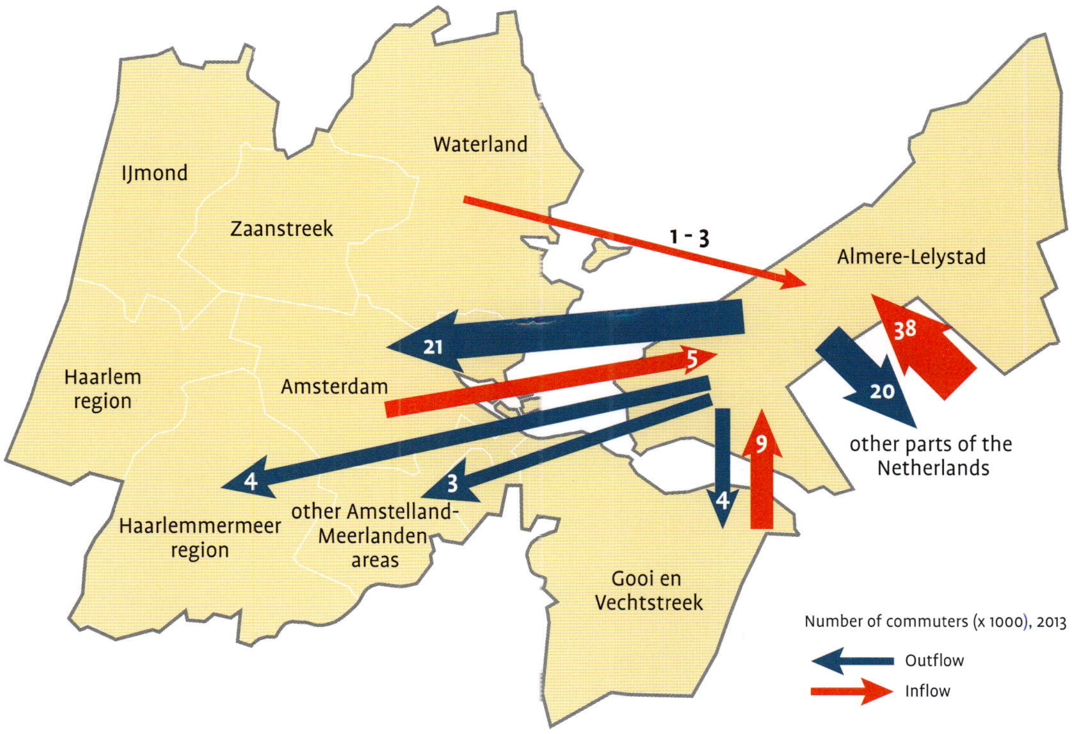

Sources: City of Almere/Onderzoek en statistiek (map) / Sociale Atlas Almere 2013 / Statistics Netherlands, PBL Netherlands Environmental Assessment Agency: Regionale prognose 2013-2040 (graph) (3); Economische Verkenningen Metropoolregio Amsterdam 2015 (4)

© Noordhoff Uitgevers

New residential areas

In 1984, the city council launched its slogan *Amsterdam heeft 't* (Amsterdam has got it), to much scorn. Even so, no one can deny that the city has had much to offer in recent decades. The 1970s plans to turn the inner city into a metropolis, demolish the old neighbourhoods and replace them with flats were scrapped and urban renewal became the new buzzword. Amsterdam had to become compact again, with facilities for working, living and shopping. New districts were built in Zuidoost, Nieuw-West and the Oostelijk Havengebied. Urban planners and architects made sure the developments kept a human scale, substituting monotony for imagination and experimentation. Amsterdam has got it again. The mass exodus to nearby areas has ended and the population is once again over 800,000.

❶ Expansion since 1950

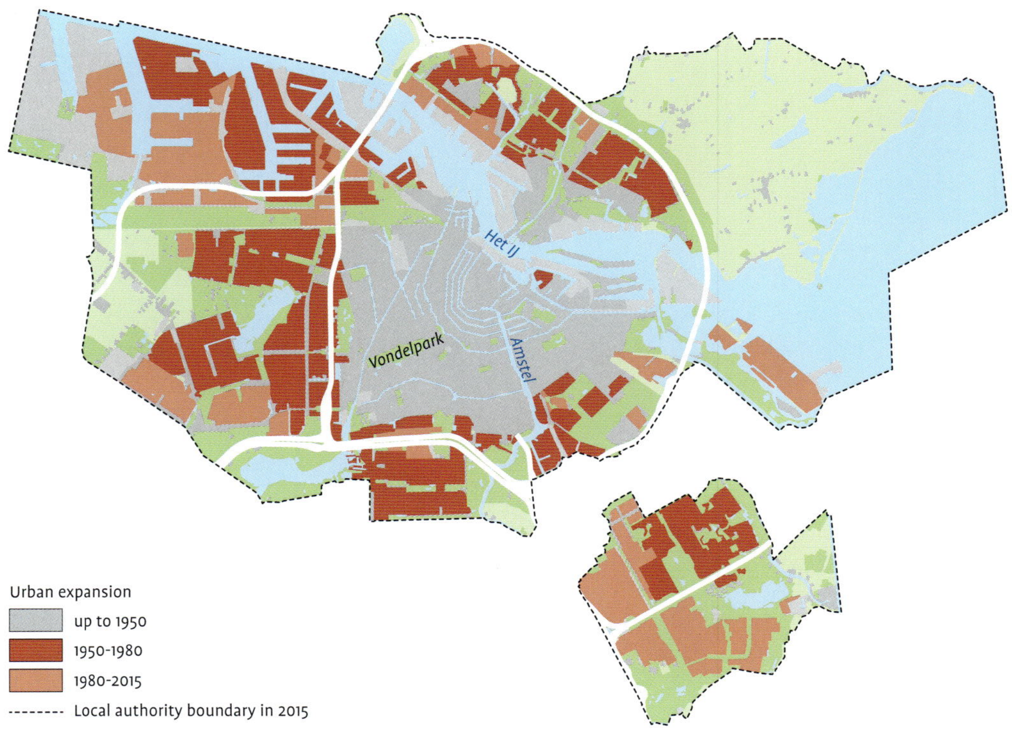

❷ IJburg

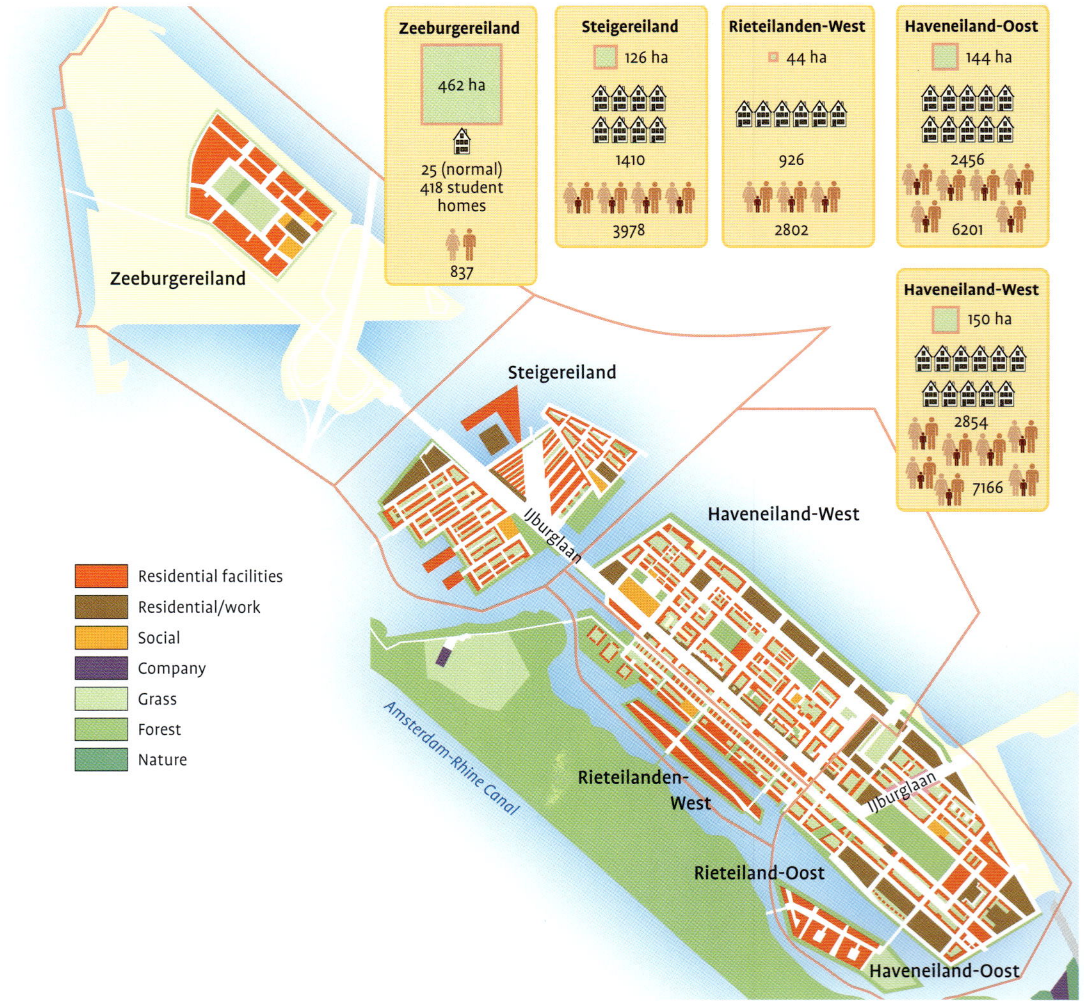

❶ Popular Amsterdam
From 1980, social housing construction was once again prioritised, partly thanks to the aldermen Jan Schaefer and Enneüs Heerma, who felt that Amsterdam should revert to being a city for living and working. That vision has come true. Between 1990 and 2015, the population rose from 702,000 to over 820,000 and the housing stock also increased substantially.

❷ Seven islands
In 2002, the first residents moved into their homes on IJburg, a combination of seven artificial islands. The Steigereiland, Haveneiland and Rieteilanden developments are now almost complete. The islands differ greatly. Social housing on Haveneiland accounts for nearly 50% of all homes, compared with just 13% on Rieteiland-West. Rieteiland-Oost, on the other hand, consists completely of DIY building plots for detached villas. Some 35% of the 20,000+ IJburg residents are aged under 18.

Sources: City of Amsterdam (1); Ruimtelijkeplannen.nl (2)

© Noordhoff Uitgevers

❸ - ❻ On the waiting list

Around 15,700 new homes were built between 2009 and 2014, most of them in the Nieuw-West and Oost areas. An impressive number, but not enough. About 44,000 Amsterdammers are on the waiting list for a home. On average, they wait 11 years, so Amsterdam still has a huge housing shortage. Although this is bad news, there is also an upside. It seems that Amsterdam is now a very attractive place to live, unlike in the 1960s and 1970s.

❼ The next step

Amsterdam has a very strong image and therefore exerts a magnetic attraction. That will not change for the time being. After all, the city has many trump cards up its sleeve, including a maritime port, Schiphol airport, Internet companies, financial institutions, museums, universities and colleges. Policymakers expect the city's housing stock to have to increase by at least 70,000 homes between now and 2040. However, space is at a premium in Amsterdam and citizens have become more assertive, demanding ever higher standards for their home and living environment. Basically, Amsterdam is facing an enormous challenge.

❸ Housing stock

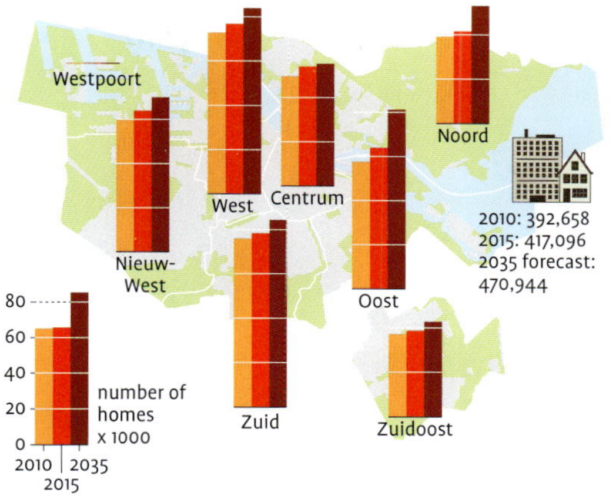

❹ Homeseekers

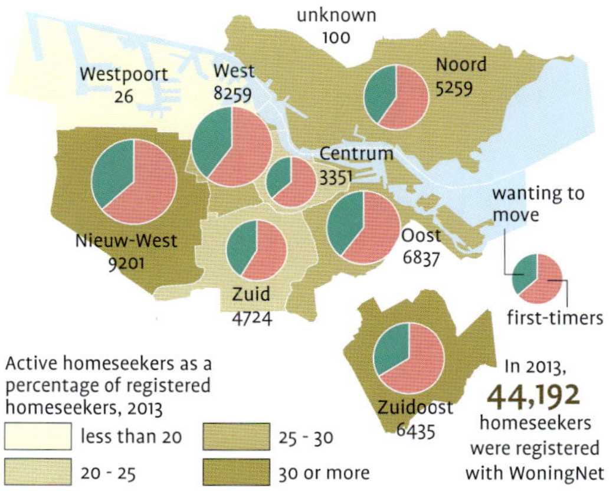

❺ Change in housing stock

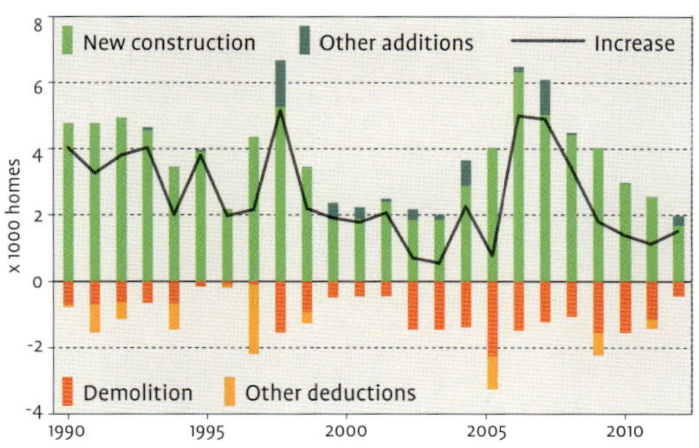

❻ Ownership of housing stock

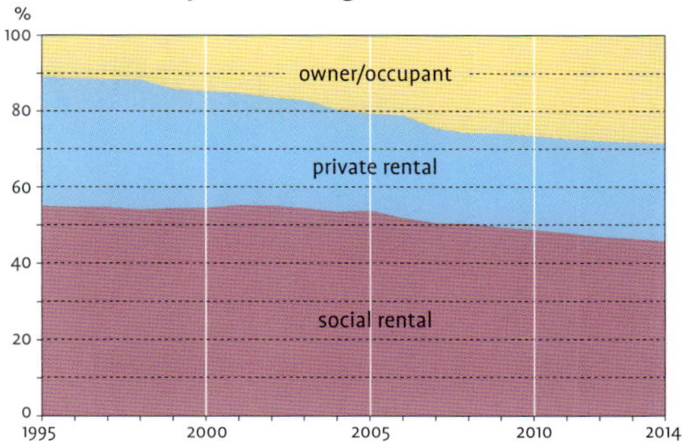

❼ Development plans up to 2030

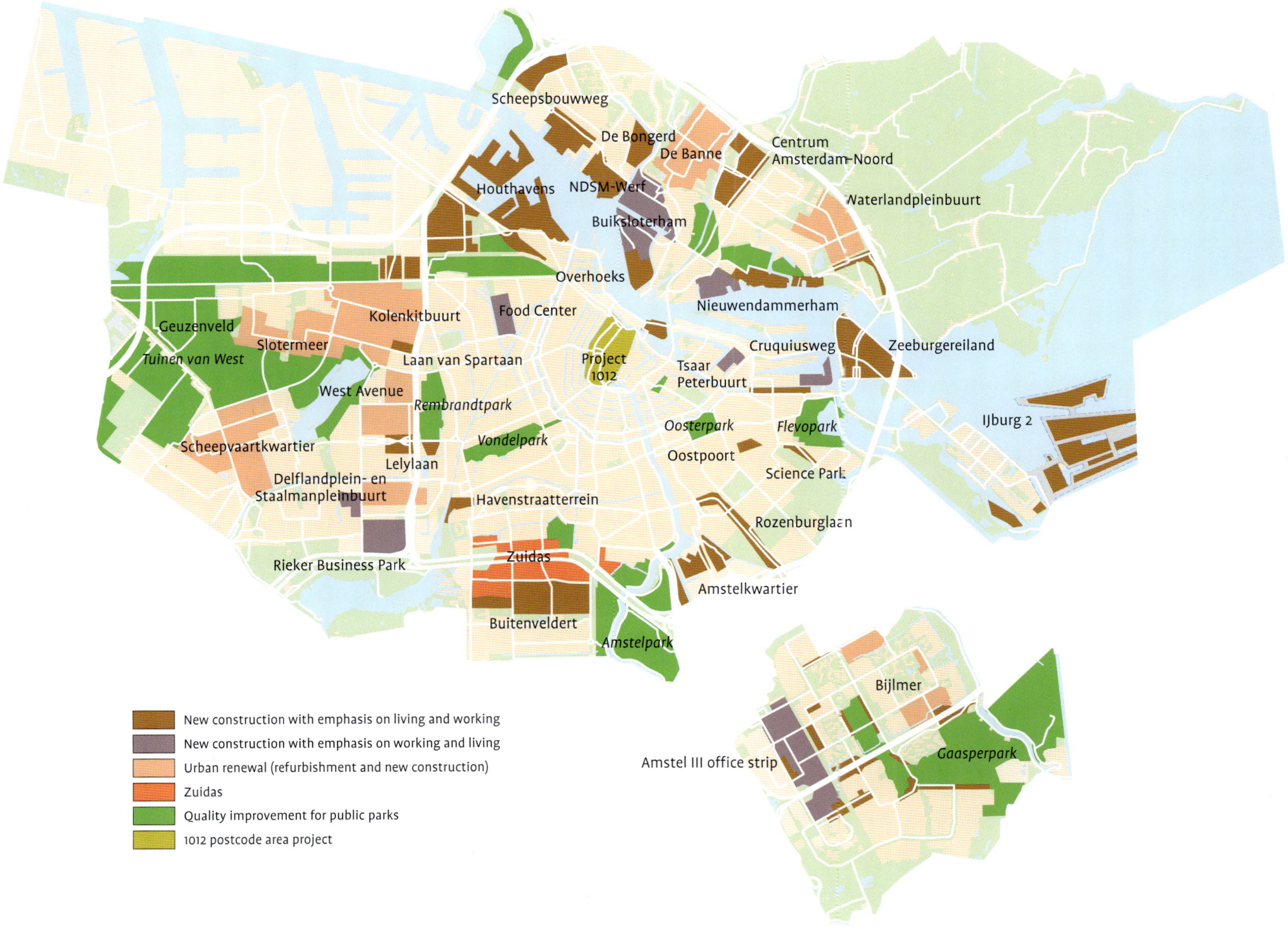

Sources: OIS, Research, Information and Statistics, City of Amsterdam (3-6); City of Amsterdam, Faseringsbeelden (7)

© Noordhoff Uitgevers

Amsterdam of yesteryear

❶ The old town hall
At a time when work on the new town hall was in full swing, a major fire razed the mediaeval town hall on the Dam to the ground in 1652. Even though many art treasures were lost, few people regretted the fire, since the town hall, a jumble of structures that had evolved over time, had already been earmarked for demolition. The two main parts were the tower, which was once crowned by a beautiful spire, but fell into disrepair and had to be demolished in 1616, and the Vierschaar tribunal. The council of four mayors, the true rulers of the city, used to meet in the tower, while the Vierschaar tribunal was where the city sheriff and aldermen used to pronounce death sentences. This painting by Jan Beerstraten shows the Vierschaar on the left-hand side. It had barred windows so the public could follow the court proceedings from the outside.

❷ The Weesperpoort
The city expansions of the 17th century made the late mediaeval city wall superfluous, so it was demolished and replaced with a 6-metre-wide moat (today's Singelgracht). A new city wall with 26 bastions and five major access gates was built around the extended periphery of the city. The four gates of the Vierde Uitleg expansion (Leidsepoort, Utrechtsepoort, Weesperpoort and Muiderpoort) were built in the 1660s, all using the same design so as to keep costs down. The Weesperpoort was demolished in 1885, with the Utrechtsepoort and Leidsepoort suffering the same fate soon after. Only the Muiderpoort was spared. Like the other gates, it had a large square for carts immediately on the inside, which was used for transferring goods transported from the outside in large carts to smaller means of transport. The square was surrounded by numerous livery stables, forges and inns. Leidseplein, Frederiksplein and Weesperplein still remind us today of these squares.

❸ The Goudsbloemgracht
Around 1850, Amsterdam's dignitaries realised that they had to do something about the appalling housing conditions of the poorer classes. Helping other people was a moral duty, but they were also motivated by their fear of disease, crime and rebellion. In 1852, a number of the dignitaries founded the 'Vereeniging ten behoeve der Arbeidersklasse', or Association for assisting the Working Classes, which started to buy plots of land along Goudsbloemgracht, a canal that was more or less an open sewer flanked on both sides by paths and a few rickety houses. It was reputed to be the most unhealthy area of the city. The residents hung around on the street all day, fought each other, spoke their own language and adhered to their own morals. In 1856-1857, the canal was filled in and renamed Willemsstraat after King William III, the association's patron. Over the next fifteen years, the association built new workers' homes on most of the land between Willemstraat and Palmstraat.

Photos: © Amsterdam Museum (1); © Rijksmuseum Amsterdam (2); © Amsterdam City Archives (3)

© Noordhoff Uitgevers

❹ The Paleis voor Volksvlijt

In 1851, Samuel Sarphati visited the Great Exhibition in London, which was held in the Crystal Palace, and he was deeply impressed by what he saw. In 1852, he founded the 'Vereeniging voor Volksvlijt', or Association for Public Industriousness, with the aim of furthering industry by exhibiting products made in the Netherlands. To this end, he built an industrial palace that was intended to rival the Crystal Palace. The Paleis voor Volksvlijt opened in 1864 on Frederiksplein. In 1881, an arcade housing luxurious boutiques was added on to the main building. Since it proved not financially viable to run the palace purely for exhibitions, the main exhibition hall was converted into a concert hall and theatre in 1890. During the night of 17 to 18 April 1929, the palace burned to the ground and only a small section of the arcade survived. In 1960, this remnant was demolished to make way for De Nederlandsche Bank's new building.

❺ Vlooienburg

During the Tweede Uitleg expansion in the late 16th century, the island of Vlooienburg was created in the Amstel river. It was surrounded by the Amstel, Zwanenburgwal, and the Leprozengracht and Houtgracht canals. Over the years, more and more Jewish Amsterdammers moved to Vlooienburg, so it ultimately became part of the 'Jodenbuurt' area. In 1882, the two canals were filled in and Waterlooplein was constructed. Immediately afterwards, the city council ordered the Jewish street traders operating on and around Jodenbreestraat to move their businesses to the new square. This marked the start of the Waterlooplein market, known to locals as the second-hand or flea market. Post-war Vlooienburg was abandoned and had been thoroughly looted. The first proposals for razing the area to the ground in order to build a new town hall date back to 1949. However, it would be years before the demolition teams could start work. The doors of the Stopera complex only opened in 1986.

❻ The Maupoleum

The construction of Burgemeester Tellegenhuis on Jodenbreestraat was part of the plan to demolish the run-down 'Jodenbuurt' area and make room for office buildings, the metro and a wide thoroughfare between the city's Centraal and Amstel railway stations. Architect Piet Zanstra's colossal, four-storey, almost 200-metre-long structure was completed in 1971. It was soon baptised Maupoleum, a combination of mausoleum and Maup (Caransa), the name of the real estate developer responsible for letting and managing the building. A few years later, after major protests by local residents, the city council abandoned the plan to demolish the neighbourhood and instead, rebuilt it as part of the urban renewal programme. As a result, Amsterdam was stuck with a building that had been designed for an environment that was never actually completed. Having been declared the ugliest building in the Netherlands, the Maupoleum was demolished in 1994.

Photos: © Rijksmuseum Amsterdam, Wegner & Mottu (4); © ANP Photo (5); © Amsterdam City Archives (6)

© Noordhoff Uitgevers

2

Amsterdammers

<
Museumplein
Photo Karel Tomeï

2 Introduction

A varied population
The inhabitants of a city are just as important as its streets, canals and buildings. Who are today's Amsterdammers?
That is not an easy question to answer as the population is hugely varied. For example, we find no less than 180 nationalities among the over 800,000 residents of the city. Around half are native, i.e. they have two Dutch parents, but even that group is not homogeneous – the differences in prosperity and lifestyle are considerable.

Growth
Amsterdam's population has certainly started to grow again in recent years. This is striking, because the city entered a phase of contraction in the 1960s when many young families moved to newly built residential areas in Purmerend, Hoorn, Diemen, Lelystad and Almere. The number of inhabitants dropped below 700,000 and the trend only reversed in 1985. The population of Amsterdam is expected to exceed 900,000 people in 2035 – more than ever before.

Young and single
Some 53% of today's Amsterdammers live alone (36% countrywide). This is partly due to the many students living in the city. They make Amsterdam one of the Netherlands' 'youngest' cities. After graduating, they generally stay on for several years until they find a good job elsewhere, or have their first child. New young people then come to the city in their place. Incidentally, Amsterdam has become more 'family-friendly' in recent years and the number of households with children is increasing.

Born and bred in Amsterdam
With all these moves, it is hardly surprising that less than half of the city's inhabitants (44%) were born and bred in Amsterdam. And even those who were born in the city no longer fit the stereotypical image of the working-class Amsterdammer, with a distinctive accent, rough humour and penchant for traditional pubs with Persian tablecloths. Many of today's born-and-bred Amsterdammers are in fact the children of immigrants

Museumplein
Many residents of Amsterdam do not think that Museumplein is a very nice place to socialise. Even so, it regularly takes on the role of an urban living room where all sorts of Amsterdammers get together. During political demonstrations, for example, or during cultural festivals like the Uitmarkt, or – in this case – the 2015 Keti Koti Festival, celebrating the abolition of slavery in 1863.

and live outside the ring road. The old working-class districts inside the ring road have become the domain of yuppies, hipsters, cargo-biking parents and self-employed professionals.

Today's Amsterdammer

So who is today's typical Amsterdammer? No longer just the prankster that loves singers like Tante Leen or René Froger, that much is clear. Today's Amsterdammer can just as easily have Moroccan, Surinamese, Ghanaian or Russian roots, or may even be a well-paid expat who will return to New York or New Delhi after spending a few years in Amsterdam. In any case, he or she is likely to be young and single, and to have been born elsewhere.

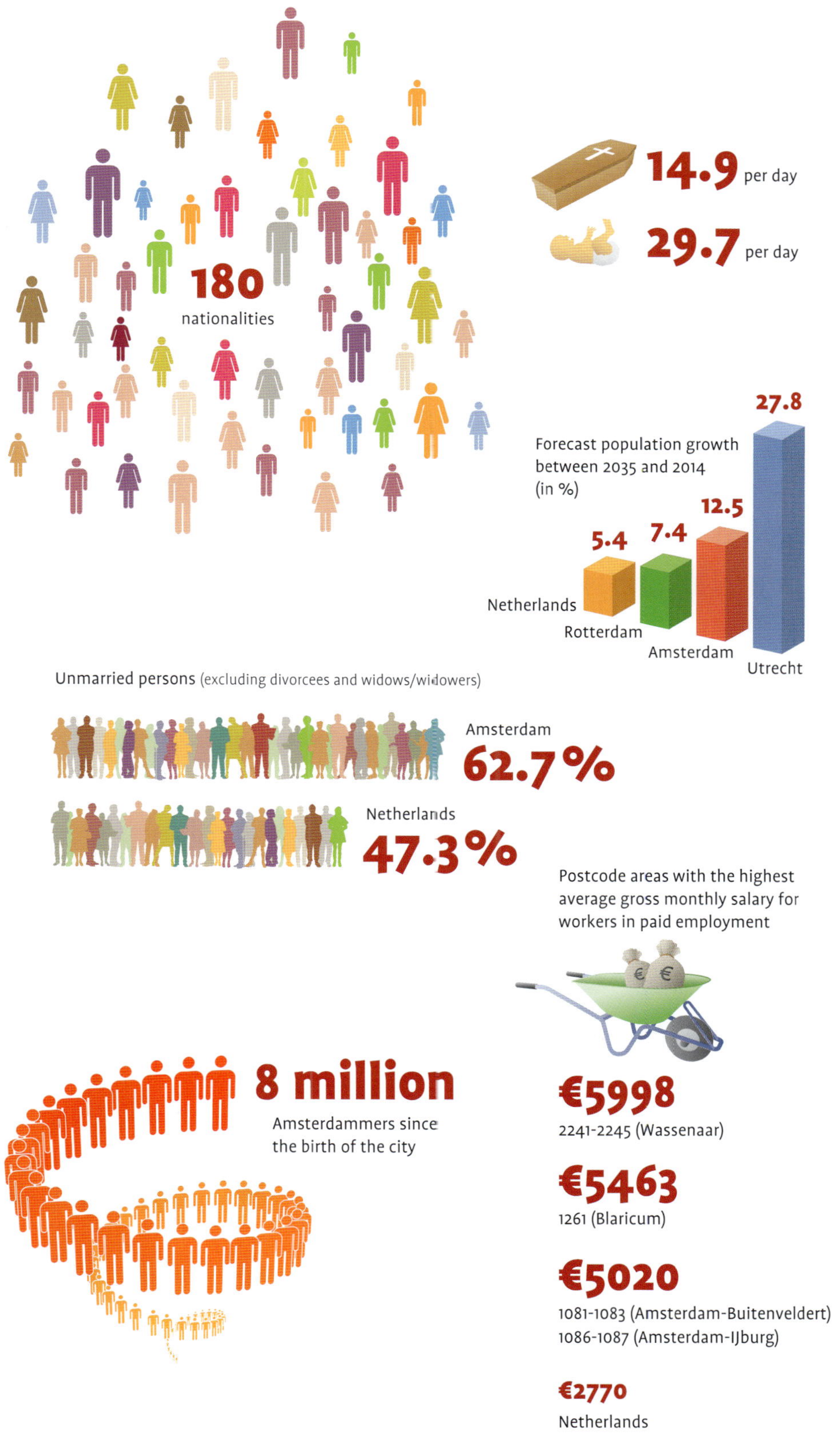

Sources: OIS, Research, Information and Statistics, City of Amsterdam; www.z24.nl

© Noordhoff Uitgevers

A growing population

City life is popular all over the world, and that is certainly also true of Amsterdam, the Dutch city with the most inhabitants. From 2008 to 2015, the city's population grew by 75,000 – more than during the baby boom just after World War Two. The current growth phase started in 1985 with the reunification of migrant workers with their families. This was followed by an influx of Surinamese and Ghanaians, and more recently, people from other European countries above all, once Europe's internal borders had been opened. Young people have always flocked to Amsterdam, to study for instance, but their numbers are growing. Even after studying elsewhere, Amsterdam is a good place to look for work, and has become a temporary home, where many people spend part of their lives before moving on. The population is highly diverse and international, with no single ethnic group forming a majority any longer.

❶ Population growth

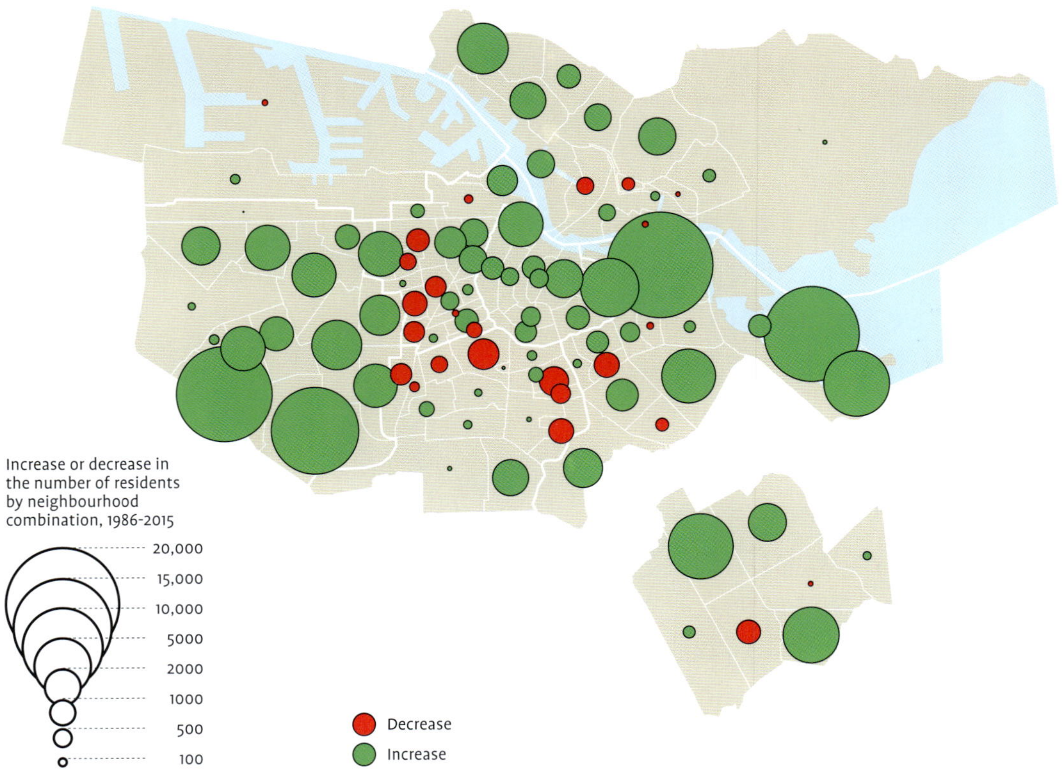

❶ Compact city

A policy change has enabled cities to grow again. The idea of the compact city first emerged in 1991. New homes were no longer built only in the growth concentrations outside the city, but also inside cities and on their peripheries. Amsterdam's IJburg is a good example of one such district, commonly known as a 'Vinex' district.

❷ Sustained growth?

The current phase of population growth was preceded by a period of contraction. From 1965 onwards, many tens of thousands of Amsterdammers left their small, barely adequate flats for newly constructed homes outside the city. Population growth started again in 1985 and shows a sustainable trend, even though it is slowing. The record of 872,000 inhabitants, which dates back to 1959, is set to be broken in 2020. However, Amsterdam's success in constructing enough homes is the main cause of uncertainty in this forecast. On top of that, we cannot be sure whether today's preference for an urban living environment, rather than the quiet and spaciousness of rural areas, will continue.

❷ Population development

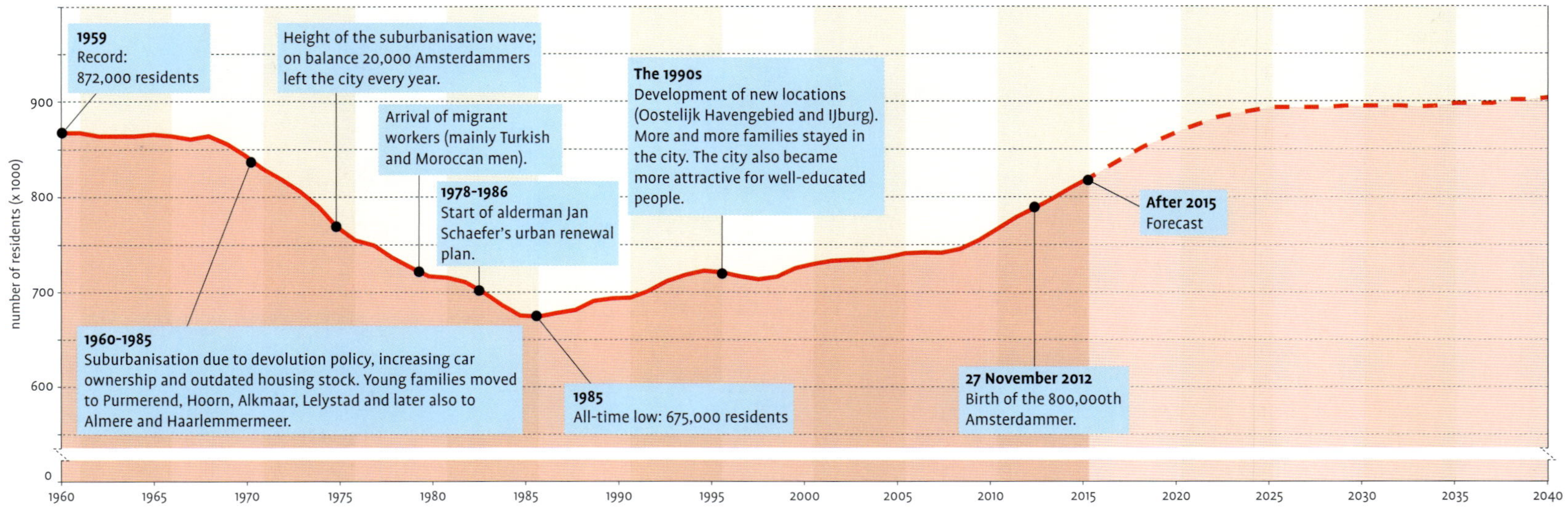

Source: OIS, Research, Information and Statistics, City of Amsterdam (1, 2)

© Noordhoff Uitgevers

❸ Young people

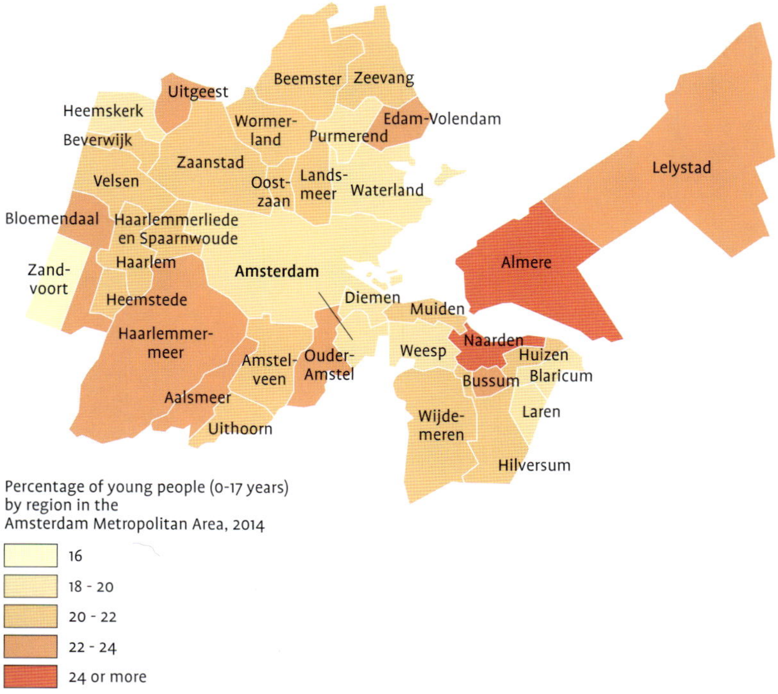

❹ Elderly people

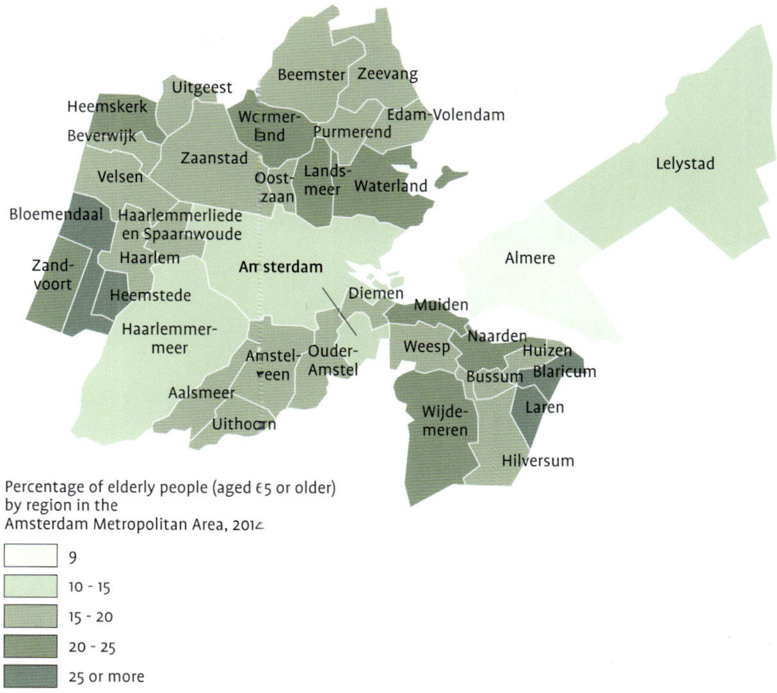

❸ Over eighteen

Although Amsterdam is a young city, relatively few children live there – people only come to the city once they are eighteen or older to study, find employment and look for a partner.

❹ Young and old

In the 1960s and 1970s, many young people moved away from Amsterdam. They are now growing old in the surrounding country areas. Their departure, together with the major influx of young people, means that population ageing is much slower in Amsterdam than in the Netherlands as a whole.

❺ Large city, small households

Cities have long been a good place for small households, as they have an ample supply of compact, affordable accommodation, with special facilities and plenty of places to socialise. However, the growth of small households in Amsterdam has come to a halt. The city has become attractive for families again and financial considerations force single people to share a home increasingly often.

❻ Room for everybody

Amsterdam is a tolerant city that is accepting of a range of different lifestyles. Specific groups find others of the same persuasion here, which explains why over a quarter of all same-sex marriage ceremonies take place in Amsterdam, even though this group accounts for less than 5% of the Dutch population.

There are more native Dutch women aged 18 to 24 years old in the city than there are men, and in Amsterdam-West the ratio is even 156 to 100. This is because girls outperform boys at school so there are more female students.

Average life expectancy in Amsterdam is one year shorter than in the rest of the Netherlands. This is partly due to lifestyle and living environment, combined with income and level of education. The difference is reducing rapidly due to the changing composition of the city's population.

❺ Single-person households

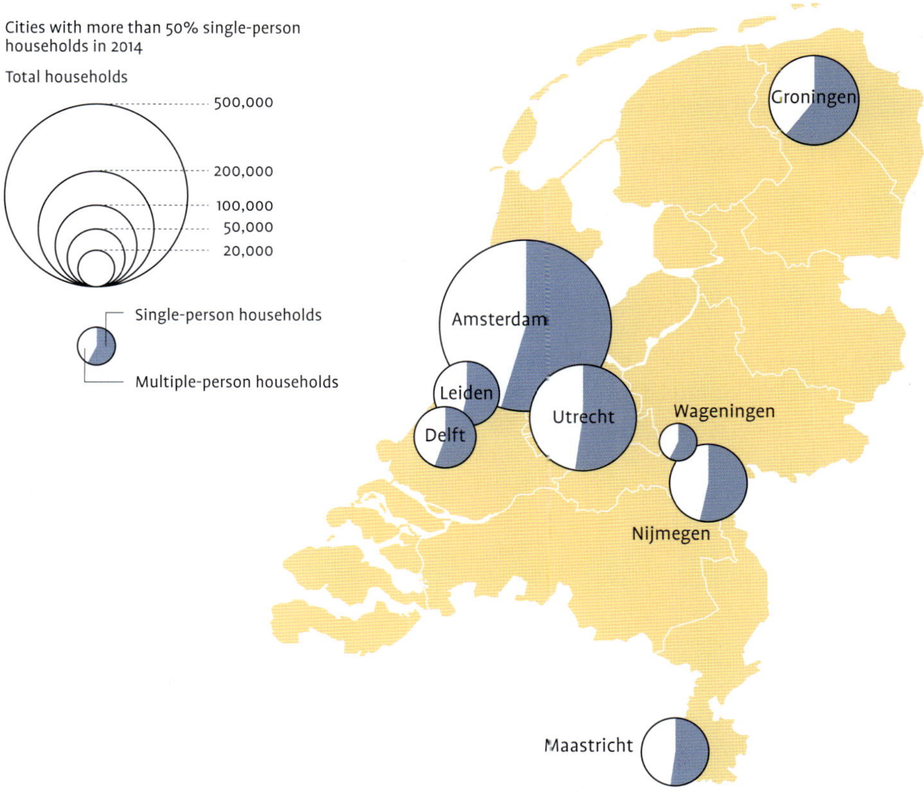

❻ Statistics on Amsterdam's population

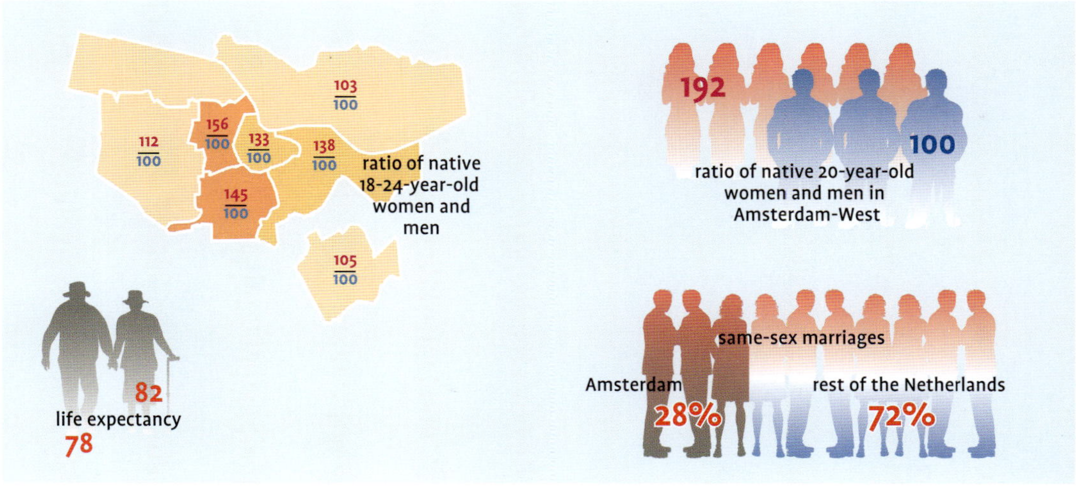

© Noordhoff Uitgevers

Born and bred in Amsterdam

Who do we actually class as Amsterdammers? Only people born in Amsterdam who have always lived there ? Or all residents? What about people in the city temporarily, like commuters, day trippers and tourists – do they count too? One thing we know for sure is that some eight million people have lived in the city since 1275, whether they were born there or not. Amsterdam has also become a city where people come and go, with few people living there all their lives. In this atlas, we have decided to class everybody who lives in Amsterdam as an 'Amsterdammer'.

❶ Born in Amsterdam

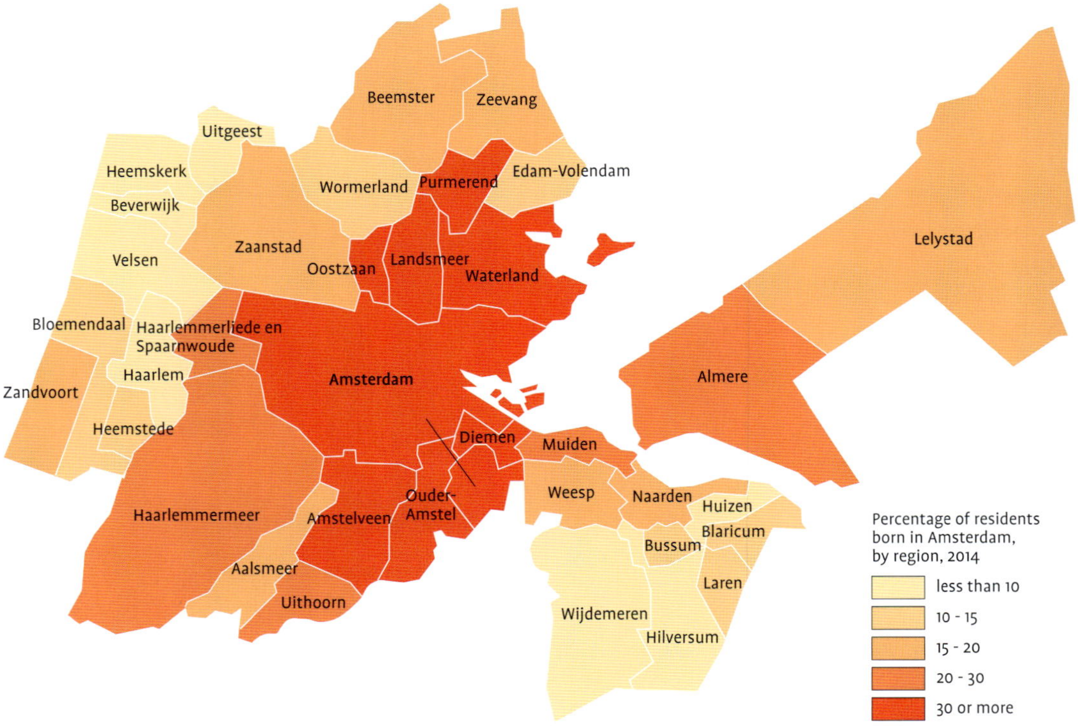

❶ Regional distribution
More people born in Amsterdam currently live in Landsmeer (52%) and Diemen (48%) than in the capital city itself (41%). This is a lot more than in Velsen, Beverwijk and Heemskerk (5%).

❷ Changing population structure
Native Amsterdammers were the largest group in the city up to the start of the 21st century, but their percentage has reduced rapidly in recent decades. However, this downward trend has levelled out since the 2008 economic crisis.
For a considerable time, population growth in Amsterdam was largely driven by what is now the largest group, the non-Western immigrants.

In recent years, native Dutch people born elsewhere in the Netherlands and Western immigrants have also contributed to growth.

❸ Distribution through the city
Nearly a quarter (23%) of all Amsterdammers were born in Amsterdam to two native parents. That figure is over 50% for some of Amsterdam-Noord's garden villages.
People moving to the city from elsewhere really want to live in the pre-war areas, but this is not always possible. Young people often start in Zuidoost and many families settle in IJburg. Non-Western immigrants born in Amsterdam generally grow up in the outer suburbs.

❷ Amsterdam's population by ethnic origin

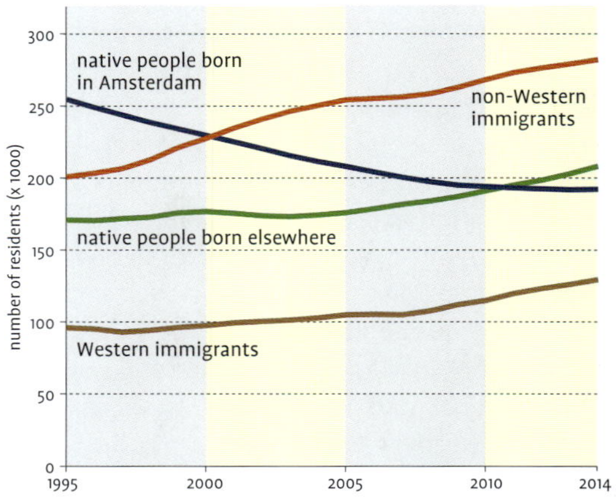

❸ Amsterdammers

Native and born in Amsterdam

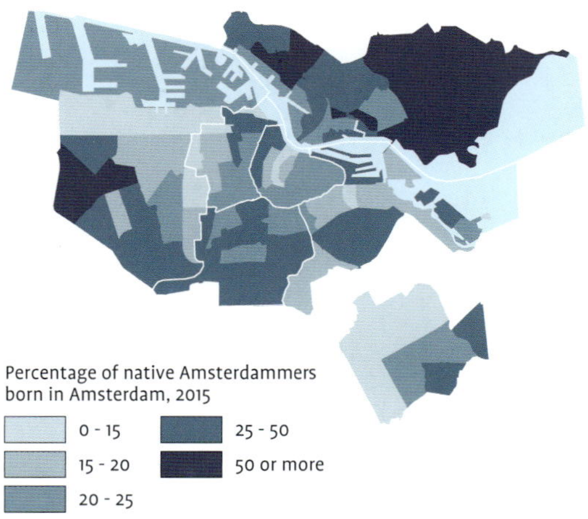

Born in the Netherlands, but outside Amsterdam

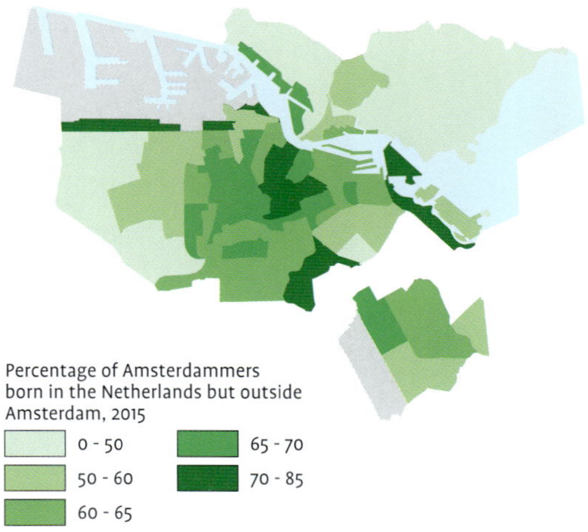

Second-generation non-Western immigrant

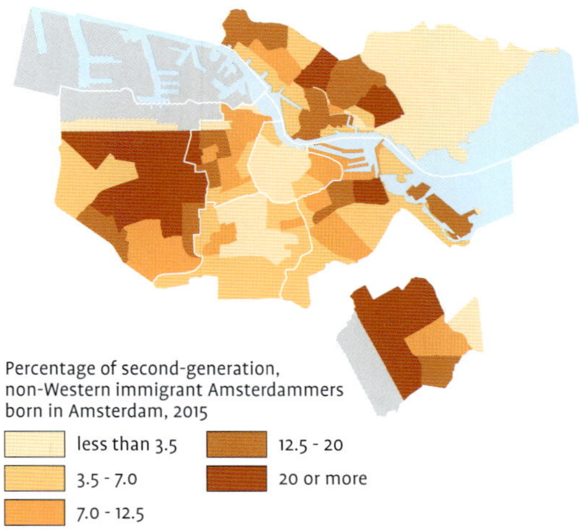

Sources: OIS, Research, Information and Statistics, City of Amsterdam (1, 3); www.nul20.nl / OIS, Research, Information and Statistics, City of Amsterdam (2)

© Noordhoff Uitgevers

❹ Great inhabitants of Amsterdam

Amsterdam has had an almost endless list of famous, notorious and remarkable residents during its over 700-year history. Many became famous in Amsterdam without being born there, while others, such as politician Willem Drees, were born in Amsterdam, but are hardly associated with the city. Baruch Spinoza, perhaps the most quoted son of Amsterdam, did not live there all his life.

By no means all of these Amsterdammers have been of specific importance for the city, but those who have include administrators (Witsen, Den Tex, De Vlugt, Lammers), architects (Berlage, De Klerk, Merkelbach), people who improved living conditions in the city (Van Lennep, Ter Meulen, Went) and entrepreneurs (Asscher). Samuel Sarphati is without a doubt the most impressive Amsterdammer in this category, leaving his mark on the city in a way emulated by few others. He was responsible for putting an end to the self-centredness that was so commonplace in Amsterdam in the 19th century and his numerous initiatives greatly improved the living conditions of the largely impoverished city population. The 'Paleis voor Volksvlijt', a building constructed on Sarphati's initiative, burned to the ground in 1929.

❺ From Gijs to Hailey

Nowadays, new-born children are by no means always given a traditional name. Names go in and out of fashion, and popular artists and leading sportsmen and women have a major influence on the choice of names for new babies. However, social and cultural differences have an impact too, with parents in Zuid choosing different names to those in Noord or Zuidoost.

❻ City slang

Language creates identity and distinctively characterises groups of people, neighbourhoods or cities. The 'nozems' (the Dutch equivalent of the Teddy Boys), people from the Jordaan area, dock workers, migrants and, last but not least, the large pre-war Jewish community have enriched the Dutch language with words typical of Amsterdam. Modern rappers continue this tradition with street-slang terms such as *fittie* (argument) and *fatoe* (joke).

❹ Famous people born in Amsterdam after whom a street has been named

❺ Most common names given to new-born Amsterdammers

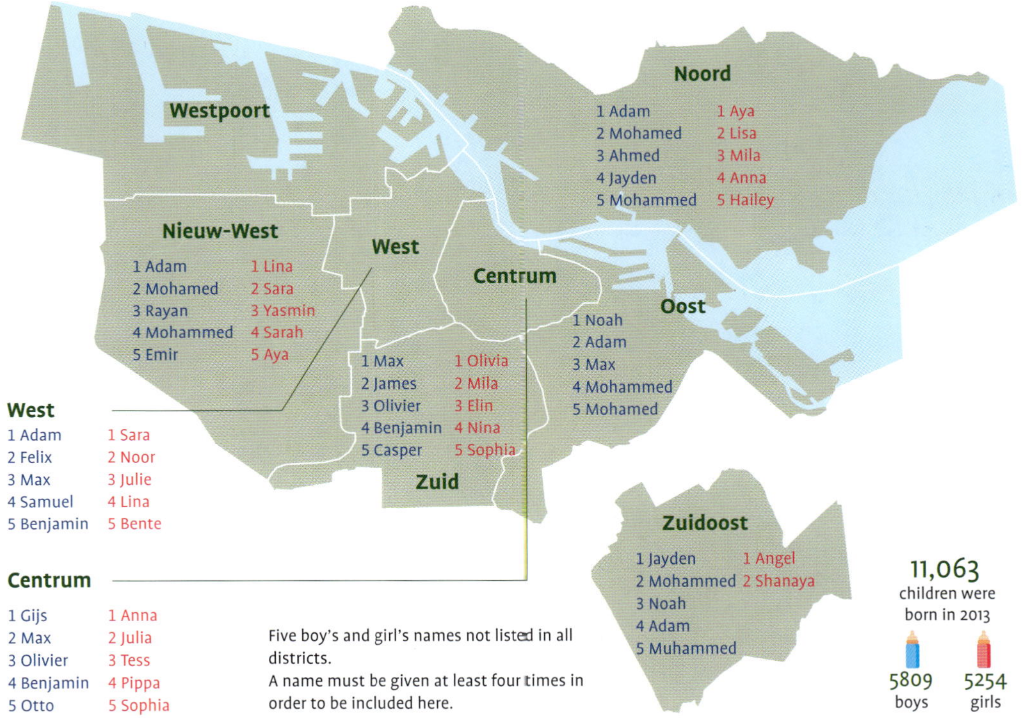

Five boy's and girl's names not listed in all districts.
A name must be given at least four times in order to be included here.

❻ Typical Mokum slang

Sources: *Sociale Verzekeringsbank / Statistics Netherlands (5); www.mokums.nl (6)*

© Noordhoff Uitgevers

Multicultural Amsterdam

Amsterdam has always had a high migrant population and tens of thousands of migrants came to the city after the conquest of Antwerp in 1585, bring along knowledge and capital in their quest for (economic) freedom. Even today, many Amsterdammers are descended from migrants. Making up around 35% of the population, the non-Western migrants are or are the children of people from the former colonies, migrant workers from the Mediterranean, refugees and newer migrant groups such as the Ghanaian Amsterdammers. The Western migrants mainly come from neighbouring countries and, following expansion of the European Union, from Eastern and Central Europe. Migrants often create and use their own facilities, such as shops and churches, just like in former times. Many Jewish Amsterdammers lived near their synagogues and the French Protestants built their own Walloon churches.

❶ Ethnic origin by neighbourhood

Native Amsterdammers

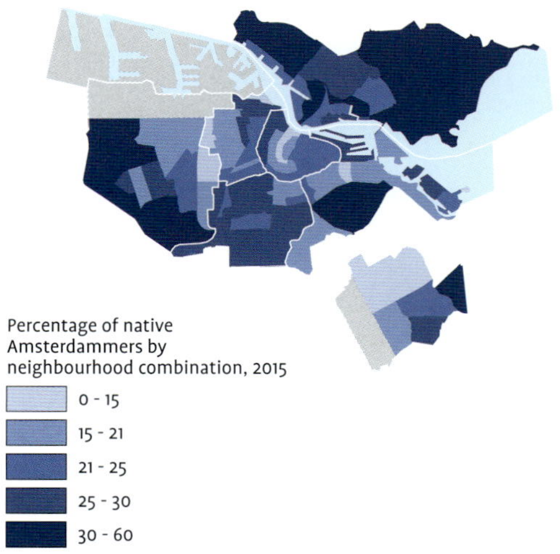

Amsterdammers with a Western immigrant background

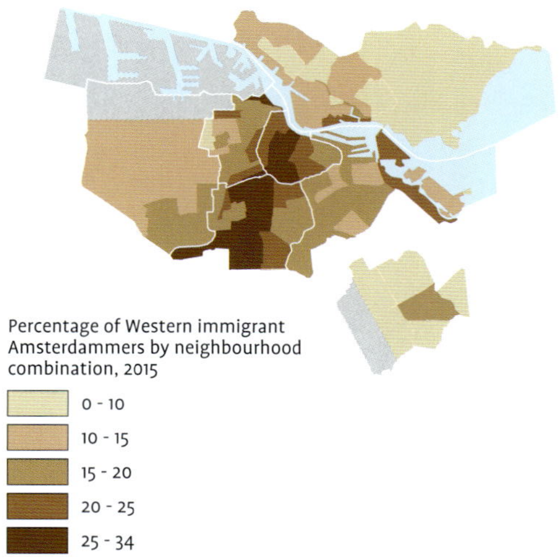

Surinamese and Antillean Amsterdammers

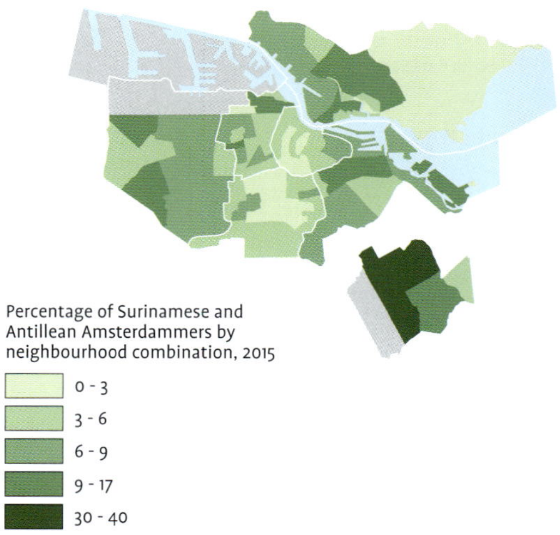

Moroccan Amsterdammers

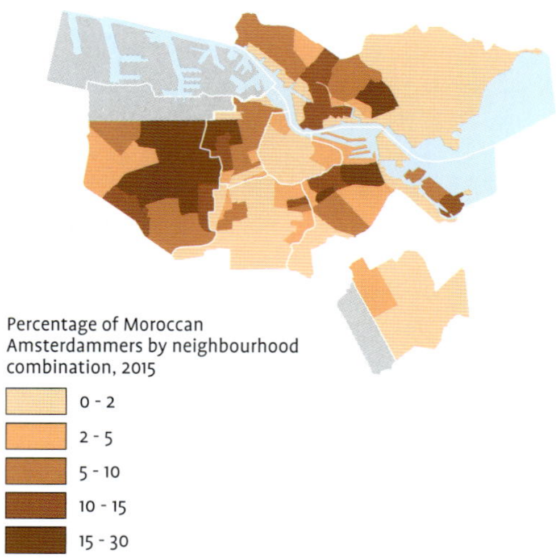

Turkish Amsterdammers

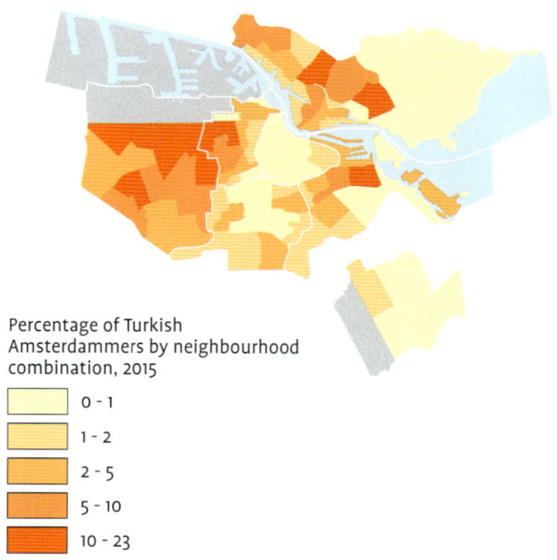

Ghanaian Amsterdammers

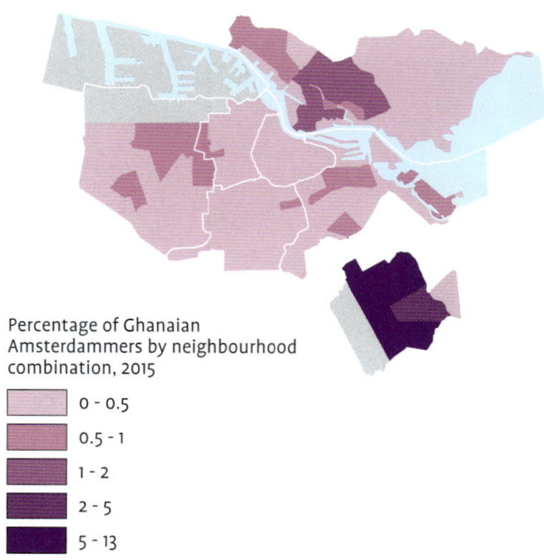

❶ Population group distribution

The location to which population groups gravitate in the city is determined by the time when they arrive, their motives and ambitions and, obviously, their financial resources. For example, the Oostelijk Havengebied and the Watergraafsmeer areas are attractive for young, well-educated, double-income families, while Western migrants prefer the Centrum and Zuid districts, because they can afford the to buy or rent one of the private-sector homes there. The three large non-Western migrant groups are generally reliant on the extensive social rented housing sector. New migrant groups on a low income often start in areas that are not so popular, such as the Ghanaian community in Zuidoost.

Source: OIS, Research, Information and Statistics, City of Amsterdam (1)

© Noordhoff Uitgevers

❷ Chinatown – a microcosm in Amsterdam

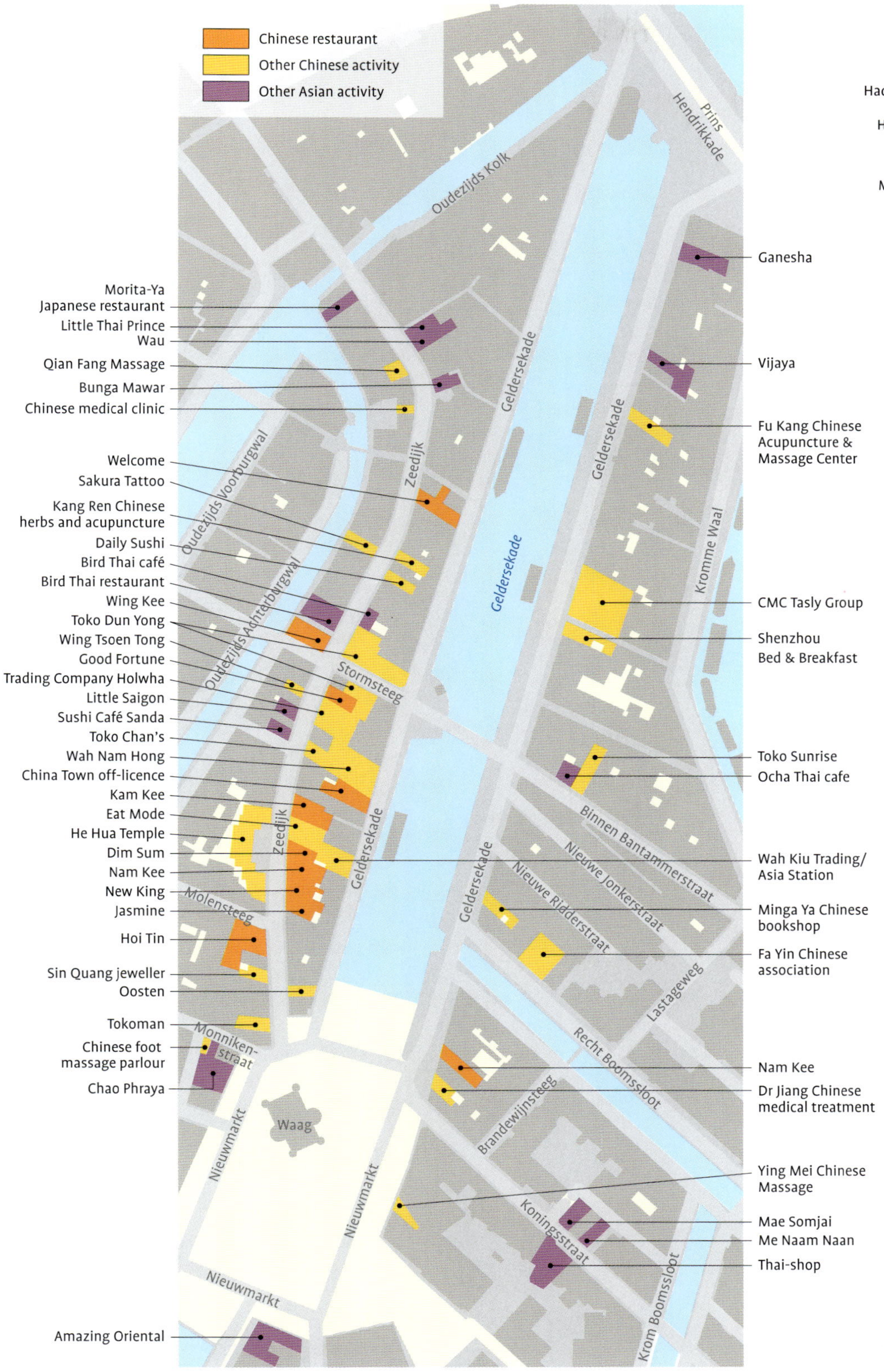

❸ Hustle and bustle on Javastraat

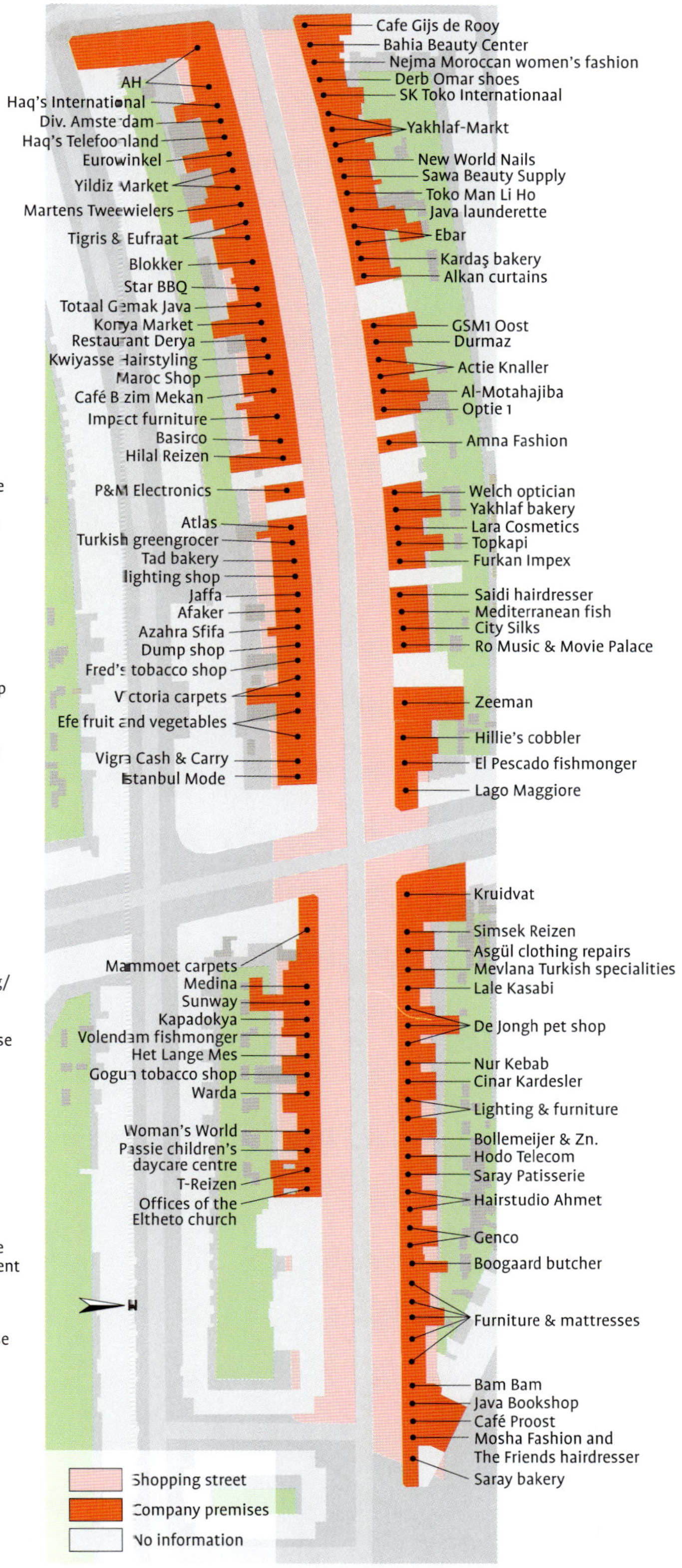

❷ Chinatown

The first Chinese came to Amsterdam on sea-going ships just before World War One and stayed in the city, either by choice or because that same war prevented them from returning home. They lived around Geldersekade and Zeedijk, where a Chinatown eventually emerged, with well-known restaurants such as Nam Kee. Thai and Japanese entrepreneurs also settled in this area later on. These days, numerous Chinese companies also operate in the Zuidas area.

❸ Javastraat

Service providers based in the 19th-century ring cater to specific groups and niches. Amsterdam-Oost's Javastraat is home to specialist hairdressers, Indian bridal wear shops, meat and fish specialists, restaurants and Asian grocers, alongside familiar Dutch brands such as Albert Heijn, Blokker and Zeeman.

❹ Growing diversity

As the diversity of the city's population increases, so too does the number of mixed marriages. One in five of the native population marries someone with at least one parent born outside the Netherlands. Mixed marriages are still extremely rare in the Turkish and Moroccan communities, where it is customary to marry someone from the home country. Within the relatively small group of Antillean Amsterdammers, mixed marriages are the rule rather than the exception.

❹ Mixed marriages

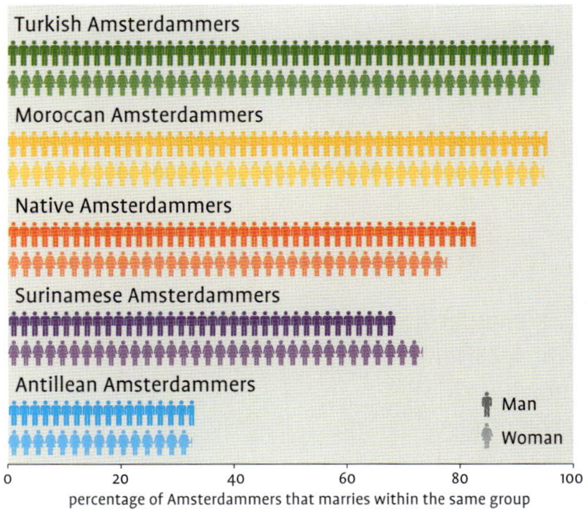

Source: OIS, Research, Information and Statistics, City of Amsterdam (2, 3, 4)

© Noordhoff Uitgevers

Ethnic origin of the people of

There are almost as many different nationalities in Amsterdam as there are countries in the world — one or more Amsterdammers come from 180 of the 196 official countries.

Of the 811,185* Amsterdammers, one third holds a foreign nationality, including those with dual nationality

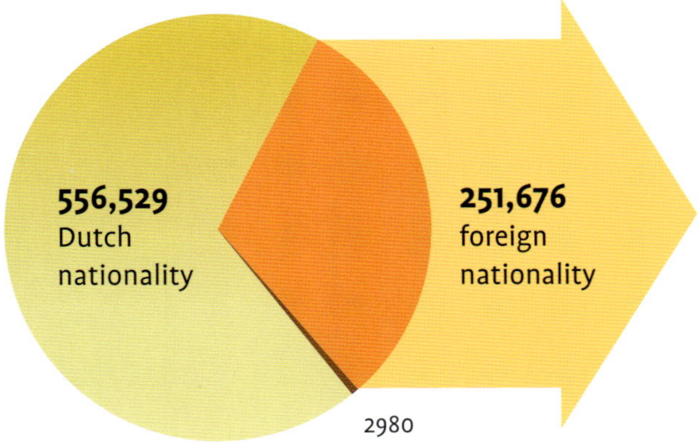

** Reference year 2014*

Top 20 nationalities

1	Morocco	72,251
2	Turkey	41,392
3	UK	12,012
4	Germany	9089
5	Italy	6981
6	Ghana	6636
7	USA	6509
8	France	6037
9	Suriname	5437
10	Spain	5283
11	Egypt	4694
12	Poland	3668
13	Portugal	3408
14	Pakistan	3179
15	Bulgaria	2958
16	Belgium	2637
17	India	2487
18	China	2374
19	Iran	2232
20	Romania	2116

Dual nationality

Of the people with a foreign nationality, 148,688 hold both the Dutch and a foreign nationality.

1	Moroccan-Dutch	60,749
2	Turkish-Dutch	31,775
3	Surinamese-Dutch	4129
4	British-Dutch	4020
5	Egyptian-Dutch	3970
6	Ghanaian-Dutch	3669
7	German-Dutch	2857
8	Pakistani-Dutch	2412
9	French-Dutch	2189
10	American-Dutch	2181
	People with more than two passports	4099

Migration and growth of the city

5000 BC to 1000 AD
Small settlements. The archaeological finds are 4600 years old and include finds from the Roman era.

Starting in the year 1000, the areas surrounding the mouth of the river Amstel were cleared little by little. The number of residents increased slightly.

Trade in wood and grain over the Baltic Sea flourished fro the 14th century onwards. There were extensive contacts with people from Latvia, Estonia, Lithuania, Poland, Germany and Denmark.

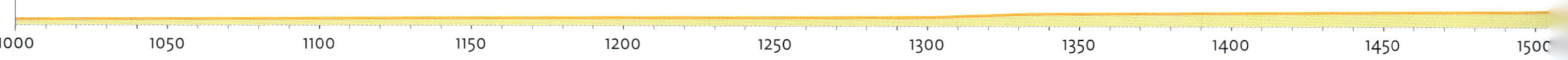

Sources: OIS, Research, Information and Statistics, City of Amsterdam / E. Kuijpers, Migrantenstad: immigratie en sociale verhoudingen in 17e-eeuws Amsterdam

Amsterdam

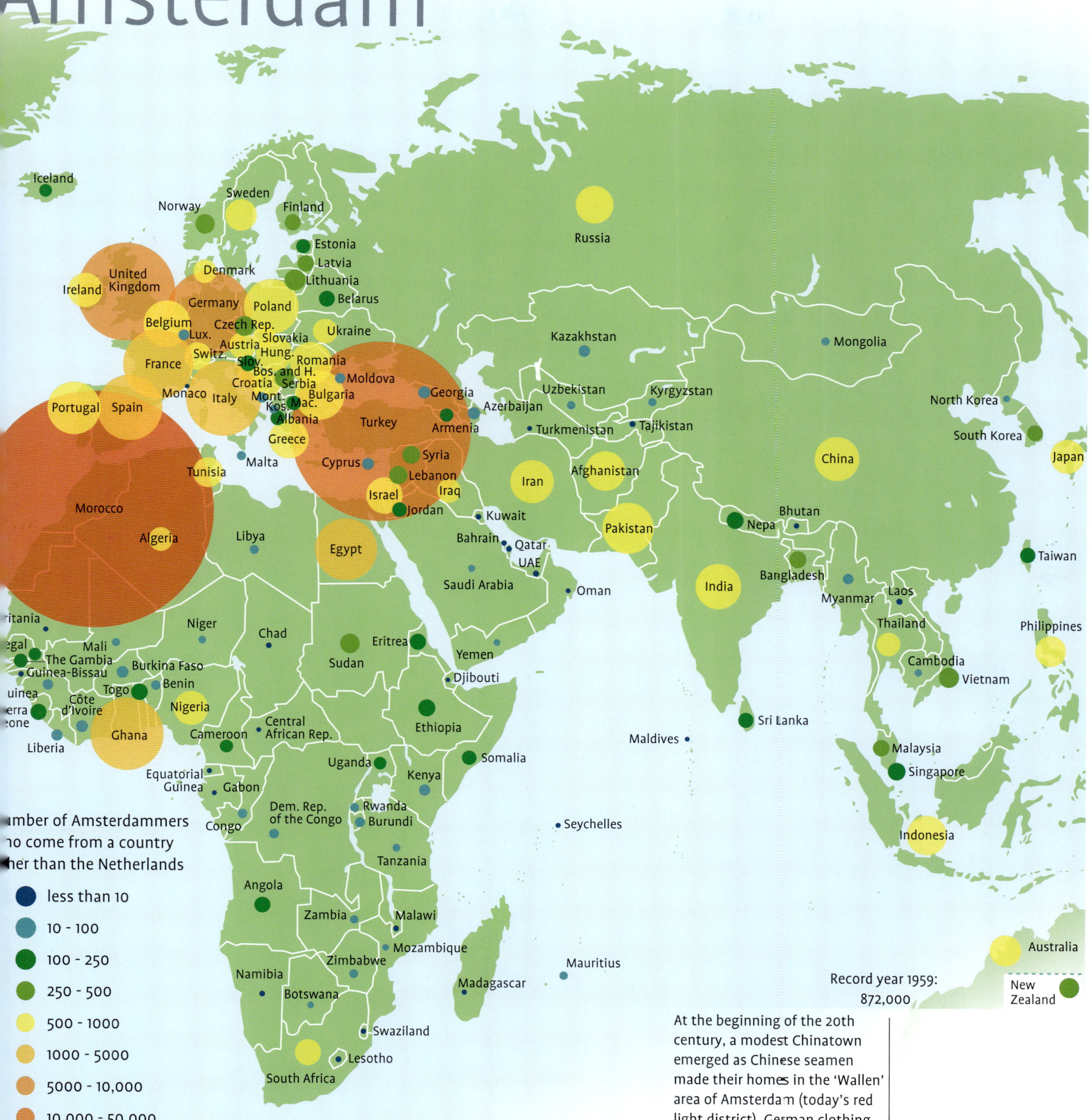
Iceland
Norway
Sweden
Finland
Estonia
Latvia
Lithuania
Belarus
Russia
Denmark
Ireland
United Kingdom
Germany
Poland
Belgium
Lux.
Czech Rep.
Slovakia
Ukraine
France
Switz.
Austria
Hung.
Slov.
Romania
Moldova
Croatia
Bos. and H.
Serbia
Monaco
Italy
Mont.
Kos.
Mac.
Bulgaria
Albania
Greece
Portugal
Spain
Turkey
Georgia
Armenia
Azerbaijan
Malta
Tunisia
Cyprus
Syria
Lebanon
Israel
Iraq
Jordan
Morocco
Algeria
Libya
Egypt
Kuwait
Bahrain
Qatar
UAE
Saudi Arabia
Oman
Kazakhstan
Uzbekistan
Kyrgyzstan
Turkmenistan
Tajikistan
Mongolia
North Korea
South Korea
Japan
China
Iran
Afghanistan
Pakistan
Nepal
Bhutan
India
Bangladesh
Myanmar
Laos
Taiwan
Thailand
Philippines
Cambodia
Vietnam
Sri Lanka
Maldives
Malaysia
Singapore
Indonesia
Seychelles
Mauritius
Australia
New Zealand
Record year 1959: 872,000
Mali
Niger
Chad
The Gambia
Guinea-Bissau
Burkina Faso
Benin
Togo
Côte d'Ivoire
Liberia
Ghana
Nigeria
Cameroon
Central African Rep.
Sudan
Eritrea
Yemen
Djibouti
Ethiopia
Somalia
Uganda
Kenya
Equatorial Guinea
Gabon
Congo
Dem. Rep. of the Congo
Rwanda
Burundi
Tanzania
Angola
Zambia
Malawi
Mozambique
Zimbabwe
Namibia
Botswana
Madagascar
Swaziland
Lesotho
South Africa
umber of Amsterdammers
10 come from a country
her than the Netherlands
less than 10
10 - 100
100 - 250
250 - 500
500 - 1000
1000 - 5000
5000 - 10,000
10,000 - 50,000
50,000 - 100,000

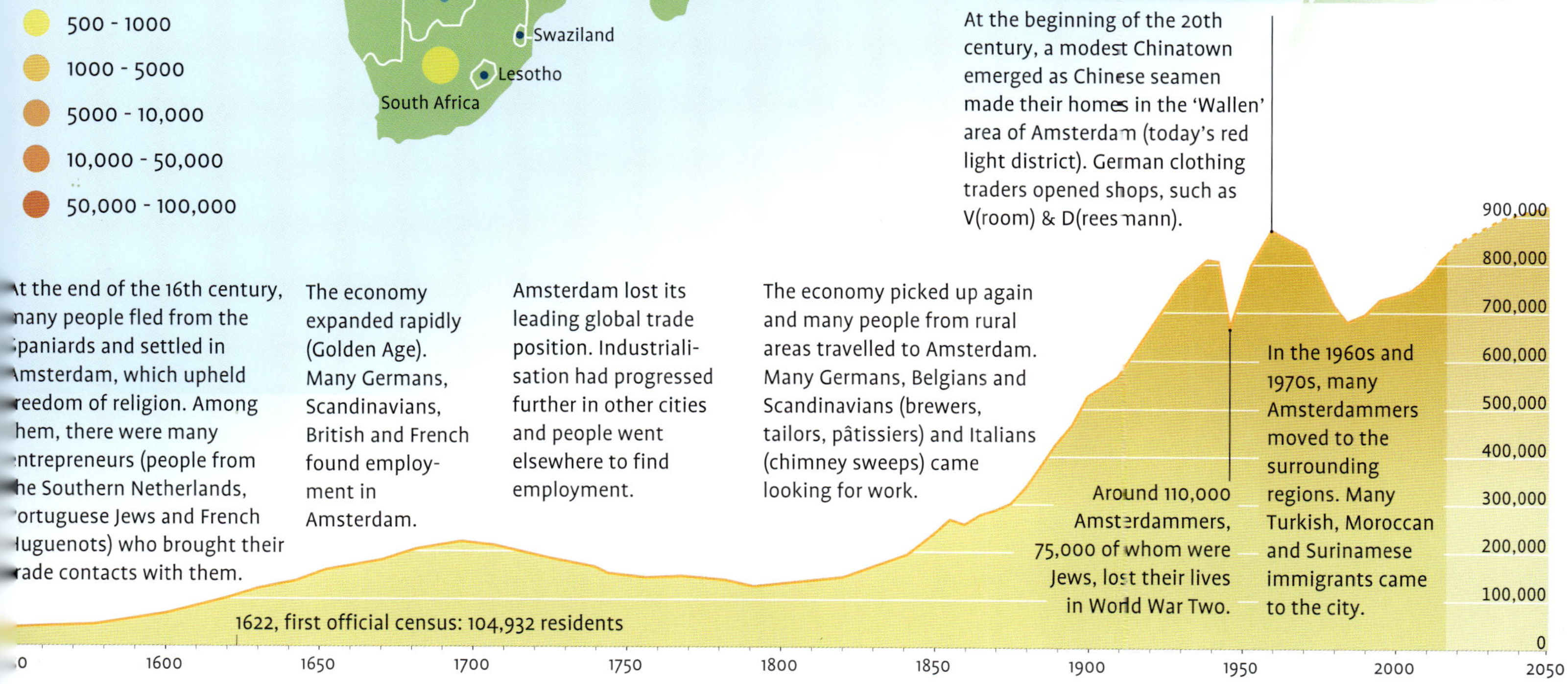
At the beginning of the 20th century, a modest Chinatown emerged as Chinese seamen made their homes in the 'Wallen' area of Amsterdam (today's red light district). German clothing traders opened shops, such as V(room) & D(reesmann).
At the end of the 16th century, many people fled from the Spaniards and settled in Amsterdam, which upheld freedom of religion. Among them, there were many entrepreneurs (people from the Southern Netherlands, Portuguese Jews and French Huguenots) who brought their trade contacts with them.
The economy expanded rapidly (Golden Age). Many Germans, Scandinavians, British and French found employment in Amsterdam.
Amsterdam lost its leading global trade position. Industrialisation had progressed further in other cities and people went elsewhere to find employment.
The economy picked up again and many people from rural areas travelled to Amsterdam. Many Germans, Belgians and Scandinavians (brewers, tailors, pâtissiers) and Italians (chimney sweeps) came looking for work.
Around 110,000 Amsterdammers, 75,000 of whom were Jews, lost their lives in World War Two.
In the 1960s and 1970s, many Amsterdammers moved to the surrounding regions. Many Turkish, Moroccan and Surinamese immigrants came to the city.
1622, first official census: 104,932 residents
900,000
800,000
700,000
600,000
500,000
400,000
300,000
200,000
100,000
0
1600
1650
1700
1750
1800
1850
1900
1950
2000
2050

© Noordhoff Uitgevers

The ties with Suriname

In 1683, Amsterdam obtained a third of the shares in Suriname. This South American colony and Amsterdam have had close ties ever since.

Until 1795, Amsterdam remained a colonial power in Suriname, earning a fortune from the plantations and slave trade. Many canal-side properties, including the current official residence of the Mayor of Amsterdam, were built or occupied using funds obtained from the activities in Suriname.

Before World War Two, there were less than one thousand Surinamese living in the Netherlands, many of them students or artists. The flow of migrants grew steadily after the war.

By the late 20th century, Surinamese people made up nearly 10% of the population of Amsterdam. This is evident in the many restaurants, the street slang, the interest in the history of slavery and the statue of resistance fighter Anton de Kom. Various Surinamese Amsterdammers have also earned respect and acclaim in sport, culture and society.

❶ Plantations owned by residents of Amsterdam in 1863

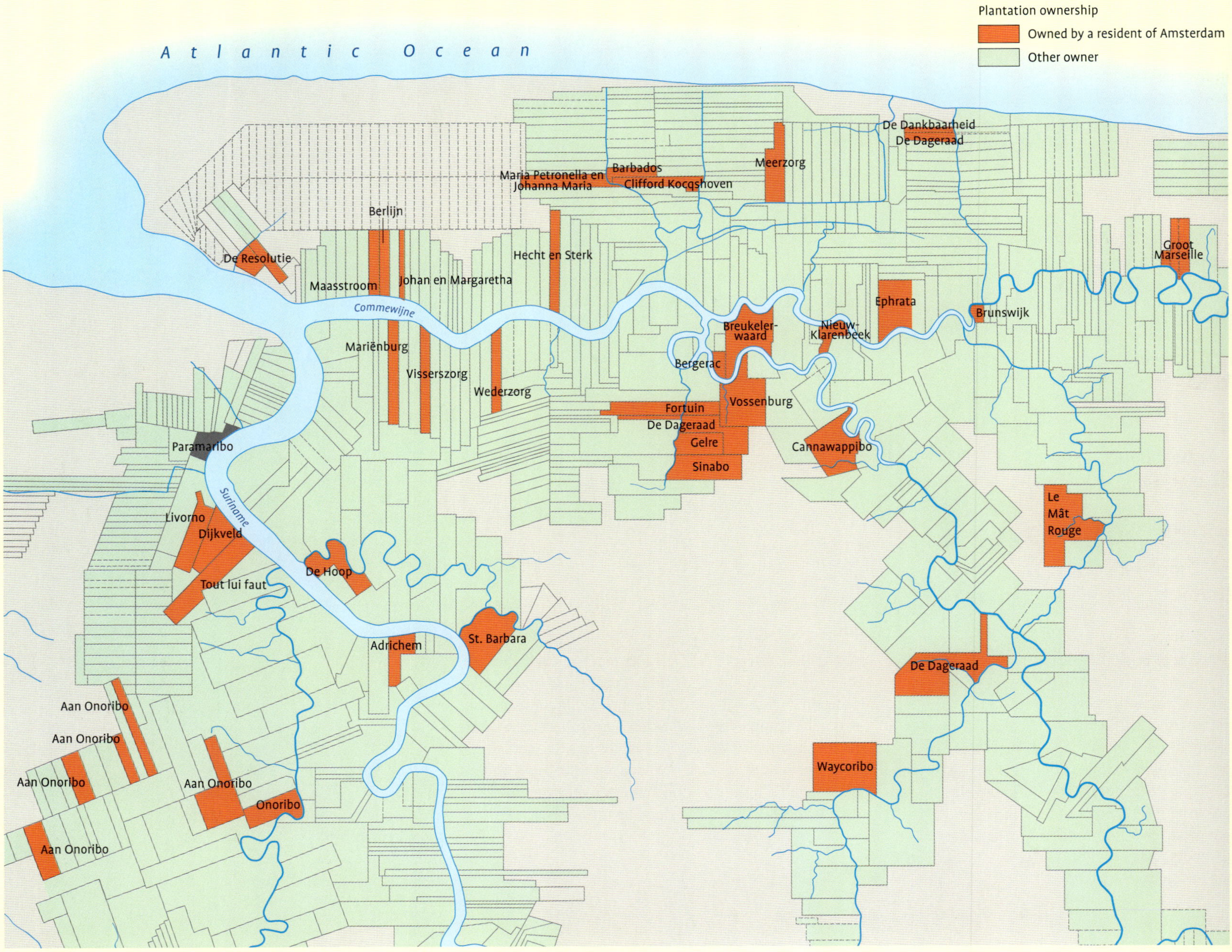

Sources: *University of Amsterdam / Koninklijk Instituut voor de Tropen / D. Hondius, VU University Amsterdam / National Archives of the Netherlands / Amsterdam City Archives*

© Noordhoff Uitgevers

❶ Amsterdam's plantations
On 1 July 1863, some 35,000 people were freed from slavery in Suriname. In return, they were expected to carry on working on the plantations for very modest payment for the next ten years.

❷ Two peaks
Suriname was declared independent in 1974, triggering a strong wave of migration. Desi Bouterse's coup d'etat in 1980 once again resulted in an exodus to the Netherlands. Today, around 40% of all Surinamese live in the Netherlands, approximately 350,000 people.

❸ - ❹ An attractive alternative
In the early 1970s, there were plenty of large and affordable homes in the Bijlmermeer area, so a lot of migrants moved there. Later on, Almere became an attractive alternative for them and many other Amsterdammers. Today, slightly more Surinamese still move from Amsterdam to Almere than vice versa, but the differences are not as great as in the past.

❺ - ❽ Surinamese groups
All of the population groups in Suriname are pretty much equally represented in the flow of migrants that came to the Netherlands, but they are not distributed equally across the country. For example, 60% of the Surinamese in Amsterdam are Creoles, as opposed to only 13% in The Hague. In The Hague, three quarters are Indo-Surinamese compared to only a quarter in Amsterdam.

❷ Migration between Suriname and the Netherlands

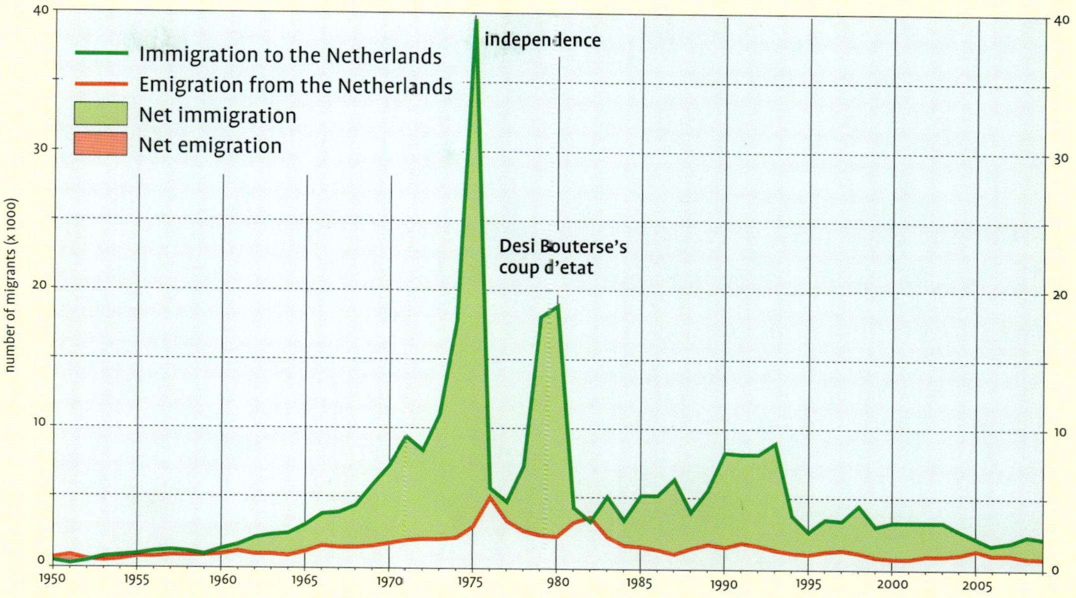

❸ Surinamese in Amsterdam and Almere

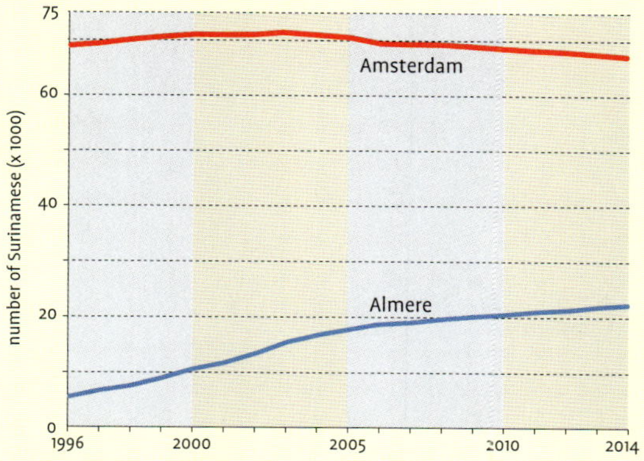

❹ Surinamese migration: Amsterdam-Almere

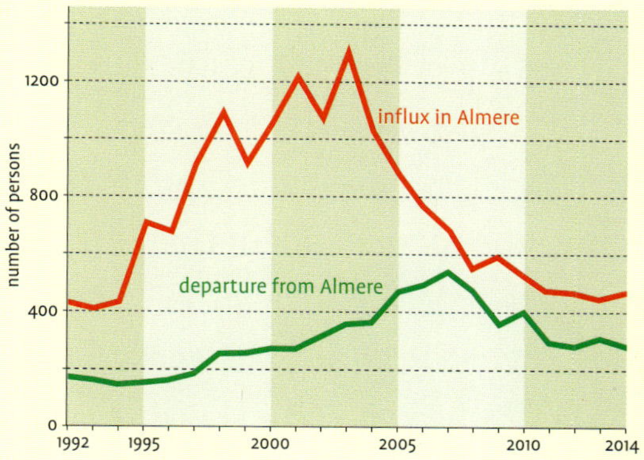

❺ Surinamese population groups in the major cities

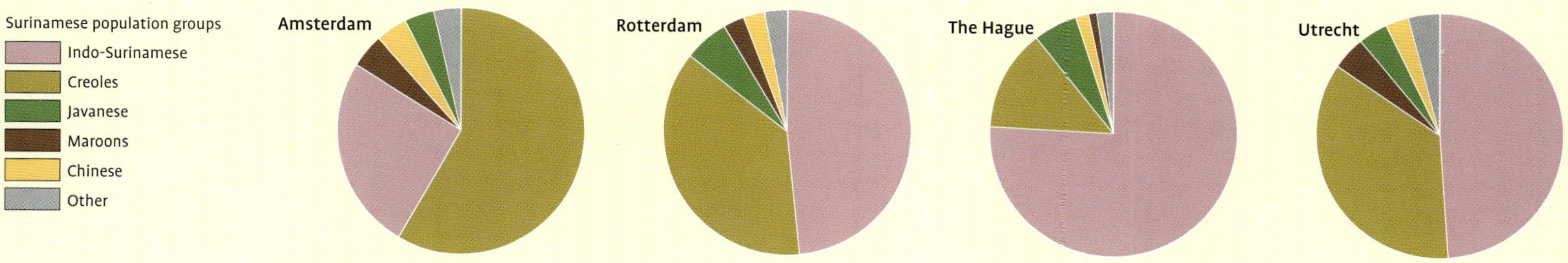

❻ Indo-Surinamese

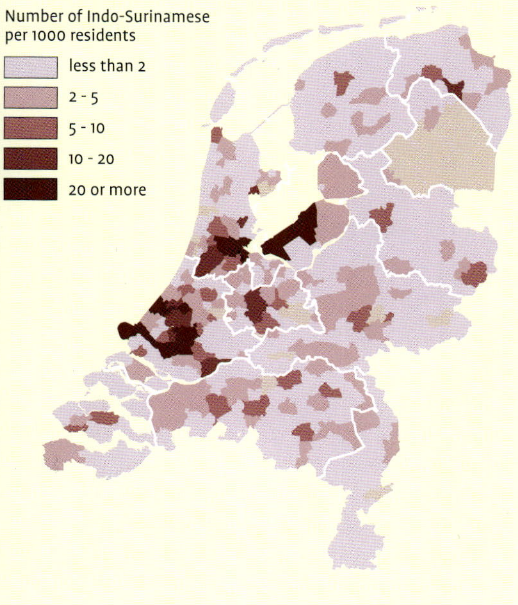

❼ Creoles

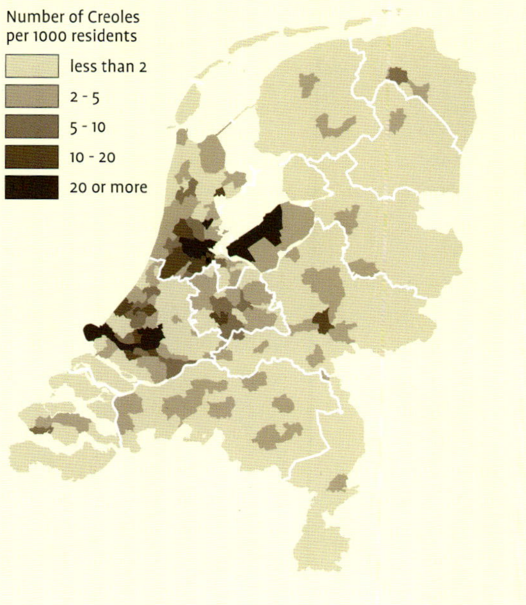

❽ Javanese

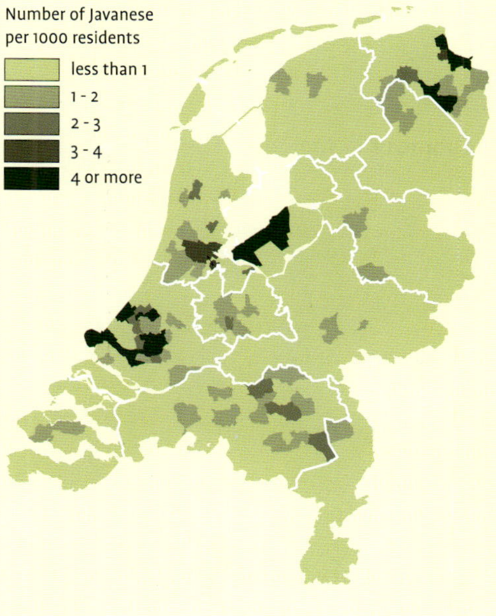

Sources: Statistics Netherlands (2); OIS, Research, Information and Statistics, City of Amsterdam (3, 4); Statistics Netherlands (5-8)

© Noordhoff Uitgevers

Students and yuppies

Amsterdam's magnetic attraction for young people can largely be attributed to the city's higher education facilities. The two universities in the city and the countless professional courses on offer attract more than one hundred thousand students. These students are almost equally distributed between the universities and higher professional education colleges.

After completing their studies, many students stay in the city as they also find their first job there. Graduates also come to Amsterdam from elsewhere in order to further their career. This obviously affects the social fabric of the city – an increasing number of young, well-educated single people or couples move into some neighbourhoods. An early example of one of these districts is the Jordaan, a run-down area until the late 1960s, which then became very popular. Bos and Lommer is currently the trendy district, while the Van der Pekbuurt in Amsterdam-Noord may well be the next.

❶ Student housing

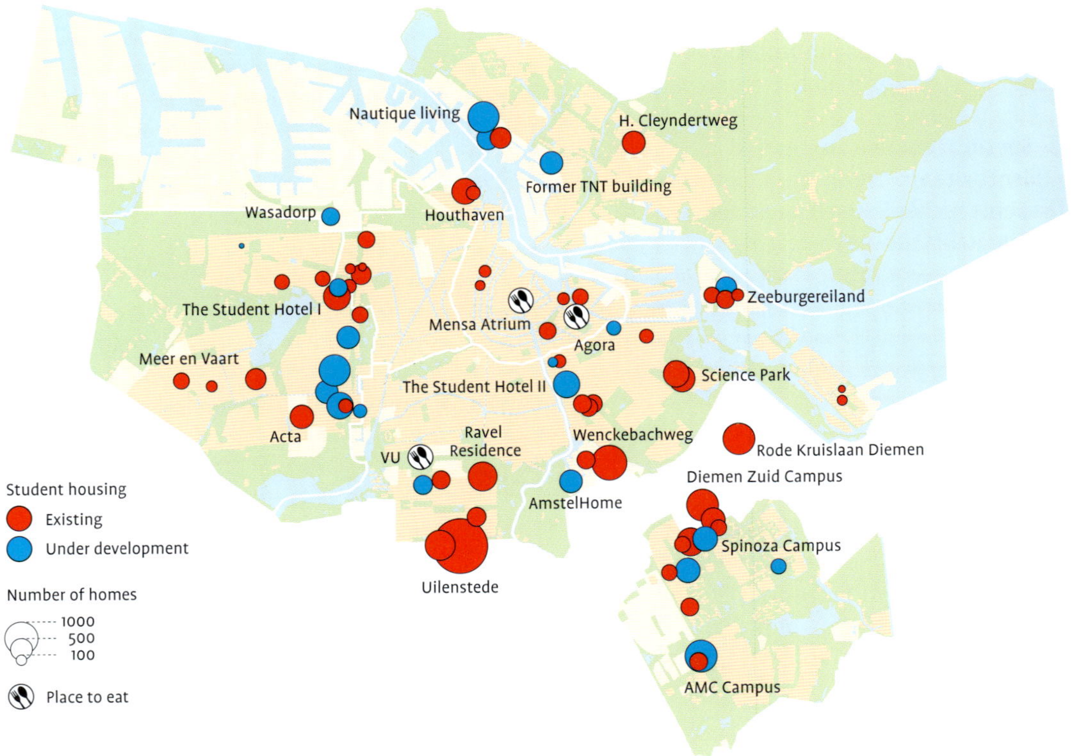

❷ Student societies and sports clubs

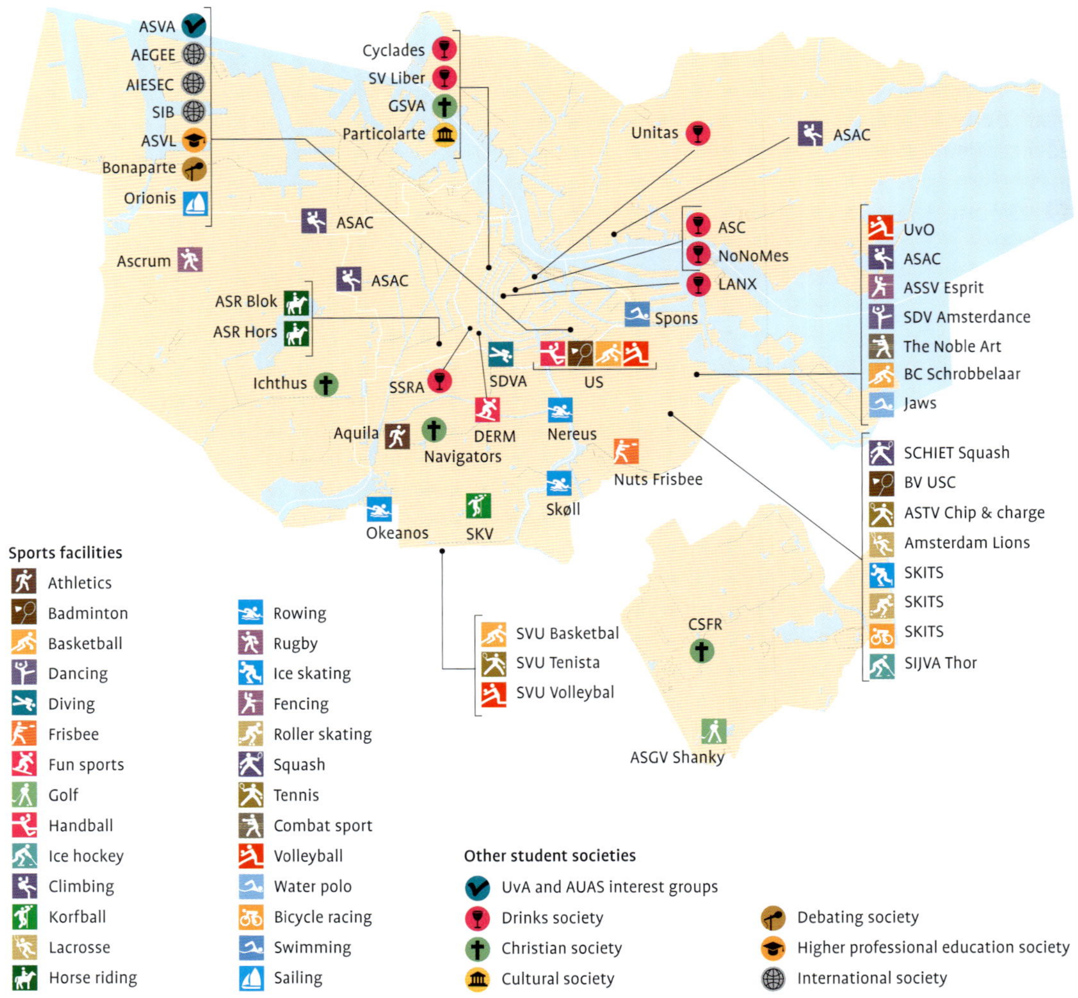

❸ At home or in shared accommodation

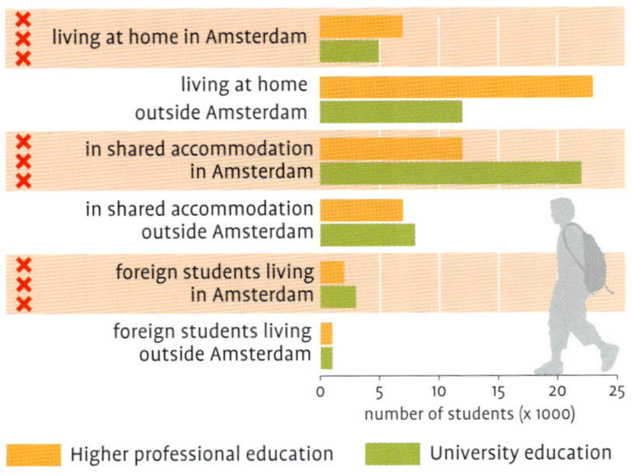

Sources: City of Amsterdam (1); student societies (2); OIS, Research, Information and Statistics, City of Amsterdam (3)

© Noordhoff Uitgevers

❶ Flats, sea containers and private studios
Nearly half of Amsterdam's students find accommodation through a housing association or student housing organisation. As well as traditional student flats like Uilenstede, locations such as the Science Park offer newly built accommodation. Students increasingly rely on sea-container homes (e.g. those at the NDSM site in Amsterdam-Noord), modularly constructed homes (like those on the Spinoza Campus in Zuidoost) or student hotels and privately owned studio apartments, in former office buildings for example.

❷ Special facilities
Students share most facilities with other city dwellers and also have several dedicated facilities of their own. These are mainly sports facilities, but also include pubs, student societies and other meeting places.

❸ Staying at home
Due to the limited availability and high costs of accommodation, not all students leave home right away. Over half of the Dutch students at Amsterdam's higher professional education colleges, and one third of those at university, still live at home.

❹ Districts on their way up
When a district becomes more popular, it attracts more and more well-educated, affluent residents, and rents and house prices increase as a result. This process takes many forms and the classical form is displacement, whereby the original residents are unable to pay the increased living expenses and have to move elsewhere. When successful people continue to live in the area where they started out as first-time buyers on a low income, growth comes from within. Succession takes place when the original residents grow old and die, making way for well-educated newcomers.

❺ Rise and decline of neighbourhoods
In practice, all forms of upgrading take place simultaneously in Amsterdam's neighbourhoods. There is however a tendency towards displacement in high-status neighbourhoods like Amsterdam-Zuid. In low-status neighbourhoods, like Amsterdam-Oost, growth comes more from within.

❻ Working and looking after the children
The rising social status of neighbourhoods is closely associated with *young urban professionals* (yuppies) – well-educated young people who find employment in knowledge-intensive sectors and live in the city. Yuppies now tend to stay in the city more often, even when they start a family, becoming 'young urban professional parents'. They form households with a city lifestyle and two incomes, and both parents have a roughly equal share in working and looking after the children. Yuppies need to have facilities nearby, as this allows them to combine family life, work and a city lifestyle. The city's central areas are best suited to the group's needs.

❹ Different models underpinning the rise of districts

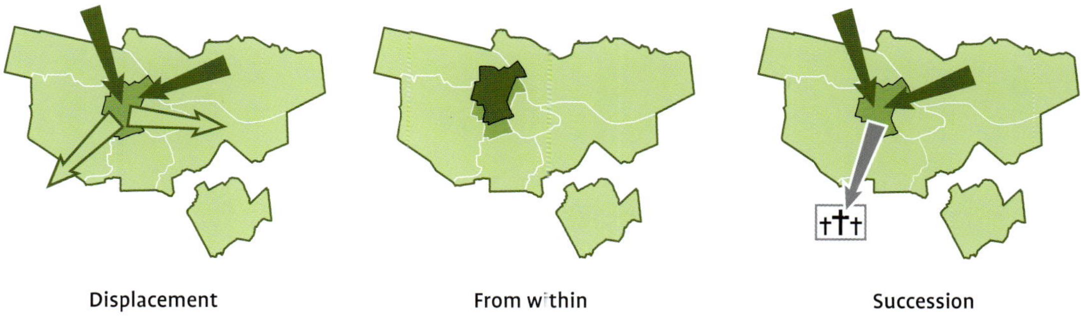

❺ Rise and decline of neighbourhoods, 2004-2011

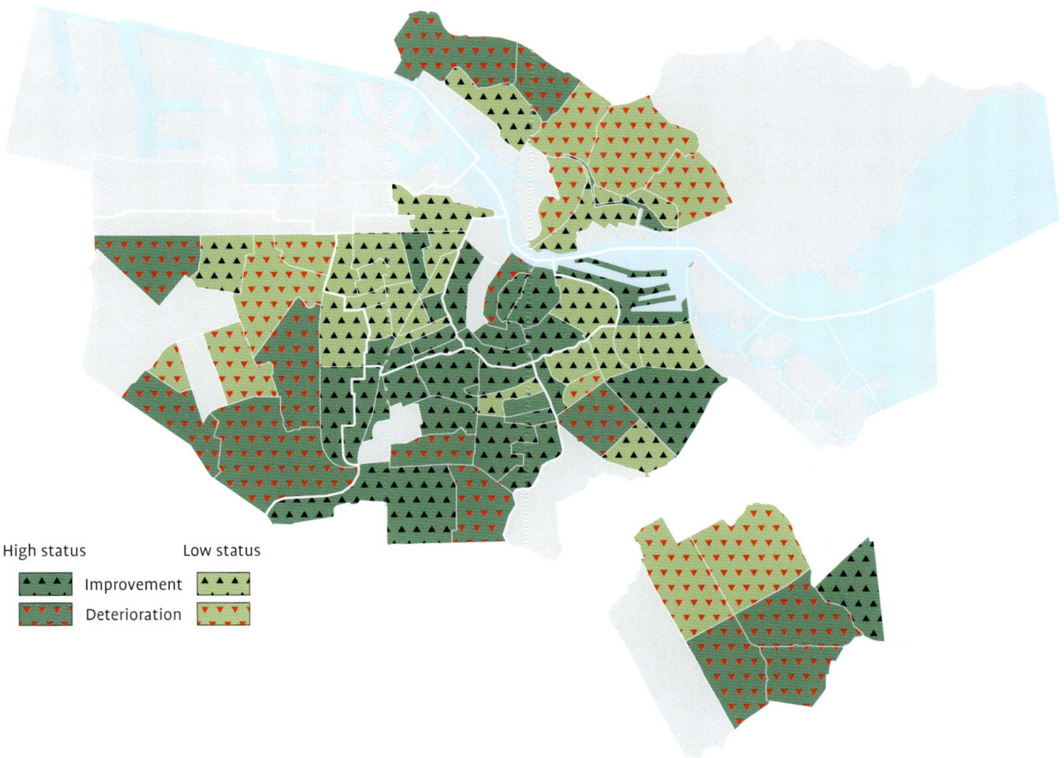

❻ Differences in working hours within households

Sources: C. Hochstenbach and W. van Gent, An anatomy of gentrification (4, 5); PBL Netherlands Environmental Assessment Agency / Statistics Netherlands / W. Boterman & L. Karsten, De opmars van het stadsgezin (6)

© Noordhoff Uitgevers

Rich and poor

Amsterdam is a city of striking contrasts. Wealthy cosmopolitans and well-educated double-income families live next door to newly arrived migrants and single parents who have had to live on a minimum income for years. The differences in income in the city are increasing and this is also reflected in the districts. Some neighbourhoods are among the country's richest, while others are among the poorest. The mixture of income groups, for which Amsterdam is known internationally, is under pressure due to the liberalisation of the housing market and other factors. The proportion of high earners has risen sharply this century, particularly in the area between the river IJ and the A10 ring road. Many more less well-educated people and households with an income close to the poverty line (around 22,000 euros per year for a family with two children) live outside that area. The facilities on offer reflect these differences. As well as the luxurious shops on P. C. Hooftstraat, Amsterdam has an extensive network of shelters for the homeless.

❶ Income

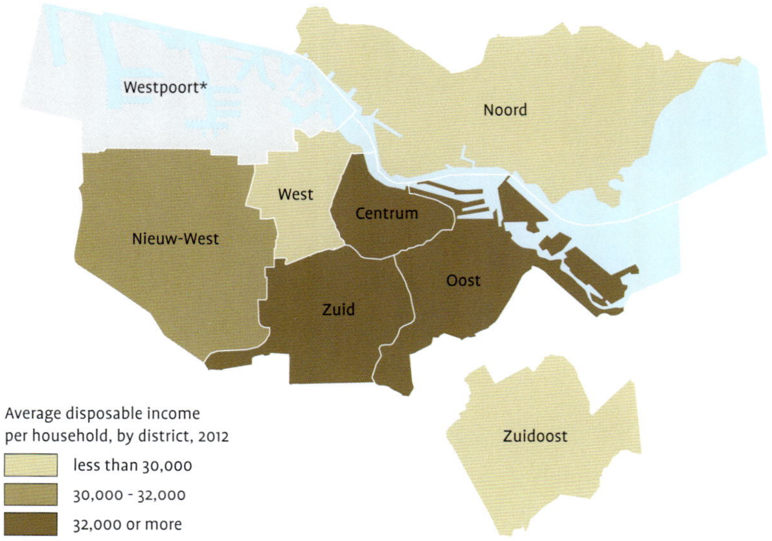

Average disposable income per household, by district, 2012
- less than 30,000
- 30,000 - 32,000
- 32,000 or more

* Westpoort is disregarded here

❷ Wealthiest neighbourhoods

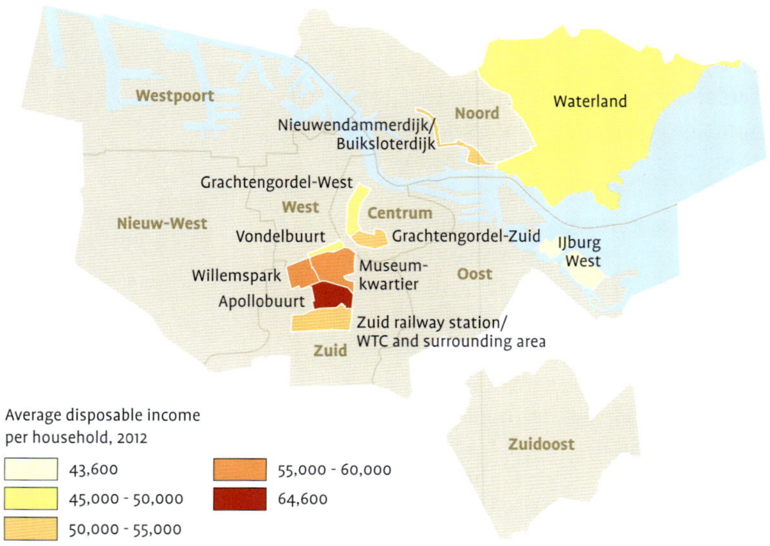

Average disposable income per household, 2012
- 43,600
- 45,000 - 50,000
- 50,000 - 55,000
- 55,000 - 60,000
- 64,600

❸ Property value

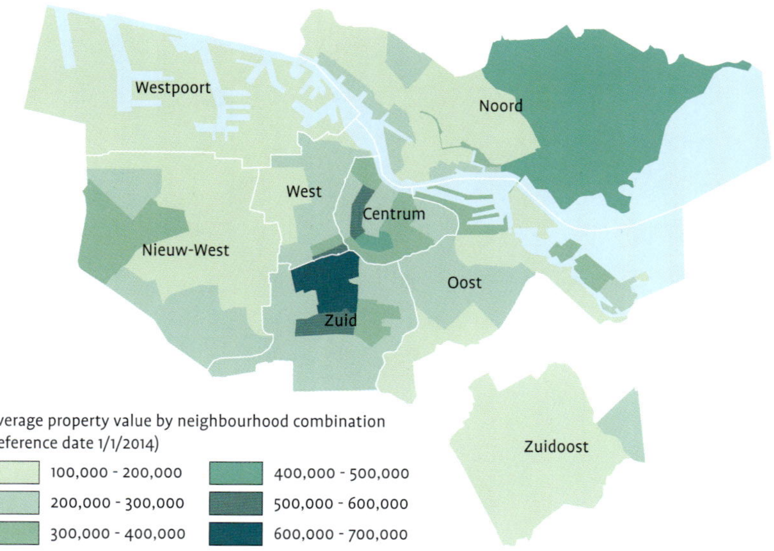

Average property value by neighbourhood combination (reference date 1/1/2014)
- 100,000 - 200,000
- 200,000 - 300,000
- 300,000 - 400,000
- 400,000 - 500,000
- 500,000 - 600,000
- 600,000 - 700,000

❹ Poorest neighbourhoods

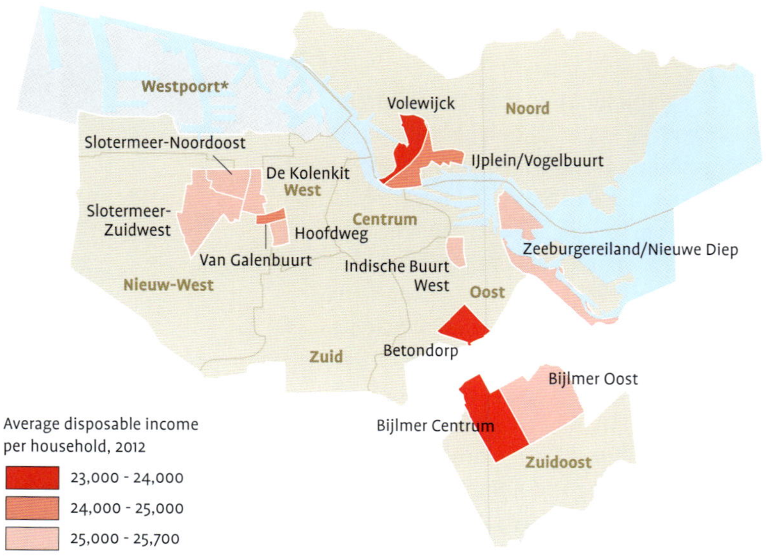

Average disposable income per household, 2012
- 23,000 - 24,000
- 24,000 - 25,000
- 25,000 - 25,700

* Westpoort is disregarded here

Sources: Statistics Netherlands (1, 2); OIS, Research, Information and Statistics, City of Amsterdam (3); Statistics Netherlands (4)

© Noordhoff Uitgevers

❶ More high incomes
The average disposable income of households in Amsterdam has currently almost returned to the level of the Netherlands as a whole, but the differences within the city are considerable. Disposable income in Zuidoost is 10,000 euros lower than in Zuid.

❷ Affluent districts
Amsterdam's most affluent districts are situated in Berlage's Plan Zuid area, with the 'Apollobuurt' as the clear front-runner. Nieuwendammerdijk and Buiksloterdijk in Noord, with their characteristic dike houses, and the Zuidas area, with its luxurious apartments, are completely different but no less desirable living areas.

❸ Rising house prices
Many Amsterdammers have benefited from rising house prices and built up capital in this way, especially in the areas surrounding the city centre.

❹ Poor districts
Amsterdam's poorest districts are located in the outer suburbs, which have a very high proportion of less well-educated households, from both native and migrant backgrounds. Over a quarter of all households in Amsterdam have to make ends meet on an income close to the poverty line.

❺ Caring for the poor
Amsterdam has a long tradition of social care, as the numerous historic almshouses for widows and the elderly in the city centre attest. However, caring for the poor has changed significantly. Only the Stadsbank van Lening, a city lending institution founded 400 years ago, still exists today.

❻ Luxurious shopping street
Leading international fashion brands have shops on P. C. Hooftstraat. Situated between the Vondelpark and the major museums, it is a popular backdrop for wealthy women from Het Gooi, professional footballers and other people who enjoy being seen in public.

❼ Rich and poor
Despite the increased gap between Amsterdam's rich and poor, few homeless people have to sleep on the streets.

❼ Wealth and poverty

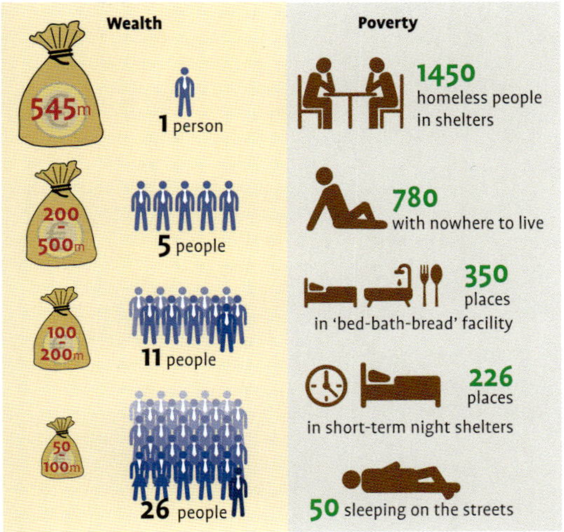

❺ Facilities for the less fortunate

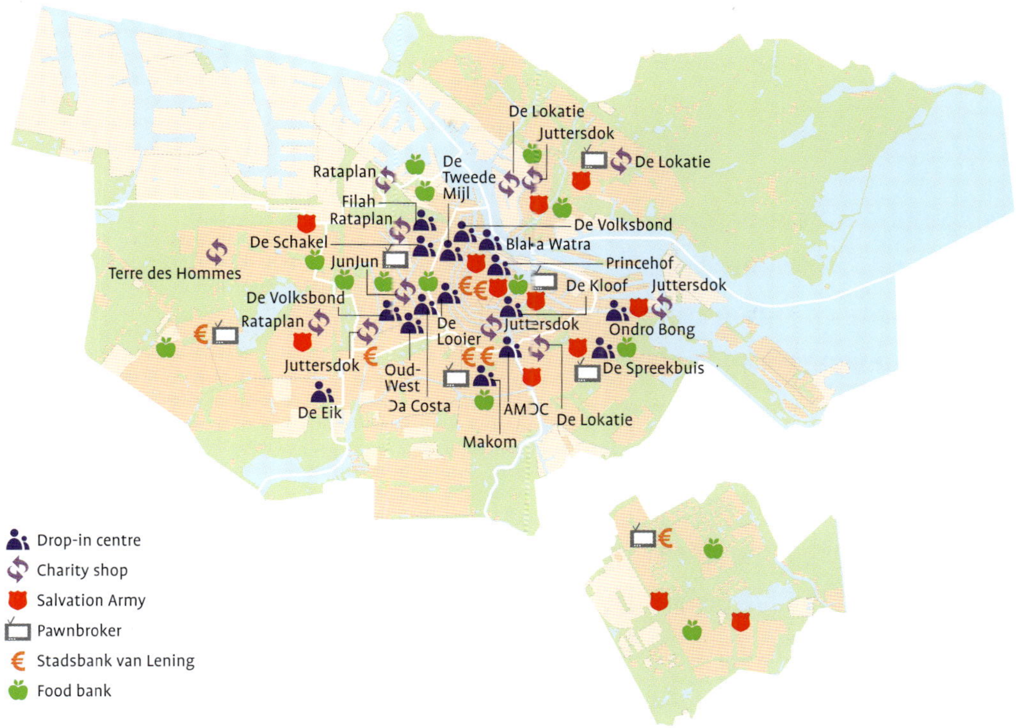

❻ P. C. Hooftstraat – a microcosm in Amsterdam

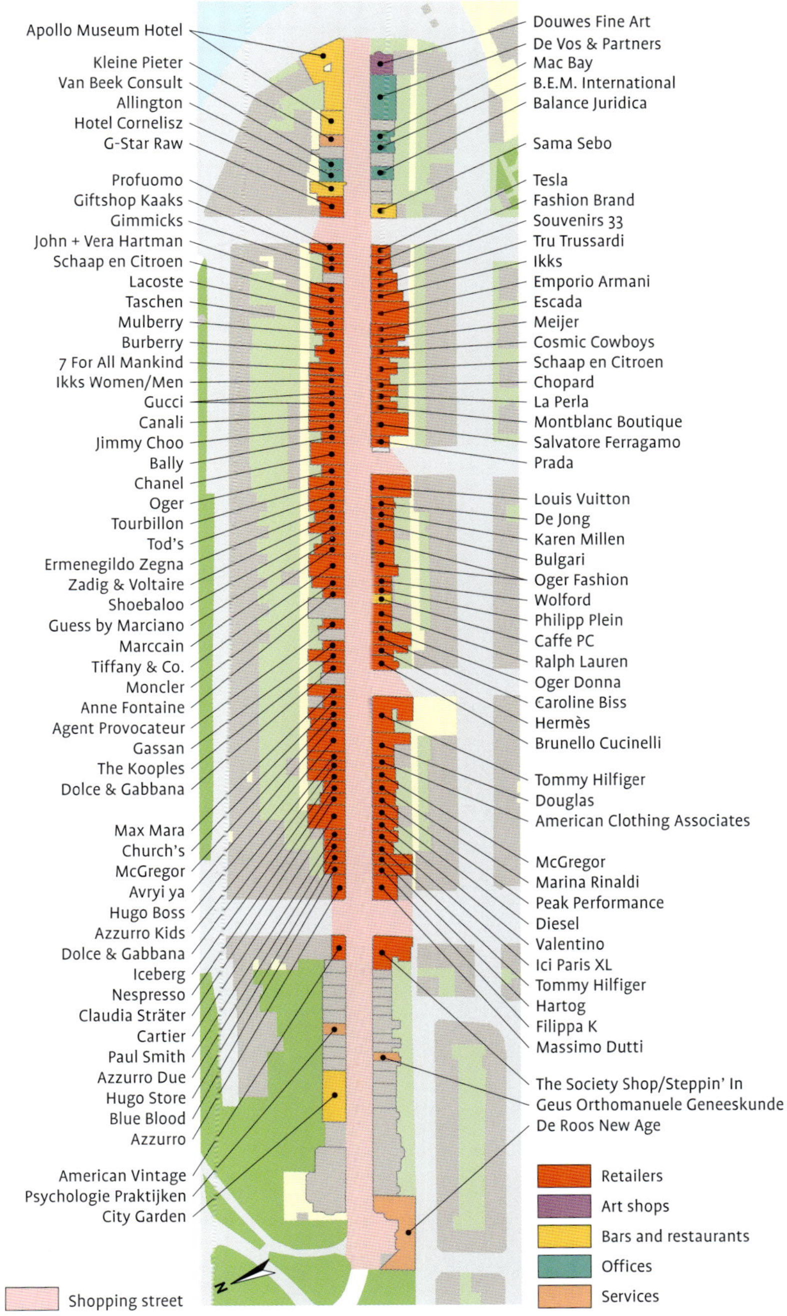

Sources: City of Amsterdam (6); Quote 500 / City of Amsterdam (7)

© Noordhoff Uitgevers

Commuters and expats

Some 800,000 Amsterdammers live in Amsterdam, and many other people 'use' the city. Take commuters for example. Even though we do not refer to them as 'Amsterdammers', they are still a definite part of the city, if only because of their numbers – more than half of the people who work in Amsterdam live elsewhere. Expats are another group of 'temporary Amsterdammers' that are inextricably linked to the city. They are well-educated, well-paid foreigners who come to Amsterdam for a temporary position, generally for a few years. The city has a relatively high number of expats and their presence gives the city an international feel.

❶ Top 15 commuter routes

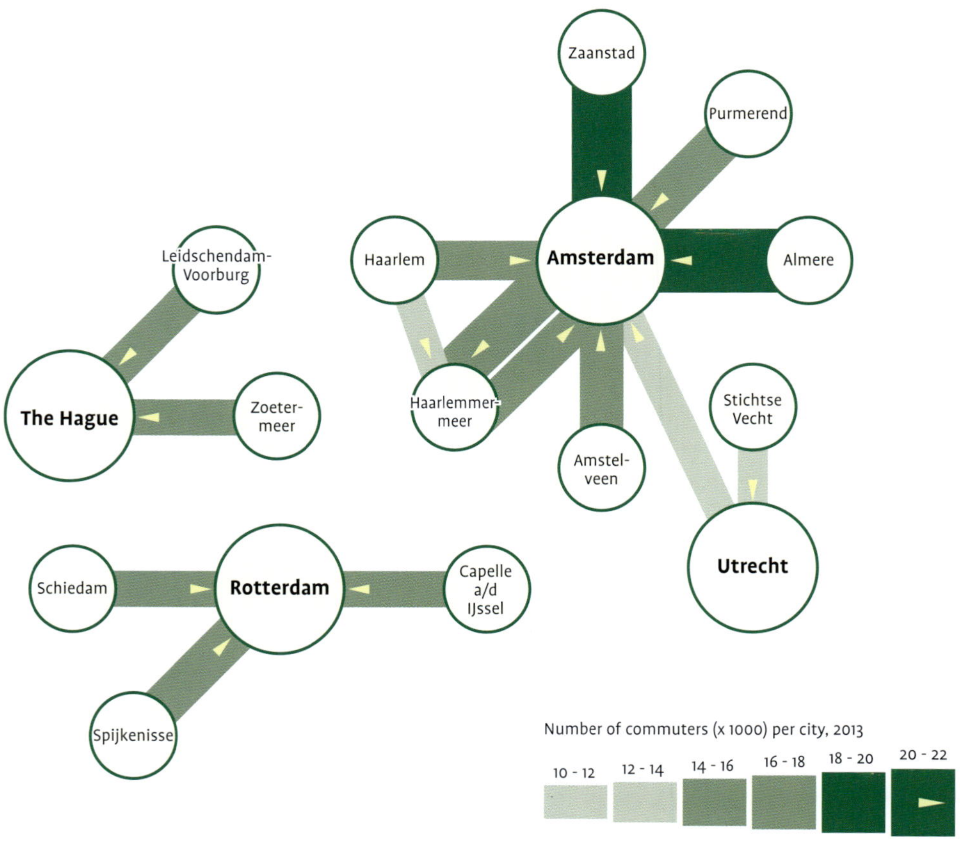

❷ Amsterdam's commuter flows within the Amsterdam Metropolitan Area

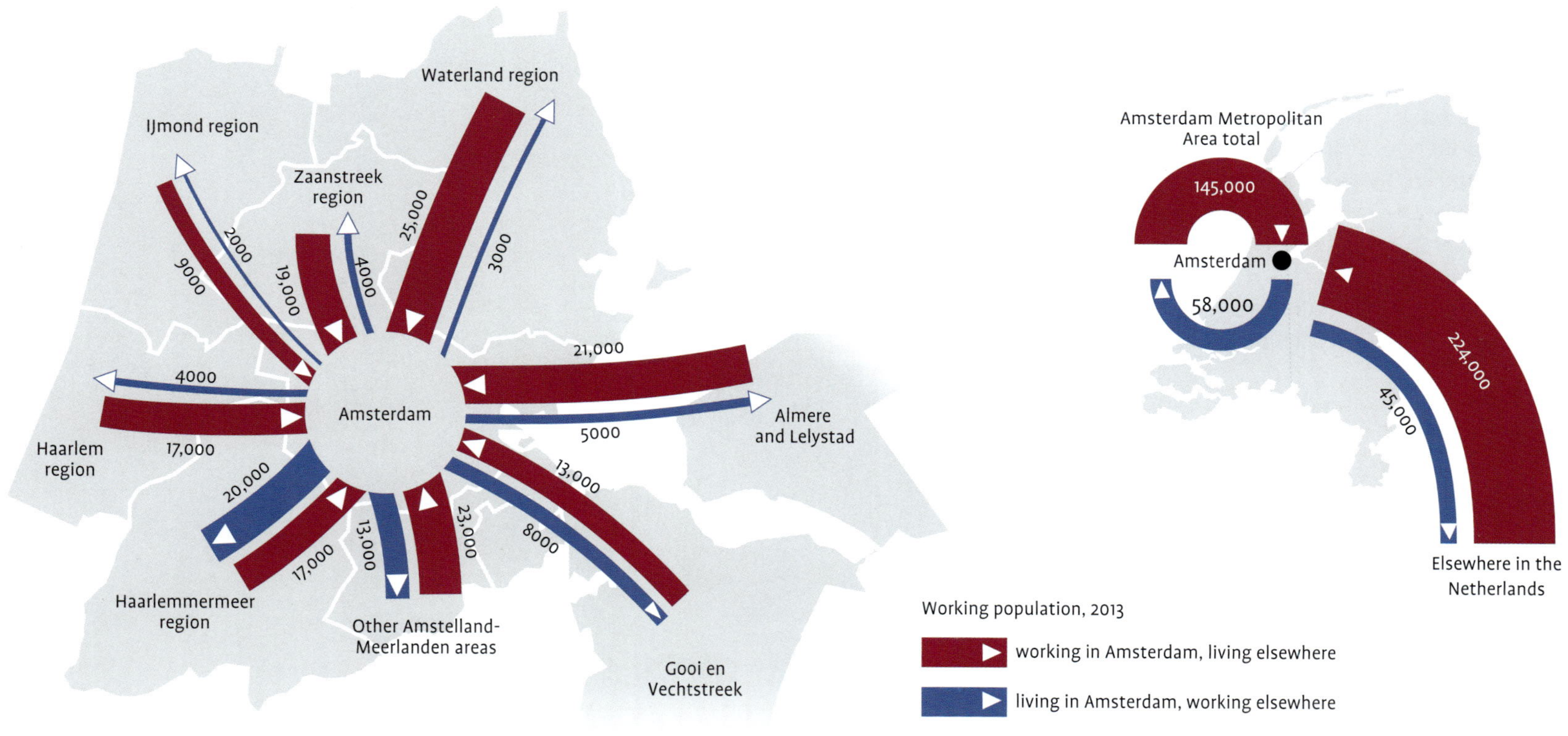

Sources: *Statistics Netherlands (1); Statistics Netherlands, TNO adaptation (2)*

© Noordhoff Uitgevers

❸ Expats in the Randstad

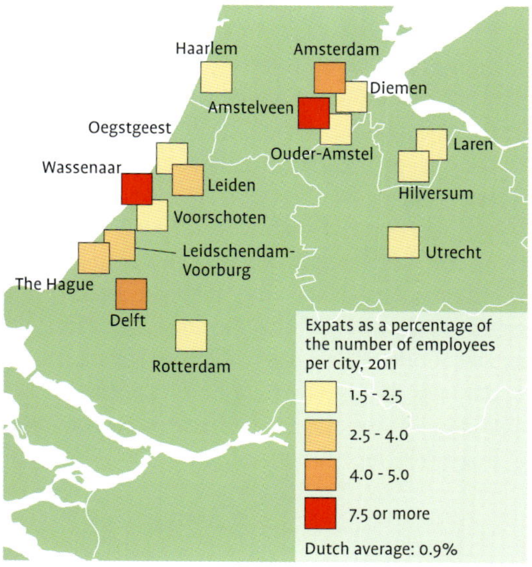

❹ Expats

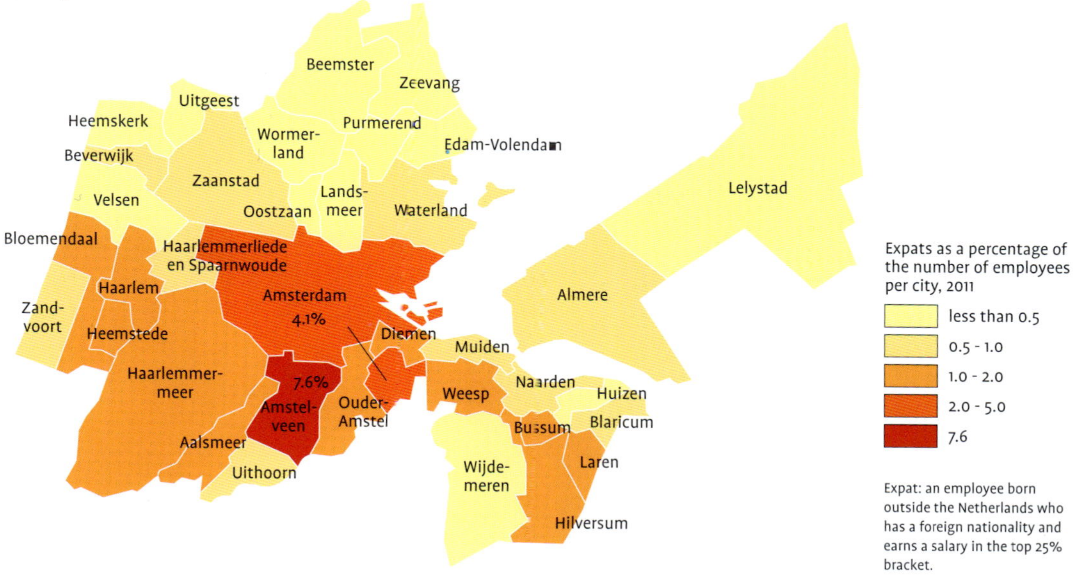

❶ Busy areas around Amsterdam

Amsterdam features high in the rankings of cities with the most commuter traffic. Most of the people who work in Amsterdam come from Almere, followed by Zaanstad in second place.

❷ Commuting more popular than relocation

Of the more than 650,000 people who work in Amsterdam, 57% live outside the city. Nearly a quarter of a million people even travel to Amsterdam from outside the metropolitan area.

❸ Expats in the Randstad

International companies often bring in staff from abroad, who are known as expats. They are not Dutch nationals, they came to the Netherlands aged 18 or above and they are among the highest earners in their industry. Many expats are also employed by knowledge institutes and international organisations.

❹ Expats in the Amsterdam region

Over 4% of all employees in Amsterdam are expats, a figure that rises to nearly 8% in Amstelveen, where many Japanese expats live. The country-wide figure is 1%.

❺ International schools

Expats' children often go to international schools. There are large ones in Hilversum and Amstelveen, but more and more are opening in Amsterdam. These schools are sometimes very small, focusing on specific groups.

❻ A relatively international focus

Expats are mainly employed by foreign companies, of which Amsterdam has a high percentage compared with the rest of the country. Only 1% of all companies in the Netherlands are foreign-owned, compared to nearly 3% in Amsterdam. They are often large consulting firms and ICT companies. Altogether, foreign companies in Amsterdam provide 20% of the jobs in the city – not just for expats of course.

❺ International schools

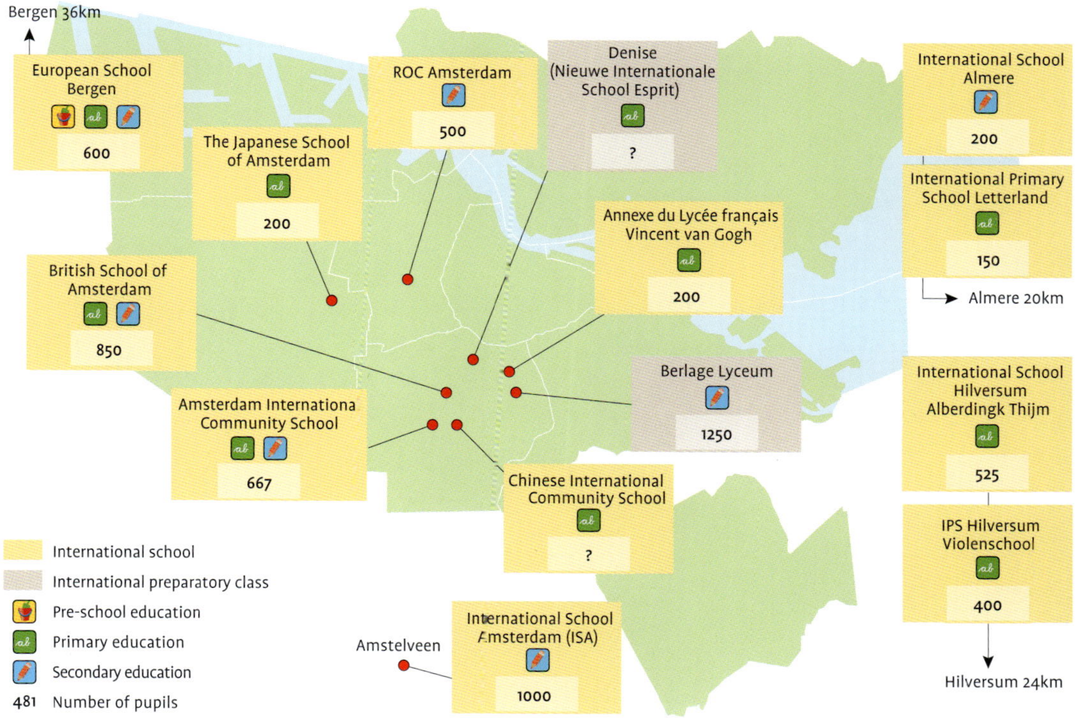

❻ Large foreign companies

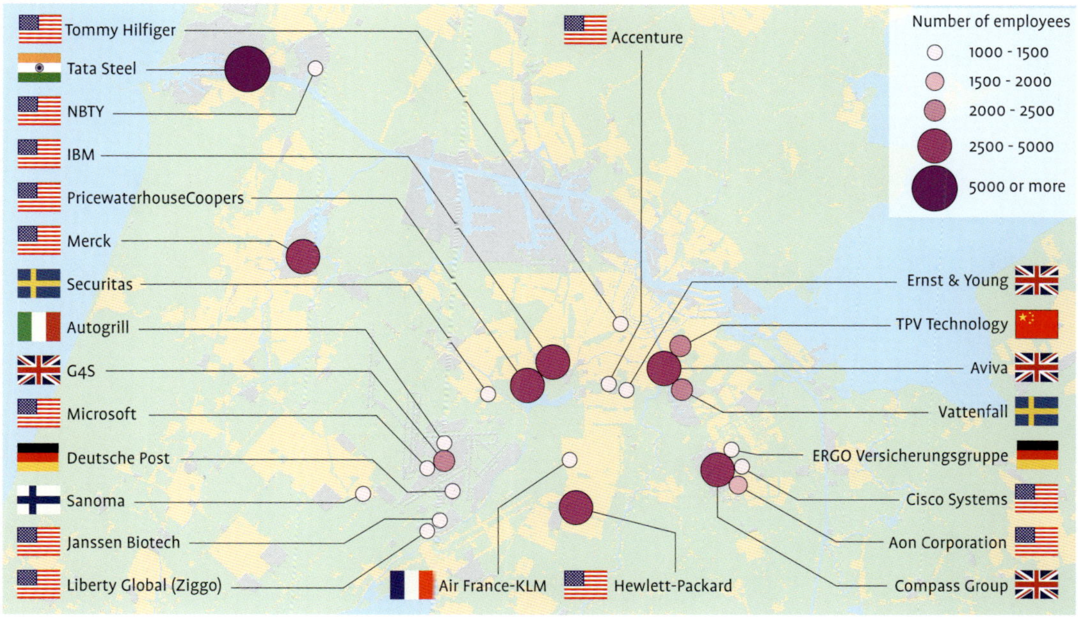

Sources: PBL Netherlands Environmental Assessment Agency / Statistics Netherlands (3-4); OIS, Research, Information and Statistics, City of Amsterdam / Foundation for International Education in The Netherlands (5); PBL Netherlands Environmental Assessment Agency / OIS, Research, Information and Statistics, City of Amsterdam (6)

© Noordhoff Uitgevers

Group portraits

❶ Catholic through and through
In the Middle Ages, Amsterdammers were Catholics through and through. They organised their lives according to the rhythm of the ecclesiastical calendar and prayed to Mary and other saints for protection, healing and grace. The annual procession, pictured here on a painted tapestry dating from 1555, was a special event. This procession commemorates the Miracle that took place in March 1345. A sick man had vomited a piece of sacramental bread which was then thrown into the burning hearth and subsequently retrieved without signs of scorching or damage. In 1578, Amsterdam finally had to abandon its Catholic nature following a change of power on the city council.

❷ Wealth and care
During the Golden Age, the influx of people, knowledge and capital helped Amsterdam to become the world's most important trading centre. The city was ruled by merchants, some of whom had amassed immeasurable wealth. These 'regents' realised that many of their fellow townspeople were less fortunate, so they set up and maintained an extensive system of facilities for the sick, for orphans, for the elderly and for the poor. They did so for religious reasons and also to keep beggars off the streets. They were also prone to vanity – members of the ruling class often commissioned portraits of themselves, such as these female regents of the hospital for lepers. This canvas was painted in around 1668 by Ferdinand Bol.

❸ Enlightened citizenry
In 1777, the wealthy citizens of Amsterdam founded the Felix Meritis ('happy through merit') fellowship. The fellowship's aim was to promote the arts and sciences in Amsterdam. Its founders had been inspired by the Age of Enlightenment, a period during the 18th century that emphasised the value of knowledge and reason. The Felix Meritis building on Keizersgracht was completed in 1788, an event which Adriaan de Lelie recorded for posterity in this painting dating from around 1800. The building was the city's main concert hall until the Concertgebouw took over this role in 1888. The Felix Meritis fellowship was disbanded in the same year. The building still stands today and has been home to the Communist daily newspaper *De Waarheid* and the Shaffy Theater, to name but a few.

Photos: © Amsterdam Museum (1); © Rijksmuseum Amsterdam (2); © Amsterdam Museum (3)

© Noordhoff Uitgevers

❹ Labourers and construction workers
Industrialisation did not start in the Netherlands until the late 1800s, when Amsterdam was in the middle of its 'Second Golden Age'. The lethargy that had dominated the city for many years was shrugged off and building work started all over Amsterdam. Brewer Gerard Heineken was one of the first entrepreneurs to have a new factory built outside the city walls in 1867. Many striking buildings were erected, ranging from the Amstel Hotel to the Centraal railway station. People from all over the country travelled to Amsterdam to start work in construction or in the factories. They ended up in districts such as De Pijp, with its narrow streets and mediocre housing. However, their difficult living and working conditions became increasingly apparent, to artists (such as Hendrik Breitner, who photographed these workers on Van Diemenstraat around 1900), but also to members of the city council.

❺ Provos
The Provo movement emerged in Amsterdam in the mid-1960s. It was a protest movement consisting of young people who advocated a kind of pacifist anarchism and primarily challenged the establishment. Luud Schimmelpennink, Rob Stolk, Robert Jasper Grootveld and Roel van Duijn were some of the most notorious Provos. They attracted national attention by organising anti-smoking demonstrations around the Lieverdje statue on the Spui, handing out free currants in the street and promoting the 'Witkar'. They also became known internationally after they triggered a smoke bomb during the royal wedding of Claus van Amsberg and Princess Beatrix. Although the movement disbanded in 1967 after only two years, Amsterdam's reputation as a 'magic centre' had been firmly established.

❻ Influx of foreign workers
The first migrant workers came to the Netherlands in the late 1960s, initially from southern Europe and later also from Morocco and Turkey. They had been brought to the Netherlands by employers who were looking for cheap labour and nearly all of them were young single men. At first, they found accommodation in substandard homes and boarding houses, but they were later reunited with their families or married someone from their home countries. They relocated to Nieuw-West or Noord, where they could move into larger homes. People getting together in parks for a barbecue has since become a familiar sight in a diverse city which now only consists of minorities.

Photos: © Rijksmuseum Amsterdam, George Hendrik Breitner (4); © Amsterdam City Archives, Cor Jaring (5); © ANP Photo (6)

© Noordhoff Uitgevers

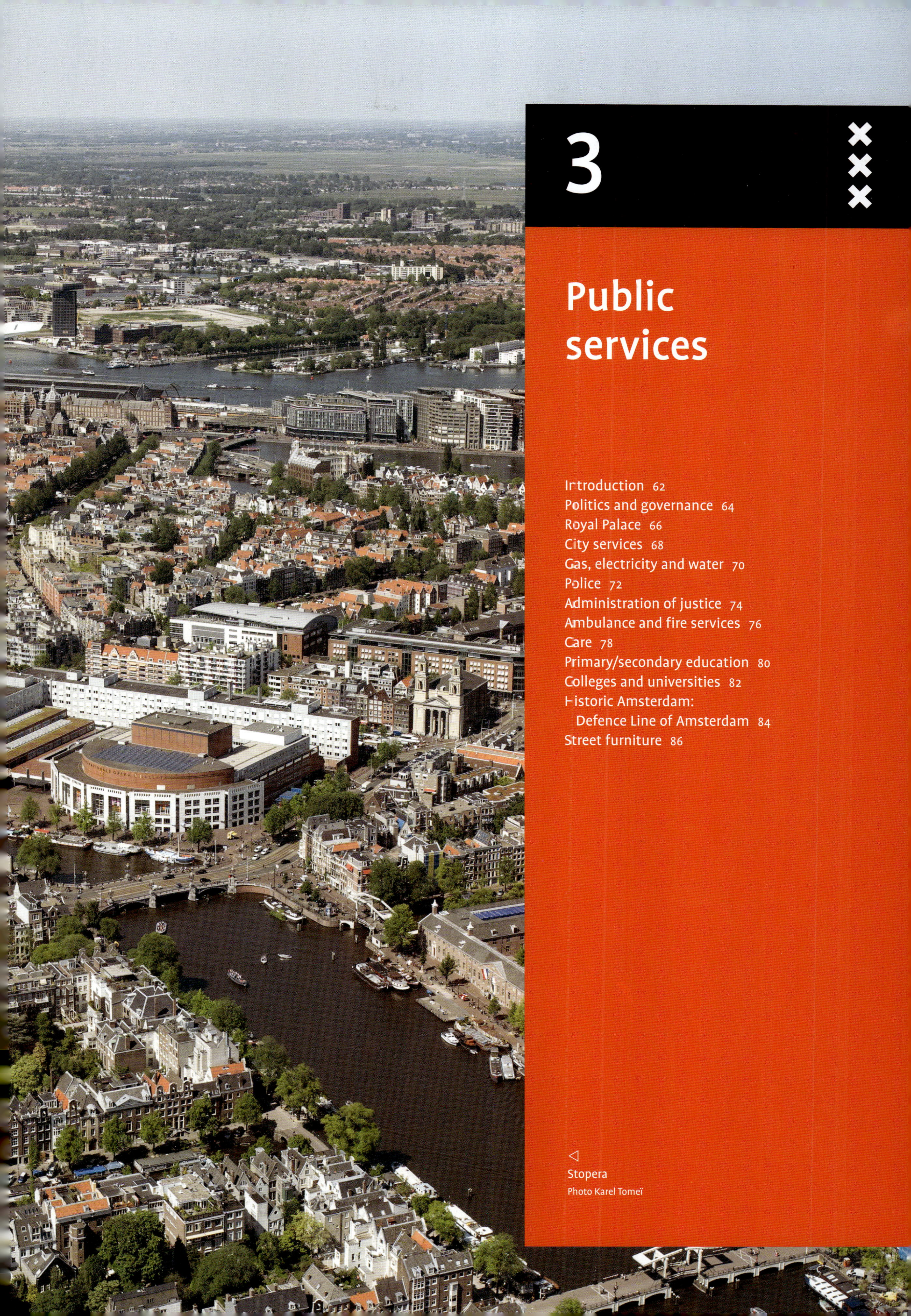

3

Public services

◁
Stopera
Photo Karel Tomeï

3 Introduction

Government versus market forces

Modern people have extensive needs. In addition to food and safety, they need a trustworthy legal system, medical care and education. They need to be able to live in a clean environment and drink the water that comes out of the tap. When accidents and fires occur, immediate assistance must be available, and the power supply may not fail under any circumstances.

Until recently, the government was responsible for organising most public services of this kind. The City of Amsterdam once had its own water company, power company, university and giro payment system. The latter two were the only ones of their kind in the Netherlands. None of these organisations still exist today, at least not in the same form. They have either been privatised or made independent. Whatever the case, they are no longer managed by the city council.

Safety

Other public tasks are still controlled by the government. The legal system and the armed forces are two examples. Traditionally, these public tasks were organised locally. Until 1795, cities had their own laws, judges and city militias and Amsterdam was no exception. Later on, the national government took control of these tasks. Even so, Amsterdam still had a special place within national defence policy. At the end of the 19th century, a separate defensive structure called the Defence Line of Amsterdam was built around the capital.

Public order

Maintaining public order is another traditional government task. Since the mayor plays a central role in this task, it can be considered a city responsibility. However, economies of scale have left their mark in this field and Amsterdam's policemen are now part of a national police force. Even ambulances operate within a supra-urban network these days.

Local authorities

Despite this trend towards scaling-up, the local authorities still provide extensive public services. They maintain the city's personal records

The Stopera

The local authorities are based in the Stopera, a combined town hall and opera house. The building has an eye-catching location at a bend in the river Amstel. The semi-circular Dutch National Opera & Ballet is both eye-catching and impressive; the wings of the town hall behind it (1988) are less striking. Incidentally, many civil servants work in the districts rather than at town hall.

database, clean the streets, take care of the parks and gardens, work to ensure welfare and combat poverty, and do a great deal more besides. All of these activities are managed by the local authorities, i.e. the mayor, the aldermen and the city council. They are assisted in their duties by seven governing committees, one for each district, and a large team of civil servants.
The current town hall's architecture is typical of the image that the local authorities aim to project today – solid and sober. The contrast with its 17th-century predecessor on the Dam could not be greater. The latter is such a prominent showpiece that it has been used as a royal palace since 1808.

PvdA mayors for the last **70** years

13,777
civils servants employed by the city council (16.8 per 1000 residents)

97,398
recorded crimes in 2013

1 in **5** PhDs
gained in Amsterdam

per 100,000 residents
5.2 Amsterdam
4.3 Netherlands

Sources: City of Amsterdam / OIS, Research, Information and Statistics, City of Amsterdam / Ambulancezorg Nederland / VSNU

© Noordhoff Uitgevers

Politics and governance

The city council is Amsterdam's highest political and governing body. It is elected by the people of Amsterdam and has 45 members. Generally, the council meets once every three weeks. Everybody is free to attend the council meetings in the public gallery. City council elections are held every four years and the last one was in 2014. The council determines the general outlines of city policy and the mayor and aldermen implement these outlines under the council's watchful eye. They are aided in this task by all kinds of administrative departments and seven governing committees, which have replaced the former district councils.

❶ Result of the 2014 city council elections

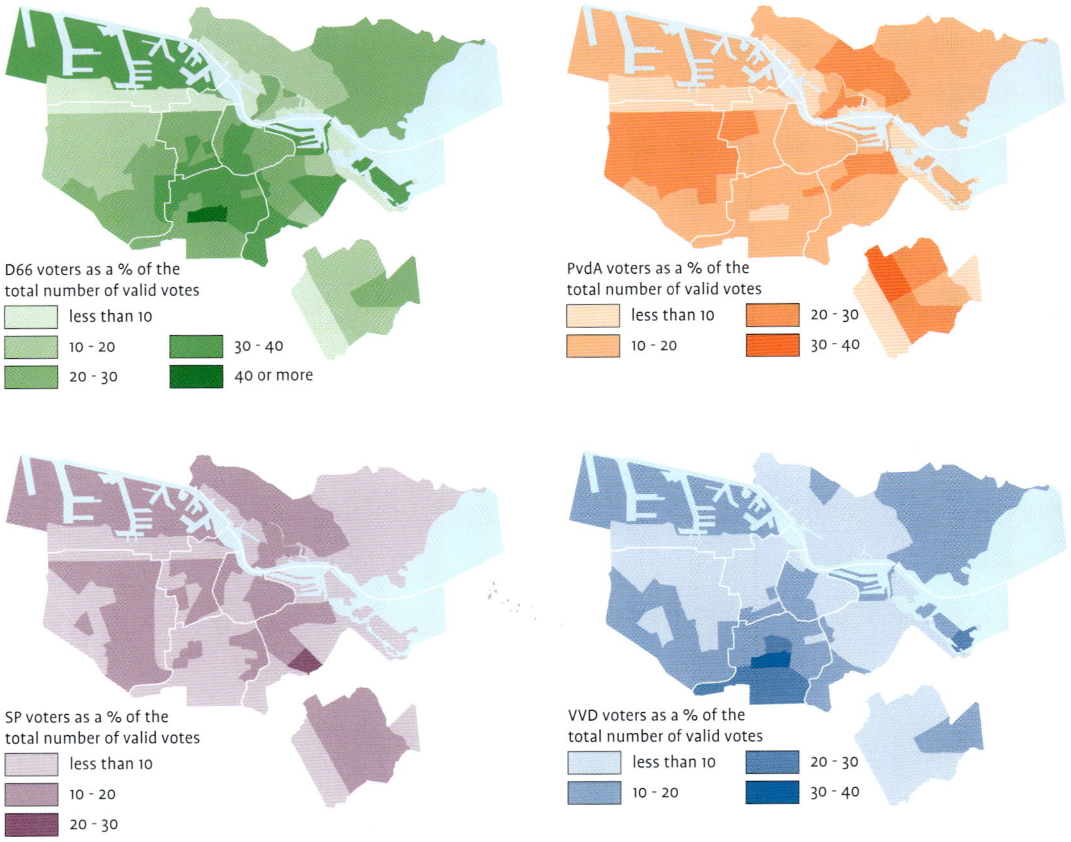

❷ Local parties in the Amsterdam and Rotterdam city councils

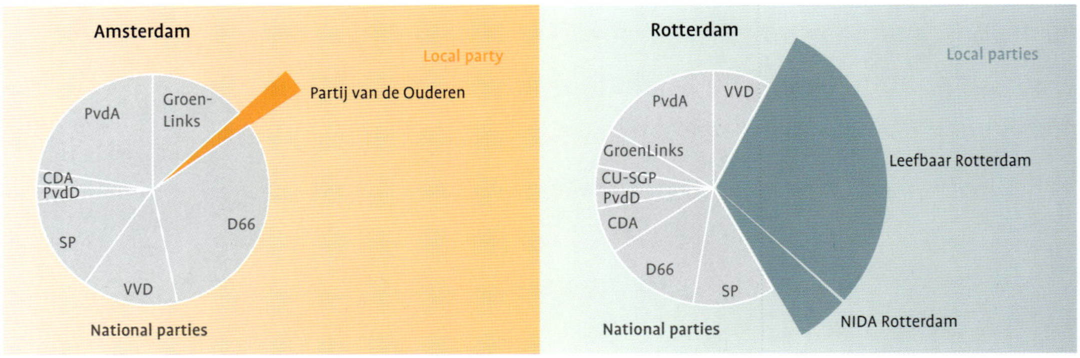

❸ Voting trends

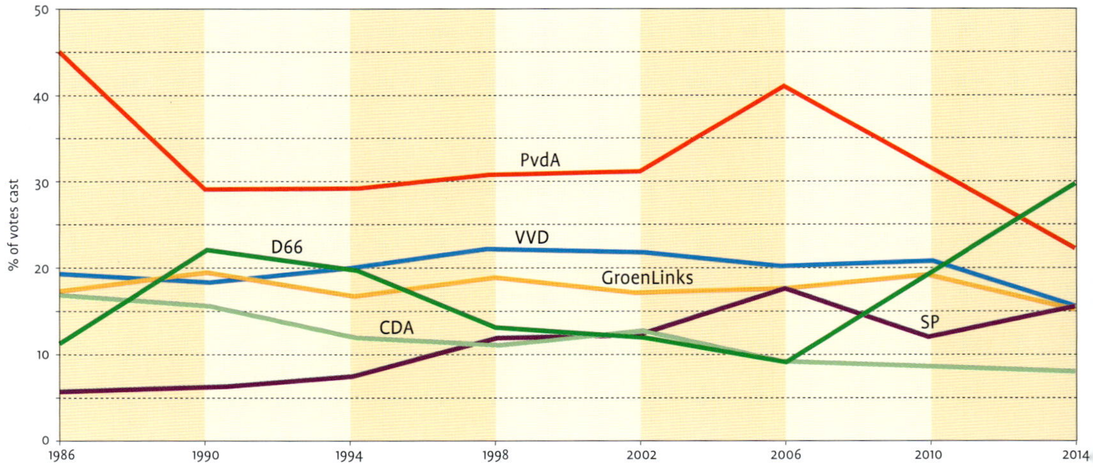

❶ Green displaces red
In the March 2014 city council elections, 310,649 of the 604,583 Amsterdam residents who were eligible to vote made their way to the polling stations (51.4%). It was a landslide election. The PvdA, the largest political party in the city for decades, had to relinquish its position to D66.

❷ Dominant national parties
Around thirty parties participated in the 2014 elections and eight of them won one or more council seats. All of them except the local Partij van de Ouderen are national parties. Local parties in Rotterdam achieved much better results, with Leefbaar Rotterdam (27.5%) and NIDA Rotterdam (4.8%) winning 16 of the 45 seats. Lokaal Amsterdam, on the other hand, did not even win 1% of the votes.

❸ The undisputed winner
With almost 27% of all votes cast, D66 was the undisputed winner of the 2014 elections. After lengthy negotiations, D66, the VVD and the SP signed a coalition agreement. This was the first time since World War Two that none of the aldermen were PvdA members.

Sources: OIS, Research, Information and Statistics, City of Amsterdam (1, 3); City of Amsterdam / City of Rotterdam (2)

© Noordhoff Uitgevers

❹ Governing committees

On 19 March 2014, Amsterdammers were given the opportunity of voting for the members of their district's governing committees for the first time ever. The governing committees have replaced the former district councils and their members are nominated by the city council based on election results. The committees have fewer powers than the former district councils, as the national government wanted to put an end to this fourth governance layer at district level. Accordingly, as of 2015, the governing committees no longer have their own budgets and the members only receive payment for each meeting. The thirteen to fifteen committee members have a lot of meetings – the Oost district had no less than 59 meetings between March 2014 and March 2015.

❺ Expenses and revenue

Each autumn, the city council has to approve the annual budget for the following year. This is a complex task – the budget proposal is more than 400 pages long and all expenses and revenue ultimately have to balance. The City receives significant income from the national government's dedicated fund. Amsterdam has a 'city debt' of 4.7 billion euros (2014), which is largely the result of investments in infrastructure such as bridges and buildings.

❻ - ❼ National public figures

Rather than being elected, the mayor is appointed for a period of six years by the Crown. Since 1946, all mayors of Amsterdam have been members of the same political party, the Partij van de Arbeid. The aldermen are elected by the political parties that form the governing coalition. Amsterdam currently has eight aldermen – four from D66 and two each from the VVD and the SP. Serving as the mayor or an alderman of the capital city generates a great deal of prestige, which explains why a relatively high number of Amsterdam's former mayors and aldermen are later appointed to high positions in national, provincial and local politics.

❹ Local government organisation

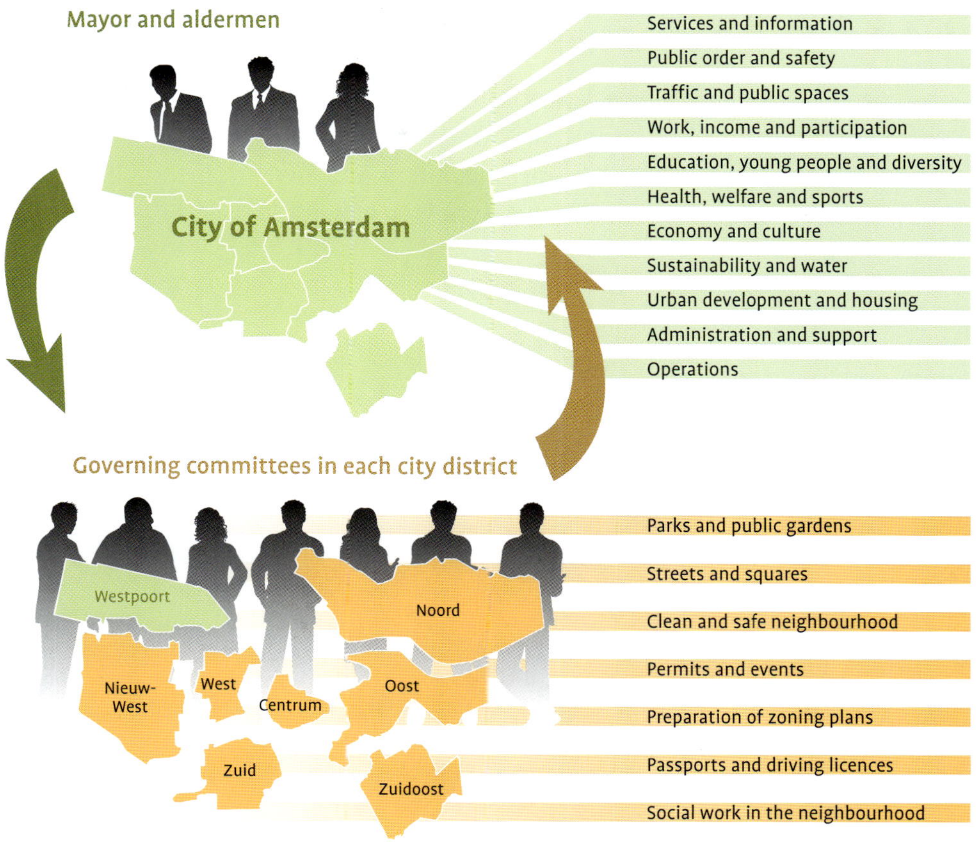

❺ City budget for 2015

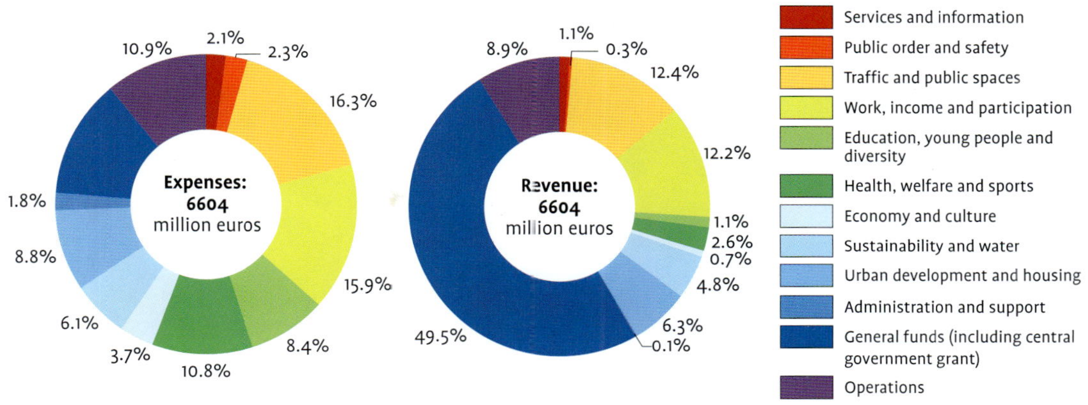

❻ Mayors since 1900

2010-	Eberhard van der Laan	PvdA
2001-2010	Job Cohen	PvdA
1994-2001	Schelto Patijn	PvdA
1983-1994	Ed van Thijn	PvdA
1977-1983	Wim Polak	PvdA
1967-1977	Ivo Samkalden	PvdA
1957-1967	Gijs van Hall	PvdA
1946-1957	Arnold Jan d'Ailly	PvdA
1945-1946	Feike de Boer	LSP*
1941-1945	Edward Voûte	Liberaal
1921-1941	Willem de Vlugt	ARP
1915-1921	Jan Willem Tellegen	VDB*
1910-1915	Antonie Röell	Liberaal
1901-1910	Wilhelmus Frederik van Leeuwen	Liberaal
1891-1901	Sjoerd Vening Meinesz	Liberaal

*LSP = Liberale Staatspartij 'De Vrijheidsbond', VDB = Vrijzinnig-Democratische Bond

❼ Alderman in Amsterdam – springboard to higher office

Joop den Uyl, Prime Minister
Gausje ter Horst, Minister of the Interior and Kingdom Relations
Frank de Grave, Minister of Defence
Lodewijk Asscher, Minister of Social Affairs
Eric Wiebes, State Secretary for Finance
Enneüs Heerma, State Secretary for Public Housing

Han Lammers, Queen's Commissioner in Flevoland
Roel de Wit, Queen's Commissioner in North Holland

Cees de Cloe, Mayor of Almere
Wim Polak, Mayor of Amsterdam
Pauline Krikke, Mayor of Arnhem
Freek Ossel, Mayor of Beverwijk
Thomas Elsenburg, Mayor of Geleen
Mark van der Horst, Mayor of Heemskerk
Ernst Bakker, Mayor of Hilversum
Geert Dales, Mayor of Leeuwarden
Harry Groen, Mayor of Noordwijk
Ahmed Aboutaleb, Mayor of Rotterdam
Hester Maij, Mayor of Zandvoort

Source: *City of Amsterdam (4-7)*

© Noordhoff Uitgevers

Royal Palace

The current Royal Palace dates from the 17th century and was built as a representative accommodation for the city council. The design and furnishings were so luxurious that architect Jacob van Campen's creation soon became known as the 'eighth wonder of the world'.

Present use
Palace used by the Royal Family to receive dignitaries. During state visits, heads of state and the accompanying delegations sleep here.

When the Royal Family is not using it, the palace is open to the public six days a week.

Exhibitions are organised in the palace twice a year.

Visitors since the opening in 2009

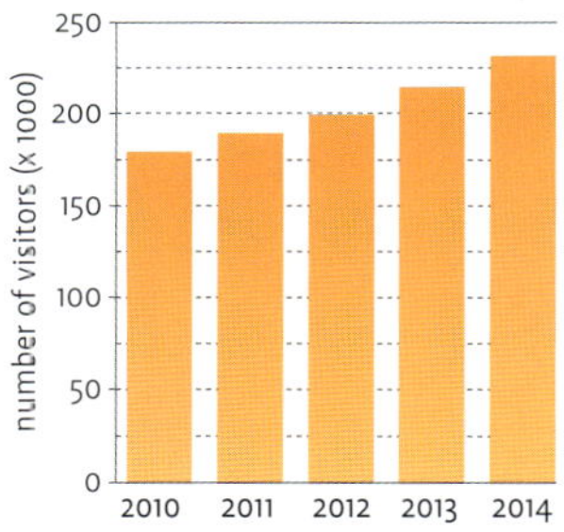

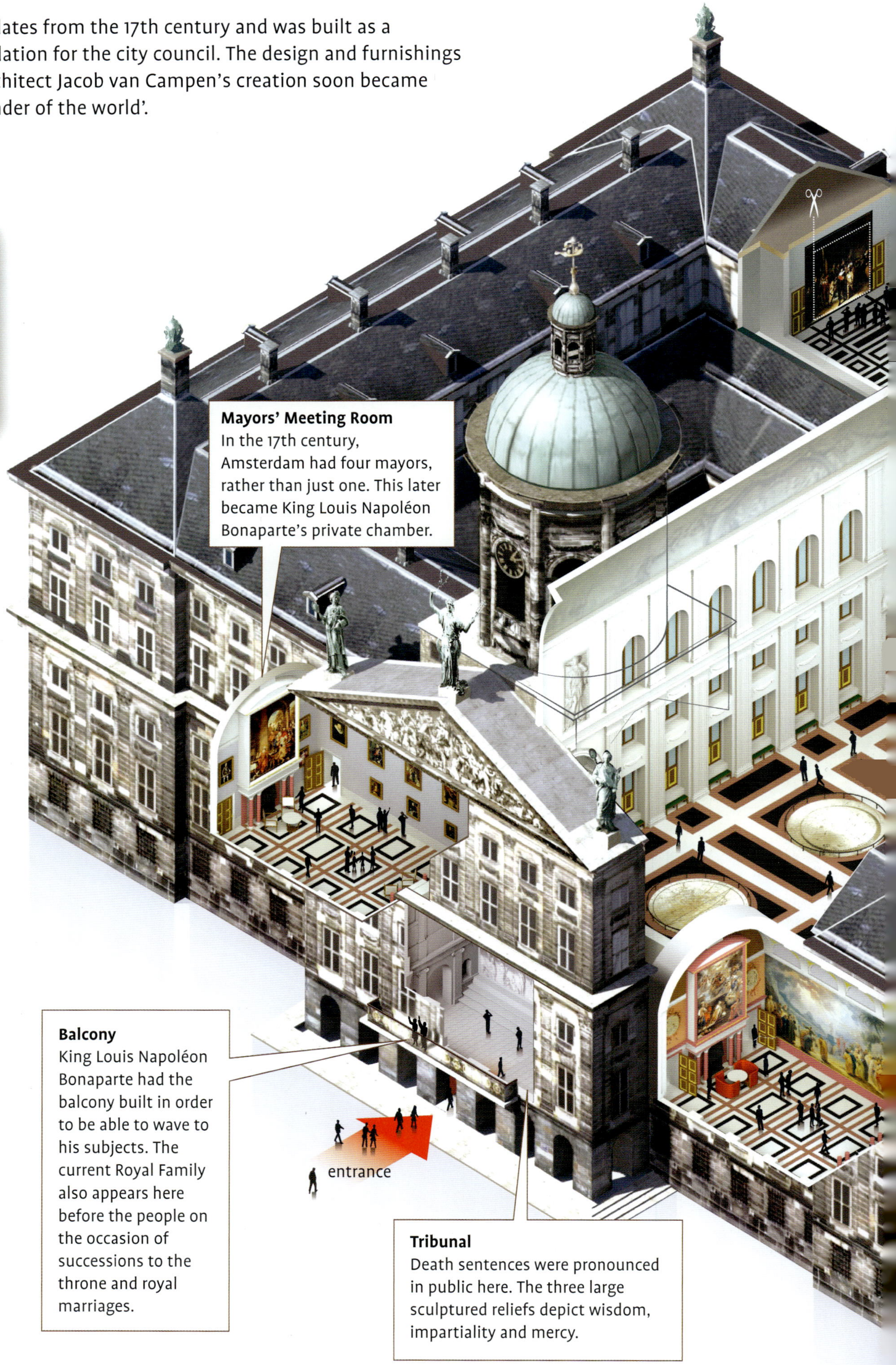

Structural alterations

In 1808, King Louis Napoléon Bonaparte turned the town hall into his palace: the arcades were converted into rooms, statues disappeared behind canvases, a balcony was built and new furniture installed. The latter items are still there.

The palace was used very little after Louis' departure.

In 1936, the state bought the buil for 10 million guilders, around €10 million in today's money.

Source: Royal Palace Amsterdam; Photo: © Hollandse Hoogte

Small War Council Room
Rembrandt's *Night Watch* hung on the wall in this room from 1715 to 1808. The canvas did not fit between the doors so it was decided to trim it down.

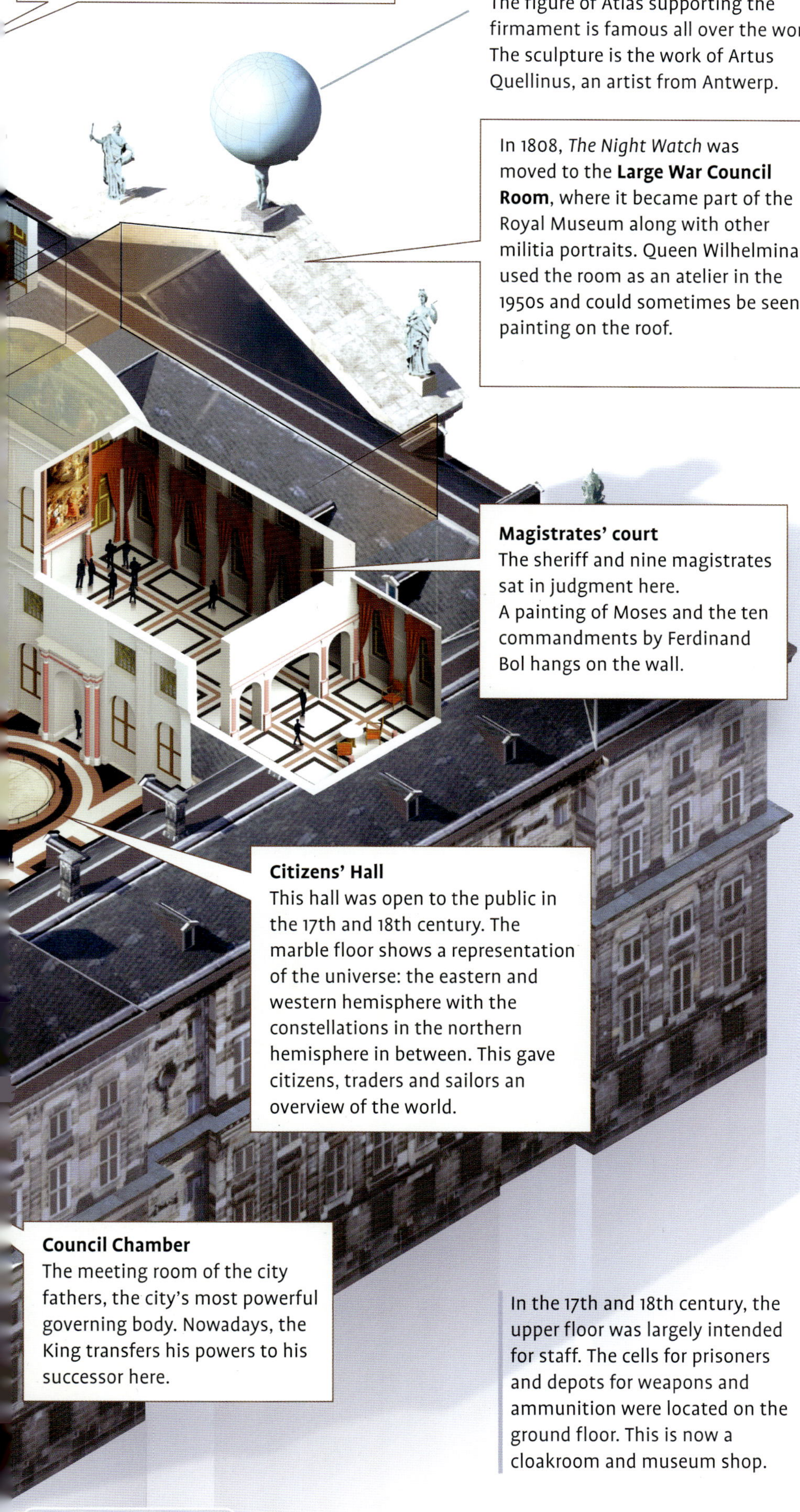

The style of the building is referred to as Dutch classicism, which is based on Greco-Roman architecture.

The figure of Atlas supporting the firmament is famous all over the world. The sculpture is the work of Artus Quellinus, an artist from Antwerp.

In 1808, *The Night Watch* was moved to the **Large War Council Room**, where it became part of the Royal Museum along with other militia portraits. Queen Wilhelmina used the room as an atelier in the 1950s and could sometimes be seen painting on the roof.

Magistrates' court
The sheriff and nine magistrates sat in judgment here.
A painting of Moses and the ten commandments by Ferdinand Bol hangs on the wall.

Citizens' Hall
This hall was open to the public in the 17th and 18th century. The marble floor shows a representation of the universe: the eastern and western hemisphere with the constellations in the northern hemisphere in between. This gave citizens, traders and sailors an overview of the world.

Council Chamber
The meeting room of the city fathers, the city's most powerful governing body. Nowadays, the King transfers his powers to his successor here.

In the 17th and 18th century, the upper floor was largely intended for staff. The cells for prisoners and depots for weapons and ammunition were located on the ground floor. This is now a cloakroom and museum shop.

Seat of the city council

- *From the 14th century*
  Old town hall on the site of the current palace.
- *7 July 1652*
  Major fire in the old town hall. City council took up residence in the **Prinsenhof** (a former monastery) pending completion of the new town hall.
- *29 July 1655*
  Inauguration of the **new town hall on the Dam.**

- *1808*
  The city council moved back to the **Prinsenhof**, because King Louis Napoléon Bonaparte requisitioned the town hall.
- *1813*
  After the departure of the French, the council was unwilling to move again and remained at the **Prinsenhof**.
- *1988*
  Council moved into the **Stopera**.

Collection

Upon leaving the palace in 1810, King Louis Napoléon Bonaparte left the following behind:
- the largest collection of Empire-style furniture outside France
- various silver objects
- a museum on the 2nd floor, the basis for today's Rijksmuseum

Restorations

1914: restored as far as possible to how it was prior to 1808	1960: partly opened to the public	2005-2009: restoration and refurbishment of the guest accommodation	2009: cleaning of the facades	June 2009: most of the palace opened to the public again

© Noordhoff Uitgevers

City services

The city council and the mayor and aldermen are responsible for political decision-making. However, civil servants are responsible for the preparation and implementation of those decisions. For many years now, Rotterdam and Amsterdam have together employed more civil servants per thousand residents than any other of the 393 local authorities in the Netherlands (as of 1 January 2015). A major restructuring exercise started in 2014. This is intended to create a more flexible and result-focused organisation and reduce the number of civil servants to 12,000 in 2016. Most civil servants currently work in four clusters, which are subdivided into 38 departments. The civil servants in the seven districts largely focus on operational tasks such as collecting refuse and maintaining public spaces.

❶ City organisation

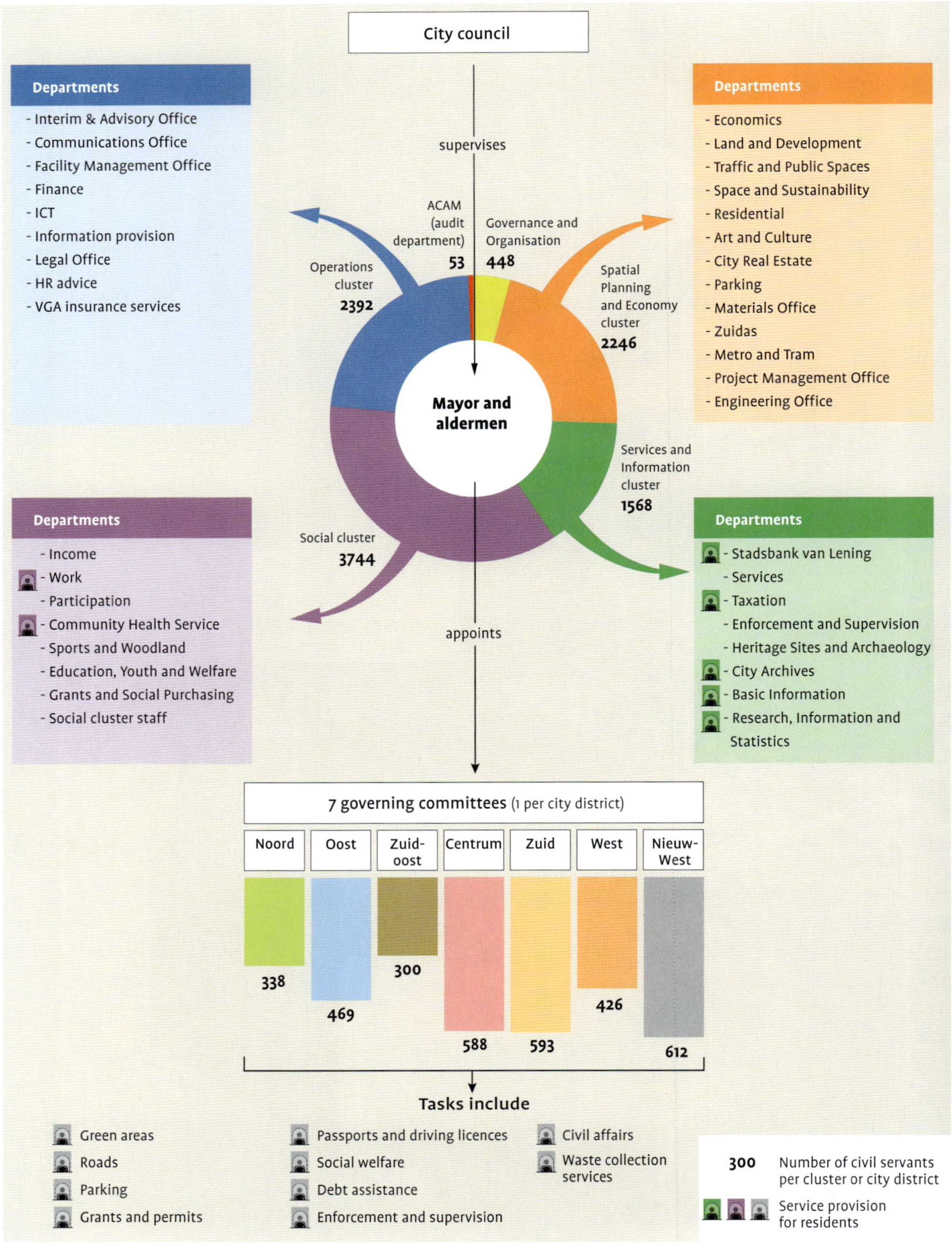

❶ - ❷ Seventeen per thousand

On 1 June 2015, Amsterdam employed 13,777 civil servants, slightly more than seventeen per thousand residents. The Social cluster has the most civil servants and they support Amsterdammers with matters relating to public health, employment and reintegration, poverty, youth and adult care services, education and sport. More than a third of the city budget is reserved for implementation of initiatives in these fields.

❷ Civil servants

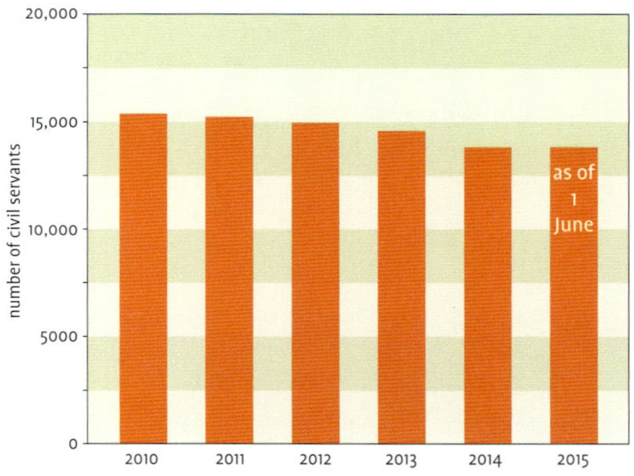

❸ City residential charges in 2015

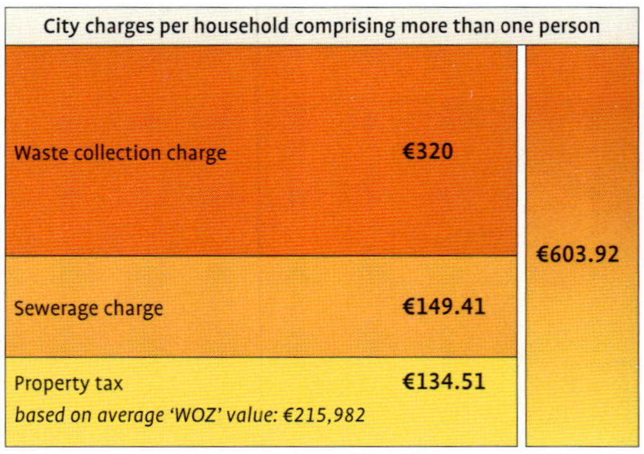

Sources: City of Amsterdam (1, 2); Vereniging Eigen Huis (3)

© Noordhoff Uitgevers

❹ Waste recycling

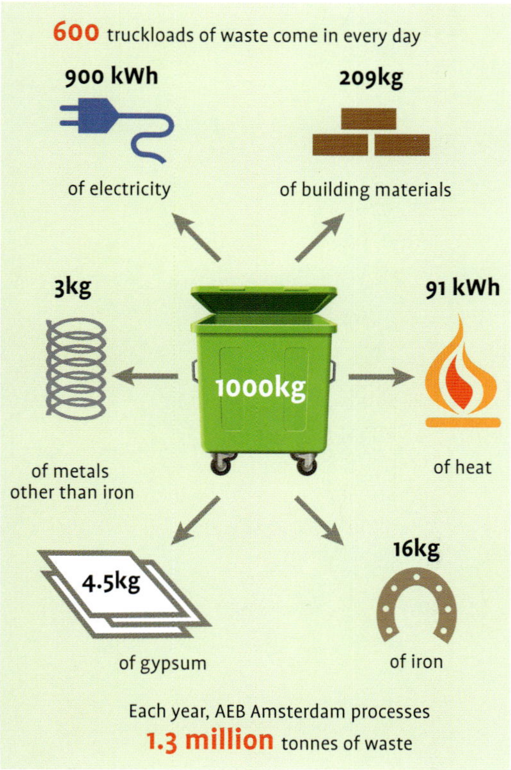

❺ Household waste collection

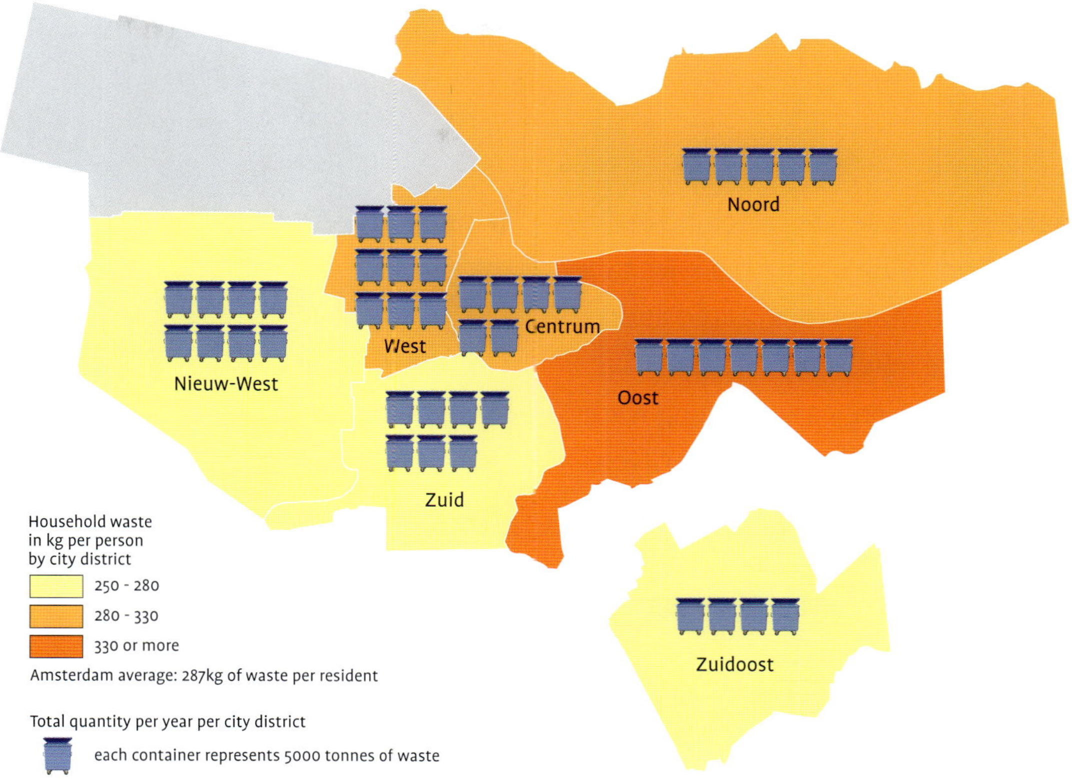

❸ Revenue and expenses

Each year, home owners and tenants in Amsterdam have to pay residential charges to the City. These charges are relatively low compared with neighbouring Diemen, for instance, where residents pay 398 euros for waste collection and 206 euros for sewerage.

❹ - ❺ Keeping Amsterdam clean

The City spends about 450 million euros each year on waste collection and processing, sewage sludge purification and water treatment. It recovers much of that expenditure through the taxes levied for waste collection services and water and sewage treatment and the profit generated by AEB Amsterdam.
This independent waste and power company runs a waste-to-energy plant, a high-efficiency power station, a hazardous waste depot, a regional sorting centre for domestic appliances and consumer electronics and six collection points where residents can dispose of their bulky waste. Together with Nuon, AEB also supplies heat to the residents of West and Noord through the district heating network. AEB has 400 employees.

❻ City with the most elms in Europe

Like waste collection, taking care of green areas is also the responsibility of the districts. The 75,000 elms in the city – more than any other city – put Amsterdam in a class of its own. There are fifty varieties.

❼ Wealth of information

The Dutch Public Records Act requires local authorities to keep their records. In Amsterdam, this task has been assigned to the City Archives. Since 2007, this department has been based in De Bazel, the Nederlandsche Handel-Maatschappij's former head office, which was built from 1919 to 1926 and designed by K. de Bazel.

❻ Green areas

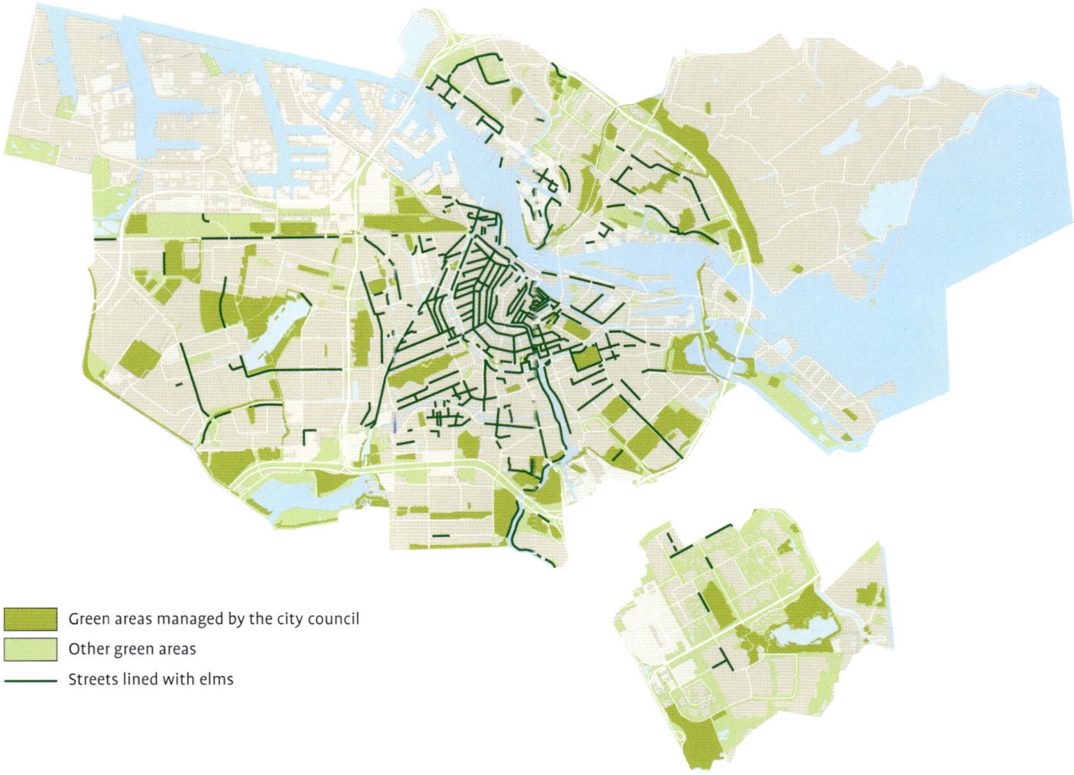

❼ Amsterdam City Archives

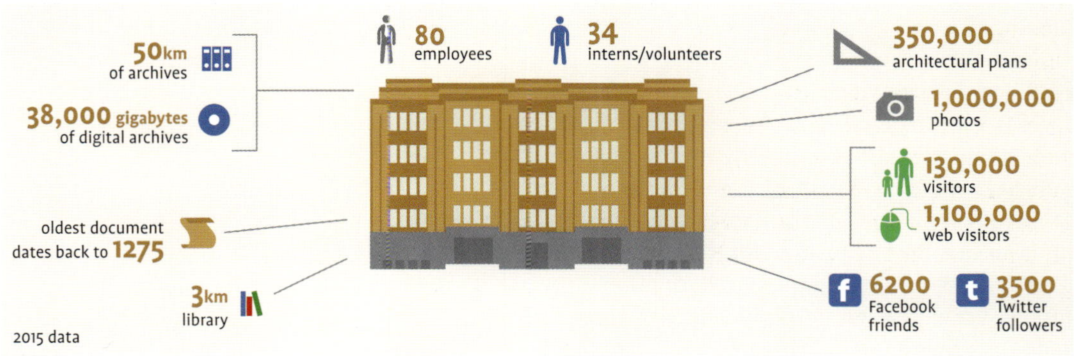

Sources: AEB Amsterdam (4-5); City of Amsterdam (6); Amsterdam City Archives (7)

© Noordhoff Uitgevers

Gas, electricity and water

Lighting a gas stove, switching on the lights or turning on the tap – we take all of these things for granted and only realise how dependent we have become on energy and running water when something goes wrong. Given the vital importance of these utilities, the government has long retained responsibility for generating and supplying energy and producing drinking water. However, the energy market was recently liberalised and different competitive companies are now authorised to transport and supply energy. Water, on the other hand, is still the City's responsibility. Controlled by the City of Amsterdam and the Amstel, Gooi en Vecht regional public water authority, the local government company Waternet not only supplies adequate drinking water, but is also responsible for flood control and rainwater and sewage processing.

❶ Gasworks and power stations

In 1898, the City's Gemeentelijk Gasbedrijf took over the operation of Amsterdam's private gasworks. One year later, the Gemeentelijke Electriciteitswerken was founded. The two utility companies merged in 1941 to form the Gemeentelijk Energiebedrijf. At the time, Amsterdam had three coal gasworks and one power station, but the gasworks had to close down after natural gas was discovered in Groningen.

❷ Subsurface network

There is a vast network of cables, pipes and conduits below street level, and if anything breaks, the street has to be dug up, which of course causes a lot of bother. A man-high underground tunnel is therefore being used for the Zuidas development. All gas, electricity, telecommunications, water, sewage and district heating pipes and cables run through this tunnel.

❶ Sites of current and former utility companies

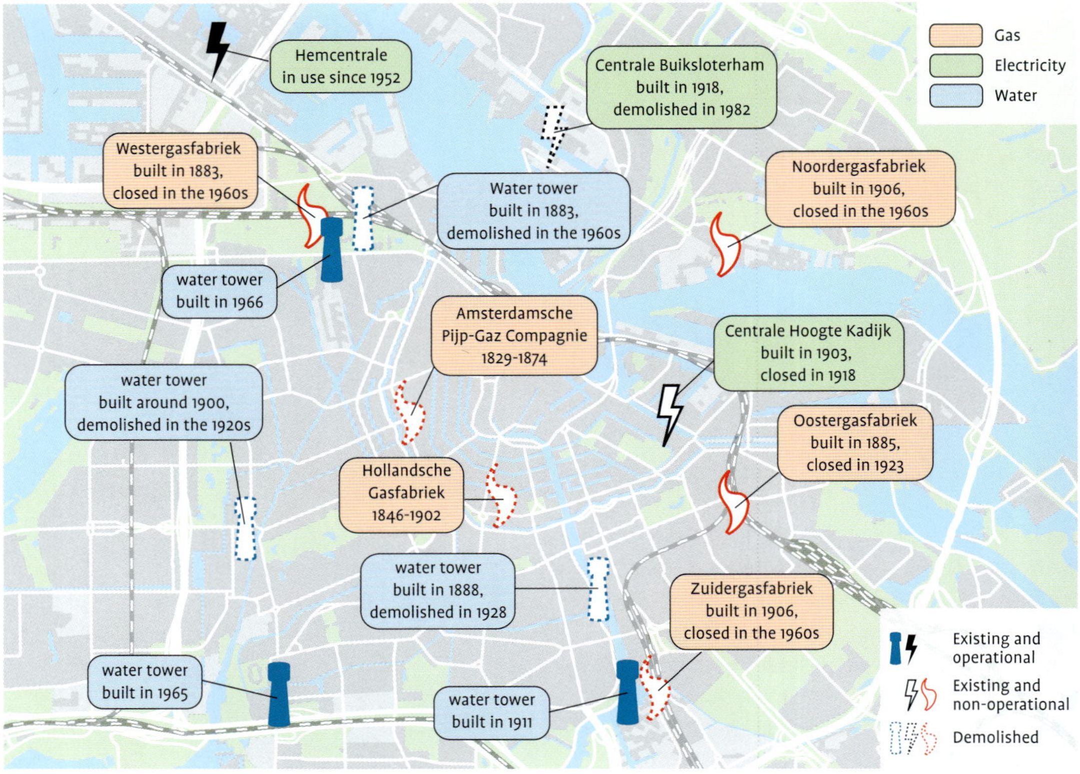

❷ High-voltage network

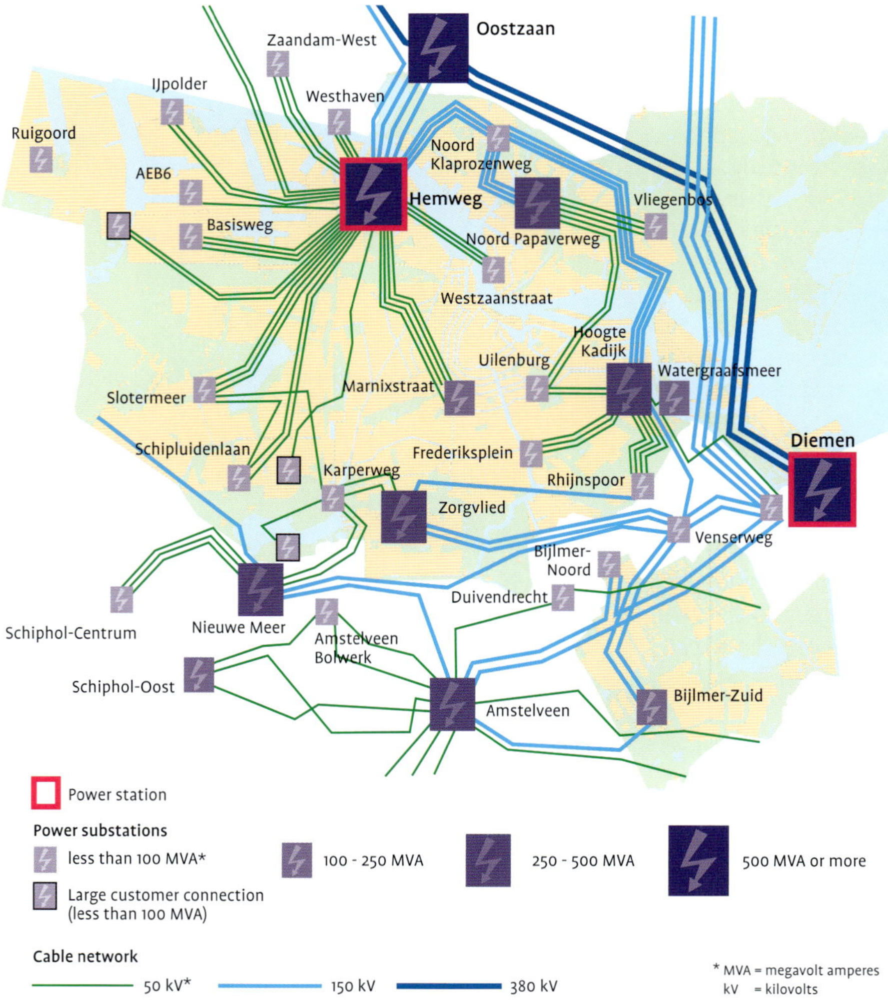

Source: Alliander (2)

© Noordhoff Uitgevers

❸ Millions of cubic metres

Households and companies in and around Amsterdam use 90 million m3 of drinking water each year. All that water is produced at two locations – Leiduin (70%) and Weesperkarspel (30%) – and then distributed using a pipe network with some 2000km of pipes in total.

❹ Excess water

Most of Amsterdam's rainwater and waste water is collected in a 50km-long sewer system and transported to the treatment facility in the Westelijk Havengebied. The city centre and pre-war city neighbourhoods still use a common sewer system for both types of water. One major disadvantage of this is that heavy rainfall can cause the sewers to overflow. These neighbourhoods therefore have large underground basins that buffer excessive volumes of water. Four supplementary pumping stations ensure that the waste water ultimately reaches the treatment plant, which processes an average of 200,000m^3 of waste water every day.

❺ A well-designed water system

The water in Amsterdam's ditches, waterways and lakes usually flows into the IJsselmeer and the North Sea via the river Amstel and the canals. During periods of heavy rainfall and high water levels in the North Sea, the Zeeburg pumping station discharges excess water into the IJmeer and the Markermeer. This pumping station is also used to renew the water in the canals, which happens a few times a week during the summer.

❸ Amsterdam Water Supply Dunes

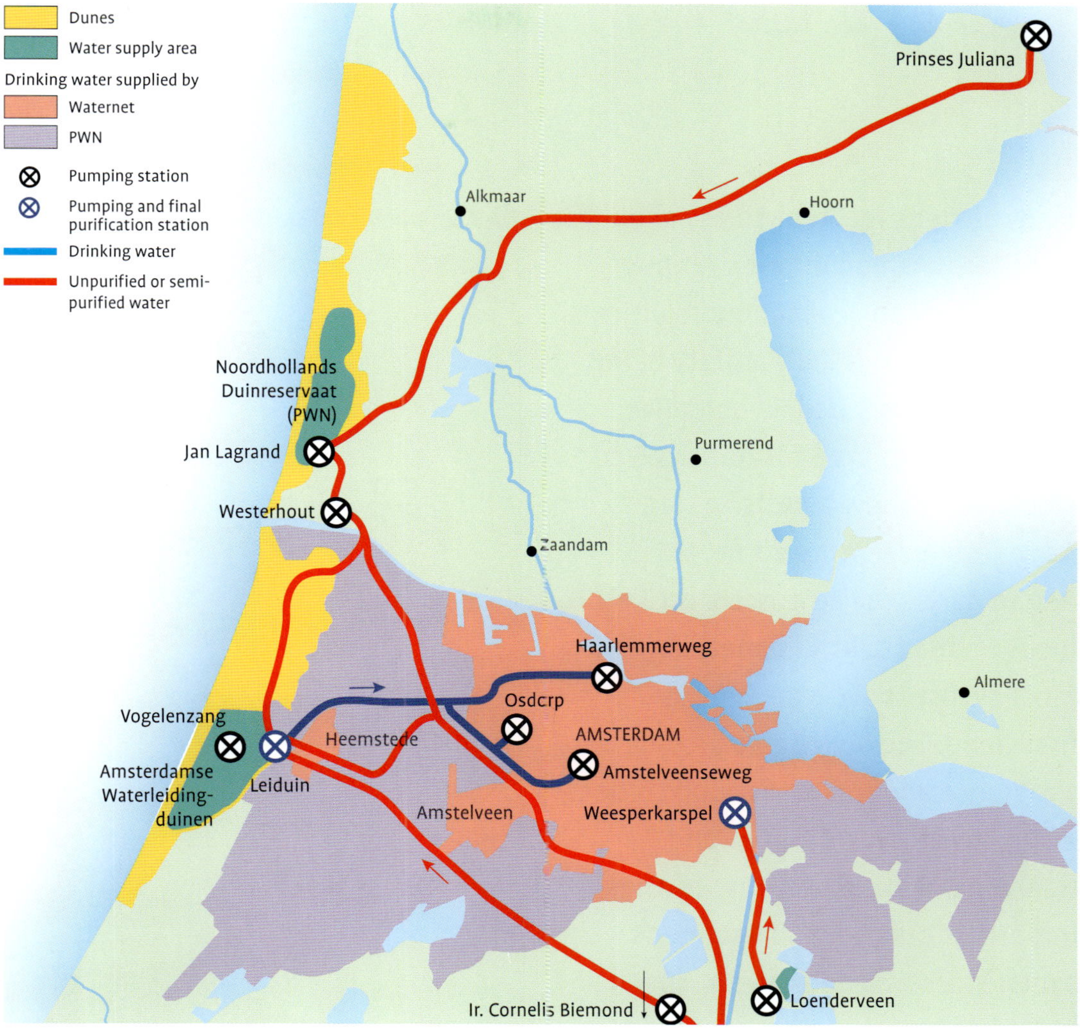

❹ Sewage systems

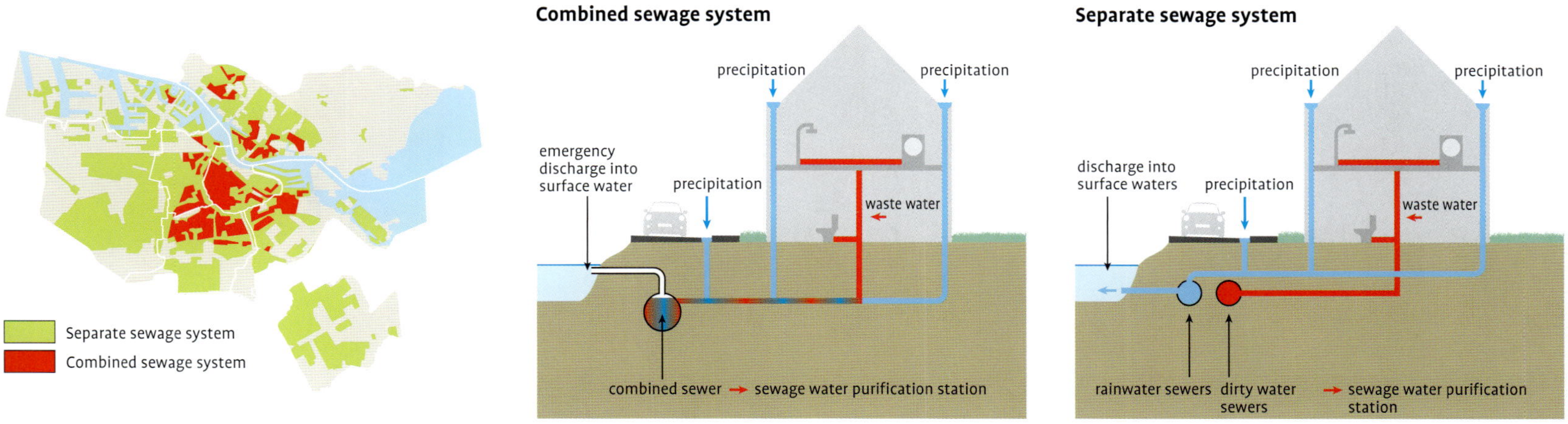

❺ Water renewal system inside the ring road

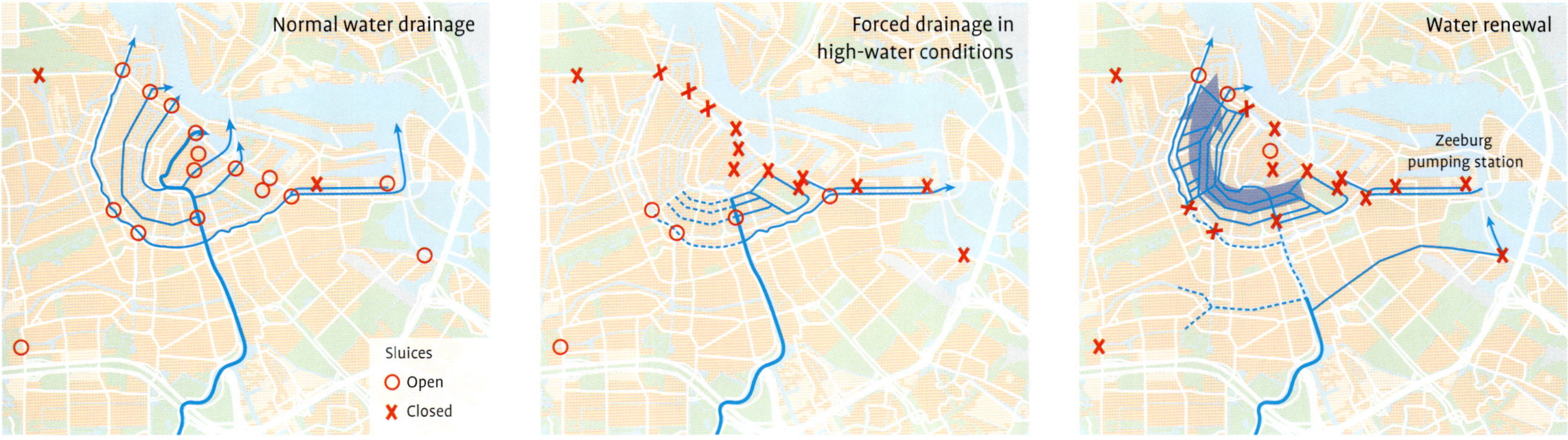

Sources: City of Amsterdam, Waternet, Amsterdam Waterbestendig (3-5)

© Noordhoff Uitgevers

Police

Many citizens feel that safety should be politicians' top priority. Among other things, the call for 'more officers on the street' has led to safety being constantly measured, in objective terms and also in terms of perceived safety. Both show a positive trend. As well as preventing crime, Amsterdam's police officers actively focus on road safety, something that most cyclists have experienced first-hand. The police also provide assistance and maintain public order, while investigating crimes and tracking down suspects are further important tasks. Appie Baantjer's experiences as a detective at the Warmoesstraat police station provided enough inspiration for nearly 70 blood-curdling thrillers.

❶ Community police officers in the Amsterdam regional unit

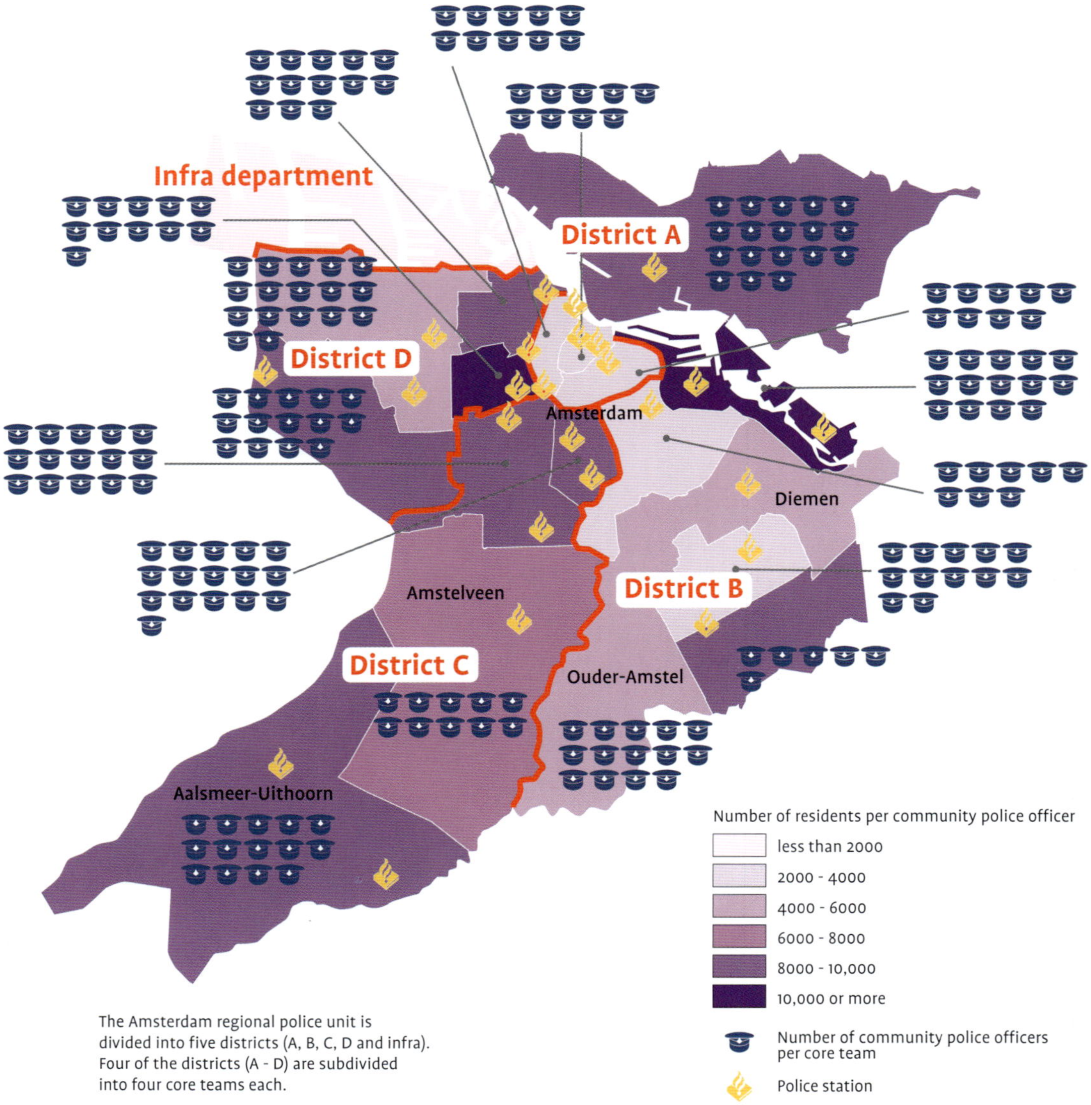

The Amsterdam regional police unit is divided into five districts (A, B, C, D and infra). Four of the districts (A - D) are subdivided into four core teams each.

❶ Policeman on the beat
For many Amsterdammers, community police officers are the eyes and ears of their neighbourhood. Former Chief of Police Jelle Kuiper (1997-2004) called them neighbourhood coordinators, or more affectionately the 'neighbourhood chiefs of police'. However, community police officers are under pressure – now that the Amsterdam constabulary has become part of a single national police force, it is easier to obtain a position in the 'provinces'. As a result, the remaining community police officers often have to take on tasks outside their formal responsibilities.

❷ Little chance of being caught
Cyclists are not permitted to do many things for their own safety and the safety of others. However, they are not likely to be fined if they do something wrong, as booking cyclists is not a top priority. The police fined 5527 people for cycling at night without lights in 2011, as opposed to a 'mere' 1700 in 2014.

❷ Bicycle-related offences and faults and the associated fines

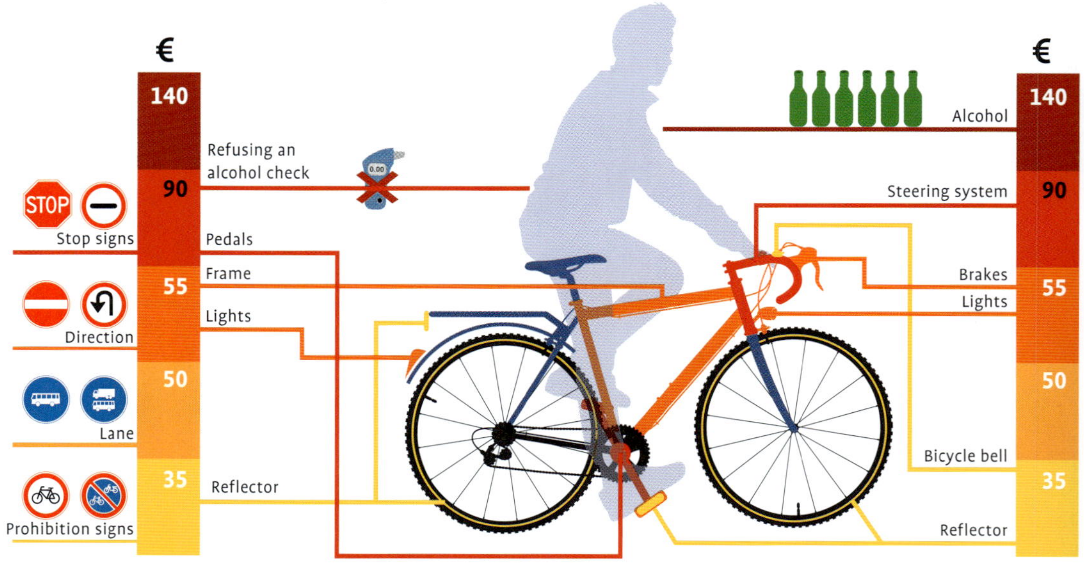

Sources: OIS, Research, Information and Statistics, City of Amsterdam (1); Veilig Verkeer Nederland (2)

© Noordhoff Uitgevers

❸ Objective safety index

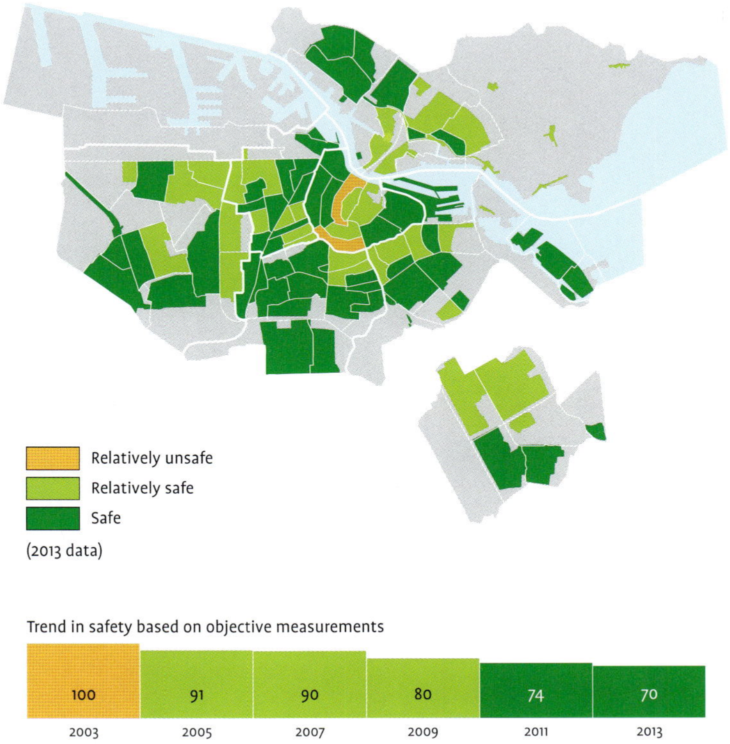

❹ Subjective safety index

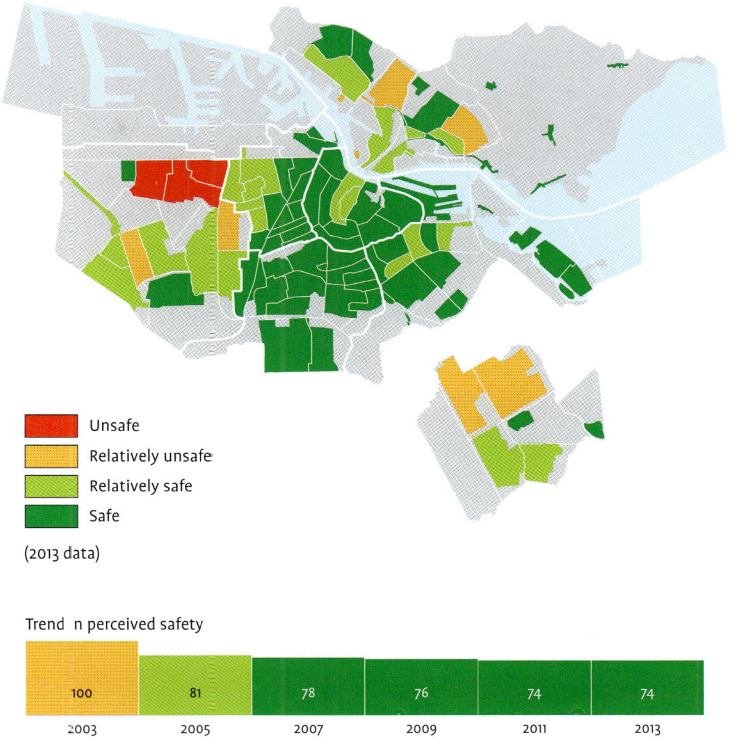

❸ - ❹ Objective and subjective

The city council regularly investigates the safety of neighbourhoods and the residents' perception of that safety. Police statistics and reports are used in the first case (objective), while surveys are used in the second (subjective). The two methods produce different results. The objective figures indicate that, with the exception of the city centre, Amsterdam is becoming an increasingly safer city. In 2013, some 97,000 offences were reported to the police, compared to around 93,000 in 2014, most of which involved property offences, like pickpocketing and burglaries. Even so, residents of certain neighbourhoods, particularly Nieuw-West and Zuidoost, do not feel that there has been any improvement. They think their neighbourhood is not safe, even though there is no objective reason for this. Residents of some areas in Centrum, on the other hand, have a more positive perceptions than the objective results warrant.

❺ Appie Baantjer

In 1945, Albert (Appie) Baantjer (1923-2010) joined Amsterdam's police force. In 1955, he was transferred to the Warmoesstraat station where he worked as a detective, staying there for 38 years. His experiences inspired him to write dozens of detective novels with a detective called De Cock as the main character. His books led to a successful television series called Baantjer. Nearly all of his books refer to a specific crime scene in the centre of Amsterdam. TV producer Peter Römer, with whom Baantjer collaborated intensively in his final years, opened the Appie Baantjer Museum in 2008. It is situated on Warmoesstraat, in the basement of Cafe Heffer, just a stone's throw away from the former police station. There are also special Appie Baantjer tours.

❺ Baantjer's Amsterdam

Sources: *OIS, Research, Information and Statistics, City of Amsterdam (3-4); A. C. Baantjer, 'De Cock' series / A. P. Scholten (5)*

© Noordhoff Uitgevers

Administration of justice

The mayor is responsible for public order and the emergency services, but not for the preservation of law and order – this is the public prosecutor's responsibility. Together with the chief police officers, the mayor and public prosecutor form the 'triumvirate', which decides on the deployment and tasks of the regional police force. Many different crimes are punished by criminal law, ranging from simple shoplifting to manslaughter or even targeted murder. Once a suspect has been arrested, it is up to the court to decide whether or not he is guilty. Incidentally, most of the cases processed by the courts involve civil law rather than criminal offences.

❶ Dispensation of justice

❷ Drug-related crimes

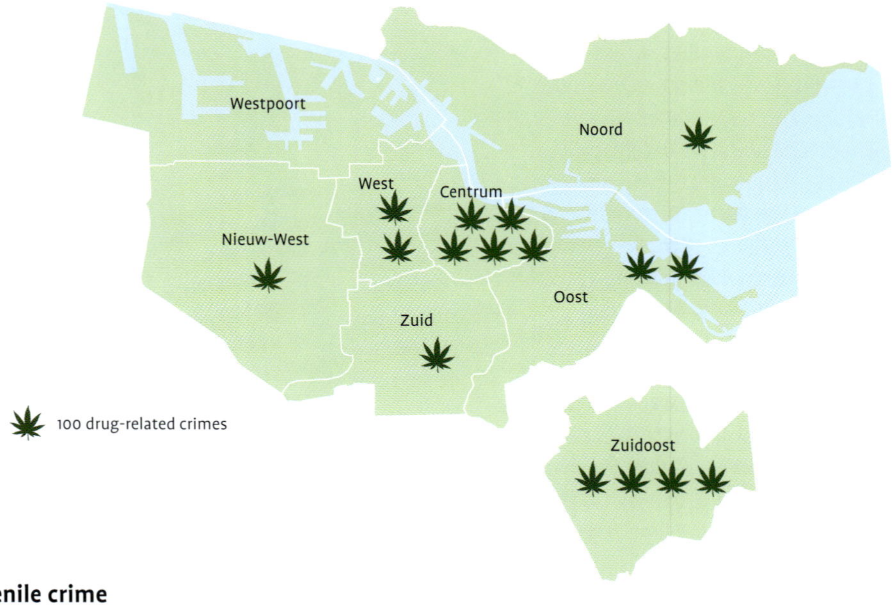

❸ Juvenile crime

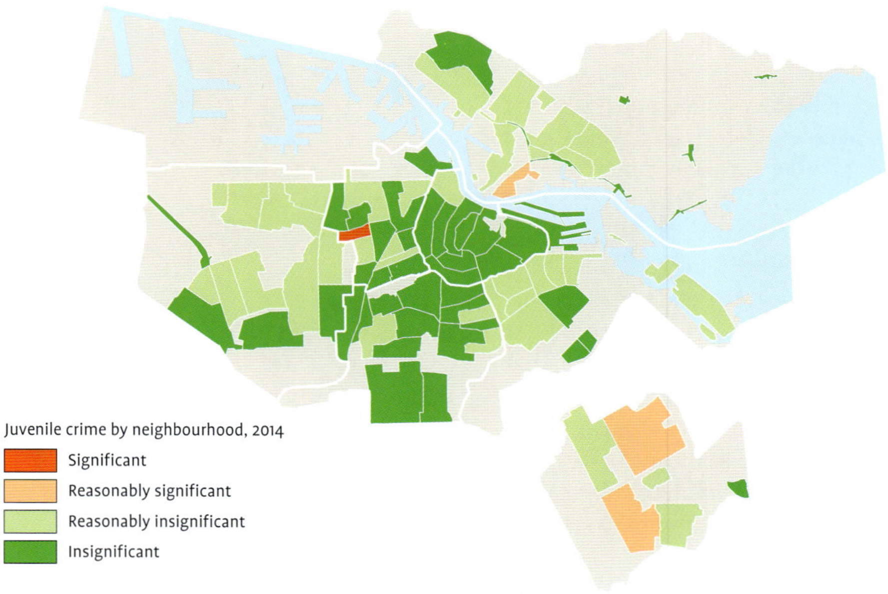

❶ Court cases
Around 200 judges and 800 civil servants work for the court of Amsterdam. Most hearings, generally subdistrict court cases, are held in the courthouse on Parnassusweg. Special criminal cases are heard in the high-security courtroom, nicknamed the Bunker, in Osdorp. Once the 'Bijlmerbajes' has closed in 2016, Amsterdam will only have one prison left – the 'Penitentiaire Inrichting Amsterdam' on Tafelbergweg.

❷ Crimes
In 2014, the police took note of almost 94,000 crimes, nearly half of which involved theft and pickpocketing. 'Only' 1561 were drug-related crimes, such as the illegal sale of drugs, extortion and drug money laundering.

Source: OIS, Research, Information and Statistics, City of Amsterdam (1-3)

© Noordhoff Uitgevers

❸ Young offenders

In 2007, 16,300 young people aged 12 to 24 were suspected of a criminal offence, compared with 11,550 in 2014. The juvenile crime rate is therefore falling, except in Zuidoost, where nearly 6% of young people were apprehended as suspects in 2014. This high percentage reflects the major risk factors in this part of the city – many households on the breadline, single-parent families, early school leavers and a high rate of absence from school. The 'Van Galenbuurt' is shown in red because the Work and Income department has a homeless persons office there. Around 60 homeless people are registered at the facility, but they do not live there.

❹ - ❺ Murderous city

In 2014, the Amsterdam regional police unit (formerly known as the Amsterdam-Amstelland police region) recorded 357 cases of manslaughter or attempted manslaughter and 25 cases of murder (23 in Amsterdam, 2 in Amstelveen). The national figure in that year was 137.
The police made 305 arrests in connection with the 382 Amsterdam cases. In the 1990s, there were 250 murders a year in the Netherlands on average. The number of murders is therefore declining, but the use of violence does seem to be on the increase.

❻ War on drugs

Shots were fired at a car with four passengers of Moroccan descent in the 'Staatsliedenbuurt' during the evening of 29 December 2012. Two were killed, but the other two managed to escape. This targeted killing was the first visible sign of a feud that had raged for some time between the Moroccan drug trafficking gangs after a delivery involving a large amount of cocaine had gone wrong in Antwerp a few months earlier. The shooting sparked off a chain reaction of targeted killings. In 2014, at least five men who could be linked to the murders in the 'Staatsliedenbuurt' in one way or another were killed. Quarrels and conflicting interests in other areas of Amsterdam's underworld are also resulting in violent reprisal killings increasingly often. Sometimes shots are simply fired at random without attempting to avoid innocent bystanders.

❹ Murders

❻ Murders and targeted killings

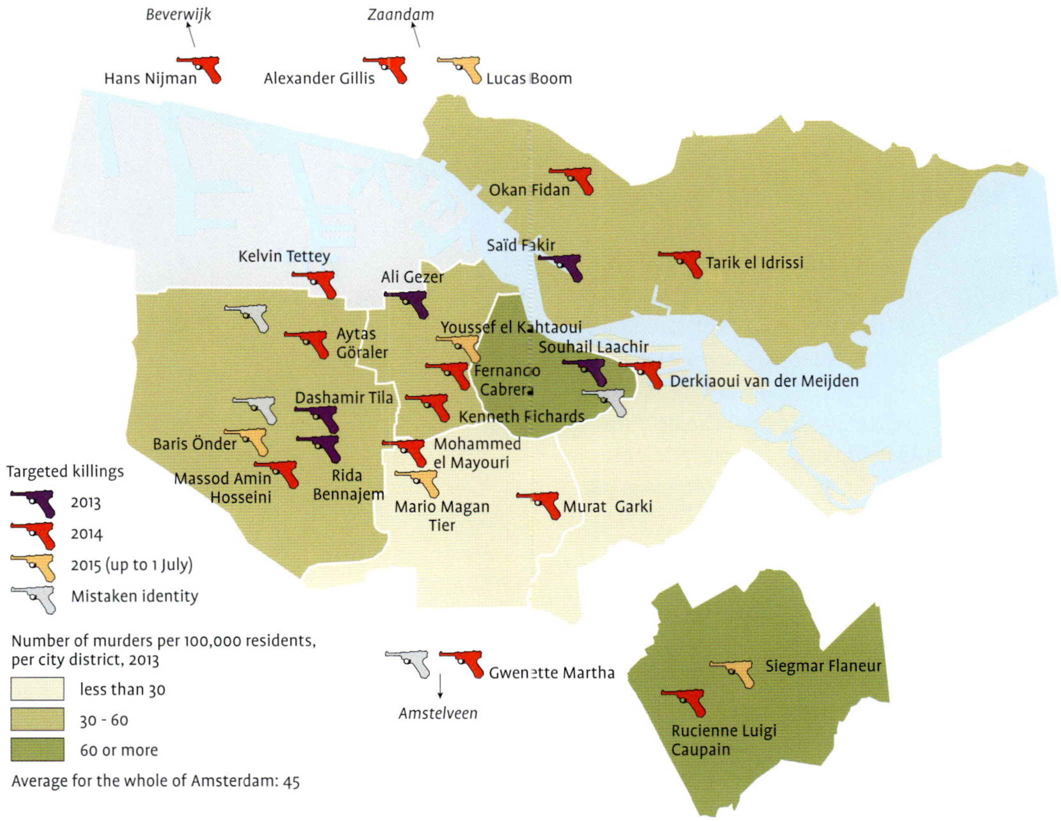

❺ Murders by category

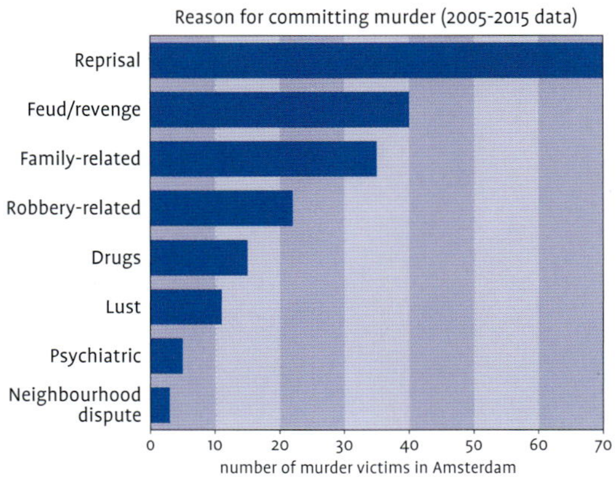

© Noordhoff Uitgevers

Ambulance and fire services

The many hundreds of men and women who man the ambulances and fire engines are on call and ready to respond to emergencies throughout the day and night. The organisation of both emergency services has changed drastically since the introduction of the Amsterdam-Amstelland safety region, which consists of six local authority areas. The six separate fire brigades have been merged to form a single fire-fighting service, known as Brandweer Amsterdam-Amstelland. In addition, there is now only a single ambulance service, Ambulance Amsterdam, which is responsible for transporting injured and sick people throughout the region. All calls are now channelled to a single central emergency control centre, which deploys fire engines and ambulances to the right address.

❶ Amsterdam-Amstelland ambulance region

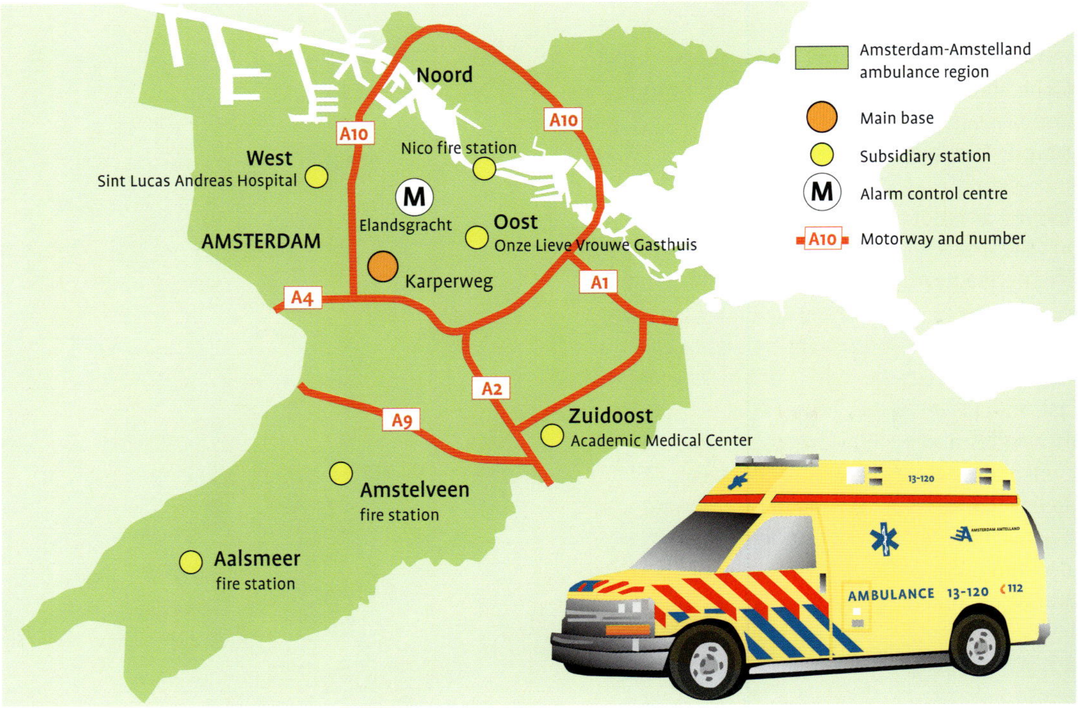

❷ Ambulance deployments

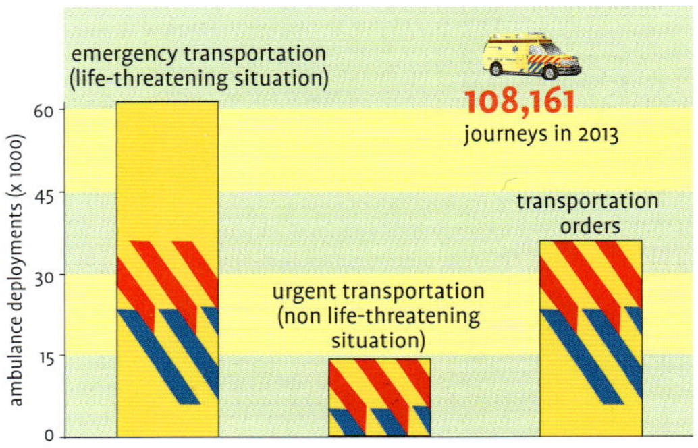

❸ Average emergency response time

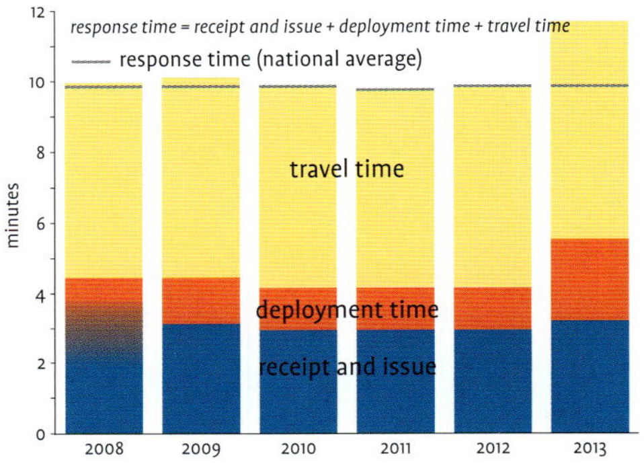

❶ Stations
As of 2014, Weesperplein, Sarphatistraat and Wibautstraat are no longer full of blaring ambulance sirens. Amsterdam's best known ambulance station, at the Public Health Service on Valckenierstraat, has closed and the ambulances are now stationed at three new sites – Onze Lieve Vrouwe Gasthuis, Sint Lucas Andreas Hospital and the Nico fire station close to the IJtunnel. The latter site is being used temporarily until the ambulance station at BovenIJ Hospital is ready.

❷ - ❹ Within fifteen minutes
The aim is to get an ambulance to the scene within 15 minutes of receiving a request for emergency assistance. In 2014, this was achieved in nearly 94% of all cases. The ambulance service also offers 'plannable' ambulance care for people who are not in immediate mortal danger, but who do have to be transported in a reclining position.

❹ Transporting patients to and from hospitals

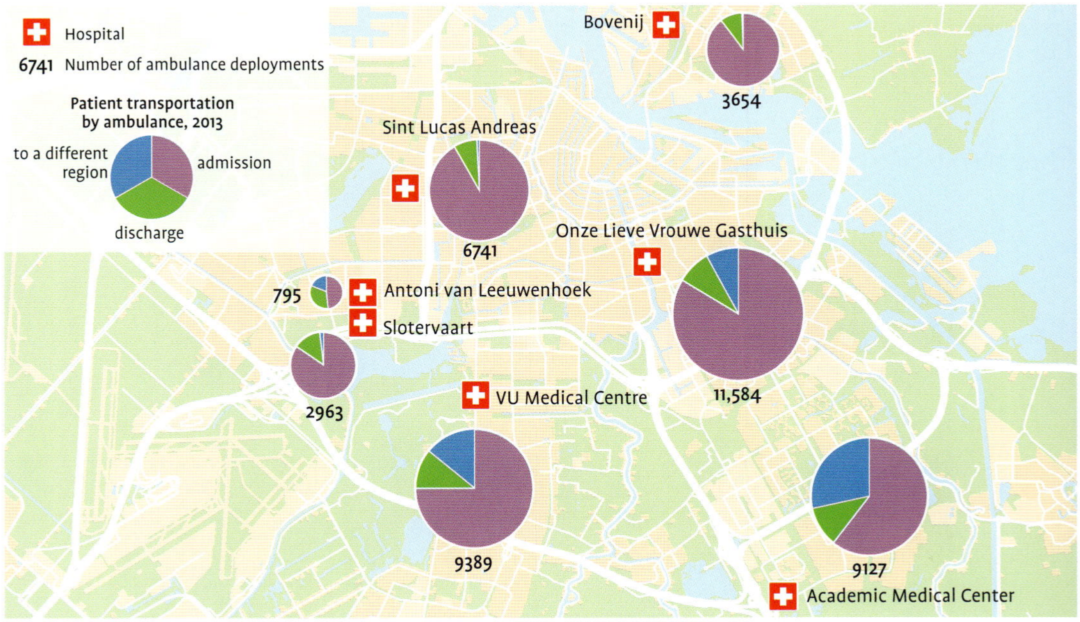

Sources: *Ambulance Amsterdam (1-4); Ambulancezorg Nederland (3)*

© Noordhoff Uitgevers

❺ N for Nico

Brandweer Amsterdam-Amstelland (BAA) operates nineteen fire stations, thirteen of which are located in Amsterdam itself. Traditionally, each fire station is given a boy's name, the first letter of which often corresponds to the first letter of the street or location where the oldest station was situated. A professional fire brigade was first set up in Amsterdam in 1874. Fire station 'N' was housed in the weighing house on Nieuwmarkt, hence the name Nico. In 1890, Nico station relocated to De Ruijterkade, but kept its name. In 1973, it moved again, to the IJtunnel this time. The building on De Ruijterkade was earmarked for demolition, but Stichting Oud-Nico successfully prevented the building's destruction and it was restored in 2011.

❻ Deployment

In 2014, the BAA responded to over 12,000 calls, nearly 8500 of which related to incidents in Amsterdam itself. They ranged from storm damage, car crashes, animals in distress and flooding to vehicles in the canals, resuscitation and, of course, fires. In total, the fire brigade had to be deployed in the region on 547 occasions to extinguish a house fire. 487 were in Amsterdam. They also had to hoist sick persons down out of their homes on almost three times as many occasions.

❺ Former Nico fire station (De Ruijterkade)

① Main entrance
② Bay
③ Stables
④ Waiting room
⑤ Canteen
⑥ Chief fireman's living quarters
⑦ Chief fireman's room
⑧ Kitchen
⑨ Office
⑩ Dormitory for firemen on duty
⑪ Bathroom
⑫ Washroom
⑬ Climbing area
⑭ Hose store
⑮ Spiral staircase to bay
⑯ Corridor
⑰ Attic

❻ Fire service deployments

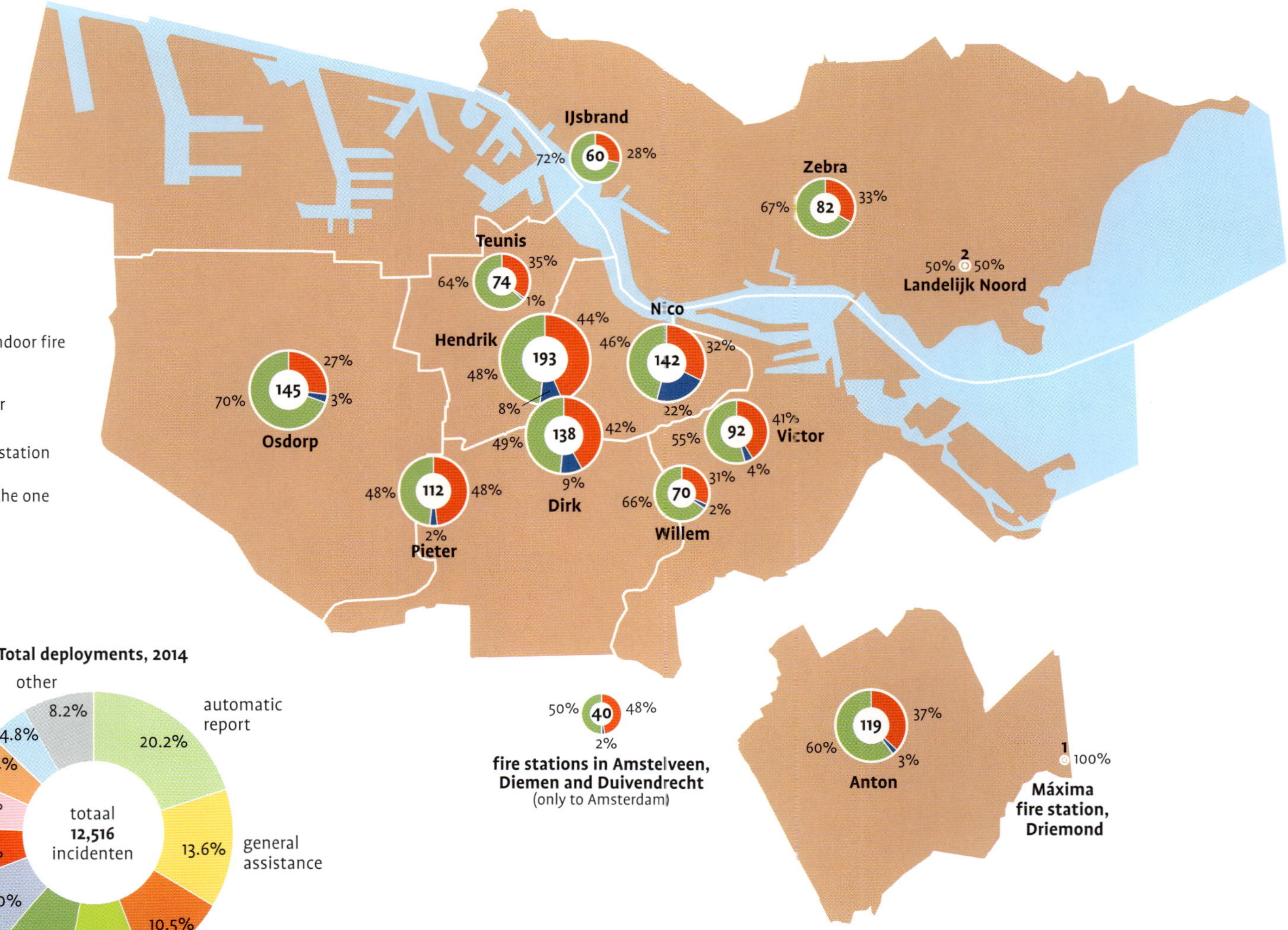

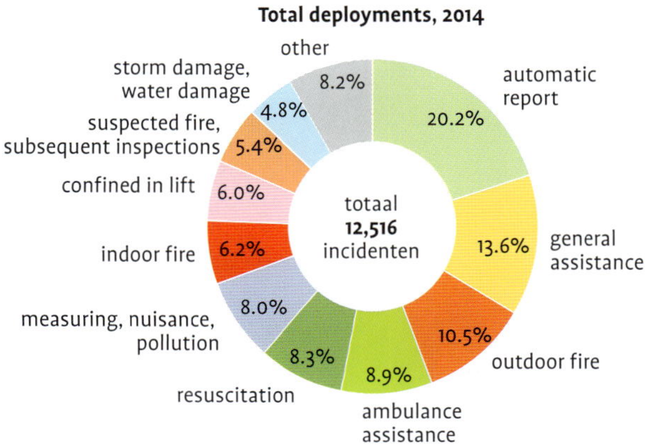

Source: Brandweer Amsterdam-Amstelland (6)

© Noordhoff Uitgevers

Care

With seven hospitals, dozens of other care institutions and a GP within walking distance almost everywhere in the city, Amsterdammers have no reason to complain about the provision of medical, social and mental care in the city. This is reflected in the average Amsterdammer's high level of satisfaction with the local care facilities. Whether this situation will continue remains to be seen.
In its efforts to manage costs, the national government wants elderly people to live at home for longer. This has resulted in the closure of numerous care and nursing homes. On top of that, the city council was assigned responsibility for youth care and care for handicapped people living at home in 2015, a further major change whose effects are not yet fully apparent.
Amsterdammers feel reasonably healthy and are also living longer and longer. However, the city's Public Health Service is concerned by the fact that the number of smokers is no longer falling, as well as by the alarmingly high number of overweight or obese young people, the excessive intake of fat and salt and the lack of exercise. Accordingly, cardio-vascular diseases are the second highest cause of death in Amsterdam.

❶ Care institutions

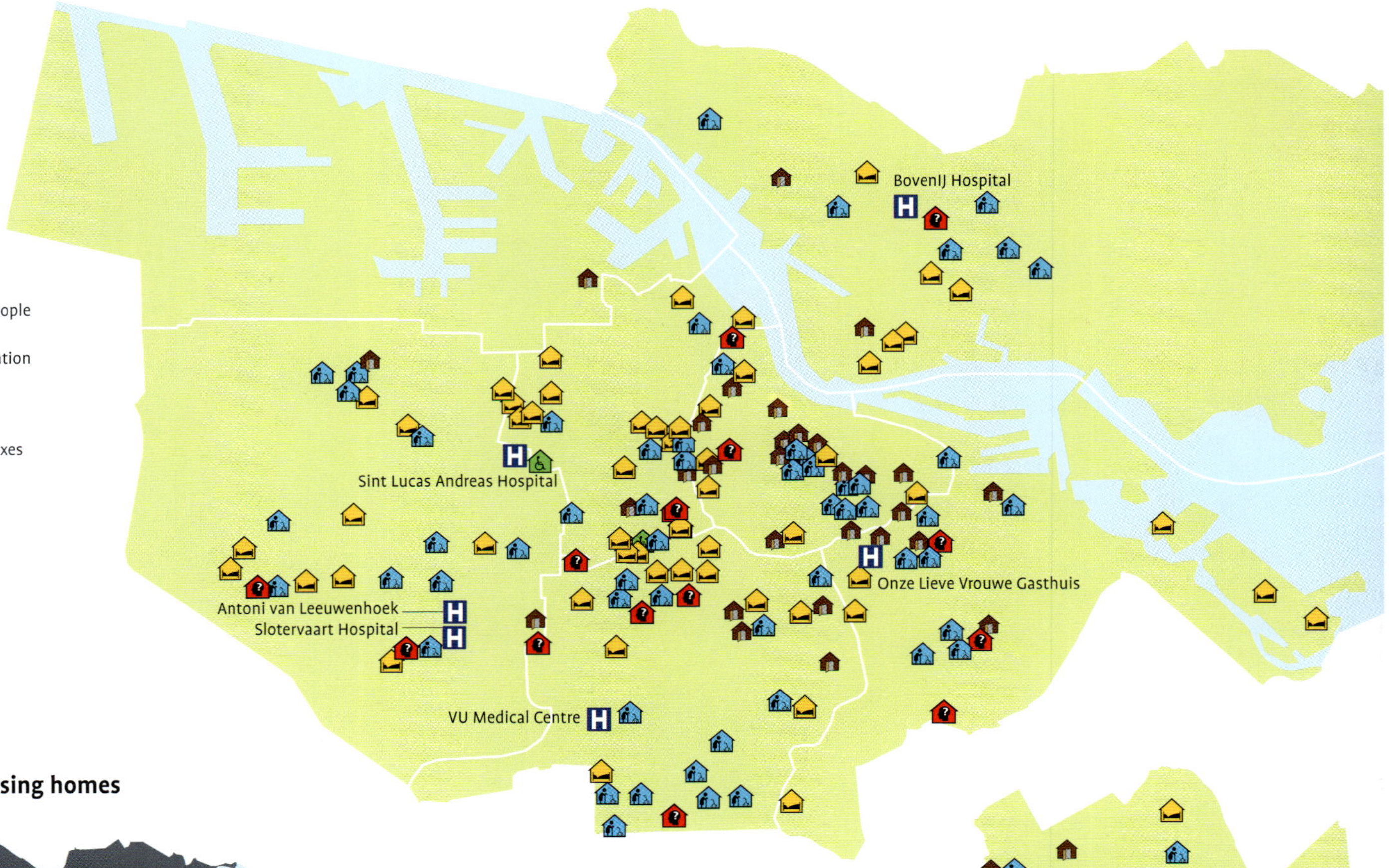

❷ Beds in care and nursing homes

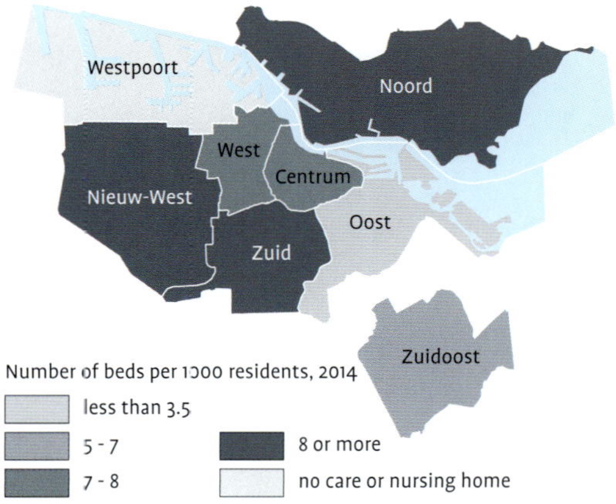

Source: OIS, Research, Information and Statistics, City of Amsterdam (1, 2)

© Noordhoff Uitgevers

❸ Distance to a GP

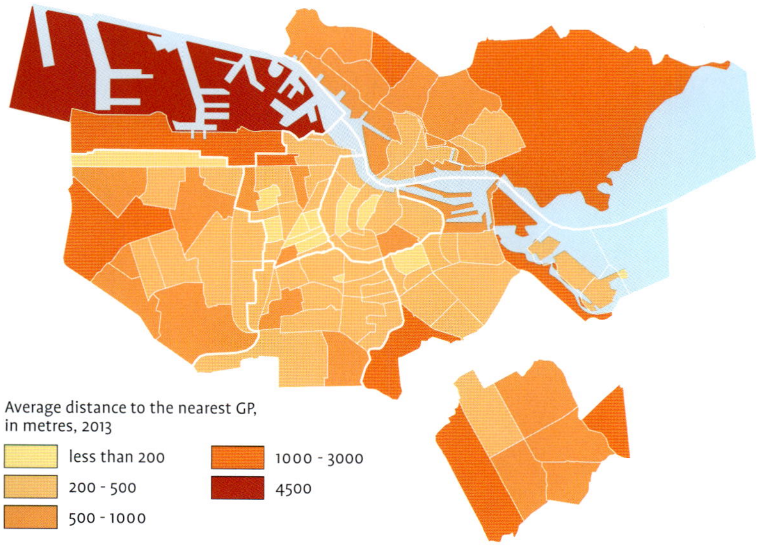

❹ First-line health care

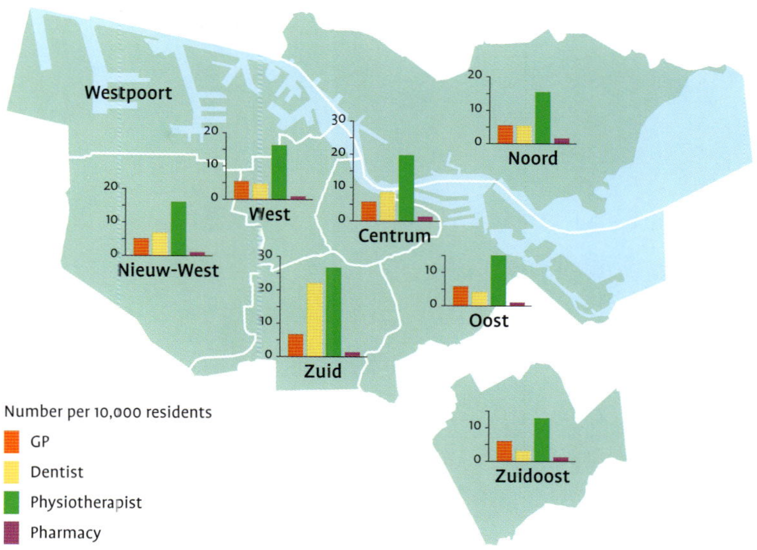

❺ Perceived level of health in the Amsterdam Metropolitan Area

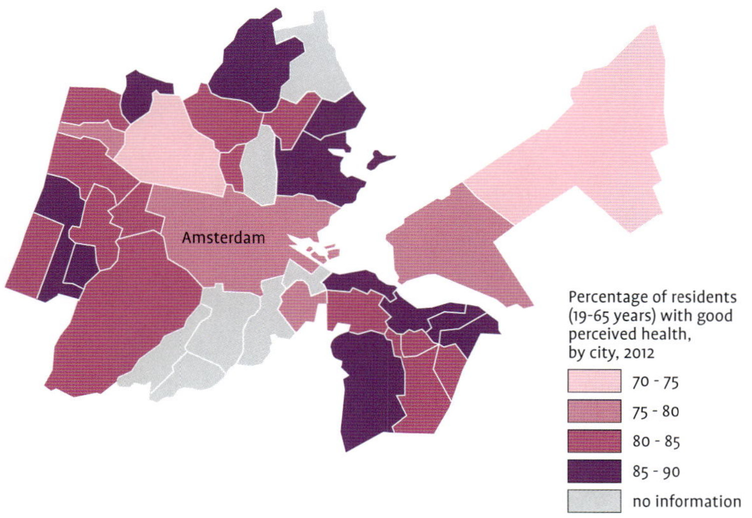

❻ Heavy smokers in the Amsterdam Metropolitan Area

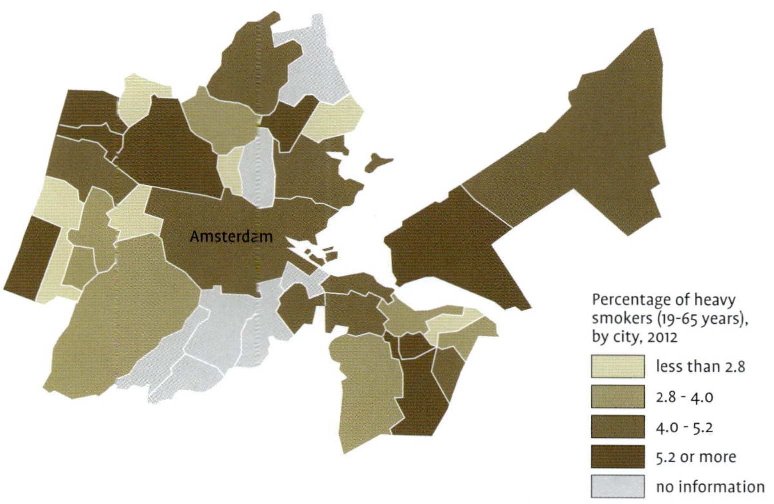

❶ - ❷ Care home places harder to obtain

The national government wants people to live at home for longer, even if they need care, and expects their immediate circle of family and friends to take greater responsibility for caring for them. As a result, obtaining a place in a care home or nursing home has become much more difficult. The number of care institutions in Amsterdam (currently around 75) is expected to drop by one third over the next few years and Sint Jacob, Wittenberg and Bernardus have already closed.

❸ - ❹ Making an appointment

In 2014, 451 GPs, 687 dentists and 1443 physiotherapists were seeing patients in Amsterdam. People living inside the ring road can walk or cycle to their appointments. In that area, there is almost always a GP practice within 500 metres.

❺ Reasonably satisfied

The Public Health Service regularly investigates how Amsterdammers perceive their level of health. The 2012 survey indicates that three quarters of the population feel reasonably healthy. It also reveals that residents of Noord, Nieuw-West and Zuidoost suffer from more mental and chronic conditions than average and are more likely to be overweight. Loneliness is also a growing problem that affects some 65,000 Amsterdammers.

❻ Difficulty with quitting

In 1994, 42% of Amsterdam's population were smokers. Since then, that percentage has gradually decreased to 28% in 2012. The national rate that year was just 23%.

❼ - ❽ Living longer and longer

The average life expectancy increased from 55 to 80 years over the last century. In 1900, only 5% of Amsterdam's population was aged 65 or above, compared to 12% in 2014. Noord has the most elderly residents – 7% of people living there are aged over 75 compared to only 3% in West. Even so, population ageing is not excessive in Amsterdam – 17% of the total Dutch population is aged 65 or above. As for the causes of death, Amsterdam hardly differs from the national statistics.

❼ Life expectancy

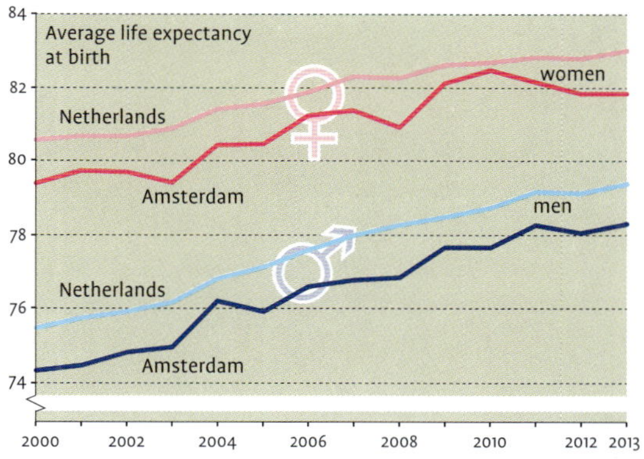

❽ Causes of death in major cities

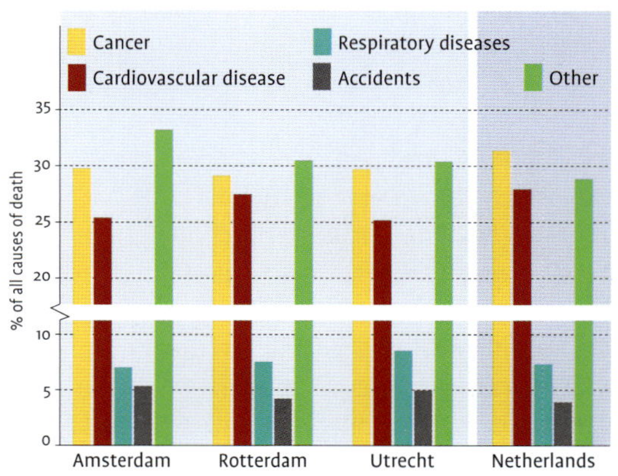

Sources: Statistics Netherlands (3); OIS, Research, Information and Statistics, City of Amsterdam (4); Public Health Service of Amsterdam / Statistics Netherlands (5-6); OIS, Research, Information and Statistics, City of Amsterdam (7); Statistics Netherlands Health Monitor (8)

© Noordhoff Uitgevers

Primary/secondary education

By law, children in the Netherlands must go to school from the ages of 5 to 16. Anybody who fails to gain a basic qualification in that time (at least a level-2 senior secondary vocational education diploma), has to stay at school until the age of 18. School attendance officers enforce compliance with compulsory education, by taking action to reduce absenteeism, for example. This has varying degrees of success in Amsterdam.

There are still major socio-economic differences between school types. This is apparent at primary school level and continues in secondary education. For instance, more children born to native parents go to pre-university schools than those whose parents come from non-Western countries. Gender is also a major factor in determining where school pupils in Amsterdam end up.

❶ Primary schools

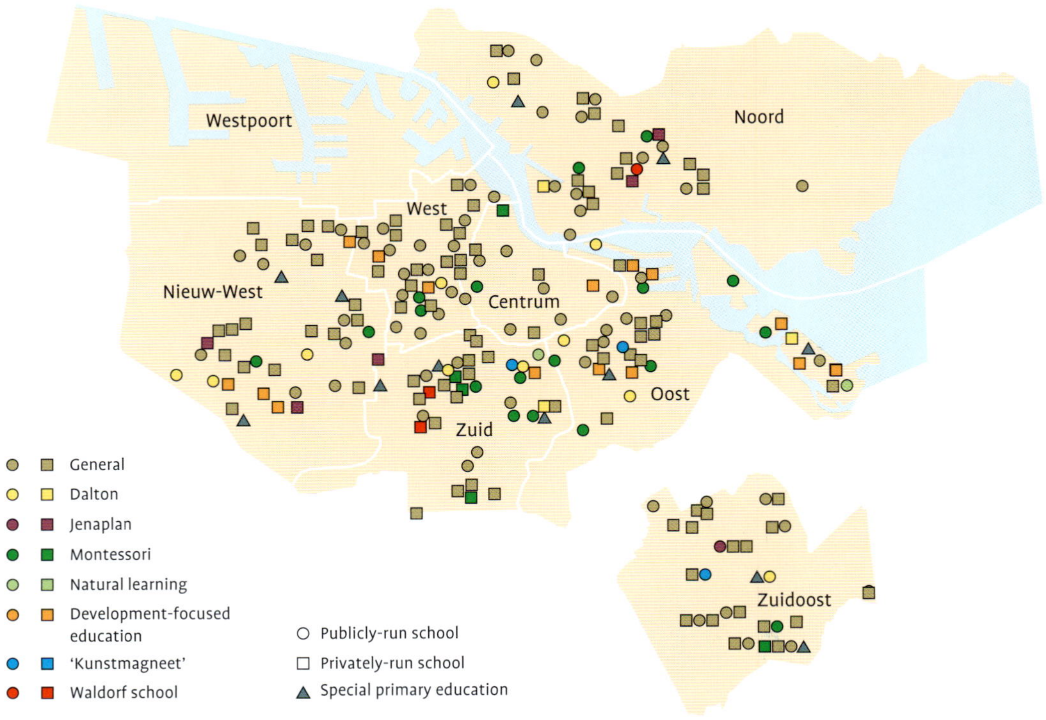

❷ Districts and primary schools by socio-economic status

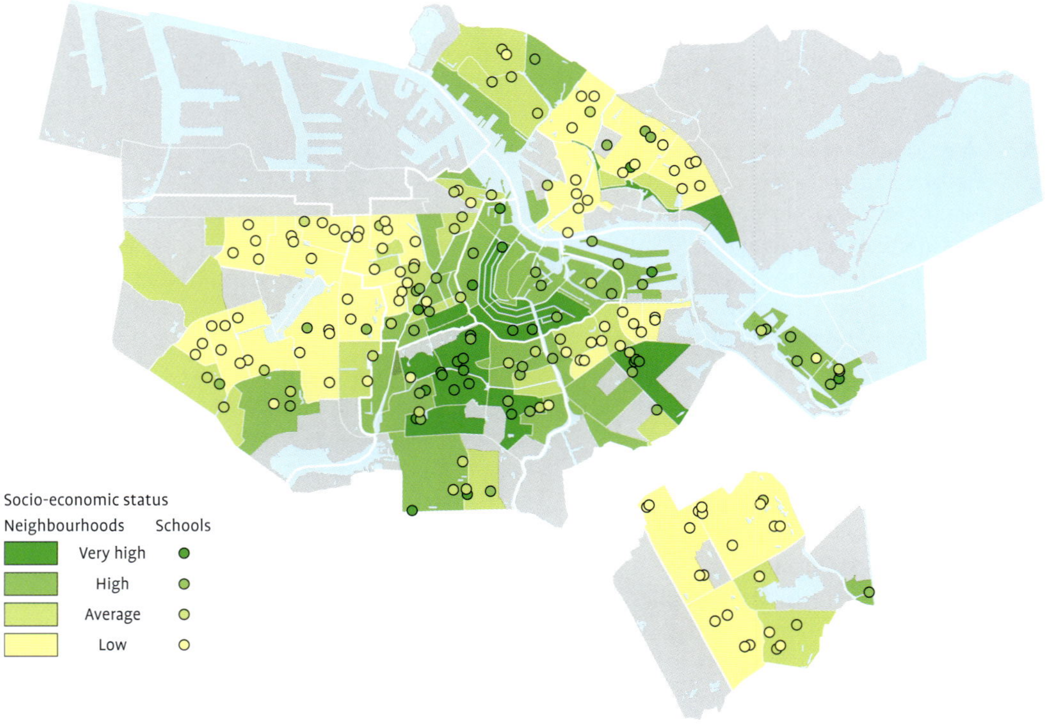

❶ Publicly and privately-run schools

There are 210 primary schools in Amsterdam, 98 of which are publicly run and 112 privately. Publicly-run schools have 312 pupils on average, and privately-run schools 279. A total of almost 62,000 children are registered, most of them in Nieuw-West (over 12,000) and Oost (over 11,000). All schools use the same application and registration procedure. Parents have freedom of choice and may apply to any school, but only have priority at eight schools in the immediate vicinity of their homes.

❷ - ❸ Privileged and underprivileged

Pupils from the Centrum and Zuid districts score highest in their primary school leavers' tests – 540 on average – whereas children from West and Zuidoost achieve an average score of 531. Around 80% of the children from Centrum receive a senior general secondary education or pre-university recommendation compared to 30% of those in Zuidoost.

❸ Schools and pupils in the 2014-2015 academic year

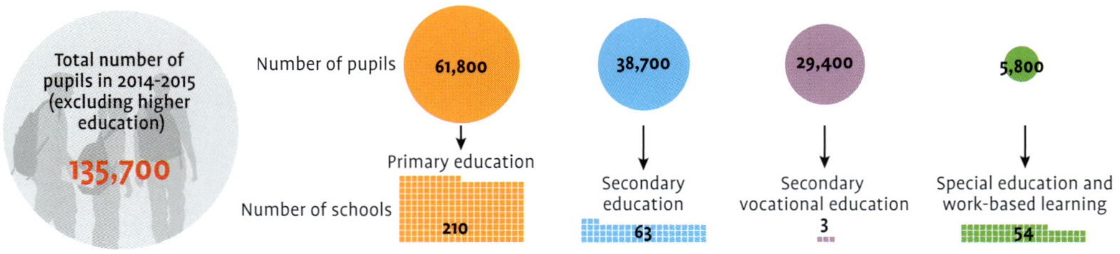

Sources: *City of Amsterdam (1); OIS, Research, Information and Statistics, City of Amsterdam (2, 3)*

© Noordhoff Uitgevers

❹ The next step

After primary school, all pupils have to attend secondary education. Parents and pupils can choose from 63 secondary schools in Amsterdam. As of 2015, each new pupil is given a number for each school. If too many pupils apply to a specific school, a draw is held for pupils who do not have priority. Pupils not assigned a place in the draw are given a place at their second-choice school. Civil servants call this 'central matching'.

❺ Strict rules

'Bureau Leerplicht', on Jodenbreestraat, with branch offices in each district, enforces compliance with compulsory education obligations. The rules are strict. Pupils are only excused from attending school in special situations. If the rules are broken, the school attendance officer can draw up a formal written report, register the pupil with the youth care department, refer the pupil to the HALT organisation for a study order or community service order, or, in the worst case scenario, take legal action. Even so, the absenteeism rate has still risen in recent years, particularly in Noord and Zuidoost, although this is probably partly due to improved registration.

❻ Matching

Secondary education is offered at several levels: learning support (lwoo), preparatory secondary vocational (vmbo), senior general secondary (havo), pre-university (vwo) or community school (brede school). The level at which children attend school is strongly dependent on their socio-economic background. Some 67% of vmbo pupils come from a non-Western immigrant background, whereas three out of four vwo pupils have native parents. The twenty secondary vocational education institutions present the same picture.

❼ ROCvA, ROC TOP and Mediacollege

ROC van Amsterdam, ROC TOP and Mediacollege are the main providers of secondary vocational education (mbo). Pupils can choose from three hundred different vocational courses, which are subdivided into different domains. However, the mbo sector is going through a rough patch, as a relatively large number of pupils leave their courses prematurely, especially at levels 1 (28%) and 2 (14%).

❹ Schools for secondary education and secondary vocational education

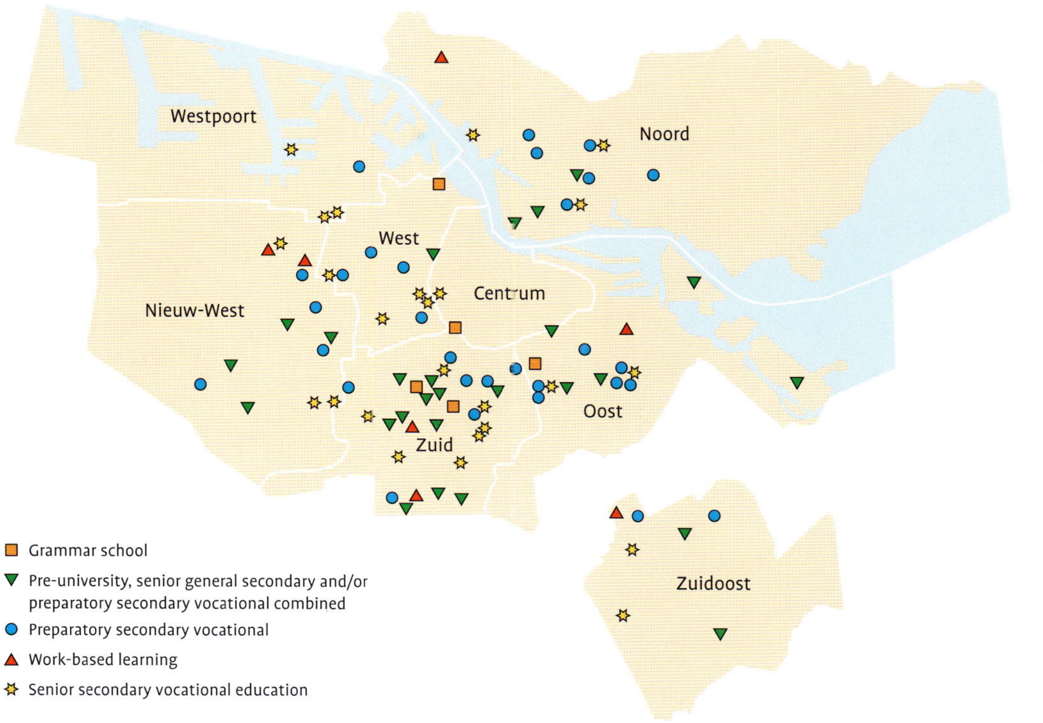

❺ Absenteeism trends

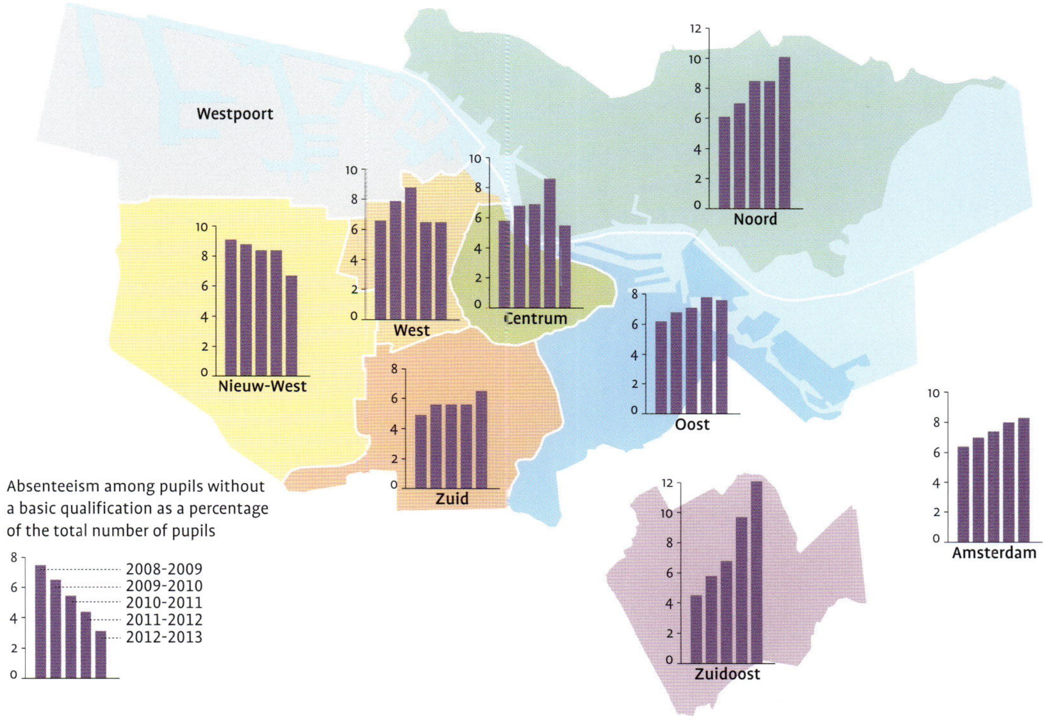

❻ Secondary education

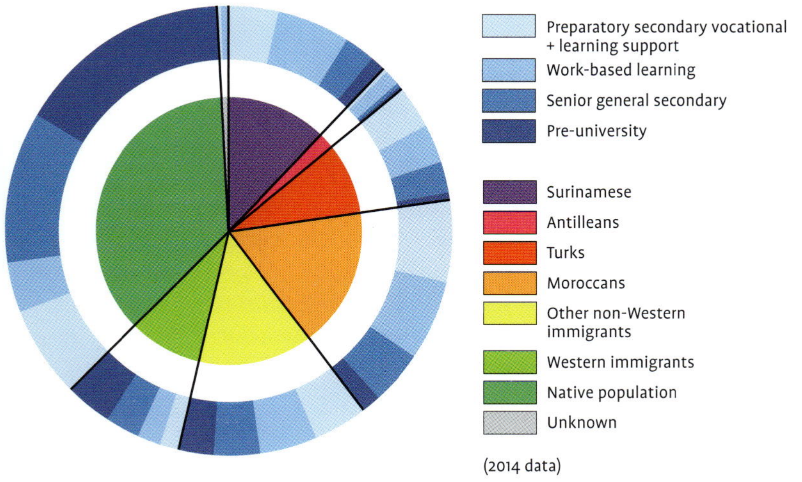

(2014 data)

❼ Secondary vocational education

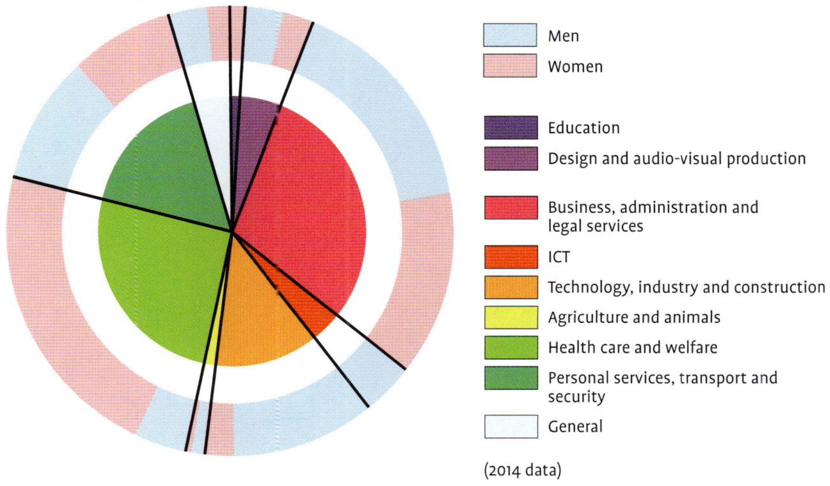

(2014 data)

Sources: City of Amsterdam (4); OIS, Research, Information and Statistics, City of Amsterdam (5-7)

© Noordhoff Uitgevers

Colleges and universities

Amsterdam is a student city. In 2013-2014, nearly 110,000 students were registered at the University of Amsterdam (UvA), the VU University Amsterdam (VU) and the four universities of applied sciences. Many of them still live with their parents, partly because there is a shortage of student accommodation, but also because living at home is convenient and much less expensive.

The two universities are highly regarded and the University of Amsterdam is even ranked 77th in the world's top 100 universities. This attracts both Dutch and foreign students and gives Amsterdam much prestige.

❶ Higher professional education students

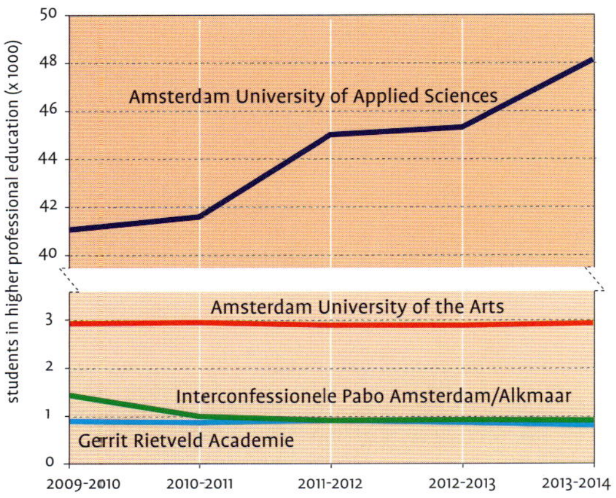

❷ Higher education in Amsterdam

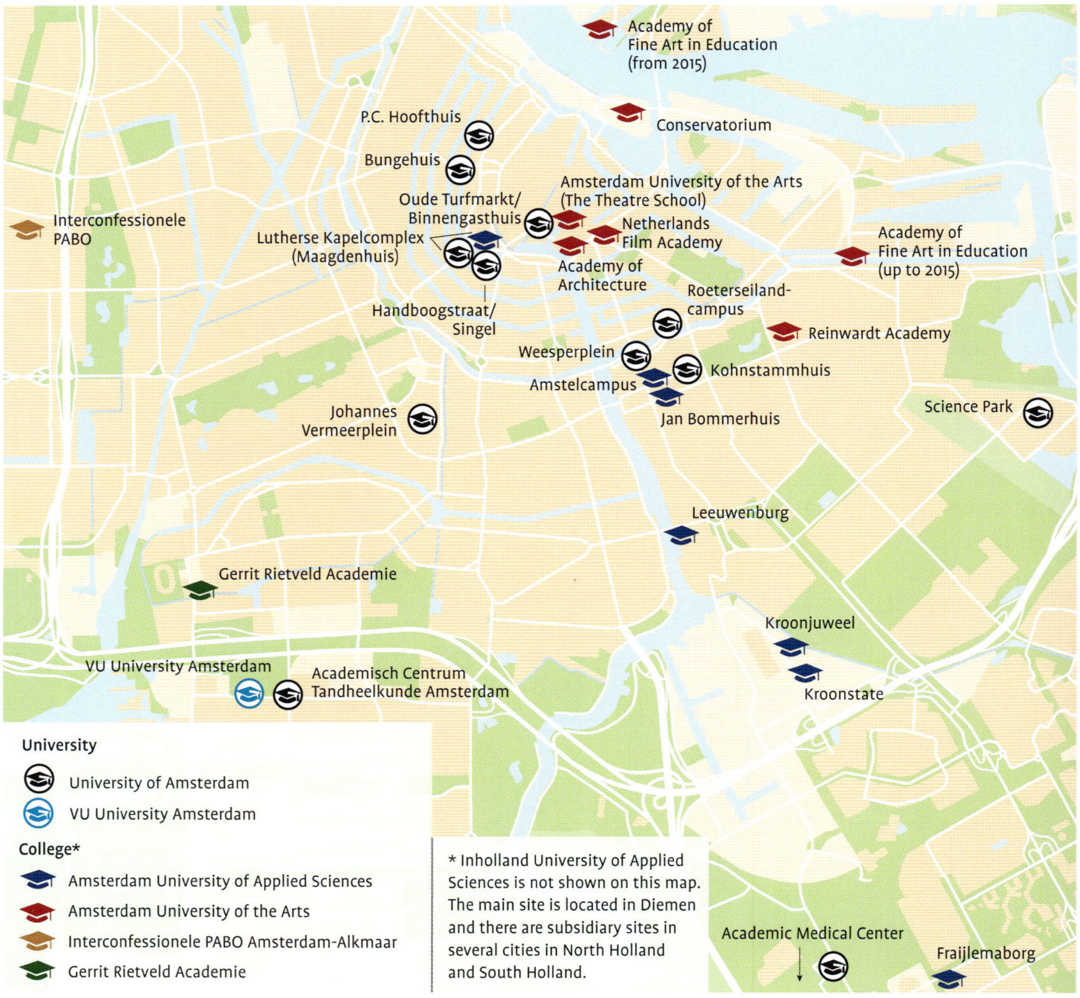

❸ Amstel Campus

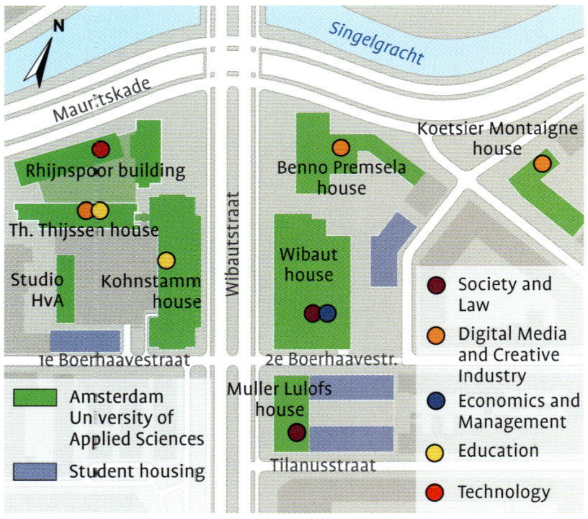

❶ More students

Until the late 1960s, only the upper classes had the opportunity of studying at university. The 1968 Dutch Secondary Education Act changed that. The number of students is still increasing, both in higher professional education and at the universities and the number of students attending Amsterdam University of Applied Sciences (HvA) rose by 17% during a period of five years.

❷ Scaling-up

Universities and colleges have different faculties or domains, which in turn are subdivided into subjects. Until recently, many subjects had their own dedicated site, but there has been a tendency in recent years to bring the different subjects together at a single site or campus.

❸ Together in one place

Amsterdam University of Applied Sciences is attended by more than 50,000 students and employs 3590 people. It has four campuses – the Business Campus in Zuidoost, the Health Campus at the AMC, the Sport and Nutrition campus in Osdorp and the new Amstel Campus on Wibautstraat. The final touches are currently been made to the latter, and around 13,000 students will attend their lectures there in 2018.

❹ Concentration

The UvA is also attempting to concentrate faculties and subjects. The campuses at the Academic Medical Center (AMC, medical studies) and the Science Park (science courses and research) are already in use, while work on completing the Roeterseiland and Binnengasthuisterrein campuses is in full swing.

Sources: City of Amsteraam (1); Amsterdam University of Applied Sciences (3)

© Noordhoff Uitgevers

❹ Science Park

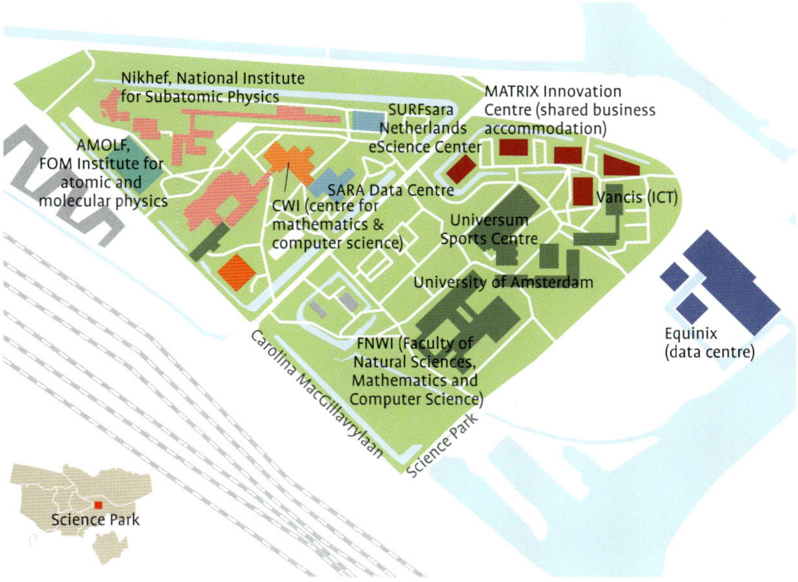

❺ VU campus and VU medical centre

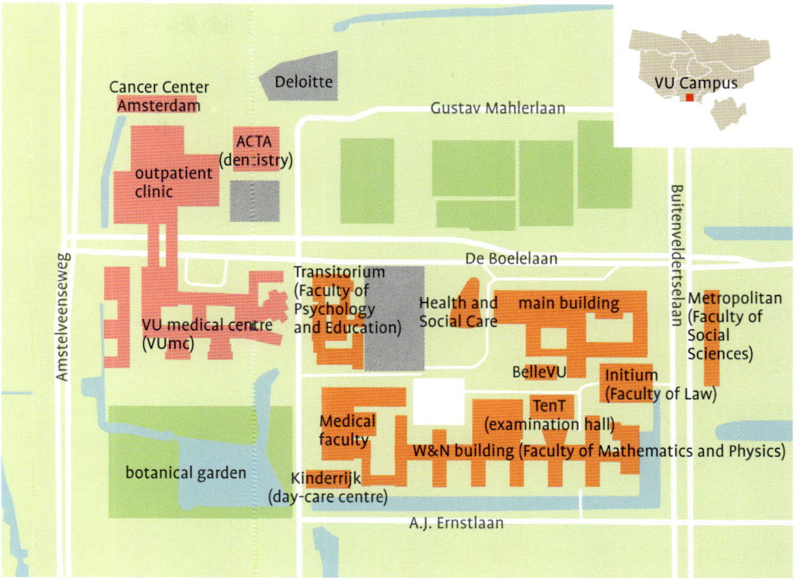

❻ University of Amsterdam students

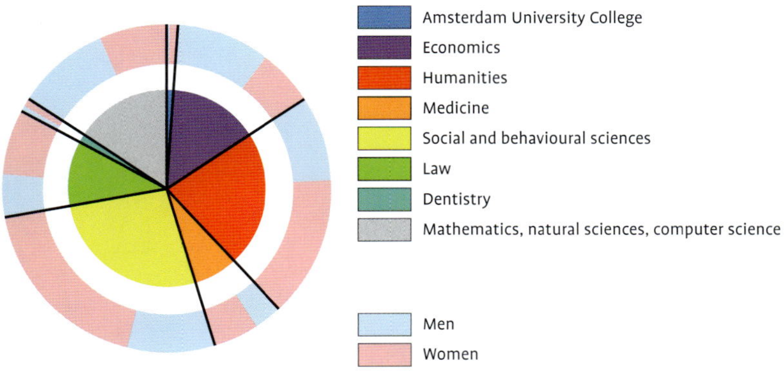

❼ VU University Amsterdam students

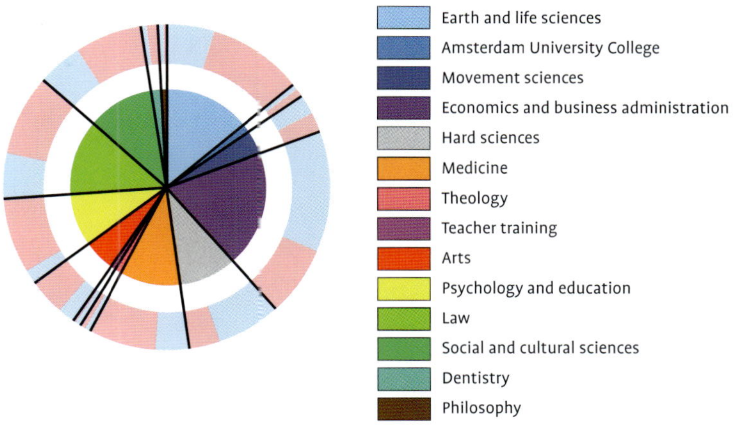

❽ Foreign students at the University of Amsterdam and VU University Amsterdam

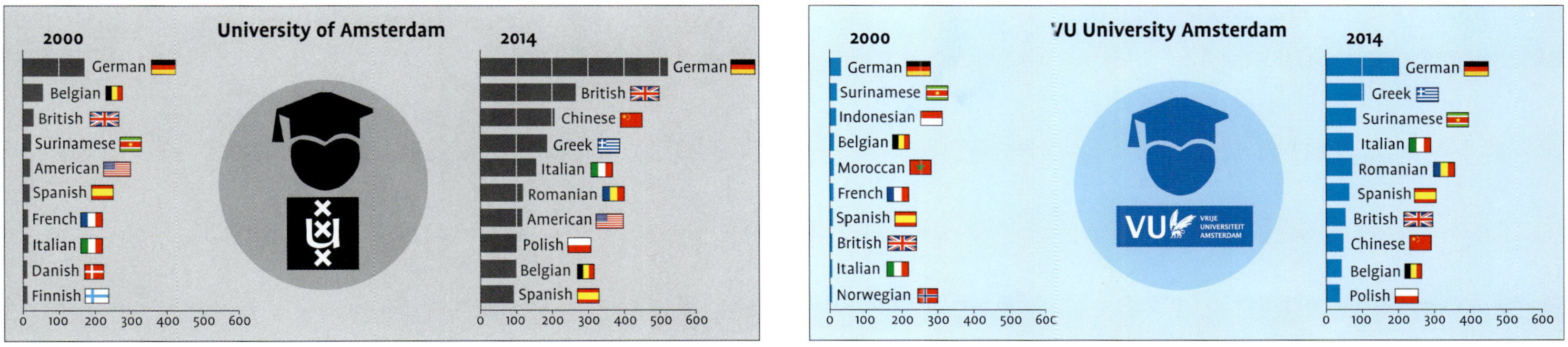

❾ Street names commemorating Amsterdam's scientists and academics

❺ De Boelelaan

In the 1960s, the VU University Amsterdam relocated from Keizersgracht to De Boelelaan in Buitenveldert. Since then, nearly all of its education and research facilities, including the medical centre, have been based at a single site.

❻ - ❼ Ideological foundations

In the 2013-2014 academic year, 23,656 students were registered at the VU and 31,180 at the UvA. Both institutions offer a broad range of courses. Although the VU has Protestant origins and the UvA is neutral, this difference is hardly evident in their academic profiles. For instance, Theology is one of the smallest faculties at the VU.

❽ Cross-border collaboration

The days of universities being self-contained islands are long gone. The UvA, VU and HvA collaborate in many areas and internationalisation is a buzzword nowadays. In order to compete with other leading academic institutions, Amsterdam's universities and colleges swap professors and host foreign students.

❾ Pride

Higher education attracts young people to the city, while high-profile scholars give it a certain prestige. Amsterdam is proud of its prowess in this area, so numerous streets in the city are named after its famous scientists and academics.

Sources: Amsterdam Science Park (4); University of Amsterdam (5); OIS, Research, Information and Statistics, City of Amsterdam (6, 7); University of Amsterdam, VU University Amsterdam (8)

© Noordhoff Uitgevers

Defence Line of Amsterdam

In 1874, the Dutch House of Representatives approved a major upgrade of the Netherlands' defences. As a result, Amsterdam was given its own defence line.

The use of extremely powerful artillery determined the outcome of the Franco-Prussian War (1870-1871) and this made politicians realise that the Netherlands' defences needed to be upgraded. The Dutch Fortifications Act of 1874 was based on the principle that only the western part of the Netherlands would be defended. This took the form of two defensive lines – the Dutch Waterline and the Defence Line of Amsterdam. If the enemy succeeded in breaking through the former, the army would regroup within the latter. Once in this position, it could withstand a siege of nine months, which would be more than enough for allies to come to the rescue – or so it was hoped.

❶ The Defence Line of Amsterdam

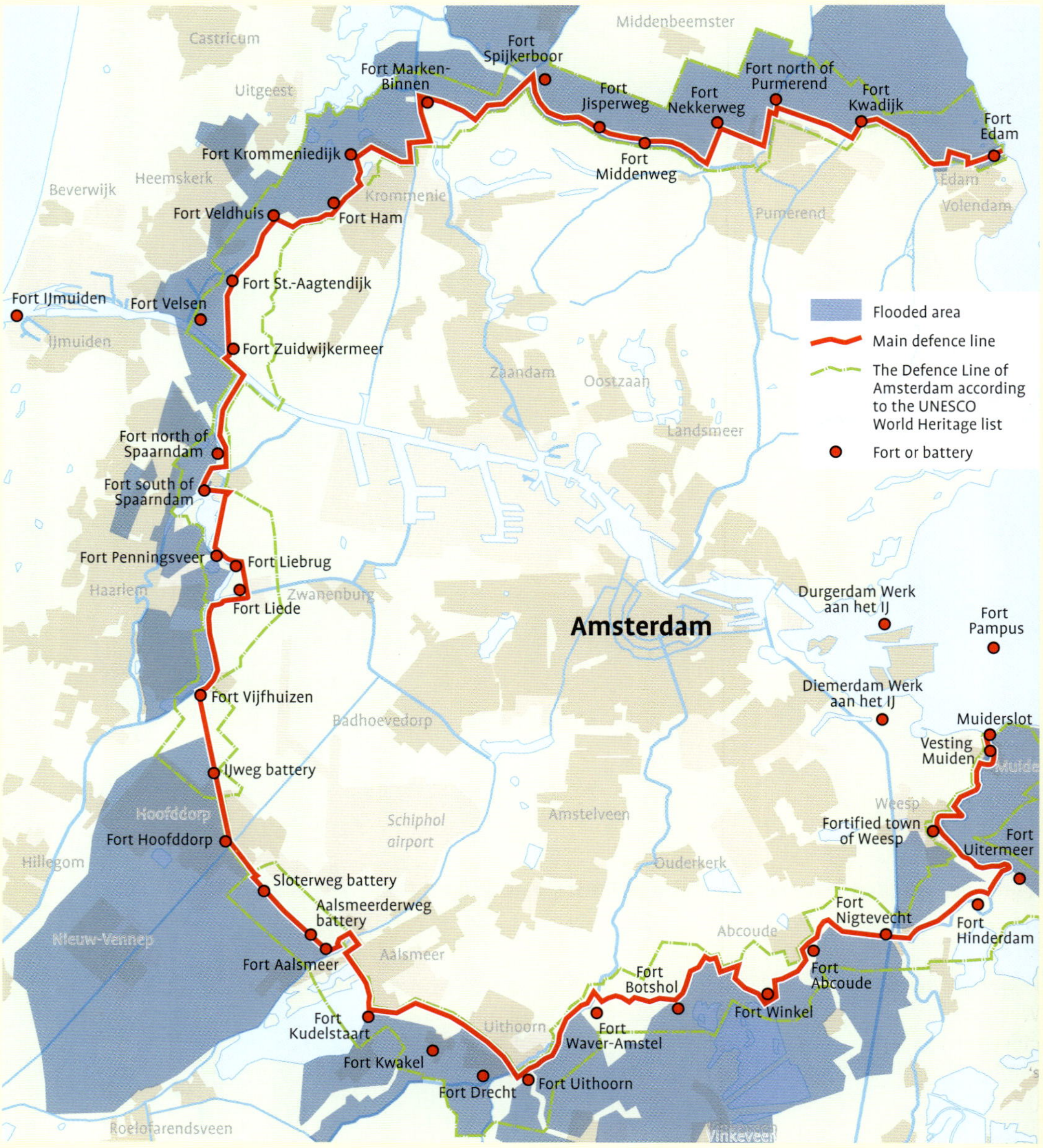

❶ - ❷ A ring of water and forts
In 1880, work started on constructing the Defence Line, an ingenious system of concrete forts, batteries, dikes, locks and canals around Amsterdam. The basic design principle was to allow controlled flooding of the territory around the Defence Line to a depth that was just too shallow for boats, but just too deep to wade through.
Forts were built in the areas that were too high to be flooded, or where railway tracks, rivers, canals or roads intersected the defence line.
The fort on Pampus island and the IJmuiden coastal fort at the mouth of the North Sea Canal were intended to control access to the port of Amsterdam. The 135-kilometre defence line had almost been completed by 1914, which was just in time, since World War One broke out that summer.

❷ Fort on Pampus island

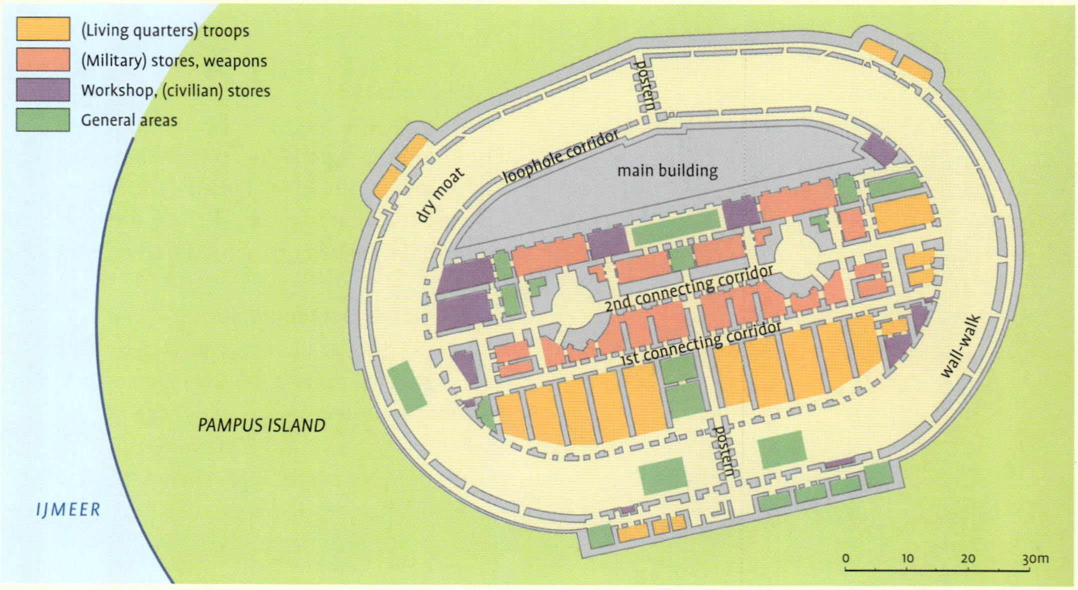

© Noordhoff Uitgevers

❸ Barracks, storehouses and other military buildings, 1918

❸ Combat readiness

On 31 July 1914, the government announced a general mobilisation and the forts around Amsterdam were brought to a state of combat readiness. Amsterdam itself also prepared for the worst. Soldiers were billeted all over the city and stores were stockpiled in strategic positions, e.g. grains in the Korthals Altes silo on the tip of the Westerdoksdijk, millions of peat logs in sheds close to the former Hembrug bridge and fuel in the petroleum harbour. Separate cages were set up for carrier pigeons in the government carrier pigeon station at Artis to allow communication with the outside world in emergencies.
However nothing happened. When the war ended four years later, not a single shot had been fired around Amsterdam, the locks remained unopened and no land had been purposely flooded. It was now clear that all that work had been for nothing. New long-range guns and bomber aircraft had rendered the Defence Line completely useless, so it was decommissioned in 1922, although the forts remained off-limits to the public for a considerable time after. In 1996, the Defence Line was added to UNESCO's World Heritage List.

❹ A storehouse of soldiers

Built between 1810 and 1813, the Oranje-Nassau-kazerne on Sarphatistraat was commissioned by Napoleon, but paid for by the people of Amsterdam. All of the city's residents had to pay a one-off fee equivalent to 5% of the rental value of their homes. Anybody who was unable, or unwilling, to do so had to take in French soldiers. The 278-by-16-metre complex, which is supported on 3300 piles, was designed to accommodate 2400 soldiers. Ironically, the French departed shortly after its completion. Napoleon's coat of arms on the front facade and the French eagles were replaced by the House of Orange coat of arms and Dutch lions. The name of the barracks also changed from Quartier Saint-Charles to Oranje-Nassau-kazerne. The building was used as a military barracks and a place where young men were tested for military service until 1987. Following thorough restoration, the ground floor has been converted for commercial use, while 150 social-sector rented homes have been created on the upper floors.

❹ Oranje-Nassaukazerne

Source: P. Vesters (red.), Harnas voor de hoofdstad. De Stelling van Amsterdam (3)

© Noordhoff Uitgevers

Street furniture

❶ 'Amsterdammertjes'
The reddish-brown 'Amsterdammertjes' still exist, but their numbers are decreasing each year. In 1985, there were around 100,000 of these anti-parking bollards inside the Singelgracht periphery, costing 250 guilders each (including installation) and 50 guilders to straighten them again after a collision. The initial bollards were longer, hollow inside and driven deep into the ground, but this design was no longer feasible due to the enormous expansion of the underground cable network. The newer bollards had a base plate and were only driven into the ground to a depth of 30 centimetres. More stringent parking enforcement made the 'Amsterdammertjes' superfluous some time ago, so they are removed each time the streets are renovated. In 2003, there were only 40,000 left, and the redundant bollards have since become a popular collector's item. Many people born and bred in Amsterdam – even those who live elsewhere – have them in their gardens.

❷ Curved urinals
As a measure against public urination, the city council decided to install public urinals for men in around 1870. In 1916, Jan van der Mey, a well-known Amsterdam School architect, was asked to come up with a new design for these urinals. The result was the familiar curved iron structures with perforations at the top and a partially open bottom section. This design made it possible to see at a glance whether the urinal was occupied and whether it was being used for improper purposes. Since then, all kinds of different variants have been devised, including a concrete unit with a double curve. Most of the curved urinals have now disappeared, but there are still 32 in the city centre. Toilet kiosks, small but often striking buildings which offered facilities for women as well, appeared in the 1920s, but they too have largely disappeared or been adapted for other uses.

❸ 'Waterhappertje' drinking fountain
In 1896, the city council became owner of the Netherlands' oldest water company, the privately owned Amsterdamsche Duinwater-Maatschappij (1851). This acquisition reflected a desire to provide running water all over the city within a relatively modest timeframe. The installation of drinking fountains, known as 'waterhappertjes', in public places was part of this ambitious programme. The first 'happertje' – a cast-iron post supporting a basin and fountain that provided a continuous flow of drinking water 24 hours a day – was installed in 1903. Around one hundred of these fountains still exist in the city. In the autumn, they are either removed by Waternet or the water supply is turned off. In spring, the fountains are made fully operational again. All of the 'happertjes' together consume about 35 million litres of water a year, equating to a cost of around 43,000 euros for the water alone. To avoid waste, Waternet now also provides drinking fountains with a push-button.

Photos: © Wolverlei/Martin Stevens (1-3)

© Noordhoff Uitgevers

❹ Giro boxes

The City of Amsterdam broke new ground when it introduced its own giro payment system, the Gemeentegiro, in 1917. The similar service provided by Postcheque- en Girodienst was only set up one year later. By 1930, the Gemeentegiro already had 30,000 private account holders, who deposited their giro transfer orders into one of the many blue giro boxes in the city without using an envelope. City architect Peter Lucas Marnette designed the first giro boxes in 1918. They were upright, cast-iron, 1.60-metre-tall pillar boxes, embossed with Amsterdam's coat of arms and marked with 'Gem. Girokantoor' in a business-like font. From 1926 onwards, these rather impractical pillars were replaced by smaller boxes that were attached to the wall and also made of cast iron. In 1979, the Postgiro took over the Gemeentegiro service (which had 300,000 account holders by then) and the boxes were no longer required. Members of staff were permitted to take a box home.

❺ Lampposts

In 1669, Jan van der Heyden approached the city council with a proposal to replace the street lights of the time, which used wax candles, with oil-fuelled lighting that he had invented. The council agreed and 2300 of his lampposts were erected in Amsterdam that same year. They were the first of their kind anywhere in the world. In the 19th century, his lampposts were replaced with two types of gas lighting – the octagonal lamppost (1867) and the crown lamppost (1883). There are only a few of the former left in the city centre, but around 3000 crown lampposts still survive, most of them on the banks of the canals. In 1917, the gas mantles in these lampposts were replaced with incandescent light bulbs. As for Van der Heyden's lampposts, only one original has been preserved and it can now be seen in the Amsterdam Museum. However, there are replicas in various parts of the city, such as on Amstelveld, near the Sint Olofskapel and, since 2005, also on the Magere Brug.

❻ Climbing frames

Anybody who grew up in post-war Amsterdam will probably have played on one of the climbing frames designed by architect Aldo van Eyck (1918-1999) at some time or other. Before World War Two, there were no public playgrounds, only playground associations, which children had to be members of in order to use the facilities. After the war, growing traffic density made playing on the street increasingly dangerous. In 1949, the Public Works Department commissioned the young Van Eyck to design playgrounds and playing areas. He spent almost 30 years at Public Works and designed no less than 860 playgrounds during that period. The sandbox and various aluminium climbing frames, of which the igloo is the best-known, were permanent features of his designs. Most of Van Eyck's playgrounds have now disappeared or been adapted to meet today's strict safety rules. Some original examples of Van Eyck's playground equipment were recently placed in the gardens of the Rijksmuseum.

Photos: © Wolverlei/Martin Stevens (4-6)

© Noordhoff Uitgevers

4

Economy

◁
Westelijk Havengebied
Photo Karel Tomeï

4 Introduction

Exceptional
Amsterdam is exceptional within the context of the Dutch economy. While the overall economy in the Netherlands is service-based, this is even more pronounced in Amsterdam. The commercial services sector is particularly well-developed.

Capital city effect
The presence of trade, transport, banks and insurers has historical roots to a certain extent – Amsterdam was the focal point of colonial trade in the 1600s and the leading financial centre of the Western world until well into the 1700s. The Zuidas can therefore be seen as a distant relative of the Dutch East India Company and the Dutch West India Company.

Amsterdam also benefits from the 'capital city effect' – financial institutions like to set up in the country's largest city and attract numerous lawyers, ICT specialists, accountants and consultants in their wake. Creative service providers such as advertising agencies, graphic designers and architects follow their example.

Non-profit sector
Amsterdam has quite a large non-profit service sector, but national government is hardly present at all. While other capital cities have big government ministries within their boundaries, Amsterdam does not, since it is not a centre of government. The main entities in the non-profit service sector are therefore the City itself and educational and health-care institutions that often play a regional role.

Metropolitan area
That regional role is a key element in understanding the city's economy. The city actually provides services within in a large and varied network – the Amsterdam Metropolitan Area. For example, industrial companies and building contractors are few and far between in the city itself, as most of them have relocated to the surrounding areas which offer better accessibility.
Two important economic drivers are located completely outside the city limits – Schiphol *airport* and the flower auction in Aalsmeer (*greenport*). The port area bordering the

Westelijk Havengebied
The Port of Amsterdam lies well over the horizon for most Amsterdammers, but its discreet presence does not make it any less important for the regional economy. Amsterdam has the largest petroleum port in the world. The oil storage tanks are concentrated between the Petroleumhaven (the curved port on the left) and the Jan van Riebeeckhaven (on the right). The entrances to the two Coen tunnels are located directly behind.

North Sea Canal (*seaport*) also pays little regard to the city's borders. The newest 'port', the *dataport*, is the only one actually concentrated in Amsterdam itself – the huge servers and data centres that keep the Internet up and running are located close to major customers like banks and universities.

I amsterdam

The business activity most strongly associated with the city is the tourist industry. Each year, millions of foreigners visit Amsterdam to admire the wonders of the inner city. The resulting jobs are of immeasurable value and Amsterdam is exceptional compared to the rest of the Dutch economy in this respect too.

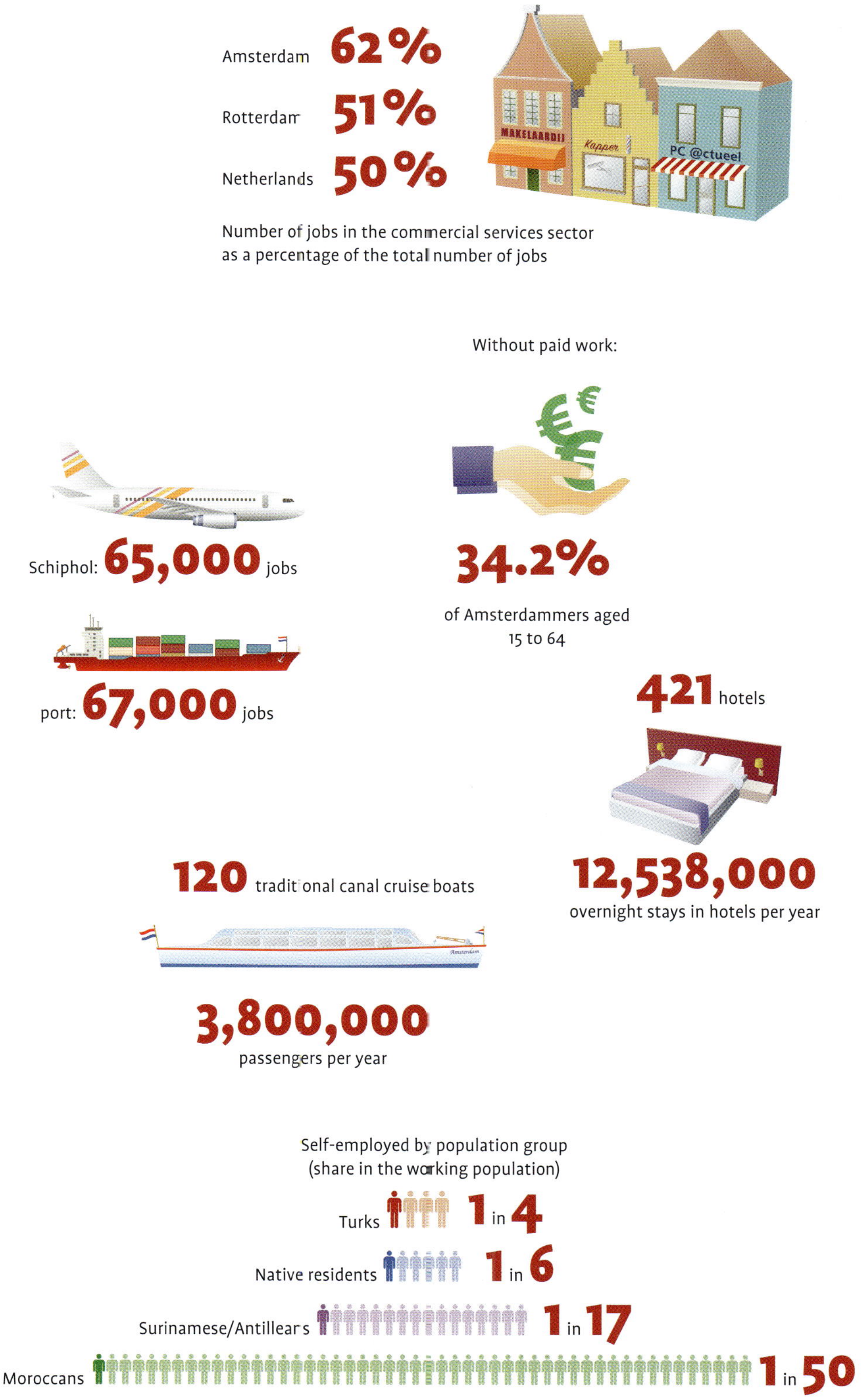

Sources: OIS, Research, Information and Statistics, City of Amsterdam / Schiphol Group / Port of Amsterdam

© Noordhoff Uitgevers

Amsterdam Metropolitan Area

The Amsterdam Metropolitan Area (AMA) is a collaboration between the city of Amsterdam, 35 other regions and the provinces of North Holland and Flevoland. The idea behind this alliance is to speed up decision-making and exert influence on national politics in The Hague. The alliance aims to strengthen the AMA's competitive position compared with other European metropolitan areas, and seems to be rather successful. The AMA is one of Europe's five strongest economic regions. Hundreds of thousands of people work there, making a significant contribution to the Dutch economy.

❶ Working and living areas

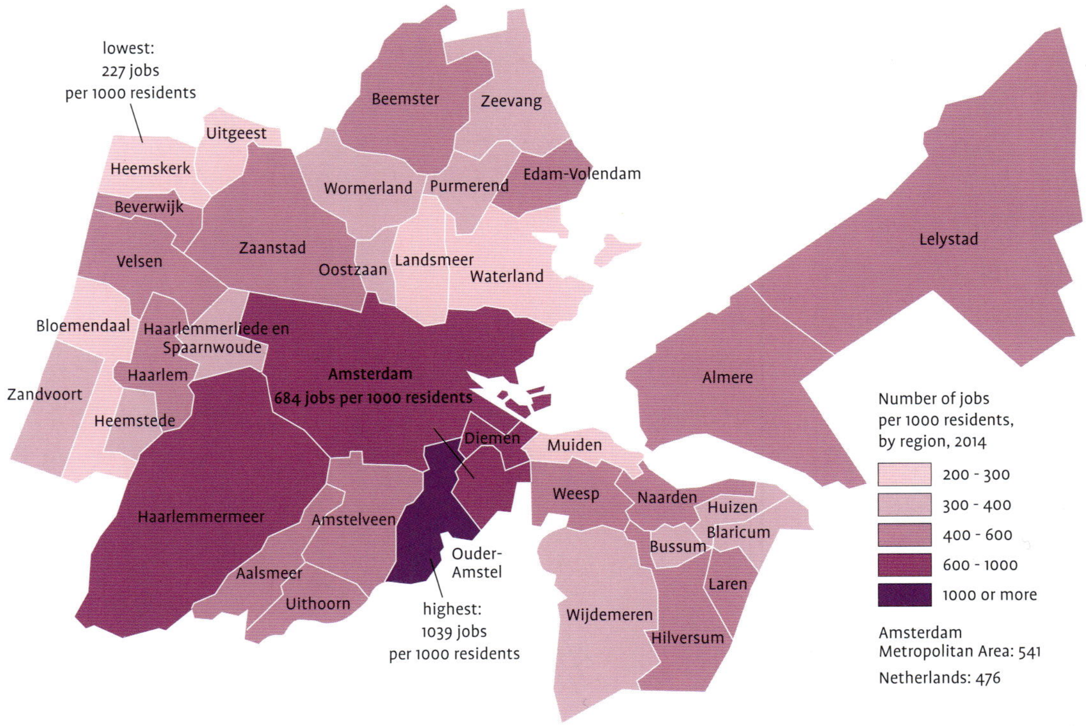

❷ Employment in the primary sector

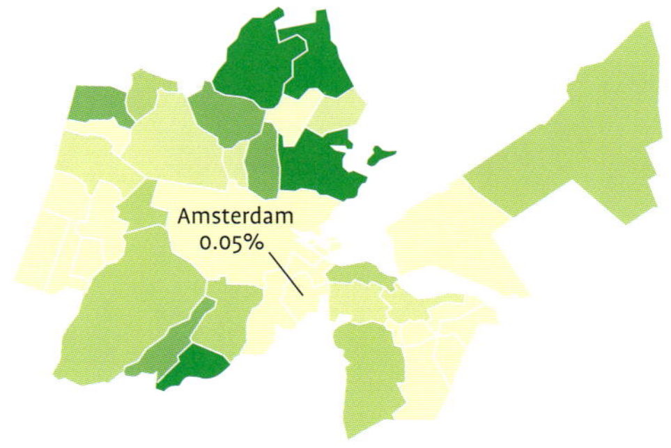

Number of people employed in the primary sector as a percentage of the total number of people employed, by region, 2013

less than 0.5 | 0.5 - 1.0 | 1.0 - 2.0 | 2.0 - 5.0 | 5.0 or more

❸ Employment in the quaternary sector

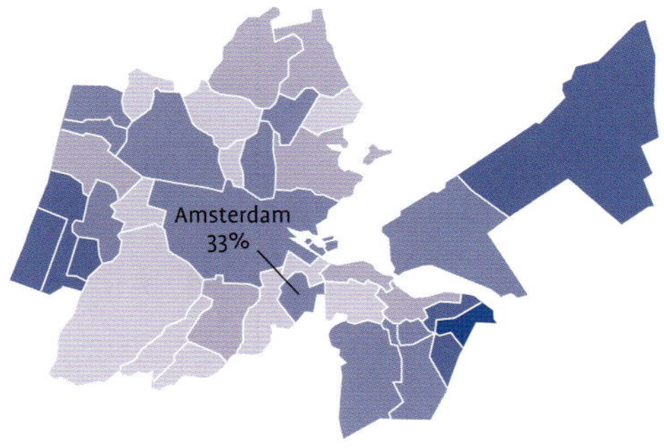

Number of people employed in the quaternary sector as a percentage of the total number of people employed, by region, 2013

less than 20 | 20 - 30 | 30 - 40 | 40 - 50 | 50 or more

❶ Centres of employment

Some 237,000 businesses – 18% of the country-wide total – are based within the AMA. However, employment is not distributed evenly – some regions (Ouder-Amstel, Haarlemmermeer and Amsterdam) are characterised by relatively high levels of business activity, whereas others are mainly residential areas. These differences result in large numbers of commuters. For instance, of the nearly 200,000 people who work in the 'Schiphol region' of Haarlemmermeer, only 60,000 actually live in the region itself.

❷ - ❺ Economic sectors

The vast majority of the working population is employed in commercial and non-commercial services (tertiary and quaternary sectors). Agriculture and fishing (the primary sector) have almost completely disappeared, and cows can only be seen grazing in the meadows on the outskirts of the area. Employment in the secondary sector, industry, has also contracted strongly, with only one in ten residents still working in this sector. At 14.5%, the health-care and welfare sector is the largest employer.

❹ Employment in the tertiary sector

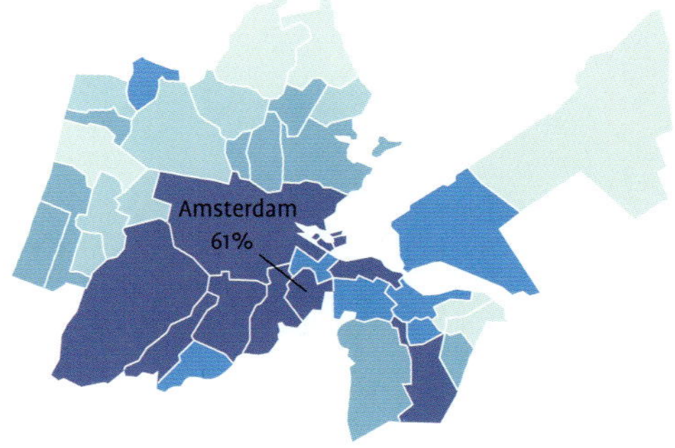

Number of people employed in the tertiary sector as a percentage of the total number of people employed, by region, 2013

less than 45 | 45 - 50 | 50 - 55 | 55 - 60 | 60 or more

❺ Tertiary sector breakdown

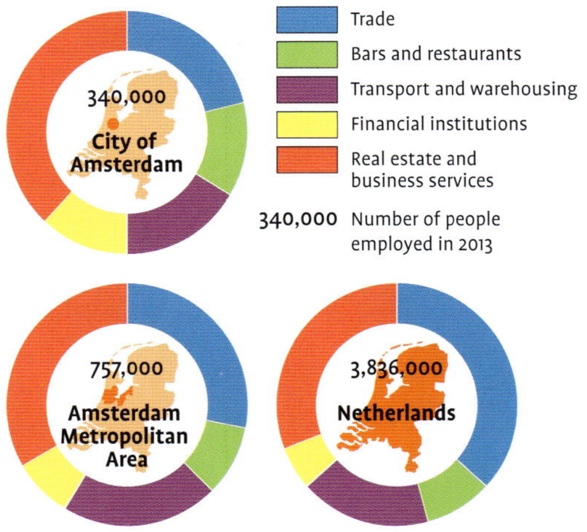

Sources: LISA / OIS, Research, Information and Statistics, City of Amsterdam (1); OIS, Research, Information and Statistics, City of Amsterdam (2-5)

© Noordhoff Uitgevers

❻ - ❼ Big money

In 2013, the gross domestic product of the Netherlands (the value of all goods and services produced/provided in the country in one year) amounted to approximately 643 billion euros. of which around 118 billion euros (18%) came from the Amsterdam Metropolitan Area. Another commonly used way of measuring the importance of a certain economic sector in a country, region or city is to determine the 'value added' – the market value (selling price) of goods and services minus the value of the associated raw materials and consumables. The total value added in the Netherlands amounted to 579 billion euros in 2013, 107 billion of which in the Amsterdam Metropolitan Area. Within the latter figure, the tertiary sector (commercial services) accounted for the largest portion. The value added for business services, ICT and the wholesale sector amounted to nearly 18 billion (16.7%), 14.4 billion (13.5%) and 13.4 billion euros (12.6%) respectively. The value added in the industrial sector, on the other hand, was just 6.5%.

❽ Large institutions

The city council has been Amsterdam's largest employer for many years. The University of Amsterdam (including the AMC medical centre) is the second largest, with around 13,000 employees, some 4400 of whom are members of the academic and teaching staff.
The largest commercial businesses are banks, but the 2008 crisis hit the financial sector hard. Due in part to scaling effects and automation, the number of jobs in this sector reduced from 3829 in 2007 to 3122 in 2015. The number of businesses dropped significantly too.

❻ Employment in the Amsterdam Metropolitan Area and the Netherlands

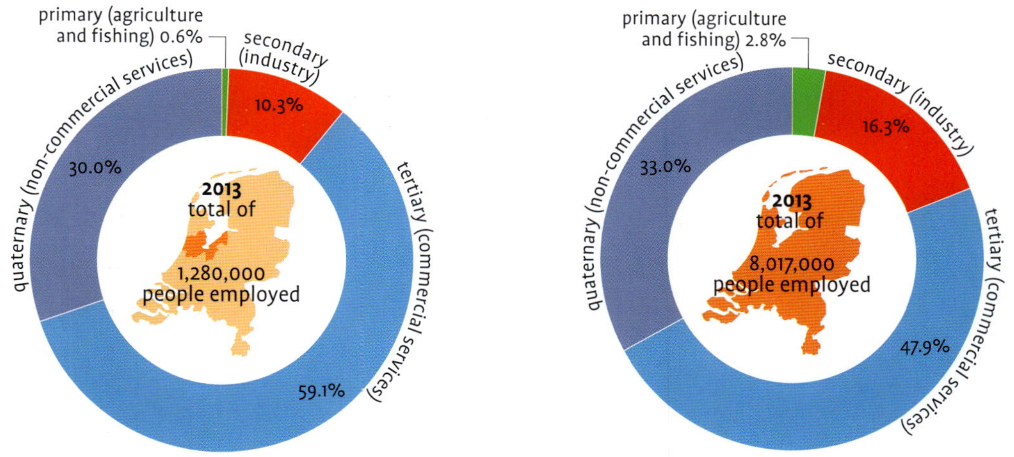

❼ Value added

❽ Largest employers in Amsterdam

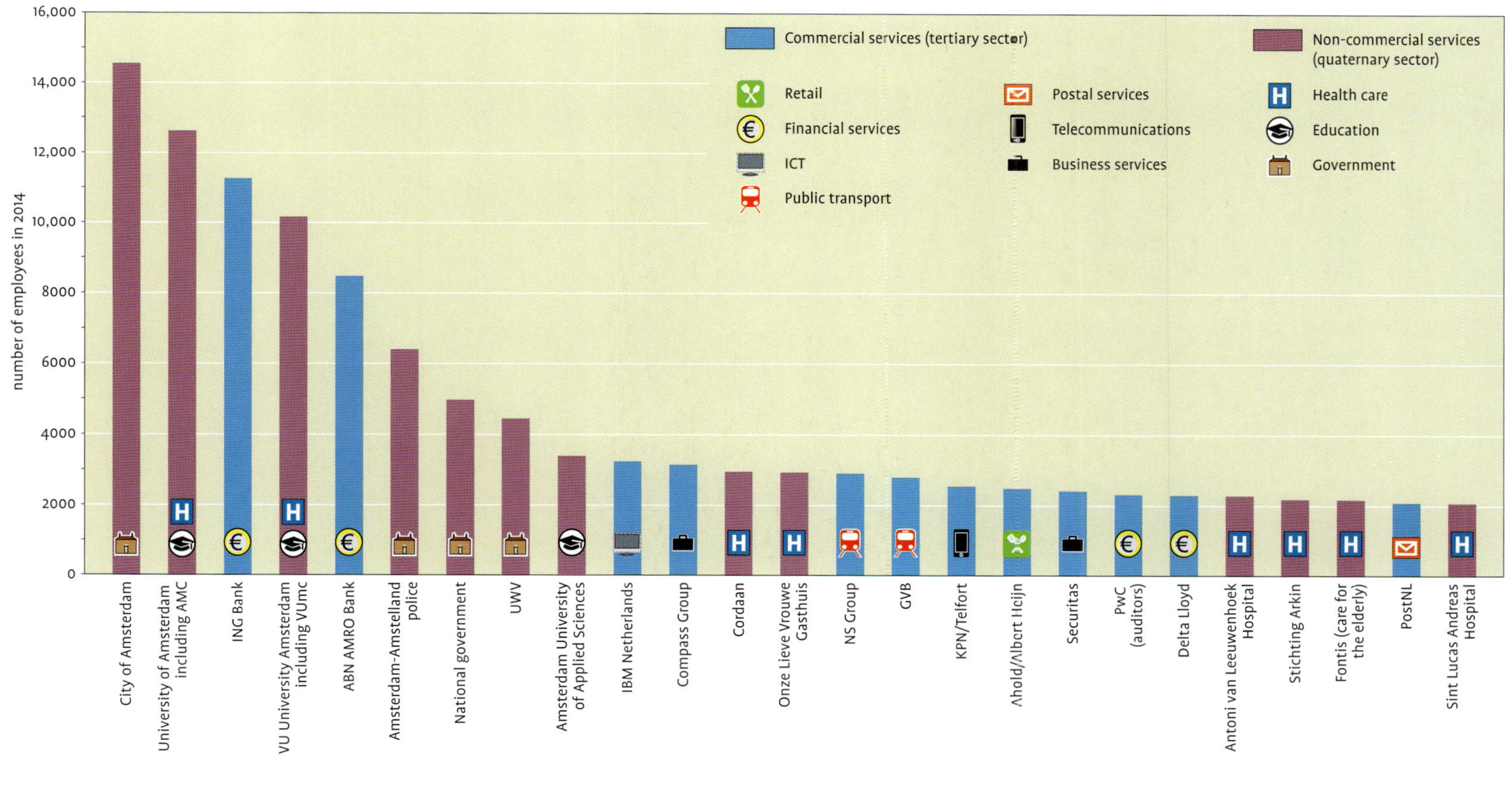

Source: OIS, Research, Information and Statistics, City of Amsterdam (6-8)

© Noordhoff Uitgevers

Industry

Industry was once extremely important in Amsterdam, with shipbuilding and the steel industry in particular providing employment for tens of thousands of Amsterdammers. Those days are long gone. Only a small percentage of Amsterdam's working population is still employed in the sector and industrial activities are largely concentrated in the Westelijk Havengebied. Industry and construction also only contribute modestly to the Amsterdam Metropolitan Area's total gross regional product.

❶ Jobs in industry and construction

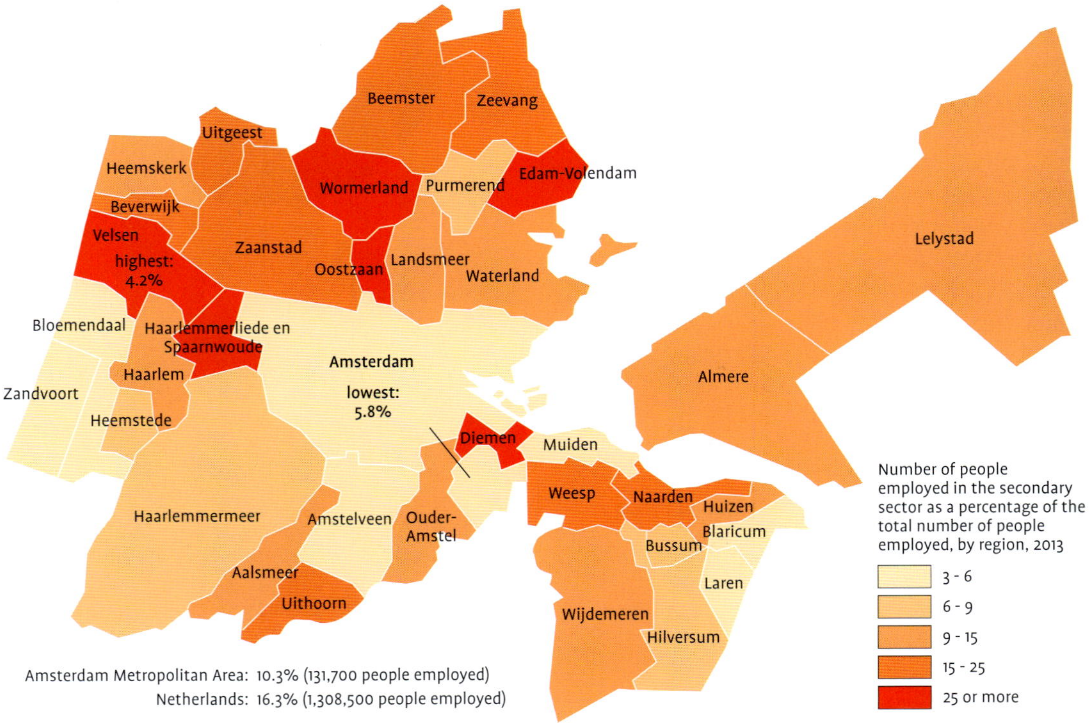

Amsterdam Metropolitan Area: 10.3% (131,700 people employed)
Netherlands: 16.3% (1,308,500 people employed)

❷ Total employment along the banks of the North Sea Canal

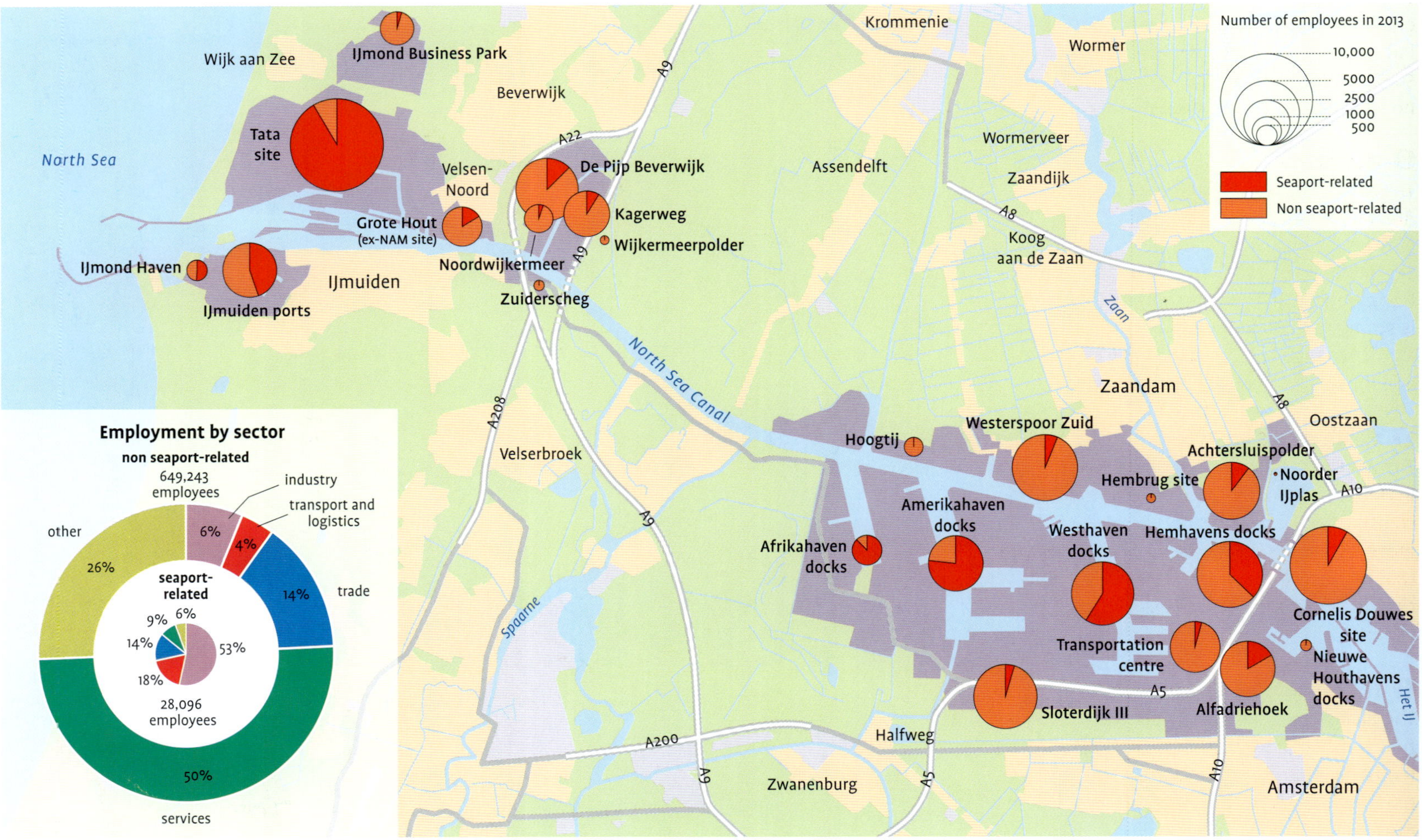

Sources: OIS, Research, Information and Statistics, City of Amsterdam (1); Monitor werkgelegenheid & Bedrijventerreinen Noordzeekanaalgebied (2)

© Noordhoff Uitgevers

❸ Average company size in the industrial sector

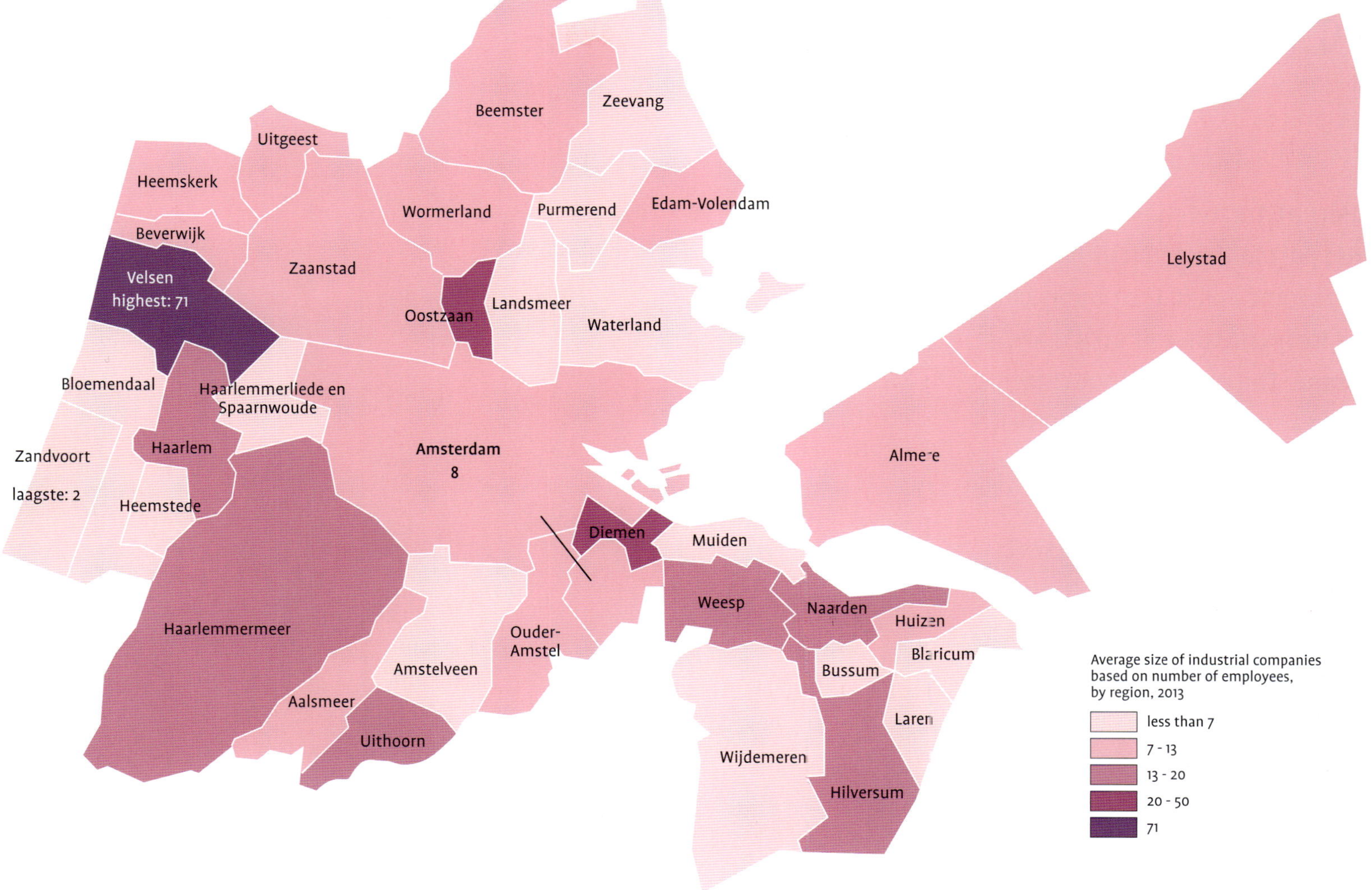

❶ Small scale

Some 82,000 people were employed by around 7000, mainly small-scale, industrial businesses in the AMA in 2014. In Amsterdam itself, only twelve industrial plants employed more than one hundred people. The region's construction industry is also small-scale – in 2014, just under 50,000 construction workers were employed by no less than 18,700 businesses.

❷ Vital artery

The North Sea Canal is a vital artery for Amsterdam's business community and particularly for industry. With more than 9000 employees, Indian steel company Tata Steel (formally Hoogovens) is the largest employer. The company is strongly dependent on the seaport and the North Sea Canal for the supply of raw materials and for shipping out finished products.

❸ Mainly small and medium-sized businesses

The nearly 7000 industrial businesses registered in the metropolitan area only make a modest contribution to its economy – a mere 7% of the gross regional product is generated by the industrial sector. The average company is small, other than in Velsen where Tata Steel Europe boosts the average figure.

❹ Still extensively industrialised

The Zaanstreek region was once a major industrial area. Despite the greatly diminished level of industrial activity, 13.2% of the working population is still employed in industry today (3.4% in Amsterdam).

❹ Zaanstad's largest industrial businesses

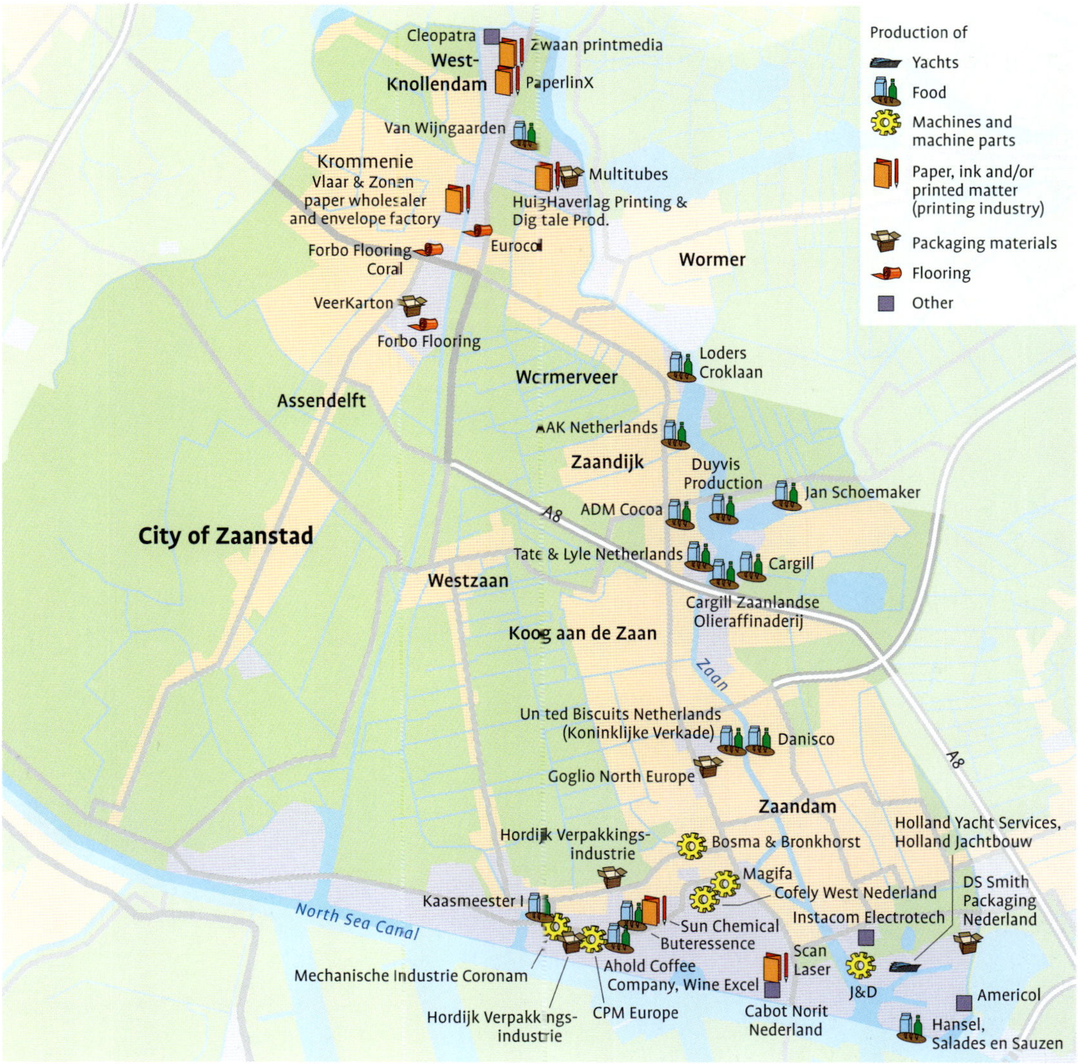

© Noordhoff Uitgevers

Seaport

The Port of Amsterdam is the fourth largest port in Western Europe. It is an important link in the supply chain to the Netherlands and inland areas of Europe. The port has four core activities – handling raw materials and energy (petrol, coal and biofuels), handling agricultural and food products (cocoa beans), fertilisers, minerals and scrap, handling large items of cargo (cars, containers and machines) and attending to the needs of cruise ships. It is the world's largest shipping hub for petrol and kerosene, the largest importer of cocoa beans in the world and the second largest transshipment port for coal in Europe. As a result, the port is an immensely important economic driver for Amsterdam, providing direct employment for around 34,000 people and indirect employment for another 33,000.

❶ The docks area

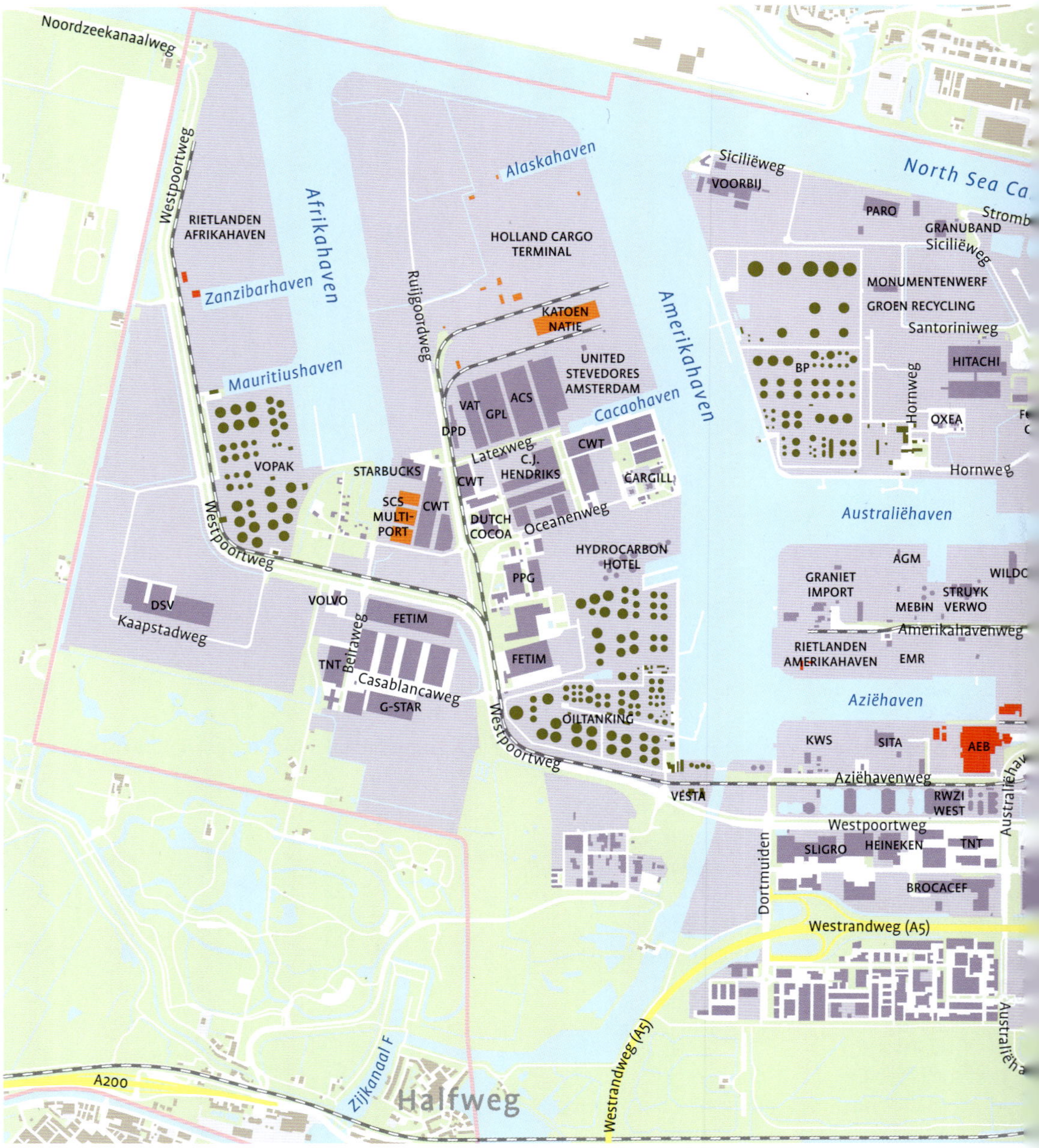

❶ - ❸ Growth prospects
Compared to its three closest competitors, Rotterdam, Antwerp and Hamburg, the port of Amsterdam is only a small player. However, Amsterdam is expected to be able to improve its competitive position after 2019 when the new sea lock in IJmuiden will come into operation. Large seagoing vessels, which currently have to divert to other ports, will then be able to moor in Amsterdam.

❹ - ❺ Oil and coal
In 2014, 7486 ships called at the North Sea Canal ports, 4927 of which sailed into the port of Amsterdam – a slight drop on 2013. Even so, the transshipment volume rose to nearly 100 million tonnes, of which nearly 70% related to imported goods and 30% to export. Raw materials for energy and energy products accounted for over three quarters of the total transshipment tonnage.

❸ Main import and export countries

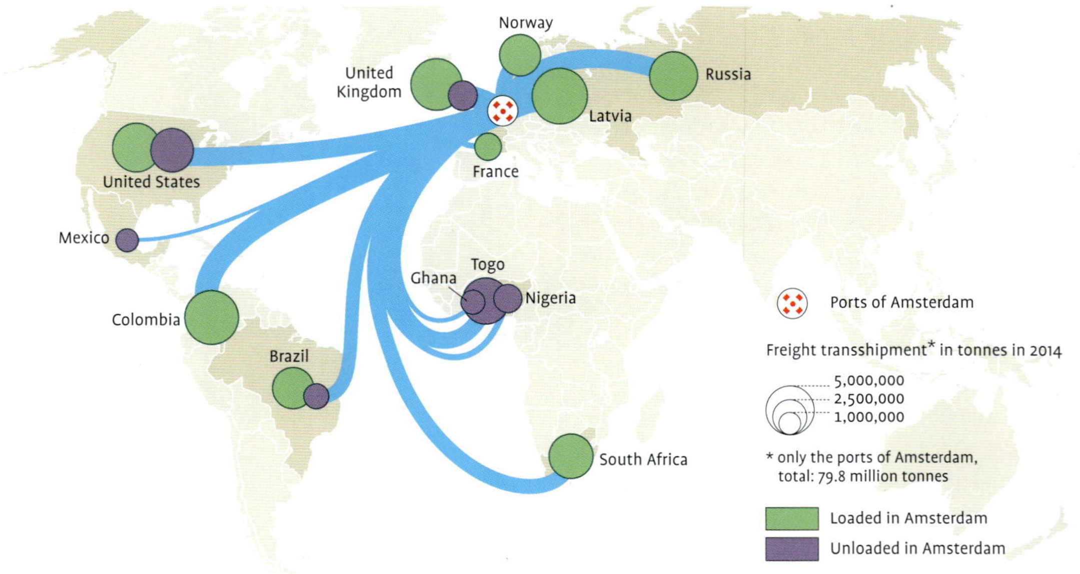

Source: Port of Amsterdam (1-3)

© Noordhoff Uitgevers

Port area
- Industrial estate
- Liquid bulk
- Dry bulk
- General cargo and containers
- Other activities

Outer port area
- Industrial estate
- Building

General
- Park, woodland, agriculture
- Water
- Surfaced or disused land
- Motorway
- Other road
- Railway
- Municipal boundary

❷ Position of the Amsterdam port region*

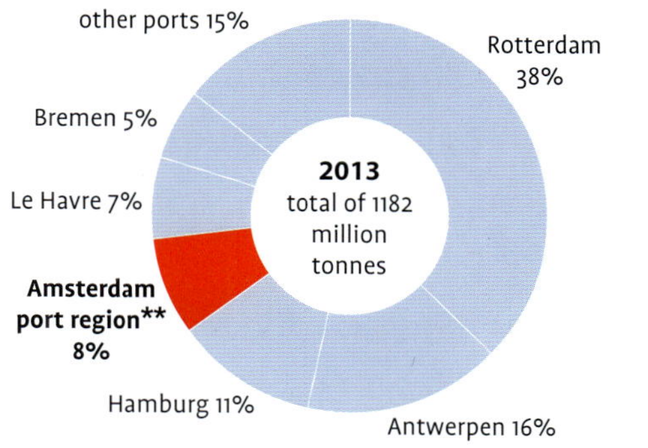

* Market share relative to turnover in the ports of north-western Europe
** Amsterdam, Beverwijk, Velsen/IJmuiden and Zaanstad

❹ Seagoing ships and goods

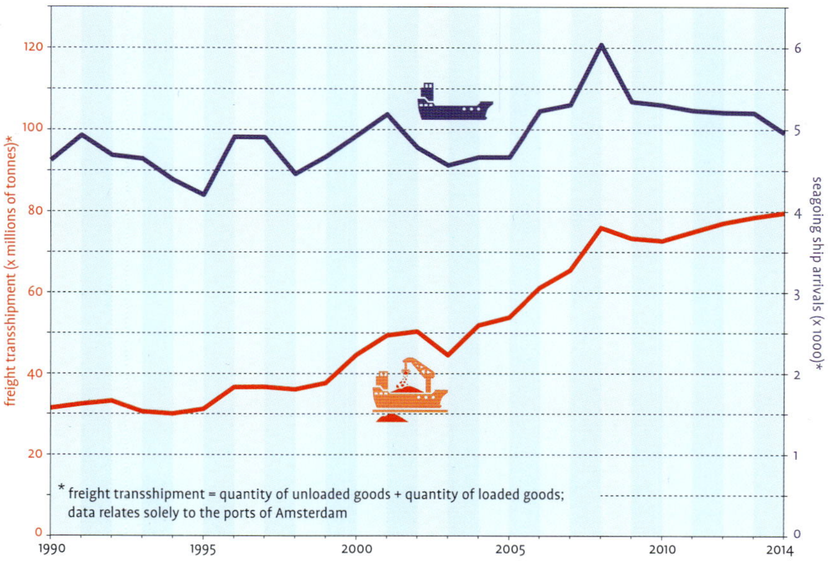

* freight transshipment = quantity of unloaded goods + quantity of loaded goods; data relates solely to the ports of Amsterdam

❺ Transshipment of goods (unloaded-loaded)

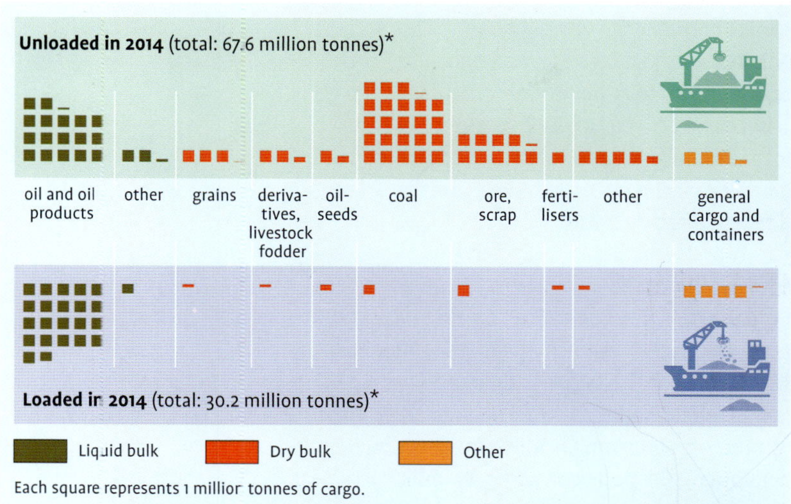

Each square represents 1 million tonnes of cargo.

* including the ports of Beverwijk, Velsen/IJmuiden and Zaanstad

Sources: OIS, Research, Information and Statistics, City of Amsterdam (4); Port of Amsterdam (5)

© Noordhoff Uitgevers

VOC and WIC

In early 1660, the Dutch East India Company (VOC) laid the first foundation stone of the East India Warehouse on Oostenburg. The enormous building was completed within a single year.

Founded in 1602 and 1621 respectively, the VOC and the Dutch West India Company (WIC) were intended to strengthen the Netherlands' trading position compared to other European trading nations. The VOC mainly traded in spices, tobacco, tea and coffee, and the WIC in sugar, salt, tropical wood, gold and slaves. While the VOC contented itself with setting up trading posts, the WIC pursued a deliberate policy of expansion and founded colonies in North America, the Caribbean and South America.

❶ An immense structure
The VOC constructed its operational buildings on an artificial island in Amsterdam called Oostenburg. The East India Warehouse was a huge 225-by-25-metre structure, with four floors, 124 doors and 710 windows. On 13 April 1822, the building collapsed due to neglect.

❷ Factories
The VOC wanted to trade profitably rather than conquer overseas territories, which was too risky and costly. The company negotiated with the local inhabitants and rulers from fortified trading posts (factories) in coastal locations to arrange delivery of trade goods.

❸ Colonisation
In 1621, the WIC was granted an exclusive right to trade between West Africa and the Americas. Large areas of the latter had already been colonised by Spain and Portugal. In the struggle to take control from these countries, the WIC also pursued a policy of active colonisation. As a result, part of the Portuguese colony of Brazil was conquered between 1630 and 1637.

❶ VOC company site on Oostenburg, 1750

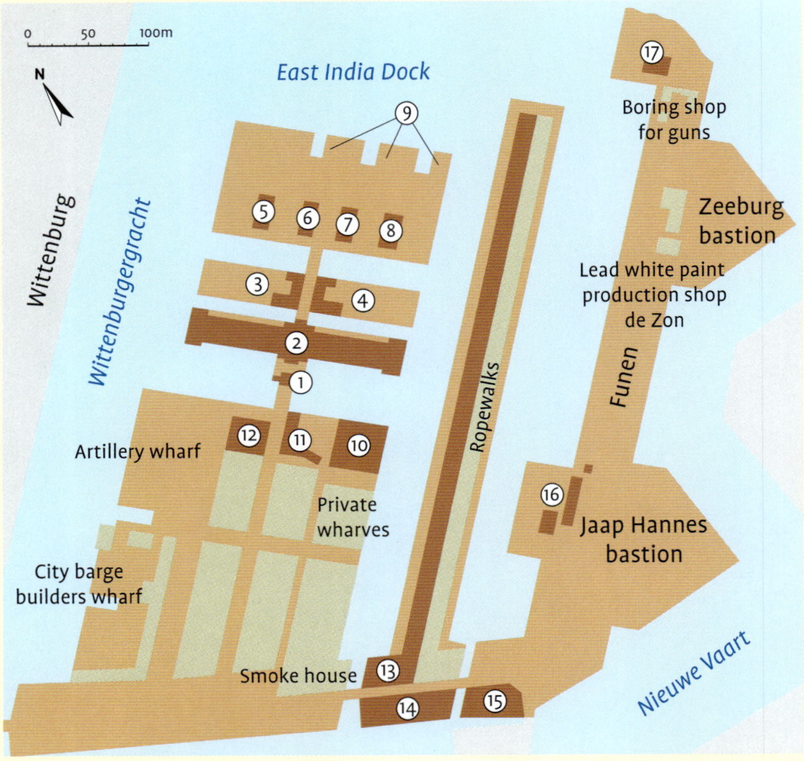

VOC land
VOC building
Other land
Other buildings

1. Guardhouse, lodgings for weighers and overseers
2. East India Warehouse
3. Production area for rigging, blocks and barges
4. Production area for gun carriages, reels and skewers
5. Nail store
6. Smithy
7. Production area for nails, boatswain's office, pharmacy
8. Ship carpentry shop
9. Slipway
10. Warehouse (1720) for storing sugar, saltpetre and other goods
11. Sail-making area, meat store (1752)
12. Master carpenter's quarters
13. Ropewalk (warehouse) and boatswain's quarters
14. Anchor wharf
15. Ballast wharf
16. Wood sawmill with sheds
17. Tar house

? Wood stove (location unknown)

❷ VOC trading posts and trade goods, 1602-1799

Sources: *R. van Gelder and L. Wagenaar, Sporen van de Compagnie (1); F. Gaastra, Bewind en beleid bij de VOC 1672-1702 / J.P. de Korte, De jaarlijkse financiële verantwoording in de Verenigde Oostindische Compagnie (2)*

© Noordhoff Uitgevers

❸ WIC monopoly area, 1621-1791

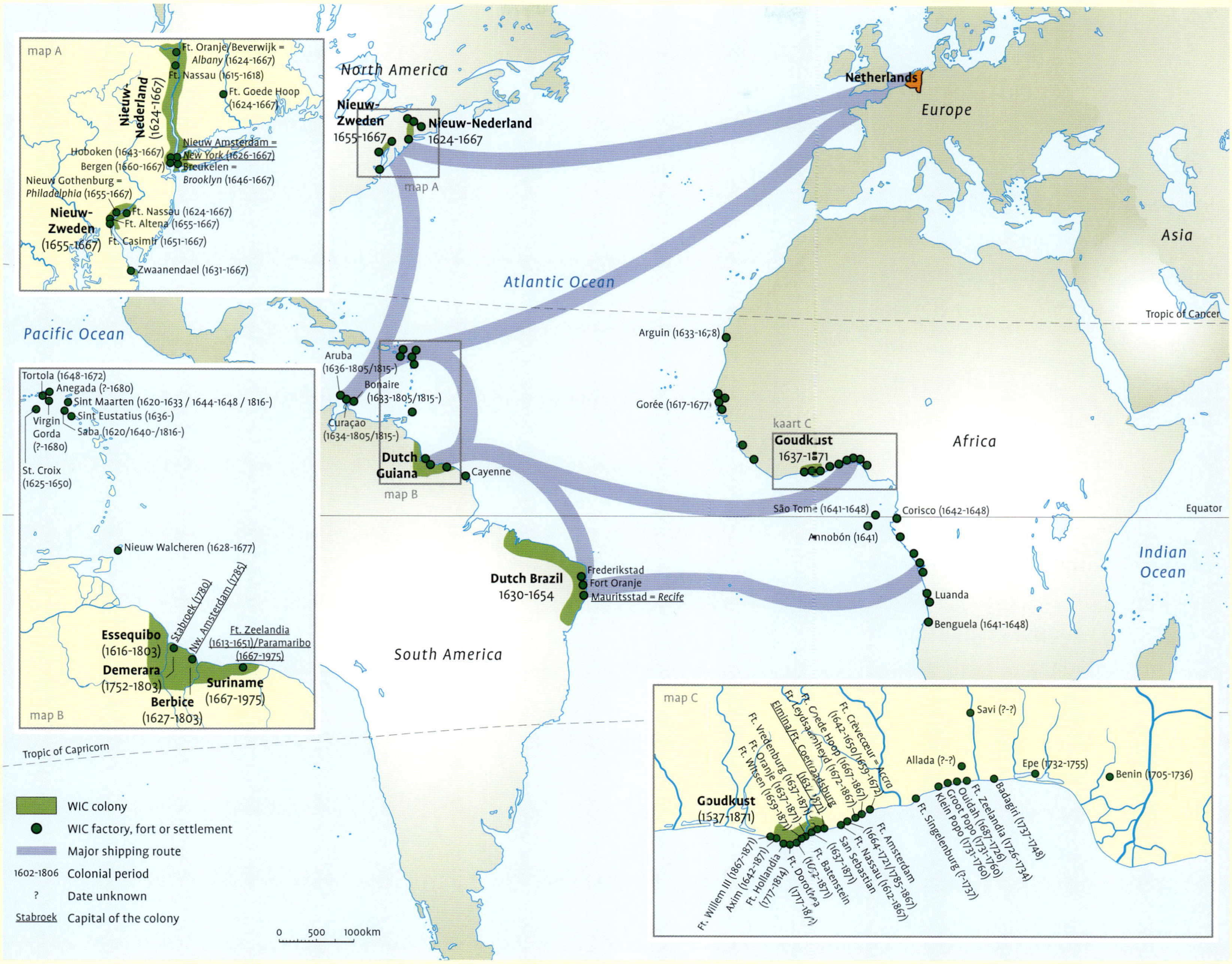

❹ - ❺ Slave trade

The Portuguese had introduced a system of forced labour on the sugar plantations in Brazil, with the work done by African slaves. Following the WIC's conquest of the territories in Brazil, the Dutch continued this form of exploitation and also based the economy in Suriname and on the Antilles on slave labour. To ensure a continuous supply, the WIC had a series of trading forts constructed along the length of the West African coast. When the Netherlands outlawed the slave trade in 1816, Dutch ships had already transported around 550,000 slaves to America. Slavery itself was not abolished until 1863.

❻ The end

The WIC was dissolved in 1791. Eight years later, the VOC went bankrupt and the government acquired all of its assets and liabilities. Today, various buildings in Amsterdam still remind us of these two once so powerful companies.

❹ Purchase and sale prices for WIC slaves

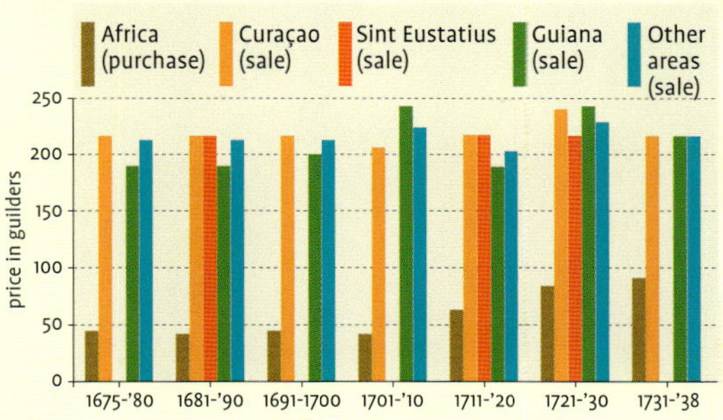

❺ Export of slaves from West Africa by the WIC

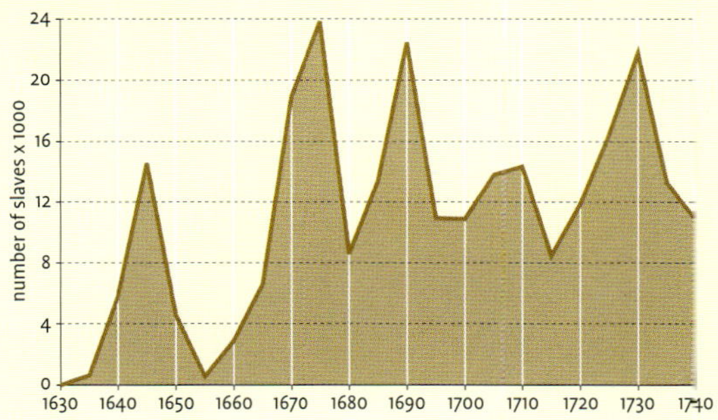

❻ VOC and WIC monuments

Sources: H. den Heijer, *De geschiedenis van de WIC* (3, 5); H. den Heijer, *Goud, ivoor en slaven* (4)

© Noordhoff Uitgevers

Schiphol Airport

In just a few decades, Amsterdam Airport Schiphol has become one of the main aviation hubs in Europe. Home to KLM, Corendon, Transavia and ArkeFly, the airport provides jobs for tens of thousands of people and business premises for hundreds of companies. It operates around the clock in order to serve the millions of arriving and departing passengers, turn cargo aircraft around and offer facilities to airlines. KLM is the largest customer.
The Schiphol Group is responsible for operating and managing the airport. The State of the Netherlands owns 69.8% of the shares in the group, the City of Amsterdam owns 20%, and France and Rotterdam own 8% and 2.2% respectively.

❶ Operational buildings by function

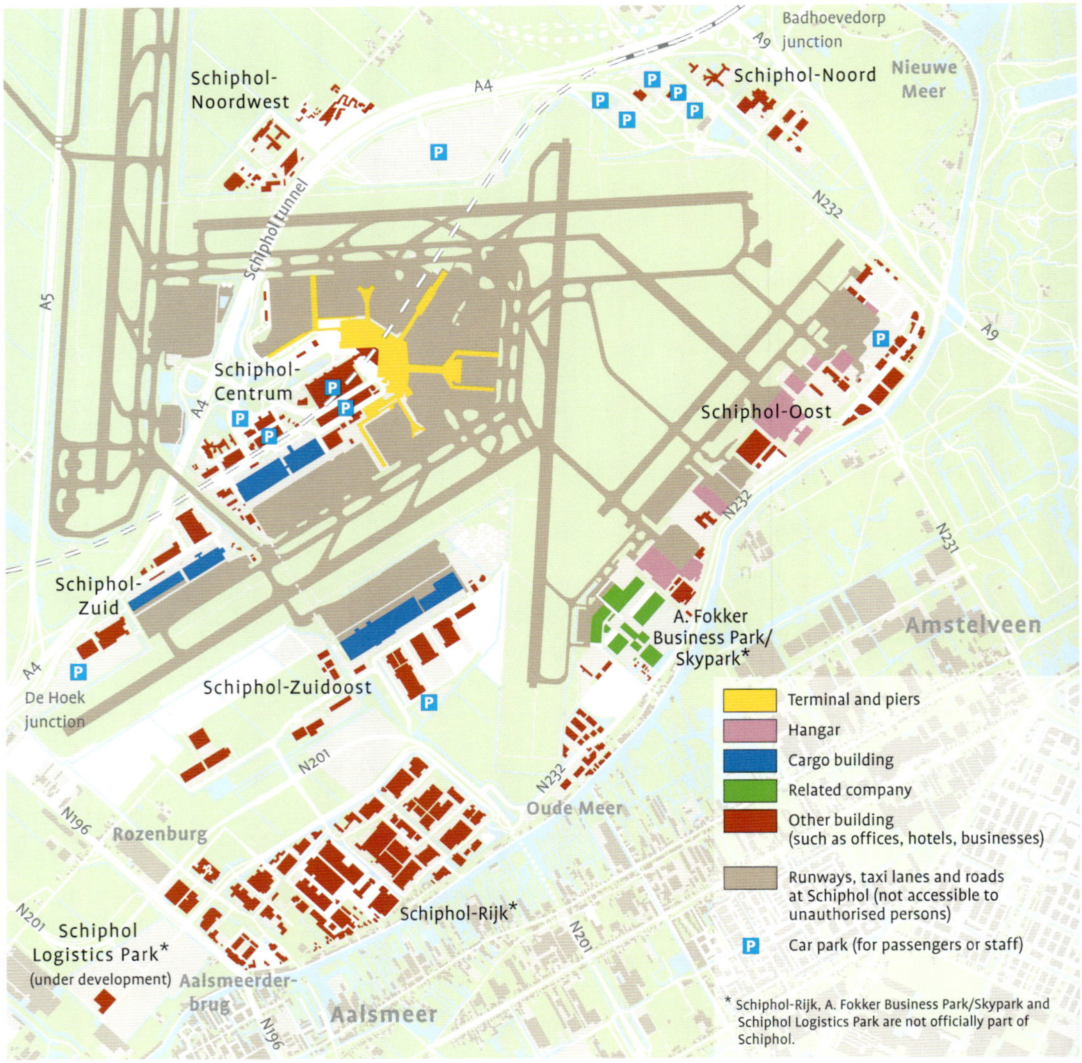

❷ Commercial statistics

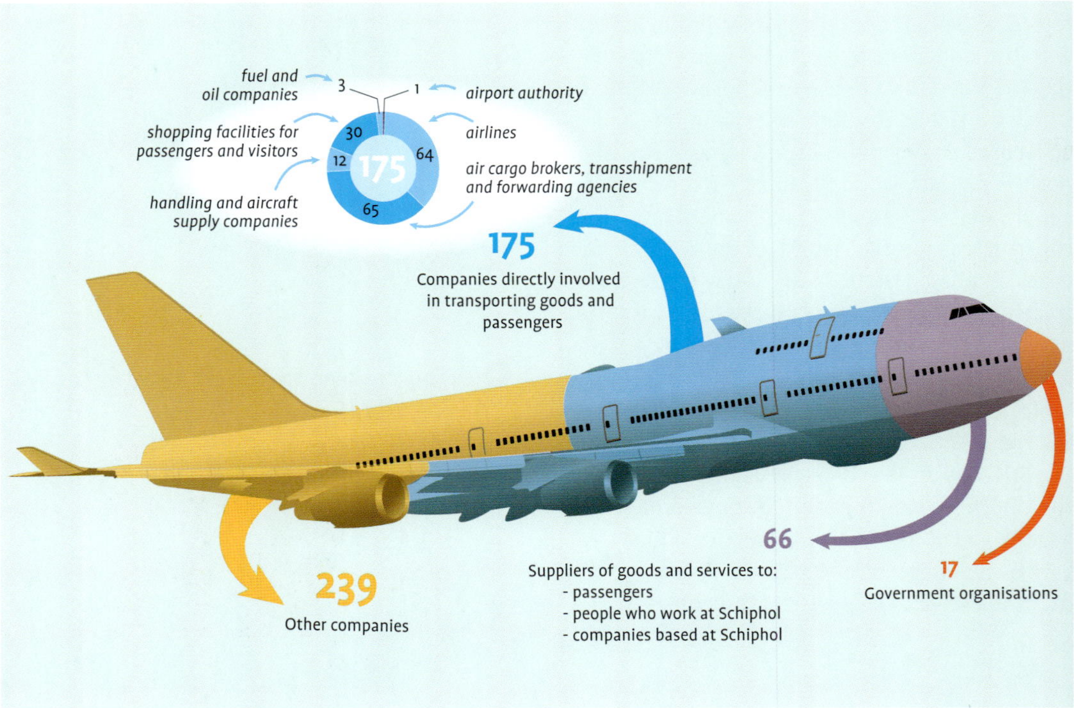

❶ A city in itself

Covering a surface area of 2787 hectares, Schiphol is larger than Amsterdam-Zuidoost. It is a city in itself, where many activities other than handling aircraft traffic take place. For example, there are hotels and the offices of international companies all over the airport. Refurbishment and new construction work takes place constantly at Schiphol. In 2014, the airport itself invested no less than 396 million euros.

❷ Millions of items of baggage

Of the 65,000 people employed at Schiphol, 63% are directly involved in air transport. They work for airlines, freight forwarders and handling organisations. Some 2000 people work in the baggage handling department. In 2014, they processed a total of 47 million items of baggage, and as many as 180,000 items on peak days. The conveying system is around 30 kilometres long and the longest route a suitcase can take at Schiphol is 2.5 kilometres.

Source: Regioplan Beleidsonderzoek: overzicht werkgelegenheid luchthaven Schiphol (2)

© Noordhoff Uitgevers

❸ Big business

Around 560 companies are based at Schiphol. With more than 24,000 employees, KLM is the airport's largest employer, but cutbacks may lead to job losses in future years as the company wants to outsource various activities. Microsoft is another major employer. In 2008, this ICT giant moved into a brand-new office building, The Outlook, with a floor area of 38,000m².

❹ Taking off

Schiphol has really taken off over the last 50 years. Whereas it provided employment for around 16,000 people in 1970, that figure has risen to 64,000 45 years later. Accordingly, most of the approximately 26 billion euros that aviation contributes to the Dutch gross national product is earned at Schiphol.

❺ - ❻ Operational 24 hours a day

The lights never go out at Schiphol and the airport operates around the clock. Although Schiphol Plaza, the ground-side shopping area, closes at 10pm, the shops after passport control only close once the last passenger has checked in and open again when the first passengers arrive. Some of the restaurants and bars stay open all night. In 2014, the airport welcomed 55 million passengers. On average, they spent 14.50 euros on purchases, 3.80 euros on refreshments and 7.80 euros on parking.

❼ From far and wide

The roads to and from Schiphol are extremely busy. This is partly due to heavy commuting traffic – of the 64,000 people who work at Schiphol, only a few live in the Haarlemmermeer area itself, 13% live in Amsterdam and the rest come from the metropolitan area or further afield. Arriving and departing passengers also add to congestion. Nearly 40% of them use public transport, 26% are given a lift and 14% drive, parking their cars in one of the 22,000 parking spaces at the airport.

❸ Employers and employees

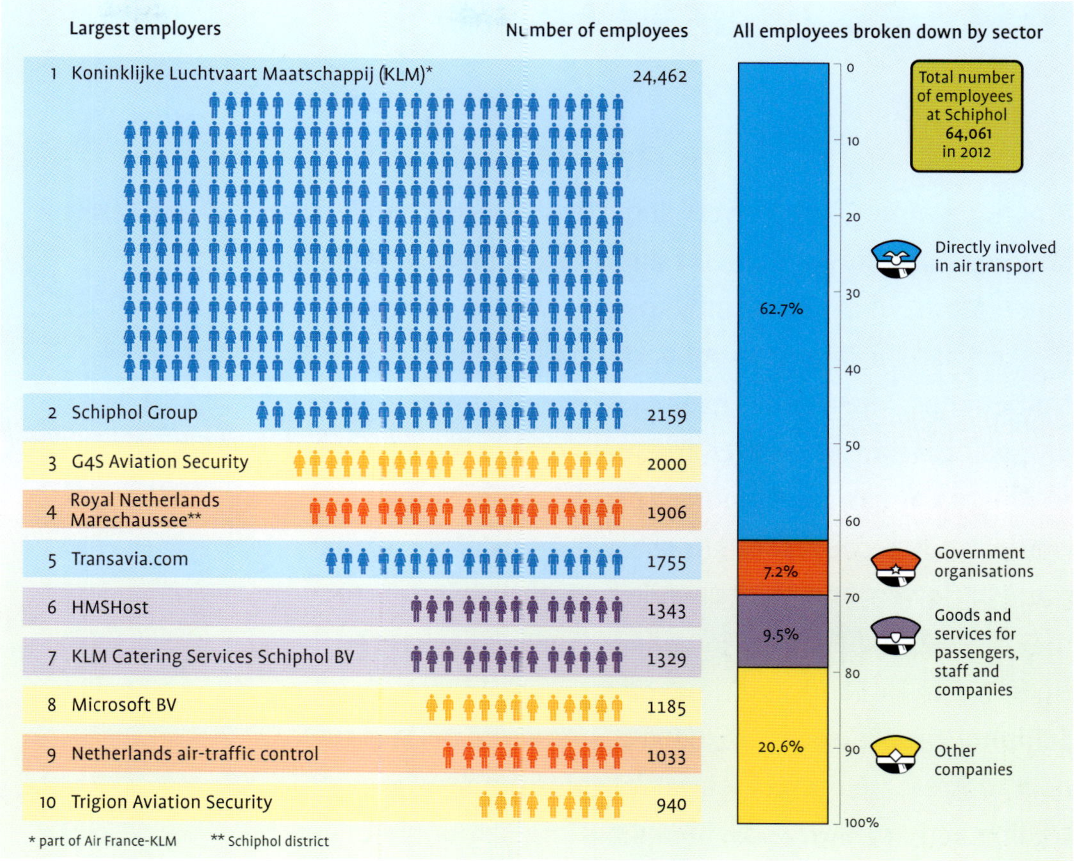

❹ Employment trends

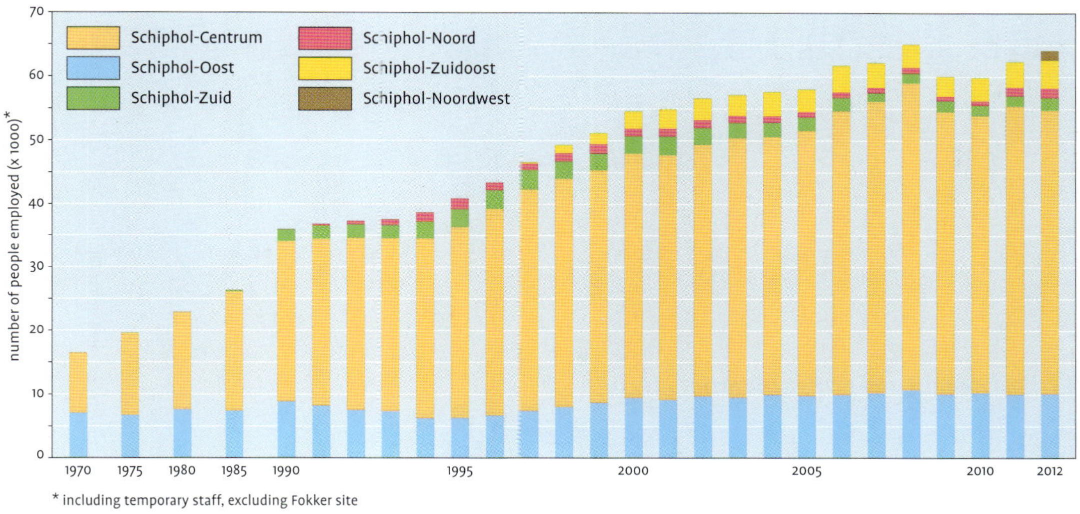

❺ Work locations

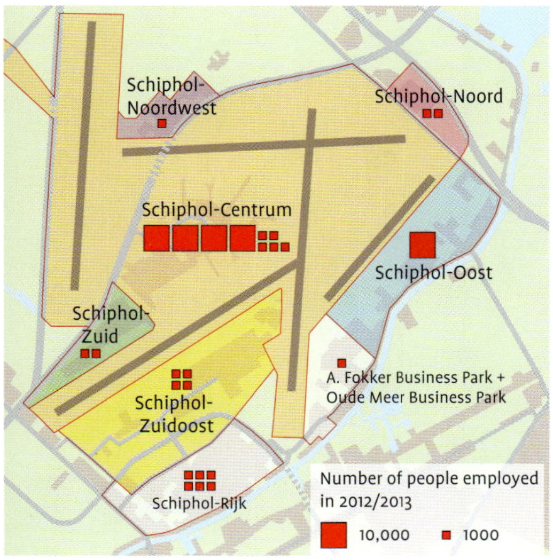

❻ Working hours

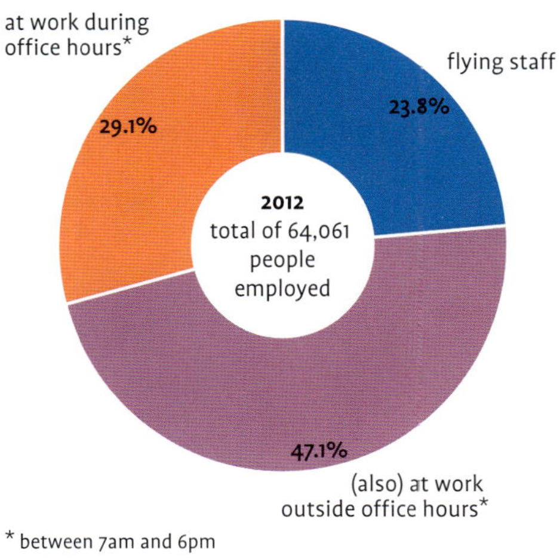

❼ Home towns

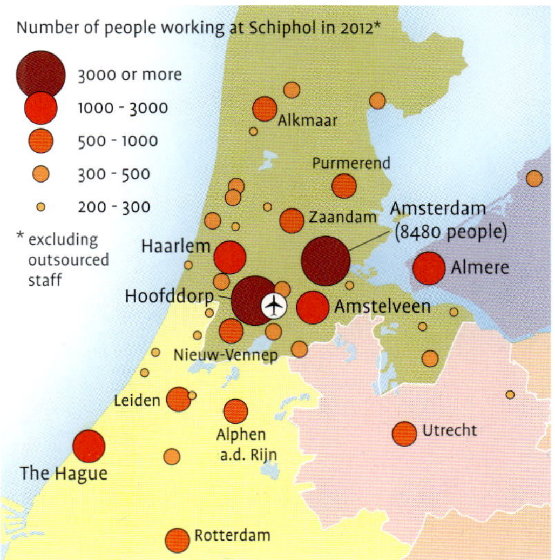

Sources: Schiphol Group (3); Regioplan Beleidsonderzoek: overzicht werkgelegenheid luchthaven Schiphol (4, 6, 7); Schiphol Group / City of Haarlemmermeer (5)

© Noordhoff Uitgevers

Greenport

Amsterdammers love flowers and like to give each other bouquets of tulips and, increasingly often, roses as well. Amsterdam, which is the only town with its own flower market, has the largest number of flower stalls in the Netherlands. The city has even organised a Floriade event on two occasions. However, the main reason for referring to Amsterdam as a greenport is purely economic. The Netherlands accounts for almost two thirds of the global trade in flowers and plants, while four of the world's ten major seed producers are located in 'Seed Valley' at the tip of North Holland. The flower auction in Aalsmeer and Schiphol airport, each located in the Amsterdam Metropolitan Area, are both essential for this immense 'green' trading activity. Every day, incredibly large amounts of cut flowers and plants are transported to Aalsmeer from the Dutch bulb fields, greenhouses and gardens. Cargo aircraft full of foreign consignments of flowers for auction in Aalsmeer land at Schiphol every day too.

❶ Bulb fields

Surface area devoted to flower bulbs and tubers as a percentage of the total utilised agricultural area*, by region, 2014

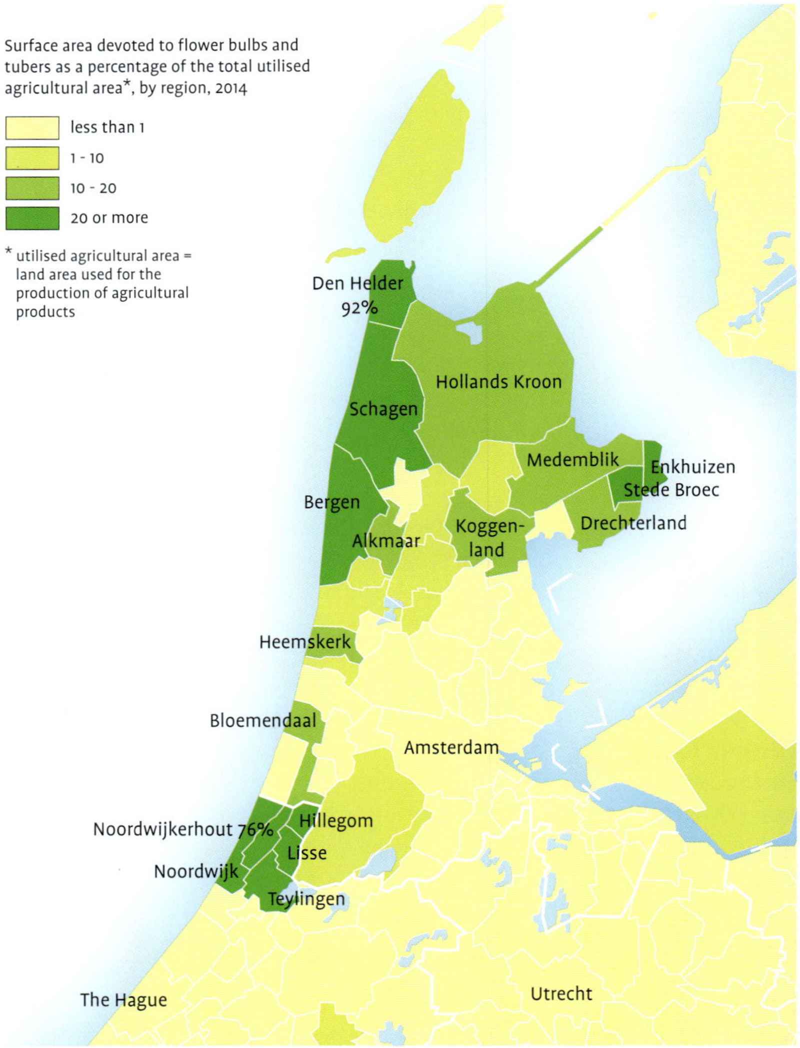

❷ Main import and export countries

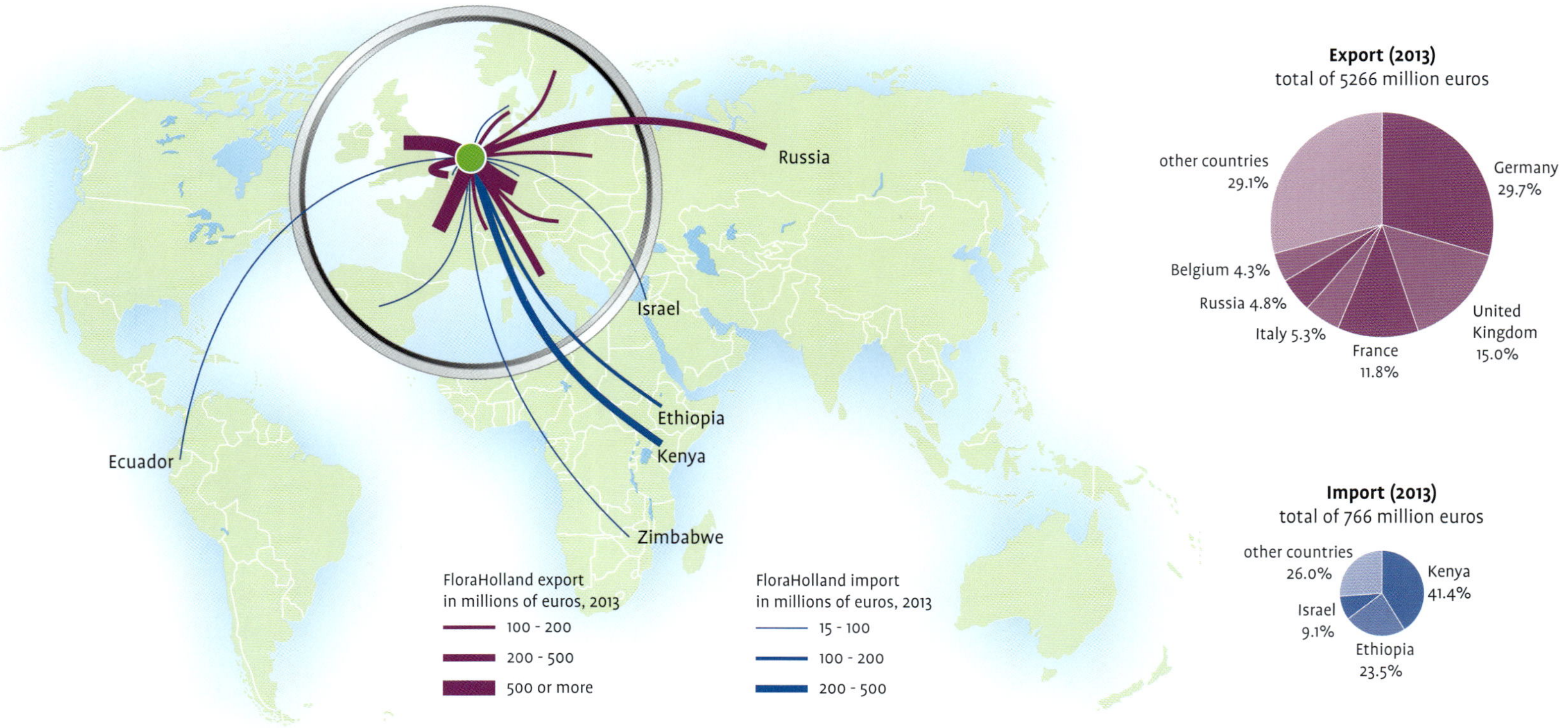

Sources: Statistics Netherlands (1); FloraHolland (2)

© Noordhoff Uitgevers

❸ Size of the Aalsmeer flower auction

❹ FloraHolland* flower traders

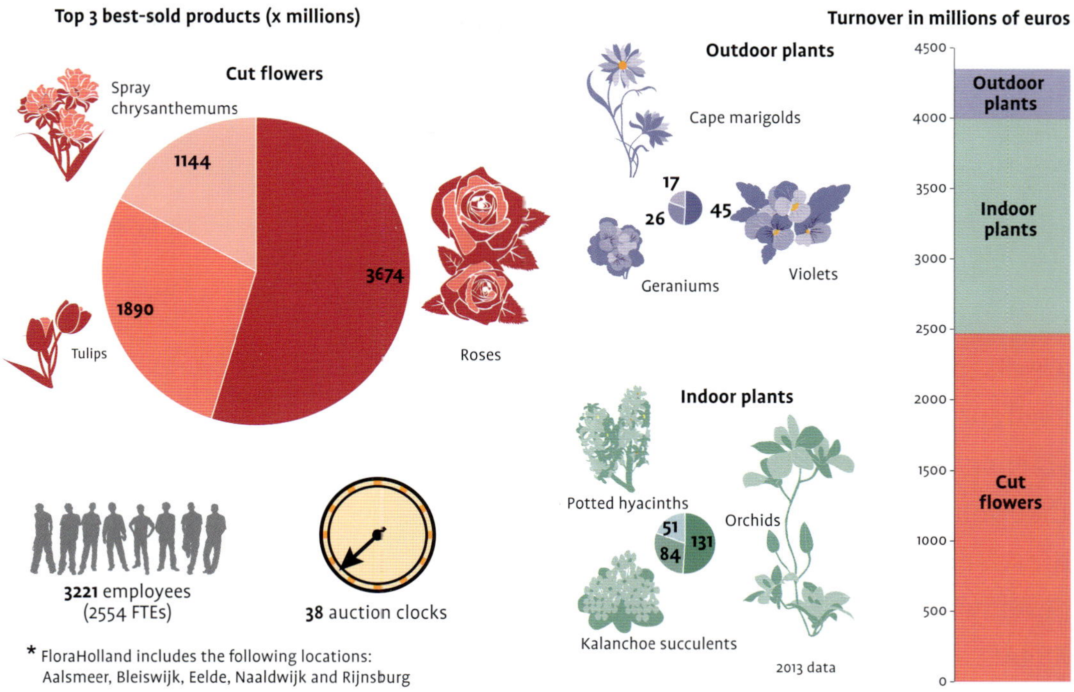

* FloraHolland includes the following locations: Aalsmeer, Bleiswijk, Eelde, Naaldwijk and Rijnsburg

❶ Bulb fields

Around 23,300 hectares of land are used for growing flower bulbs in the Netherlands. Tulip bulbs are cultivated on almost half of that area of land. In West-Friesland and the surrounding area, almost 90% of the bulb fields are used for cultivating tulips.

❷ FloraHolland

The trade in floriculture products is dominated (90% share) by FloraHolland, a co-operative growers' association with around 4,500 members. Of those members, 750 work in foreign countries.

❸ - ❹ Impressive numbers

With a floor area of 1,287,813m², the Aalsmeer auction complex is the largest building in the Netherlands. It has 14 auction clocks, which processed an average of 44,550 transactions a day in 2014. Among other products, those transactions included 3.3 billion cut flowers and 174 million indoor plants. The rose is by far the most traded flower variety and many roses are imported from abroad, particularly from Kenya. Despite these impressive figures, the auction complex's future is anything but rosy, as the Internet has made it increasingly easier for growers and customers to deal with each other directly.

❺ Two Floriade events

In 1972, Amsterdam had the privilege of organising the second Floriade event, a world horticultural exhibition of the highest standard. The exhibition site covered an area of 700,000m² and included two parks created especially for the occasion – Amstelpark and Beatrixpark. Numerous facilities remained behind after the exhibition ended, including a narrow gauge railway, a rose garden and an orangery. Amsterdam hosted the event again in 1982, in Gaasperpark on this occasion. Since then, a Floriade event has been organised in the Netherlands every 10 years. The next event will be held in Almere in 2022.

❺ Amstelpark (Floriade site, 1972)

Sources: FloraHolland (3-4); www.amstelpark.info (5)

© Noordhoff Uitgevers

Dataport

The Internet has irreversibly changed the world. Whereas familiar facilities such as CD shops and travel agencies are disappearing from our living environment, new businesses are starting up, for example companies that build Internet websites. Amsterdam became involved in this development at a very early stage and XS4ALL was founded in the city as one of the first public providers. After Germany's DE-CIX exchange ('Frankfurt'), the Amsterdam Internet Exchange (AMS-IX) is the world's second largest company for Internet traffic. Amsterdam has also been home to the Netherlands' fastest computer – currently the SURFsara facility – for a very long time. In other words, the city is an ICT-friendly environment, which has become home to Internet companies such as Booking.com and digital specialists like TomTom.

❶ Digital fast lane

The Internet is a global system of computer networks that communicate with each other. 'Internet exchange points' have been built in various places to ensure reliable distribution of the billions of data items that are sent over the digital highway every day. One of the largest exchanges is located in Amsterdam.

❷ Storage and processing

Data centres provide data storage capacity and processing power. Most of them are directly connected to an Internet exchange, and large institutions and companies have their own data centres. The other data centres rent capacity to companies and individuals. The city of Amsterdam alone is home to more than 40 data centres.

❶ International Internet traffic by city

Internet traffic by city in 2012

- 10 Global top 10
- 20 Global 11 - 20
- 30 Global 21 - 30
- Other Internet exchanges

In 2012, 19 of the 30 cities with the highest level of international internet traffic were located in Europe. There is usually more than one Internet traffic company operating in a single city.

Of the top 10, seven are in Europe and the other three in the United States (no. 5: New York, no. 6: Miami and no. 8: Los Angeles).

Main data flows (the thicker the line, the greater the volume of data)

❷ Data centres

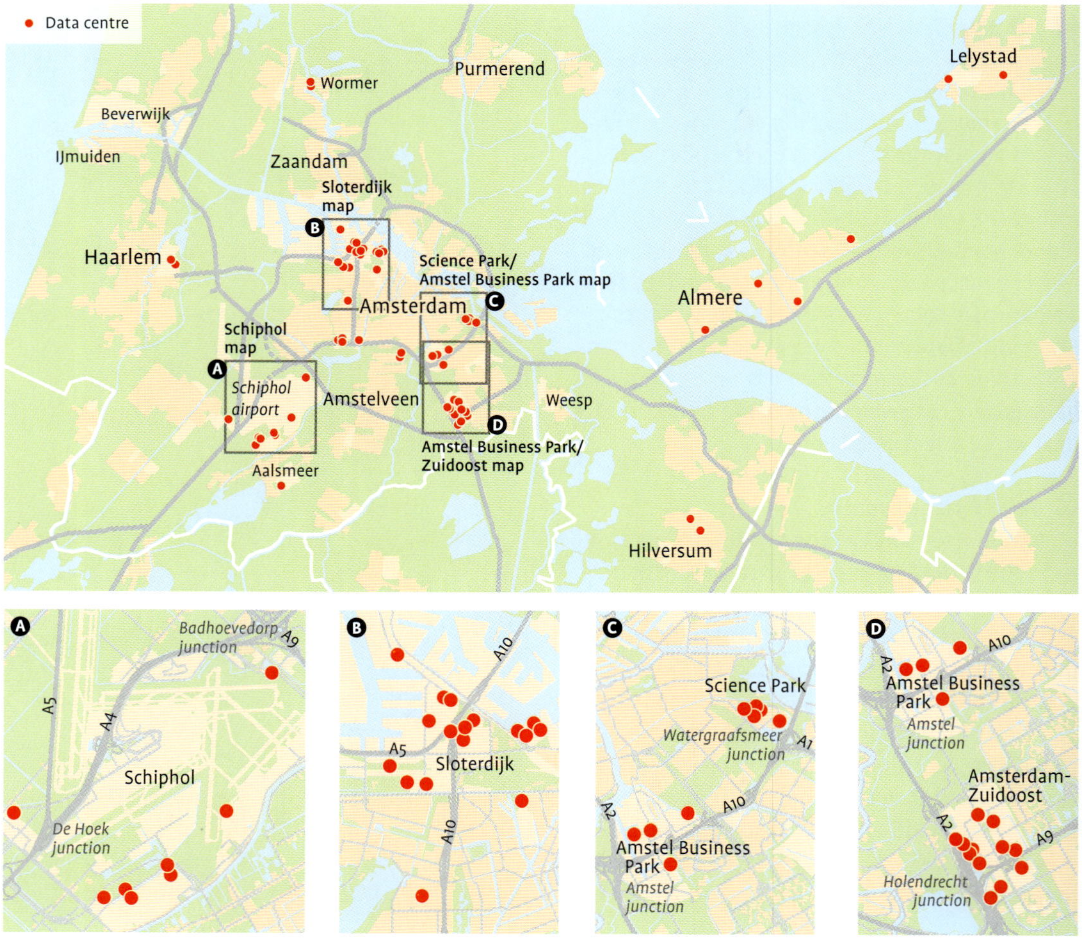

© Noordhoff Uitgevers

❸ - ❹ ICT

Since the financial crisis ended, the information and communications technology sector (ICT) has started to grow again rapidly. In 2013, 4.4% of all Dutch companies and nearly 4% of the country's total working population were active in this sector. For comparison purposes – the 18,193 ICT companies based in Amsterdam provided around 56,000 jobs in January 2015, nearly 8% of all jobs in the city.
Growth in the ICT sector is driven by a succession of new applications and the increasingly intensive use of ICT capabilities. In 2012, for example, 4.3 billion text messages were sent, but that number has since reduced drastically, due to the arrival of new media such as WhatsApp, Facebook and Twitter. Whereas only 21% of the Dutch population had a smartphone at the start of 2010, that figure had risen to 81% by early 2015.

❺ Amsterdam's showpiece

Founded in 1994, the Amsterdam Internet Exchange (AMS-IX) has become the world's second largest Internet traffic-handling company in just 20 years – and one of the city's largest energy consumers. The company's digital infrastructure is spread across twelve sites in the city. They are linked in such a way that if a fault occurs at one location, the other sites automatically assist. Over 700 customers use AMS-IX including Microsoft, XS4ALL and Netflix.

❸ Employment in ICT in the Netherlands

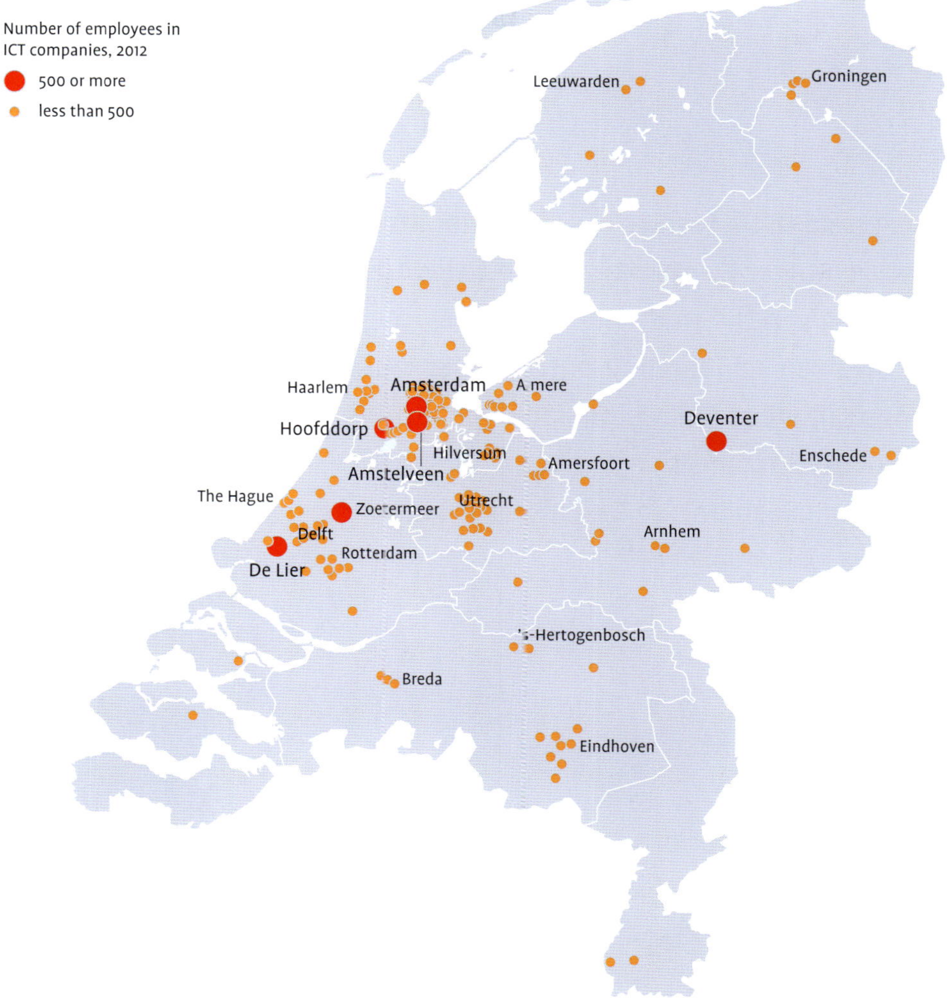

❹ Employment in ICT in Amsterdam

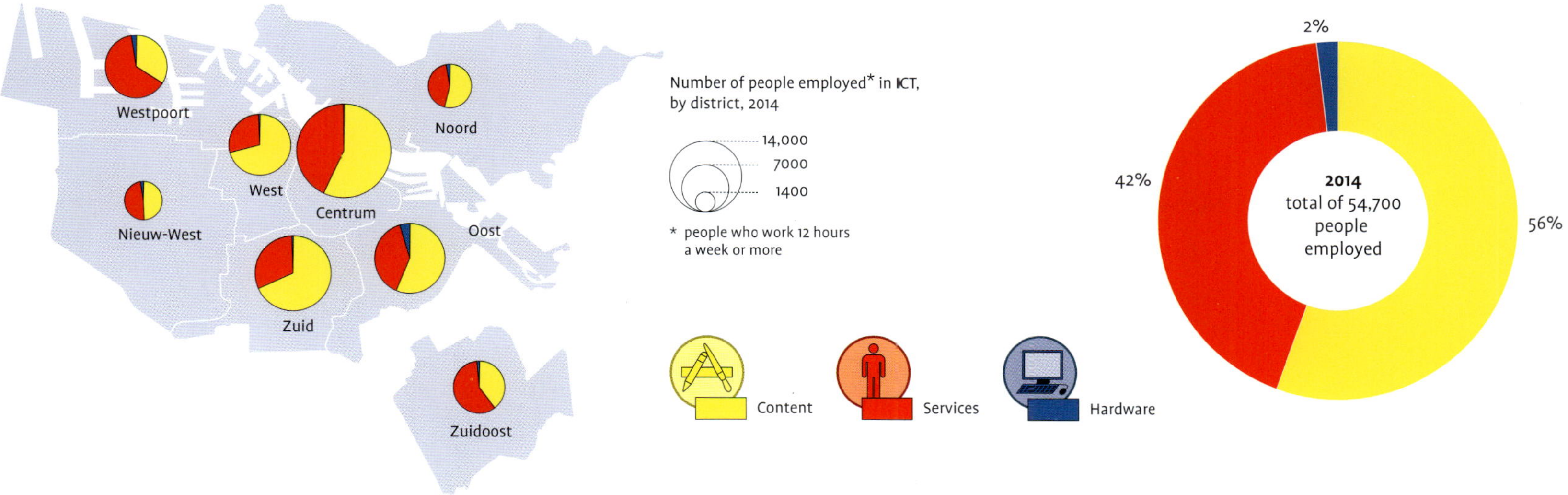

❺ Statistics relating to the ICT sector in Amsterdam

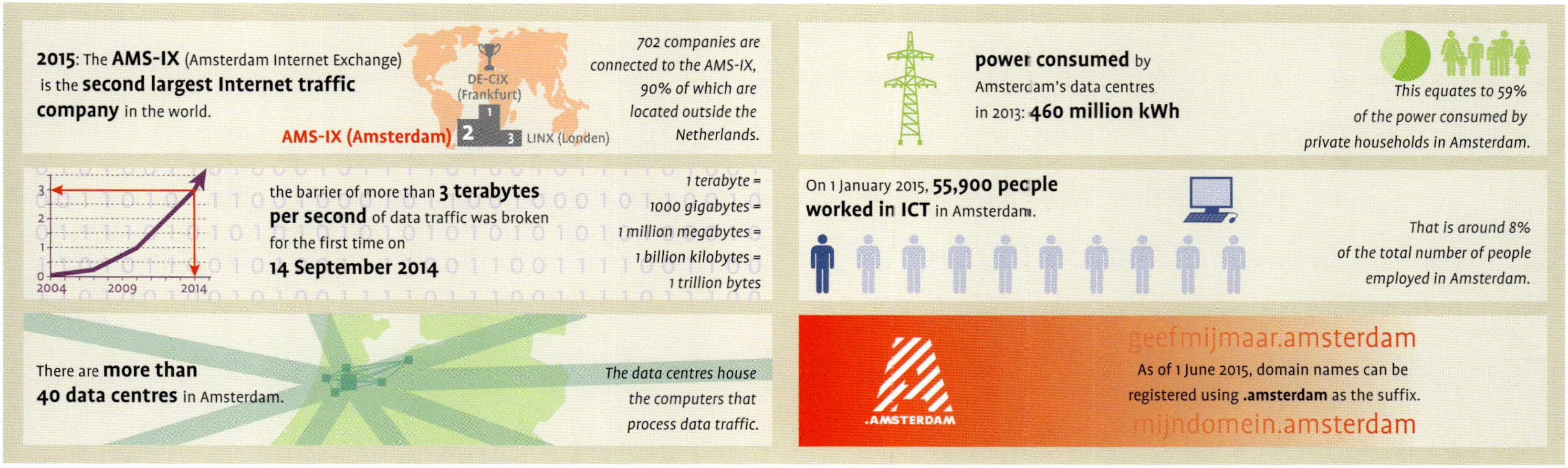

Sources: Stichting Amsterdamse Innovatie Motor (3); OIS, Research, Information and Statistics, City of Amsterdam (4, 5)

© Noordhoff Uitgevers

Creative industry

Amsterdam is proud to be seen as the most vibrant and versatile creative 'hotspot' – perhaps not in the whole of Europe, but certainly in the Netherlands. The creative sector is very diverse, including not only the arts, but also media and entertainment (television, radio, publishing, gaming) and creative business services (advertising, design, architecture, fashion). This chapter focuses on services, while chapters 7 and 8 look at the arts and entertainment in detail. The large number of business start-ups and failures and the small-scale approach are typical of this sector. More than 80% of the companies are one-man businesses and only 4% employ more than five people. Their distribution across the city is extremely inconsistent, but the majority are based in Centrum and Zuid.

1 Advertising agencies

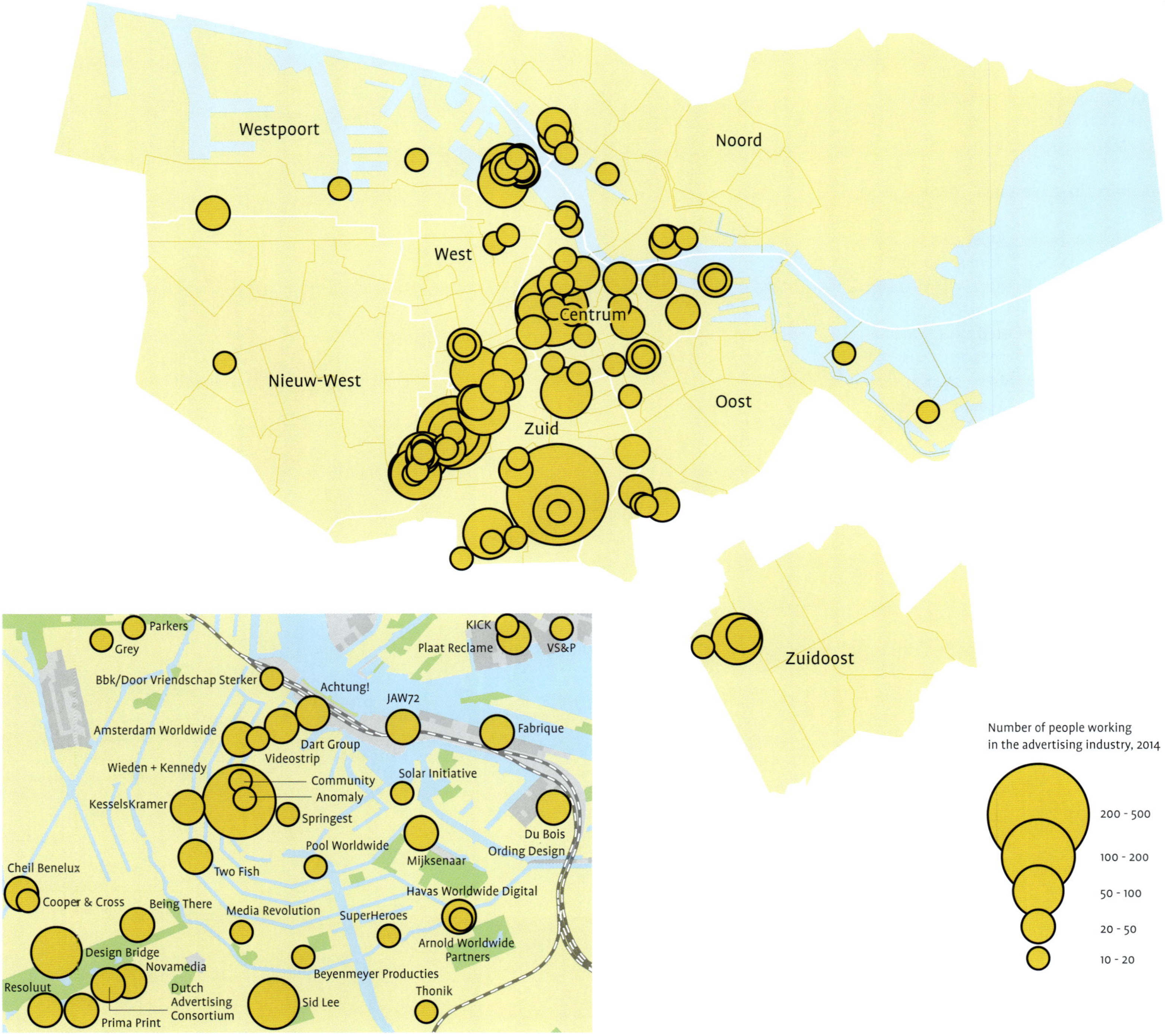

Source: OIS, Research, Information and Statistics, City of Amsterdam (1)

© Noordhoff Uitgevers

❶ Gouden Loekies

There are hundreds of advertising agencies in Amsterdam – numerous small ones and a few very large agencies such as TBWA\NEBOKO. This company's well-known customers include Albert Heijn, KLM, Unox, Pearle and McDonald's. The dominance of Amsterdam's advertising community is illustrated by the fact that the 'Gouden Loekie' – an award for the best TV commercial – went to a company in Amsterdam almost every year out of the last ten.

❷ City of fashion

Amsterdam is a force to be reckoned with in the international world of fashion designers and the Amsterdam Fashion Institute (AMFI), a four-year higher professional education course, is highly regarded. In 2012, there were some 1640 fashion design companies in Amsterdam, including Viktor&Rolf. However, this sector only employs around 2300 people.

❸ Famous architects

Although Amsterdam is definitely not the architectural heart of the Netherlands, various major architects are based in the city, including Ton Alberts, Jan Benthem, Mels Crouwel, Ben van Berkel, Pi de Bruijn, Herman Hertzberger, Max van Huut, Roberto Meyer, Liesbeth van der Pol, Herman Zeinstra and Jeroen van Schooten. Their firms are generally larger than those of graphic and industrial designers and in the latter case, the average staffing level is only 1.4.

❹ - ❺ Leader in digital media

Between 2008 and 2012, the creative digital media sector grew spectacularly in Amsterdam, at an average rate of 17% a year. This makes Amsterdam the undisputed leader in the sector – the figure for the Netherlands as a whole is only 8%. This strong growth can largely be attributed to new media. The demand for websites, games and apps – and therefore creative ICT specialists – seems never-ending. Traditional media (TV, newspapers), on the other hand, are struggling in the face of declining turnovers and contracting markets.

❷ Fashion

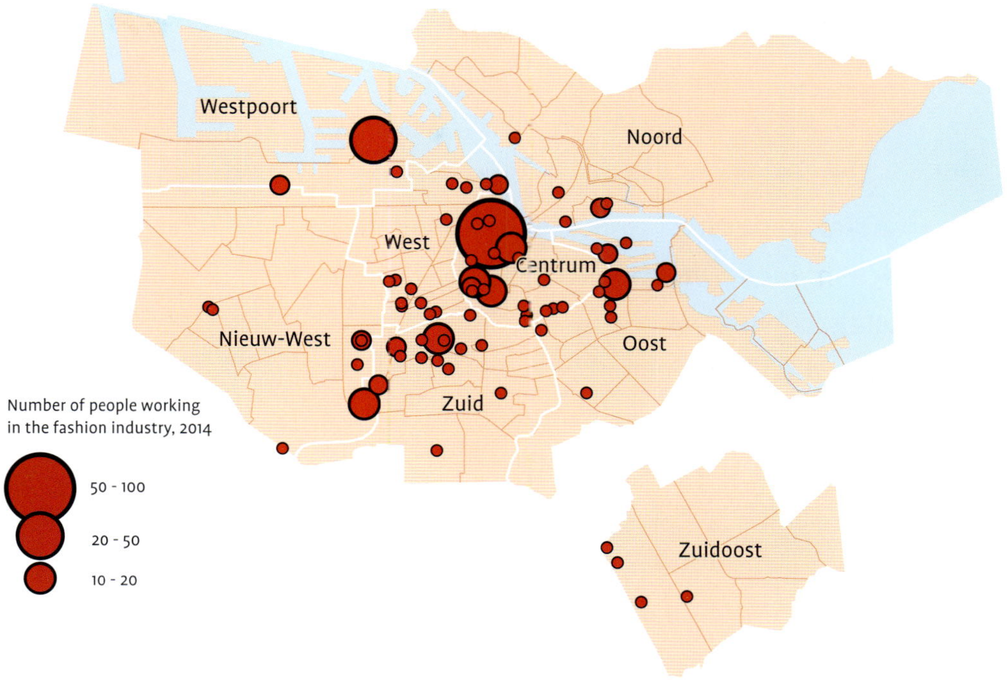

❸ Design and architecture

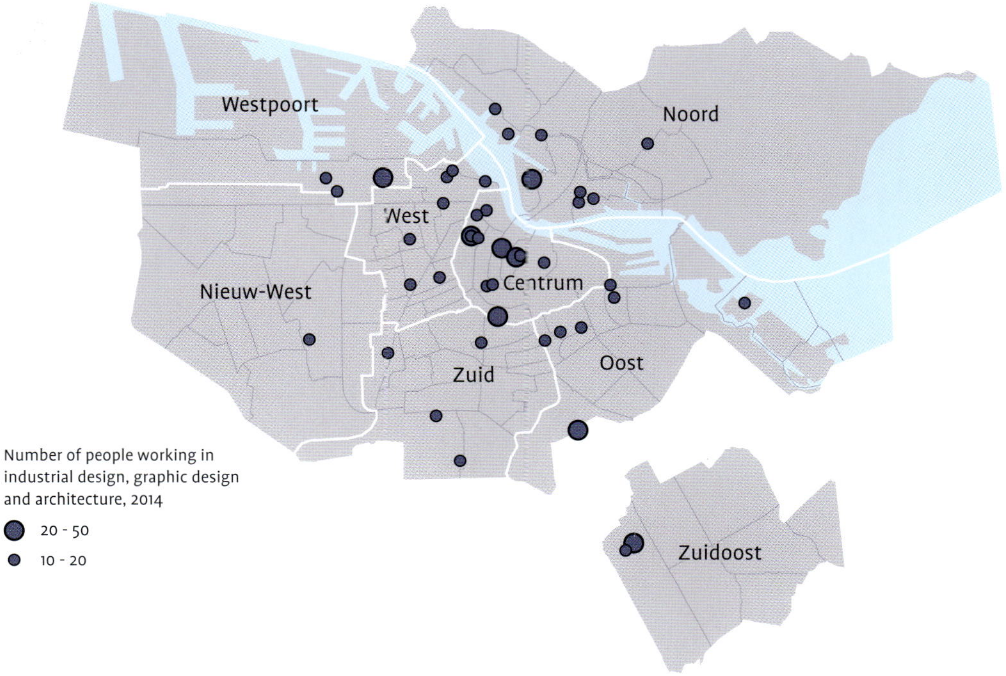

❹ Gaming in the Netherlands

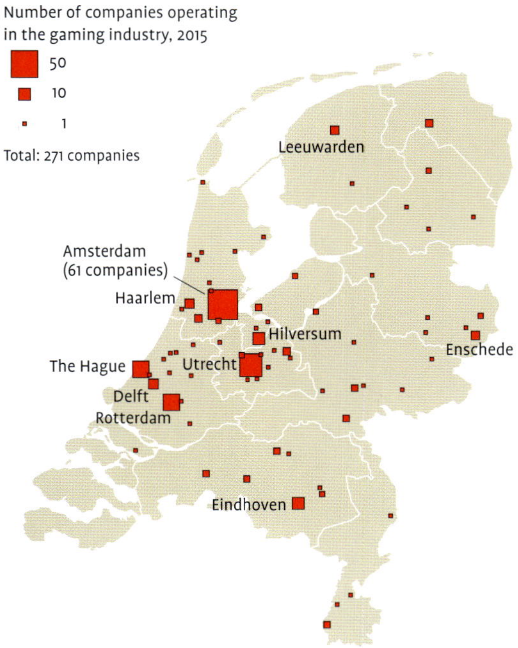

❺ Digital media

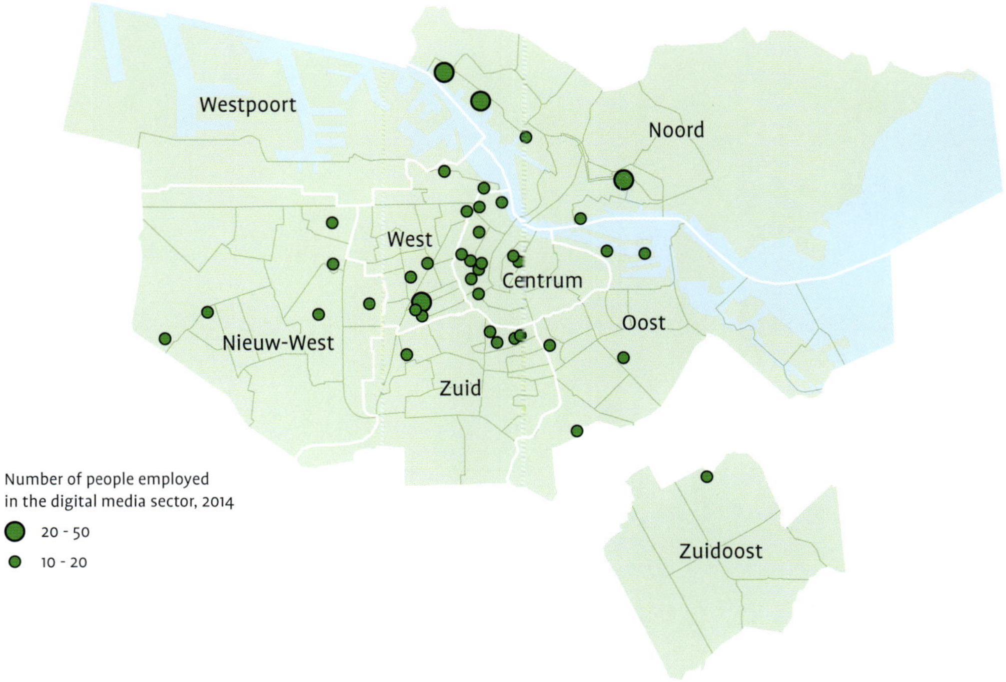

Source: OIS, Research, Information and Statistics, City of Amsterdam (2-5)

© Noordhoff Uitgevers

Retail trade

The Dutch retail trade is going through a difficult period. Due to population ageing, depopulation and the rapid increase of online shopping, small businesses in particular have had to close their doors. The recent recession and the resulting fall in disposable income have led to a further increase in the number of vacant shops. Amsterdam has been less affected by these factors, as young people continue to flock to the city to study, work and raise families. Amsterdam also remains a favourite destination for day trippers and tourists who spend a significant amount of their time shopping or paying visits to the market.

❶ Markets

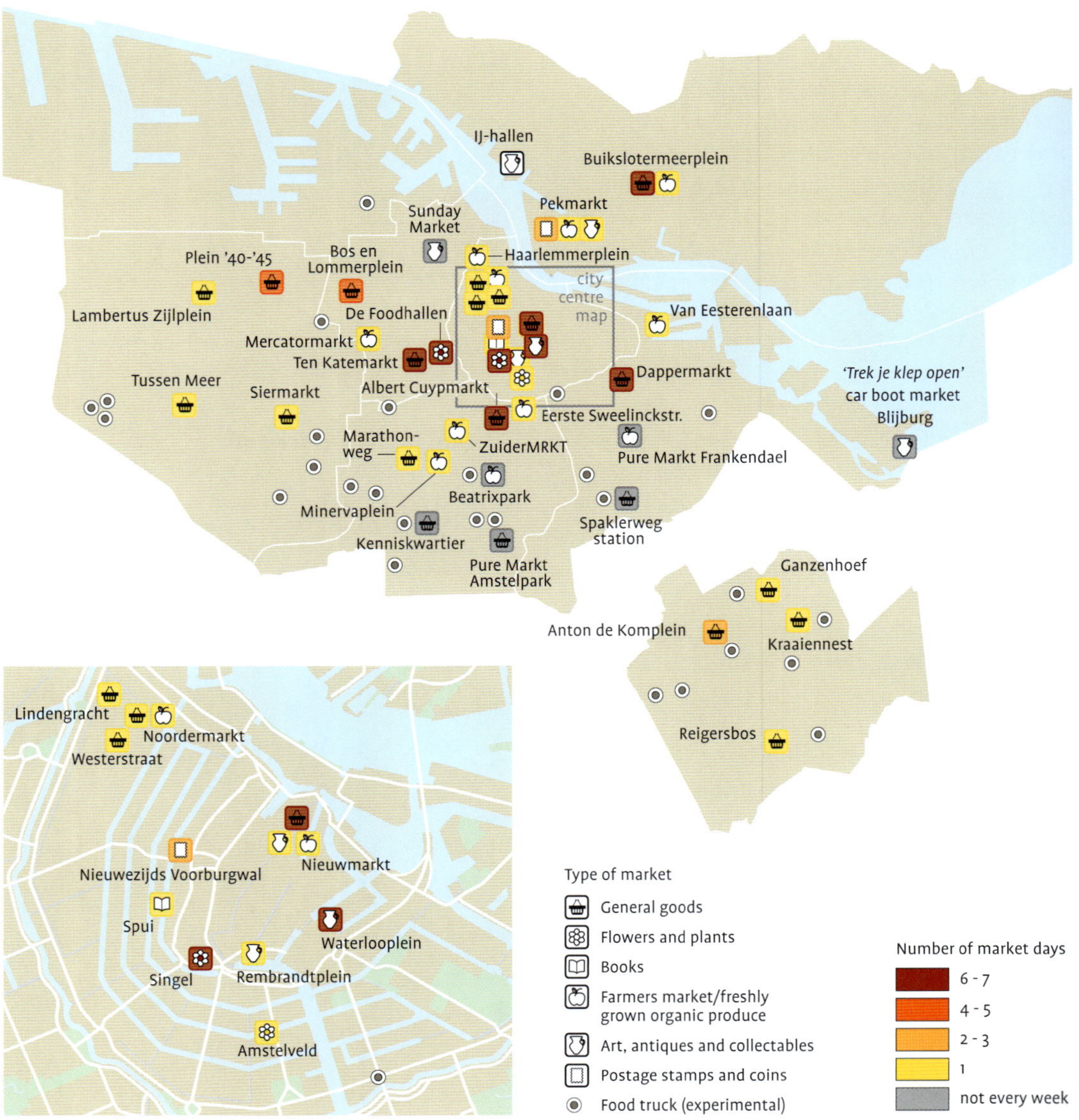

❷ Largest markets

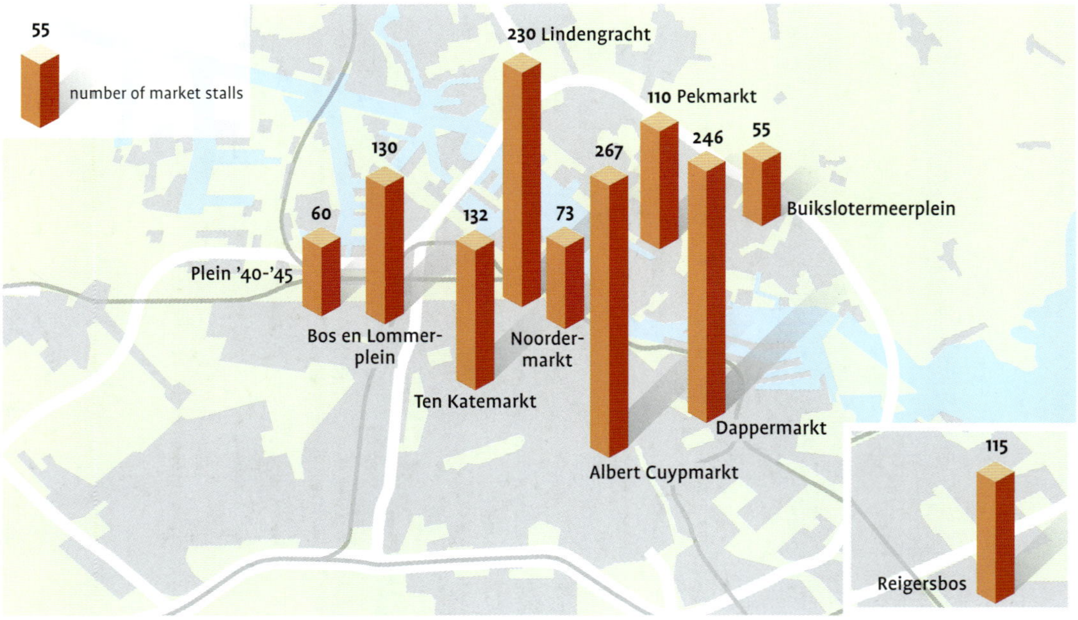

Comparison of most visited markets
(Percentage of all market-goers)

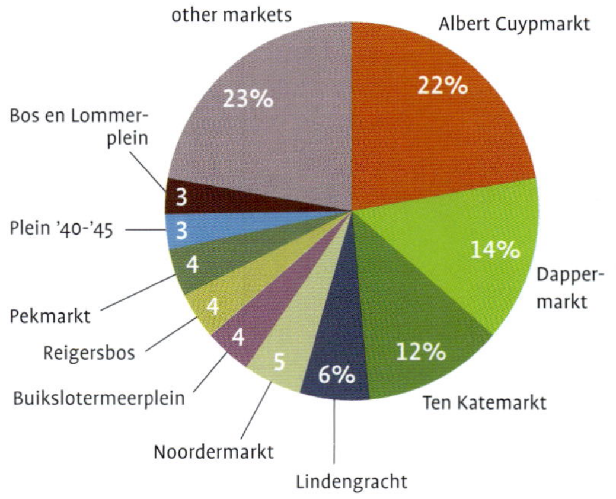

Source: OIS, Research, Information and Statistics, City of Amsterdam (1-2)

© Noordhoff Uitgevers

❸ Retail sectors

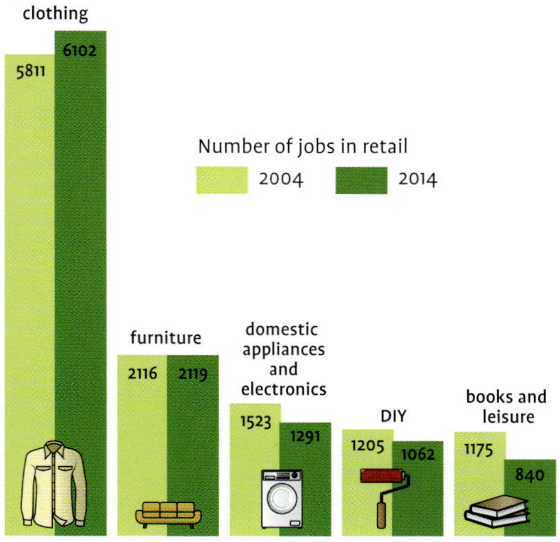

❹ Shops for non-everyday items

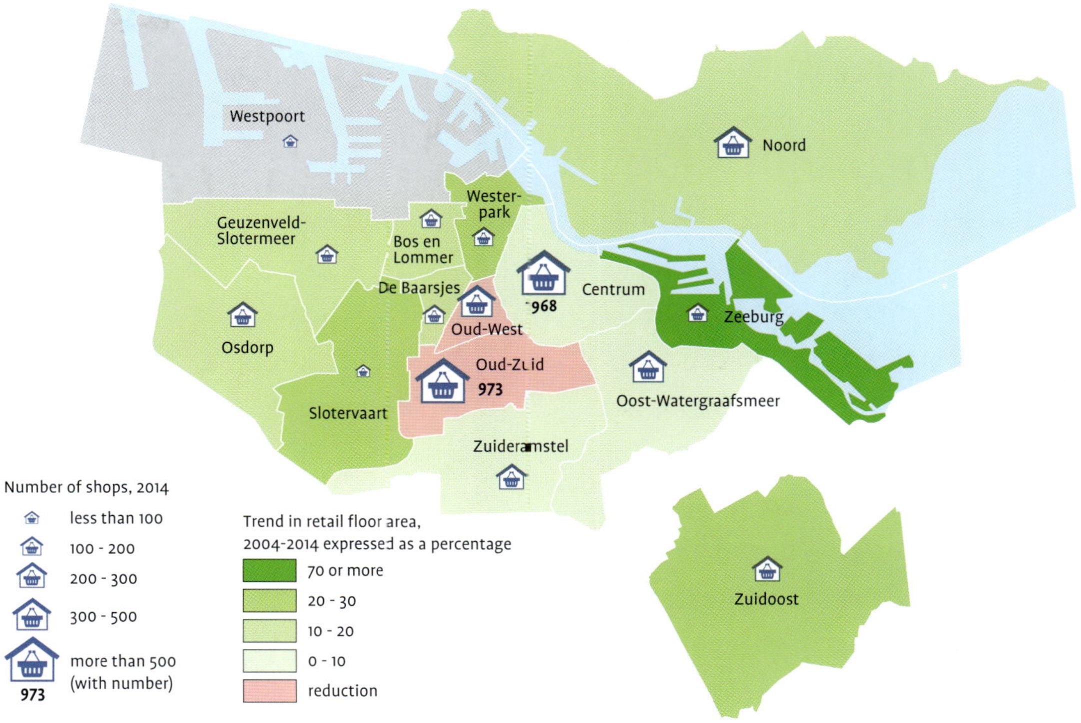

❶ - ❷ Off to the market

Seven out of ten Amsterdammers go to the market now and then. City-centre residents, the over-50s and those on a relatively low income are the most frequent shoppers, spending around 22 euros per visit on average. The Albert Cuyp, Dapper and Ten Kate markets are the busiest in Amsterdam. However, the markets in Noord and Zuidoost have the most loyal visitors.

❸ Part-timers

Despite the decline in the number of shops, the number of jobs in retail increased between 2004 and 2014, from 34,500 to 37,100. Most of the new jobs are part-time ones in the food sector due to the increase in the number of supermarkets and extended opening hours.

❹ Fewer shops, greater surface area

Between 2004 and 2014, the number of retail shops in Amsterdam decreased from 6080 to 5668. Most of the closures took place in Nieuw-West. At the same time, the retail floor area increased, which indicates that smaller shops are being displaced by larger competitors, a trend that is also evident to varying degrees elsewhere. The number of shops in the city centre has fluctuated around the 2000 mark for the last ten years.

❺ Loyal to their home town

Almost all Amsterdammers (98%) do their daily shopping in Amsterdam itself, generally in their own neighbourhood or at the market. Nearly a quarter buy non-everyday items in a different city (11%) or online (11%). Kalverstraat is still the main shopping street, and Amsterdammers spend as much as 10% of their total available budget for non-everyday items there.

❻ Limited exodus

Around 9% of Dutch retail properties are empty. In Amsterdam, that figure is 'only' 4.5%, much less than in Rotterdam and The Hague, where 10% of retail premises are empty.

❺ Shopping behaviour for non-everyday items

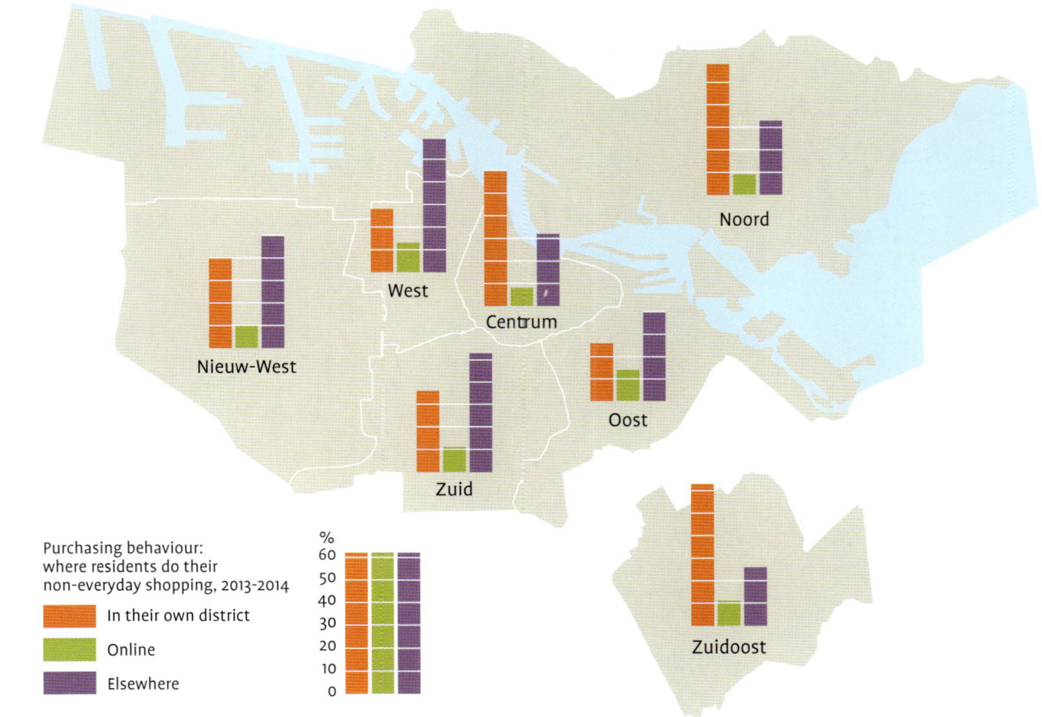

❻ Empty retail premises

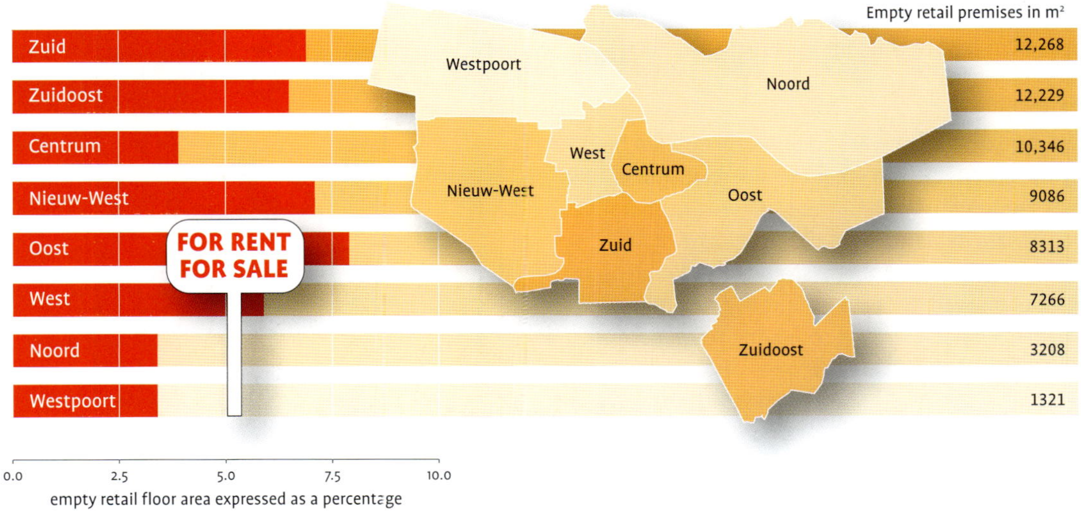

Source: City of Amsterdam (3-6)

© Noordhoff Uitgevers

Financial centre

Even though Amsterdam is no longer the financial centre of the world, as it was in the 17th and 18th centuries, it still plays a pivotal role in the Netherlands, as the city's banks and insurance companies make a major contribution to the Dutch economy. In fact, this sector is one of the largest employers in the Amsterdam Metropolitan Area and accounts for a significant portion of the more than 100 billion euros that are earned in Amsterdam each year.
Amsterdam is also home to the Dutch stock exchange. The main yardstick, the AEX, is an indicator of developments in the Dutch economy.

❶ Financial institutions

❷ Financial institutions in the southern Canal Ring

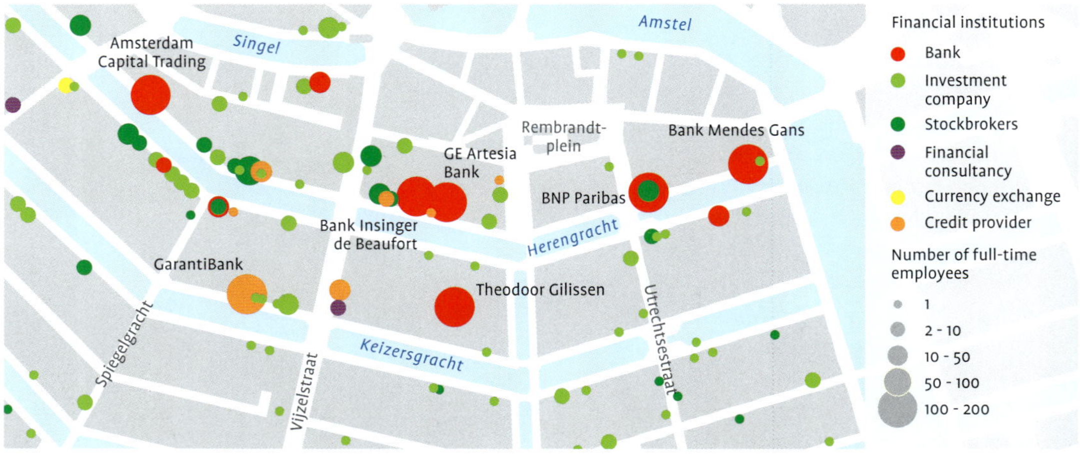

❶ - ❷ Migration to the periphery

In former times, banks operated from stately mansions along the canals, but the large Dutch banks have now moved most of their staff to impressive bank buildings on the outskirts of the city in Zuid and Zuidoost. Today, it is largely the branches of foreign banks that line Amsterdam's canals. In 2014, 3122 financial institutions were based in Amsterdam, 132 of which were banks. More than half of these institutions were based in the Centrum (790) and Zuid (970) districts.

❸ Recovery

Amsterdam's financial sector has been hard hit by the credit crisis in recent years, resulting in mass redundancies and the closure of numerous bank branches. However, the first signs of a recovery are now apparent. Nearly 44,000 people were employed by the sector at the beginning of 2015, a small increase compared to 2014. Zuidoost offers the highest level of employment (around 15,700 jobs). This is noteworthy as significantly fewer financial institutions (about 190) have a branch there than in Zuid and the Zuidas development.

❸ Jobs in the financial sector (by field of activity in 2014)

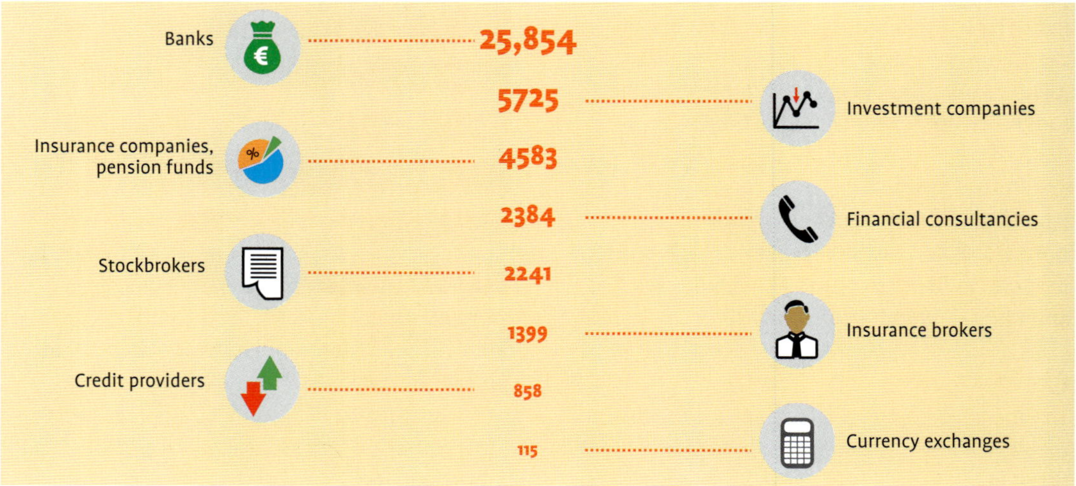

Source: OIS, Research, Information and Statistics, City of Amsterdam (1-3)

© Noordhoff Uitgevers

❹ Financial sector in the Netherlands

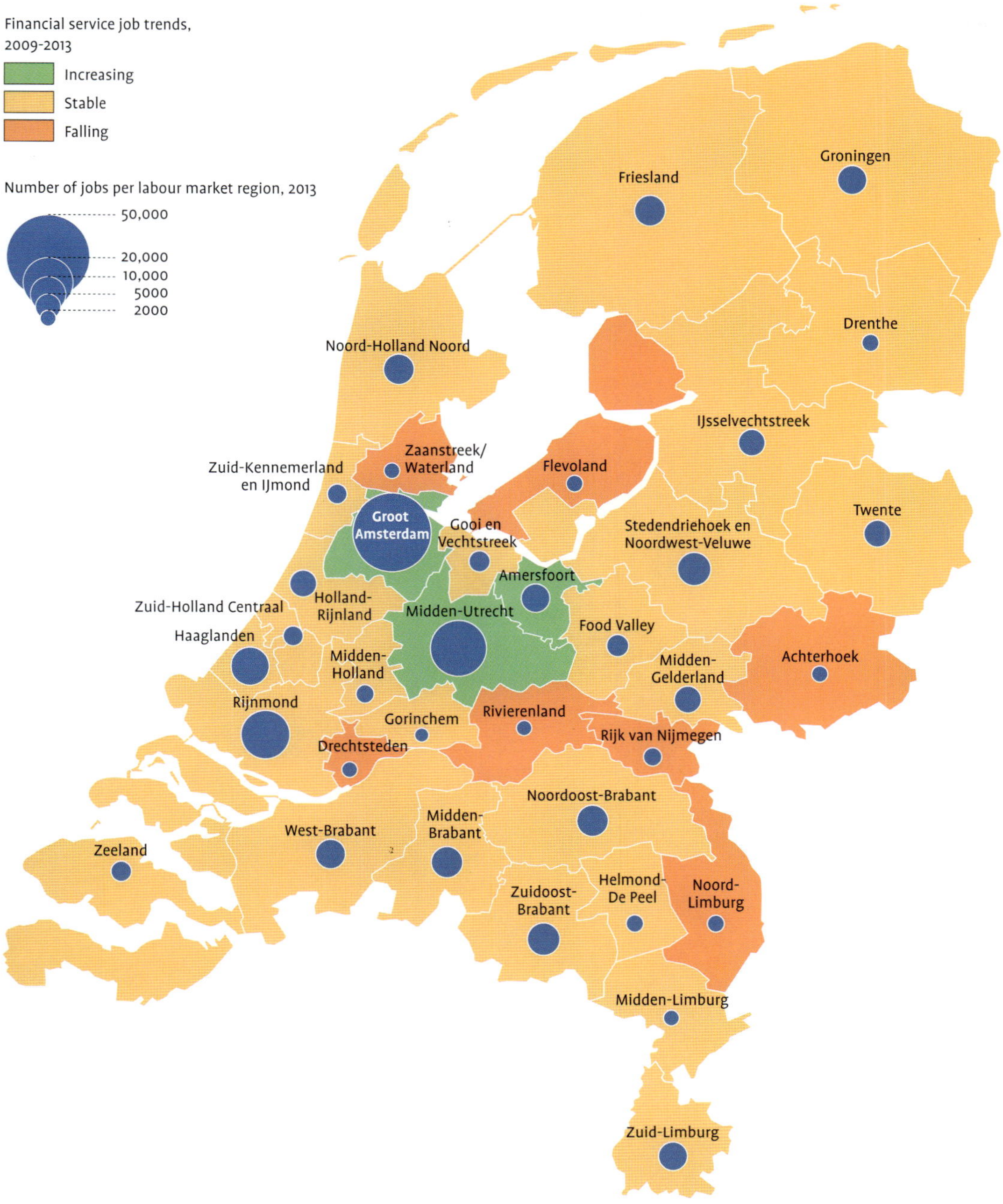

❺ Importance of the financial sector

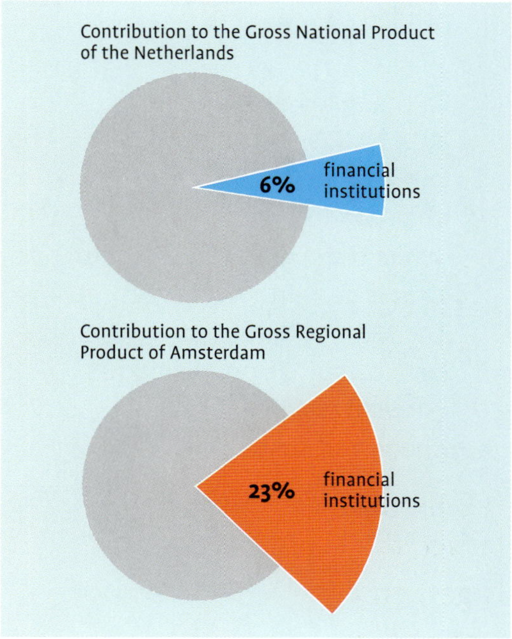

❻ Share price trend

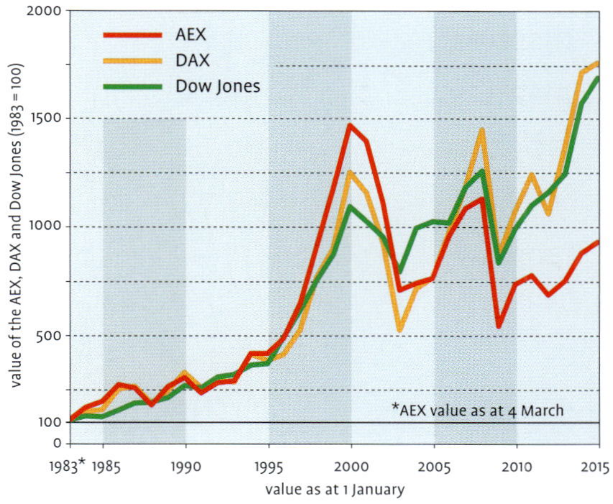

❼ AEX shares: largest companies in the Netherlands

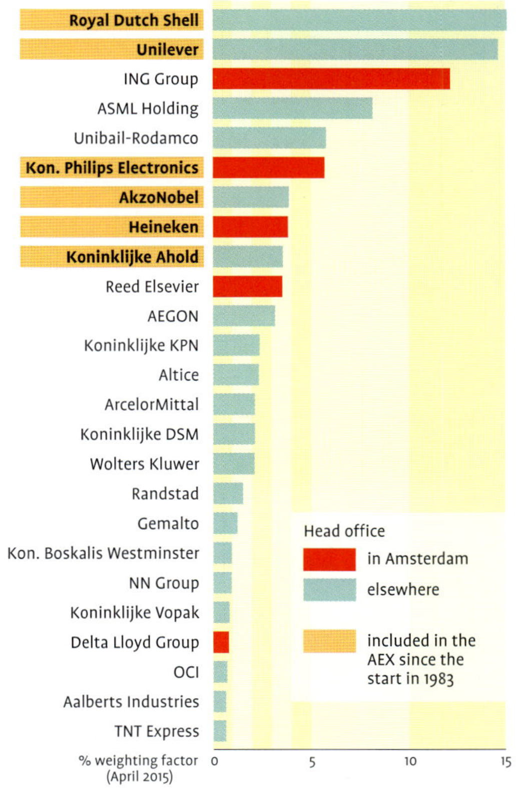

❹ - ❺ Profit and loss

At 8.2%, the financial sector's share in the Dutch economy is higher than the average for all 27 countries in the European Union (5%). Even though the banks and insurance companies are now making profit again after a few difficult years, employment continues to decline. Between 2005 and 2014, the number of jobs reduced from 276,000 to 248,000. In Greater Amsterdam, employment in this sector reduced by 15% to around 50,000 jobs. The loss of jobs is expected to continue in the years to come. Of the three major Dutch banks, Rabobank, ING and ABN AMRO, the latter two have their headquarters in Amsterdam. Together, they account for 85% of the loans held by Dutch households and 60% of business lending.

❻ - ❼ A handy number

The Amsterdam Exchange Index, usually called the AEX index, is a handy number that expresses the value of the 25 most traded share funds on the Amsterdam stock exchange. It is seen as an indicator of the level of confidence in the Dutch economy. If confidence is high, the AEX increases; if not, it reduces.
The composition of the AEX changes regularly due to splits, mergers or disappointing results. Since its introduction in 1983, only six funds have succeeded in maintaining their position – Ahold, AkzoNobel, Heineken, Philips, Shell and Unilever. Together, the five largest stock funds determine 50% of the index, which explains why movements in the price of these shares determine the index's value. The AEX reached its highest closing value – 701.56 points – on 4 September 2000. Up to that point, the world had had boundless faith in the emerging Internet economy, but after the bubble finally burst, share prices in Amsterdam never again rose to the same level, as the AEX index line relative to 1983 shows. The AEX was recalculated to reflect the euro (divided by 2.20371) on 4 January 1999.

Sources: UWV (4); OIS, Research, Information and Statistics, City of Amsterdam (5); AEX / www.1stock1.com (6); www.beursaex.nl (7)

© Noordhoff Uitgevers

The Zuidas

In the 1980s, the World Trade Center (WTC) and ABN AMRO took up residence next to the new A10 motorway. This marked the start of a business centre that was intended to compete with London and Paris. While that objective has yet to be achieved, this area is currently the largest business centre in the Netherlands. Today, the emphasis lies on a combination of working, (stylish) residential facilities, shops and sustainability.

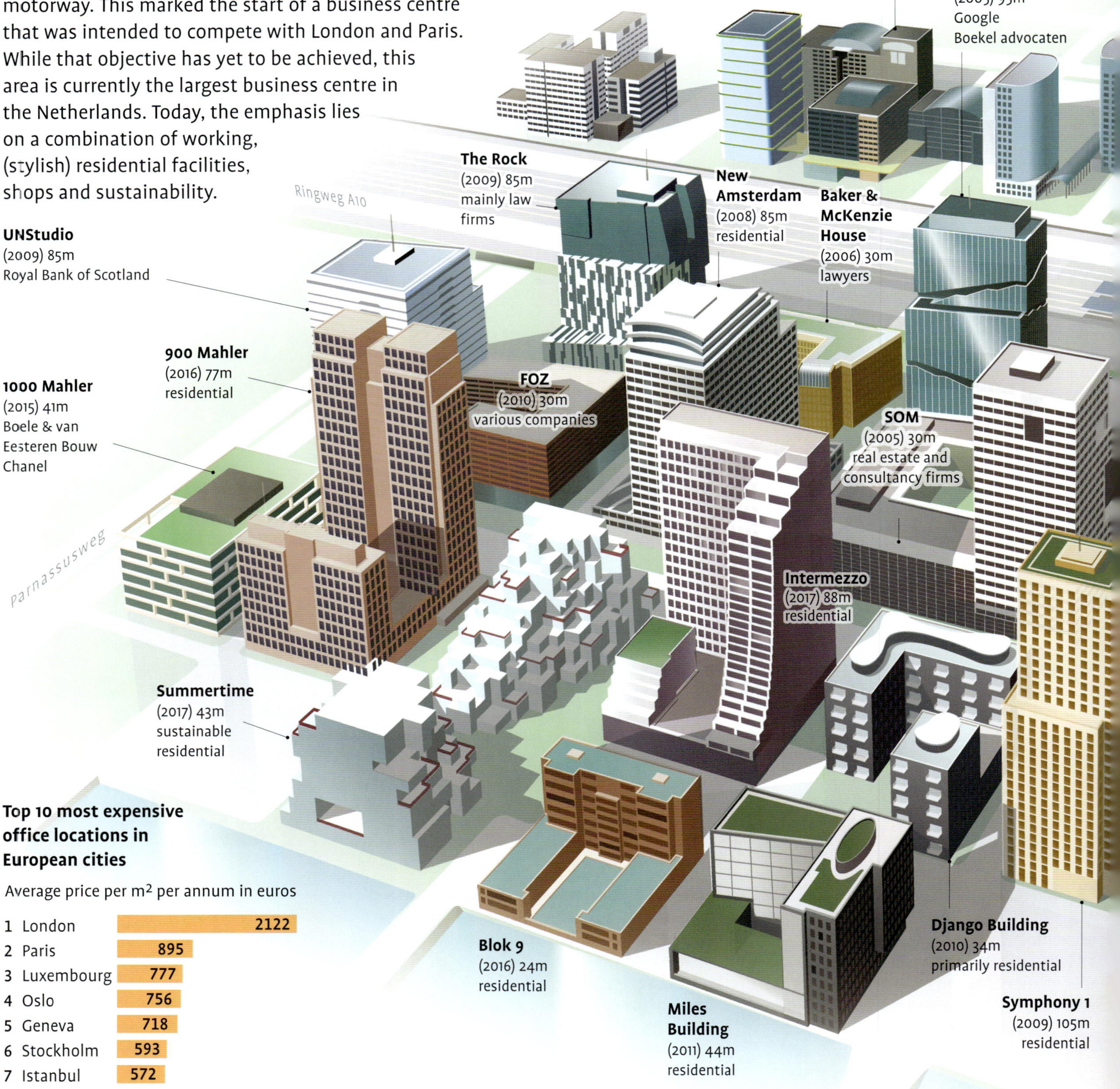

Top 10 most expensive office locations in European cities

Average price per m² per annum in euros

1	London	2122
2	Paris	895
3	Luxembourg	777
4	Oslo	756
5	Geneva	718
6	Stockholm	593
7	Istanbul	572
8	Milan	556
9	Munich	540
10	**Amsterdam**	506 **Zuidas**

Global top 5

1	London	2122
2	Hong Kong	1432
3	Beijing	1027
4	Tokyo	1003
5	New York	993
22	**Amsterdam**	506 **Zuidas**

Floor space in the Zuidas

The total office floor space is growing and the number of empty premises is falling.

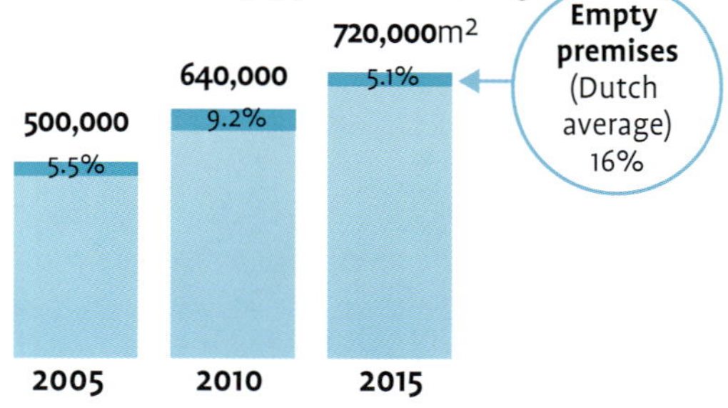

Who occupies the office space in the Zuidas?

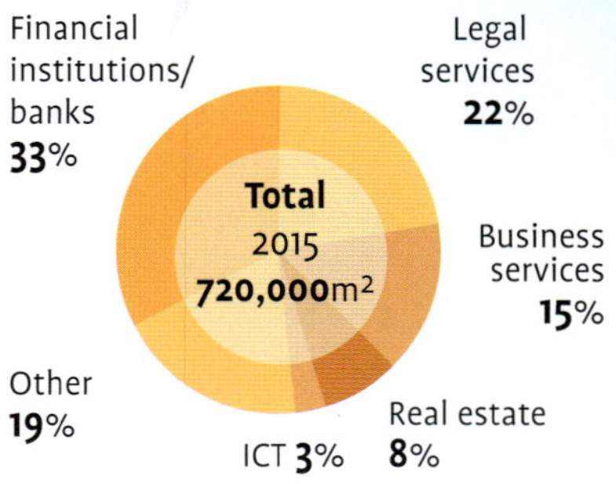

Sources: Cushman & Wakefield / JLL kantorenmarktmonitor / JLL Zuidas office monitor / City of Amsterdam

Residential facilities

More homes are being built in order to make the Zuidas area more attractive.

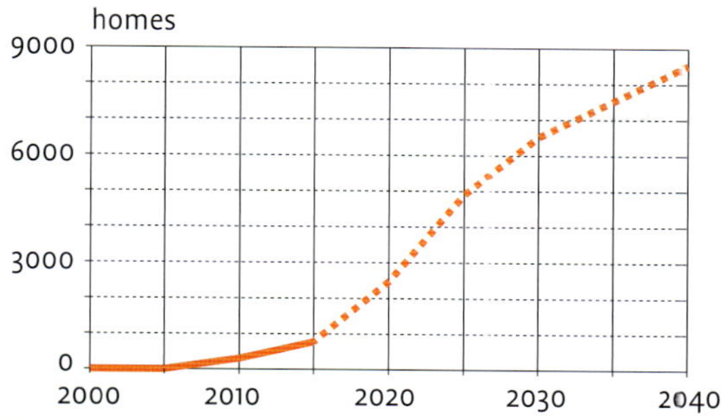

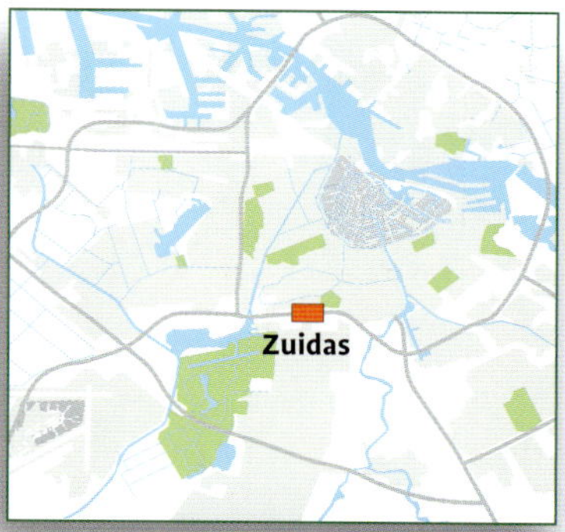

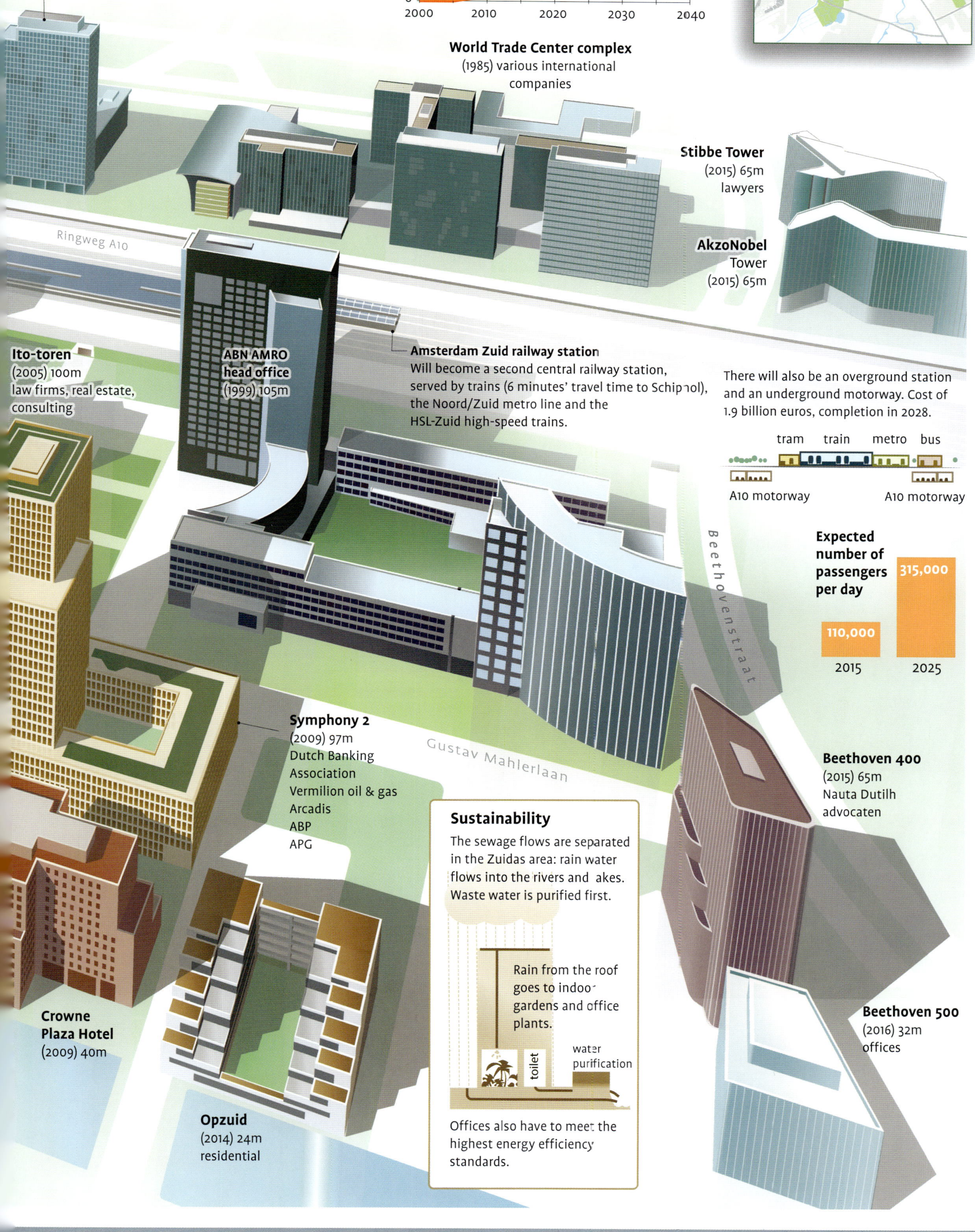

Amsterdam Zuid railway station
Will become a second central railway station, served by trains (6 minutes' travel time to Schiphol), the Noord/Zuid metro line and the HSL-Zuid high-speed trains.

There will also be an overground station and an underground motorway. Cost of 1.9 billion euros, completion in 2028.

Expected number of passengers per day

Sustainability

The sewage flows are separated in the Zuidas area: rain water flows into the rivers and lakes. Waste water is purified first.

Offices also have to meet the highest energy efficiency standards.

© Noordhoff Uitgevers

Tourism

Amsterdam is a major tourist attraction, setting new records every year. Whereas some tourists only visit for one day, others stay overnight in a hotel, bed and breakfast, Airbnb facility or youth hostel, or at one of the five campsites. Tourists find Amsterdam so appealing because of its pleasant atmosphere, its numerous and varied shops and above all because it offers some of the world's finest attractions. A cruise along the canals and through the port is still the most popular way of getting to know the city, but tourists have also been able to tour Amsterdam by pedicab for some years now. This is a fast, comfortable and environmentally friendly way of getting around.

❶ Four-star and five-star hotels and their beds

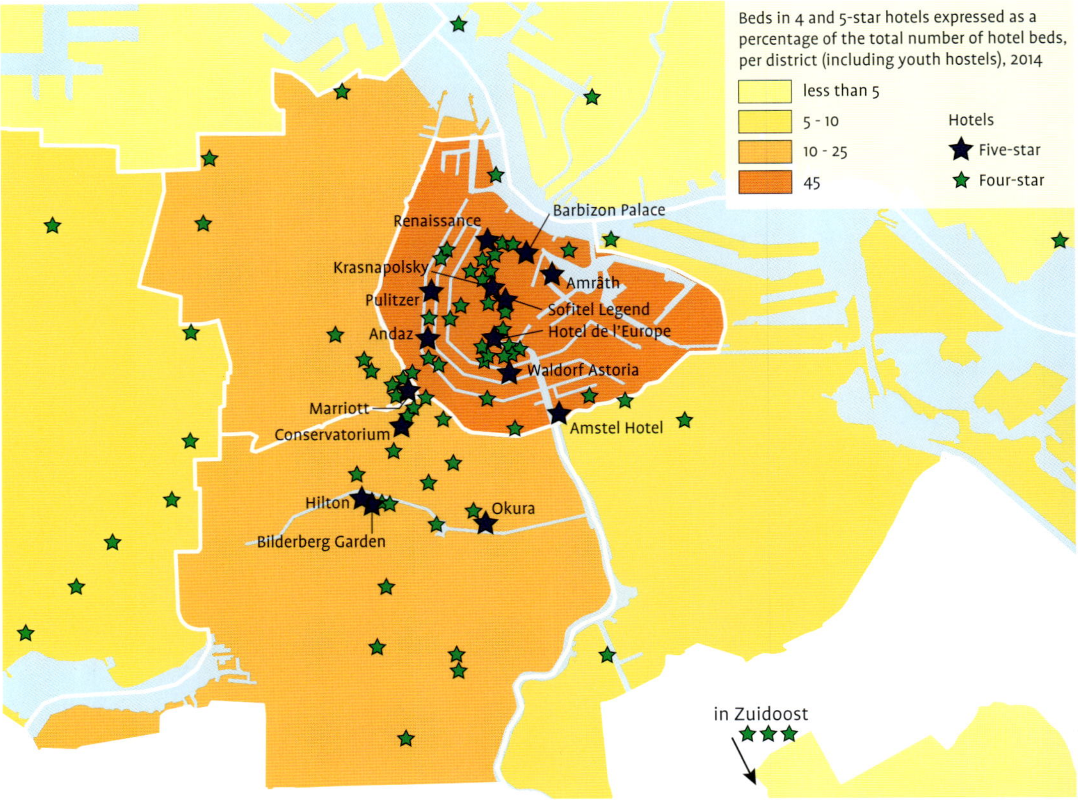

❷ Jobs and beds

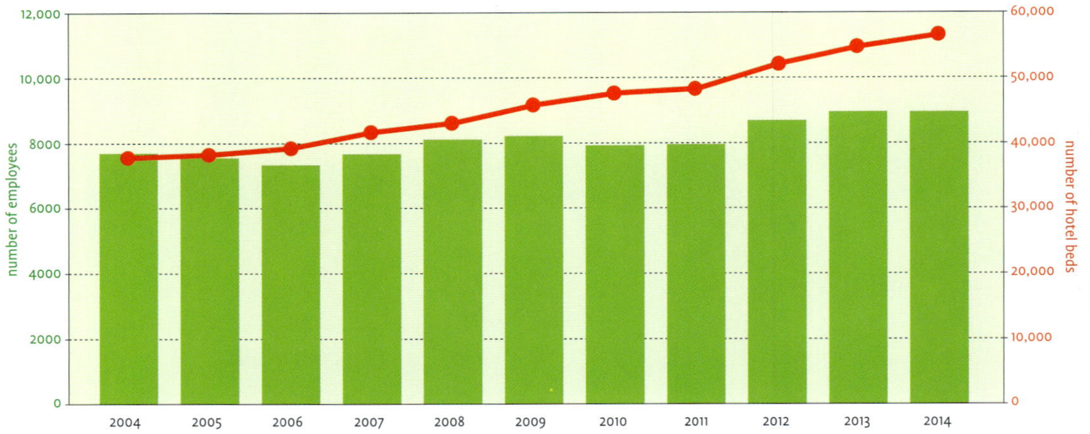

❸ Tourism statistics

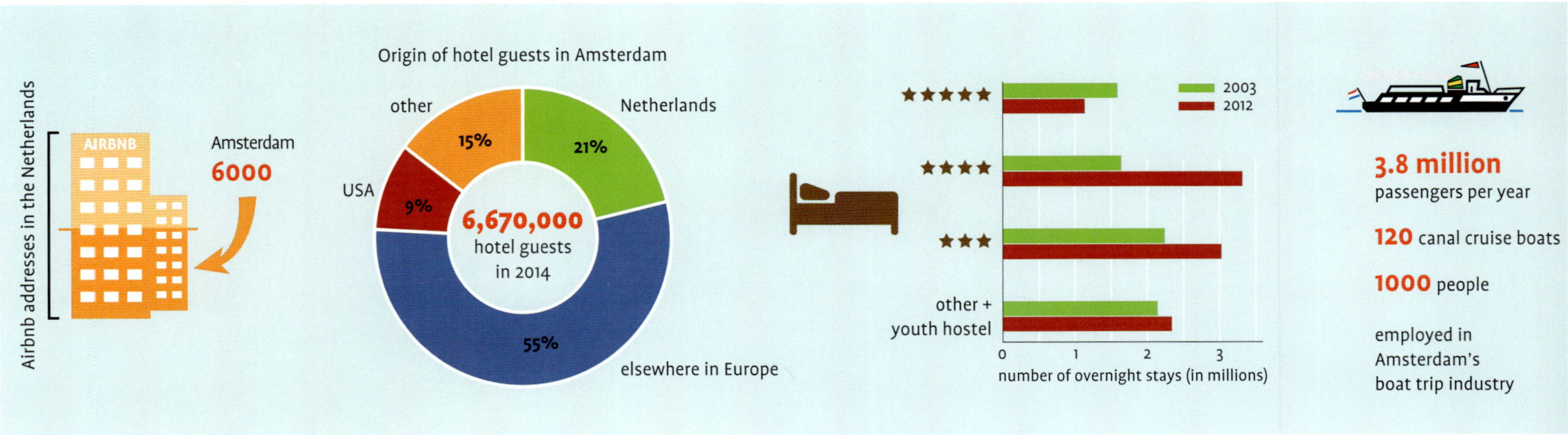

© Noordhoff Uitgevers

❹ **Pedicabs**

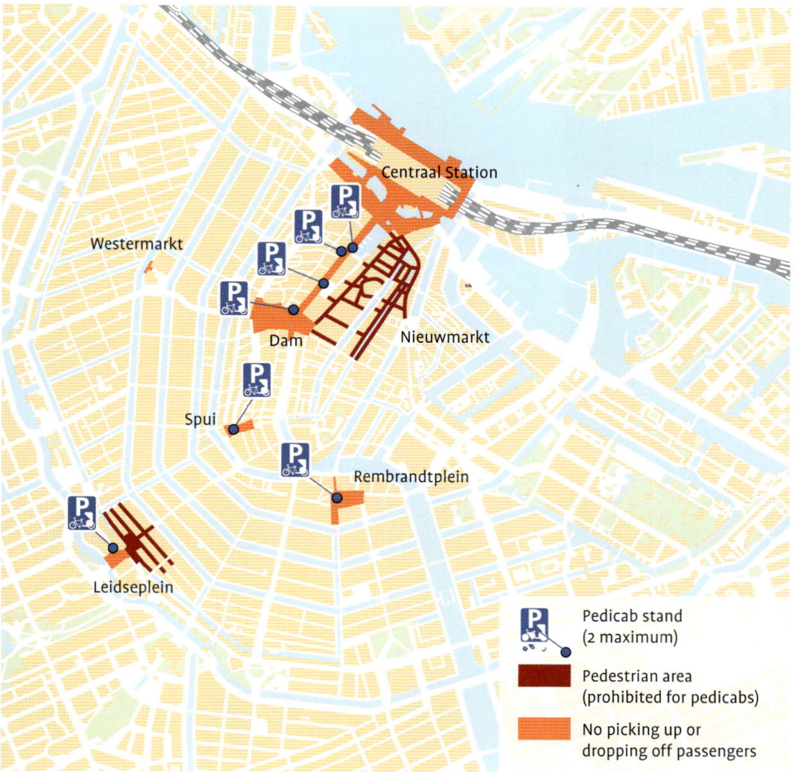

❺ **Boat trips**

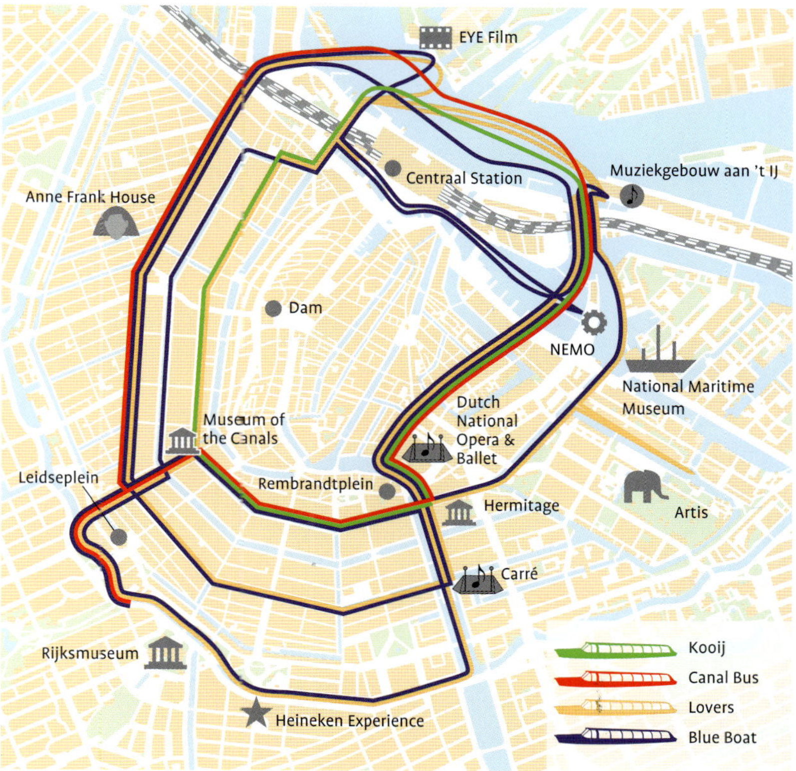

❶ - ❷ Hotels and beds

A wide range of overnight accommodation is available. Between 2004 and 2014, the number of hotels increased from 338 to 421, including 14 five-star and 68 four-star hotels. The number of rooms rose from 17,728 to 26,287 and the number of beds from 37,763 to nearly 57,000. As you would expect, Centrum has the most hotels (253) and Zuidoost (7) the least.

❸ A new record

With slightly more than 6 million hotel guests, 2013 set a new record, albeit one that was broken just one year later. In 2014, 6,670,000 people stayed in Amsterdam's hotels, an increase of 11%. Many Amsterdammers are afraid that the city will succumb to its own success if this trend continues. Even so, the economy in Amsterdam certainly benefits from this explosive growth. Between 2010 and 2014, the number of businesses in the tourist sector rose from 6974 to 7836. The sector also provides employment for around 55,000 people.

❹ Alternative transport

Providing a memorable way to travel through the city, pedicabs have been operating in Amsterdam for some time now. The city council has issued licences to around 110 pedicab operators, who take both tourists and ordinary Amsterdammers to areas that cannot be reached by bus or boat. However, they are not allowed to cycle in certain parts of the city, such as the red light district, and they are not allowed to stop everywhere. A 1.5-hour journey costs between 40 and 60 euros.

❺ Primary attraction

Some 3,800,000 tourists took a boat trip in Amsterdam in 2014, which makes the trip the city's most popular tourist attraction. Around 120 cruise boats sail on the canals, the Amstel and the IJ. However, the water has become increasingly crowded in recent years because around 18,000 Amsterdammers now also have a pleasure craft. As a result, the city council has decided to ban cruise boats longer than 20 metres from 2020 onwards.

❻ Plenty to experience

Long queues for the Rijksmuseum, the Anne Frank House or the Van Gogh Museum have become an everyday sight. In 2014, the Rijksmuseum attracted nearly 2.5 million visitors; an average of just under 7,000 people a day. Undisturbed enjoyment of *The Night Watch* or *The Jewish Bride* is almost impossible nowadays.

❻ **Amsterdam's day trip attractions in the top 50 of the Netherlands**

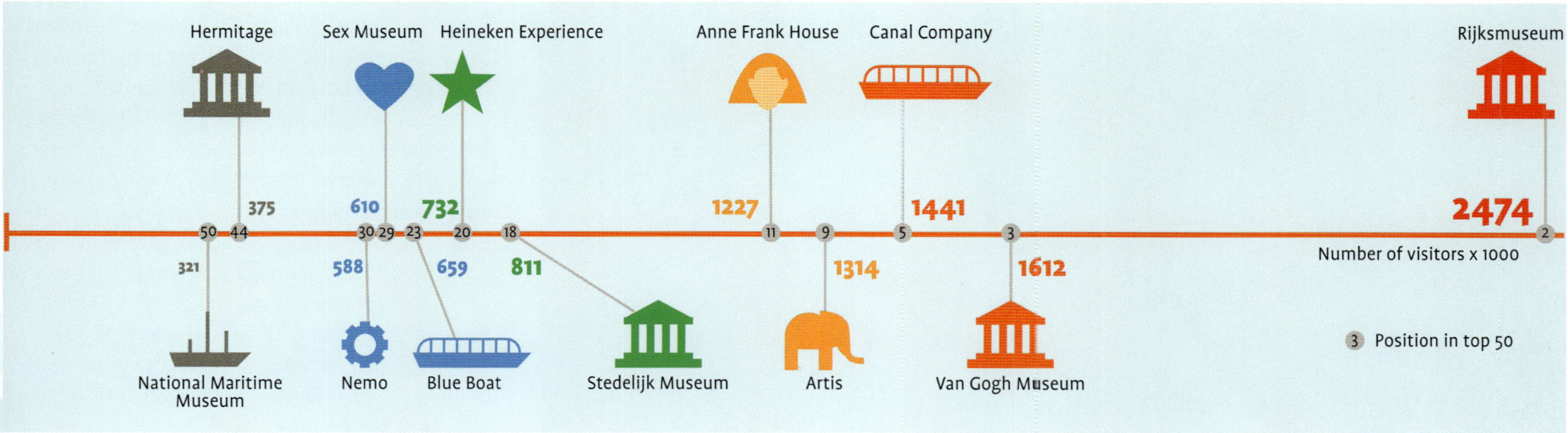

Sources: City of Amsterdam (4); various ship-owners (5); NBTC Holland Marketing 2014 (6)

© Noordhoff Uitgevers

Working in Amsterdam

❶ Tough guys
The city council is Amsterdam's largest employer, providing work for around 13,500 people. That number includes a few hundred city cleaners, who keep public spaces clean and collect household refuse and items of bulky waste. In 1990, the duties of the city's cleaning service (Gemeentelijke Stadsreinigingsdienst, founded in 1877) were transferred to the districts, which explains why each district has its own rules and schedules. Most neighbourhoods have large waste containers above and below the street surface, but in the city centre, plastic refuse bags are still put out on the pavement for collection, alongside huge piles of cardboard. The dustcart drives around twice a week, with tough men and the odd woman at the wheel and clinging to the back. They were recently given new overalls with Amsterdam's coat of arms on the sleeves and trousers.

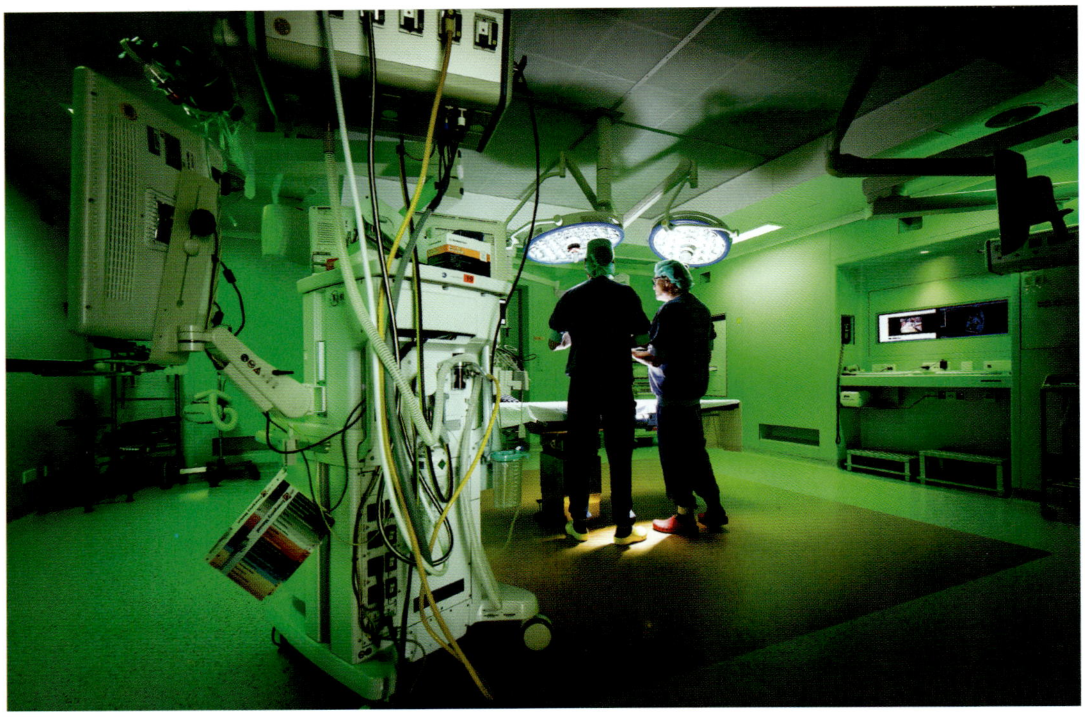

❷ Academic health care
The Academic Medical Center opened in Zuidoost in 1983, replacing the Binnengasthuis and Wilhelminagasthuis facilities, which were extremely outdated. In 1988, the Emma Children's Hospital also moved to Zuidoost. The AMC comprises the Academic Hospital and the University of Amsterdam's Faculty of Medicine and therefore has three primary tasks – patient care, scientific medical research and the training of medical staff. Among other disciplines, the AMC's specialities include the treatment of cardiovascular disease, infectious and metabolic diseases, paediatrics and reproductive medicine. In 2014, the AMC employed 6944 people, including 1379 nurses and care providers (84% women) and 207 professors. In the same year, 2220 medical students were enrolled at the university. In order to guarantee quality, the AMC annually invests millions of euros in new facilities such as this operating theatre, which has been in use since 2014.

❸ Drie Dwaze Dagen
Department store de Bijenkorf occupies 20,000m² of floor space, making it one of Amsterdam's largest shops. Its stylish appearance and expensive products are mainly aimed at more affluent buyers, including many wealthy Russians and Chinese in recent years. However, during its annual Drie Dwaze Dagen or Three Crazy Days event, de Bijenkorf opens its doors to all and sundry. For three whole days, the department store is besieged by bargain hunters flocking in their hundreds of thousands to buy specially sourced, but unbelievably cheap, branded items. Different products are on offer each day. 'Crazy' promotions are organised and musicians perform during the event, which is always opened by a celebrity. In 2014, the choice fell on actress Joanna Lumley, one of the stars of popular television series *Absolutely Fabulous*. Yellow and black have been the dominant colours ever since the event was first held in 1984. The photograph shows employees busily wrapping mannequins in yellow and black.

Photos: © Hollandse Hoogte (1); © ANP Photo (2); © Hollandse Hoogte (3)

© Noordhoff Uitgevers

❹ Herengracht killzone
Developing computer games has been a rapidly growing activity for many years now. In 2010, around 150 companies in the Netherlands were involved in designing, producing and marketing games, and 40 of them were located in Amsterdam. Four years later, 330 companies in the Netherlands were operating in this sector, over one hundred of which in the Amsterdam Metropolitan Area. Most of these companies are one-man businesses, but the exceptions include IJsfontein, based in the Westergasfabriek with 35 employees, and Guerrilla Games, a very successful company with some 270 developers at its Herengracht site. The latter was founded in 2000 following a merger of three smaller companies. Sony Computer Entertainment acquired Guerrilla Games in 2005, after the latter had made a name for itself worldwide in 2004 as the developer of *Killzone*, a PlayStation 2 game. Since then, various versions of this game have been developed.

❺ Challenge for higher education
VU University Amsterdam, Amsterdam University of Applied Sciences and the University of Amsterdam provide higher education for more than 115,500 students. Together, these three educational institutions employ nearly 13,000 people in educational, research, support and management roles. As a result, the higher education sector is a major employer in the city. One significant problem faced by all three institutions is the large number of first-year students who drop out or change course during their first year of study. On average, around 30% do this, with occasional peaks of up to 70%. In order to combat this problem, the University of Amsterdam has organised matching days for secondary school students wishing to enrol at the university since 2014. Prospective students attend lectures, thus gaining first-hand experience of the course of their choice. They also have to take a test, based on which they receive a course recommendation.

❻ National pride
The Dutch are proud of KLM, their national airline. Founded in October 1919, KLM is the oldest airline in the world that still operates under its own name. It currently has a fleet of around 115 aircraft, which serve over 130 destinations. The home base is Schiphol airport, which handled 438,296 aircraft movements in 2014. With 221,178 movements, KLM accounted for almost half of that total, followed after a considerable gap by Transavia (a KLM subsidiary since 1991) and Easyjet with 28,411 and 25,837 flights respectively. In 2004, to the shock and dismay of many Dutch people, KLM decided to strike up a partnership with Air France. Due to fierce competition, the group has had a hard time in recent years and will probably have to make significant cuts.

Photos: © ANP Photo (4); © Hollandse Hoogte (5); © ANP Photo (6)

© Noordhoff Uitgevers

CRYSTAL TOWER

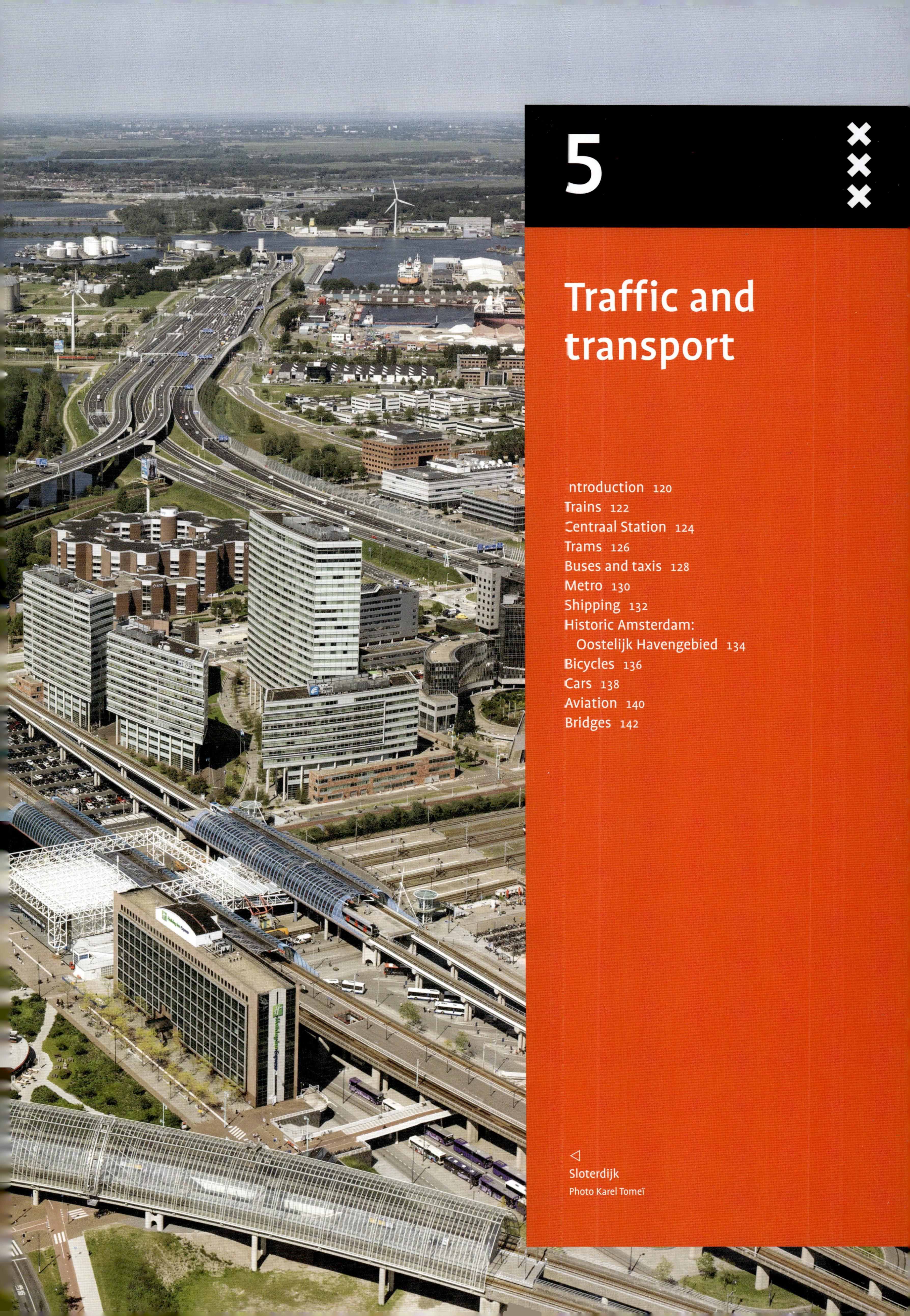

5

Traffic and transport

◁ Sloterdijk
Photo Karel Tomeï

5 Introduction

Amsterdam's hub function

Amsterdam owes its existence to its location on major traffic routes. In the Middle Ages, the routes were mostly waterways. While the waterways are still very important for transporting freight, they now have to compete with railways and roads. Every day, cars, buses and trains transport large quantities of goods and many commuters into the city.

Few cars

Surprisingly, cars are not so important to Amsterdammers themselves. At less than 25 cars per 100 residents, the city has the lowest level of car ownership in the whole country. Although this is a phenomenon typical of large cities, the effect is especially pronounced in Amsterdam.
This is certainly due in part to the relatively young (student) population, but the city council's parking policy is another factor. Parking spaces are limited, parking charges are high and the waiting time for a parking permit in the inner city area is several years.

Bicycles

The bicycle is far more suitable for journeys in the city and Amsterdam is known as Europe's top cycling city with good reason. The number of journeys by bicycle is still rising, but this mode of transport is in danger of succumbing to its own popularity in the city. The council has therefore taken action in recent years to combat the bicycle parking problem and other bicycle-related problems, with varying degrees of success.

Trams, metro and city buses

The tram and the metro are good alternatives for people unwilling or unable to cycle. Constructing the first metro line was a painful process, so it was a long time before politicians recognised the need for a new underground connection. However, the Noord/Zuid metro line is likely to be completed in 2017 after all. GVB, the city's transport company, also maintains an extremely dense bus and tram network, which even continues to operate at night – Amsterdam is the only city in the Netherlands where night buses run all week and not just at the weekend.

Sloterdijk
Sloterdijk is a busy traffic junction on the west side of Amsterdam. Its railway station is split between two physical sites, both of which are covered over. Every day, hundreds of trains depart from this station to Amsterdam Centraal, Haarlem, Zaandam and Schiphol. The motorways you see in the distance lead to the two Coen tunnels. Even though the area is easy to get to, the demand for office space has been overestimated and Sloterdijk is struggling with overcapacity.

Trains, regional buses and aircraft
There are also good public transport facilities for longer distances. Ten railway stations are located within the city itself and most regional buses also depart from these stations. These buses are extremely important for daily commuting between Amsterdam and the surrounding towns.
Schiphol, Europe's fourth busiest airport, helps passengers get to foreign destinations and is just 20 minutes away from central Amsterdam by train.
Thanks to good regional and international public transport connections, fewer people in Amsterdam feel the need to own a car than anywhere else in the Netherlands.

number of bicycles

per hundred residents

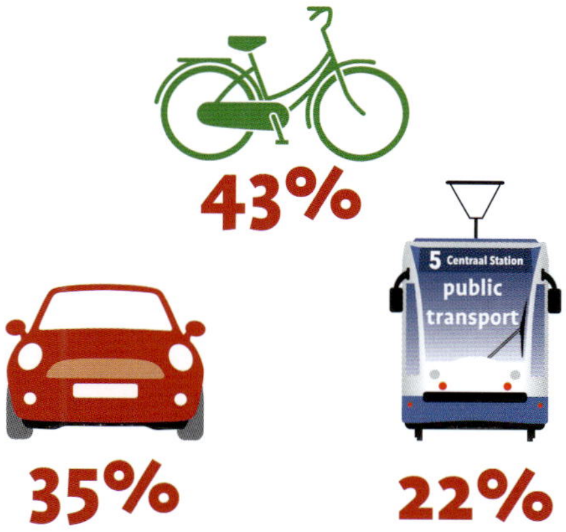

journeys within Amsterdam

annual parking income

Sources: I amsterdam / Statistics Netherlands, OViN / City of Amsterdam / Schiphol Group

© Noordhoff Uitgevers

Trains

After Utrecht, Amsterdam is the biggest hub in the Dutch railway network. It has ten stations – more than any other Dutch city – without even counting Duivendrecht, Diemen and Diemen-Zuid, which are outside the city's boundaries. Work on constructing the railway network around Amsterdam has been ongoing since 1837 and seven stations have actually been closed during that period. Many metro, bus and tram lines start and end at Centraal Station, so the square in front of the station is the busiest in the city during the day. It is expected to get even busier, especially when the Noord/Zuid metro line opens in 2017. In anticipation of this, the station and station square are undergoing extensive remodelling, which is due to be completed in 2018.

❶ Stations in the Amsterdam area

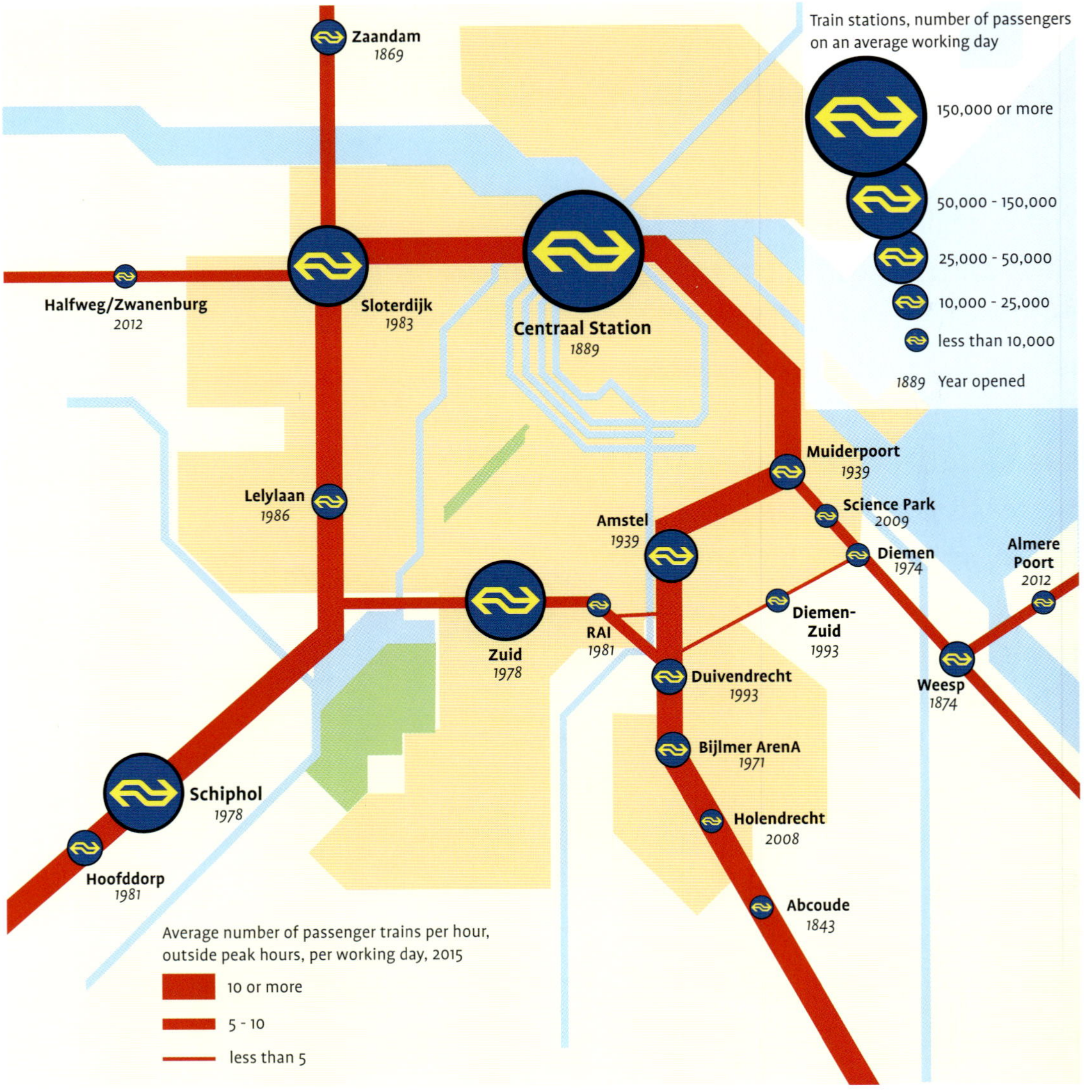

❷ Development of the railway network

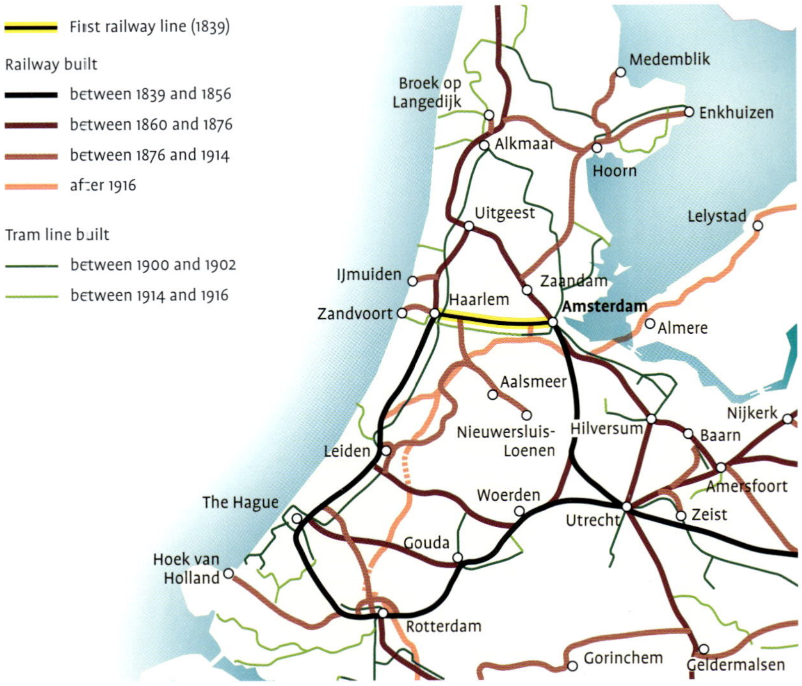

❸ Bygone stations

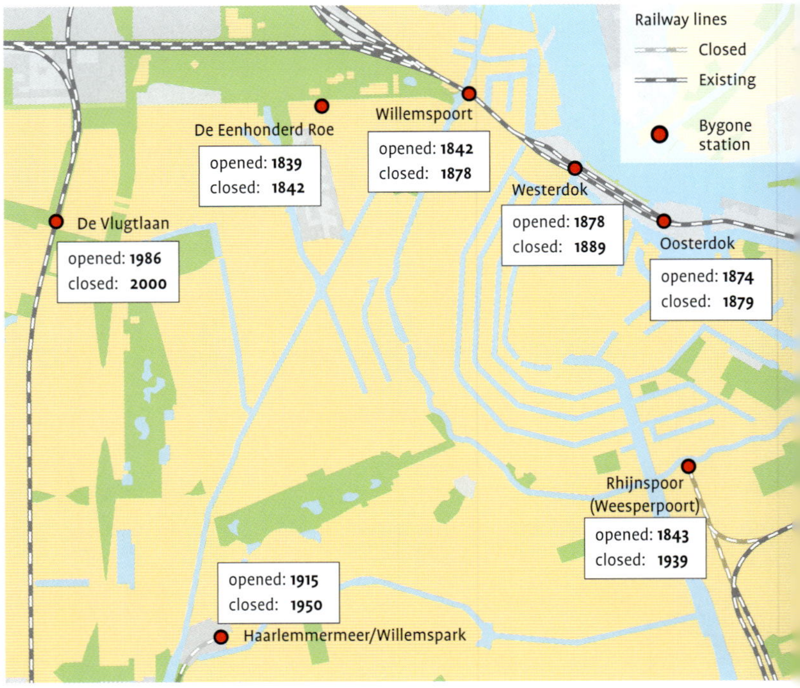

Sources: GVB (1); Nederlandse Spoorwegen (2); www.stationsweb.nl (3)

© Noordhoff Uitgevers

❶ Zuid station expected to grow
There are ten stations in Amsterdam, more than in Rotterdam seven, Utrecht seven and The Hague six. Some 185,000 passengers use Centraal Station every day and Sloterdijk is the second busiest with 54,000 passengers. Zuid will become more important in the near future after completion of the Noord/Zuid line and the Zuidas project. In 2012, a decision was made to expand the station and cover over the A10 motorway. This is due to be completed around 2030.

❷ Railway network in the making
The first railway connection in the Netherlands, between Amsterdam and Haarlem, was completed in 1839 and the railway network in and around Amsterdam has expanded steadily since then. The first railway lines were run privately but the government took control of the railways in 1860, resulting in a rapid increase in the number of lines. The Netherlands currently has the most frequently used railway network in Europe.

❸ Stations of yesteryear
Seven Amsterdam stations have closed over the years. The oldest, near the De Eenhonderd Roe inn, only existed for three years, while Willemspoort, Westerdok and Oosterdok disappeared following completion of Centraal Station. 1939 saw Rhijnspoor terminal station superseded by Muiderpoort and Amstel, and Haarlemmermeer also closed following the dissolution of the Haarlemmermeer railway lines. In 2000, the NS decided to close De Vlugtlaan because too few people used it.

❹ and ❺ Restructured station island
Every day, 250,000 people cycle or walk across the square in front of Centraal Station and along the bank of the IJ at the rear. This area can barely handle these volumes, so work is ongoing to change the layout of the entire area around the station.
Traffic will be restricted on Prins Hendrikkade, the buses will run from the IJ side of the station rather than the city side and four large bicycle stores, with space for a total of 10,000 bicycles, should put an end to the parking chaos. Last but not least, road traffic will be diverted under the new bus station through an underground tunnel bordering the IJ from 2015 onwards. The map shows the situation in 2015.

❹ Amsterdam Centraal Station in figures

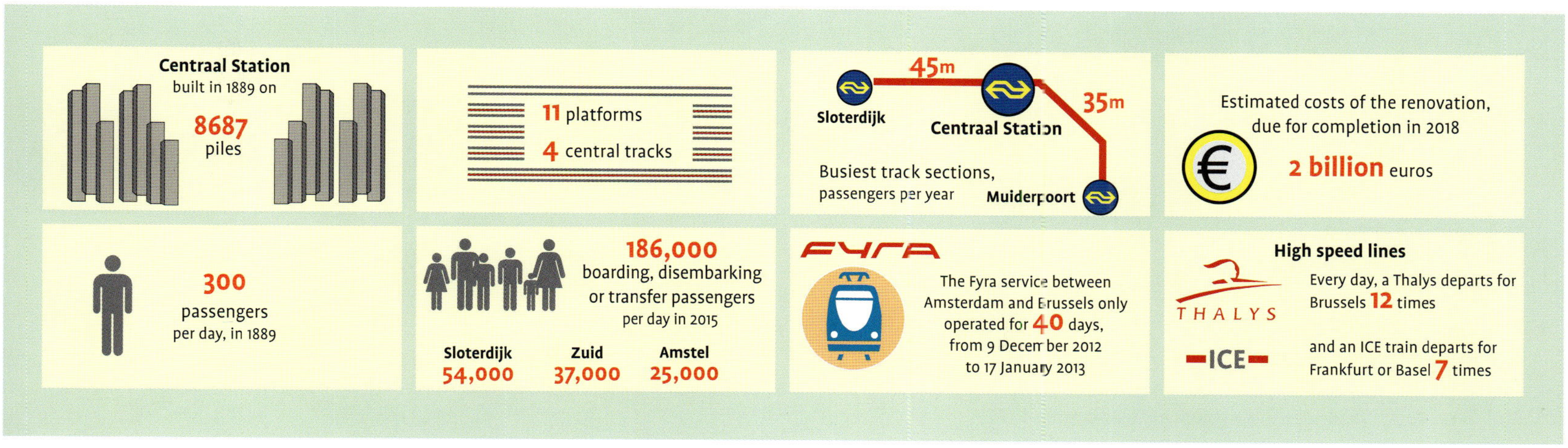

❺ Centraal Station and the surrounding area

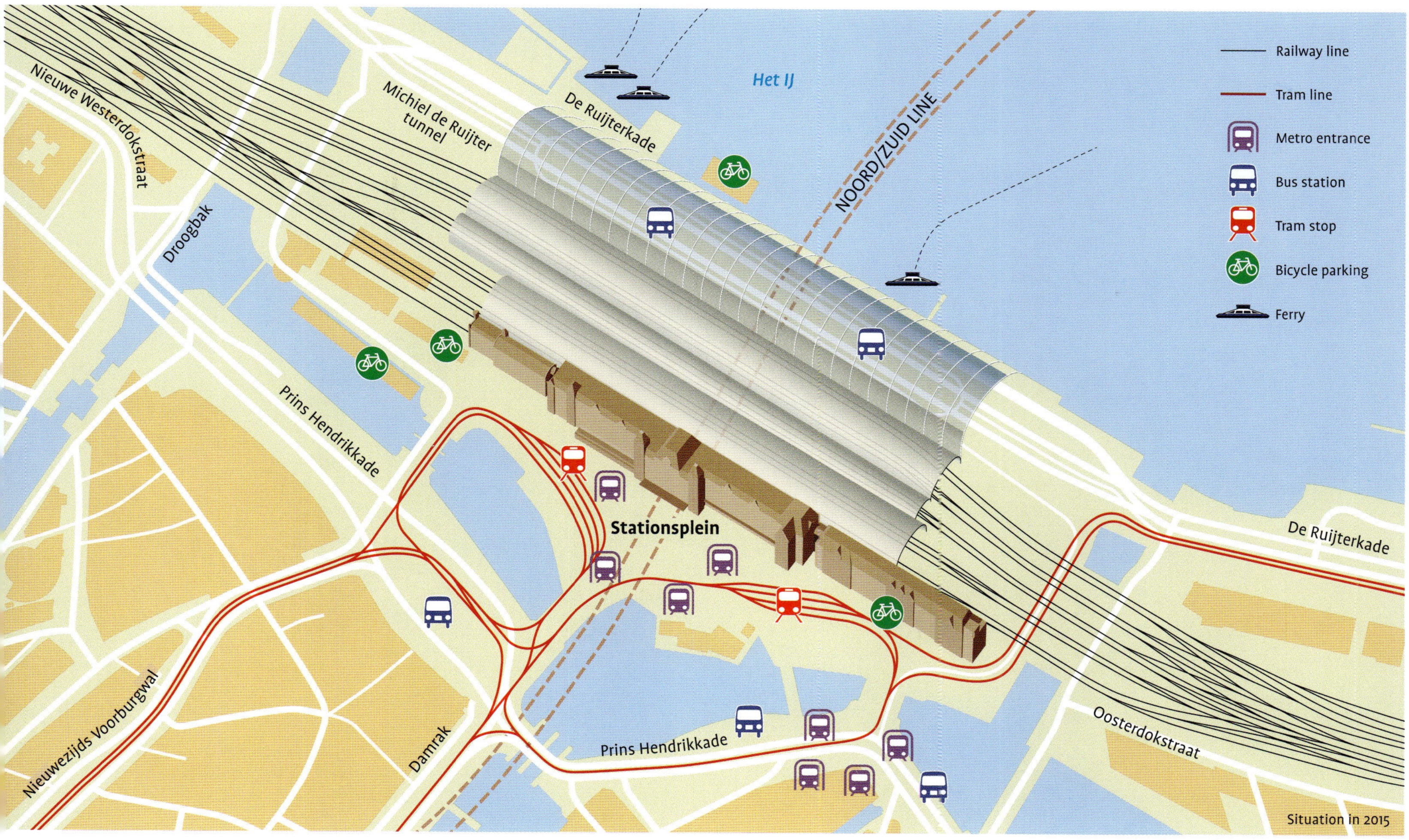

Sources: Nederlandse Spoorwegen / Prorail (4, 5)

© Noordhoff Uitgevers

Centraal Station

Amsterdam Centraal is the second busiest station in the Netherlands, and the number of people passing through is expected to grow considerably, partly due to the new Noord/Zuid line. The new bus station at the rear will ensure that pedestrian flows are more evenly distributed.

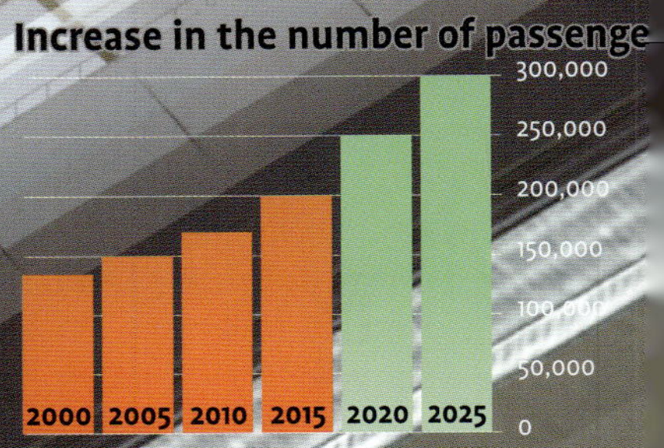

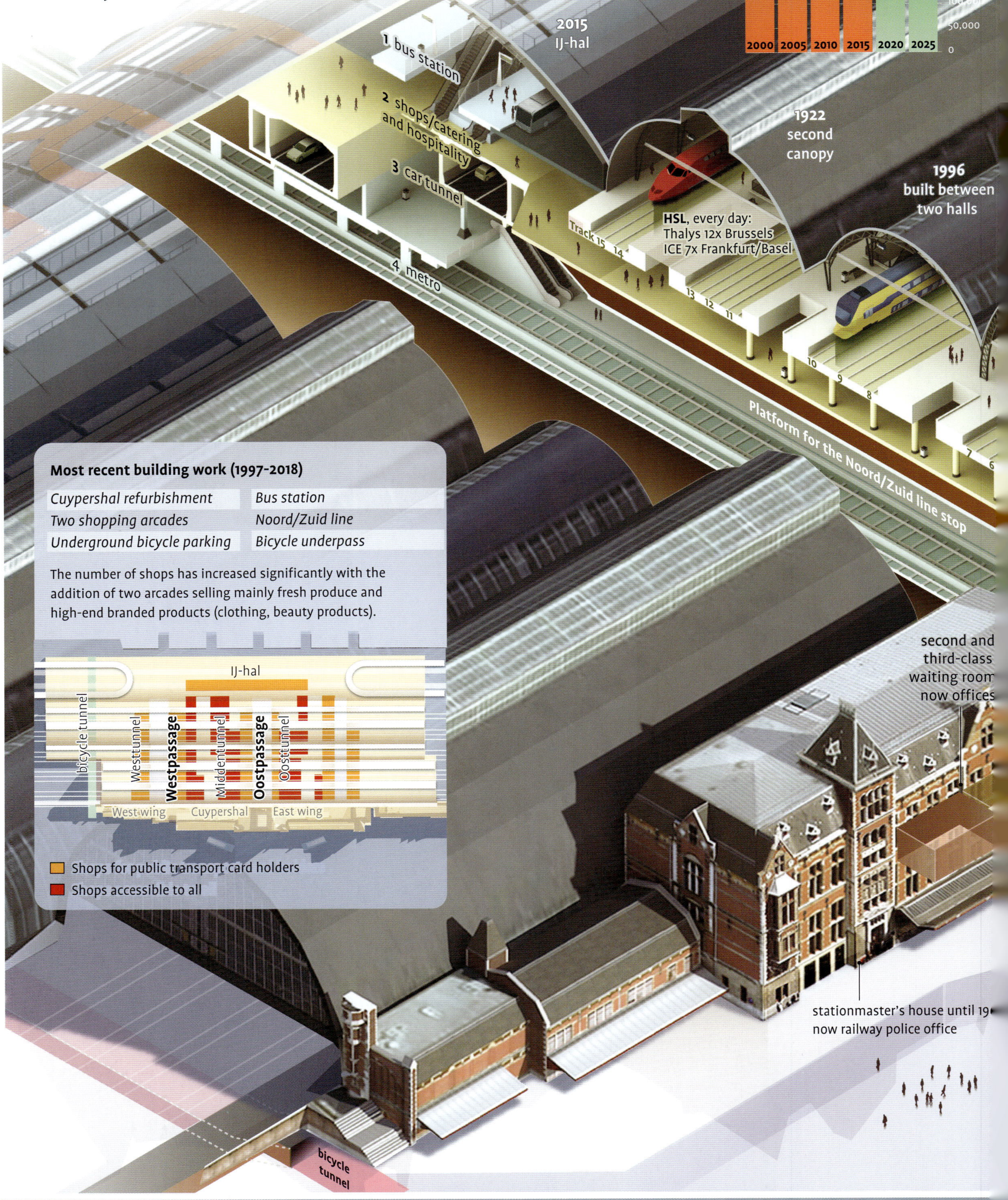

Most recent building work (1997-2018)

Cuypershal refurbishment	*Bus station*
Two shopping arcades	*Noord/Zuid line*
Underground bicycle parking	*Bicycle underpass*

The number of shops has increased significantly with the addition of two arcades selling mainly fresh produce and high-end branded products (clothing, beauty products).

Shops for public transport card holders

Shops accessible to all

Sources: PrcRail / Nederlandse Spoorwegen / City of Amsterdam; Photos: © Hollandse Hoogte (Royal waiting room, Cuypershal), © ANP Photo (International Lounge)

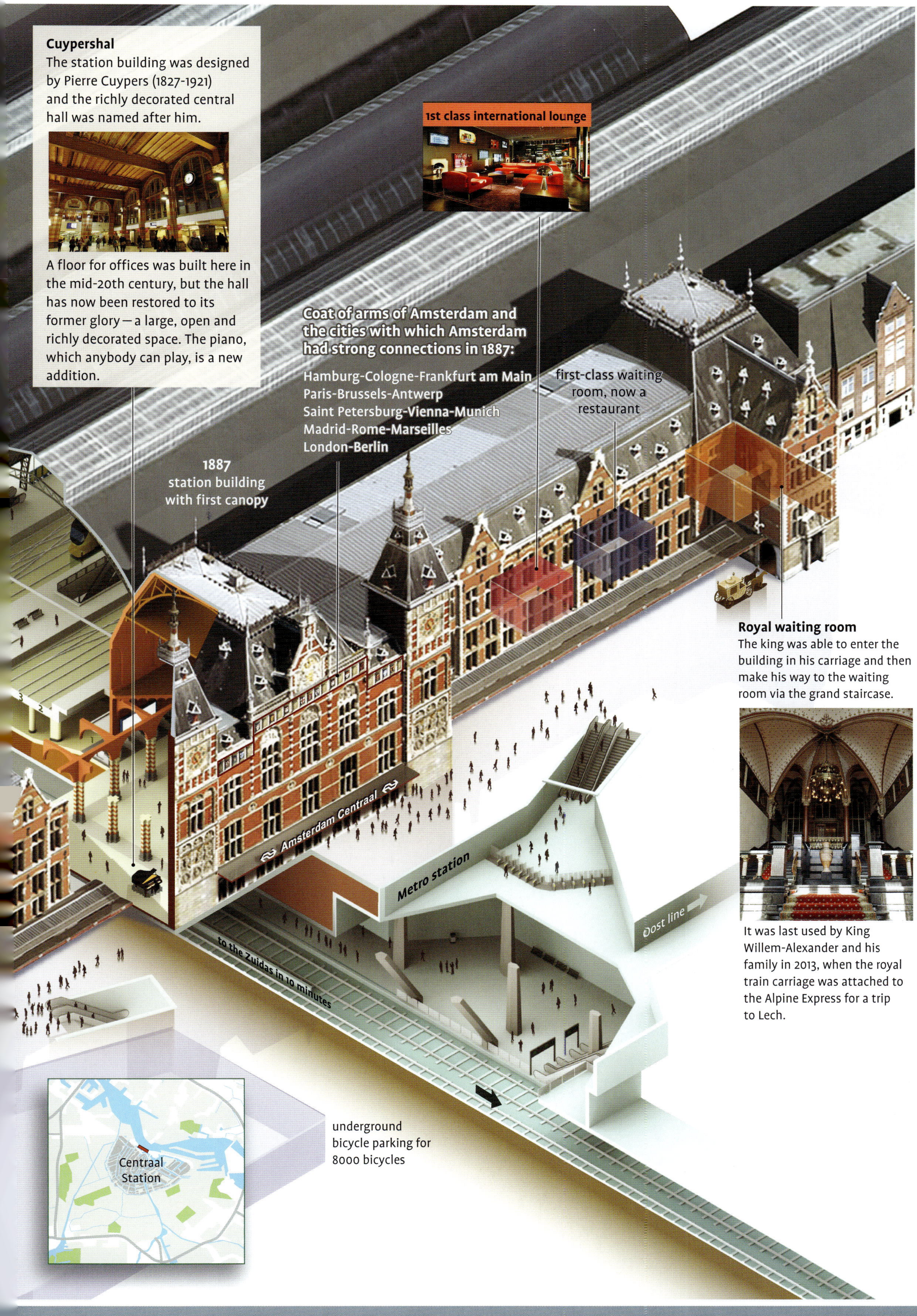

Cuypershal

The station building was designed by Pierre Cuypers (1827-1921) and the richly decorated central hall was named after him.

A floor for offices was built here in the mid-20th century, but the hall has now been restored to its former glory—a large, open and richly decorated space. The piano, which anybody can play, is a new addition.

Royal waiting room

The king was able to enter the building in his carriage and then make his way to the waiting room via the grand staircase.

It was last used by King Willem-Alexander and his family in 2013, when the royal train carriage was attached to the Alpine Express for a trip to Lech.

© Noordhoff Uitgevers

Trams

Amsterdam, Rotterdam, The Hague and Utrecht are the only cities in the Netherlands that still have trams. Amsterdam has the most lines, but not the longest length of track. The tram is a key part of Amsterdam's public transport services and is used a lot by residents, more than buses or the metro. That even applies in the city centre, where trams sometimes experience long waits at junctions such as Leidseplein. Amsterdammers love their trams, as demonstrated by the level of protest in 2013 when line 25 was discontinued. It also shows in the way they care for the city's tram heritage. Two associations of volunteers take excellent care of the old twin axle and 3-axle units, operating their own tram museum during the summer.

❶ Tram lines

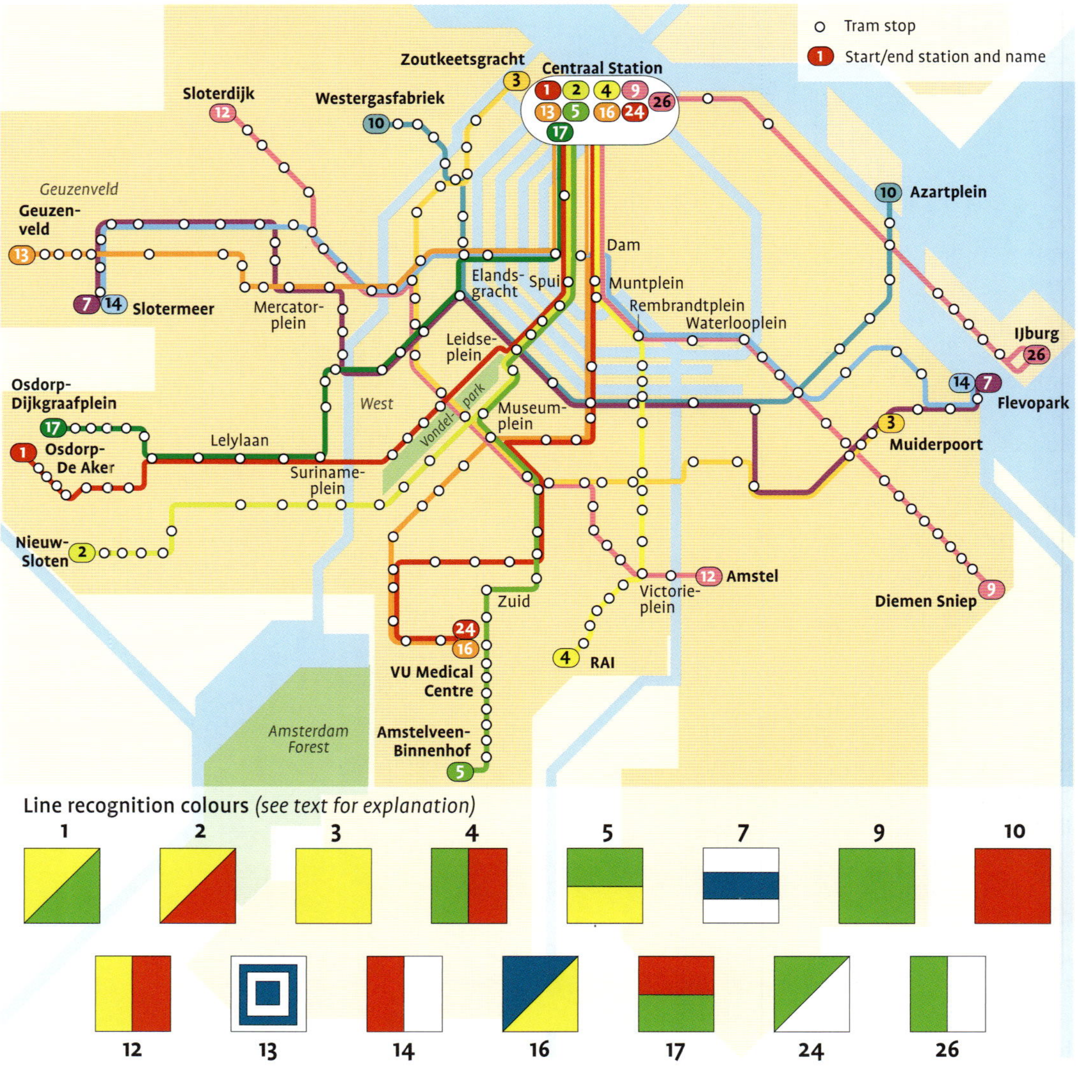

❷ Tram networks in Amsterdam, Rotterdam and The Hague

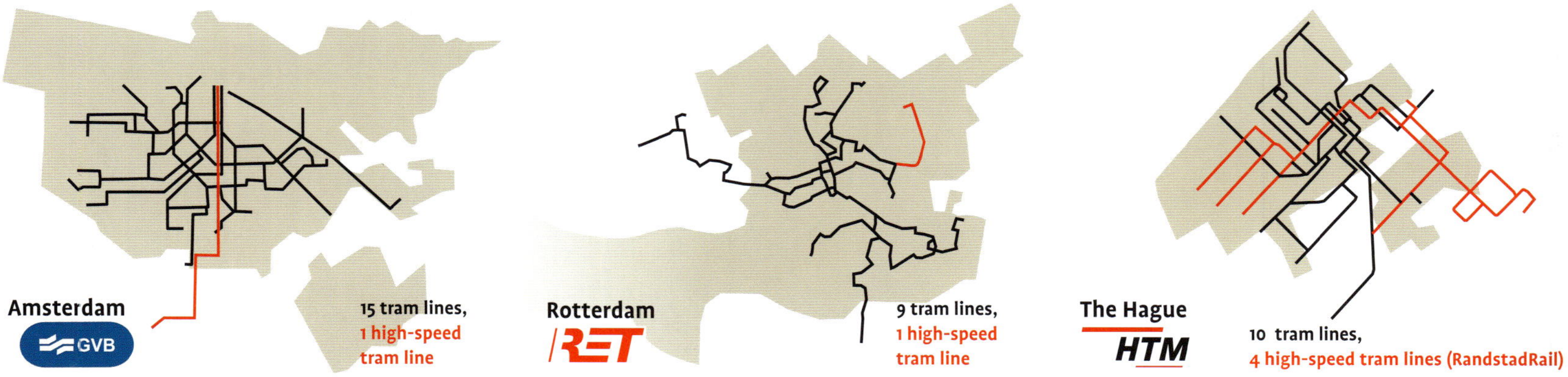

The Utrecht-Nieuwegein/IJsselstein high-speed tram line has been disregarded here.

2013 data	Year of first tram	Number of trams	Tram tracks length in km	Maximum speed kilometres per hour	Punctuality as a percentage	Customer satisfaction scale 0-10 (0=low, 10=high)	Fare dodgers as a percentage	Kilometres travelled in millions	Revenue from operations total, millions of euros	Net result total, millions of euros
Amsterdam (GVB)	1875	213	200	70	86	7.3	1.9	290	439	0.3
Rotterdam (RET)	1879	118	194	60	82	7.6	1.6	114	421	10.9
The Hague (HTM)	1864	201	336	70	95	7.1	3.0	376	273	15.5

Sources: GVB (1); GVB / RET / HTM (2)

© Noordhoff Uitgevers

❶ and ❹ Numbers and colours

GVB operates fifteen tram lines. At 6.1km, line 4 is the shortest, while lines 7 and 14 are the longest (12.5km). Amsterdam's trams are special because they still have a line colour as well as a line number. These colours were probably introduced because numbers are less easy recognisable at a distance, especially in the dark. Line colours have now fallen into disuse elsewhere.

❷ Tram cities

Amsterdam, Rotterdam and The Hague are the three main tram cities in the Netherlands (Utrecht is an exception with only one high-speed tram line). The Hague's HTM has the longest set of tram tracks, the most passengers, the best punctuality rate and also the best financial results. While Amsterdam's GVB achieves the largest turnover, it barely makes a profit.

❸ and ❻ Rolling stock heritage

Amsterdam's tramway museum has run restored trams from Haarlemmermeer station to Bovenkerk and back every summer Sunday since 1975. This is an initiative run by two private organisations – Electrische Museumtramlijn Amsterdam (EMA) and Rijdend Electrisch Tram Museum (RETM) – which take care of historic trams from various cities, including seven Amsterdam trams built between 1904 and 1960. As a collection, they clearly illustrate how trams developed over time in Amsterdam, from small, simple, twin axle units via combined traction units and trailers to long, articulated trams. True to the tradition in Amsterdam, the museum line also has its own colours – red and green separated diagonally.

❺ Leidseplein junction

Leidsestraat is a narrow street with a single-track tram line. There are often so many trams running here that they have to wait on the three bridges over the canals to allow their counterparts to pass, much to the annoyance of the motorists and cyclists whom they obstruct. Leidseplein itself is even busier, as this is where lines 1, 2 and 5 cross lines 7 and 10. On working days, no less than 1259 trams pass through this area between 6 am and midnight.

❸ Route served by tramway museum

❹ Amsterdam tram statistics

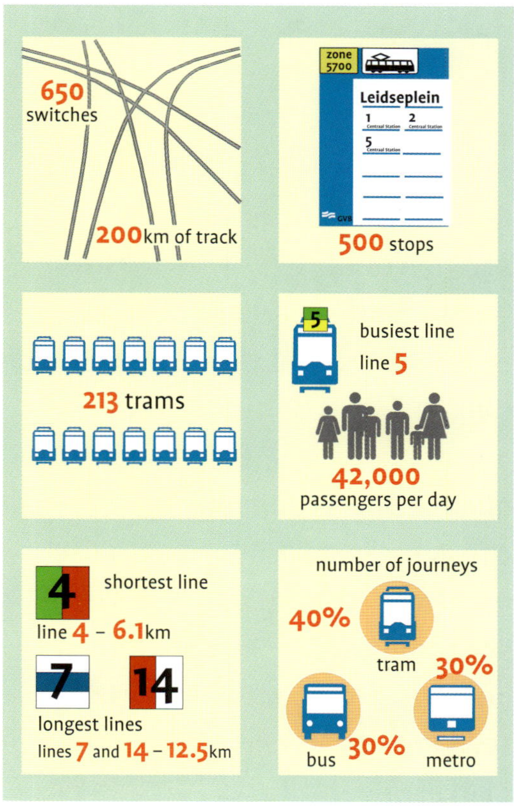

❺ Tram lines on Leidseplein

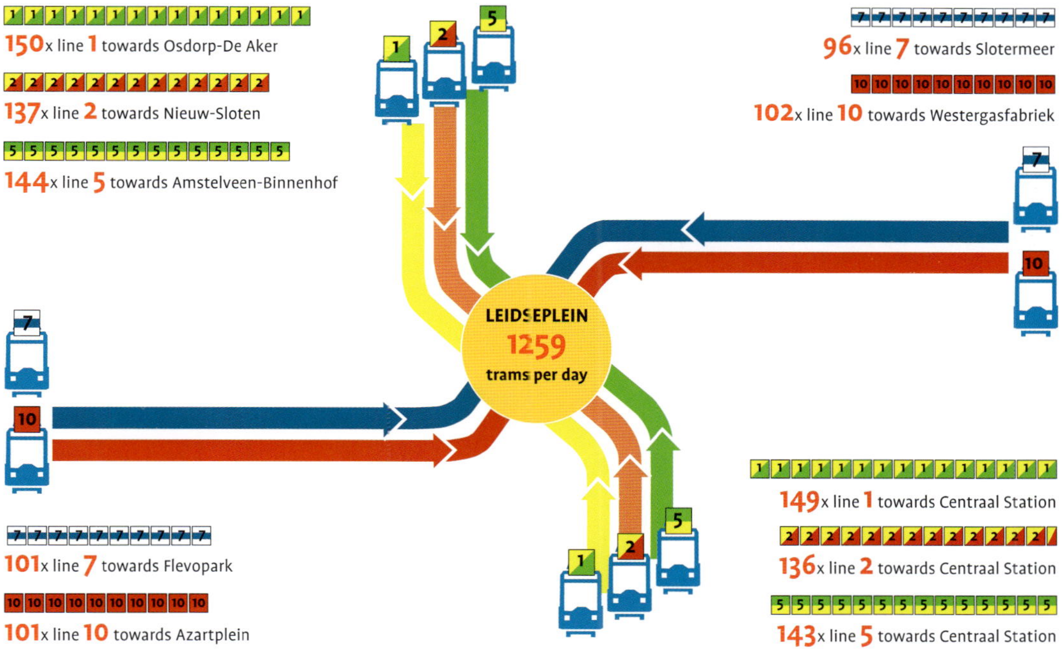

❻ Amsterdam's trams through the years

pre-war

post-war to the early 1980s

early 1980s to the 2000s

Sources: *Electrische Museumtramlijn Amsterdam (3); GVB (4); Het Parool (5); www.museumtramlijn.org (6)*

© Noordhoff Uitgevers

Buses and taxis

Buses and taxis form an extensive addition to the network of trains, trams and the metro in Amsterdam. In addition to 33 normal bus services, GVB, the city's transport service, also operates eleven night buses every night. Being a commuter and student city, Amsterdam is also serviced by numerous regional bus routes. The countless foreign tourists and business people are an interesting segment in the transportation market and their presence explains the scale of Amsterdam's taxi services, as well as the 'taxi wars' that occasionally flare up. After all, the stakes are high in the taxi sector.

❶ Bus routes, city transport

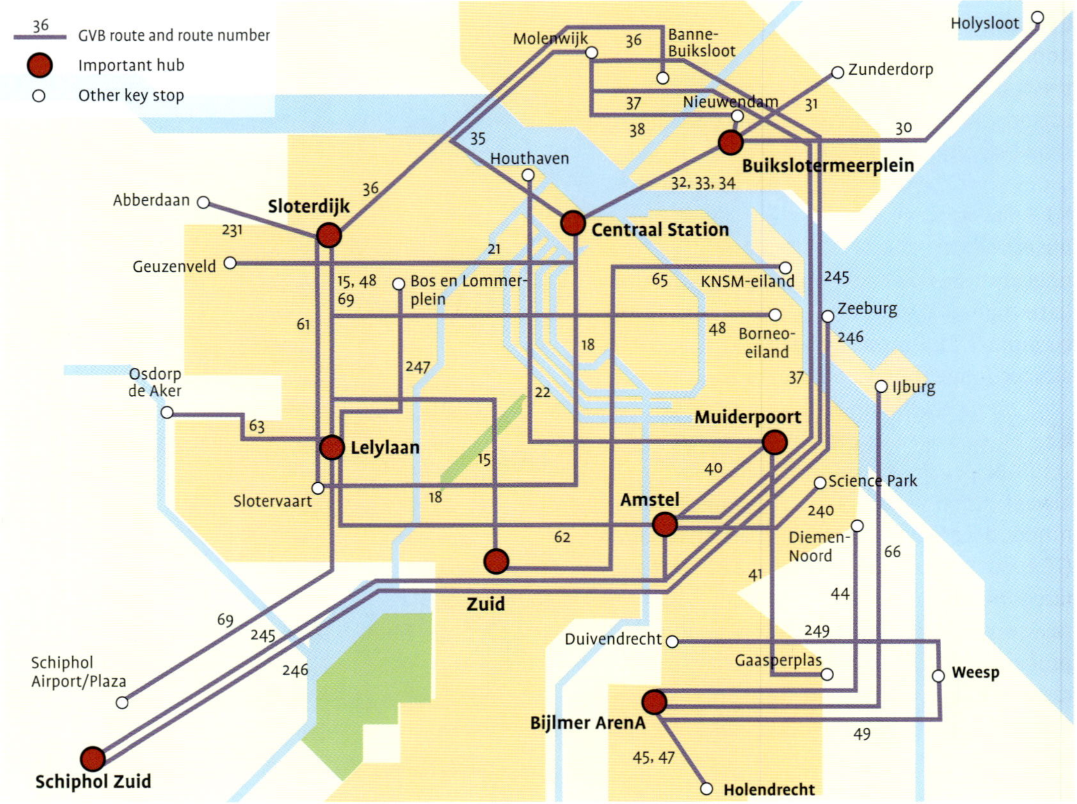

❷ Punctuality on departure

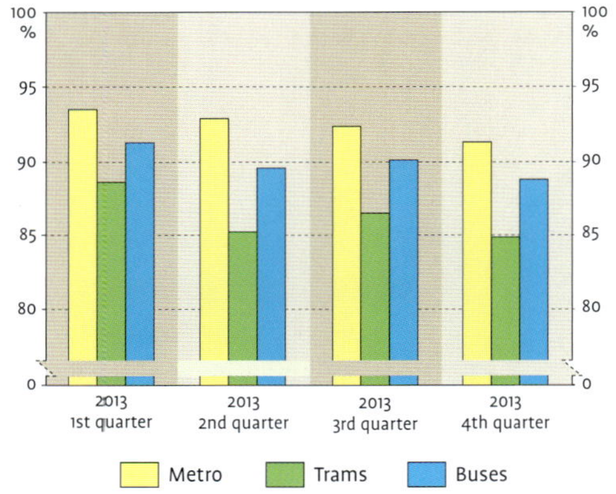

❸ Service disruptions

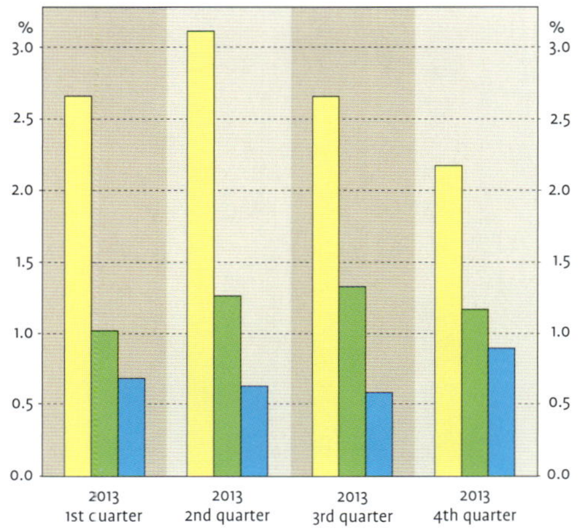

❹ Bus routes, regional transport

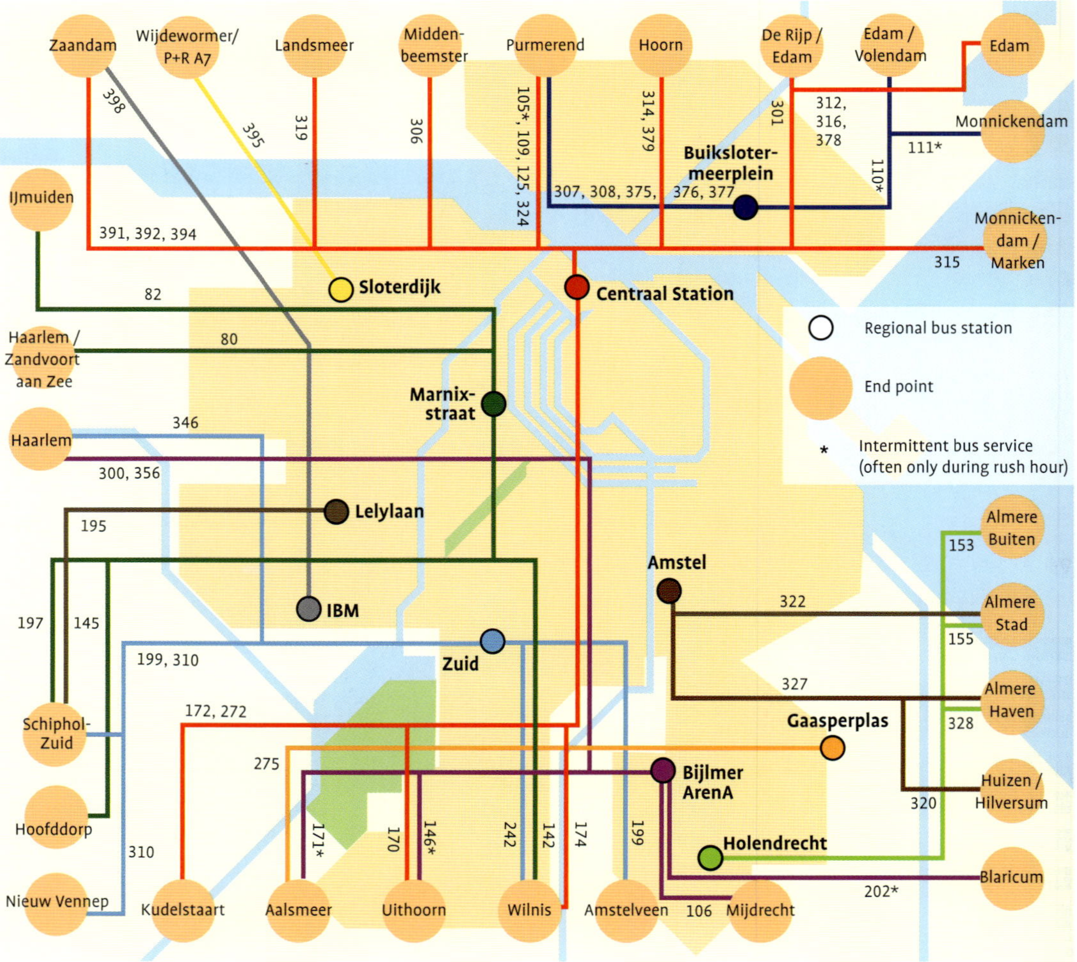

© Noordhoff Uitgevers

❶ - ❸ Satisfied bus passengers

Even though Amsterdam's city bus network is extremely extensive, the average Amsterdammer travels a much shorter distance by bus than by tram or metro. Even so, bus passengers are generally satisfied with the service, giving it a good rating. Rightly so, because service disruptions are few and far between and the buses generally run on time.

❹ Schoolchildren and commuters

Connexxion and EBS (an Israeli company) provide services to the surrounding areas from several regional bus stations and their users are mainly students and commuters.

❺ Bus services every night

Buses run at night in various Dutch cities, but only at weekends and sometimes on Thursdays (late-night shopping). Amsterdam is the only city to offer such services all week long, which it started doing in 1969.

❻ - ❽ Greater competition

Traditionally, Amsterdam's taxi drivers have always had a bad reputation, possibly due to the monopoly enjoyed by Taxicentrale Amsterdam (TCA) up to the late 1990s. With about 1500 affiliated members, TCA is still Amsterdam's largest taxi service, but it now faces competition. This probably explains why taxi drivers are given a rather positive rating these days.

❺ Night buses

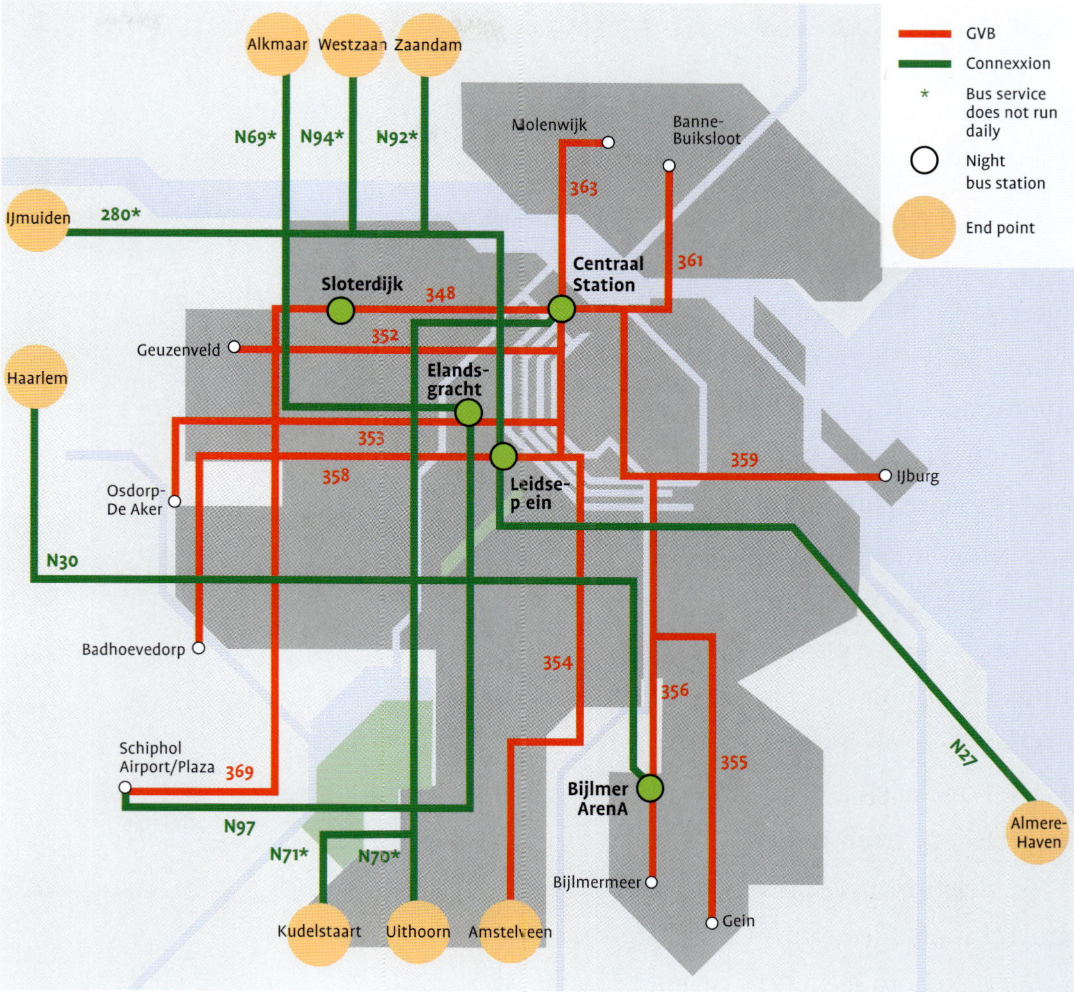

❻ Driver ratings

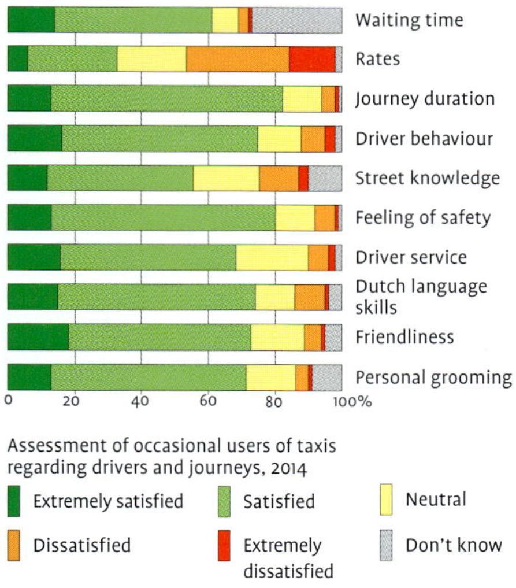

❼ Accredited taxi services with over 100 licenses

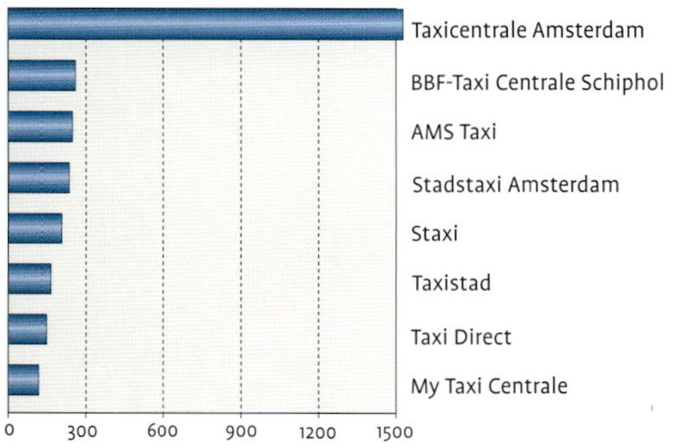

❽ Taxi ranks

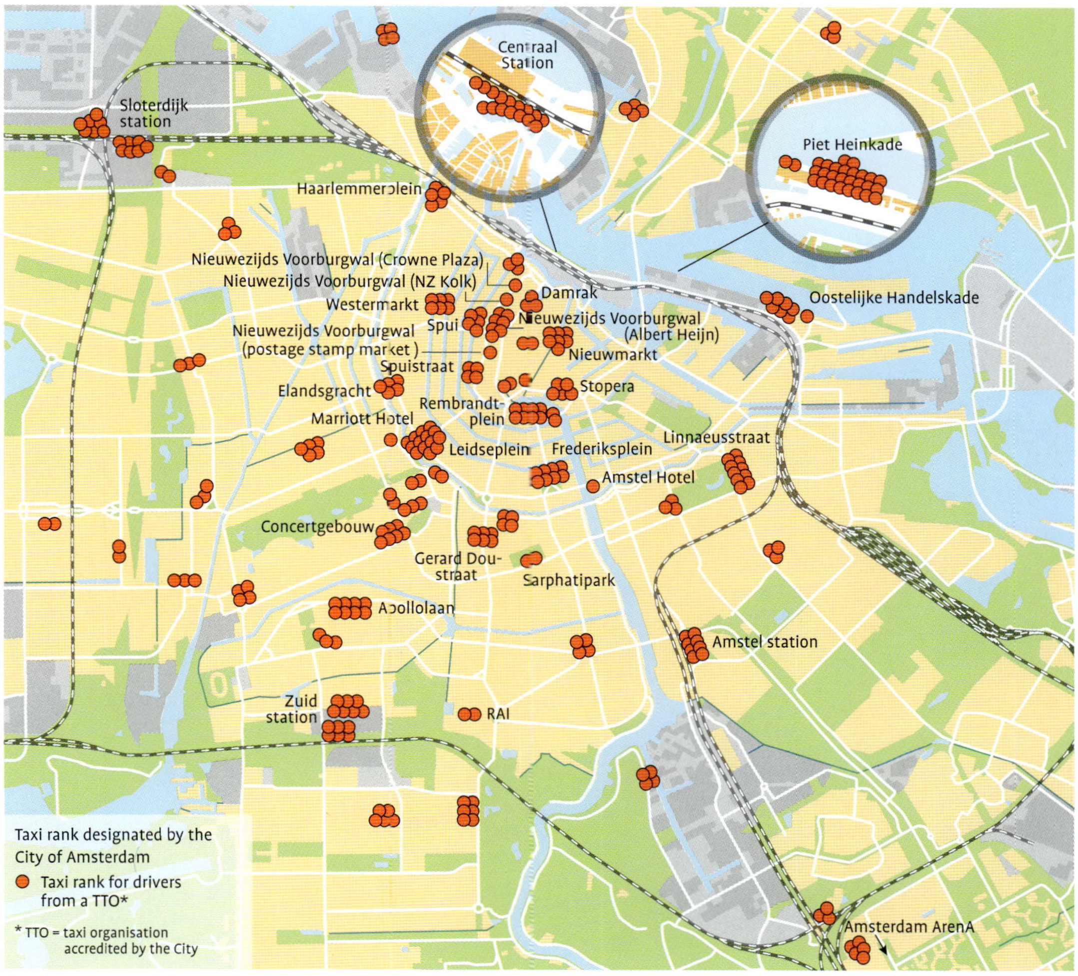

Sources: GVB / Connexxion (5); OIS, Research, Information and Statistics, City of Amsterdam (6); City of Amsterdam (7); OIS, Research, Information and Statistics, City of Amsterdam (8)

© Noordhoff Uitgevers

Metro

Compared with other capital cities, Amsterdam has a very small metro system. Even Rotterdam's metro is bigger, in terms of both length and the number of lines, stations and passengers.
Even so, construction of the metro has been a major struggle for Amsterdam's city council and the residents themselves. The problems started early on, during construction of the first line, which required demolition of part of the Nieuwmarktbuurt. This resulted in extreme riots.
The current Noord/Zuid line extension project is also fraught with problems and has been put on hold several times due to technical difficulties. Construction has turned out to be much more expensive than budgeted.

❶ Metro lines

❷ Metro systems in various major cities

	Year of first metro	Metro system length in km	No. of lines	No. of stations	Number of passengers per day (millions)
Shanghai	1993	439	14	289	8.5
London	1863	408	11	270	3.4
New York	1904	368	26	468	5.3
Tokyo	1927	329	13	282	8.0
Moscow	1935	325	12	195	6.7
Paris	1900	215	16	301	4.5
Berlin	1902	146	10	173	1.4
Rotterdam	1968	78	5	62	0.3
Amsterdam	**1977**	**43**	**4**	**58**	**0.3**
Rio de Janeiro	1979	41	2	62	1.1

❸ The metro in the Nieuwmarktbuurt

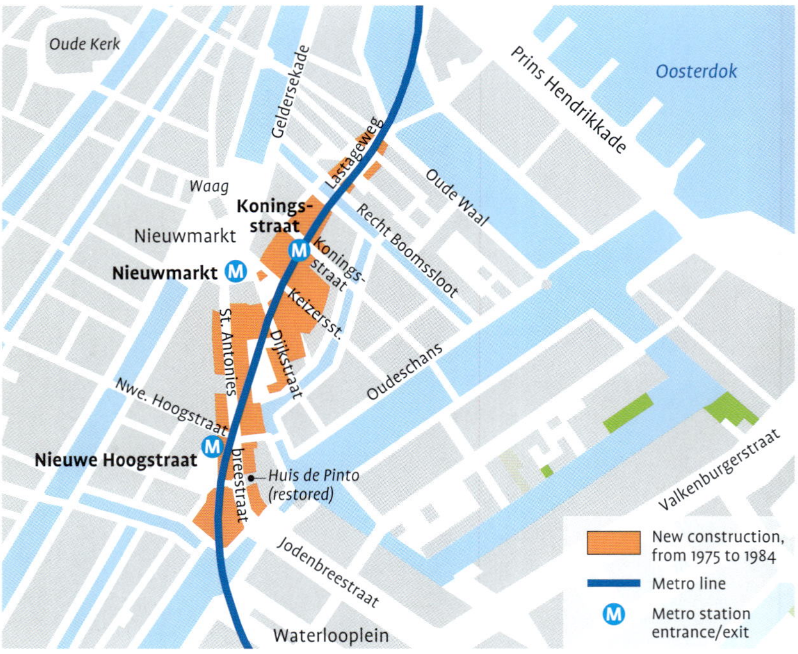

Sources: GVB (1); Wikipedia (2, 3)

© Noordhoff Uitgevers

❶ - ❷ A small system

Amsterdam's metro system currently has a length of 43 kilometres, which is not much in comparison to other major cities worldwide. What is more, only a short section is underground (between Centraal Station and Amstel station). Some people think the Amsterdam metro is hardly worthy of its name, but completion of the new Noord/Zuid line (2017) will add 9.7 kilometres to the system, 7.1km of which underground.

❸ Opposition to the metro

When constructing the first metro line, the contractors used huge concrete caissons for the section underground, even though this meant demolishing the homes above. This led to serious rioting in the Nieuwmarktbuurt in 1975 and the metro was the cause of major political disagreement for many years. When line 51 (the Amstelveen line) opened in 1990, the word 'metro' was still so controversial that GVB referred to the line as a 'high-speed tram'.

❹ - ❻ A new adventure

In 2002, the city council decided to resurrect the plan for a metro line between Amsterdam-Noord and Zuid station. In light of the lessons learned in the Nieuwmarktbuurt, the chosen approach combined tunnel boring with the use of sunken caissons in areas where this could do no harm. Unfortunately, this technique also had its problems. Leaks in the sheet piling walls caused a number of listed buildings on Vijzelgracht to subside. As a result, the authorities actually considered calling off the entire project.

❼ Pricey kilometres

If all goes to plan, the Noord/Zuid line will open in 2017. By that time, the project costs will have risen to around 3.1 billion euros, 1.9 billion of which will be paid by the already cash-strapped City of Amsterdam.

❹ Construction techniques used for the Noord/Zuid line

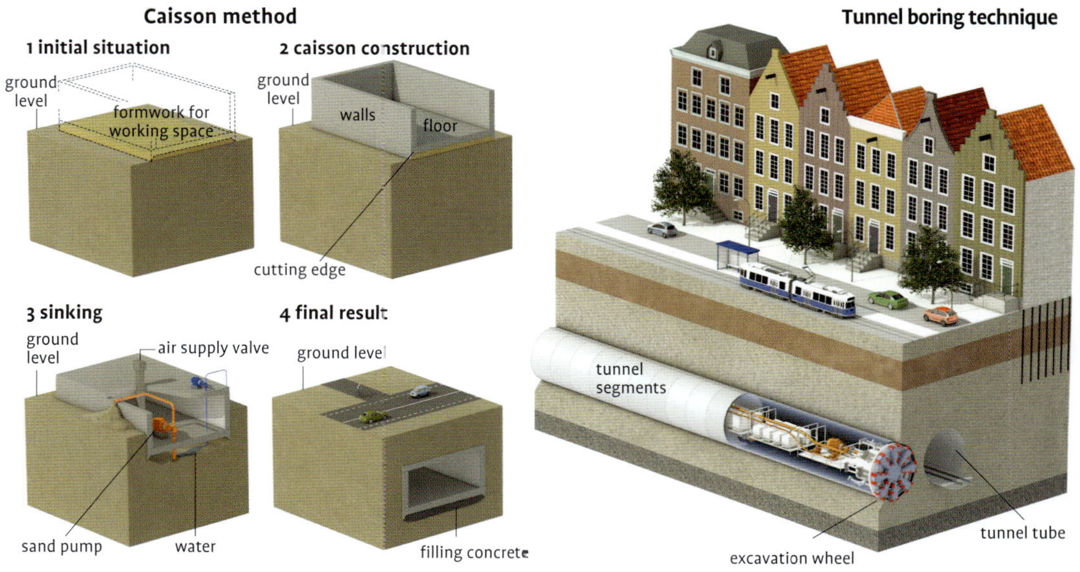

❺ Noord/Zuid line

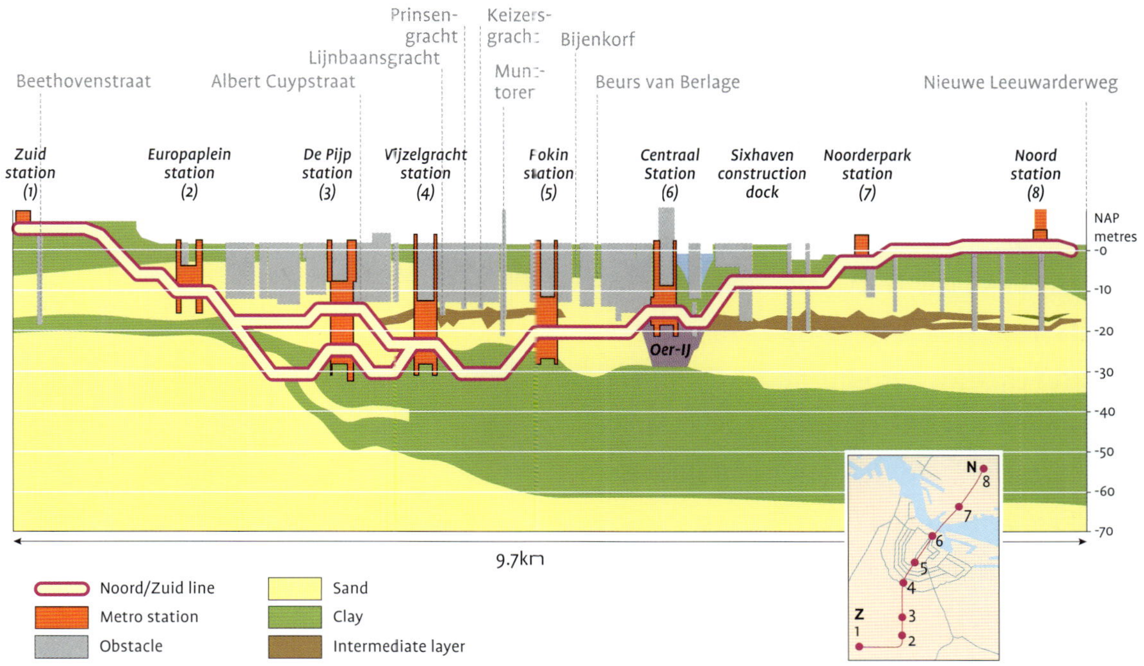

❻ Building subsidence on Vijzelgracht

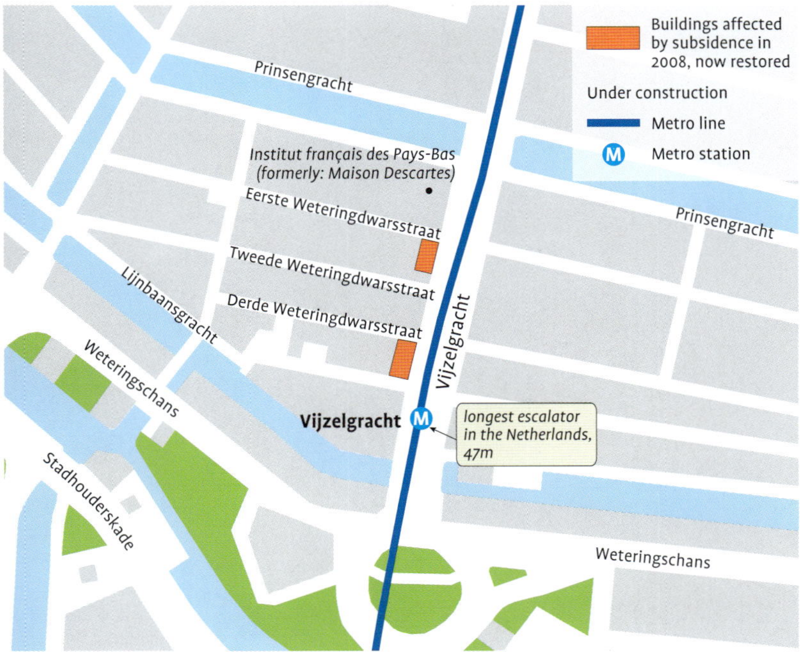

❼ Cost of the Noord/Zuid line

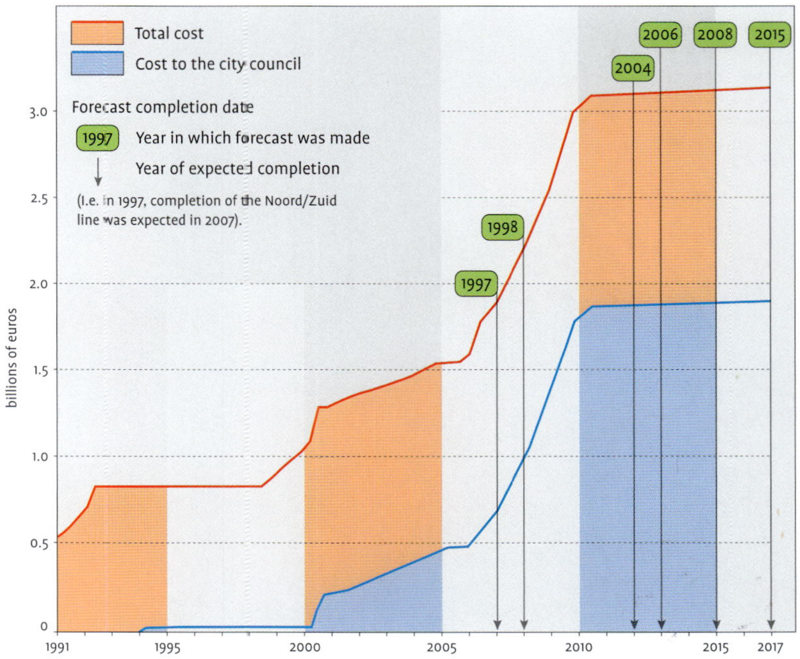

Sources: City of Amsterdam (4-5); Wikipedia (6); City of Amsterdam (7)

© Noordhoff Uitgevers

Shipping

Until the late 19th century, nearly all freight and passengers were taken to and from Amsterdam by water. The IJ, the canals for horse-drawn barges and the Amstelland-Rijnland inland waters were the main routes. Waterways such as the canals and the Binnen-Amstel were also frequently used for transportation within the city. Transportation by road only gained in importance after 1850. Today, the six ferries that carry thousands of Amsterdammers across the river IJ every day are the only regular form of passenger transportation by water. However, waterways like the North Sea Canal, with its imposing lock complex in IJmuiden, and the Amsterdam-Rhine Canal are still very significant for goods transportation. Amsterdam's canals are now barely used for transportation, so the movable bridges only open a few times a day.

❶ Goods transportation on the waterways

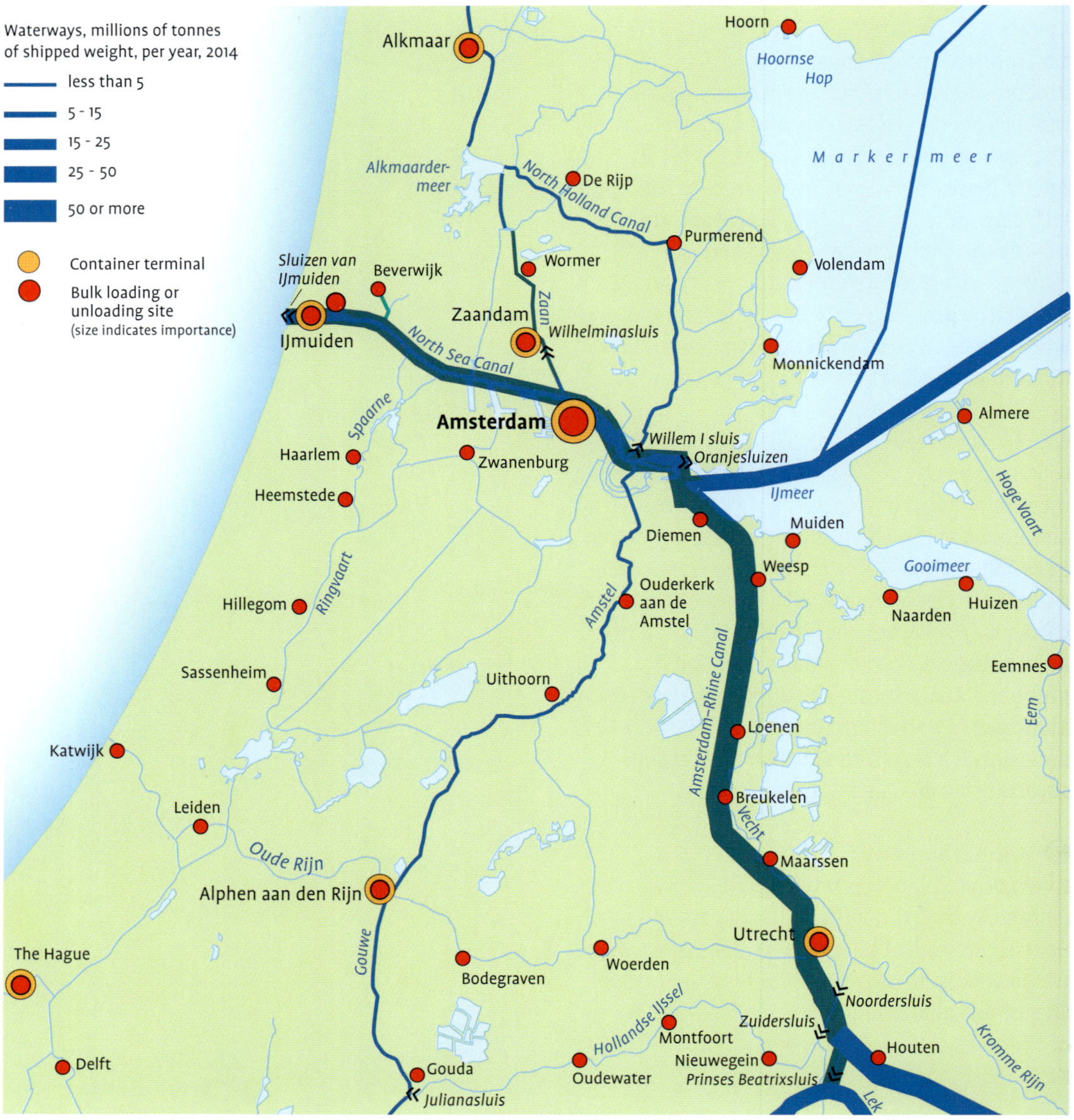

❷ Canals for horse-drawn barges around 1750

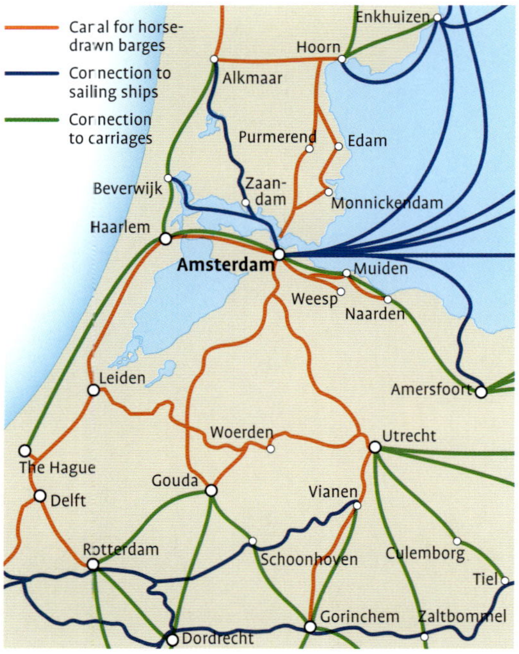

❸ New lock in IJmuiden

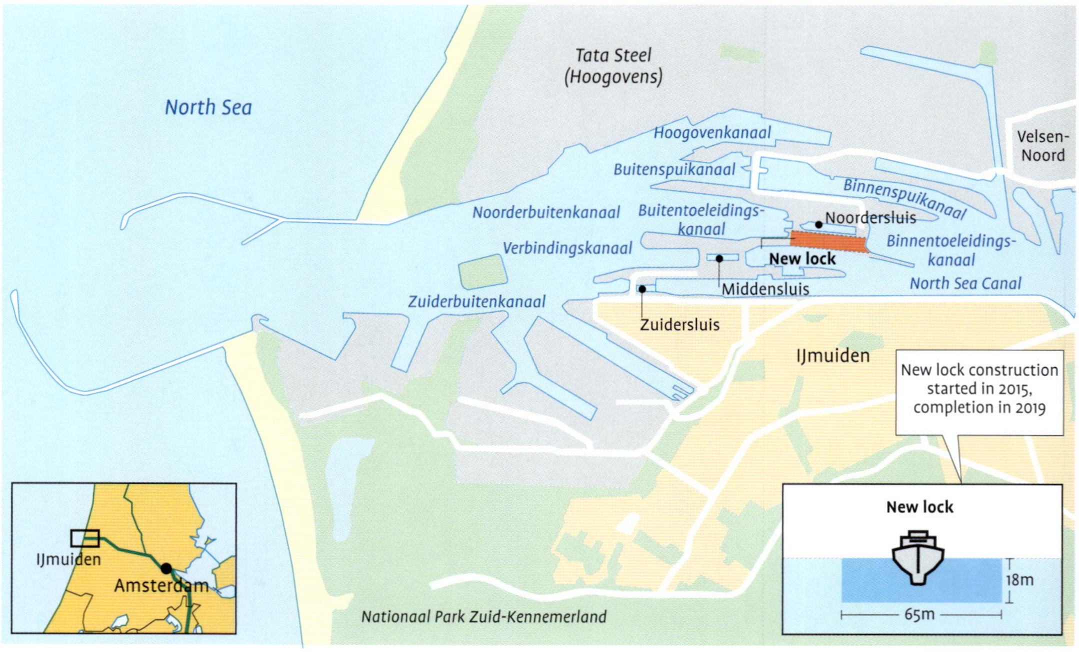

Sources: Rijkswaterstaat / Bureau Voorlichting Binnenvaart / Port of Amsterdam (1); F. H. Horsten, Doorgaande wegen in Nederland, 16e tot 19e eeuw (2); Rijkswaterstaat, Ministry of Infrastructure and the Environment (3)

© Noordhoff Uitgevers

❶ Freight transportation by water
The Port of Amsterdam owes its existence to the North Sea Canal (1876) and the Merwede Canal (1892) – modernised and renamed the Amsterdam-Rhine Canal in 1952. Every day, hundreds of sea-going and inland ships transport a few hundred thousand tonnes of freight along these canals.

❷ Transportation by water around 1750
Before the North Sea Canal and the Merwede Canal were constructed, goods were mainly transported over the river IJ and the former Zuiderzee. As of the 17th century, travellers mainly used the horse-drawn barge canals. The first one was constructed in 1632, linking Amsterdam and Haarlem, and by the end of the 17th century, there were over 400 kilometres of this sort of canal in Holland and Utrecht.

❸ A 500-metre-long lock
Since the North Sea Canal opened in 1876, its locks have been enlarged and deepened on many occasions. The Noordersluis lock in IJmuiden, which dates back to 1929, is now also too small (400 x 50 x 15m), so work started on a new lock measuring 500 x 65 x 18m in 2015. It is due to be completed in 2019 at an estimated cost of 848 million euros.

❹ A city full of bridges
Amsterdam has 1750 bridges, each with its own number. Bridge number 1, over the Singel near Muntplein, is officially called Muntsluis. For unknown reasons, Amsterdammers also refer to several other bridges as a 'sluis' or lock.

❺ - ❻ Back and forth
GVB operates seventeen ferries, providing daily services on six routes over the river IJ. The Buiksloterwegveer (line 901), better known as the Tolhuispont, transports the most pedestrians, cyclists and mopeds. Oostveer is the name of the most recent route, which has linked the KNSM-eiland and Nieuwendam since 2014.

❹ Bridges in Amsterdam

❺ Ferries

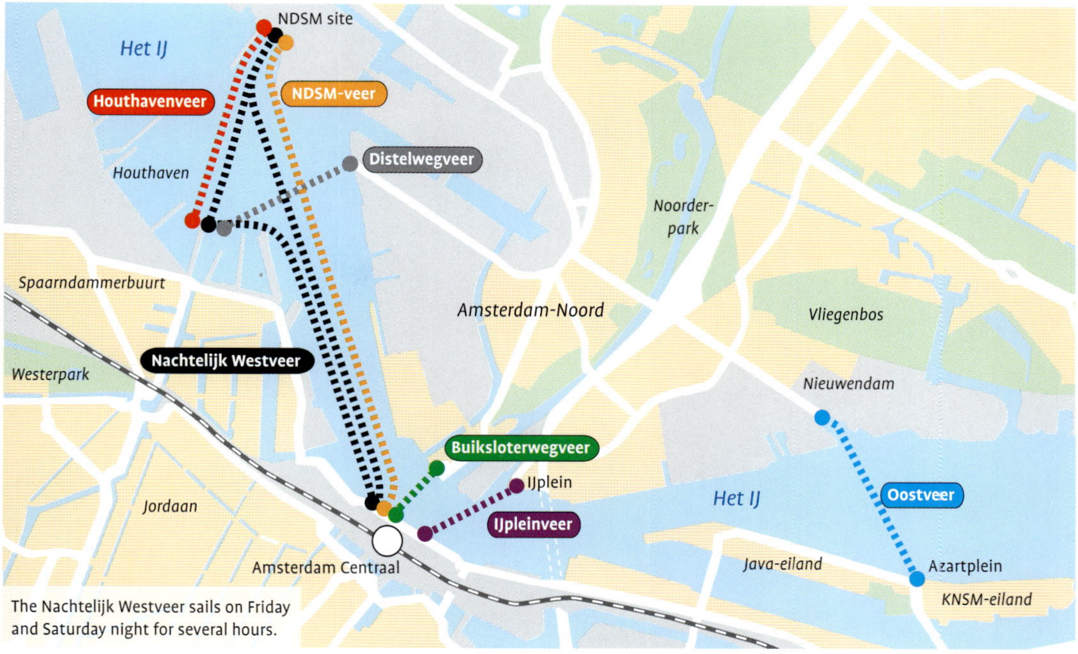

❻ Ferry passengers

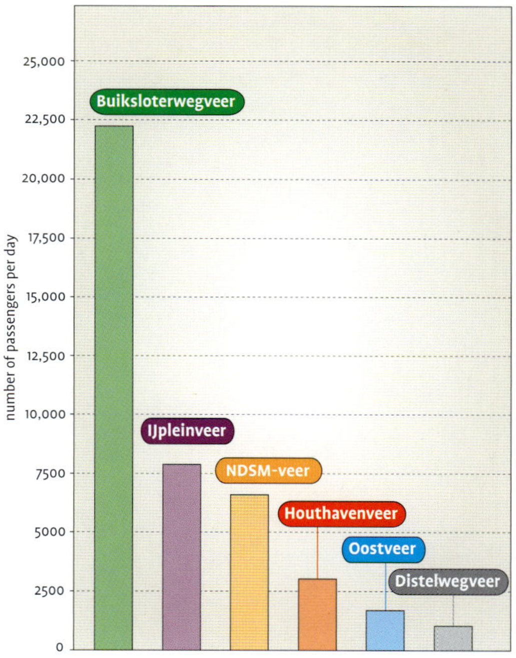

Sources: Waternet (4); GVB (5, 6)

© Noordhoff Uitgevers

Oostelijk Havengebied

In 1903, Amsterdam's largest shipping company, Koninklijke Nederlandsche Stoomboot Maatschappij (KNSM), set up operations on the 'IJ-eiland'.

This artificial island, which we now know by the names of Java-eiland and KNSM-eiland, was created to facilitate rapidly growing overseas transportation activities. It was part of the revamped Oostelijk Havengebied, with its huge expanse of docks, gigantic warehouses and the Lloyd Hotel, the place where countless emigrants started their journey across the ocean.
After 1945, the Oostelijk Havengebied fell into disrepair, partly due to increasing use of the Westelijk Havengebied. In 1980, the city council suggested building a residential area there and filling in most of the docks, but that plan was not well received. The residential area has since been built, but the infrastructure has largely been retained, including the warehouses, which have been converted into residential complexes. As a result, the Oostelijk Havengebied still provides a tangible sense of Amsterdam's transportation history around 1900.

❶ Shipping company flags and funnel colours

❷ Oostelijk Havengebied around 1930

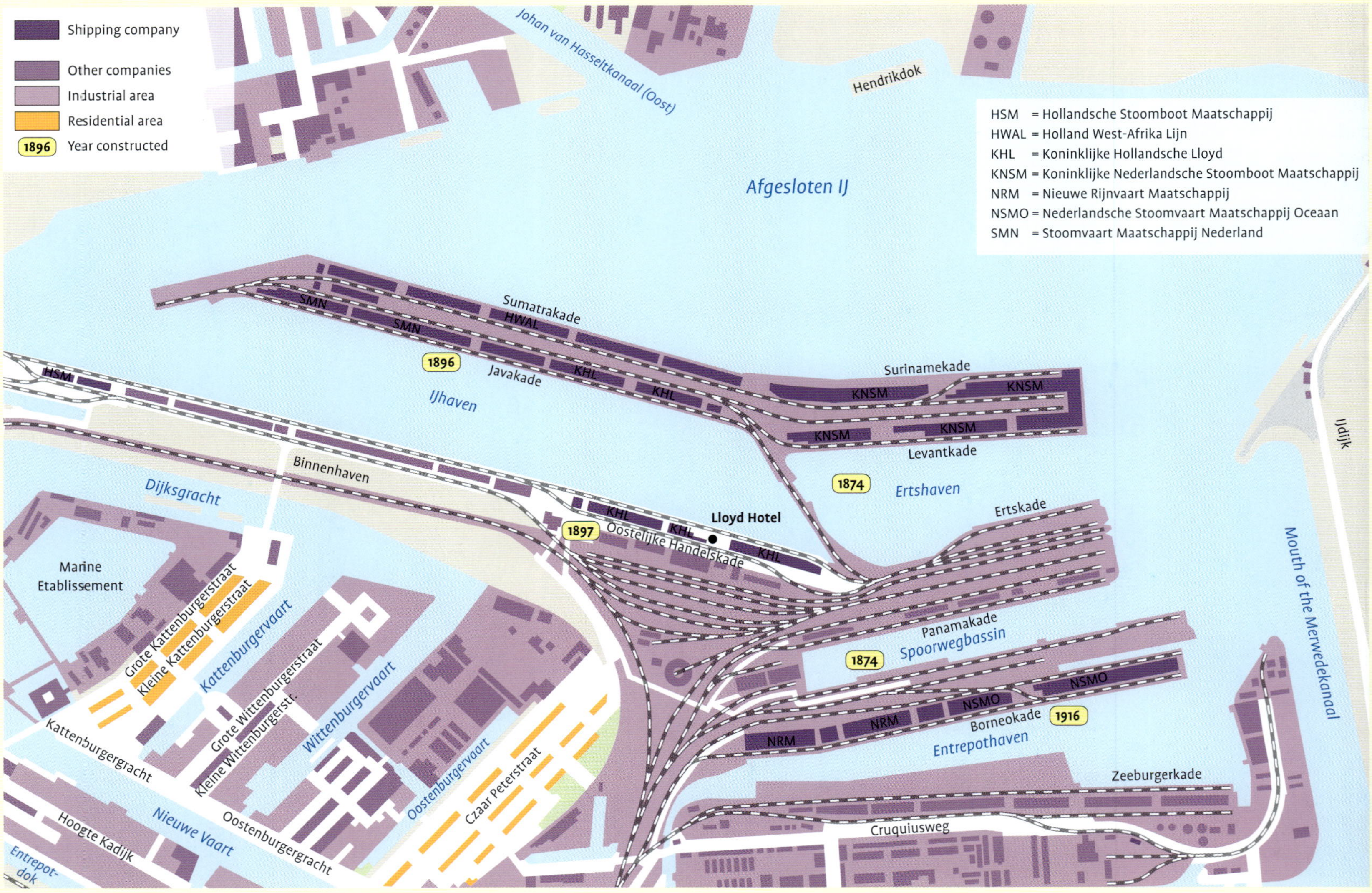

Sources: National Library of the Netherlands, Memory of the Netherlands (1); T. Heijdra, Kadraaiers & zeekastelen: geschiedenis van het Oostelijk Havengebied (2)

© Noordhoff Uitgevers

❸ Shipping companies: period of existence

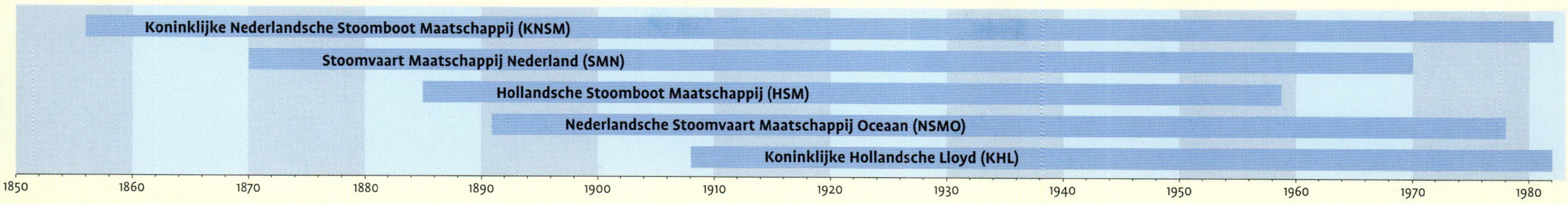

❶ and ❸ Shipping companies
Various large shipping companies had their home base in Amsterdam between 1856 and 1980. Their ships could be identified by the shipping company flag and funnel colours.

❷ Quays and harbours
In 1874, the Spoorwegbassin and the Ertshaven were excavated in the area that was known as the Rietlanden at that time. Around 1900, work started on construction of the Entrepothaven and IJ-eiland (known as Java-eiland and KNSM-eiland today). The Borneokade was completed in 1916.

❹ The Lloyd Hotel
Until 1936, the Lloyd Hotel (1921) on the Oostelijke Handelskade served as a hotel for emigrants, who waited there in large dormitories until they could make the voyage to New York. The building was subsequently used as a (juvenile) prison until 1989, and is now a three-star hotel.

❺ and ❻ Respect for the past
In the 1990s, architects Sjoerd Soeters and Jo Coenen transformed the Java-eiland and KNSM-eiland respectively into residential areas. Several old harbour buildings were preserved on the latter. City developers also left old elements intact elsewhere in the Oostelijk Havengebied. Many temporary storage warehouses in particular – built here between 1870 and 1920 – have been preserved in a recognisable form.

❹ Lloyd Hotel

❺ Java-eiland and KNSM-eiland in 2015

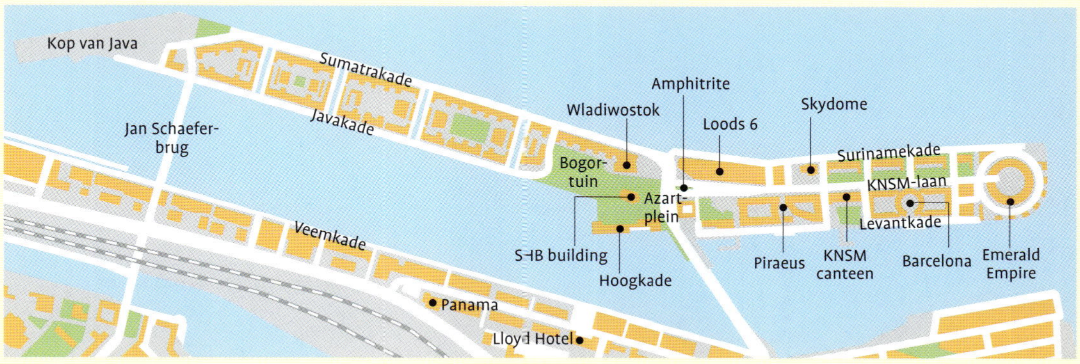

❻ Oostelijk Havengebied in 2015: historic warehouses

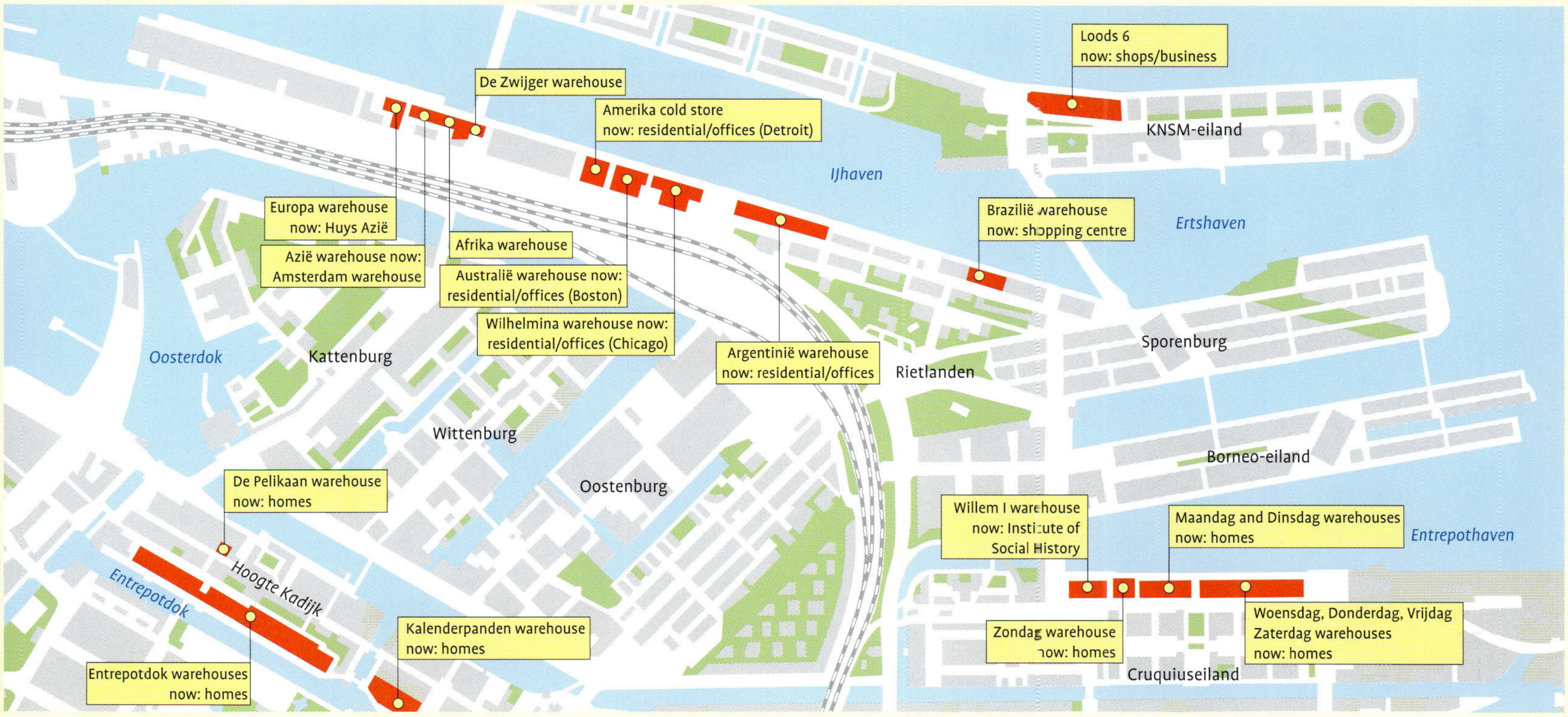

Sources: *Wikipedia (3); Oostelijk Havengebied Amsterdam (5); H. Bonke, Amsterdamse pakhuizen, 16de-20ste eeuw / Oostelijk Havengebied Amsterdam (6)*

© Noordhoff Uitgevers

Bicycles

Amsterdam has a reputation as an eldorado for cyclists and comes second only to Copenhagen in the world's top cycling cities. Every day, hundreds of thousands of Amsterdammers use their bicycles, whether they have a traditional women's or men's bicycle, a fashionable cargo bike or a folding bike.

However, all of those cyclists and bicycles inevitably cause problems. Cyclists are the most vulnerable group of road users, topping the lists of traffic accident fatalities and seriously injured road accident victims. Collisions with other road users are frequent, generally leading to aggressive exchanges of words and obscene gestures. The lack of adequate facilities for parking bicycles is also a major source of irritation and sometimes results in cluttered street scenes. This explains why every possible attempt is made to encourage Amsterdammers to park their bicycles in a more orderly fashion.

❶ Traffic safety on the busiest cycling routes

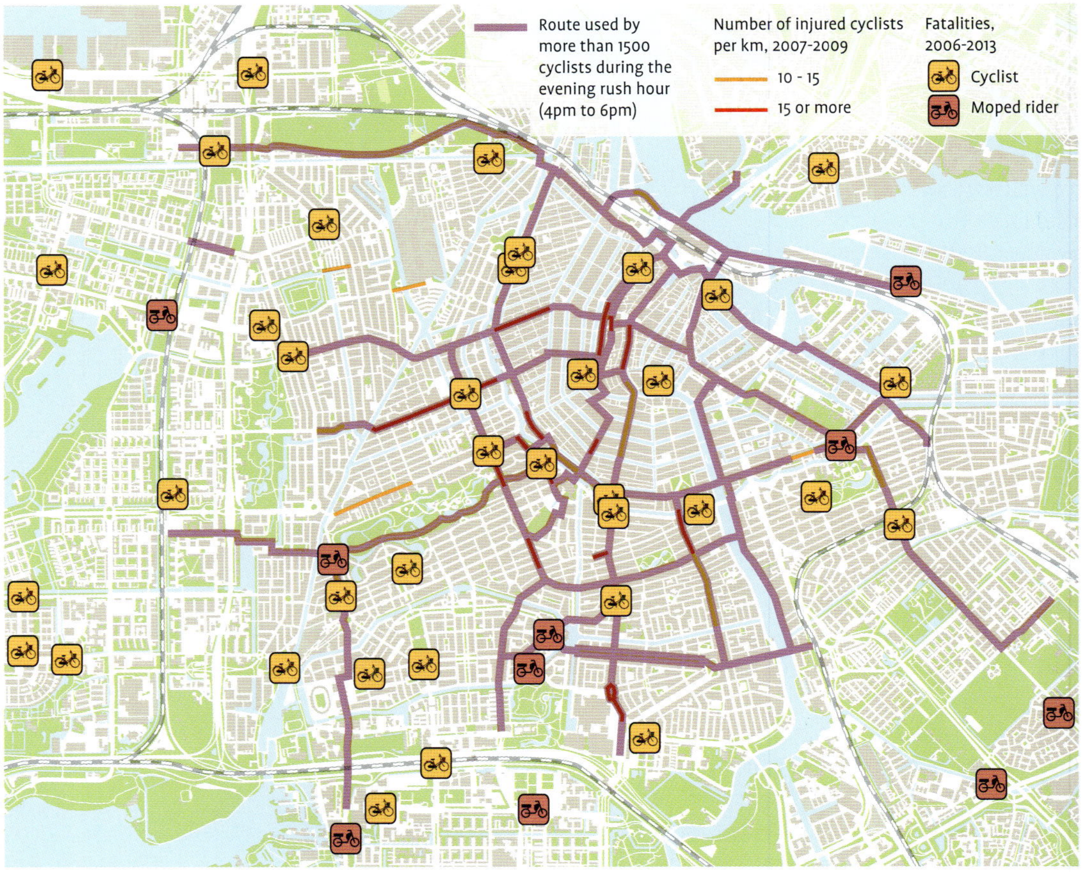

❷ Seriously injured traffic accident victims

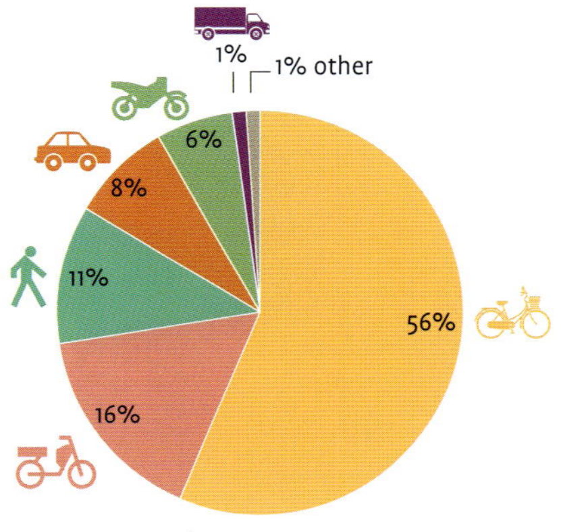

2007-2009 data, (more recent figures are not available)

❸ Traffic fatalities among cyclists and moped riders

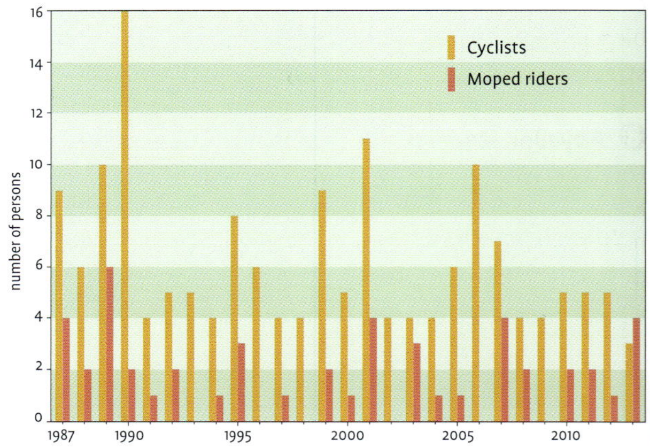

❹ Cycling in Amsterdam

There are more bicycles than Amsterdammers

73% of the city's population (over 12) has a bicycle

There are 513km of separate cycle path in Amsterdam

58% of the city's population (over 12) cycles every day

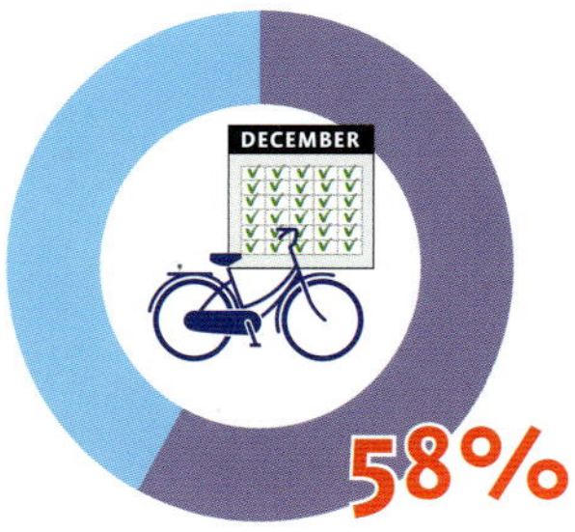

86% of the journeys are between 1 and 5km

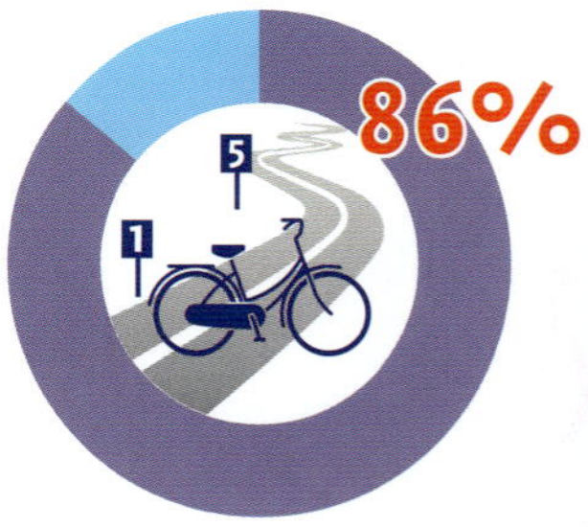

Sources: City of Amsterdam, Meerjarenplan Fiets 2012-2016 / NU.nl_Ministry of Infrastructure and the Environment (1-3); OIS, Research, Information and Statistics, City of Amsterdam (4)

© Noordhoff Uitgevers

❶ - ❸ A vulnerable group

According to estimates, there are more bicycles than residents in the city. Some residents have two or more bicycles – one for daily use and one for leisure purposes. Amsterdammers cycle around 2 million kilometres every day and the busiest routes are Marnixstraat, Weteringschans and Weesperzijde. Cyclists are the most vulnerable of all road users and of the more than eighty traffic fatalities in Amsterdam between 2006 and 2013, ten were moped riders and 37 cyclists. Cyclists also top the lists of seriously injured traffic accident victims year after year.

❺ - ❼ Problems and frustrations

All those bicycles and cyclists create a lot of problems, especially because many cyclists in Amsterdam adhere to their own traffic rules. This regularly leads to confrontations and frustration in confined public spaces.
On top of that, existing bicycle parking facilities are stretched beyond their limits, as every train user who cycles to the station knows from personal experience. As a result, serious consideration is being given to innovative solutions, such as creating bicycle parking facilities on roofs. In the meantime, civil servants in the city have a full-time job cutting through the chains of 'orphaned' and incorrectly parked bicycles and removing the offending objects. In 2014, 70,000 bicycles were removed from the streets of Amsterdam in this way.

❽ A cycling Mecca

Foreigners see Amsterdam as a Mecca for cyclists, one of the reasons being the extensive network of separate cycle paths.

❺ Bicycle parking facilities

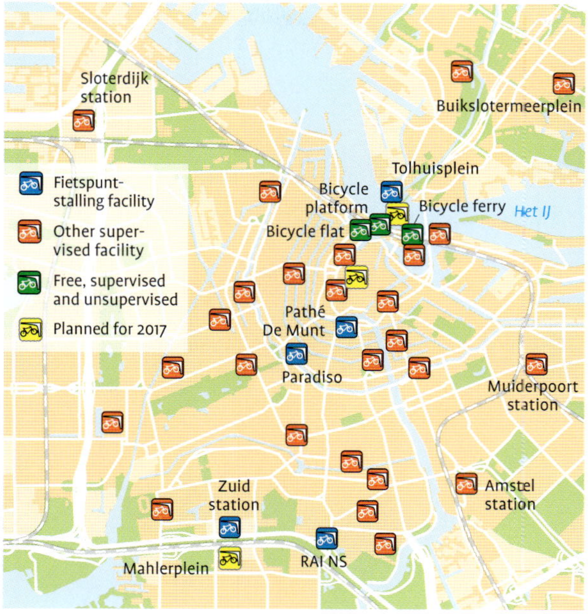

❻ Roof parking

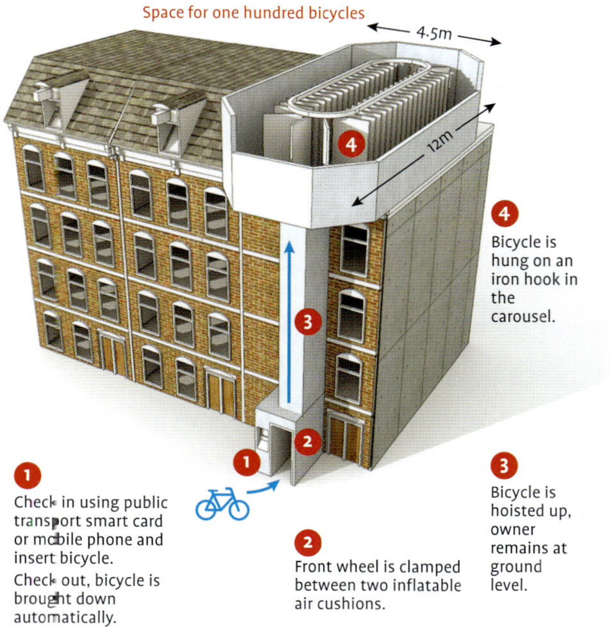

❼ Amsterdam cycling behaviour

❽ Bicycle-friendly cities

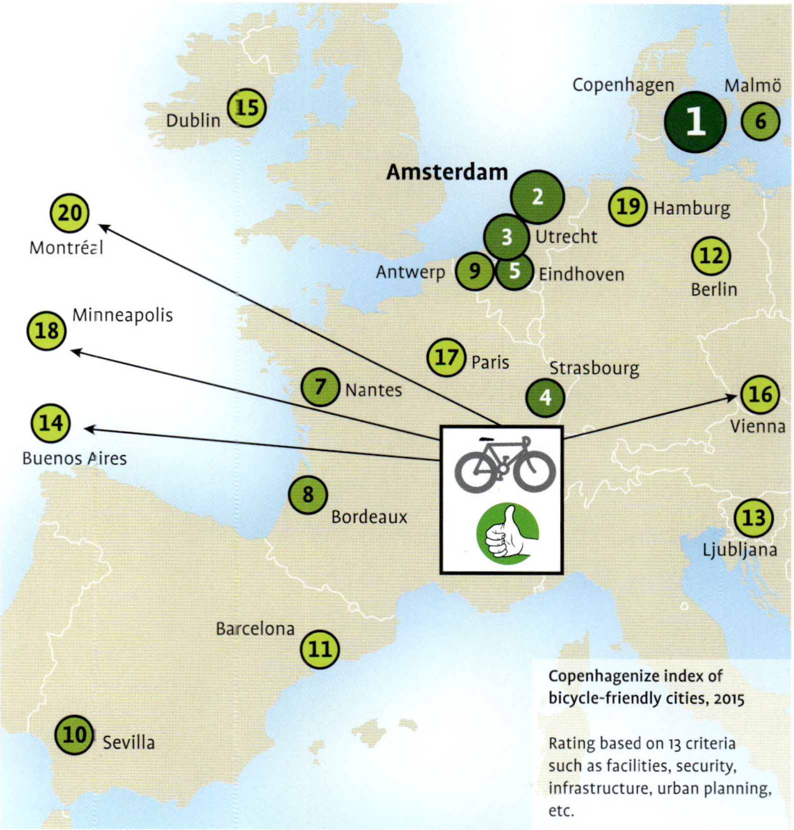

❾ Types of bicycle owned by Amsterdammers

Note: some Amsterdammers have more than one bicycle

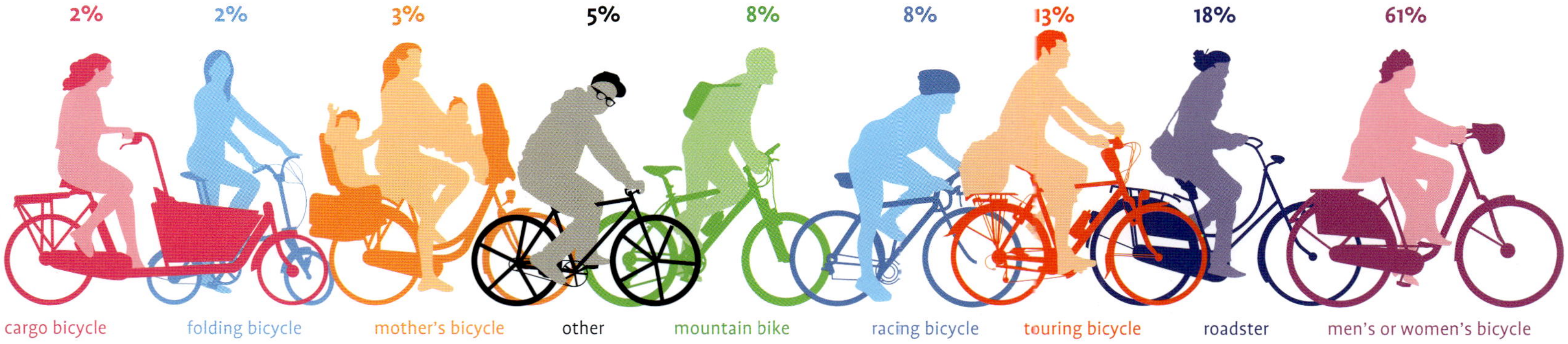

Sources: Cyclists' Union of Amsterdam / City of Amsterdam (5); Het Parool (6); www.copenhagenize.eu (8); Het Parool / City of Amsterdam (9)

© Noordhoff Uitgevers

Cars

Amsterdam has a love-hate relationship with cars. Vehicle traffic in and around Amsterdam has increased explosively since 1960, as illustrated by the rise in the number of traffic lights. However, the disadvantages soon became apparent. During rush hour, the roads into the city are often gridlocked and the city centre is equally incapable of handling large volumes of cars. There are not enough parking spaces, parking permits are difficult to obtain and parking charges are high. It is hardly surprising, therefore, that the level of car ownership is low in Amsterdam. Even so, the city's air quality is still very poor, so the council has been promoting the use of electric vehicles since 2000. Good progress is being made with installing charging stations and a large part of the city centre has been designated a low-emission zone, making it forbidden territory for 'dirty' lorries.

❶ Road traffic volumes

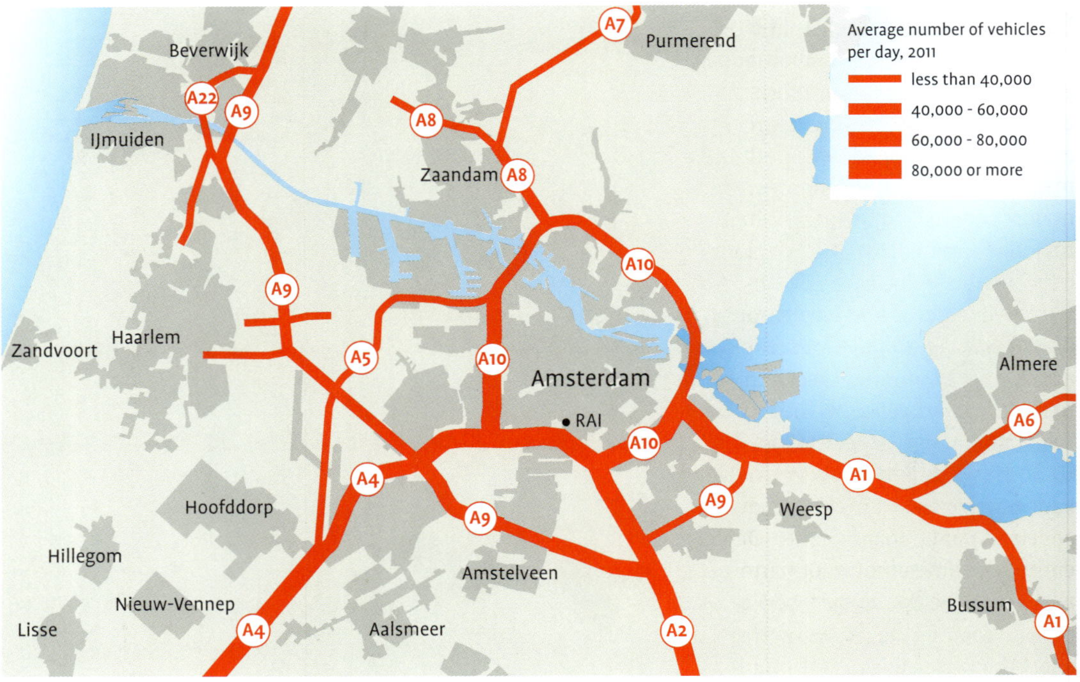

❶ The A10 ring road

The A10 ring road around Amsterdam is number 3 when it comes to roads with the most traffic jams.
During rush hour periods, the traffic jams generally start on the approach roads, particularly on the A1, A4, A7 and A9 motorways. The A10 also has a relatively high number of accidents and with 45 per week in 2014, the RAI exit is even the site of the most accidents on all Dutch motorways. The A2/A10 junction comes a close second, with 39 accidents.

❷ Increasing traffic regulation

In 1932, Amsterdam's first traffic light, on Leidseplein, attracted so many curious spectators that traffic was completely disrupted. Today, there are so many traffic lights that counting them is nearly impossible. As a result, driving through Amsterdam is a process of continuously stopping and starting. Surprisingly enough, there are only two green wave sections inside the ring road – one on Raadhuisstraat for cyclists (travelling 18km/hour) and one for cars on Wibautstraat.

❷ Traffic lights

1970

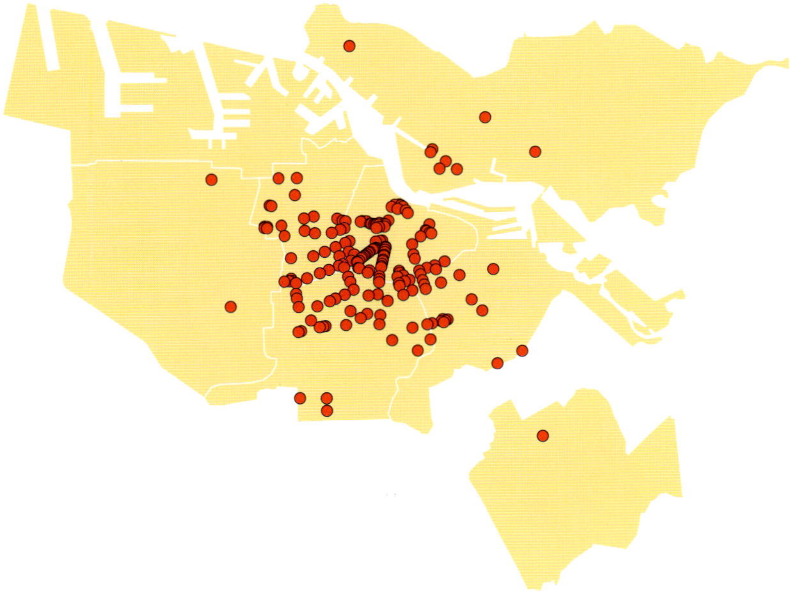

2014

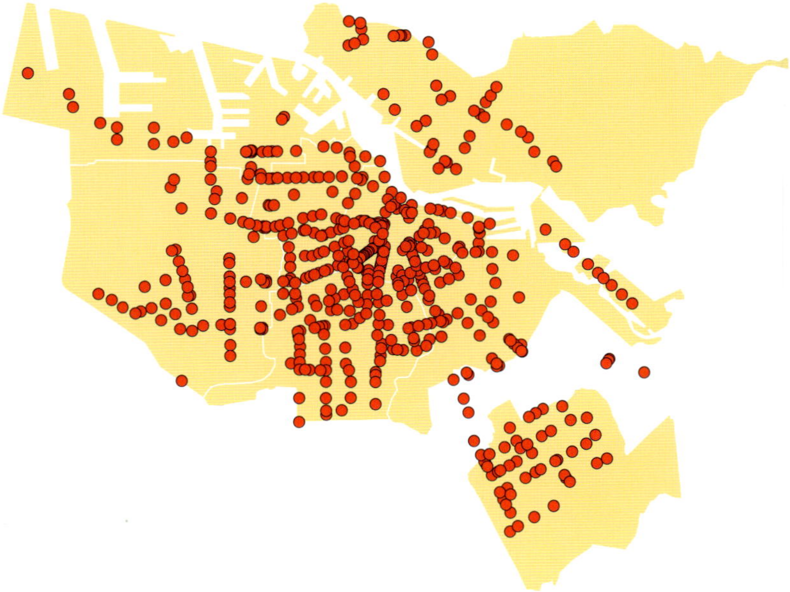

Sources: Rijkswaterstaat (1); OIS, Research, Information and Statistics, City of Amsterdam (2)

© Noordhoff Uitgevers

❸ - ❹ Parking problems
Parking spaces are at a premium in Amsterdam and even people who have a parking permit are often unable to park outside their homes. Parking charges are high for those without a permit. Together with the fact that many young people live in Amsterdam, the parking problem is a major reason why only about 231,000 Amsterdammers own a private car.

❺ and ❼ Creating a cleaner city
The city council wants to dramatically cut greenhouse gas and soot emissions. This is understandable, because according to the Public Health Service, many areas of the city do not meet environmental standards. Road traffic is a major source of pollution, so the council started to actively install charging stations for electric cars in 2000. At the start of 2015, Amsterdam had 1138 charging stations throughout the city, most of which (42) are in the Museumkwartier. Around 4000 residents use them and the aim is for 4000 to have been installed in the city by 2018.

❻ Measures against lorries and vans
Vans and lorries in particular have a significant adverse impact on air quality. One normal lorry emits the same amount of harmful substances as one hundred passenger cars on average, so policy in this field focuses on the 3200 lorries and 35,000 delivery vans that drive into the city every day. Extending the hours for loading and unloading into the evening should make an improvement and speed up circulation of lorries and vans. On top of that, the area inside the ring road has been designated a low-emission zone – by far the largest in the Netherlands. Only lorries with no diesel engine, or with a special type of diesel engine, have access to this zone.

❸ Parking zones and charges

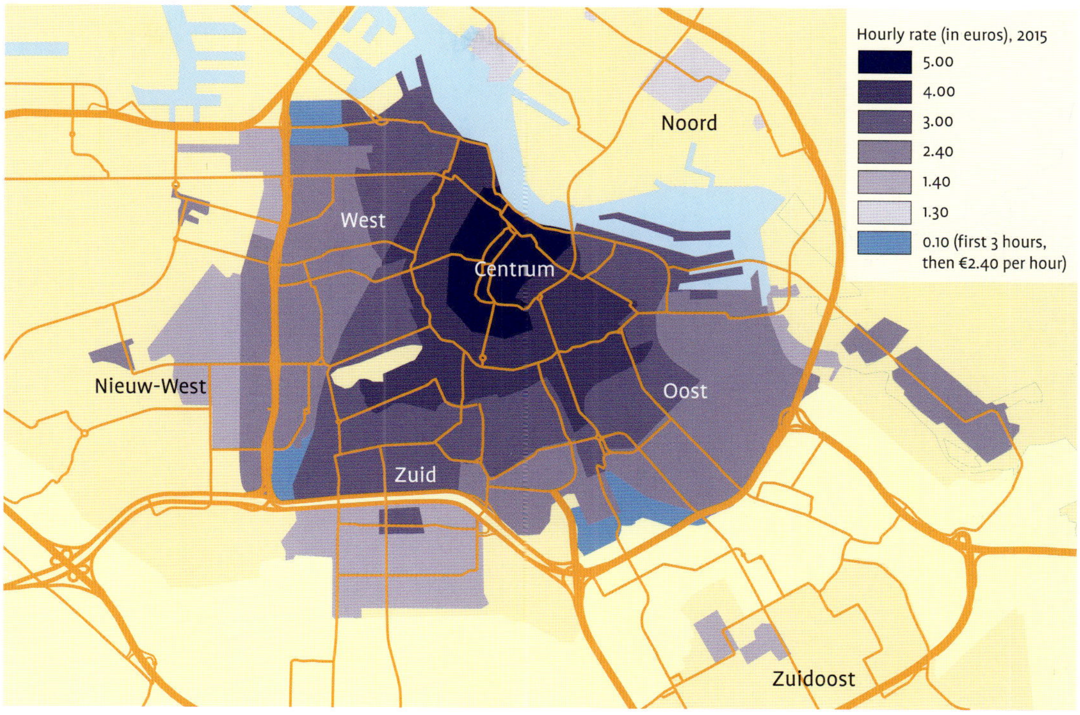

❹ Car ownership

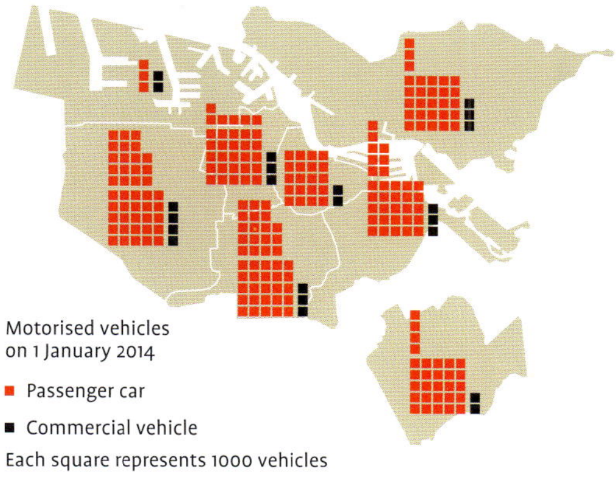

❺ Charging stations for electric cars

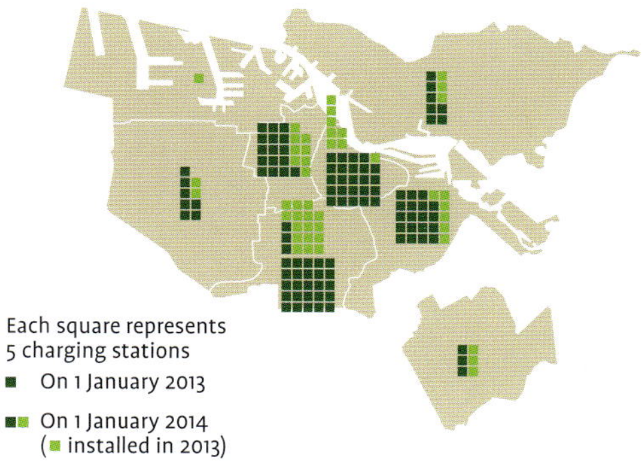

❻ Low-emission zones in the Netherlands

❼ Air pollution caused by traffic

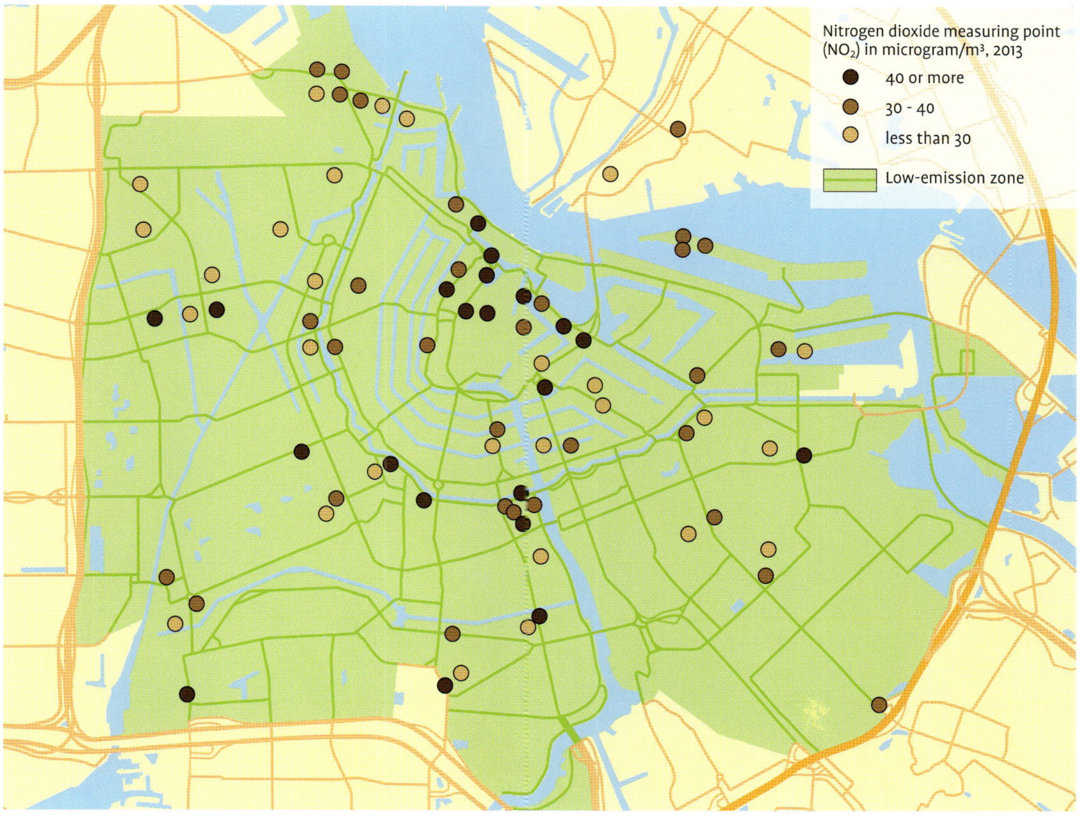

Sources: OIS, Research, Information and Statistics, City of Amsterdam (3-5); City of Amsterdam (6); Public Health Service of Amsterdam (7)

© Noordhoff Uitgevers

Aviation

During its almost one hundred years of existence, Schiphol, originally a simple grass airstrip, has now grown into a major hub and Europe's third largest airport, in terms of both the number of passengers and the number of aircraft movements. Every year, the six runways have to process more and more take-offs and landings, while passenger volumes are rising year on year. Cargo activities are also growing again, since the global economy started to recover in 2014.
However, Schiphol's success has a downside. Local residents complain about air pollution and noise, and since geese are a serious threat to air safety, Schiphol has thousands of these birds culled over an extensive area each year - much to the indignation of nature lovers.

❶ Industrial estates and runways at Schiphol

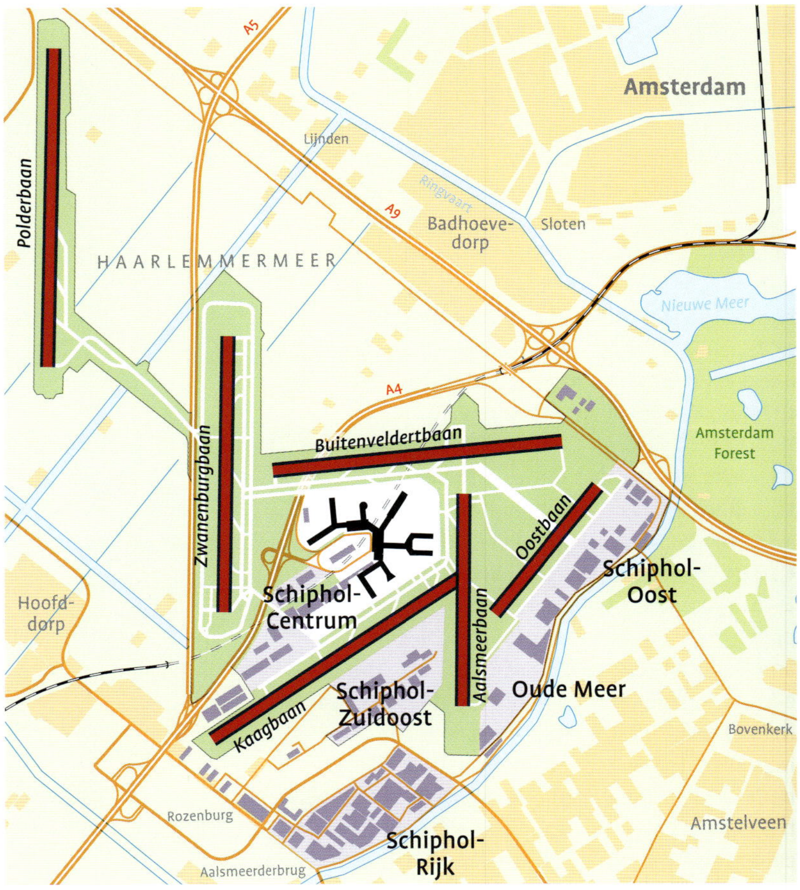

❶ Gateway to Amsterdam
Today, Schiphol airport covers an area of almost 3000 hectares and is almost 200 times larger than the small military airbase where it all started in 1916. Officially, Schiphol is outside the City of Amsterdam, but the two are closely linked, if only because the City is a shareholder.

❷ - ❹ Growth
The 2008 crisis temporarily halted the continuing increase in aircraft movements, passenger numbers and cargo volumes, but the airport is now growing again in all areas.

❺ Six runways
Schiphol currently has six runways, the longest of which is the Polderbaan, which dates back to 2003 and is 3800m long. At 2014m and dating back to 1945, the Oostbaan is the oldest and shortest and is mainly used for private aircraft.

❷ Aircraft movements

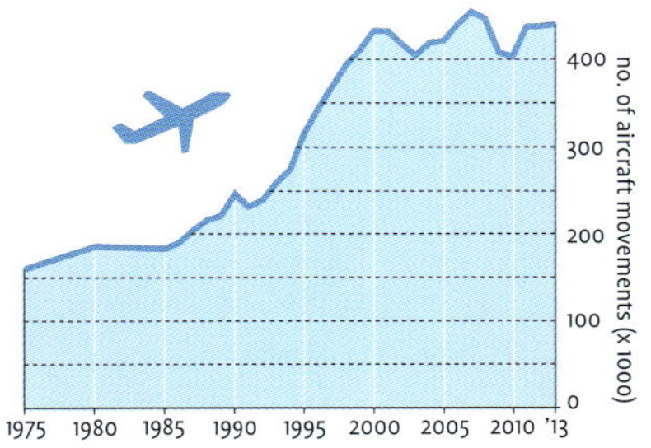

❸ Passengers

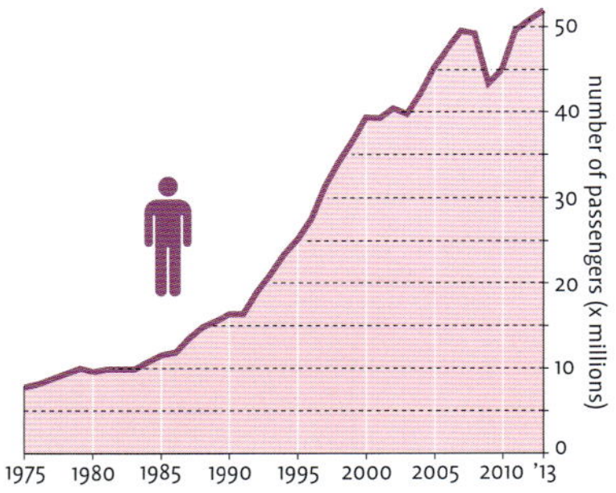

❹ Cargo

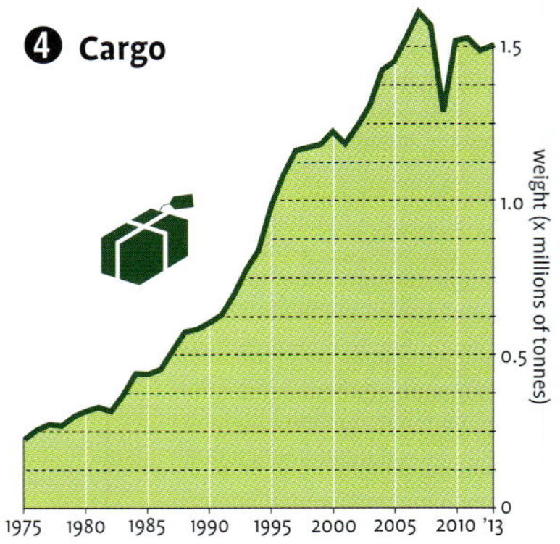

❺ Runway use

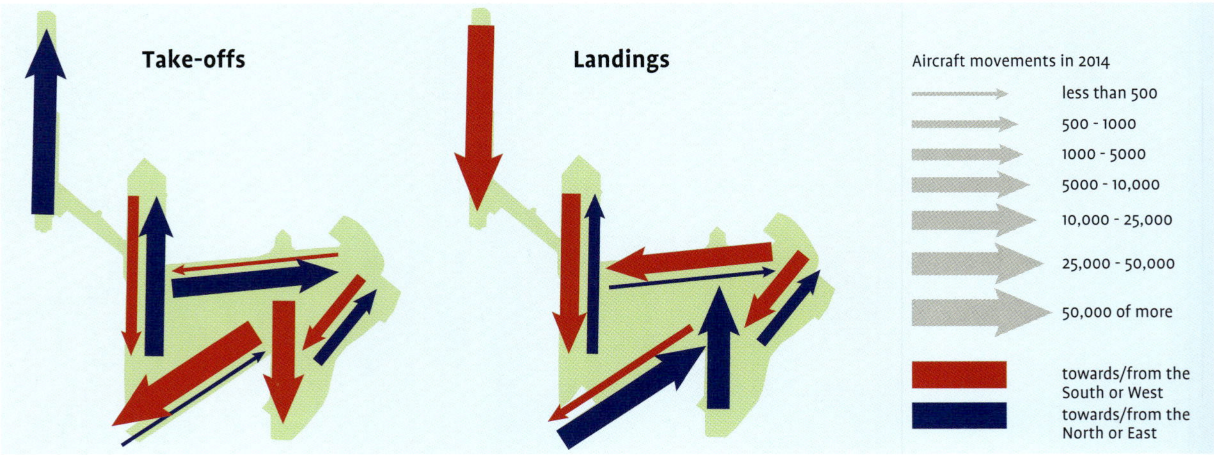

Sources: Schiphol Group (1-4); OIS, Research, Information and Statistics, City of Amsterdam / Bewoners Aanspreekpunt Schiphol (5)

© Noordhoff Uitgevers

❻ - ❼ Transit and cargo flights

Schiphol is the fourth largest European airport after London Heathrow, Paris Charles de Gaulle and Frankfurt (Germany), a position it owes to transit passengers. Nearly half of all passengers flying into Schiphol are transit passengers. In 2014, 1.6 million tonnes of cargo were transported via Schiphol, making it Europe's third largest airport when it comes to cargo transport. 39% of the cargo goes to Asia, 17% to North America and 9% remains in Europe.

❽ Noise

In May 2009, Schiphol transferred responsibility for handling complaints about noise to an organisation called Bewoners Aanspreekpunt Schiphol (BAS). In 2014, 7472 people made some 151,846 complaints to BAS. 21% of those people live within the city boundaries of Amsterdam.

❾ Geese

Every year, around 60,000 geese descend from the skies to forage at Schiphol airport and in the surrounding area. They form a hazard as they can get sucked into aircraft engines, so sixteen birdwatchers have been appointed to prevent this. In the past, they combatted this problem by shaking eggs to prevent them from hatching, but the geese are now shot, gassed or even scared off using laser beams. Even so, bird incidents occur during seven out of every 10,000 take-offs and landings.

❻ Most important airports for passengers travelling via Schiphol

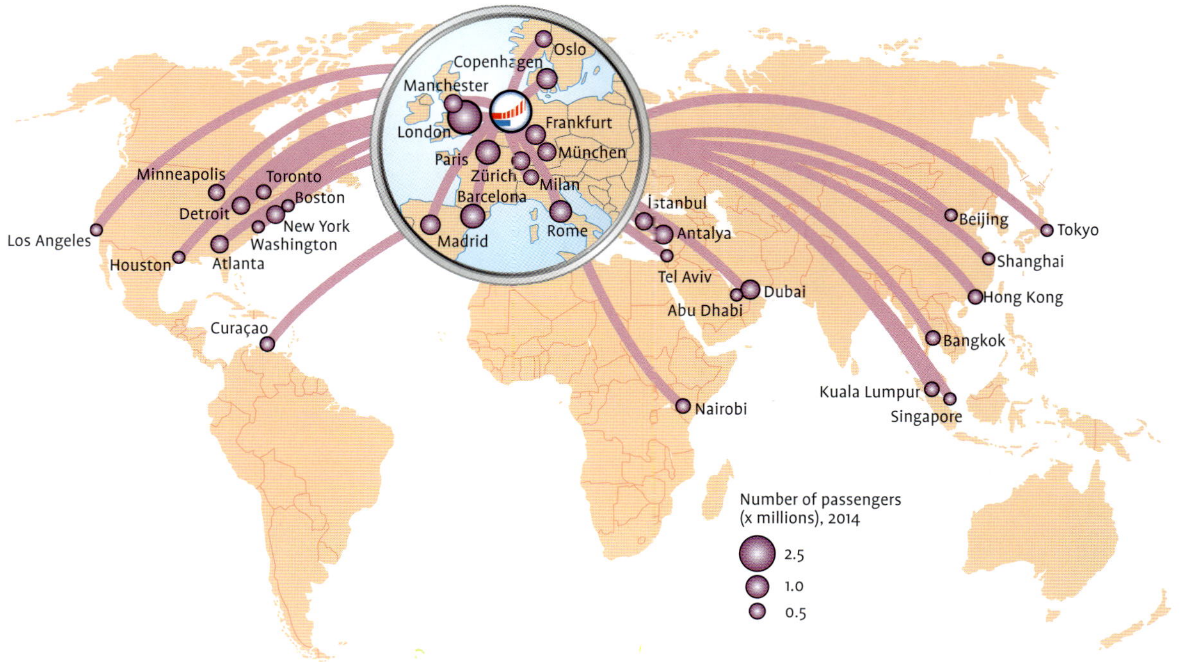

❼ Most important airports for cargo travelling via Schiphol

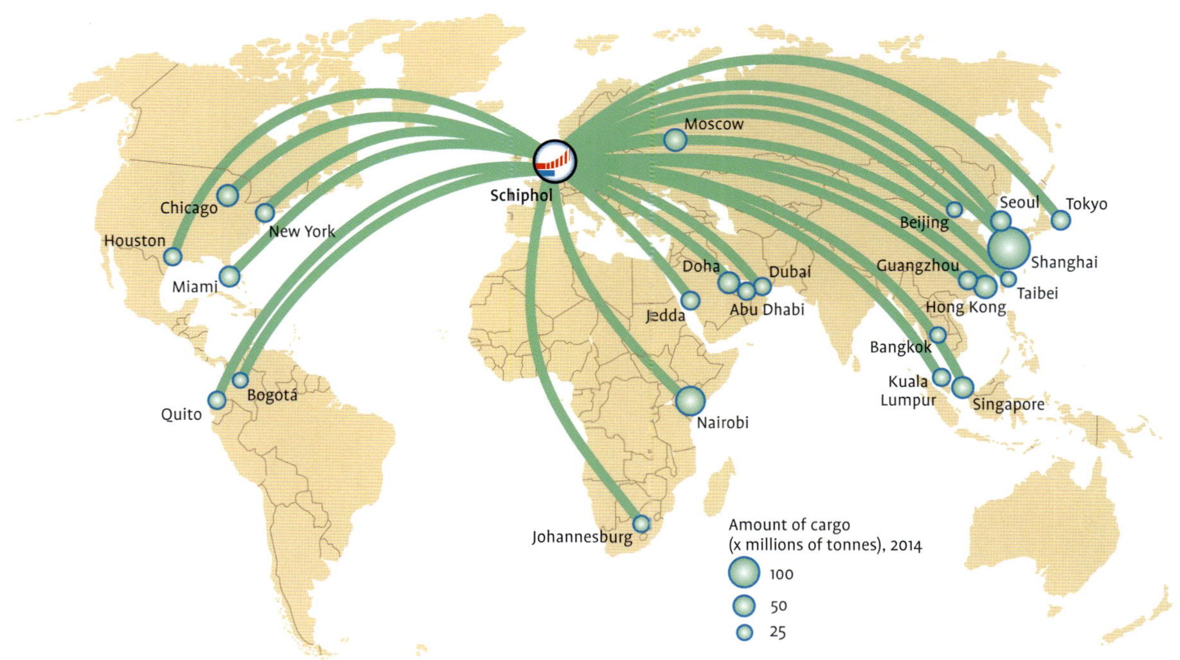

❽ Noise levels

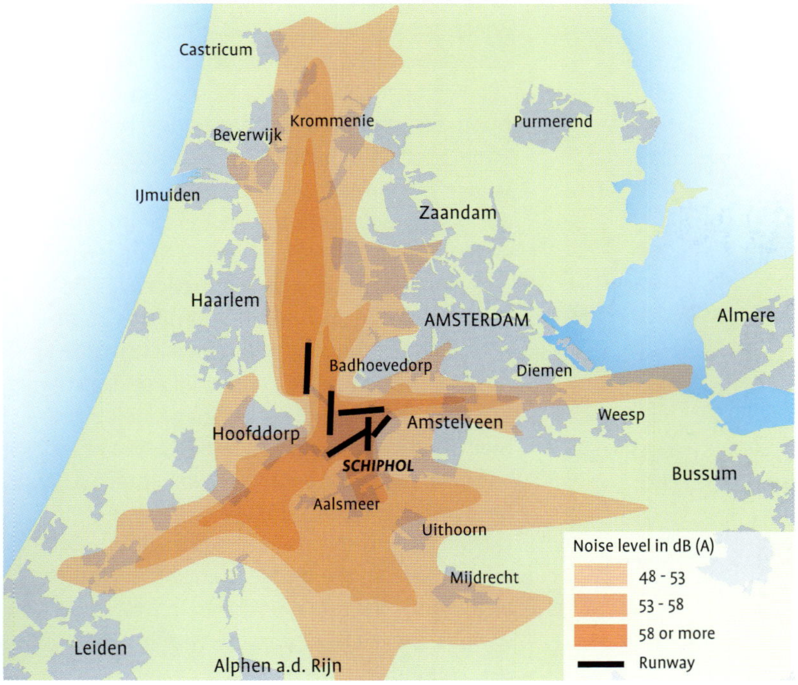

❾ Goose problem

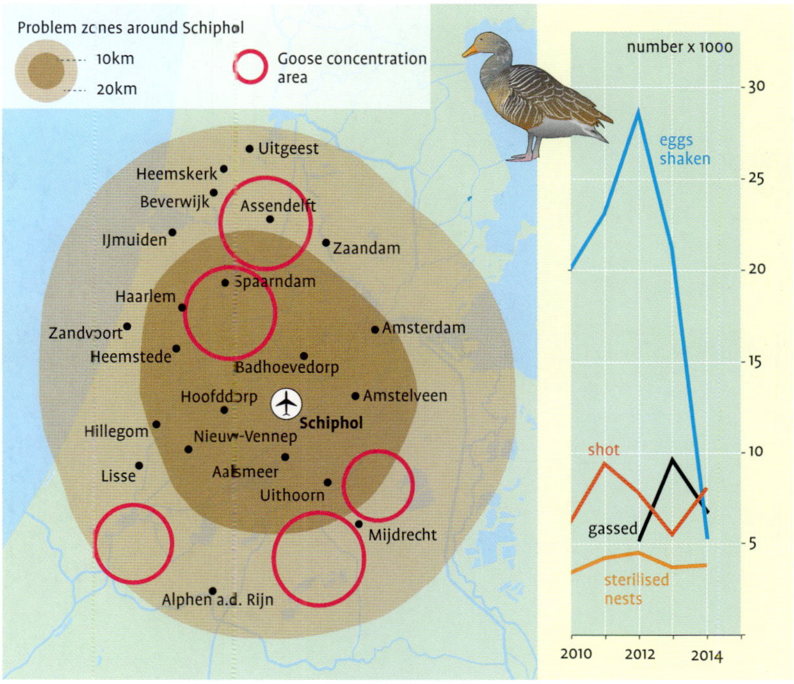

Sources: *Schiphol Traffic Review (6, 7); Bewoners Aanspreekpunt Schiphol (8); Duke Faunabeheer / Faunabeheereenheid Noord-Holland (9)*

© Noordhoff Uitgevers

Bridges

❶ '15 bridges' bridge

In the early 17th century, the city council decided to replace the existing wooden bridges with stone bridges. They were intended to give the city greater allure and also required less maintenance. In order to avoid obstructing shipping traffic on the canals, the authorities opted for arch bridges with a road surface on one or more arches. One drawback was that heavily laden carts had difficulty crossing the bridges, and this led to the creation of a new profession, the cart puller. The cart puller used a rope over his shoulder to pull the cart over the bridge.
In the 19th century, many of these arch bridges were replaced with flat steel bridges. Nowadays, the best place from which to see some authentic arch bridges is the bridge over Reguliersgracht and Herengracht. A total of fifteen bridges can be seen from this point, six over Reguliersgracht and eight over Herengracht.

❷ Magere Brug

Bridge no. 242, better known as the Magere Brug, spans the river Amstel, connecting Kerkstraat to Nieuwe Kerkstraat. A wooden bridge with thirteen water passageways was built here in 1691 and was soon nicknamed 'Magere Brug' or 'Skinny Bridge' because of its narrow road surface. In 1871, the bridge had to be replaced with a new wooden double-sided drawbridge with nine water passageways. The replacement of 1934 was designed in the old style, at the request of the city council and for a considerable period, two bridge masters were required to operate the bridge by hand. This process was somewhat dangerous, so the bridge was equipped with a motor in 1994. Since 2003, the Magere Brug has only been open to cyclists, mopeds and pedestrians. The bridge's lampposts are a striking feature. They are replicas of the lampposts designed in the 17th century by Jan van der Heyden. Together with 1800 LED bulbs, they create an enchanting scene in the dark.

❸ Blauwbrug

Bridge no. 236 is a bridge over the Amstel between Amstelstraat and Waterlooplein. Its nickname 'Blauwbrug' or 'Blue Bridge' comes from the blue colour of the original wooden bridge. When the International Colonial and Export Exhibition was held in 1883 on Museumplein, the city council decided to replace the bridge and commissioned two architects, B. de Greef and W. Springer, to design a new bridge with international allure. The final design showed great similarity to the Alexander III bridge over the Seine in Paris. The bridge's eight Swedish granite pillars are a striking feature – the middle four are shaped like a ship's hull and decorated with animal figures and masks. The pillars act as supports for two lampposts and have imperial crowns on top.
Having previously provided access to the former Jewish district, the bridge is known in Yiddish as Bloubirk, a name mentioned in a few Yiddish sayings about the impossibility of leaving your past behind you.

Photos: © Wolverlei/Martin Stevens (1-3)

© Noordhoff Uitgevers

❹ P. L. Kramerbrug
Bridge no. 400, over the Amstel canal near Amsteldijk, is named after its designer, Pieter Lodewijk Kramer. He was one of the leading architects from the early days of the Amsterdam School and specialised in designing bridges. Dating back to 1921, this bridge has characteristics that are typical of the Amsterdam School – extravagantly shaped brickwork, decorative wrought ironwork and a wealth of ornaments. The granite sculptures are the work of Hildo Krop and they are a reference to the sea, the source of Amsterdam's prosperity. They depict seals and ship worms, while the wrought ironwork with its flowing lines also refers to the sea. The city's history is also portrayed in the form of a figure of Gijsbrecht van Aemstel and a cog. The small buildings on either side of the bridge were intended for use by the city's power company and the Public Works Department's garden upkeep section.

❺ Utrechtsebrug
Bridge no. 439, which crosses the river Amstel from President Kennedylaan, provides access to the A2 motorway towards Utrecht. This explains why it is called Utrechtsebrug. The bridge was opened on 1 April 1954 together with the new motorway, which consisted of concrete slabs with tar-filled expansion joints. Together, the road and the bridge constituted the first major post-war road construction project completed. The bridge is 250 metres long, has a centre span of 56 metres and is the first bridge over the Amstel to feature prestressed concrete. The Shabbat chain attached to one of the pillars, a gift from the Jewish community, is a striking detail and forms a symbolic barrier closing the Amstel. According to Jewish law, nothing may be carried or pushed outside the city limits on the Shabbat. Closing the city in this way created an eruv (a physically enclosed area) within which carrying and pushing are permitted, so women were able to push prams with impunity inside this enclosure.

❻ Enneüs Heermabrug
Bridge no. 2001, Enneüs Heermabrug, connects Zeeburgereiland to Steigereiland and is named after Enneüs Heerma (1944-1999), a CDA politician who was born in Friesland. From 1978 to 1986, he was the alderman of Economic affairs, Port Affairs and Schiphol. Together with fellow alderman Jan Schaefer, he made a considerable contribution to Amsterdam during that period, so the whole city regretted his move into national politics in 1986.
An Englishman called Nicholas Grimshaw designed the bridge, which was opened in 2001. Grimshaw also designed bridge no. 2002, between Steigereiland and Haveneiland. The bridge consists of two main spans of 75 metres each, a bridging section measuring 30 metres and two land sections of 25 metres each. As is the custom in Amsterdam, the bridge, with its iconic double archway, was soon given a variety of nicknames, including the Bra, Cup IJ or Pam An (Pamela Anderson).

Photos: © Wolverlei/Martin Stevens (4-6)

© Noordhoff Uitgevers

6

World view

◁
Westerkerk and Anne Frank House
Photo Karel Tomeï

6 Introduction

Non-religious people in the majority
More than six out of ten Amsterdammers state that they do not have a religion. Although that percentage is higher than in Rotterdam and The Hague, it is not exceptional – more than half of the Dutch population say that they do not belong to a religious denomination.

Religious heritage
However, Amsterdam was an ecclesiastical city for many centuries. The traces of this past are still visible everywhere, mainly in prestigious church buildings, but also in care institutions, schools and cemeteries founded by Protestants or Catholics. The construction of such facilities stopped in the 20th century, when many Amsterdammers turned their backs on the church. Lots of church buildings have now been demolished or lost their original function.

Jewish Amsterdam
There was a large Jewish community in Amsterdam for many centuries. Some of the synagogues built by Jewish Amsterdammers are just as grand as the churches of their Christian fellow citizens, but even so, only a few of these buildings are still used as synagogues today. This is partly because 20th-century Jews abandoned their faith just as much as Christians, but obviously the main reason is the persecution of the Jews, which resulted in the murder of more than 70% of the Jews in Amsterdam.

New religious zeal
Historically speaking, the percentage of Amsterdammers that feel drawn to the church is lower than ever. Even so, this figure might be even lower if large numbers of foreign immigrants had not settled in Amsterdam after the war. These immigrants often still feel connected to their church or mosque and this has dramatically changed the religious landscape. The growth of Islam is the most striking phenomenon. Today, 13% of Amsterdammers are Muslims, making Islam the third largest group in the city, after the non-religious and all the Christian denominations together. Interestingly, the percentage of Muslims has hardly grown since 2000.

The Westerkerk
Amsterdam's most famous church owes its existence to the city's rapid growth in the 17th century. The old, originally Catholic, churches could not handle the flow of worshippers and a number of new church buildings, specially intended for Protestant worship, were built within a short space of time. Despite declining church attendance in Amsterdam, the 'Wester', designed by Hendrick de Keyser, is still in use as a church.

Diversity

Religion is certainly not rare in today's Amsterdam and this is mainly due to immigration from outside Europe. The immense individual freedom of choice to believe, not believe or to be sceptical is characteristic of the city. Needless to say, Amsterdam is not alone in this – it is true of the Netherlands as a whole. However, the city's scale has enabled smaller religious communities such as the Sikhs or the Syrian Orthodox Christians to build their own temples and houses of prayer here.
The presence of so many different religious facilities within one single city makes Amsterdam unique in the Netherlands.

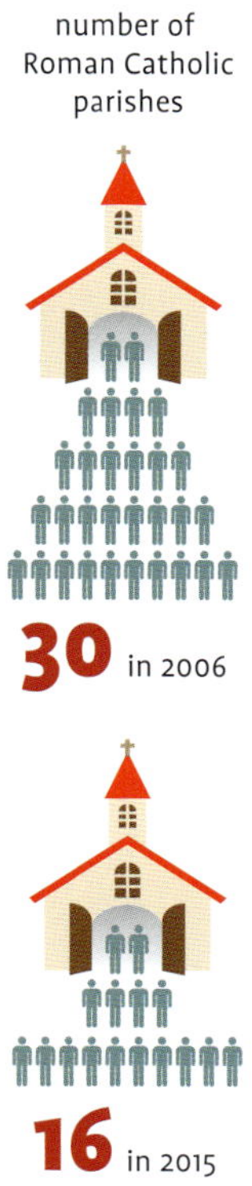

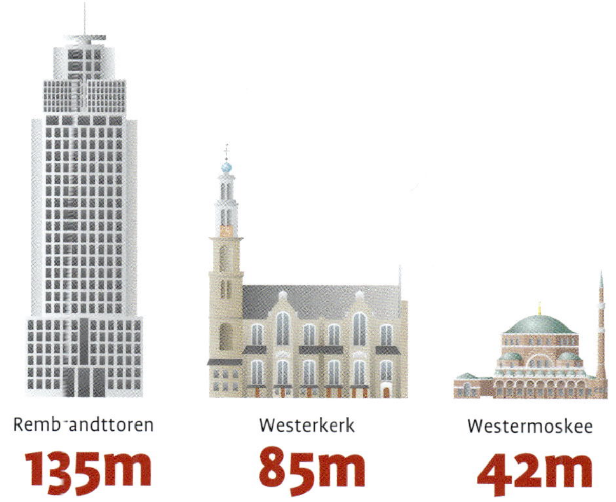

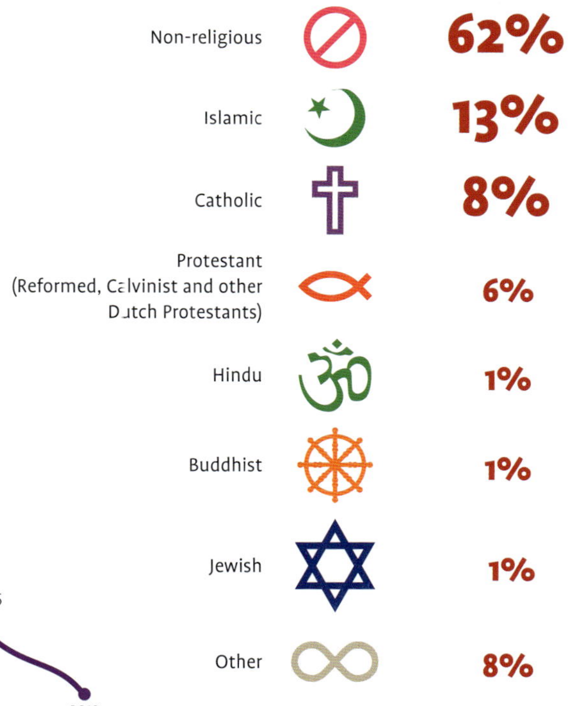

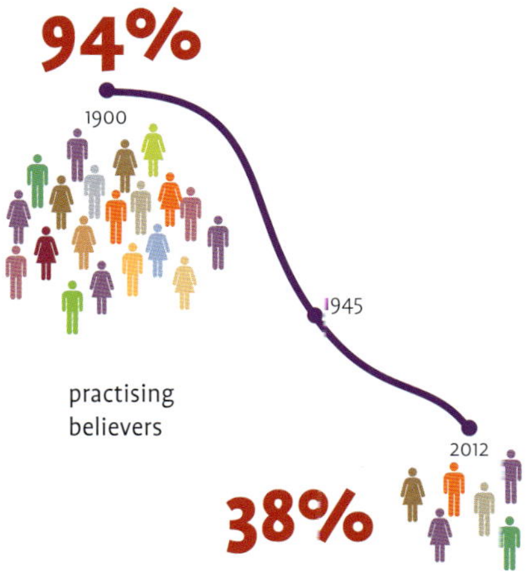

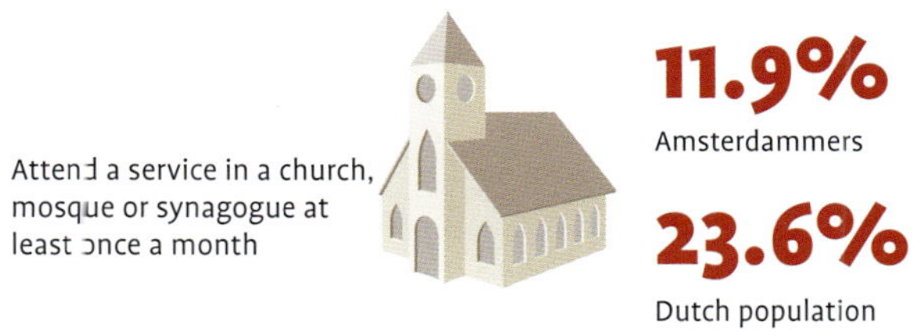

Sources: OIS, Research, Information and Statistics, City of Amsterdam / Statistics Netherlands

© Noordhoff Uitgevers

Protestants

The Protestant church is going through a difficult period in Amsterdam. For three centuries, the Protestant faith and its pastors played a leading role in the city. However, the number of members started to decrease from 1900 onwards, very gradually at first, but after the war it seemed as though the Dutch Reformed Church in particular had fallen into rapid decline.
Today, only 6% of Amsterdammers feel connected to the Protestant Church in the Netherlands (the collaborative alliance between the Dutch Reformed Church, the Reformed Churches in the Netherlands and the Evangelical Lutheran Church). The city has lost its Protestant character, which is particularly noticeable on Sundays. Gone are the numerous families wearing their Sunday best and carrying a Bible under one arm who went to church to listen to the pastor, pray and sing psalms. The Sunday has also lost its traditional function as a day of rest.

❶ Traditional Protestant churches

❷ Reformed Churches in the Netherlands up to 1795

Source: *OIS, Research, Information and Statistics, City of Amsterdam (1)*

© Noordhoff Uitgevers

❸ Noorderkerk

❶ Protestants and splinter congregations
In 2004, the leading Calvinist and Lutheran churches merged to form the Protestant Church in the Netherlands. The Amsterdam section currently has 26 churches. There are still also some churches of reformed splinter congregations that have not joined the Protestant Church in the Netherlands, but their membership is very limited.

❷ New churches
Amsterdam's Protestants initially used existing (Catholic) church buildings, but rapid population growth in the 17th century led to the construction of several new churches especially for Protestant worship – the Zuiderkerk (1611), the Noorderkerk (1623), the Westerkerk (1631), the Eilandskerk on Bickerseiland (1659), the wooden Amstelkerk (1670) and last but not least the Oosterkerk (1671).

❸ Central pulpit
The Noorderkerk is the first church in Amsterdam that was built specifically for Protestant worship. During a Protestant service, the emphasis lies on the Word of God. The Noorderkerk was built in the shape of a Greek cross (with two arms of equal length), allowing the congregation to clearly see and hear the pastor from all positions.

❹ Living in style
The leading role once played by Protestantism can still be seen in the distribution of today's Protestant residents across Amsterdam. The neighbourhoods with the highest percentage of Protestants are the old city centre and the prosperous Zuid district.

❺ High-profile pastors
Many streets and buildings in Amsterdam are named after pastors, which illustrates their importance for the city. Some pastors were also extremely influential at national level, the most famous being Abraham Kuyper, who founded the country's first political party and held the office of Prime Minister for four years.

❹ Protestant Church in Amsterdam

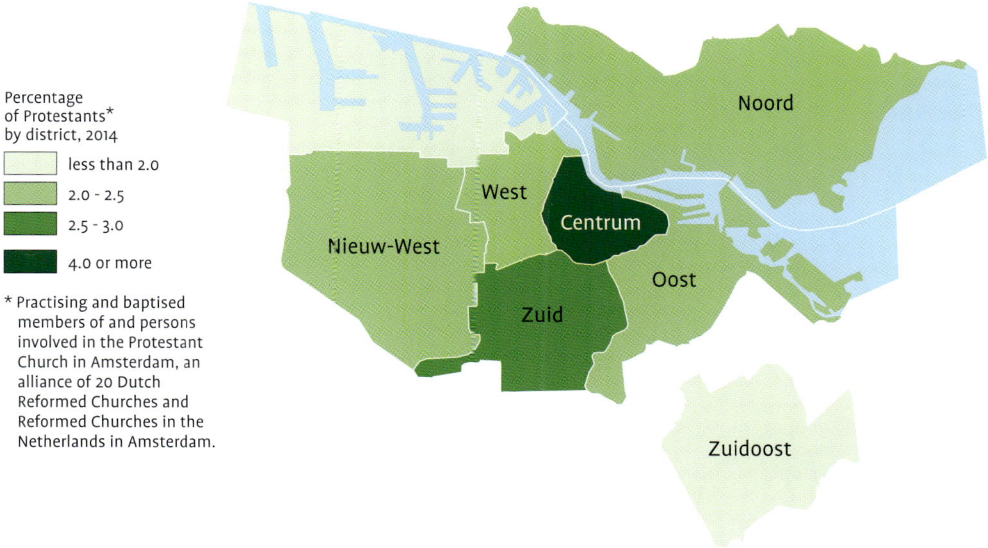

❺ Well-known Amsterdam pastors

Petrus Plancius	(1550-1622)	Opposed Arminius and his followers, the remonstrants.
Jacobus Arminius	(approx. 1559-1609)	Rejected predestination and emphasised human free will.
Caspar van Baerle	(1584-1648)	Professor of Philosophy at the Athenaeum Illustre.
Gerard Brandt	(1626-1685)	Biographer of Michiel de Ruyter and others.
Bernard ter Haar	(1806-1880)	Fiercely opposed the Catholic emancipation.
Jan de Liefde	(1814-1869)	Founder of 'Tot Heil des Volks'.
Jan ten Kate	(1819-1889)	Nicknamed the pastor-poet.
Allard Pierson	(1831-1896)	First Professor of Art History.
Abraham Kuyper	(1837-1920)	Reformed Church leader. Founder of the VU University and the Anti Revolutionary Party (ARP).
Johannes Geelkerken	(1879-1960)	Nicknamed the 'snake pastor'. Founder of the 'Gereformeerde Kerken in Hersteld Verband'.
Jan Buskes	(1899-1980)	Nicknamed the Red pastor. Very socially engaged.
Jacobus Overduin	(1902-1983)	Advocated a more human approach to the Christian faith within the reformed community.
Jan Koopmans	(1905-1945)	Openly protested against the treatment of the Jews during the war.
Nico ter Linden	(1936-...)	Author of the series *Het verhaal gaat*.
Abeltje Hoogenkamp	(1969-...)	City preacher and creator of the *De Preek van de Leek* project.

Sources: Protestantse Kerk Amsterdam (4); Photos: © Wolverlei/Martin Stevens (35)

© Noordhoff Uitgevers

Catholics

The Onze Lieve Vrouw van de Allerheiligste Rozenkrans, better known as the Obrechtkerk, is only completely full on one day in the year – Christmas Eve. During the rest of the year, the officiating priest largely sees rows of empty pews and his fellow priests elsewhere in the city experience the same lack of attendance. Just like traditional Protestantism, Catholicism finds itself in a crisis situation. The number of parishioners is decreasing each year and fewer and fewer people come to the church to celebrate mass together with the pastor or chaplain and receive communion. The Catholic faith is also increasingly disappearing from the public domain. We no longer see processions on Palm Sunday and other occasions, rows of young girls dressed like brides having received their first communion, mass spectacles and other public rituals. Only the Silent Procession still attracts thousands of participants, but it is no longer exclusively Catholic. Anybody can join in and the themes discussed have an ecumenical nature.

❶ Catholic churches and parishes

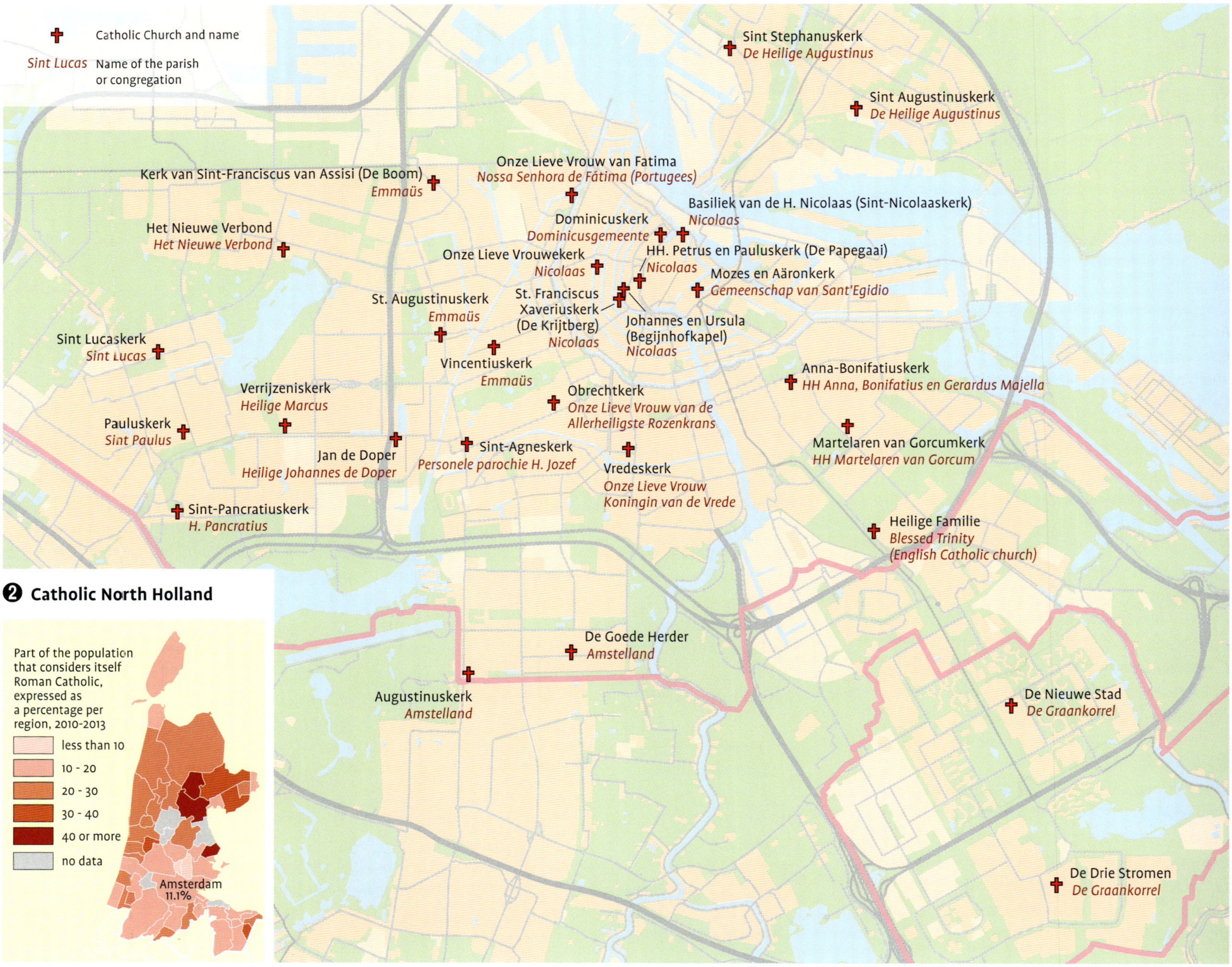

Sources: OIS, Research, Information and Statistics, City of Amsterdam (1); Statistics Netherlands (2)

© Noordhoff Uitgevers

❸ Silent Procession

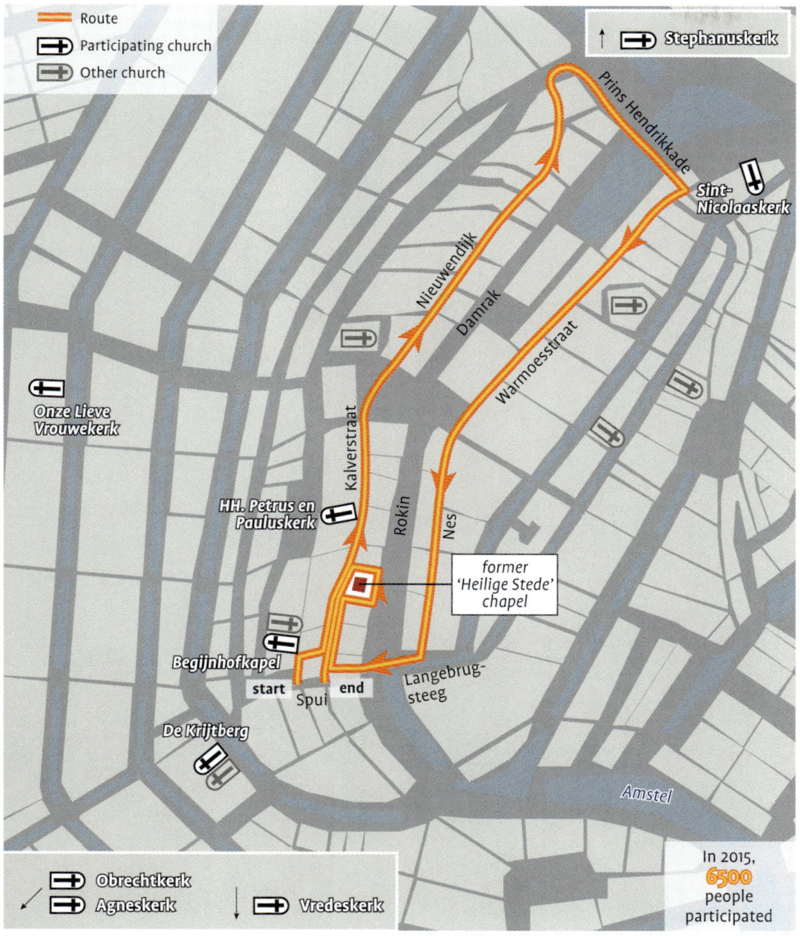

❹ Well-known Amsterdam Catholics

Joseph Alberdingk Thijm	(1810-1889)	Leader of the Emancipation of Catholic Amsterdam.
Jonkheer H.C.J.M. van Nispen tot Sevenaer	(1836-1897)	Co-founder of the 'Sint Josef Jonge Gezellenvereniging' and the Van Nispenhuis.
Lambertus Perquin	(1865-1938)	Pastor of the Dominicuskerk and founder of the KRO.
Johannes Huibers	(1875-1969)	Bishop of Haarlem 1935-1960.
Anne van Sonsbeeck	(1888-1953)	Mother Superior of Onze Lieve Vrouwe Gasthuis.
Martinus Jansen	(1905-1983)	First Bishop of Rotterdam.
Ida Peerdeman	(1905-1996)	Devout woman from Uiterwaardenstraat to whom Mary Mother of Jesus appeared on 56 occasions. Her followers gather in the Thomas van Aquinokerk on Rijnstraat.
Theodorus Zwartkruis	(1909-1983)	Bishop of Haarlem (1966-1983).
Bertus Aafjes	(1914-1993)	Author of several publications including *Voetreis naar Rome.*
Jan van Kilsdonk	(1917-2008)	Jesuit, teacher of religious studies at the Ignatius college and students' pastor.
Huub Oosterhuis	(1933-...)	Ex-Jesuit, critical believer and liturgical innovator.
Antoine Bodar	(1944-...)	Pastor in the Krijtberg (1992-1995), art historian, media personality.
Brenninkmeijer family		Important champions of the Catholic cause.

❶ Parishes
Amsterdam has sixteen parishes, but there were more until recently. The decreasing number of churchgoers has led to the dissolution or merger of parishes, such as Sint-Anna, Sint-Bonifatius and Gerardus Majella in the Oost district.

❷ Significant differences
Amsterdam is governed by the Haarlem-Amsterdam diocese, which comprises the entire province of North Holland and Almere and Zeewolde. People who consider themselves Catholic are widely spread out across the country. Most areas around Amsterdam are not more than 20% Catholic, but the figures are much higher in West-Friesland.

❸ Silent commemoration
Every March, thousands of Catholics from all over the country gather in the Begijnhof in the dead of night. They form ranks and walk in deep silence through the mediaeval city centre to commemorate the miracle of the sacramental bread which took place on Kalverstraat in 1345

❹ Roman Catholic figureheads
In 1798, the Catholics were granted freedom of religion after it had been denied to them for more than two centuries. They faced the challenge of emancipation and becoming a fully-fledged community. A number of Amsterdam's leading Catholics played a major role in this process. Catholic Amsterdammers have also figured prominently in the modernisation of Catholicism since the 1960s – Huub Oosterhuis and Jan van Kilsdonk provided their support, while the Brenninkmeijers and Antoine Bodar were – and still are – critical.

❺ The altar
For Amsterdam's Catholics, the inauguration of the Sint-Nicolaaskerk on Prins Hendrikkade (1887) was a major step forward in the emancipation process. As in every Catholic church, the high altar is positioned centrally in the choir. The priest celebrated holy mass here with his back to the congregation. Today, a simple altar stands in front of this high altar and the priest celebrates mass facing the congregation.

❺ Sint-Nicolaaskerk

Sources: *Gezelschap van de Stille Omgang (3); Photos: © National Beeldbank Amsterdam (4); © Wolverlei / Martin Stevens (5)*

© Noordhoff Uitgevers

Oude Kerk

The Oude Kerk is the oldest building in Amsterdam still in existence. In 1306, the Bishop of Utrecht dedicated the church to St Nicholas, patron saint of sailors and tradesmen. After the Alteration (transition to Protestantism), the church was no longer allowed to bear the name of a Roman Catholic saint, so the name was changed to Oude Kerk.

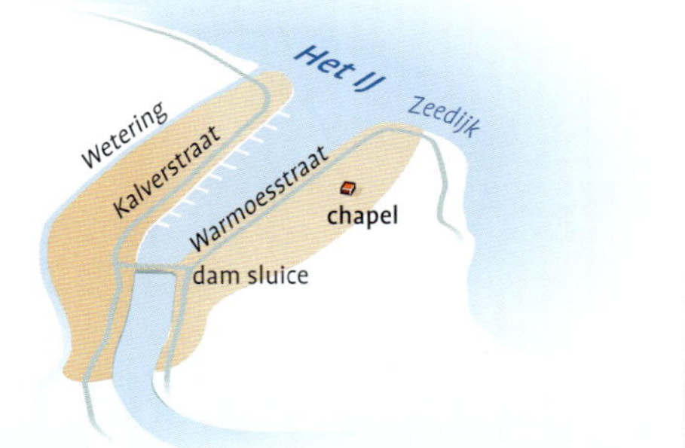

The settlement at the mouth of the river Amstel was still very small in the 13th century. The residents had a cemetery with a wooden chapel. A stone church was built on that spot around 1300.

Around 1370: choir replaced with a closed pentagonal choir.

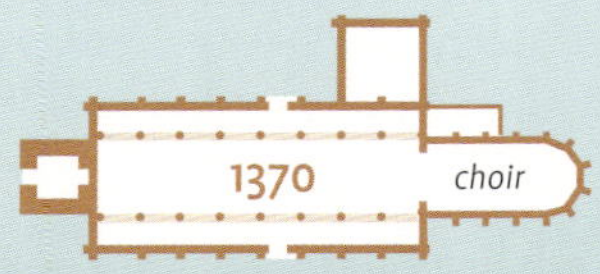

1390: two aisles completed: the church given the form of a hall church with a wooden barrel vault.

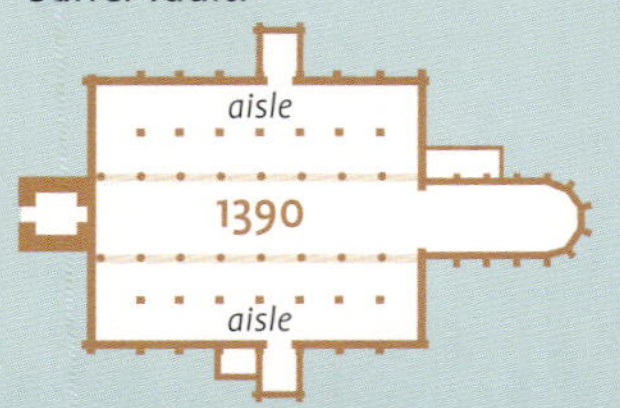

Around 1450: aisles around the choir extended.

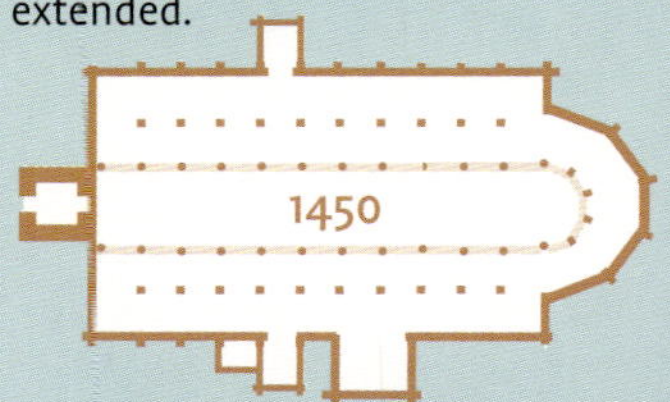

1480-1570: chapels and portals constructed. Height of the nave increased, transverse structure with clerestory and height of the choir increased. Height of the tower increased and new spire added.

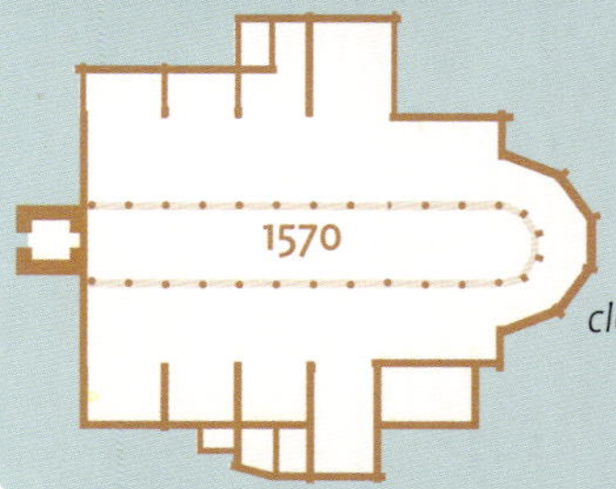

New churches were built in the city and the plans for increasing the height of the transepts were never implemented. In 1951, the church closed as it was in danger of collapse. The church was subsequently restored and is now used as a church and historic venue for contemporary culture.

Tower
This spire was installed in 1565. Due to the weak supporting surface, the spire was made of wood clad with lead.

In 1738, a new exterior wall was erected around the tower to mask its slant. The old tower is still present inside.

Main organ (1724)
54-note organ made by Christian Vater and Johann Müller, dating back to 1724. The organ is undergoing restoration and will be played again in 2017.

Baptistery with stone vault dating back to 1462. Converted into a burial chapel for Mayor Cornelis de Graeff in 1648.

Churchwarden's room (1611)
This is where the church council met and the collection money was placed in the safe here for safekeeping.

IJzeren Kapel
The city's important documents were stored here.

Entrance via the **Dodenpoortje** or Gate of the Dead (southern portal dating back to the early 16th century).

Sources: Oude Kerk / Mauritshuis / Rijksmuseum Amsterdam; Photos: © Rijksmuseum Amsterdam

Vault paintings
In 1956, the coat of black paint that had been applied after the Beeldenstorm was removed from the vaulted wooden ceiling. To everyone's surprise, paintings were discovered underneath.

(Etch: Reinier Vinkeles)

Beeldenstorm
We can still clearly see where the effigies of the apostles were forcibly removed from the pillars in the choir 450 years ago. A few sculptures, windows and choir stalls are all that remain of the original fixtures and fittings following the Beeldenstorm and the Alteration in 1578.

Service in the Oude Kerk around 1650
(Emanuel de Witte)

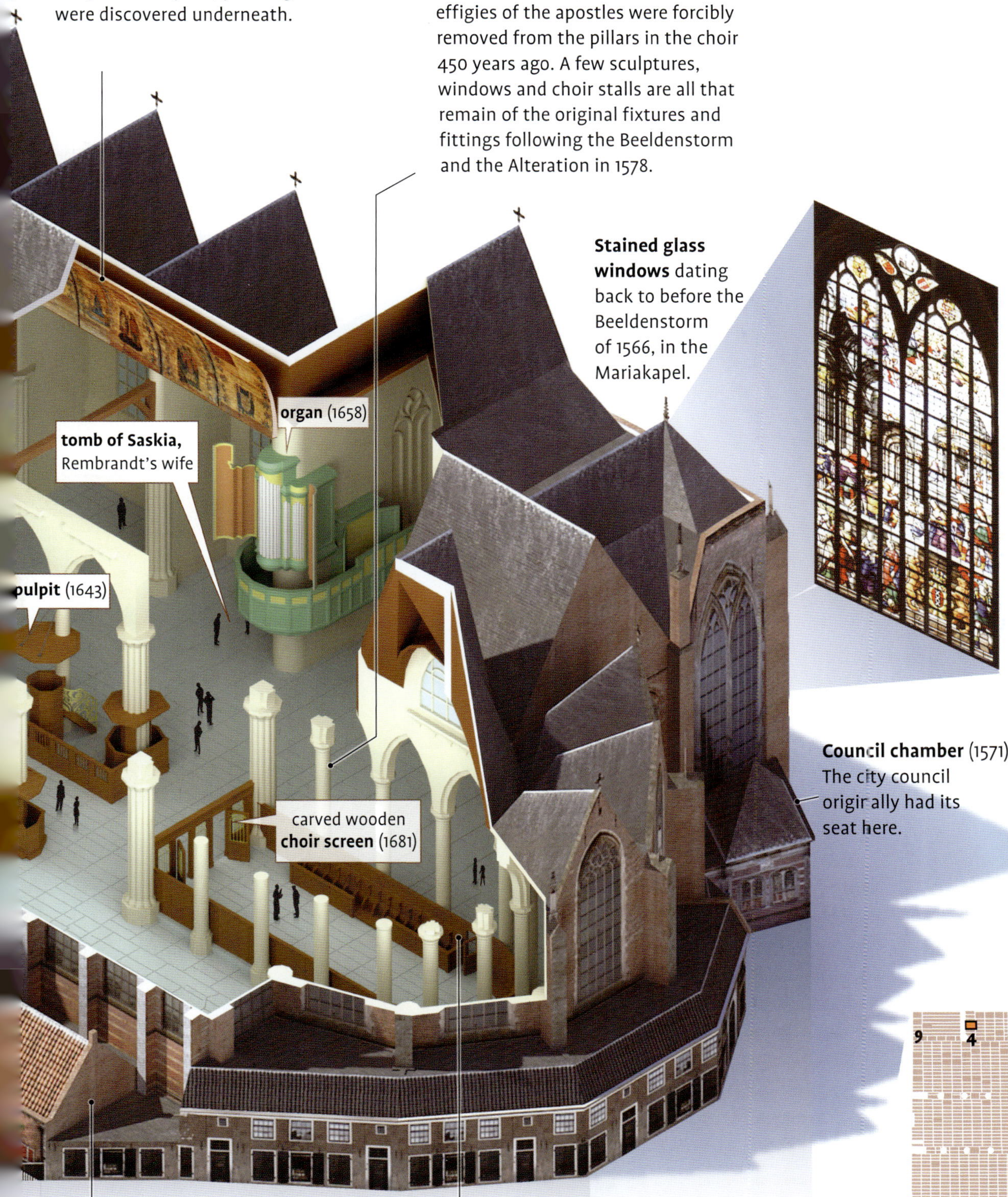

Stained glass windows dating back to before the Beeldenstorm of 1566, in the Mariakapel.

Council chamber (1571)
The city council originally had its seat here.

The **sacristy** where vestments for the services were kept. Now an area for serving coffee.

Two rows of old **choir stalls** (around 1480).

Tombs
Until 1866, people could be buried in the church. The floor consists of around **2500 gravestones.**

Famous people buried there:

1. Jan Pietersz. Sweelinck (1562-1621), composer
2. Saskia van Uylenburgh (1612-1642), wife of Rembrandt
3. Jan van der Heyden (1637-1712), painter/ inventor
4. Caspar Commelin (1668-1731), botanist
5. Daniël Raap (1702-1754), champion of political rights

Still not localised: Frans Banning Cocq (1605-1655), main character on *The Night Watch*

Funeral monuments for naval heroes:

6. Jacob van Heemskerck (1567-1607)
7. Abraham van der Hulst (1619-1666)
8. Isaäc Sweers (1622-1673)
9. Willem van der Zaan (1621-1669)
10. Cornelis Janszoon de Haan (1580-1633)

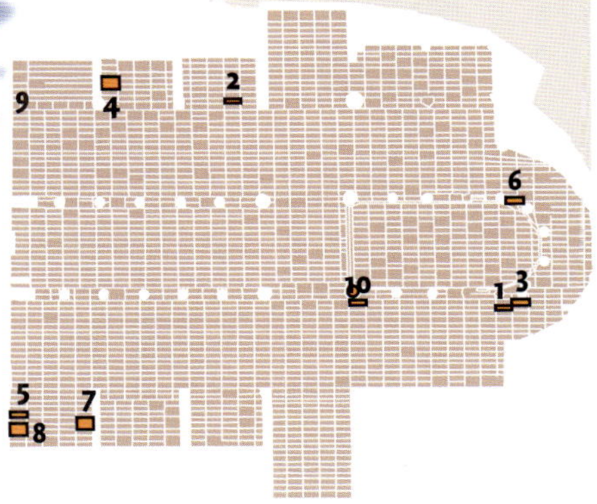

© Noordhoff Uitgevers

Jewish Amsterdam

Anybody who wants to get a taste of Jewish Amsterdam today has to search long and hard. The Jewish community had a prominent presence for centuries, but the German occupiers brought that situation to an abrupt end.
In 1940, Amsterdam had the largest concentration of Jews in the Netherlands, with around 80,000 Jewish residents (both religious and not religious). This was roughly 10% of the total population, so the city had a noticeably Jewish tint and Amsterdammers adopted many Jewish and Hebrew words and expressions.

After the war, the survivors in Mokum (Hebrew for 'place' or 'city') built a new life for themselves in Zuid, Buitenveldert and Amstelveen. A small proportion of them are practising Jews. The Dutch-Israelite Congregation has the most members, followed at a distance by the Liberal Jewish Community, the Portuguese-Israelite Congregation and some smaller religious communities. They each have their own synagogue and cemetery. The oldest Jewish cemetery is the Portuguese-Israelite Beth Haim in Ouderkerk aan de Amstel.

❶ Buitenveldert
Nearly all Amsterdam Jews feel and call themselves Jewish. However, only about 15% are members of a Jewish congregation, so most Jews rarely visit a synagogue or kosher restaurant, if at all, and do not use Jewish schools or health-care facilities. Practising Jews are usually members of the orthodox Dutch-Israelite main synagogue. Most Jews live in Buitenveldert and Amstelveen and Kastelenstraat is the main place where they go shopping on Fridays, before the start of the Sabbath.

❷ Spread over the Netherlands
Around 140,000 Jews lived in the Netherlands in 1940, but the current number is unknown. Estimates vary between 40,000 and 55,000, with most of them living in The Hague, Rotterdam, Amsterdam and Amstelveen.

❷ Jews in the Netherlands

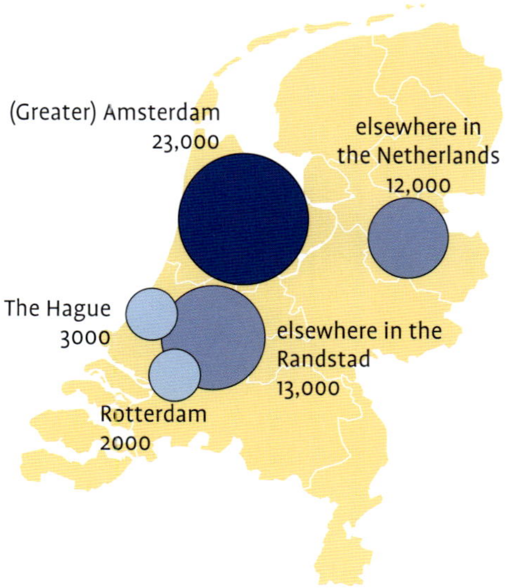

❶ Jewish institutions

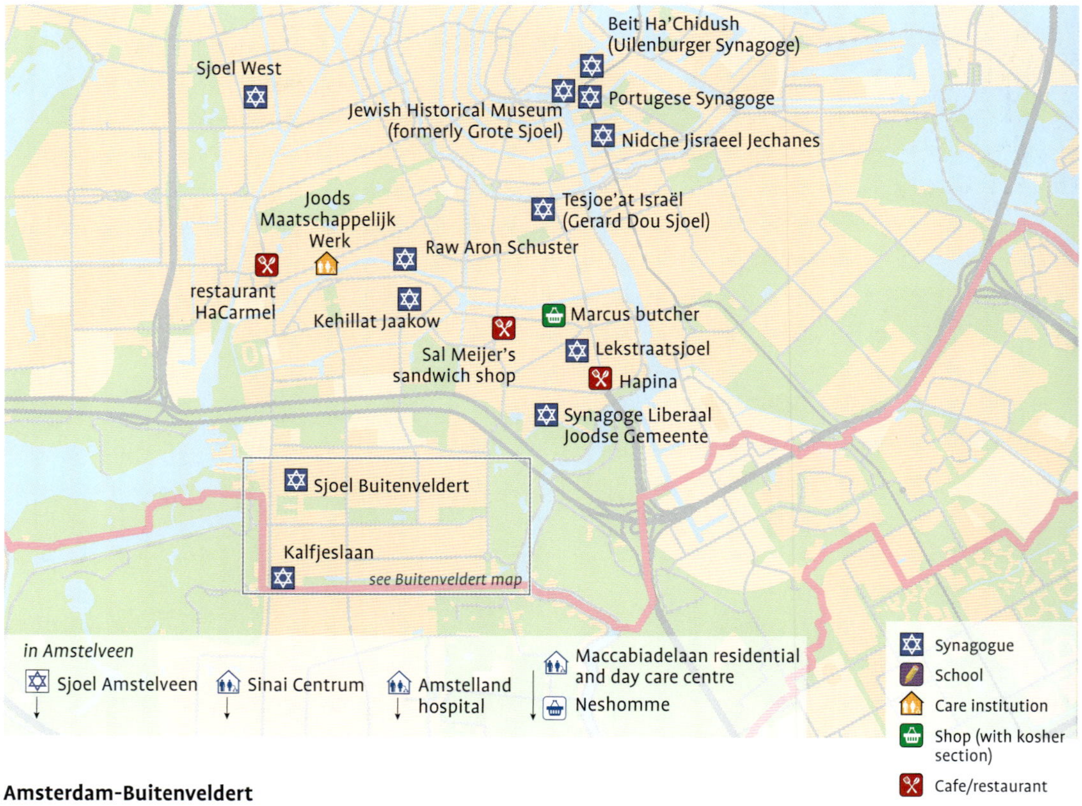

Amsterdam-Buitenveldert

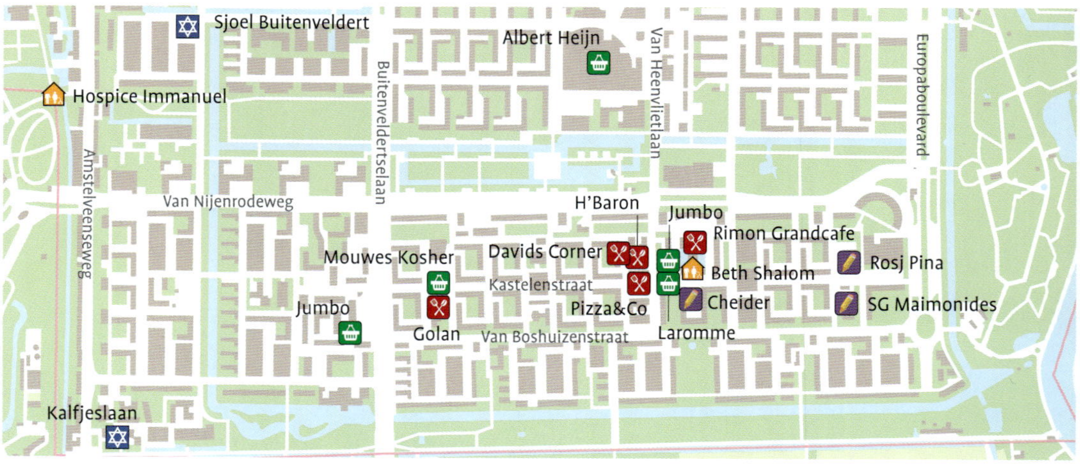

Sources: *OIS, Research, Information and Statistics, City of Amsterdam (1); Joods Maatschappelijk Werk (2)*

© Noordhoff Uitgevers

❸ Portuguese synagogue

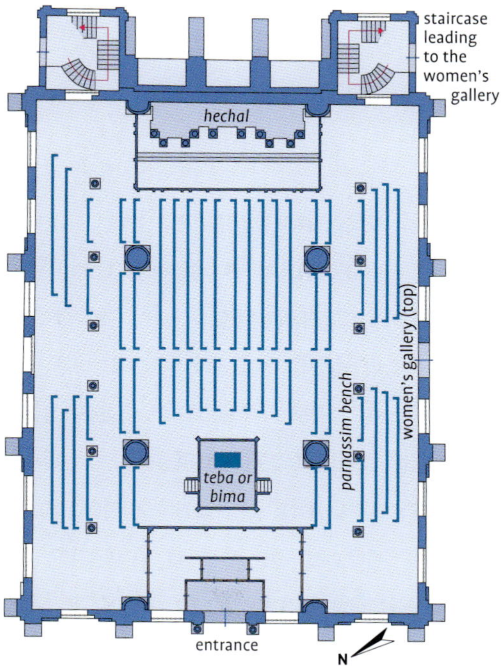

hechal = cabinet containing Torah scrolls
parnassim = administrative council
teba or bima = raised platform with a lectern for the Torah

❹ Amsterdam words derived from Yiddish or Hebrew

❸ Impressively present

In the 16th century, many Spanish and Portuguese Jews made their way to Amsterdam and their descendants inaugurated their own synagogue in 1675. The impressive building (36 x 28 x 19.5 metres) on today's Jonas Daniël Meijerplein attempted to replicate Solomon's Temple in Jerusalem.
It has hardly changed since 1675 and there is no heating and no electricity. The most important part is the 'hechal', where the rolls containing the Torah (the first five books of the Jewish Bible) are kept.

❹ Hebrew and Yiddish

There are two groups of Jews in the Netherlands – Sephardi Jews and Ashkenazi Jews. The former were once driven out of Spain and Portugal, while the latter (by far the majority) came from Germany and Central Europe. The Ashkenazi Jews spoke Yiddish, a mixture of German and Hebrew. In the 19th century, Yiddish gradually disappeared from the synagogues, but many Yiddish words have been preserved and adopted by Amsterdammers.

❺ House of Life

Beth Haim (House of Life) was created by the Portuguese-Israelite community in 1614 and is the oldest Jewish cemetery still in use in Europe.

❺ Jewish Beth Haim cemetery, Ouderkerk aan de Amstel

Sources: E. van Voolen & P. Meijer, Synagogen van Nederland (3); www.mokums.nl (4); Donkergroen Ontwerp & Advies (5)

© Noordhoff Uitgevers

Persecution of the Jews

In 1950, the Memorial of Jewish Gratitude was unveiled on Weesperstraat. Its inscription translates as "1940-1945. To the protectors of the Dutch Jews during the occupation".

The memorial was a gift from Jewish survivors to all Amsterdammers who had helped Jews during the war. However, not all members of the Jewish community welcomed this initiative.
The deportation of the Jews started during the night of 14/15 July 1942 – the first train to Westerbork left Amsterdam Centraal Station at 2.16am. Many dozens more trains carrying Jews would leave Centraal Station and Muiderpoort station after that date. On 9 September 1943, the Germans declared Amsterdam judenfrei. All that time, the tram company had made equipment available – in return for payment – and the Amsterdam police force had acted to control any unrest during the deportations. After the liberation, the Jews who had gone into hiding and those who had survived the camps found that very little was left of the Jodenbuurt. Elsewhere in the city, complete strangers had taken possession of their homes, so it is understandable that the Weesperstraat memorial evoked and continues to evoke mixed feelings.

❶ Distribution of Jews in May 1941

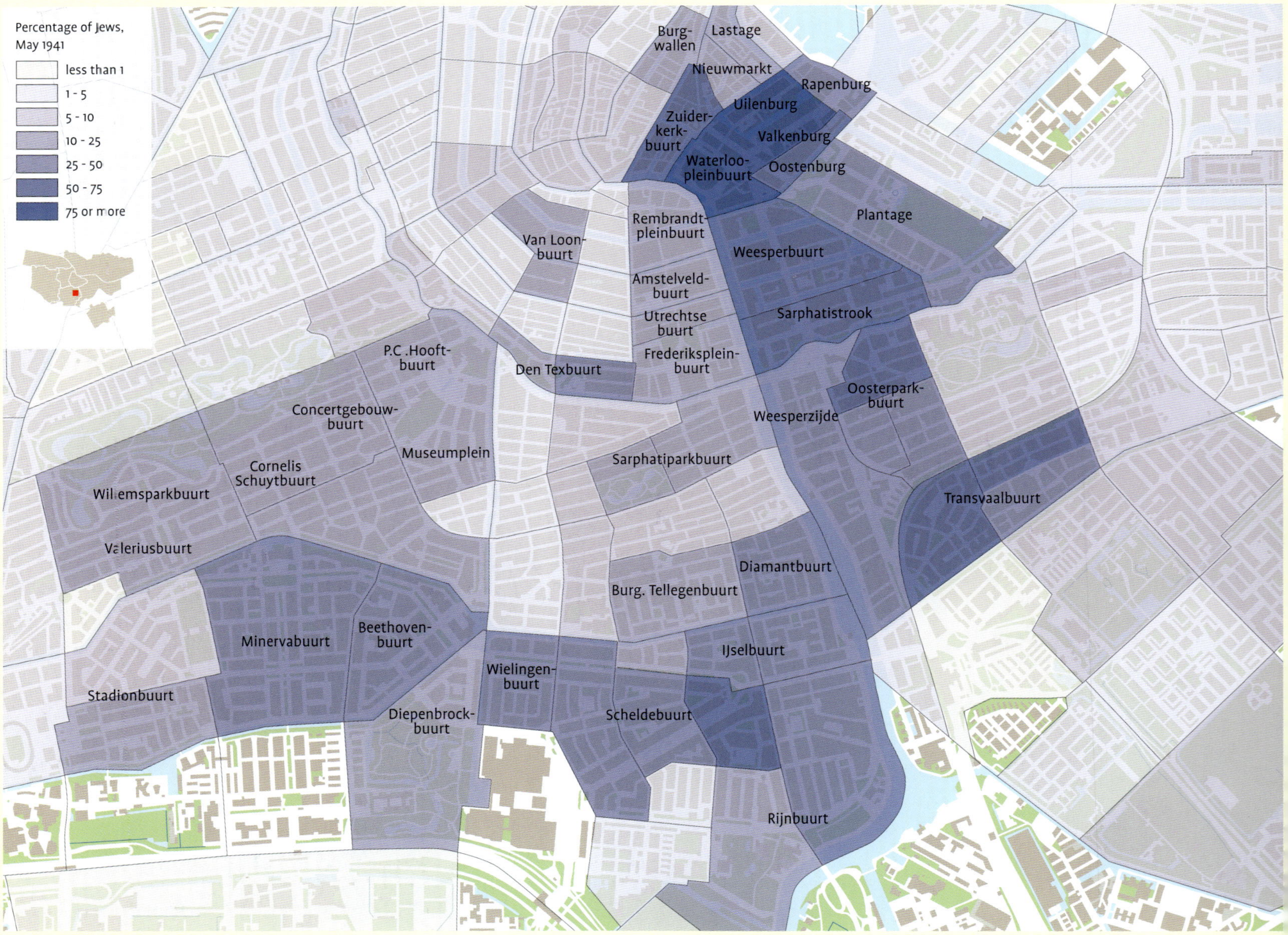

Source: *Grote Atlas van Nederland 1930-1950* (1)

© Noordhoff Uitgevers

❶ - ❷ Ten Jews per dot

In May 1941, civil registry officials drew a map of the number of Jewish residents per residential block for the German occupiers. One dot represented ten Jews and there were nearly 8000 dots on the map in total. The Germans used this map during their raids and deportation exercises, which mainly focused on the Jodenbuurt, Oost and the Rivierenbuurt.

❸ No Jewish ghetto

In 1941, the Germans wanted to turn the old Jodenbuurt into a ghetto to make 'moving' the Jews easier. This led to so much opposition that they contented themselves with putting up 'Jewish district' signs around the old Jodenbuurt. In retrospect, a ghetto turned out to be unnecessary, since the authorities in Amsterdam and the Jewish Council gave their full cooperation to the deportations. The Jewish Council was set up by the German occupying forces with the intention of having anti-Jewish measures implemented by the Jews themselves wherever possible. It was disbanded at the end of 1943 following the arrest of the last Jews in Amsterdam who had not gone into hiding.

❹ A wealthy street

Like the rest of Dutch society, the pre-war Jewish community was a class society. Impoverished Jews lived in the Jodenbuurt, the less well-off in the Transvaalbuurt, Oosterparkbuurt and Rivierenbuurt and the wealthy Jews in the Plantage and on distinguished streets such as Den Texstraat. In 1940, at least half of the residents of Plantage Middenlaan were of Jewish origin. Their favourite meeting place was the Hollandsche Schouwburg theatre where many well-known Jewish artists performed.

❷ Jews in Amsterdam, 1869-1954

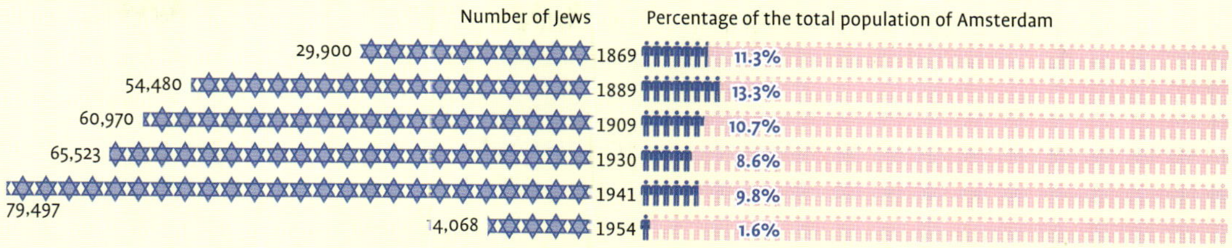

❸ Jodenbuurt in 1942

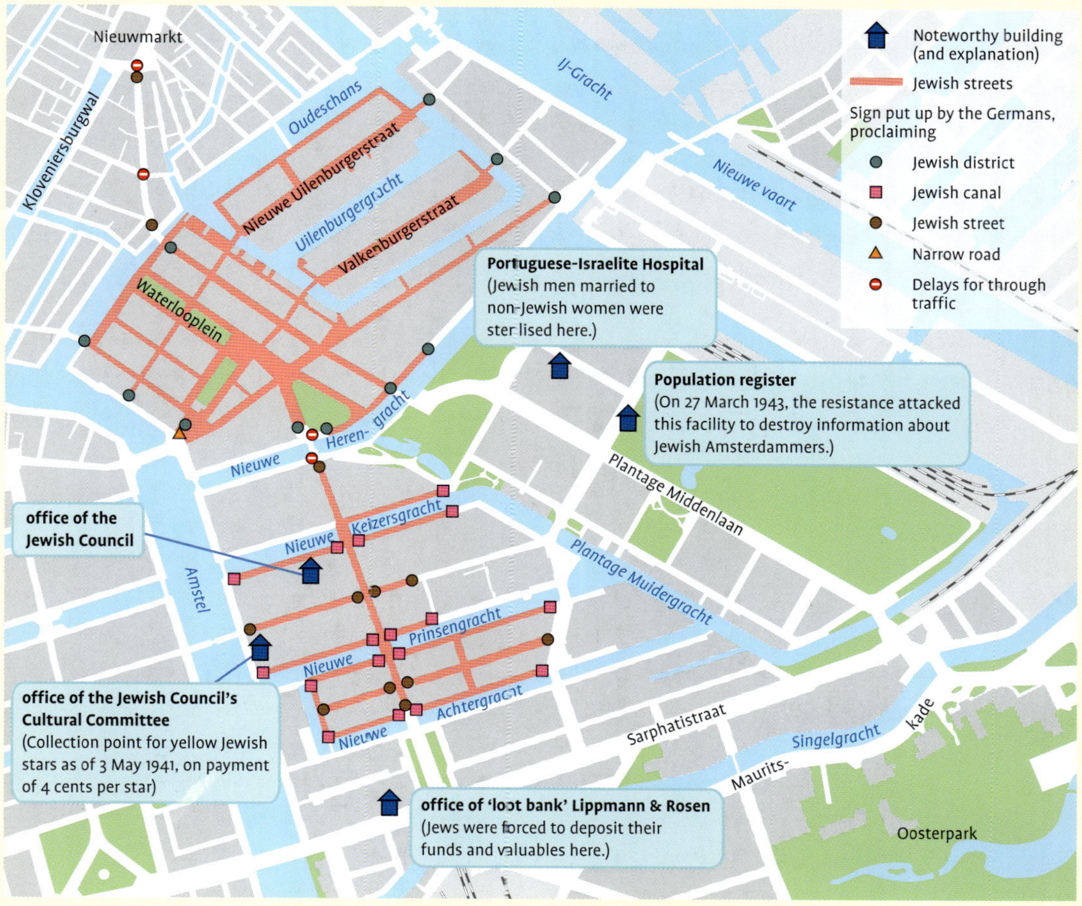

❹ Plantage Middenlaan 1941-1944

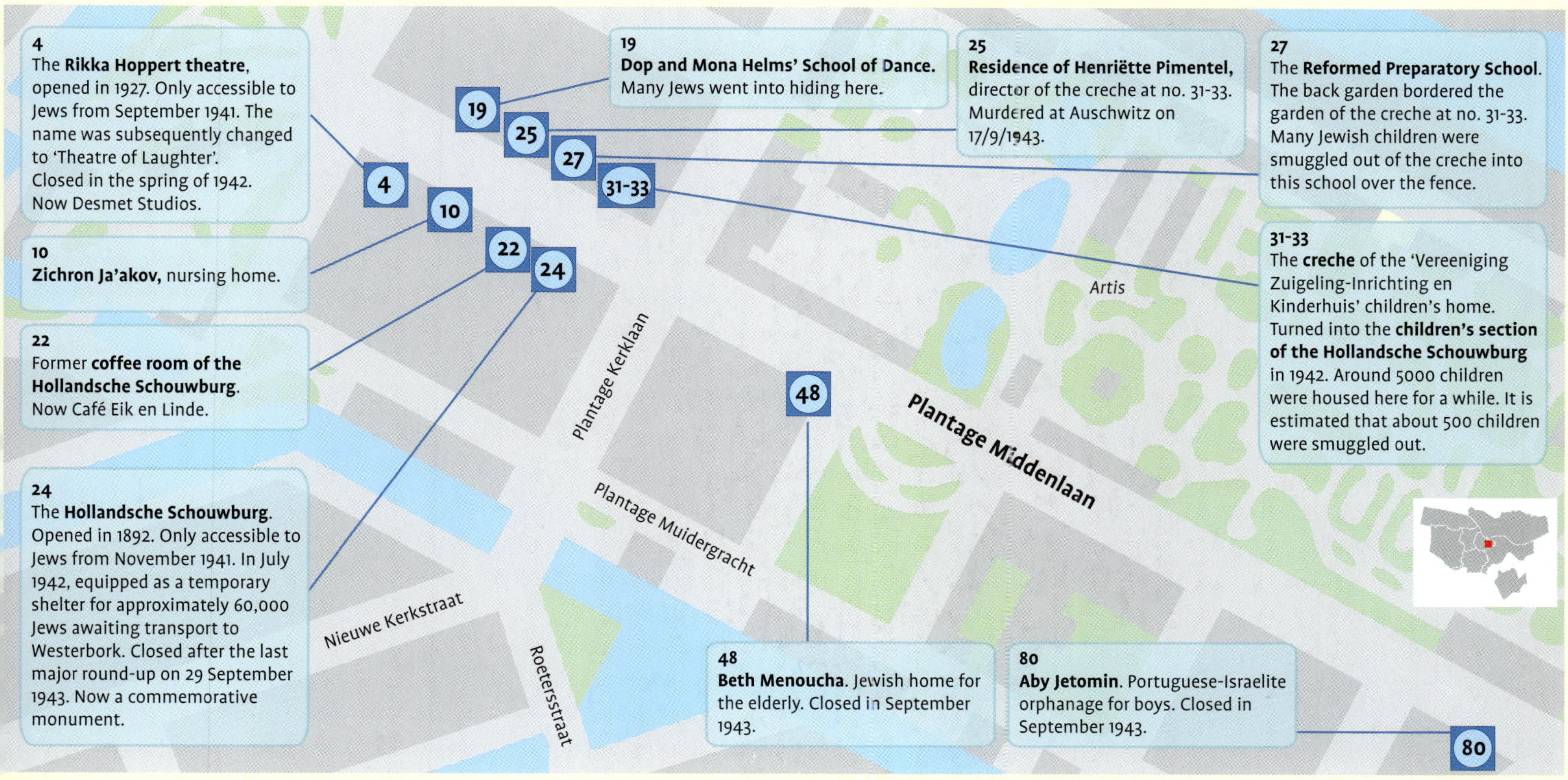

Sources: *J. Blom e.a., Geschiedenis van de joden in Nederland / www.politiekcompendium.nl (2); adapted from: Nederlands Instituut voor Oorlogsdocumentatie (3); www.joodsamsterdam.nl / www.amsterdamhistorie.nl (4)*

© Noordhoff Uitgevers

Secularisation

Surveys show that more than half of Amsterdammers do not consider themselves part of a religious denomination. However, this does not mean that they all live godless or faithless lives. Many of them probably see themselves as atheists or agnostics, but there are also people who are religious at heart and at the same time have consciously distanced themselves from organised church life. Between these two extremes, we find the supporters of what some have called 'ietsism' – the firm belief that 'something' exists between heaven and earth, without being able to describe it exactly in simple terms.

Even though the process of secularisation manifested itself in Amsterdam early on, the city is certainly not the most secularised in the whole country. However, things have certainly changed since the 1950s. Countless churches and care institutions of religious origin have closed and even been demolished. The Catholic and Protestant schools still exist, but when choosing a school, most parents are no longer swayed by its religious background. National test results and the atmosphere are more important. Last but not least, traditional church rituals are disappearing rapidly and those that do still exist (such as marriage) have been stripped of their Christian character.

❶ Demolished and re-purposed churches

Source: *Bisdom van Haarlem, Bisdom Rotterdam and Projectbureau Belvedere, Onderzoek Herbestemming kerken en kerklocaties. Een inventaris vanaf 1970* (1)

© Noordhoff Uitgevers

❷ Care institutions of religious origin

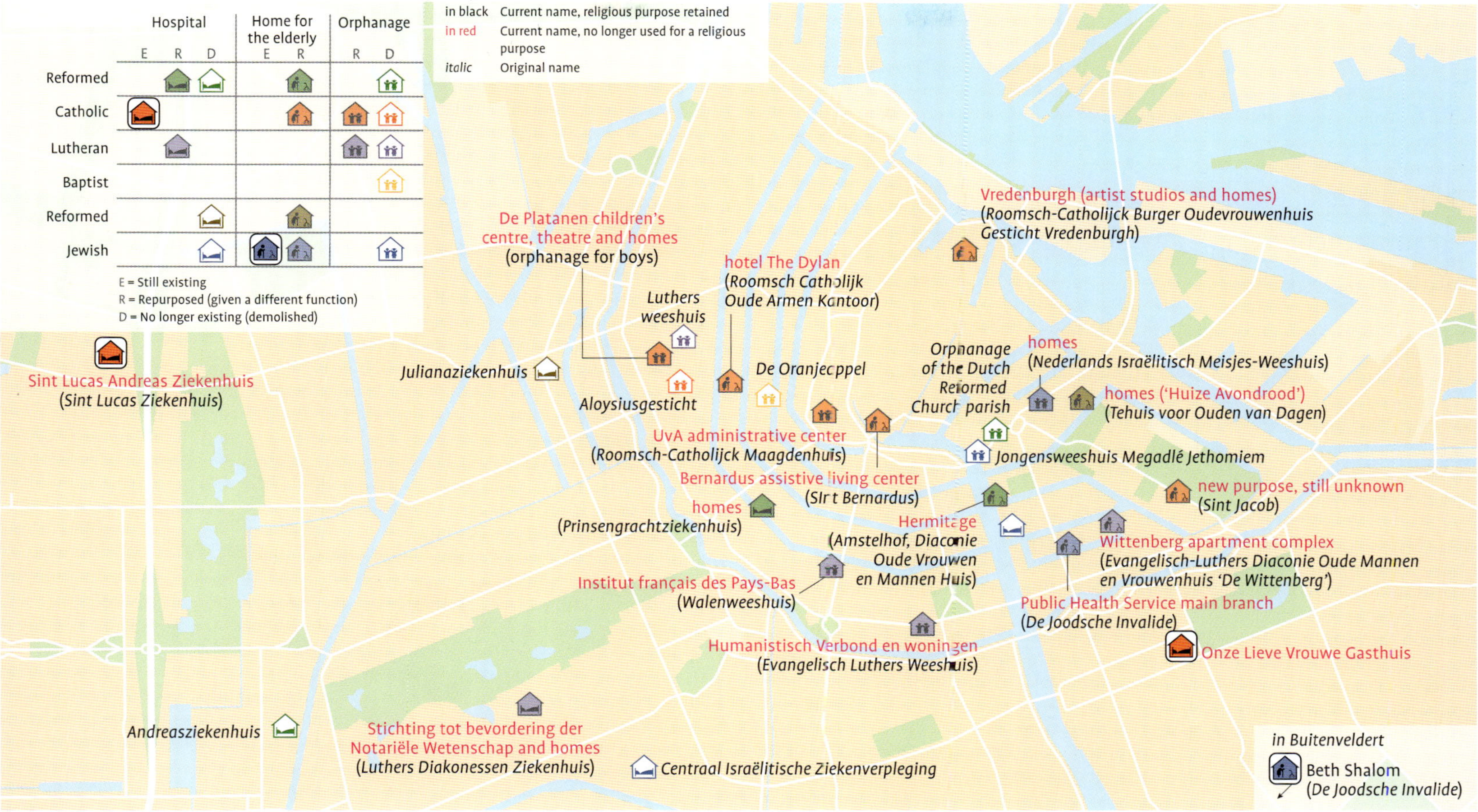

❶ Church closures

Secularisation has led to the closure and demolition of many churches, but Amsterdam takes better care of this cultural heritage nowadays. Most churches that have fallen into disuse are restored and converted for other purposes.

❷ Deaconesses, priests and nuns

In bygone times, it was customary for churches to care for their less fortunate members, so Protestants and Catholics had their own hospitals, homes for the elderly and orphanages. From the 1960s, care facilities for deaconesses, priests and nuns vanished at a rapid rate.

❸ - ❹ Secularisation

Every year, the number of Amsterdammers who consider themselves Catholic or Protestant decreases further. This process, which is called secularisation, does not occur consistently. For example, some areas of North Holland have almost no churchgoers, while other areas have many more.

❺ Sacraments

The Roman Catholic Church practices seven sacraments which are believed to have been instituted by Christ himself: baptism, Eucharist, confirmation, penance, anointing the sick, marriage and priesthood. People who receive these sacraments are supposed to be guaranteed a place in heaven, but many Catholics no longer believe in this, so fewer and fewer sacraments have been administered in recent years.

❸ Religions in Amsterdam

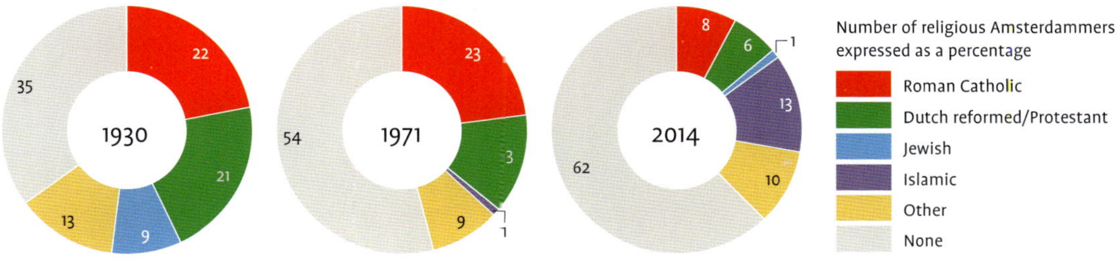

❹ Secularisation in North Holland

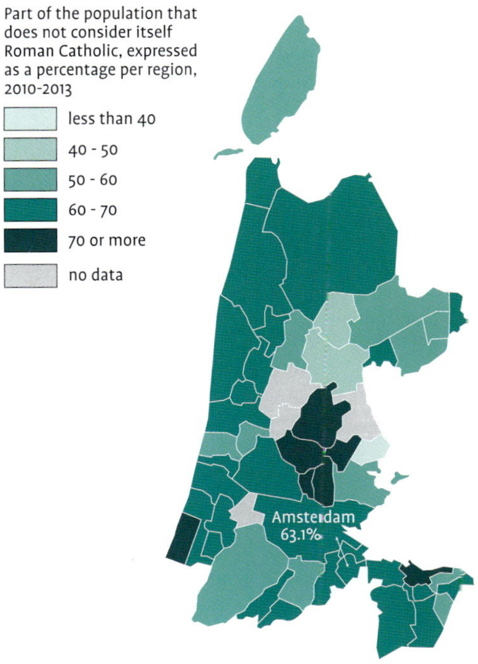

❺ Decline in Catholicism

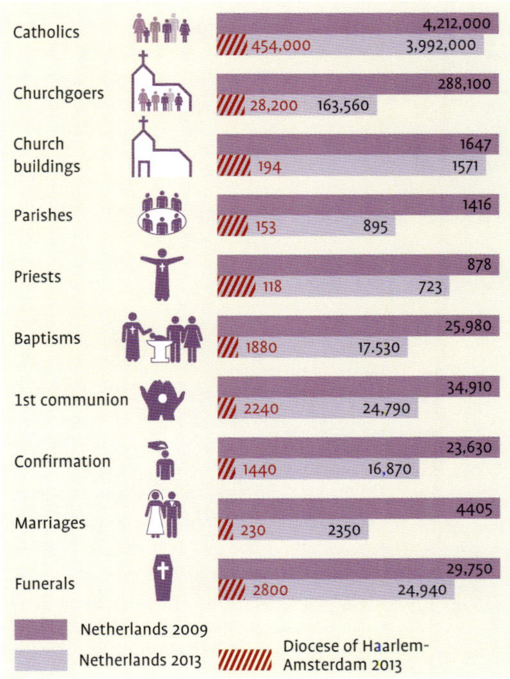

Sources: OIS, Research, Information and Statistics, City of Amsterdam (3); Statistics Netherlands (4); J. Kregting & J. Massaar-Remmerswaal, Kerncifers Rooms-Katholieke Kerk 2013 (5)

© Noordhoff Uitgevers

Muslims

Today, around 13% of Amsterdammers are Muslims. This percentage reflects a tremendous social change that has unfolded in less than 50 years – in 1971, only 1% of Amsterdam's residents were Muslims. The rise of Islam has left its mark all over Amsterdam, but particularly in Oost, West and Nieuw-West, because most Muslims live in those areas. The primitive garage mosques of yesteryear are gradually making way for fully-fledged houses of worship, and there are numerous Islamic schools and shops in Amsterdam. It is unclear whether the group of self-professed Muslims will continue to grow. While a certain degree of secularisation is apparent, many young Muslims are interested in their faith.

❶ Percentage of Muslims

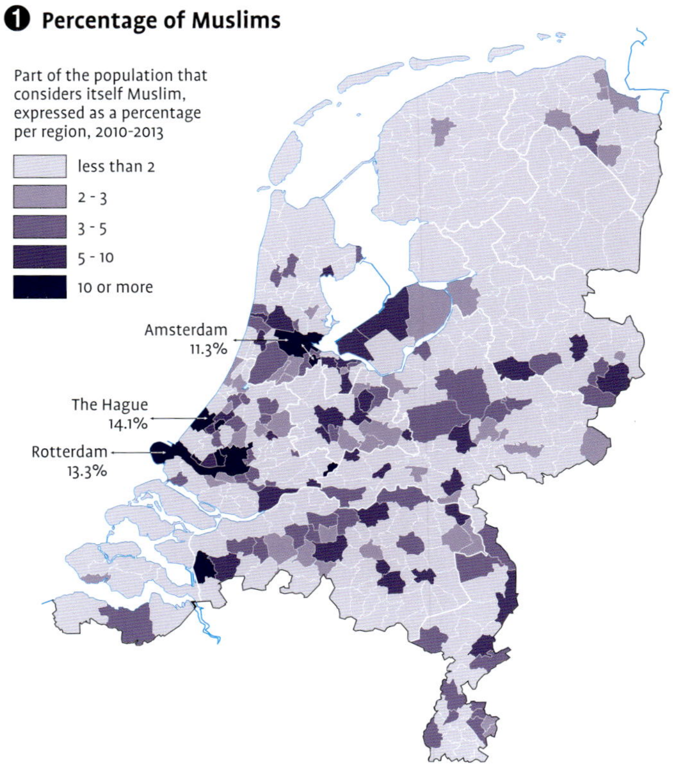

❷ Mosques

Sources: Statistics Netherlands (1); OIS, Research, Information and Statistics, City of Amsterdam (2-3)

© Noordhoff Uitgevers

❶ - ❸ Separate worlds
Most Muslims in the Netherlands live in the major cities in the Randstad area. Although Muslims claim to belong to a single *ummah* (community of all Muslims), there are different religious groups in practice. The main groups are the Sunnis and the Shiites and they disagree on the identity of the true successor of Muhammad. Most of the Turkish and Moroccan Muslims in Amsterdam are Sunni, but because of linguistic and cultural differences, they have their own mosques.

❹ Halal and haram
Like Judaism, Islam is characterised by extensive rules on slaughtering animals and eating meat. Only meat slaughtered in the correct way is *halal* (pure); all other meat is *haram* (impure) and may not be eaten. Amsterdam now has dozens of specialist Islamic butchers to meet the demand for halal meat.

❺ Largest in the Netherlands
Construction of the Turkish Ayasofya Camii mosque or Westermoskee in De Baarsjes remained controversial for nearly 20 years. The building covers a surface area of 800m² and, with room for 1700 worshippers, it is the largest mosque in the Netherlands. It has two entrances – the main entrance for men and a side entrance for women, each with their own private washroom and prayer area.

❻ Practising Muslims
Although most Amsterdammers of Moroccan and Turkish origin consider themselves Muslim, only half of them regularly attend a mosque. It is no longer only older men who do so – in recent years, mosque attendance among the second and third generation has increased. This may be down to the negative image that many native Dutch people have of Muslims (particularly Moroccan Muslims), which causes young people to feel excluded and therefore focus more on their own group. However, these young people may simply have a greater need for finding meaning in their lives, or the mosques may succeed in appealing to young people more effectively.

❻ Mosque attendance

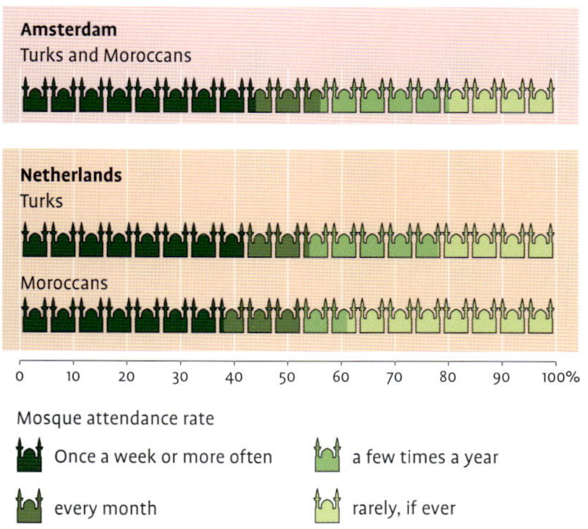

❹ Butchers

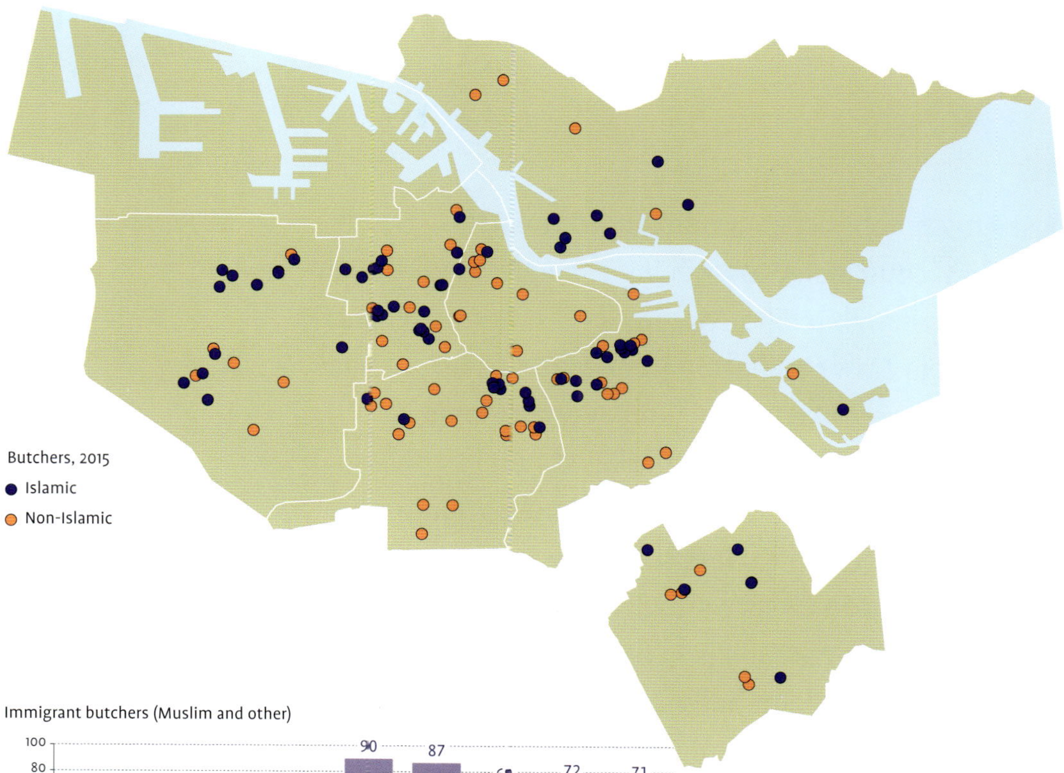

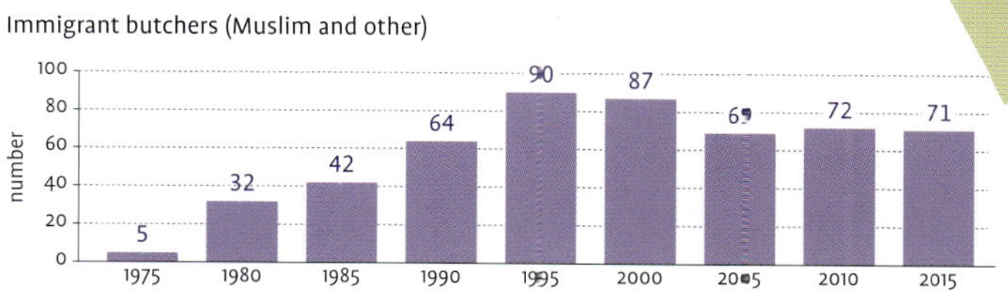

❺ Westermoskee

Sources: OIS, Research, Information and Statistics, City of Amsterdam (4); René van Asselt, Elsevier (5); OIS, Research, Information and Statistics, City of Amsterdam (6)

© Noordhoff Uitgevers

Pluralist Amsterdam

Most Amsterdammers have distanced themselves from traditional church attendance, but the need to give meaning to life through religion has not entirely disappeared. Many people draw inspiration from esoteric ideas, while others join a sect like Korean Sun Myung Moon's Unification Church or the Scientology Church. Immigration has also made a major contribution to the variety in the theological landscape. For instance, there are now more than twenty temples and institutions for Hindus, Buddhists and Sikhs in Amsterdam and the orthodox Christian faith has also taken root in the city. The growth in the number of Christian migrant churches is nothing short of spectacular. Tens of thousands of Christians who have emigrated to Amsterdam from Africa, North and South America and Asia congregate in these churches each week and their faith helps them to survive, often in the face of difficult circumstances. The density of these new churches is particularly great in Zuidoost.

1 He Hua Temple on Zeedijk

2 Oriental world view

3 Buddhist and Hindu North Holland

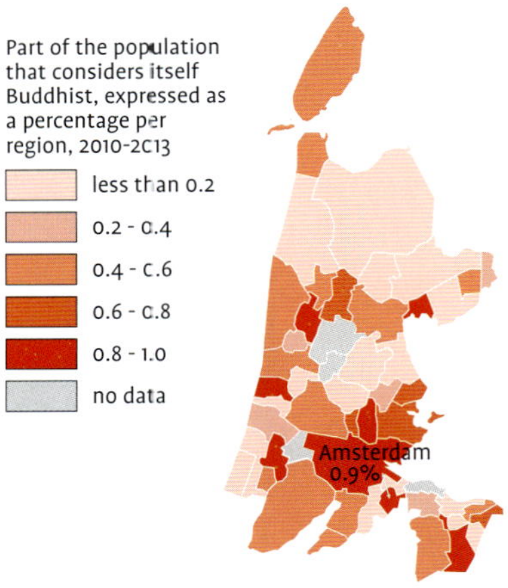

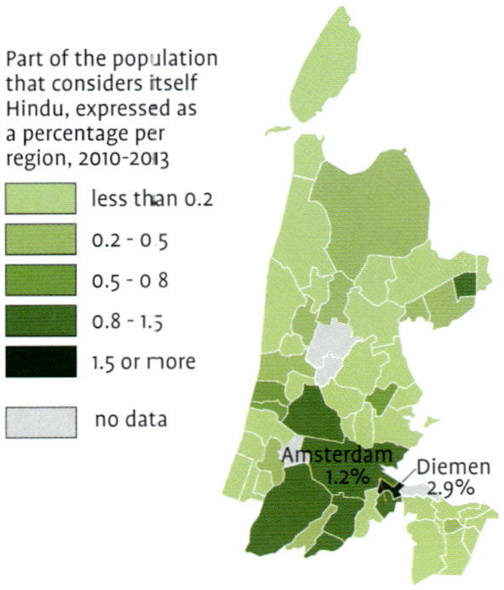

4 Hindu and Buddhist temples and institutions

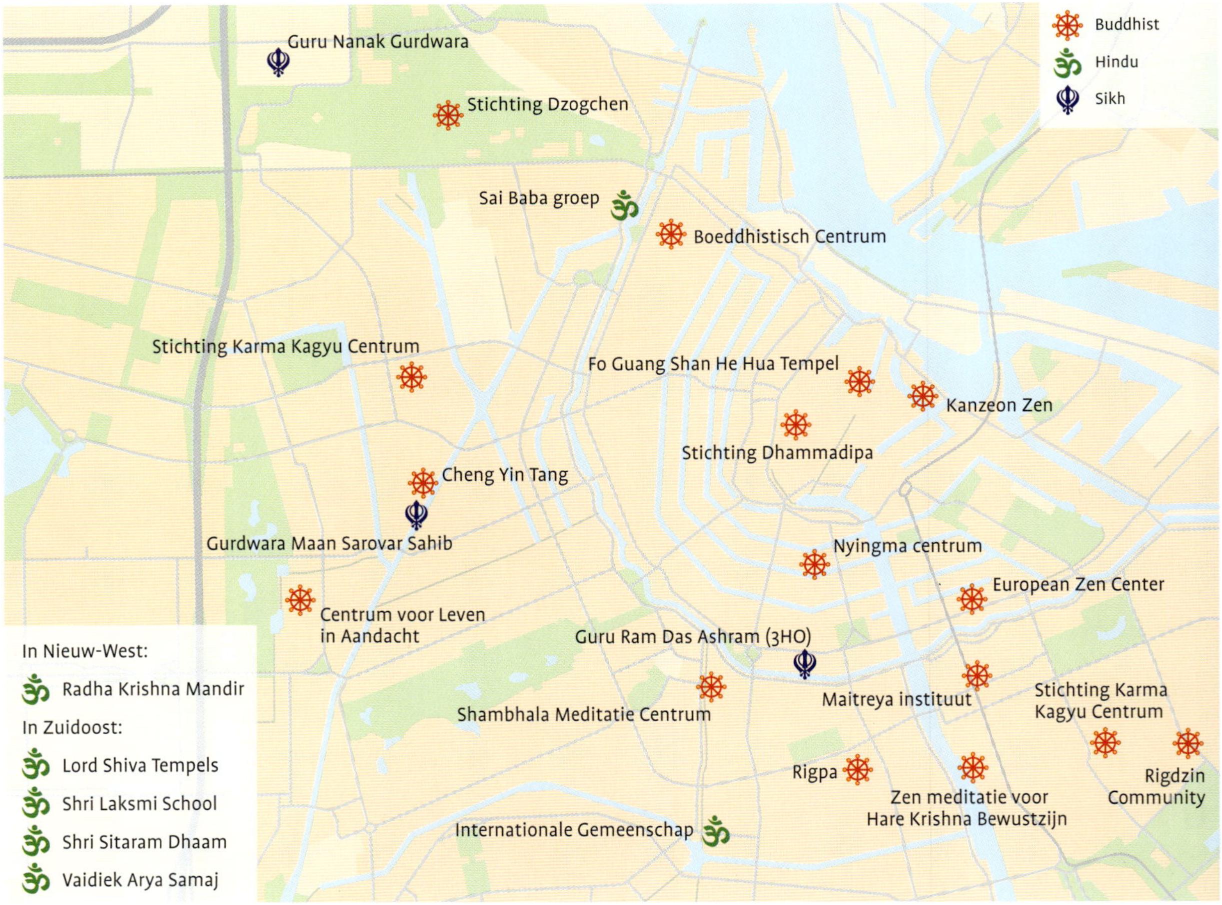

Sources: Statistics Netherlands / Ons Amsterdam / www.yogaopleiding.nl (2); Statistics Netherlands (3); www.reliwiki.nl / OIS, Research, Information and Statistics, Research, Information and Statistics, City of Amsterdam (4)

© Noordhoff Uitgevers

❺ Orthodox and new Christian migrant churches

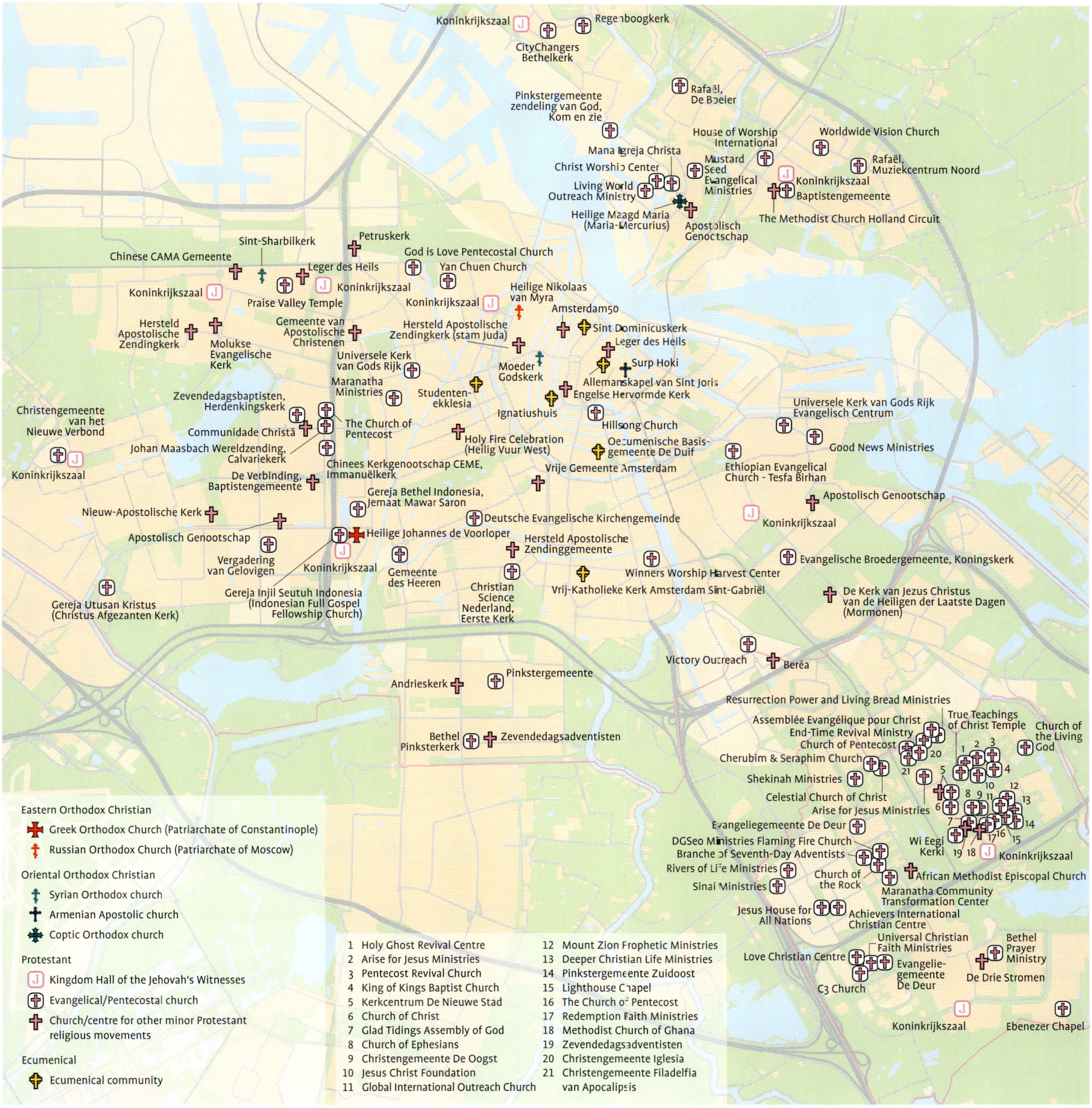

❶ Thousands of eyes

The He Hua Temple on Zeedijk is a Buddhist temple in traditional Chinese palatial style. 'He Hua' means 'lotus flower', the symbol of enlightenment and detachment. The central gate is reserved for monks and the main hall features a statue of Avalokiteshvara, with a thousand hands and eyes, who is devoted to relieving human suffering.

❷ - ❹ Oriental religions

In the 1960s, interest in mystical and Oriental religions increased a lot, partly due to the influence of the hippie movement. Buddhism, Hinduism, Zen and I Ching became fashionable, Hare Krishnas walked through the city singing as they went and Bhagwan Shree Rajneesh gained many supporters. The red or orange robed disciples of the Bhagwan are no longer a common sight and the Hindu, Buddhist and Sikh temples are mainly visited by Amsterdammers of immigrant origin.

❺ Migrant churches

It is difficult to estimate the number of migrant churches in Amsterdam, because they are largely located in inconspicuous buildings such as garages and empty industrial buildings. One thing is certain – there are a lot of them. Of all Amsterdam Christians, approximately 45% are migrants. Most of them profess an exuberant version of evangelical Christianity, with much singing, rousing sermons and an unshakeable faith in the works of the Holy Spirit. Far less numerous, but at least as unusual, are the orthodox immigrant churches from Eastern Europe and the Middle East. All of these churches offer their members a familiar environment.

Sources: www.reliwiki.nl / www.zuidoost.nl (5)

© Noordhoff Uitgevers

Burial and cremation

Funerals have long been a reflection of faith, with the deceased laid to rest in peace until the time of resurrection. Now that man, rather than God, is the focal point, funerals have become more personalised and grave designs have become more varied. Cremation has also become an option, and the number of Amsterdammers choosing to be cremated is still on the increase. This is not true of Islamic Amsterdammers, who always choose a burial ceremony, often in their country of origin. Some years ago, Westgaarde, Zorgvlied and De Nieuwe Ooster cemeteries created separate burial areas for this group so that Amsterdam's Muslims can be buried in their own city.

❶ Cemeteries and crematoria

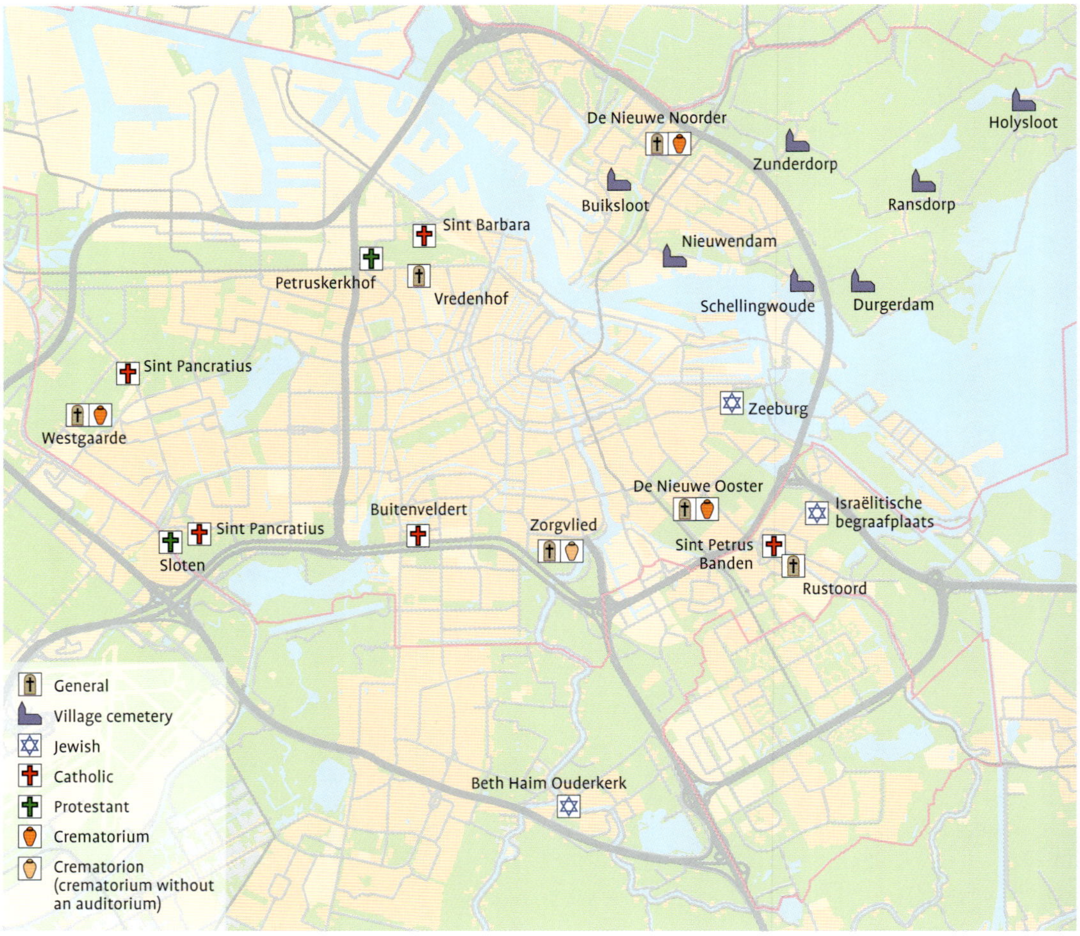

❷ Burials and cremations

Number in 2014

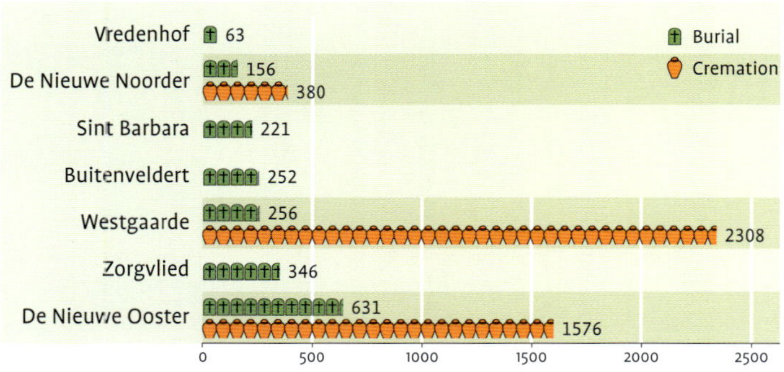

Proportion of Amsterdammers in burials and cremations in 2014

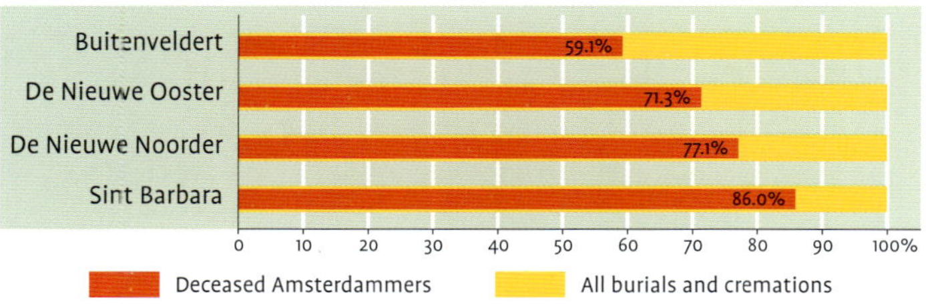

❸ Sint Barbara Roman Catholic cemetery

Sources: *M. de Roever en J. Bierenbroodspot, De begraafplaatsen van Amsterdam (1); all cemeteries mentioned (2); Sint Barbara cemetery (3)*

© Noordhoff Uitgevers

❹ Zorgvlied general cemetery

❶ On the outskirts

A prohibition on burial within built-up areas was instituted in 1829, so the cemeteries opened in Amsterdam after that date were located on the outskirts of the city. However, due to various city expansions, most of them are now surrounded by urban areas again.

❷ Preference for cremation

The Dutch government did not legalise cremation until 1955, although it was tolerated before that date. Since then, the number of cremations in Amsterdam has increased significantly and there are now more cremations than burials.

❸ Straight lines

Sint Barbara (1893, 12 hectares) on Spaarndammerdijk is a typical Roman Catholic cemetery with rectangular burial plots, strict class divisions and an exclusive area reserved for the graves of the clergy and particularly devout citizens.

❹ Prominent Dutch people

Zorgvlied (1870, 16.5 hectares) lies in Amsterdam but is officially owned by the City of Amstelveen. It has a reputation as an elitist cemetery. Although this is not the case, it is true that many prominent Dutch people are buried there.

❺ Room for everybody

De Nieuwe Ooster (1894, 33 hectares) is often referred to as the greenest memorial park in the Netherlands, due to features like its beautiful arboretum. The cemetery is managed by the city council and is intended for all Amsterdammers, regardless of their origin or religion.

❺ De Nieuwe Ooster general cemetery and arboretum

Sources: Zorgvlied cemetery (4); De Nieuwe Ooster cemetery (5)

© Noordhoff Uitgevers

Rituals

❶ Silent Procession
In 1881, two Amsterdammers resurrected the Blessed Sacrament Procession, a tradition dating back to the Middle Ages which commemorates a miracle that took place in Amsterdam in 1345. A dying man had been given the last rites. He threw up shortly afterwards and his vomit (containing the sacramental bread) was thrown into the burning hearth. The next day, the sacramental bread was found intact among the ashes. To commemorate this miracle, the city authorities decided to hold two annual processions carrying the sacramental bread through the city. This tradition came to an end in 1578.
The initiators of 1881 did not want to offend the reformed community, so they agreed to remain silent during their procession through Amsterdam. In subsequent years, more and more Catholics joined in, bringing the numbers up to more than 60,000 in the 1950s. Women were allowed to take part for the first time in 1965.

❷ The Word of God
The congregation listens attentively to every word their pastor says during a Protestant service in the Thomaskerk on Prinses Irenestraat in Amsterdam-Zuid. Together with reading the Bible and singing psalms, speaking and listening are the essence of reformed Christianity. Whereas sacred rituals (sacraments) and good deeds are very important to Catholics, Protestants focus mainly on the Word of God, which was revealed to man through the Bible. However, interpreting the words of the Bible on your own is not an easy task, so the theologically schooled preacher often explains Bible texts during the service and puts them in a contemporary context. Communal singing is also an important element of any Protestant service.

❸ Sugar Feast
Alongside the Feast of Sacrifice or *Eid al-Adha*, one of the highlights of the Islamic year is the Sugar Feast. Some Muslims prefer to use the Arabic name *Eid al-Fitr*, because the name Sugar Feast places a great emphasis on the abundance of food. Even so, enjoying good food, and especially sweet foods, is an important part of the feast.
Islamic traders make the most of this by making their confectionery look as attractive as possible. It makes sense for the Sugar Feast to be a time of enjoyment, as it marks the end of Ramadan, a period of 29 days in which eating, drinking, smoking and sex are strictly forbidden between sunrise and sunset. The standard rituals associated with the feast include visiting the mosque and family members, exchanging gifts and wearing new clothes.

Photos: © Hollandse Hoogte (1); © Protestantse Kerk Amsterdam (2); © Hollandse Hoogte (3)

© Noordhoff Uitgevers

❹ Hanukkah

During Hanukkah, the Jewish community commemorates the rededication of the Temple in Jerusalem in 165 BC after it had been desecrated by the Syrian King, Antiochus IV (175-164 BC). The celebration lasts for eight days and one of its daily rituals involves lighting a candle on the nine-branched candelabrum, the *Hanukkah menorah*, which is reminiscent of the seven-branched candelabrum that formerly stood in the Temple. A special candle is used to light the candelabrum. Other rituals include giving gifts or money to children, playing with a spinning top, the *dreidel*, and eating special Hanukkah dishes such as potato pancakes fried in oil (*latkes*) and a type of doughnut (*sufganiyah*). Hanukkah is primarily a domestic celebration, but in many large cities around the world it is also celebrated in public. This is also the case in Amsterdam, where the Hanukkah menorah is lit on the Dam each year.

❺ Diwali

1.2% of Amsterdam's population professes to be Hindu, which equates to around 10,000 people. The majority are Indo-Surinamese, but immigrants from India, Bangladesh and Sri Lanka also uphold the Hindu rituals and festivities.
One of the most important festivities takes place in October or November – the festival of lights, Diwali, also referred as Deepavali. During Diwali, Hindus celebrate the victory of light over darkness, of good over evil and of mind over matter. They light small clay lamps (diyas) full of clarified butter, in a ritual intended to move Lakshmi, the goddess of light and good fortune, to protect the devout against darkness, disaster and discord. Mainly sweet dishes are served and many Hindus adhere to a strictly vegetarian diet during Diwali.

❻ Praise the Lord

Amsterdam-Zuidoost is now well-known for its many immigrant churches. Every Sunday, hundreds of festively and smartly dressed men and women walk to church with the Bible under one arm. Their destination may be a fully-fledged church, but services also take place in simple flats, empty commercial buildings and multi-storey carparks. Many of these Christian believers are from Africa. They believe implicitly in the Bible and are convinced that only Jesus Christ can save them. They also believe in the work of the Holy Spirit and live in the expectation that the end of days is near. Their behaviour during the church service is exuberant. Passionate ministers exhort the congregation to convert while they still can, choirs sing exultantly and believers possessed by the Holy Spirit dance in ecstasy.

Photos: © Hollandse Hoogte (4-6)

© Noordhoff Uitgevers

7

Leisure

◁
Noorderparkbad pool complex
Photo Karel Tomeï

7 Introduction

Nightlife and partying
Like Rotterdam, which is known as the Netherlands' pragmatic city where actions speak louder than words, Amsterdam has made a name for itself as a city for nightlife and partying. Both perceptions are exaggerated, but people can certainly have fun in Amsterdam.

Eldorado for shoppers
Amsterdam is a true shopper's city. Some prefer the intimate atmosphere of Haarlemmerstraat or 'De 9 Straatjes' while others go for large shopping centres.
The well-off, on the other hand, appreciate the exclusivity of P. C. Hooftstraat and de Bijenkorf. Amsterdam has the fewest vacant shops (4.4%) in the Netherlands by far, which speaks volumes.

Bars and restaurants
Ranging from vending machines to Michelin-starred restaurants, Amsterdam's bars and restaurants are just as extensive and varied. Traditional neighbourhood pubs are reducing in number and being displaced by (exotic) restaurants and coffee corners where a caffè macchiato is almost run-of-the-mill. Rembrandtplein and Leidseplein are still popular with the hard-core nightlife community, but other areas, like Zuidoost, are growing in popularity. Some of Amsterdam's famous dance events also take place outside the city centre.

City of freedom
Establishments associated with Amsterdam's 'titillating' side – red light district windows, gay pubs and coffee shops – all play a prominent role, epitomising freedom for many foreign tourists. Some 23% of foreign tourists visit a coffee shop to experience for themselves Amsterdam's policy of tolerating soft drugs. The downside of that freedom is more of a concern for the city council, which is making a serious attempt to reduce the number of coffee shops and window prostitutes in the city centre.

Football and fitness training
Today's Amsterdammers also use their leisure time for other pursuits,

Noorderparkbad pool complex
Located on Sneeuwbalweg in the Noord district, the brand-new Noorderparkbad pool complex (2015) has five outdoor and four indoor swimming pools to choose from, as well as a freely accessible sunbathing area, where visitors can laze in the sun. The swimming pool is very environmentally friendly, consuming 75% less energy and an impressive 85% less water than conventional pools, partly thanks to a stainless steel screening system that captures rain water.

like sports. Despite the international fame of Ajax, football is not the most popular sport in the city – that is fitness training, something you can do on your own when it suits you. As well as gyms, Amsterdam also has a wide range of swimming pools and other facilities, including the magnificent Olympic Stadium, built for the 1928 Olympic Games.

Peace and quiet

There are also plenty of destinations for those who want to escape the hustle and bustle of the city in their free time. The Amsterdam Forest for example, or a city park, allotment, freshwater beach, or a relaxing day out at Artis with the grandchildren.

3803

bars and restaurants

6000

allotments in Amsterdam and the surrounding area

waiting list: 3000 people

number of national championship trophies (1888-2015)

Ajax **33**

PSV **22**

Feyenoord **14**

number of coffee shops

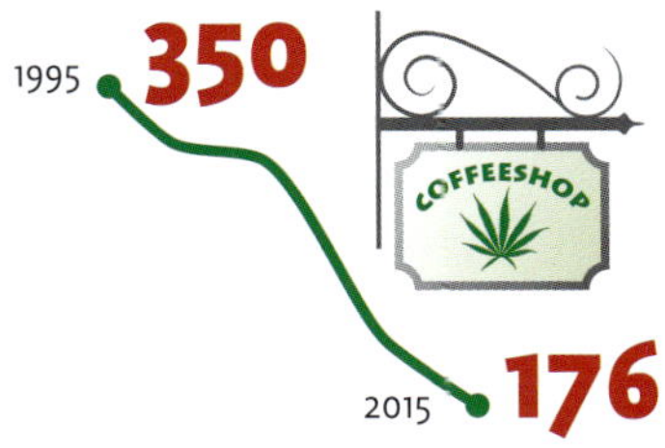

Amsterdammers do not necessarily have to travel to the coast:

there are **10** freshwater beaches

© Noordhoff Uitgevers

Shopping

Amsterdammers do not have to spend much time doing their daily shopping, as they can choose from four or five supermarkets within a one-kilometre radius. This makes Amsterdam the city with the highest supermarket density in the Netherlands. However, when it comes to recreational shopping, Amsterdammers have all the time in the world even on Sundays. The range of products on offer is overwhelming and also attracts people from outside the city. Shoppers can choose between visiting a department store, shopping centre or furniture mall, or simply stroll down one of the many picturesque shopping streets. Shops in the more expensive areas in particular offer original and sometimes very exclusive items in order to differentiate themselves. Some of these shops have a respectable history and have already survived many a crisis.

❶ Shopping streets and shopping areas

❷ Shopping on Sundays and after six o'clock

❸ Haarlemmerstraat

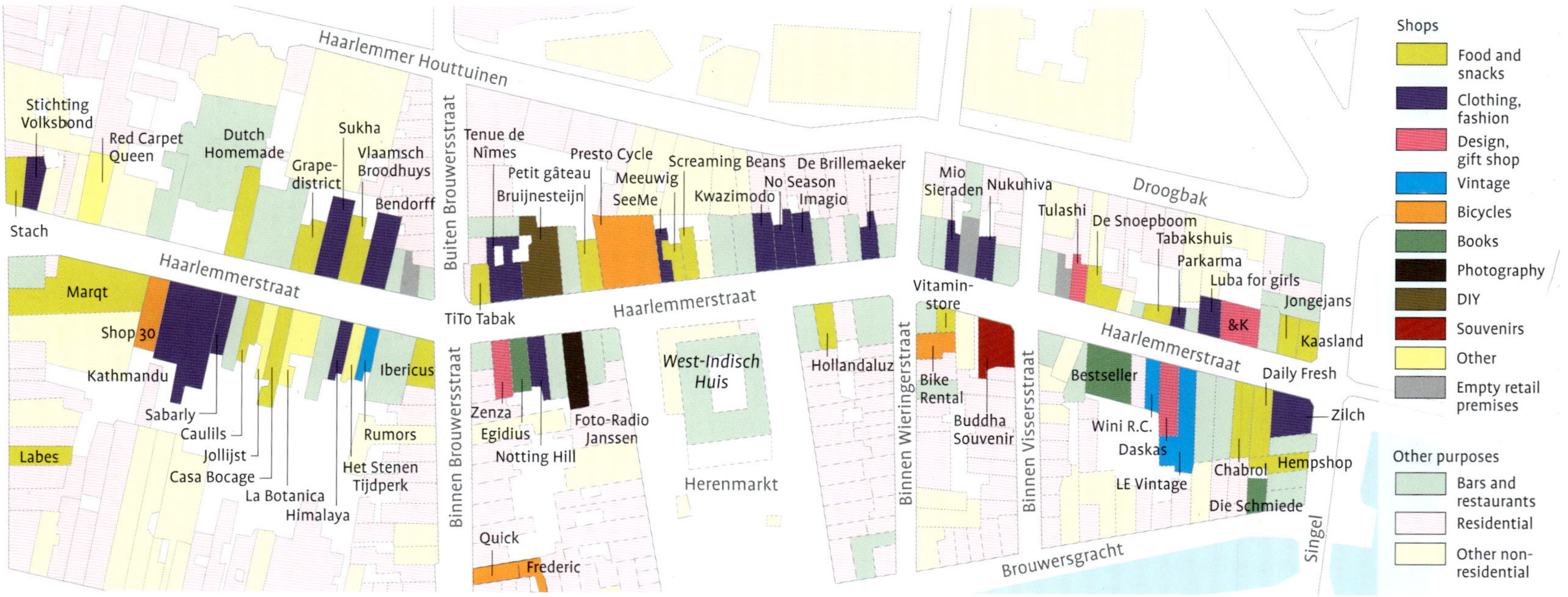

Sources: DTZ Zadelhoff, Winkelhuren Amsterdam 2014 (1); OIS, Research, Information and Statistics, City of Amsterdam (2, 3)

© Noordhoff Uitgevers

❶ Something for everyone

There are around 1520 shops selling everyday items in Amsterdam and over 4150 shops for non-everyday items. With 50,000 visitors a day on average, Kalverstraat is the busiest shopping street and also the most expensive with an average annual rental price of 2800 euros per m². However, rents are falling due to the economic crisis.

❷ Open or closed

In 2010, the entire inner city area was designated a tourist centre, enabling the shops to open on Sundays. A lot of people, including day-trippers, like to shop on Sundays.

❸ The nicest shopping street

Amsterdammers consider Haarlemmerstraat the nicest shopping street, with Utrechtsestraat and 'De 9 Straatjes' ranked second and third. Jan Pieter Heijestraat scores higher on other aspects, topping the list of the most appreciated shopping streets.

❹ Nostalgia

Around 70 shops in Amsterdam have been open for more than a century. The oldest is the W. H. van der Meulen pharmacy on Geldersekade, where pharmacists have prepared their pills and powders ever since 1696. Although pharmacies have changed significantly since then, the interior still exudes the atmosphere of days gone by.

❺ Home interior and furniture shops

ArenAPoort is the shopping and entertainment area on each side of the ArenA train station. The west side is shown below with one of the latest additions – Villa ArenA. Its fifty home and furniture shops and 75,000m² of retail space make it the Netherlands' largest furniture mall.

❹ Oldest shops still open

❺ ArenAPoort in Zuidoost

Sources: www.winkelstories.com (4); Explanation Design, Haarlem with the cooperation of NoSuchThing, Rotterdam (5)

© Noordhoff Uitgevers

Restaurants and bars

Amsterdam has plenty of restaurants, pubs and bars. There are around 1400 bars and restaurants in the city centre alone and they mainly depend on the tourist trade. The situation is rather different outside the main city canal area, where the clientele mainly consists of local residents dropping by for a beer and maybe some 'bitterbal' snacks or cheese with raw beef sausage.

When eating out, Amsterdammers either visit a pub, bar or one of the 1400 restaurants serving Dutch and foreign cuisine. On special occasions, they can reserve a table at one of Amsterdam's fourteen restaurants with one or two Michelin stars, or try a restaurant that is the latest talk of the town.

1 Hotels, bars and restaurants

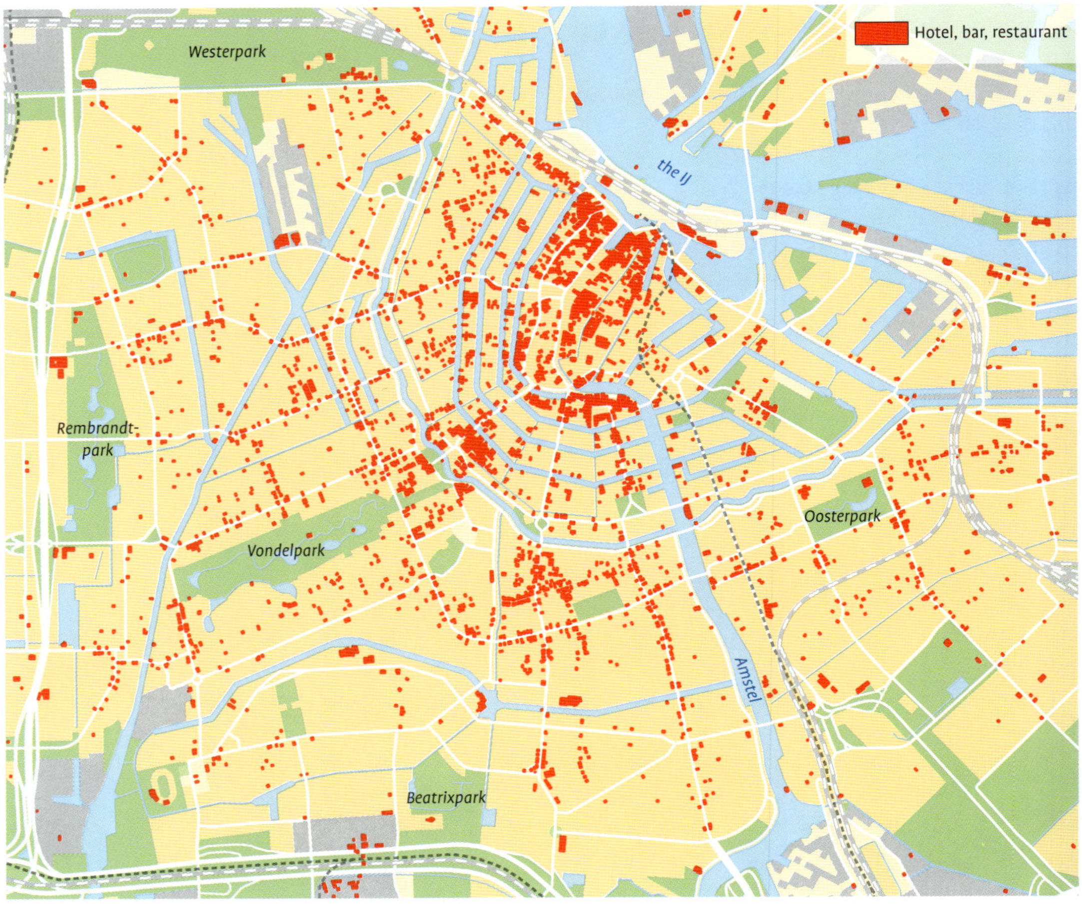

2 Hotels, bars and restaurants in Oud-West

3 Hotels, bars and restaurants in the Jordaan

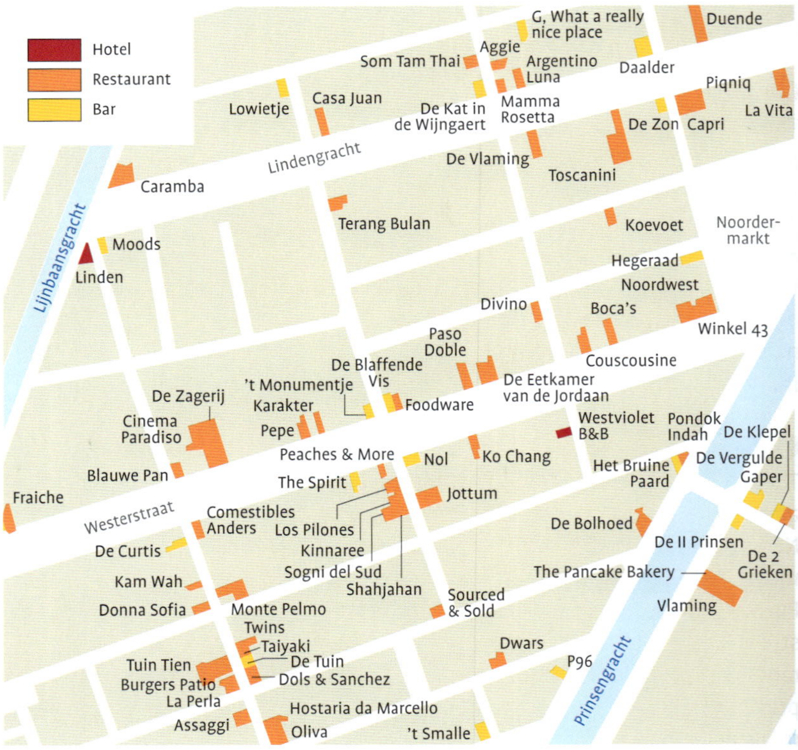

Source: OIS, Research, Information and Statistics, City of Amsterdam (1-3)

© Noordhoff Uitgevers

❹ De Hallen in West

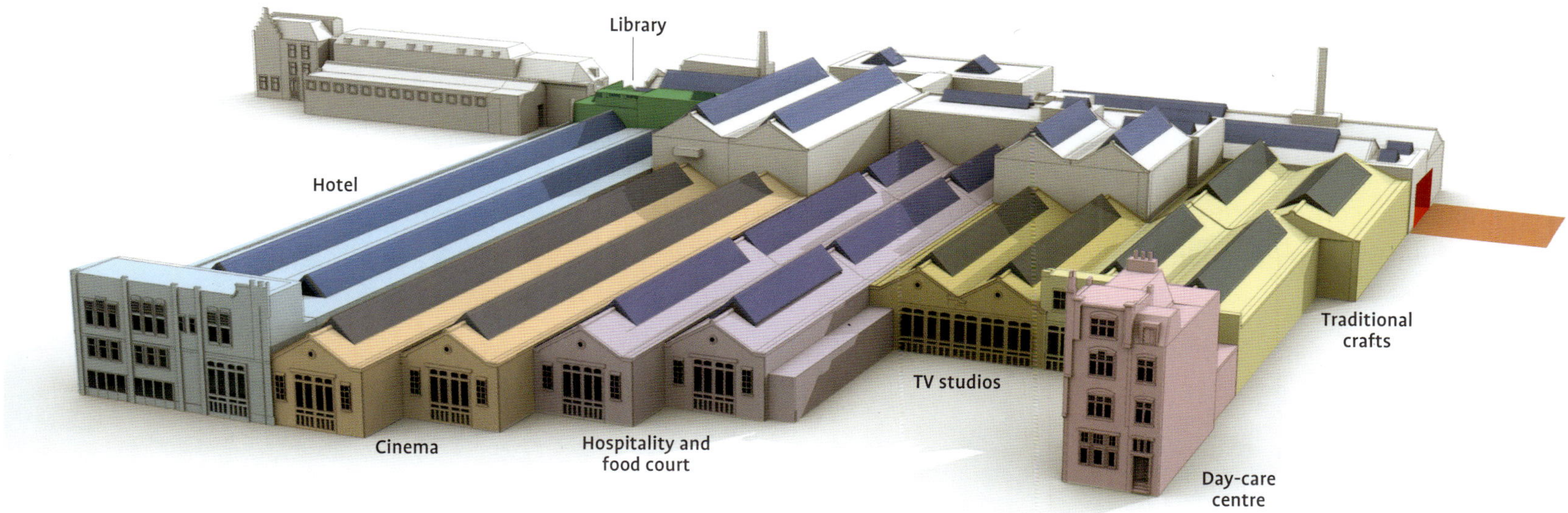

❺ Culinary delights of Amsterdam

❻ Amsterdam's breweries

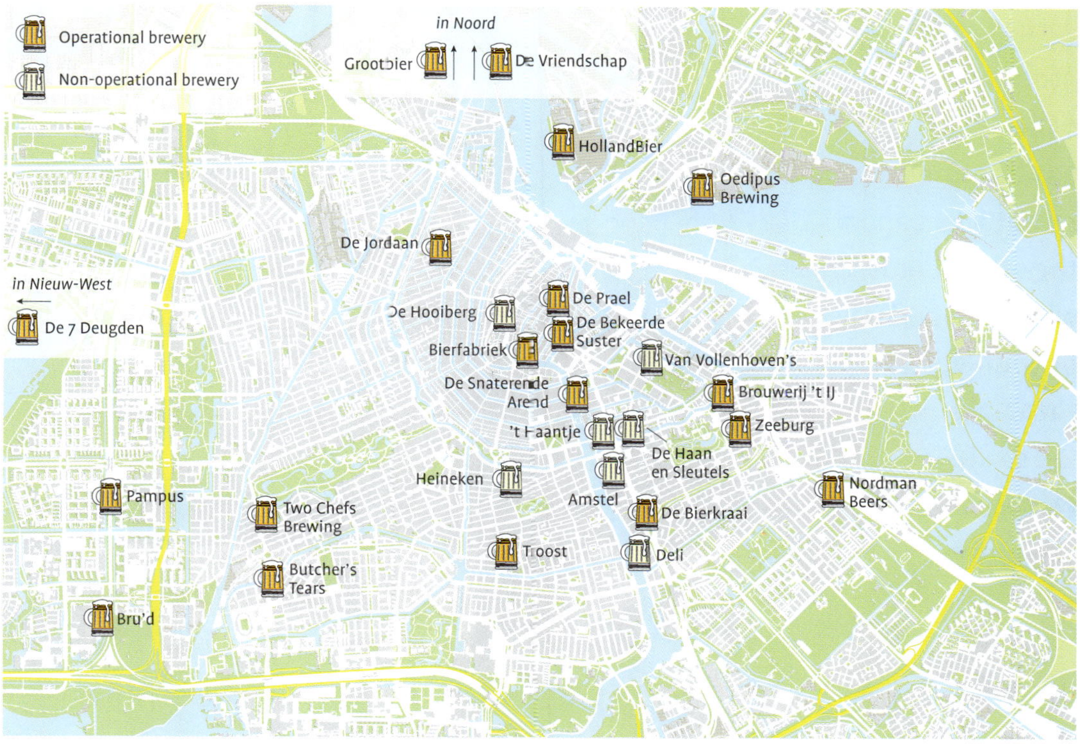

❶ - ❷ The local pub

The city has around 3800 establishments where people can go for a drink or a meal. After the city centre, the Zuid district has the most restaurants and bars, most of them near the Overtoom and Ferdinand Bolstraat, where many double-income families live. A few authentic Amsterdam neighbourhood pubs still exist, but as shown by the names on the Oud-West map, the number of modern restaurants and bars is growing fast.

❸ An area full of song

There are more songs about the Jordaan than any other working-class neighbourhood in the Netherlands. Although the Jordaan still exists, most of its original residents have moved to Purmerend or Hoorn. Even so, its nightlife is still vibrant. There are over 200 pubs and restaurants in the neighbourhood, some of which still preserve the traditional Jordaan 'levenslied' musical genre. Customers of pubs like Lowietje, Nol, De Twee Zwaantjes, Rooie Nelis and 't Monumentje are expected to sing along with the person behind the bar, or even take centre stage themselves.

❹ A stroll and a bite to eat

Since the De Hallen complex opened in October 2014, tens of thousands of curious Amsterdammers have already visited this former tram shed, which has been converted into a cultural centre. The Netherlands' very first indoor food market, the Foodhallen, is especially popular, with people pushing and shoving to get a seat near the 21 stands. Exquisite and exotic drinks and snacks are on offer, ranging from mini puff pastries, *friskas* and *temaki sushi rolls* to Italian pasta, culinary hamburgers and 'bitterballen'.

❺ Amsterdam croquettes

Amsterdammers traditionally like to eat herring and pickles, raw beef sausage sandwiches, 'halfom' sandwiches and croquettes. However, even though they like to think so, they did not invent these products. Back in 1700, the French also ate croquettes filled with poultry, potatoes or cheese. The story goes that a pastry chef called Kwekkeboom discovered this croquette in Paris around 1900 and started to sell beef croquettes upon returning to Amsterdam. Other bakers, including Van Dobben, Holtkamp and J. de Borst on Ferdinand Bolstraat (which later became famous as Febo), followed suit.

❻ New beers in Amsterdam

Following the closure of the Amstel and Heineken breweries (in 1972 and 1988 respectively), brewing in Amsterdam seemed to be finished. However, many new breweries have opened in recent years, and there are now around 20 in the city. They mainly produce beers with a highly individual taste that have been brewed using traditional methods.

Sources: Het Parool (4); www.mokums.nl / www.mokums.punt.nl (5); www.biernet.nl (6)

© Noordhoff Uitgevers

Nightlife

Amsterdam has some of the country's best nightlife and is popular with both Amsterdammers themselves and millions of tourists. After visiting museums and shops during the day, they spend the evening in the city centre, mainly near Rembrandtplein and Leidseplein. This area has many pubs, coffee shops, restaurants, theatres, cinemas and nightclubs, all within walking distance of each other. During the small hours, the dance scene takes over. Amsterdam has become a true dance city in recent years and its flagship event is the annual Amsterdam Dance Event, which attracts hundreds of thousands of young people to the city.

❶ Cultural institutions and nightlife

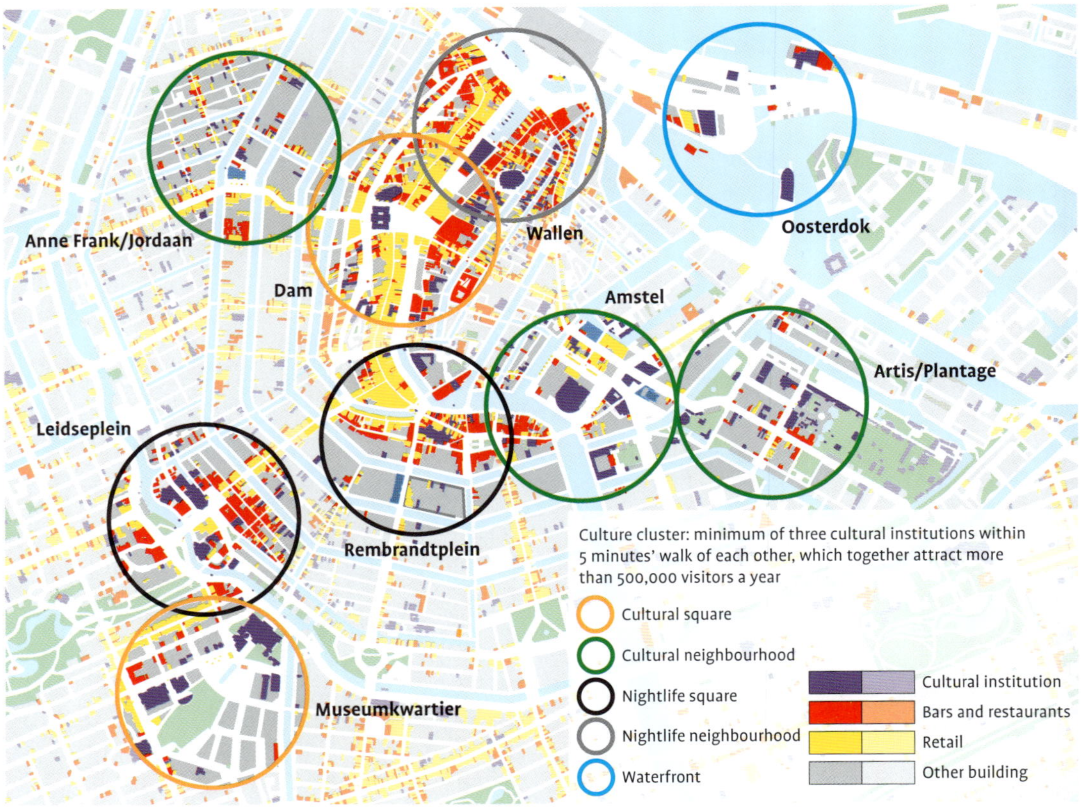

❷ Rembrandtplein

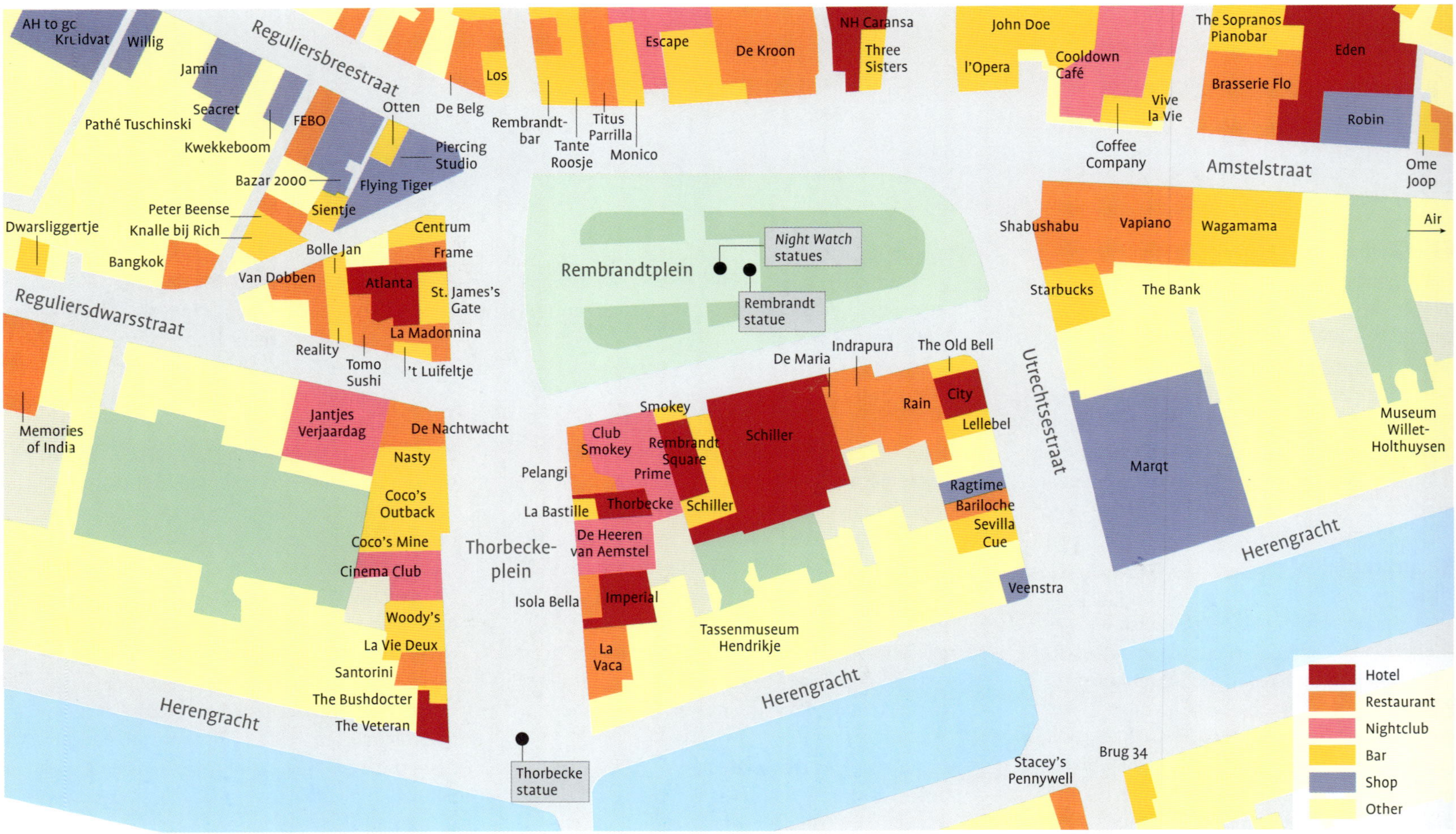

Source: O+S, Research, Information and Statistics, City of Amsterdam (1, 2)

© Noordhoff Uitgevers

❶ Different nightlife areas
Amsterdam has a wide range of nightlife venues. Whereas the restaurants and bars near major cultural institutions primarily focus on daytime services, people party until the small hours in the red light district and on the Dam, Rembrandtplein and Leidseplein.

❷ Nearly always busy
Rembrandtplein is only ever quiet in the early hours of the morning. During the day, tourists take photos of the bronze *Night Watch* statues and then stop for a drink at one of the pavement cafes. In the evening, music plays all over the square and the pubs and restaurants are full. At one time, there were five theatres and five cinemas on the square, but only Tuschinski has survived. The strip clubs on Thorbeckeplein have also disappeared.

❸ - ❹ Young people going wild
There are about 350 festivals in and around Amsterdam every year. Lovers of 'dance', a collective name for all kinds of electronic dance music, are particularly well catered for. Tens of thousands of young people, many with party drugs in their pockets, have the time of their lives at these events.

❺ Global event
The first five-day Amsterdam Dance Event (ADE), featuring 30 artists, was held in October 1995. Since then, it has become a global event, with over 350,000 ravers dancing all night long to the music of some 2200 artists.

❸ Dance festivals

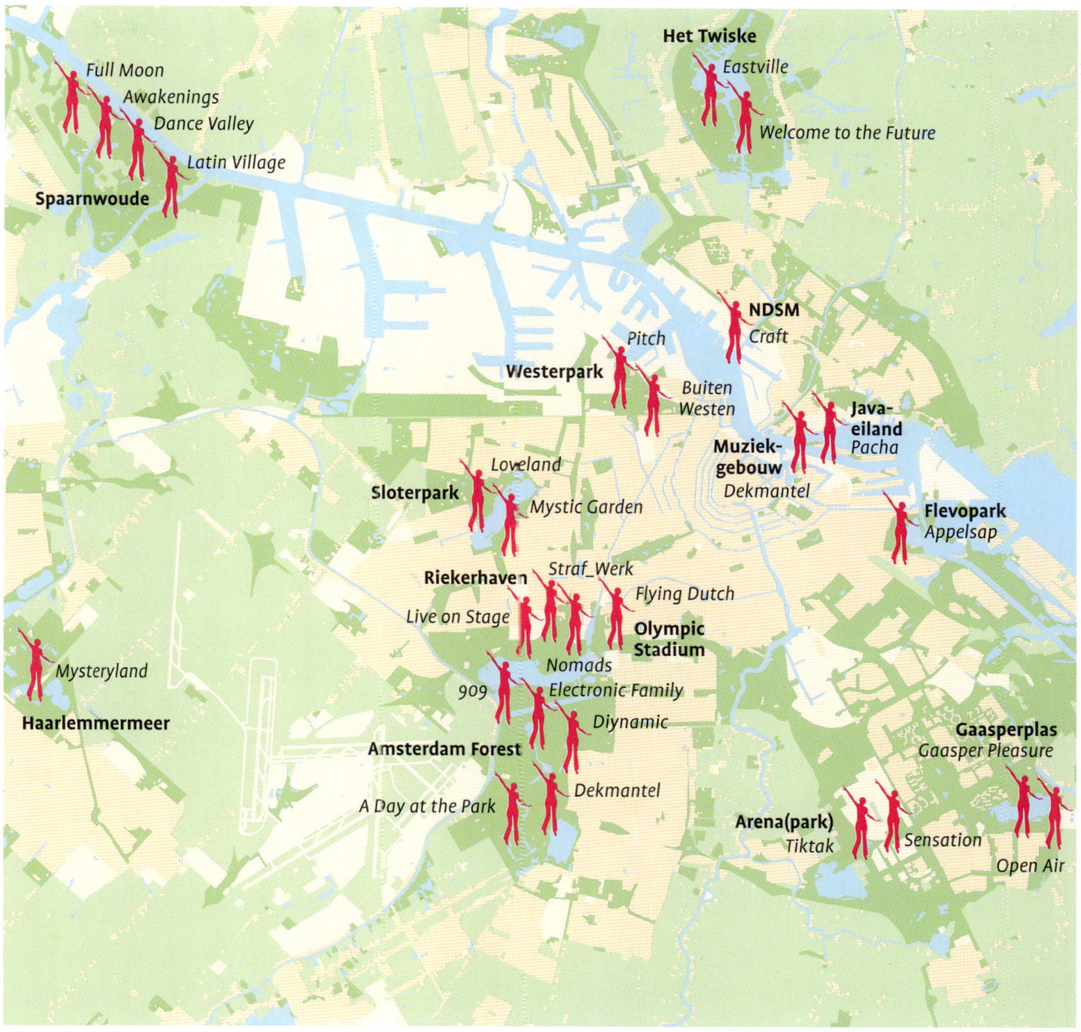

❹ Ecstasy use

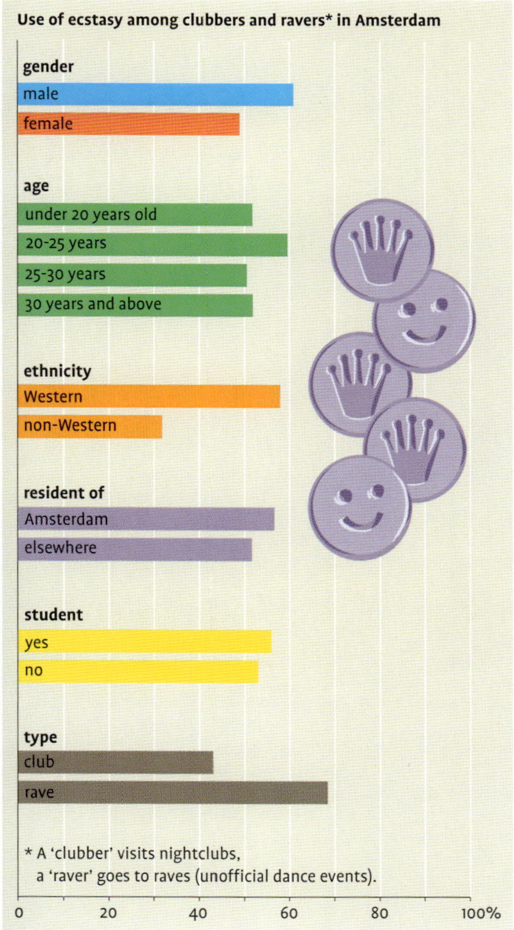

❺ Amsterdam Dance Event locations

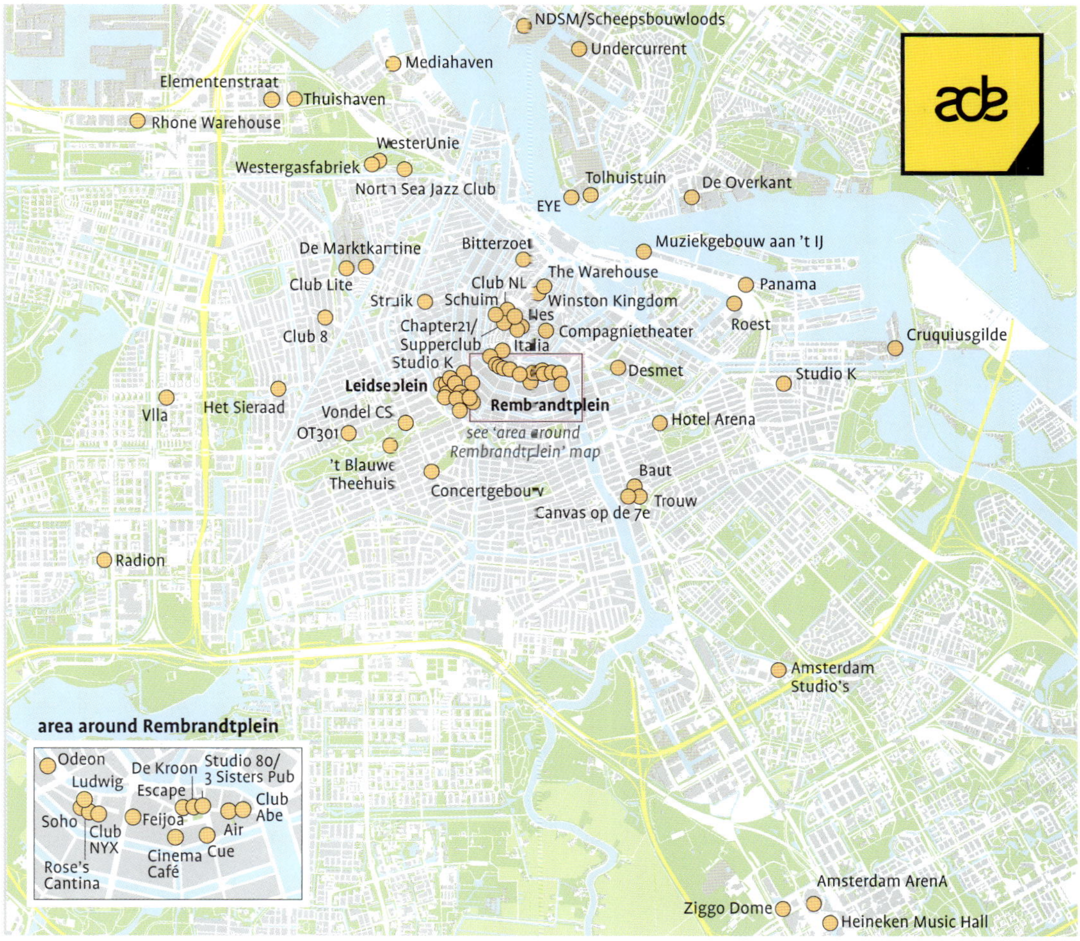

Sources: www.dance-festivals.nl (3); Jellinek, Antenne 2013 (4); www.amsterdam-dance-event.nl / Buma/Stemra (5)

© Noordhoff Uitgevers

Out in the open

Amsterdammers are highly appreciative of the parks and gardens in the city and frequently use these facilities. This is understandable, because Amsterdam is a compact city, with nearly 5000 residents per square kilometre on average. About 45% of the nearly 400,000 homes in Amsterdam date back to before World War Two. As a result, a great many Amsterdammers have to content themselves with a house smaller than sixty square metres and few people have a garden. A park or extensive garden area in the neighbourhood therefore encourages many families with children to stay in the city, or was one of the main reasons for choosing the current family home.

The Vondelpark is visited most often by far, with three quarters of Amsterdam's residents going to this park once in a while. Despite this intensive use, both people and animals find peace and tranquillity here. Herons stand calmly on the banks of the ponds looking for fish and a male and female stork have been coming to the park for several years to raise their young.
The large nature areas surrounding the city are a good alternative for anyone who finds the parks too busy. In these areas, you can walk without running the risk of being jostled by cyclists, skaters, joggers or frisky dogs. Some Amsterdammers even have allotments with ornamental flowers or home-grown vegetables.

1 Parks

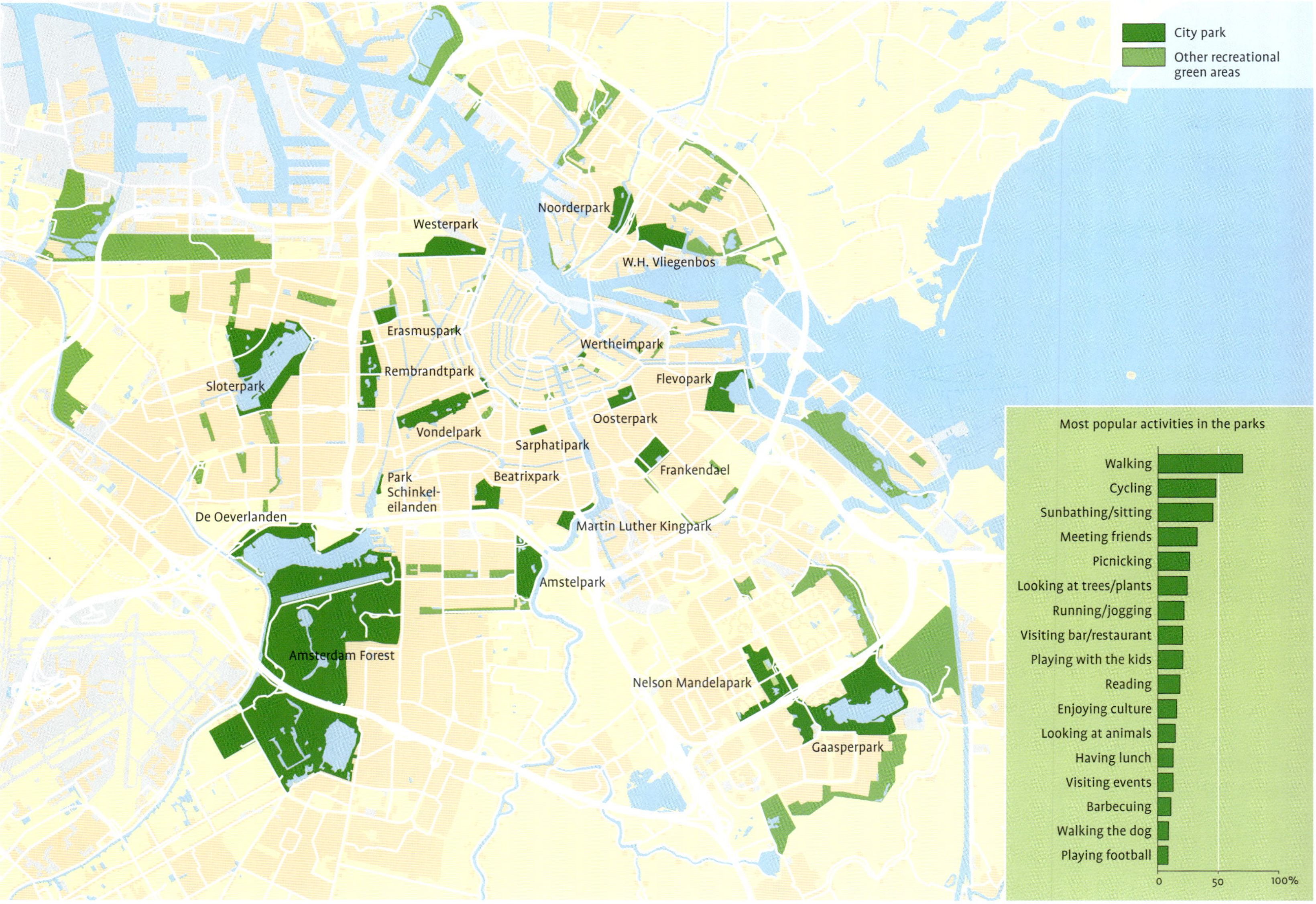

Source: *OIS, Research, Information and Statistics, City of Amsterdam (1)*

© Noordhoff Uitgevers

❷ Vondelpark

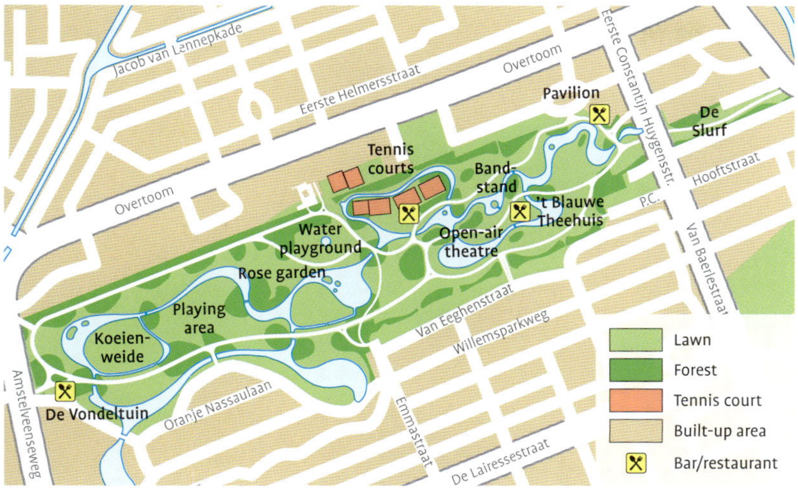

❸ Vondelpark Pavilion

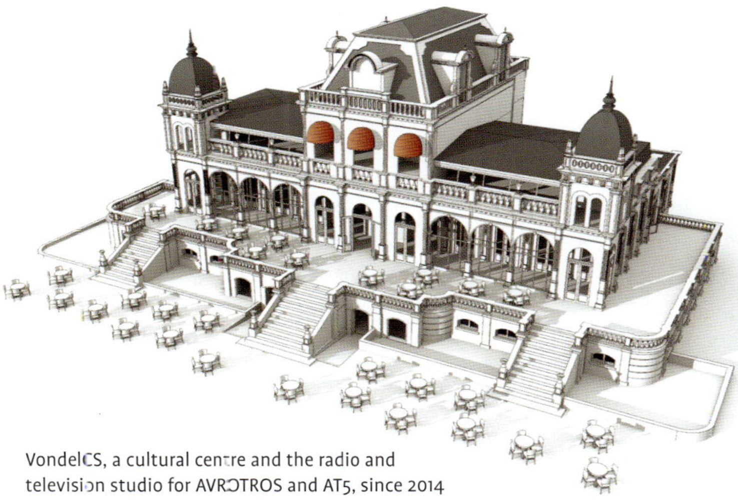

VondelCS, a cultural centre and the radio and television studio for AVROTROS and AT5, since 2014

❶ Close to home

Amsterdam covers an area of 219km^2, 25km^2 of which consist of parks, gardens, allotments or recreational areas. The three most frequently visited parks are the Vondelpark, the Westerpark and the Oosterpark. Strikingly enough, the other parks within the A10 ring road have attracted increasingly larger numbers of visitors in recent years, while less people have visited the recreational areas surrounding the city.

❷ - ❸ From posh to commonplace

The Vondelpark (nearly 49 hectares) was once created for Amsterdam's elite, who went for a stroll or a coach ride there, or relaxed in the spacious Vondelpark Pavilion. Today, the park has lost its elitist character and is used by around ten million people every year, making it the most frequently visited park in the Netherlands. It is home to nearly 5000 trees of some 55 varieties, and two of them are included on the national list of protected trees. In 1996, the entire park was designated a national heritage site.

❹ Amsterdam's *schoffies*

Amsterdam's flora and fauna are more varied than one might initially think – there are twenty-five types of mammal in the Amsterdam Forest alone. Most animals are rarely seen, with the exception of the grey heron, an excellent example of an animal that has adapted perfectly to the city. A film called *Schoffies* (rogues) was made about Amsterdam's herons in 2007 and appealed to many Amsterdammers who identified with these brazen birds that seem completely fearless.

❺ Remote gardens

Gardens are scarce in Amsterdam and the demand for an allotment is so high that people have to wait at least three years.
There are over six thousand allotments within the city's boundaries distributed across different types of garden sites. Sites specifically for allotments are small and reserved exclusively for sheds and greenhouses. Day recreation parks, on the other hand, often have small log cabins, but staying overnight is prohibited. Overnight stays *are* allowed in the sites for recreation and accommodation.

❹ Grey herons

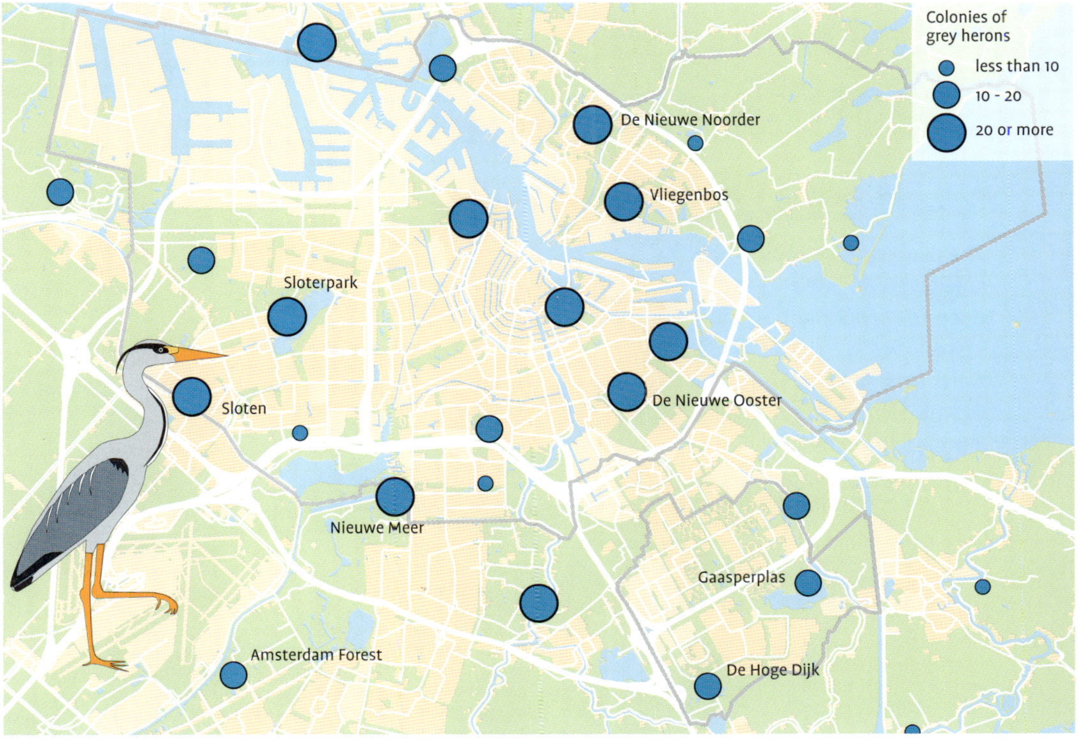

❺ Allotments

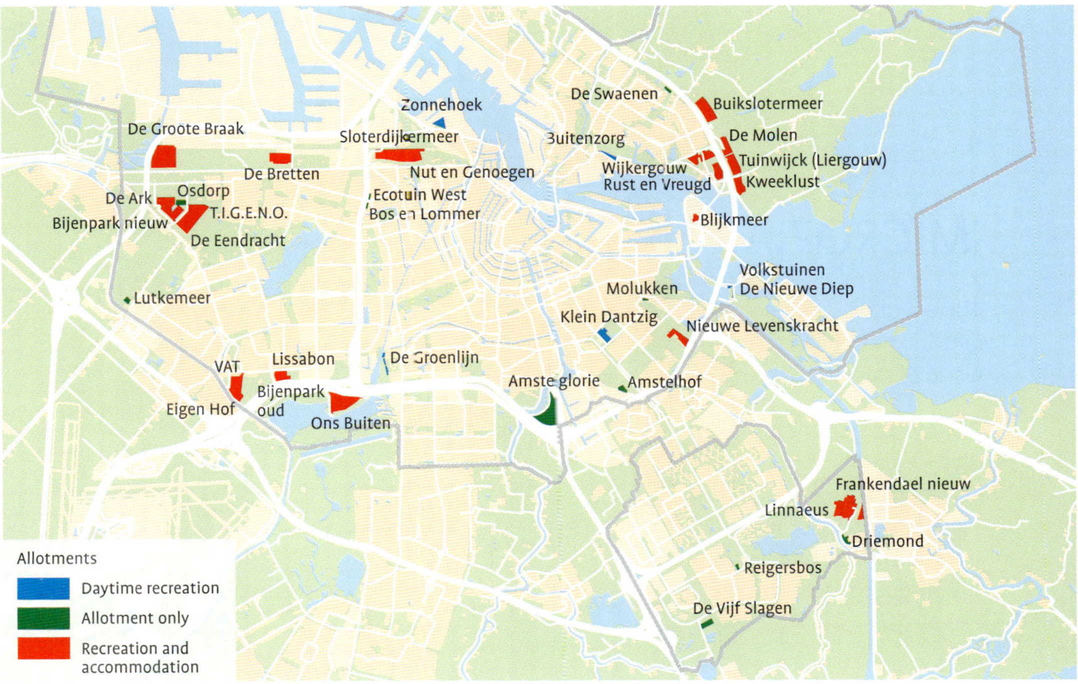

Sources: *Vrienden van het Vondelpark (2); Het Parool (3); OIS, Research, Information and Statistics, City of Amsterdam (4); City of Amsterdam (5)*

© Noordhoff Uitgevers

Artis

'Natura Artis Magistra', known simply as 'Artis', was constructed in 1838 in an attempt to bring Amsterdam's residents closer to nature. The first animals were monkeys and parrots, and the public could also see animals preserved in formaldehyde and skeletons. One year later, numerous animals were acquired from a circus and the zoo had to be extended to accommodate the elephant, bears, lions, tigers, kangaroos and other animals. Over the years, the zoo has been expanded further and modernised.

Artis collects rainwater in a 25,000 litre tank under the Vogelhuis and uses it to water the plants. This saves a great deal of water.

The planetarium depicts the solar system, but also the deep sea layer and Darwin's historic voyage to the Galapagos Islands. The 628m² dome also serves as a projection screen.

MICROPIA
shows the invisible

The world's first museum devoted to the invisible world of micro-organisms.

Did you know, for example, that:
- billions of micro-organisms live on and in our bodies?
- 50% of the Earth's oxygen is produced by microbes?

10 forgotten animals

Lions, elephants and gorillas are popular. Other animals attract far fewer spectators, so Artis has laid out a route of 10 forgotten animals.

1

pygmy marmoset

2

Macleay's spectre stick insect

Source: *Natura Artis Magistra*

Trees and plants

Artis has a collection of more than 700 trees. One of the oldest trees at Artis – and in Amsterdam itself – is an oak tree: **the Heimanseik** (A). The oak is about 275 years old and named after naturalist and nature educator Eli Heimans. Hundreds of plants are on display in the themed gardens, such as the Hollandse Tuin and the Japanse Paradijs Tuin.

Fodder for the animals is stored here. Endive, carrots, chicory and apples are the most popular foods. The lions and vultures eat the most meat, while the reptiles and aquarium animals eat 400 boxes of insects each week.

With a wingspan of 30cm, the atlas moth is the largest moth in the world.

27 Artis buildings are listed as national heritage sites. The aquarium, with its columns and unusual staircases, is one of the showpieces.

Fodder

Each year, the animals eat 37,000 kilos of fish. That is equivalent to 12 full truckloads.

Every day, 230 kilos of dry fodder are consumed.

An elephant eats more than 100 kilos a day, of which six kilos are apples...

...and produces 60-90 kilos of manure each day.

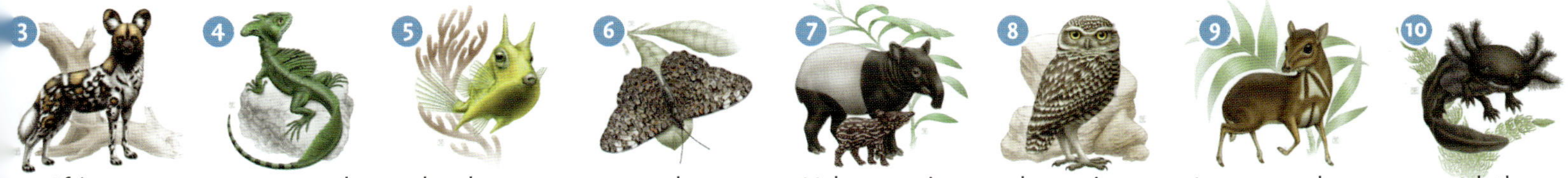

African hunting dog | green crested basilisk | longhorn cowfish | cracker butterfly | Malayan tapir | burrowing owl | Java mousedeer | axolotl

© Noordhoff Uitgevers

Sports

Two thirds of Amsterdammers exercise at least once a month and can be classed as sporty. This is not unusual, as the national average is also 66%. Only one quarter of the residents of Amsterdam belong to a sports club and consistently use one of the city's many sports grounds and complexes each week. The remainder exercise when it suits them, largely in the form of fitness training, which is the most popular sports activity in Amsterdam.

The choice of sport is strongly dependent on education, race, age and ethnicity. For example, rowing is a real student sport, while the children of more affluent parents are most likely to play hockey or tennis, or go horse riding. Young people love football, but as they grow older, they are more likely to spend their time working out in the gym or training for the Dam tot Damloop running event.

❶ Sports facilities

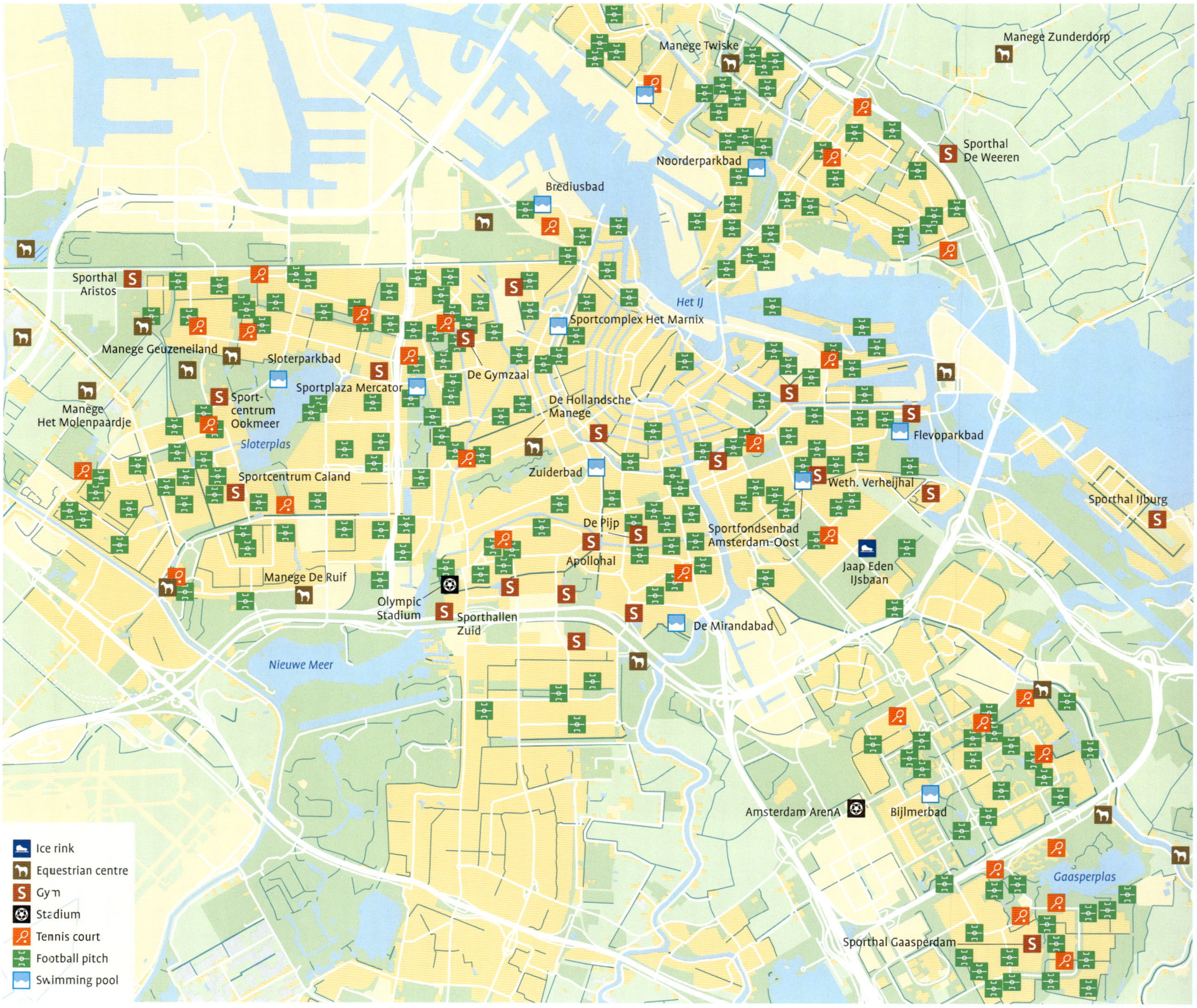

Source: OIS, Research, Information and Statistics, City of Amsterdam (1)

© Noordhoff Uitgevers

❷ Top 5 most popular sports

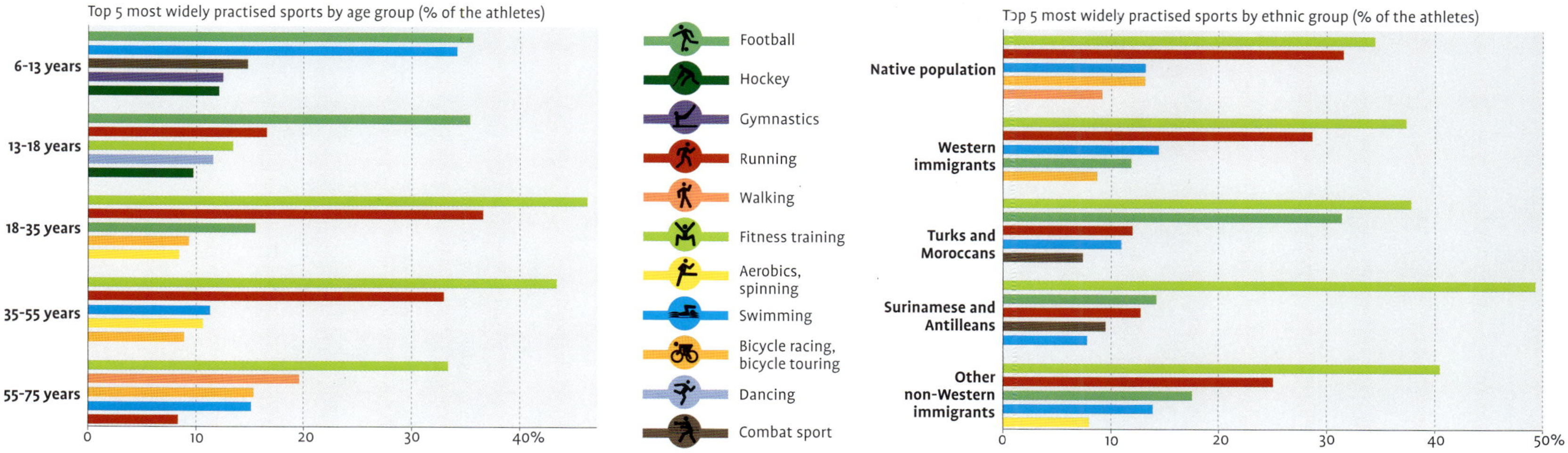

❶ Mainly football pitches

Some 145 of all the sports facilities in Amsterdam are intended for football, without even counting the training pitches. During recent decades, the number of football associations has fallen sharply, from nearly 100 in 1997 to 63 in early 2015. The increasing popularity of girls' and women's football is the main reason why the number of footballers has remained relatively stable. Amsterdammers can play tennis, swim, jog and go horse riding in all districts, except Centrum.

❷ Physical health

Football is the first choice of Amsterdam's youth. Swimming is almost as popular up to the age of 13, but interest in this sport declines strongly after that age and Amsterdammers only start swimming more regularly again later in life. Interestingly enough, a quarter of the population does not have an official swimming certificate – which does not mean that they cannot swim. Fitness training is the fastest-growing sport. Between 2003 and 2013, the percentage of Amsterdammers that went to a gym to stay in shape or improve their fitness levels increased from 19% to nearly 40%. Jogging comes in a comfortable second at 26%, which is double the percentage registered in 2009.

❸ The 10 EM

Having started out as a local running competition between Amsterdam and Zaandam, the Dam tot Damloop has become the country's second largest two-day sporting event over its 30 years of existence. In 2014, more than 87,000 people registered to run, walk or cycle between the two 'dam' cities. The event is so popular that the 50,000 starting tickets for the most important section, the 10 EM (10 English Miles), were sold out within half an hour in 2015.

❹ Open to all

Rowing as a member of a club has the reputation of being an elitist sport reserved for University of Amsterdam or VU University students with wealthy parents. However, those days are long gone and most clubs are now open to all.

❸ Dam tot Damloop

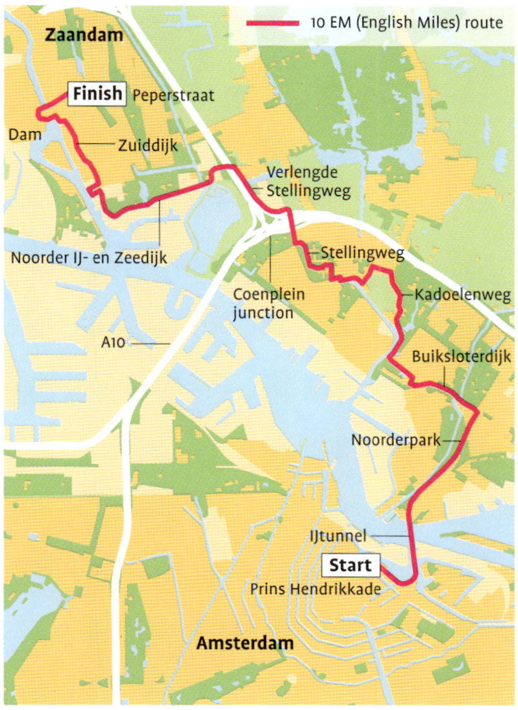

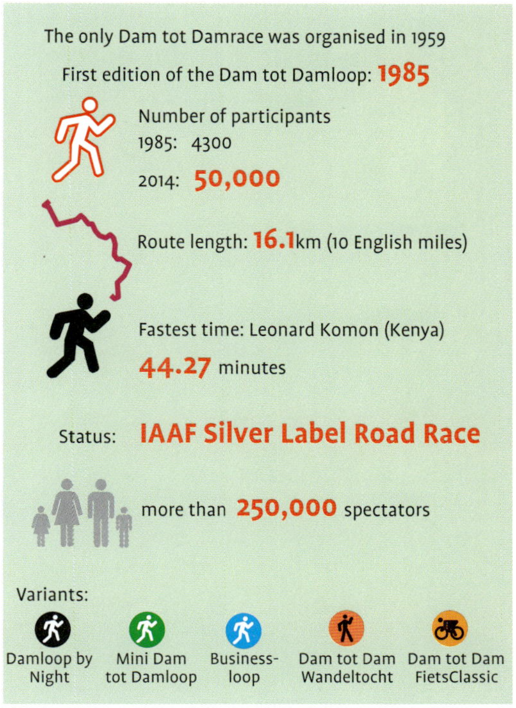

❹ Rowing clubs

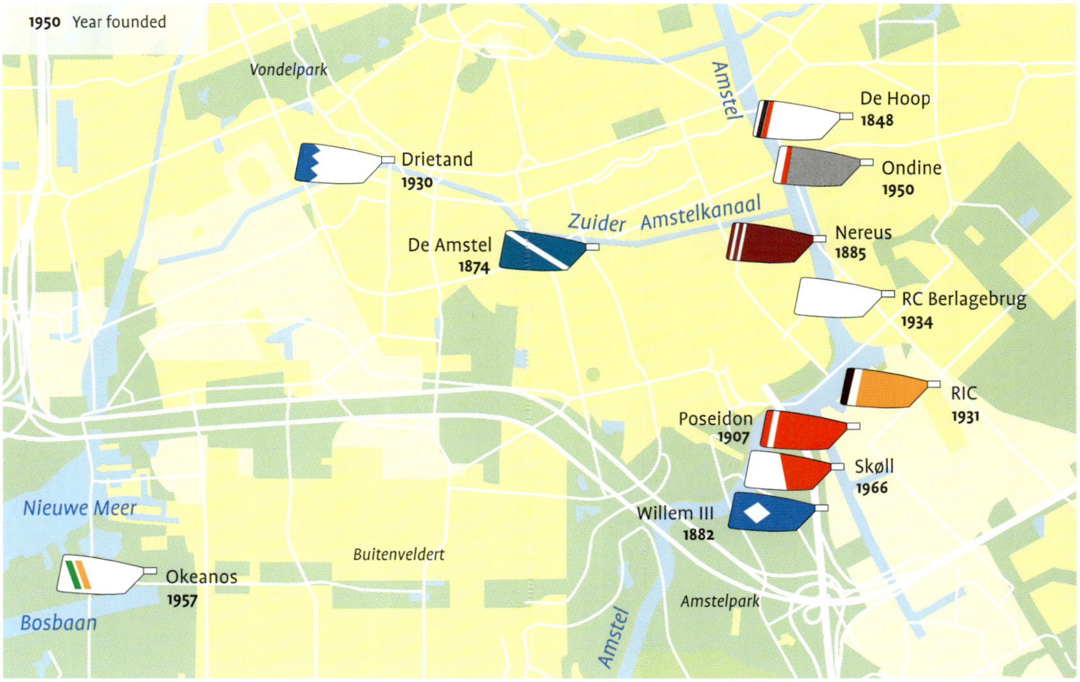

Sources: OIS, Research, Information and Statistics, City of Amsterdam (2); www.damloop.nl (3); www.nlroei.nl (4)

© Noordhoff Uitgevers

Olympic Games

On 28 July 1928, Prince Hendrik opened the Games of the IX Olympiad in the Olympic Stadium.

Television did not yet exist, but radio did. However, the organisers had forbidden a live broadcast for fear that the public would stay at home. As a result, only the 31,600 spectators in the packed Olympic Stadium were able to witness the glorious entrance of the world's best athletes.

❶ Olympic Stadium in 1928

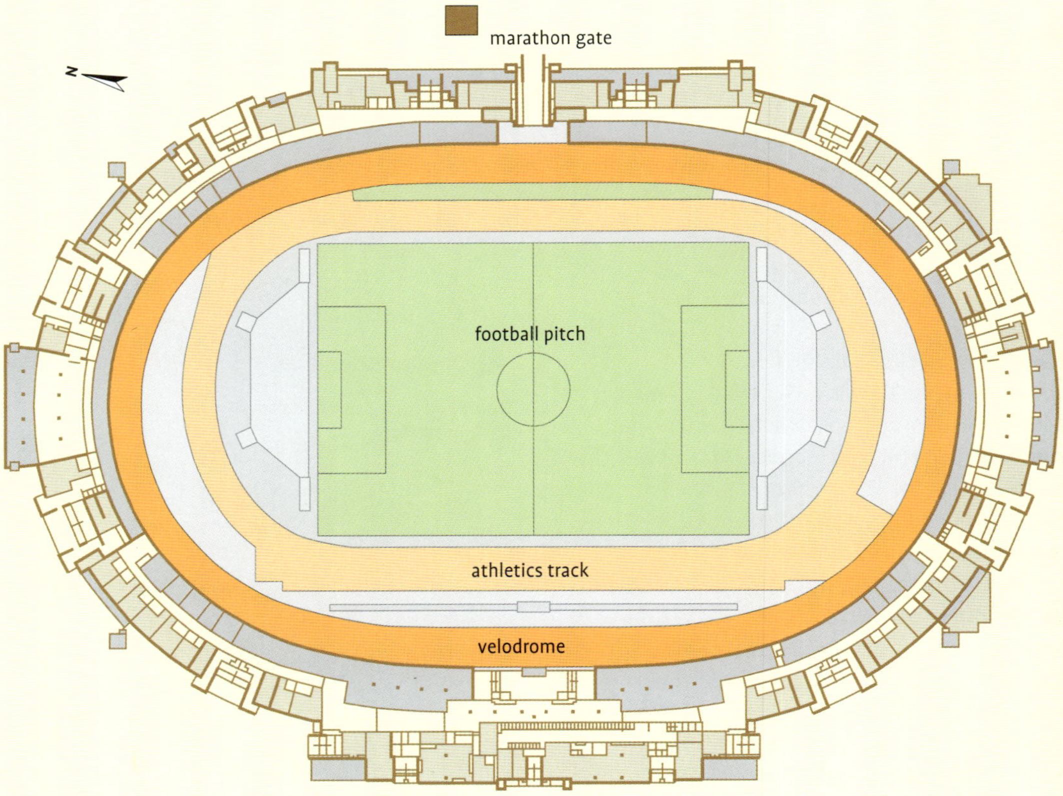

❷ The Olympic Games of 1928

The Games were opened by Prince Hendrik on 28 July 1928

The **Olympic Torch** was lit for the first time (by an employee of the gas company)

There was no Olympic village: the athletes were accommodated in primary schools (it was the summer holidays), guest houses and hotels

Number of participating countries: **46**

Number of sports: **16**

Number of events: **109**

Number of participants:

2606 men **277** women

3 demonstration sports: Frisian handball, korfball and lacrosse

A simple traffic sign was designed to indicate parking areas – a white 'P' on a blue square. It was so clear that the 'parking P' was adopted as an international standard.

P

Medal table

Country	Gold	Silver	Bronze	Total
United States	22	18	16	56
Germany	10	7	14	31
Finland	8	8	9	25
Sweden	7	6	12	25
Italy	7	5	7	19
Switzerland	7	4	4	15
France	6	10	5	21
Netherlands	6	9	4	19
Hungary	4	5	0	9
Canada	4	4	7	15

The Games were closed on 12 August 1928 by Queen Wilhelmina

❸ Olympic complex

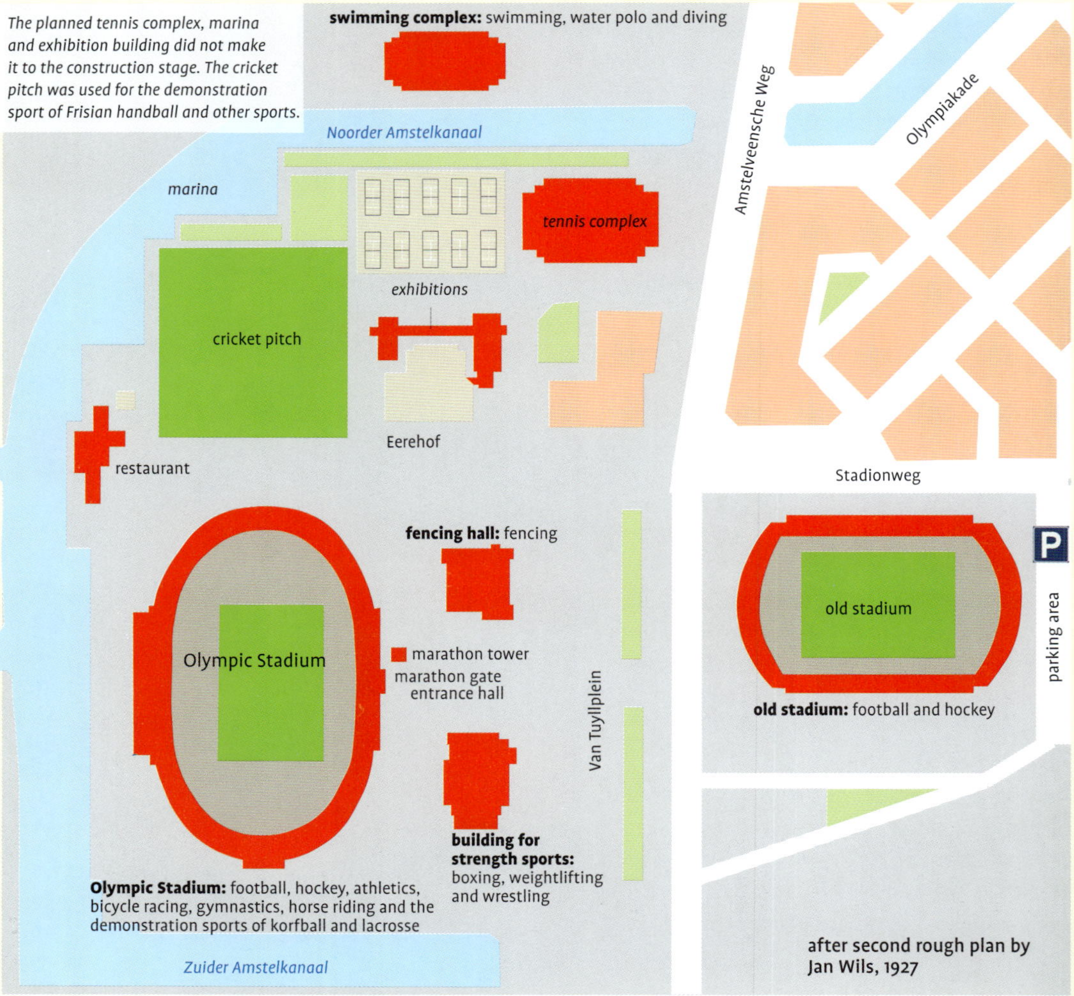

Source: NOC*NSF (1-3)

© Noordhoff Uitgevers

❶ and ❸ Two million bricks

The Olympic Stadium was designed by an Amsterdam School architect called Jan Wils. The concrete structure is hidden behind around two million bricks. The stadium and the 46-metre Marathon Tower, popularly known as 'the ashtray of Amsterdam', still exist, but all of the other sports buildings around the outside of the stadium were demolished back in the day.

❷ and ❹ Greece to the fore

In 1928, Germany was allowed to participate for the first time since World War One. Malta, Panama and Rhodesia made their début and Greece led the opening parade for the first and only time.

❺ - ❻ First women's athletic events

Women were allowed to participate in the athletics events for the first time in 1928. With a throw of 39.62 metres, a Polish discus thrower, Halina Konopacka, was the first female Olympic athletics champion. Women had already been allowed to participate in swimming events for some years, and Dutch entrant Marie Braun won a gold medal in the 100-metre backstroke with her time of 1:22.00. The 2012 women's gold medal winner swam the same distance in 58.33.

❼ Running along the Amstel

Several events took place outside the city, such as the marathon, which was a loop from Amsterdam to Uithoorn and back. The event was won by an Algerian running for France, Ahmed Boughéra El Ouafi. His time of 2:52.57 is almost one hour longer than the current winning times.

❹ Participating countries

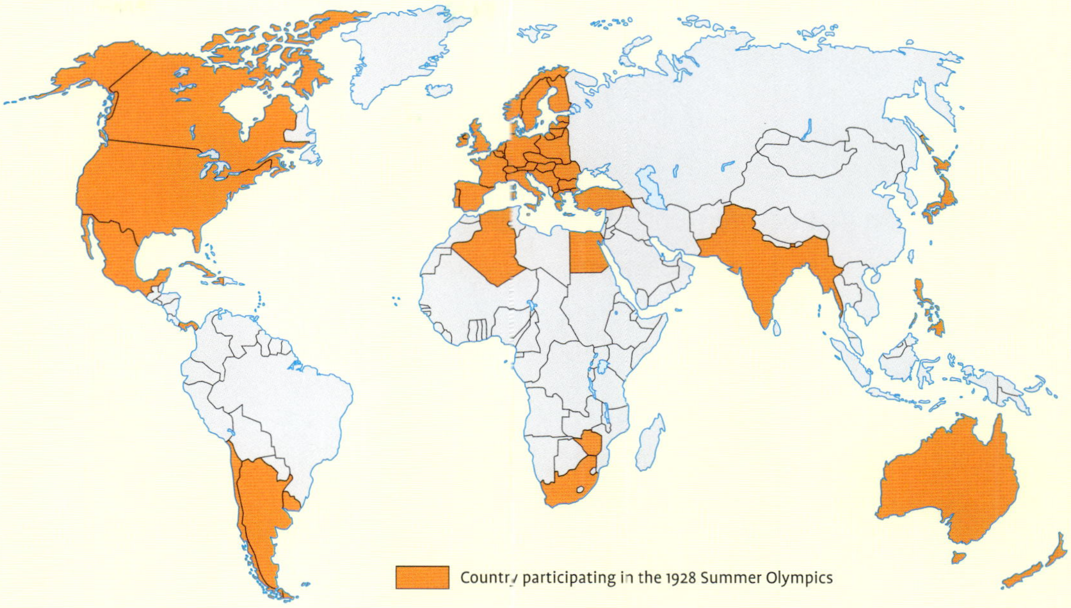

❺ 16 sports

❻ Dutch medal winners

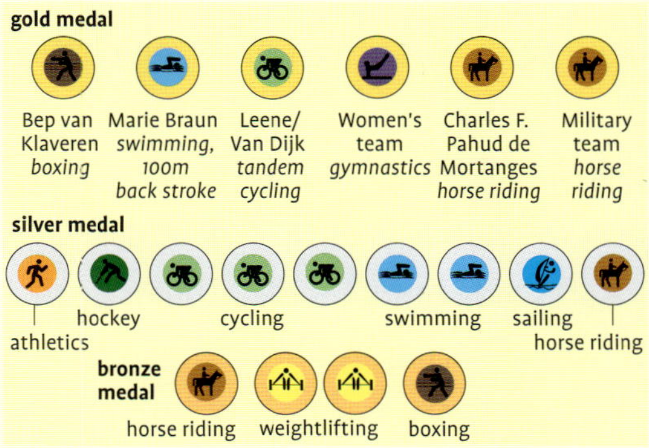

❼ Olympic events outside the city

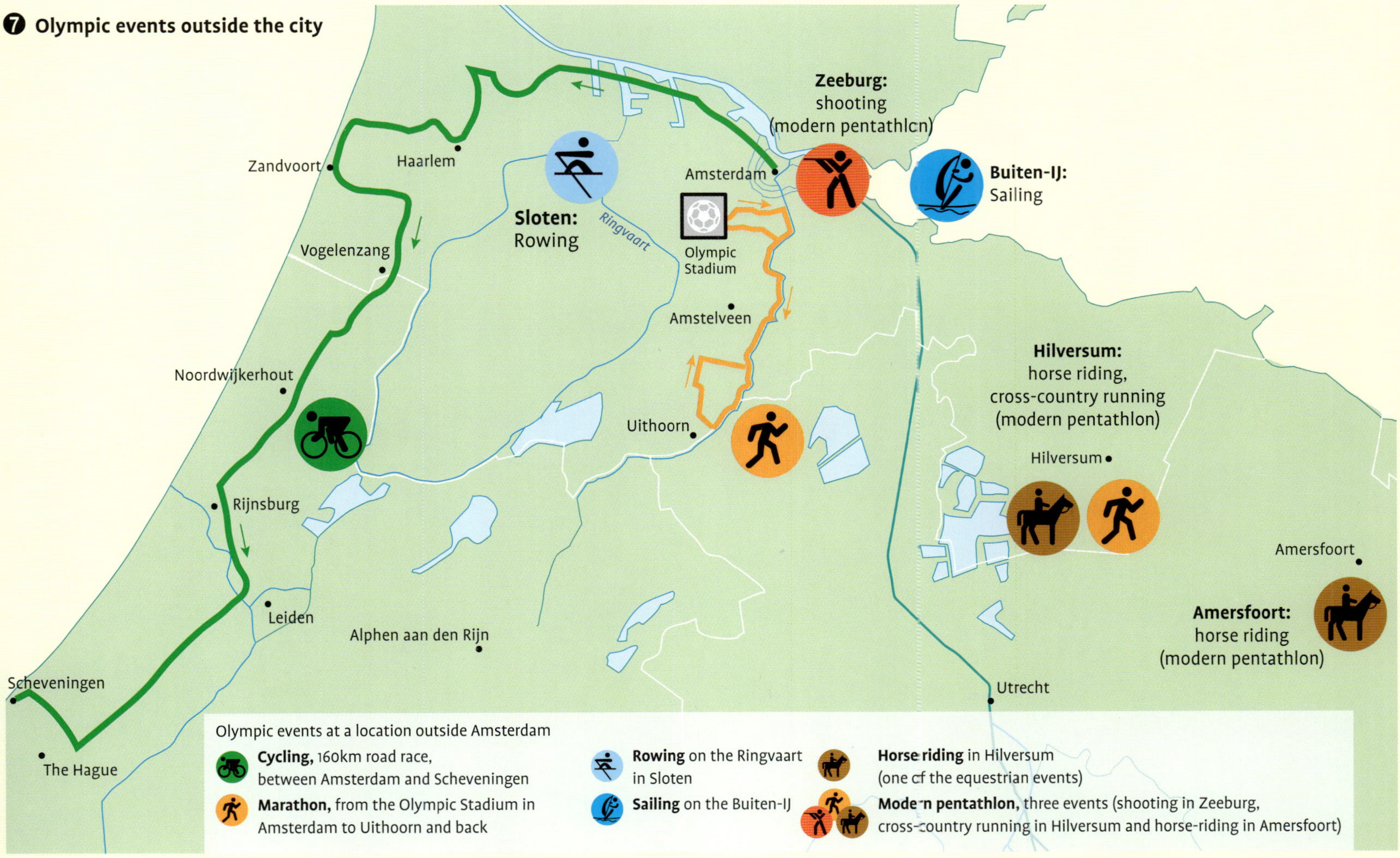

Source: NOC*NSF (4-7)

© Noordhoff Uitgevers

Ajax

With more than 95,000 members, the Ajax supporters' club is the largest in Europe. However, by no means all the supporters who cheer on or catcall their heroes in the Amsterdam ArenA are actually Amsterdammers, and the same goes for the team's line-up. The Amsterdamsche Football Club Ajax has become a listed company with a turnover of millions of euros. Even though results in recent years have been somewhat disappointing compared to the golden years of the 1970s, players are still honoured to don the Ajax shirt and managers figuratively queue up for the opportunity of managing these 'sons of the gods'. Supporters also remain faithful to the club and follow the ups and downs of 'their' players, particularly in the F-side sections 125-129 and the premium 424 and 425 sections.

❶ Ajax and Amsterdam

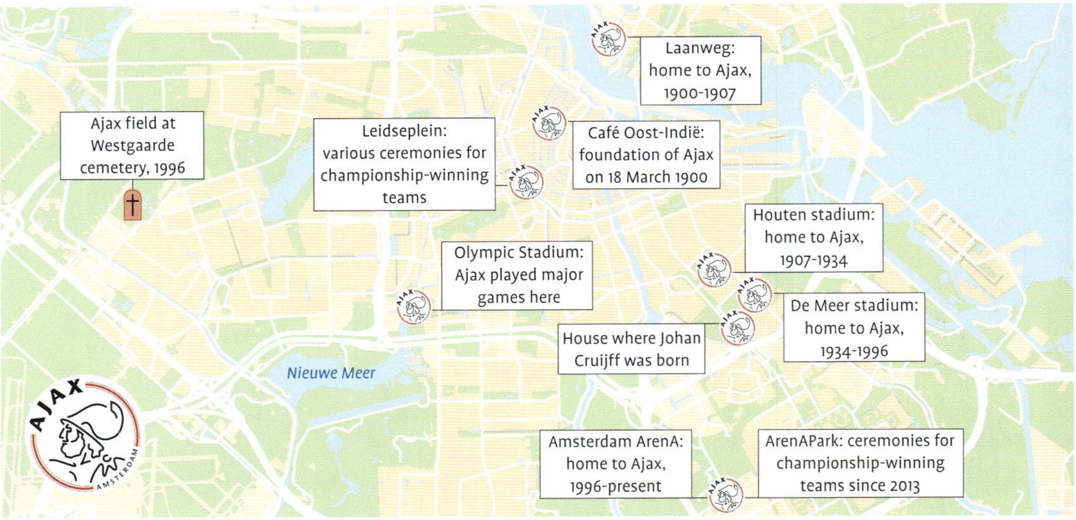

❷ Ajax's record in European finals

❸ Ajax line-ups and origin of players

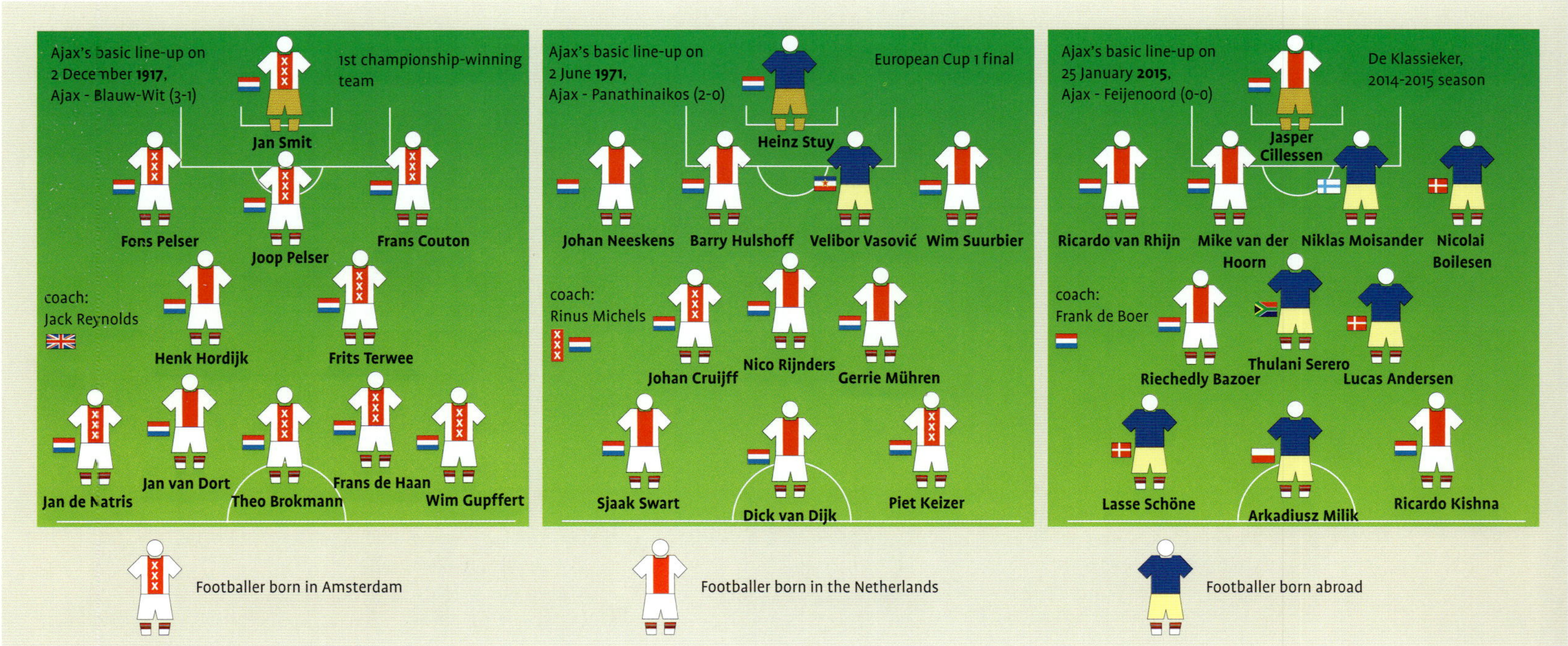

Source: AFC Ajax (1-3)

© Noordhoff Uitgevers

❶ - ❷ Triumphant successes
In the 1970s, Ajax won many games at national and European level in De Meer stadium under the leadership of 'General' Rinus Michels. The stadium closed in 1966. Part of the turf was donated to Westgaarde cemetery and is now used as an ash-sprinkling area for cremated Ajax supporters.

❸ An international team
In the early years, Ajax was still a true Amsterdam club – nearly all of the players were born in the city and only the manager was English. In the 1970s, players from Amsterdam ArenA, the Netherlands' largest stadium, accommodating 53,346 spectators.

❹ A new home
In 1996, Ajax moved from De Meer (29,500 spectators) to the Amsterdam ArenA, the Netherlands' largest stadium, accommodating 53,346 spectators. The construction costs were 96 million euros.

❺ Loyal supporters
Ajax can count on a loyal group of supporters who do not only come from Amsterdam.

❻ - ❼ Modest amounts
Ajax players earn around 400,000 euros a year on average, excluding bonuses. This is not much compared to the average annual salary of FC Barcelona players – 5,500,000 euros.

❹ Amsterdam ArenA

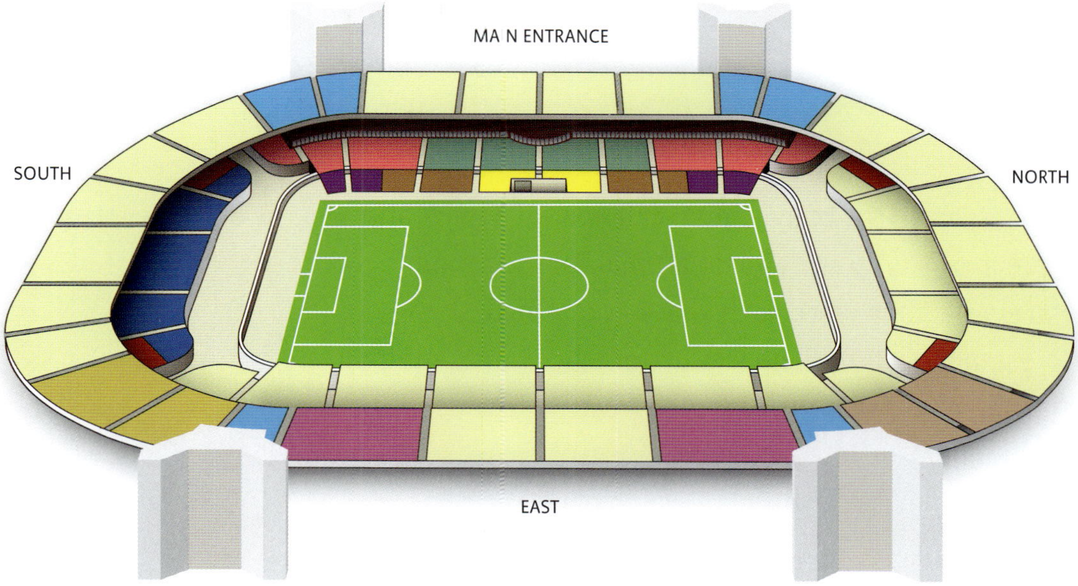

- Main stand (for board members, sponsors)
- Business seats (with special luxury chairs)
- Field seats
- Business field seats
- Dug-out seats
- Skyboxes
- F-side
- Wheelchair spaces
- Children's sections
- Ajax Kids Club
- Away-team sections (for supporters of the visiting clubs)
- Premium sections
- Other sections

❺ Ajax's market area

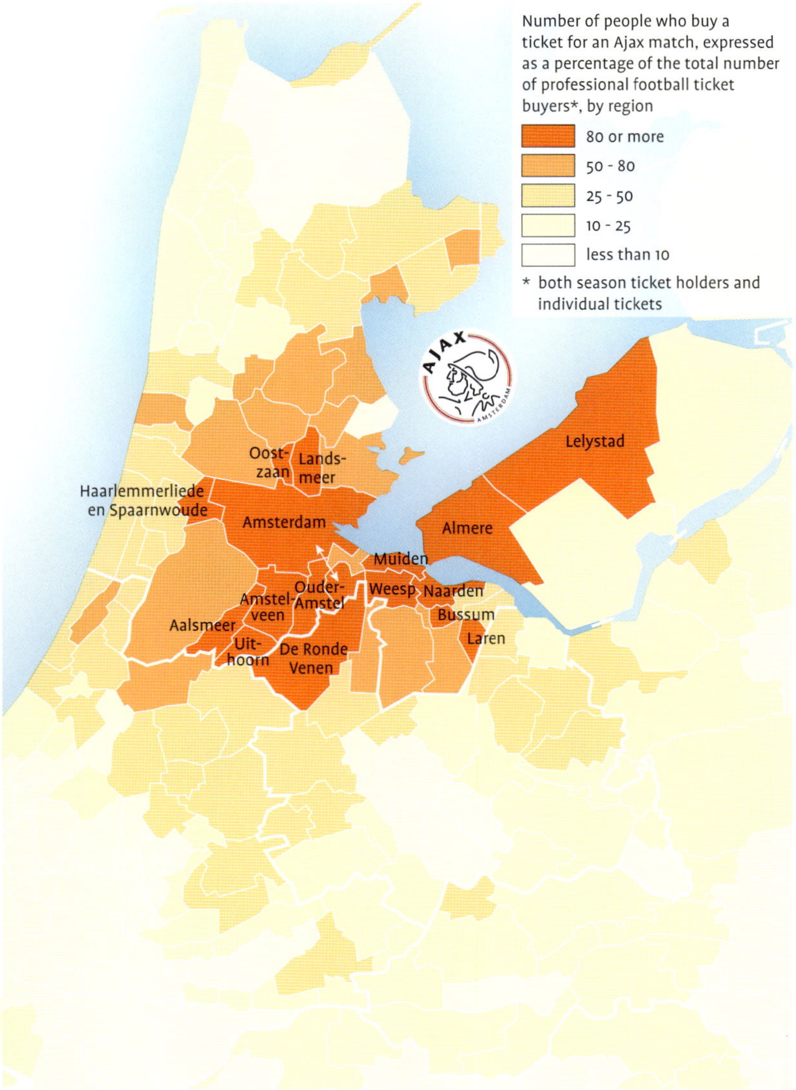

❻ Managers

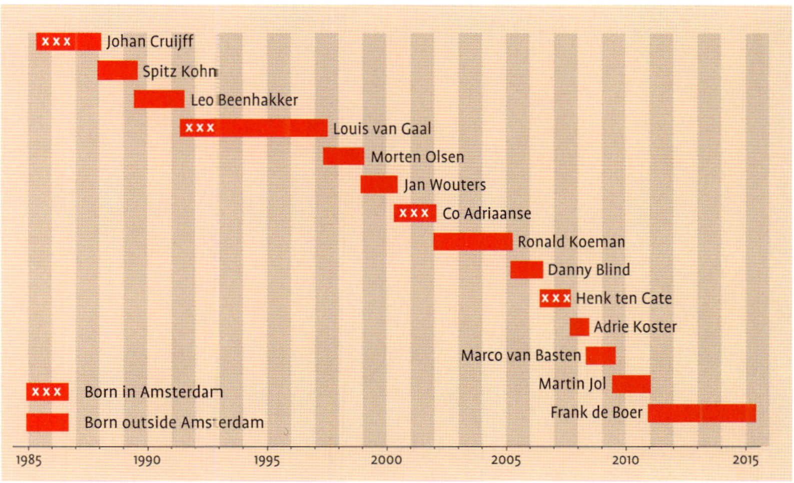

❼ Business operations

Staff

First team players	25
Youth players	39
Employees (total FTEs)	378
Players	107
Technical and medical staff	103
Other employees	168

2013/2014 season

Net turnover (euros x 1000)

Revenue from league, national cup and friendly matches	6,217
Revenue from European competitions	6,871
Bonuses from European competitions	12,080
Season tickets	11,597
Business seats and skybox seats	9,801
Indirect revenue from matches	1,866
Sponsorship	23,766
Television	19,251
Merchandising	11,029
Other income	1,302
Total net turnover	**103,780**
Wages and salaries	45.2m euros

Sources: Amsterdam ArenA (4); T. Dejonghe and S. van Hoof (5); AFC Ajax (6, 7)

© Noordhoff Uitgevers

Events

Amsterdam has a busy annual calendar of events and there is plenty to see and do all year long. Around 250 events take place each year in the Amsterdam Forest alone. The calendar is extremely diverse, ranging from one-off major exhibitions in the large museums to annual festivals and events. Some of these, such as the Holland Festival, Jumping Amsterdam and the Amsterdam Marathon, have existed for many years, while others, such as the Amsterdam City Swim, the Light festival or the Sotu festival in and around the Vondelpark, are relatively new.
Visitor numbers also vary enormously. Sail Amsterdam attracts millions of people whereas the prestigious Holland Festival, with nearly 60 productions each year and around 160 performances at 25 locations, is visited by 'a mere' 110,000 people. Many smaller events such as the Amsterdam Salsa Festival, the Pop Arts Festival (puppet theatre) and Cinedans (dance films) focus on specific market segments.

❶ Amsterdam Marathon

❷ Canal Parade/Gay Pride

❸ Sailing routes on King's Day

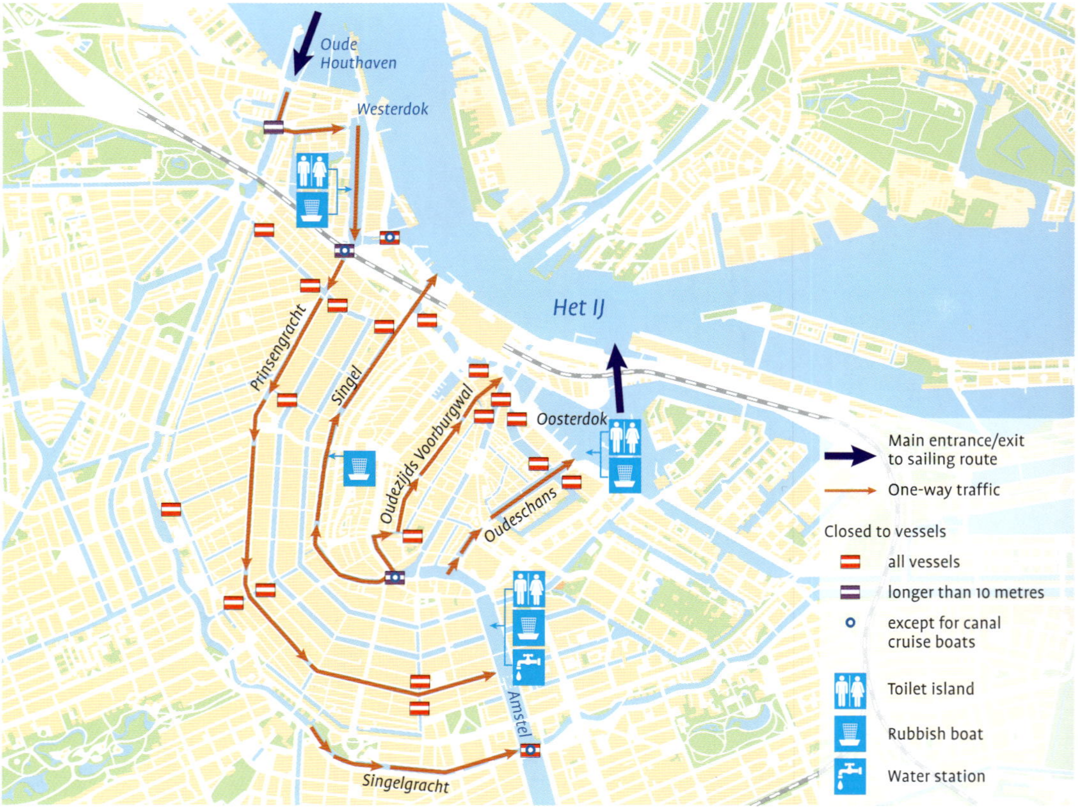

Sources: TCS Amsterdam Marathon (1); OIS, Research, Information and Statistics, City of Amsterdam / www.canalparade.nl (2); www.amsterdamkoningsdag.nl / Waternet (3)

© Noordhoff Uitgevers

❶ 42 kilometres of suffering
The 39th edition of the Amsterdam Marathon took place on 19 October 2014. Cheered on by a quarter of a million spectators, around 44,000 participants ran a half or full marathon or an 8 kilometre route. The event also resulted in 52,000 extra overnight stays.

❷ Eighty boats
The climax of the nine-day Amsterdam Gay Pride, which has been held every year since 1996, is the Canal Parade. Some eighty boats full of LGBTs (lesbians, gays, bisexuals and transgenders) and their sympathisers sail through the city.

❸ Crowds everywhere
On King's Day, hundreds of thousands of visitors from outside the city overrun the city centre and a massive influx of pleasure boats gridlocks the canals. To prevent accidents, the city council designates mandatory sailing routes and ensures large events are held on the outskirts of the city.

❹ A top event
Held for the first time in 1975 to celebrate Amsterdam's 700th anniversary, Sail Amsterdam has become one of the largest free open-air events in the Netherlands. In 2015, 2.3 million people visited Sail and the proceeds are expected to amount to around 100 million euros.

❺ - ❼ Festival city of the Netherlands
With around 350 festivals a year, Amsterdam has every right to call itself the festival city of the Netherlands. From dance to opera, film to cabaret, cooking to fashion and Surinamese dancing to the Grachtenfestival (the country's largest classical music festival) – Amsterdam has got it all.

❹ Sail Amsterdam 2015

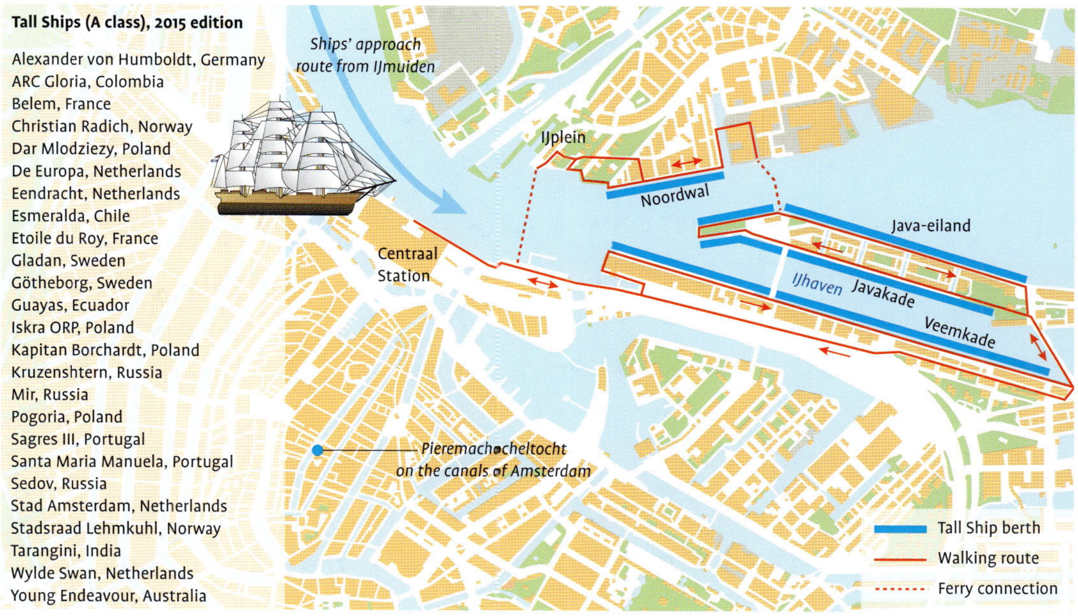

❺ Festivals

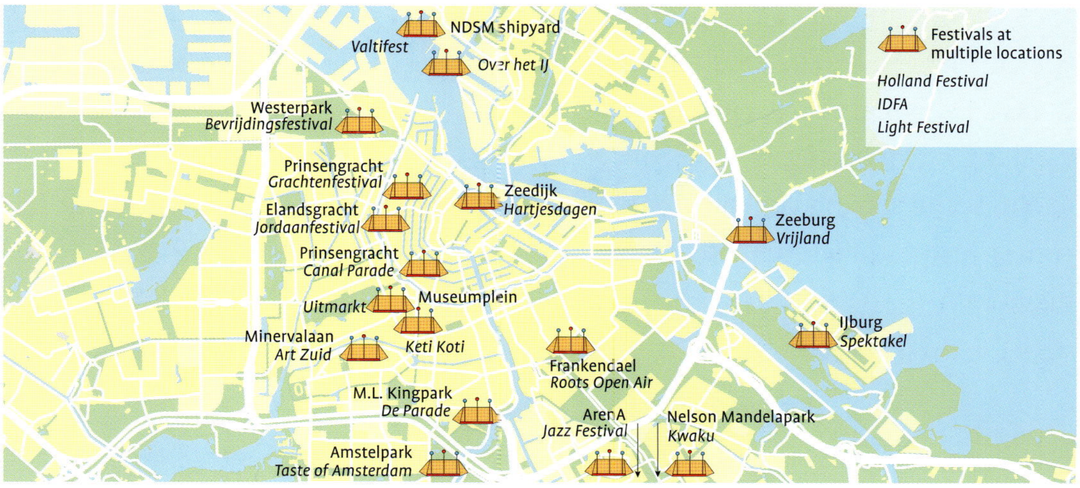

❻ The biggest events

❼ 2015 Kwaku Summer Festival, Nelson Mandela Park

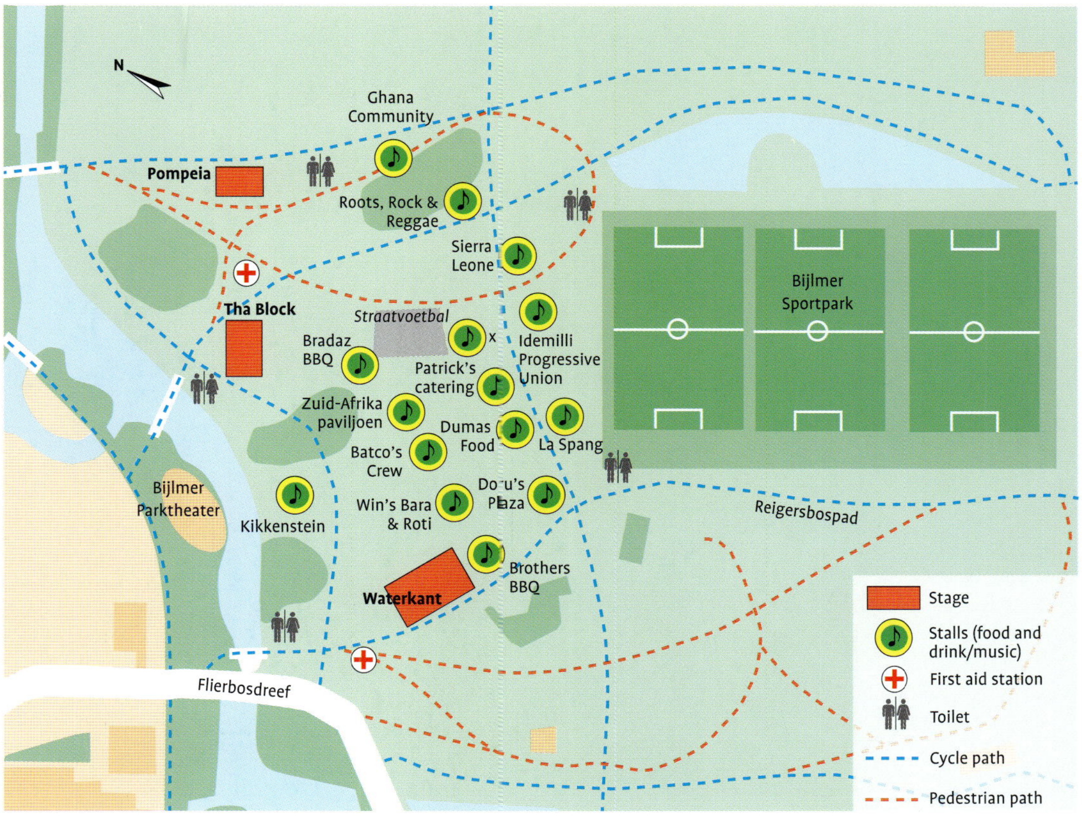

Sources: Stichting SAIL Amsterdam (4); I amsterdam (5, 6); Kwaku Summer Festival (7)

© Noordhoff Uitgevers

Amsterdam as a sanctuary

For many decades, Amsterdam had a reputation as the city that tolerated behaviour that was forbidden elsewhere. Drugs, darkrooms, window prostitution, a satanic church – almost anything was allowed. However, this policy of tolerance also had a downside. Noise, alcohol abuse, drug money laundering, real estate fraud, trafficking of women and exploitation of prostitutes all formed an increasing threat to normal life in the city centre, and particularly in the Burgwallen area, so the city council is cracking down on these issues once again. Some see this as 'self-righteous conformism', while others feel it is inevitable.

❶ Prostitution, drugs and gambling in 1012 postcode area

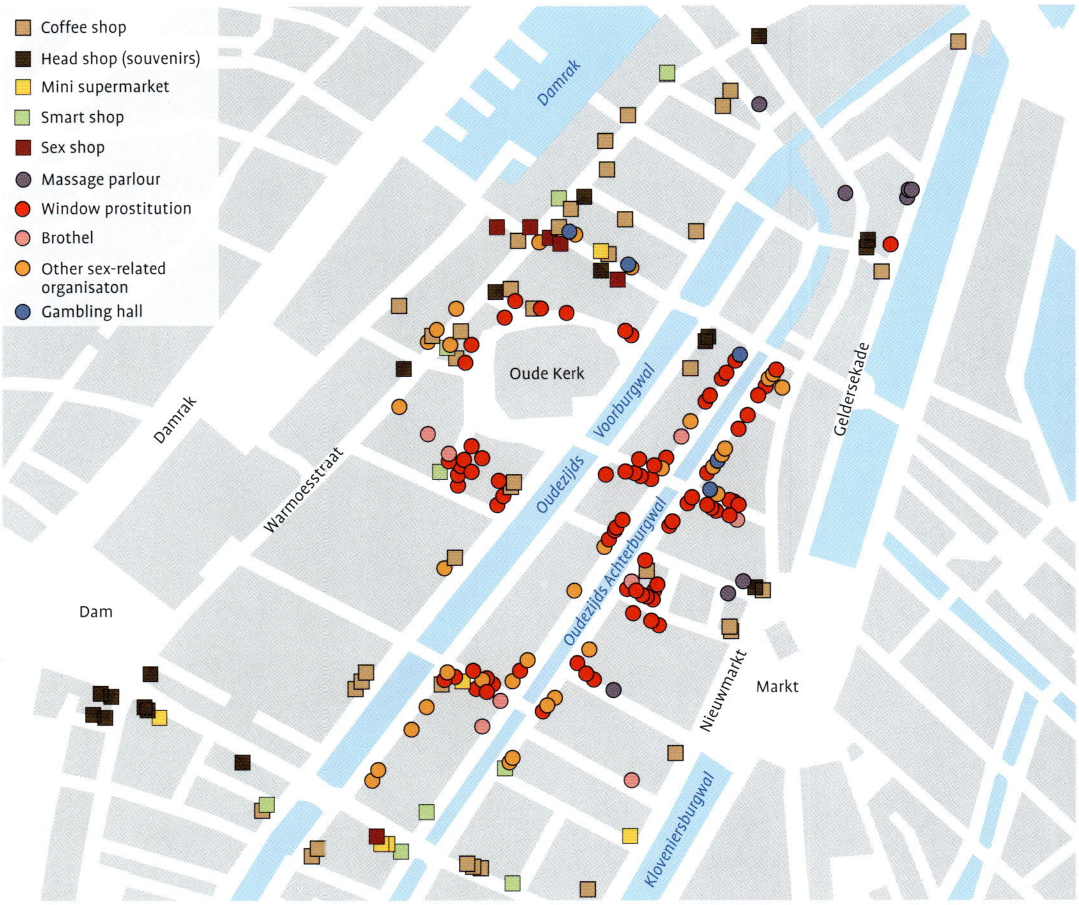

❷ Prostitution zones

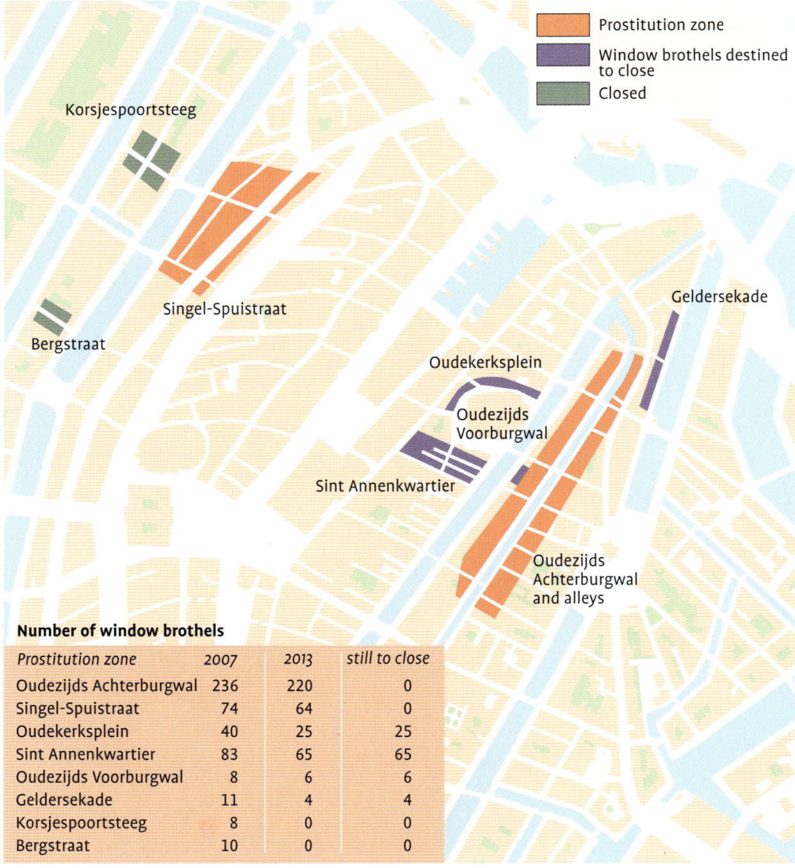

Number of window brothels

Prostitution zone	*2007*	*2013*	*still to close*
Oudezijds Achterburgwal	236	220	0
Singel-Spuistraat	74	64	0
Oudekerksplein	40	25	25
Sint Annenkwartier	83	65	65
Oudezijds Voorburgwal	8	6	6
Geldersekade	11	4	4
Korsjespoortsteeg	8	0	0
Bergstraat	10	0	0

❸ De Wallen

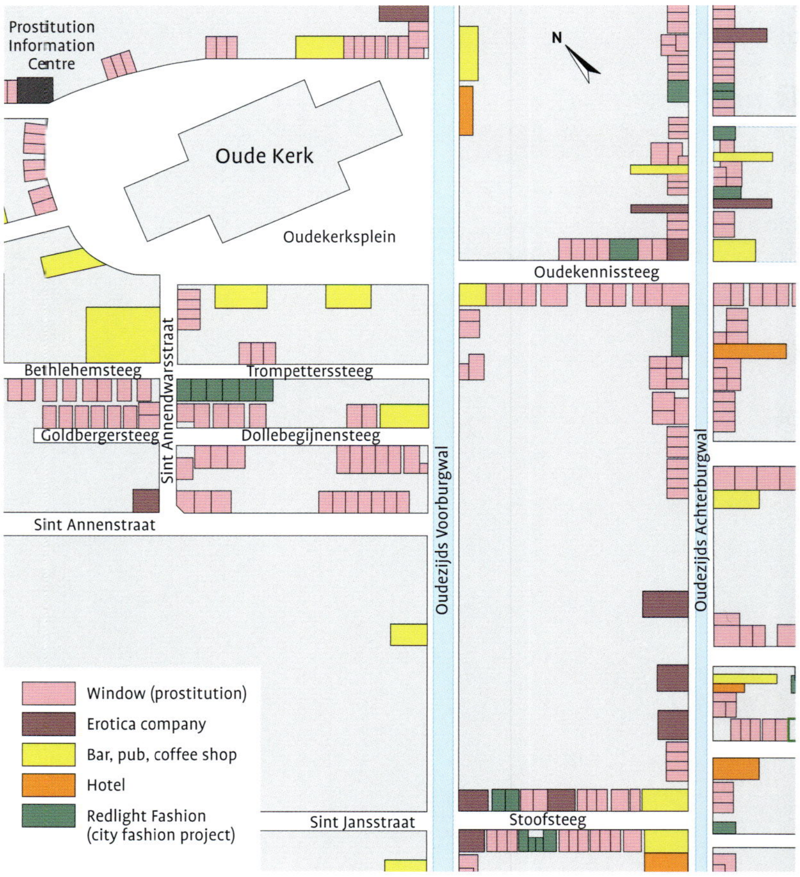

Sources: OIS, Research, Information and Statistics, City of Amsterdam (1); City of Amsterdam (2); www.raamwijzer.nl (3)

© Noordhoff Uitgevers

❶ Vulnerable to criminality
Criminal organisations are often closely linked to the drug trade and the sex industry. In order to reduce crime and boost the economy in the city centre, the city council launched an ambitious plan in 2007 called project 1012, named after the area's postcode. The plan calls for a reduction in the number of coffee shops, prostitute's windows, sex shops, gambling halls and massage parlours in order to restore a healthy balance between living, working and nightlife.

❷ - ❸ The red light district
Prostitutes used to mainly ply their trade in De Pijp (Oud-Zuid) and today's main prostitution zone, De Wallen, only started to colour red in the 1960s. Nobody knows exactly how many sex workers there are in Amsterdam, but estimates vary between 5000 and 7700, of which 1000 to 3400 are window prostitutes. The city has three prostitution zones – De Wallen, the Singel near Spuistraat and Ruysdaelkade. Nearly 70% of window prostitutes work in the De Wallen zone. Window prostitution is more integrated in the living and working environment in the other two zones.

❹ Gay Capital
Amsterdam no longer presents itself as the Gay Capital of Europe. That role has been taken over by cities like Berlin, Barcelona and London. Even so, Amsterdam remains an attractive place for homosexuals and lesbians due to the numerous nightlife facilities.

❺ Schools and coffee shops
Coffee shops have to meet ever more stringent requirements. For example, they must close down if they are situated less than 150 metres from a school (250 metres as of 1 January 2016). In 2014, this resulted in several coffee shops near a school on Nieuwezijds Voorburgwal attempting to buy out the school, but without success.

❻ Pros and cons
Despite the improved quality of life, the Burgwallen area still has the highest crime levels in Amsterdam. Even so, the residents are rather satisfied with their neighbourhood, as living in the heart of the city also has its advantages.

❹ Gay bars and clubs

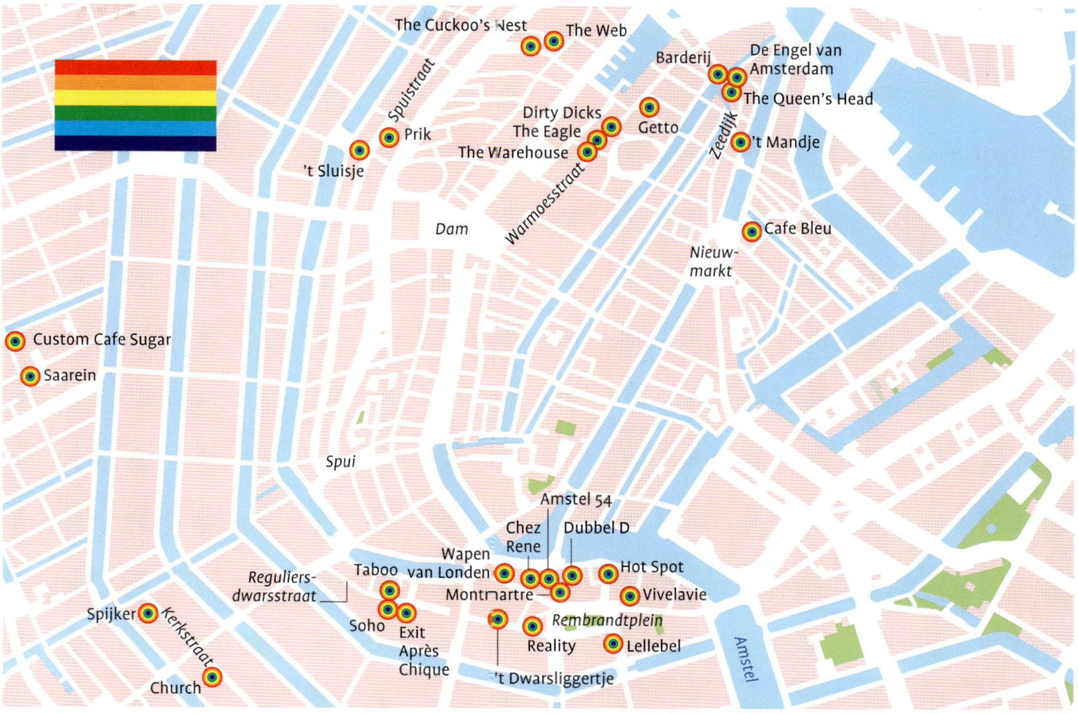

❺ Coffee shops around the Amsterdamsche School

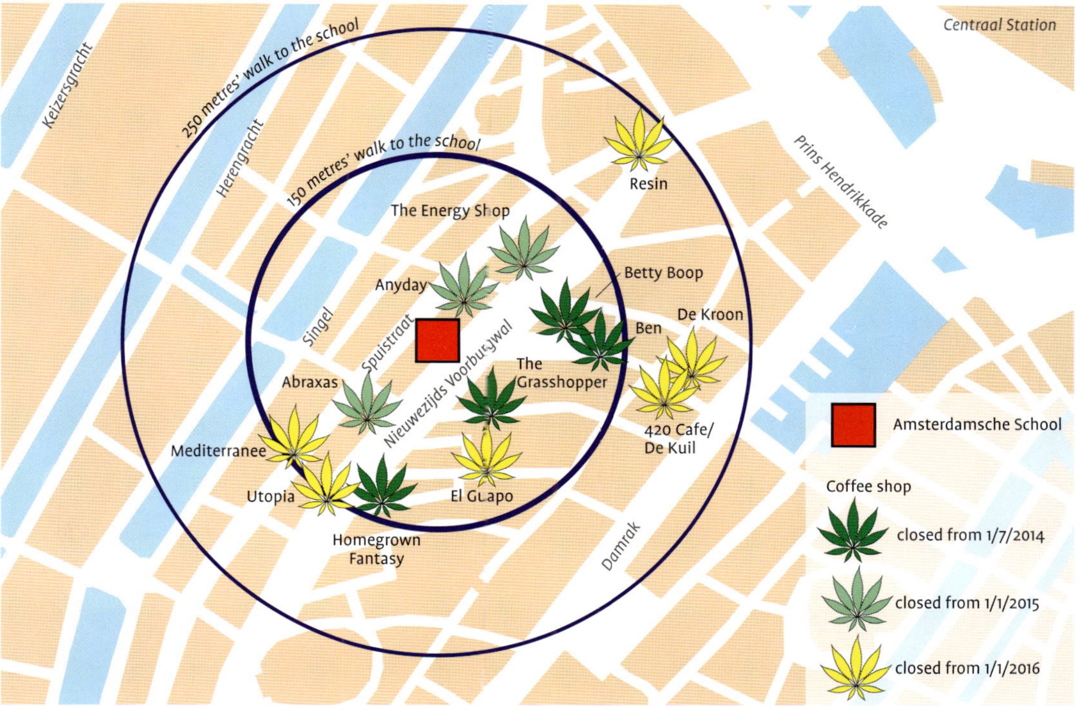

❻ Safety in the Burgwallen area

Objective safety index based on reports filed with the police (100 = average for Amsterdam in 2003, the higher the figure, the lower the level of safety)

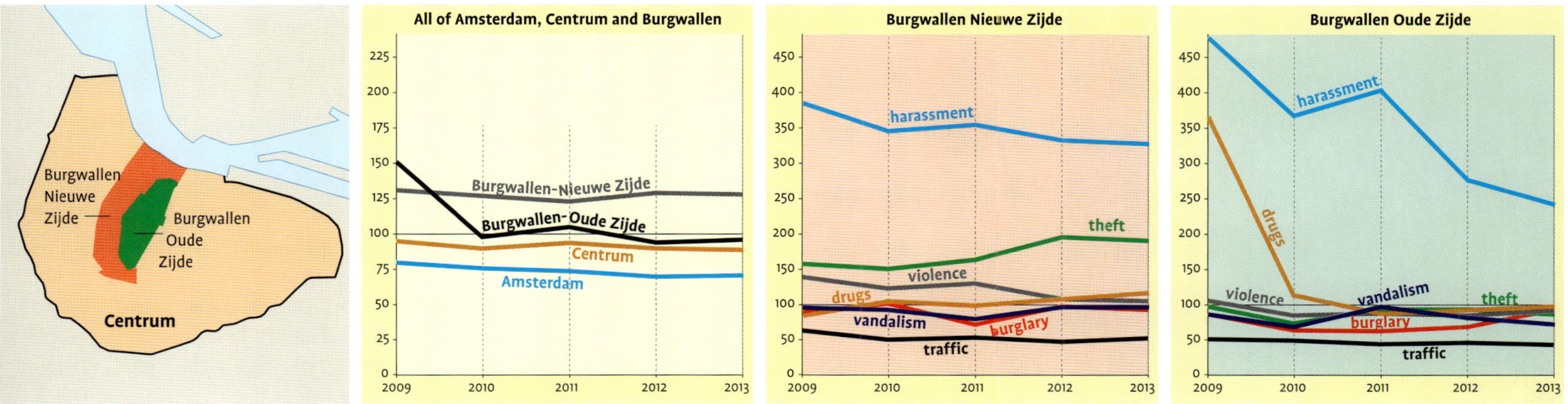

© Noordhoff Uitgevers

Singers and bands

❶ The Outsiders

Wladimir (Wally) Tax grew up in the Kadijken area and started his band, The Outsiders, at the tender age of twelve. A pub landlord in the Dapperbuurt helped Wally Tax to produce his first record in 1962. However, they only became successful after Tax's school friend, Ronnie Splinter, joined the line-up. Splinter was responsible for arranging the music, while Tax wrote the lyrics, which were mostly about love and critical of the establishment. A succession of hits followed and The Outsiders became the most hard-core beat band in the country. In 1969, at the pinnacle of his popularity, Tax left the band to embark on a career as a solo artist. Things went downhill after the death of his girlfriend and muse, Laurie Langenbach and he spent his last years living in poverty on Blasiusstraat.

❷ Ramses Shaffy

Ramses Shaffy, the son of an Egyptian diplomat and a Polish countess, started his career as a film and stage actor, singer and pianist with the Nederlandse Comedie theatre company in 1955. In 1964, he founded his own theatre company called Shaffy Chantant (later renamed Shaffy Cantate), in which he rocketed to fame in the hip Amsterdam of the 1960s together with Liesbeth List (photo), Louis van Dijk and others. In 1966, he made a successful debut as a solo artist with his first single, *Sammy*. Many classic hits followed, including the *Pastorale* duet with Liesbeth List in 1968. During the 1970s, his extravagant lifestyle and excessive drinking started to take their toll. After spending time in a Bhagwan commune, he mainly focused on acting. He died of oesophageal cancer on 1 December 2009, aged 76, and was buried in Zorgvlied cemetery.

❸ André Hazes

Johnny Kraaykamp Senior was the first person to discover singing prodigy André Gerardus Hazes — born 30 June 1951 at Gerard Doustraat 67-III — when he heard the eight-year-old singing at the Albert Cuypmarkt. A single was released, but little André's career did not take off right away. After unsuccessfully trying his hand at various trades, he was again discovered while working at pub De Krommerdt in De Baarsjes, this time as the singing bartender. Over the years that followed, Hazes evolved into the leading protagonist of the Dutch 'levenslied' musical genre. He became a Dutch celebrity, often featuring in the gossip magazines, which reported extensively on his tumultuous private life and drinking problem. However, none of this bothered the man in the long black coat and black hat. On 27 September 2004, four days after the singer's death, around 48,000 fans flocked to the ArenA where his coffin stood proudly on the centre spot. Some 5 million viewers watched the ceremony live on television.

Photos: © Hollandse Hoogte (1, 2); © ANP (3)

© Noordhoff Uitgevers

❹ De Dijk
In the 1970s, two Amsterdammers, Huub van der Lubbe and his brother Hans, were the leading artists in a pop group called Stampei. In 1981, the band changed its name to De Dijk, an ironic reference to the infamous Zeedijk in Amsterdam. The first album, which was simply called *De Dijk*, came out in 1982, but was not a big hit. However, De Dijk persisted in the face of adversity and has produced many hits since then, including *Als ze er niet is, Mag het licht uit* and *Dansen op de vulkaan*. After more than 30 years, the group still exists with the same line-up, something which is unprecedented in the history of pop – Huub van der Lubbe (lyrics and lead singer), Hans van der Lubbe (bass), Antonie Broek (drums and musical arrangement), Nico Arzbach (guitar) and Pim Kops (keyboard and guitar). Inspired by American rock, soul and rhythm-and-blues, their music appeals to older audiences in particular.

❺ De Jeugd van Tegenwoordig
In 2005, Willie Wartaal (Olivier Locadia, 1982), Vieze Fur (Freddy Tratlehner, 1983), Faberyayo (Pepijn Lanen, 1982) and producer Bas Bron decided to start a new rap group named De Jeugd van Tegenwoordig. Their first single, *Watskeburt* (street slang for 'what happened?'), was an unexpected hit and topped the Top 100 singles chart for three weeks. *Sterrenstof* is another of their hits. In 2011, the group was voted the best hip-hop group of the year by radio station 3FM. The threesome, who come from the Spaarndammerbuurt, are now an established name, playing at the biggest music festivals in the Netherlands and Flanders. Their style is characterised by humorous lyrics, bizarre language with many words of their own invention, imitations and the striking electronic synthesizer beats conceived by Bas Bron. So far, the group has released four albums comprising 64 songs and a fifth album will be released to mark their 10th anniversary.

❻ Caro Emerald
Caroline Esmeralda van der Leeuw, better known by her stage name of Caro Emerald, came into the world in Amsterdam on 26 April 1981. She graduated as a jazz vocalist from the Conservatorium van Amsterdam in 2005. Her debut album, *Deleted Scenes from the Cutting Room Floor*, including the hit *A Night Like This* (written and arranged by David Schreurs and Vince Degiorgio), was released in January 2010 and topped the Dutch Top 100 album chart for thirty consecutive weeks, an absolute record. It was also popular abroad, particularly in England, selling hundreds of thousands of copies. In November 2013, Emerald was even asked to perform for the British Royal Family. Her second album, *The Shocking Miss Emerald*, also topped the charts. She lives in Amsterdam.

Photos: © ANP (4); © Hollandse Hoogte (5, 6)

© Noordhoff Uitgevers

I amsterdam

8

Culture

◁
Rijksmuseum Amsterdam
Photo Karel Tomeï

8 Introduction

The big two

Rembrandt and Van Gogh – ask any foreigner and he will name these two painters as Amsterdam's cultural leading lights. Based on the millions of visitors to the Rijksmuseum and the Van Gogh Museum alone, Amsterdam is fully justified in calling itself an international centre of culture. However, these museums are not all the city has to offer.

Museum collections

It is hardly surprising that foreigners mainly associate Amsterdam with its museum collections and the striking buildings along the canals. The same is true of other cultural cities such as Paris and Saint Petersburg. After all, visual art is easily accessible to people who do not speak or understand the local language, unlike theatre or literature, but this is certainly not the only reason. Many of Amsterdam's museums excel at creating special exhibitions and the museums are revamped on a regular basis, even though this means that they sometimes have to close for long periods.

Global trendsetter

Amsterdam is also renowned internationally in the field of the performing arts. Ensembles and companies based in the city, such as the National Opera, the National Ballet and the Royal Concertgebouw Orchestra, are among the world's very best artists. These ensembles have lost their Amsterdam identity to a certain extent, as the dancers and musicians come from all over the world. Remarkably enough, Toneelgroep Amsterdam, an exclusive preserve of Dutch-speaking actors, has also achieved success all over the world, from Washington to Wuzhen.

National importance

Other aspects of cultural life in Amsterdam play a far less prominent role internationally, but are certainly important within the context of the Netherlands. Publishing, journalism and the film industry are all mainly based in Amsterdam, but radio and television are not – for historical reasons they are based in Hilversum. Even so, a trend towards broadcasting from locations in Amsterdam seems to be emerging, especially when it

Rijksmuseum Amsterdam
Amsterdam is indisputably the cultural capital of the Netherlands, a status to which the Rijksmuseum's presence in the city contributes significantly. Since the opening of the current accommodation in 1885, the building has been extended and revamped several times, most recently in 2013. The museum now has more than one million objects in its collection, 8000 of which are on display.

comes to talk shows and cultural programmes.

Cultural interest

Needless to say culture is not just driven by producers – consumers ultimately determine what is viable. The relatively young and well-educated residents of Amsterdam play a decisive role in that respect, visiting museums frequently and flocking to cultural events such as the Grachtenfestival and the Uitmarkt in huge numbers. When you add Amsterdam's remarkably large number of bookshops into the equation, only one conclusion is possible – Amsterdam deserves the name of 'cultural capital of the Netherlands' more than any other Dutch city.

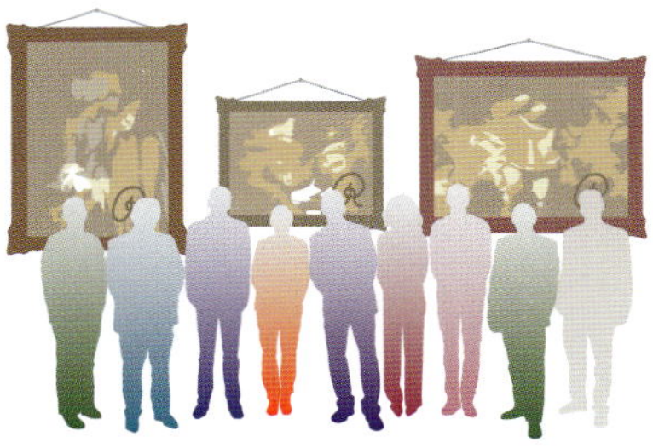

The Rijksmuseum's *Late Rembrandt* is the most expensive exhibition ever produced in the Netherlands

4,700,000 euros

520,698 visitors (= 5481 per day)

Number of items loaned by Openbare Bibliotheek van Amsterdam

2003: **5** million

2013: **3.5** million

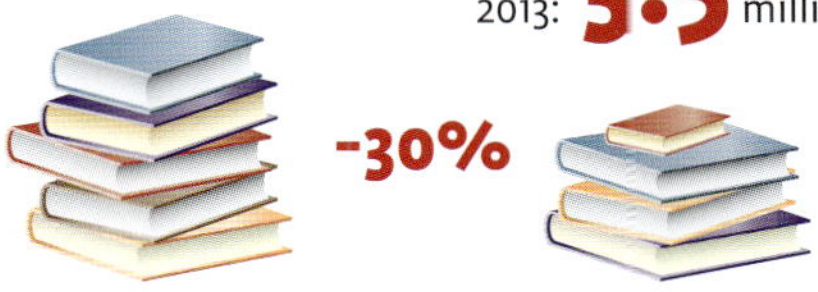

-30%

The Dutch National Ballet

99,309

attendees in 2014

More than **100** performances by De Dijk in Paradiso

30 stages

300 free performances

2000 artists

500,000 visitors

© Noordhoff Uitgevers

Museums

Five of the country's six most frequently visited museums are located in Amsterdam, along with dozens of smaller, often highly specialised, museums. In other words, Amsterdam is a true museum city. This is partly due to the at least once in 2014. However, the high density of museums also reflects the huge numbers of tourists, who not only flock to the Rijksmuseum and its Gallery of Honour, but also to many other less sophisticated exhibitions on sex, drugs and instruments of torture. Some of Amsterdam's museums, like the Anne Frank House and the Van Gogh Museum, mainly attract foreign visitors, while others focus on themes that primarily interest Dutch people, such as houseboats, old trams or the life and work of detective-turned-author Appie Baantjer. However, they all benefit from the magnetic attraction of a historical city where millions of people come to enjoy themselves each year.
In order to accommodate this still-growing group of visitors without overcrowding, some of the city's museums have recently renovated or extended their buildings. In light of reduced government funding, they are also trying to attract and retain the loyalty of a new group of visitors other than tourists, by organising special events such as the museum night and museum week.

❶ Major museums

Sources: www.amsterdam.info / OIS, Research, Information and Statistics, City of Amsterdam

© Noordhoff Uitgevers

❶ **Diversity**
There is a wide variety of museums, ranging from the Amsterdam Museum (about the city's history) to the Cat Cabinet and Museum of Bags and Purses.

❷ **Growth**
The number of people visiting a museum in Amsterdam rose from six to ten million between 2002 and 2013. The Van Gogh Museum attracted the most visitors for many years, but lost its leading position to the Rijksmuseum when the latter reopened in April 2013. New museums continue to open on a regular basis. Amsterdam has been home to a dependency of the Russian Hermitage Museum since 2009, the film museum EYE opened in 2012 and the Nationaal Sjoa Museum is due to open in 2020.

❸ **Self-generated income**
Due to cutbacks, museums will receive less government funding in the period from 2013 to 2016. As a result, they will increasingly rely on entrance fees and sponsorship funding.

❹ **and** ❺ **Representative attractions**
Many museums have been refurbished or modernised recently the best-known case being that of the Rijksmuseum, whose Gallery of Honour was closed for about ten years. Refurbishment and modernisation are prestigious projects for museums and often boost visitor numbers directly after reopening. The refurbished National Maritime Museum attracted 200,000 curious visitors in the first four months – the same as the annual total before the refurbishment.

❷ Most frequently visited museums in the Netherlands

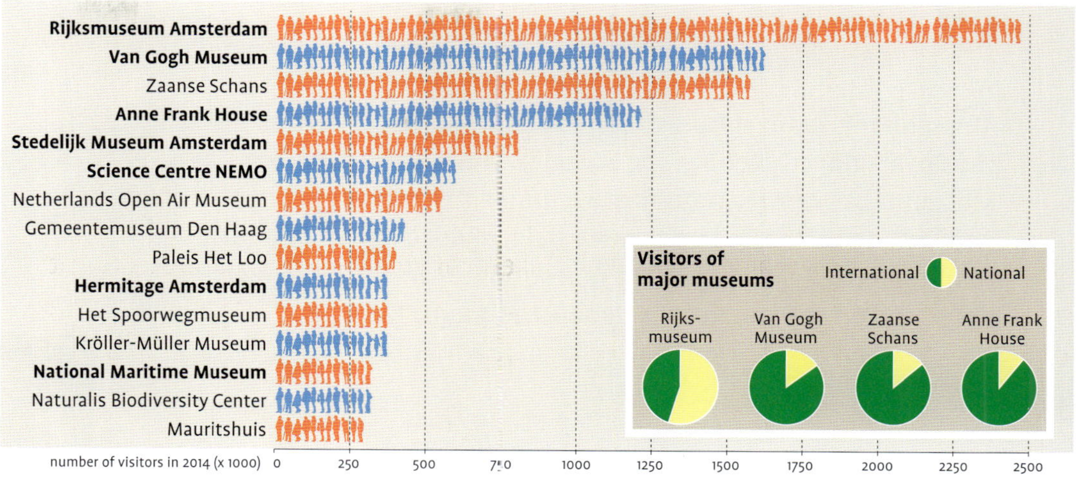

❸ Van Gogh Museum income

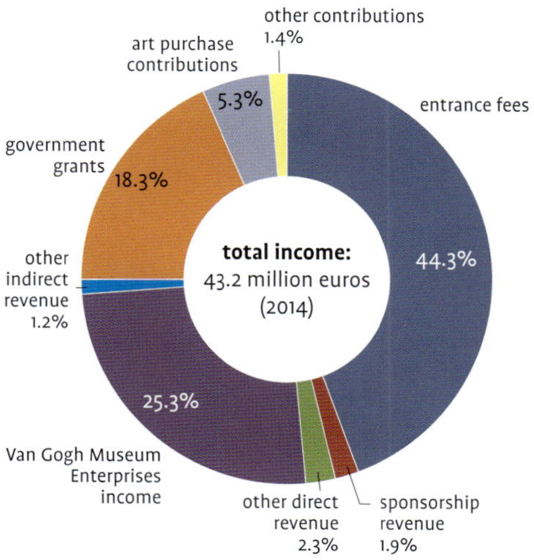

❹ Construction and refurbishment

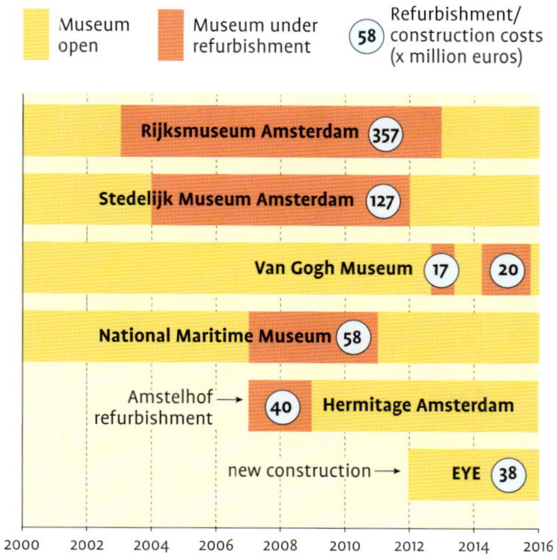

❺ The Rijksmuseum's Gallery of Honour

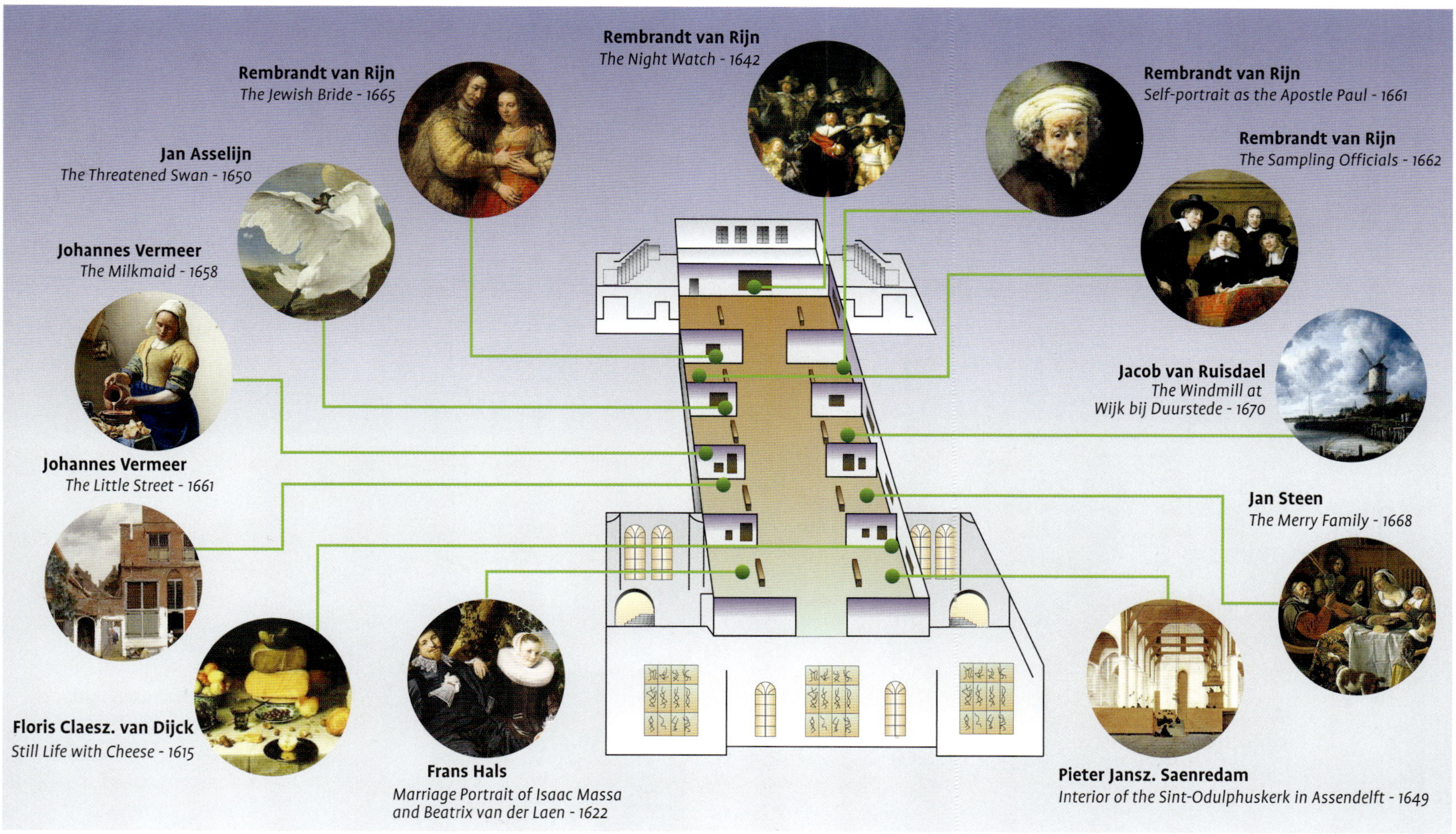

Sources: Cultural Heritage Agency / Museums Association (2); Van Gogh Museum (3); www.amsterdam.info (4); Rijksmuseum Amsterdam (5)

© Noordhoff Uitgevers

Museumplein

Amsterdam's main cultural institutions – the Rijksmuseum, the Royal Concertgebouw, the Stedelijk Museum and the Van Gogh Museum –are centred around Museumplein. For many years, this area was little more than a large grassy field, divided in two by a busy thoroughfare. Following recent renovations, cars are no longer permitted on the square, which now has more character.

Vincent van Gogh, self-portrait (1887)

Van Gogh Museum (1973)
The world's largest Van Gogh collection, also featuring works of his contemporari
Architect: G. Rietveld, in collaboration with J. van Dillen and J. van Tricht

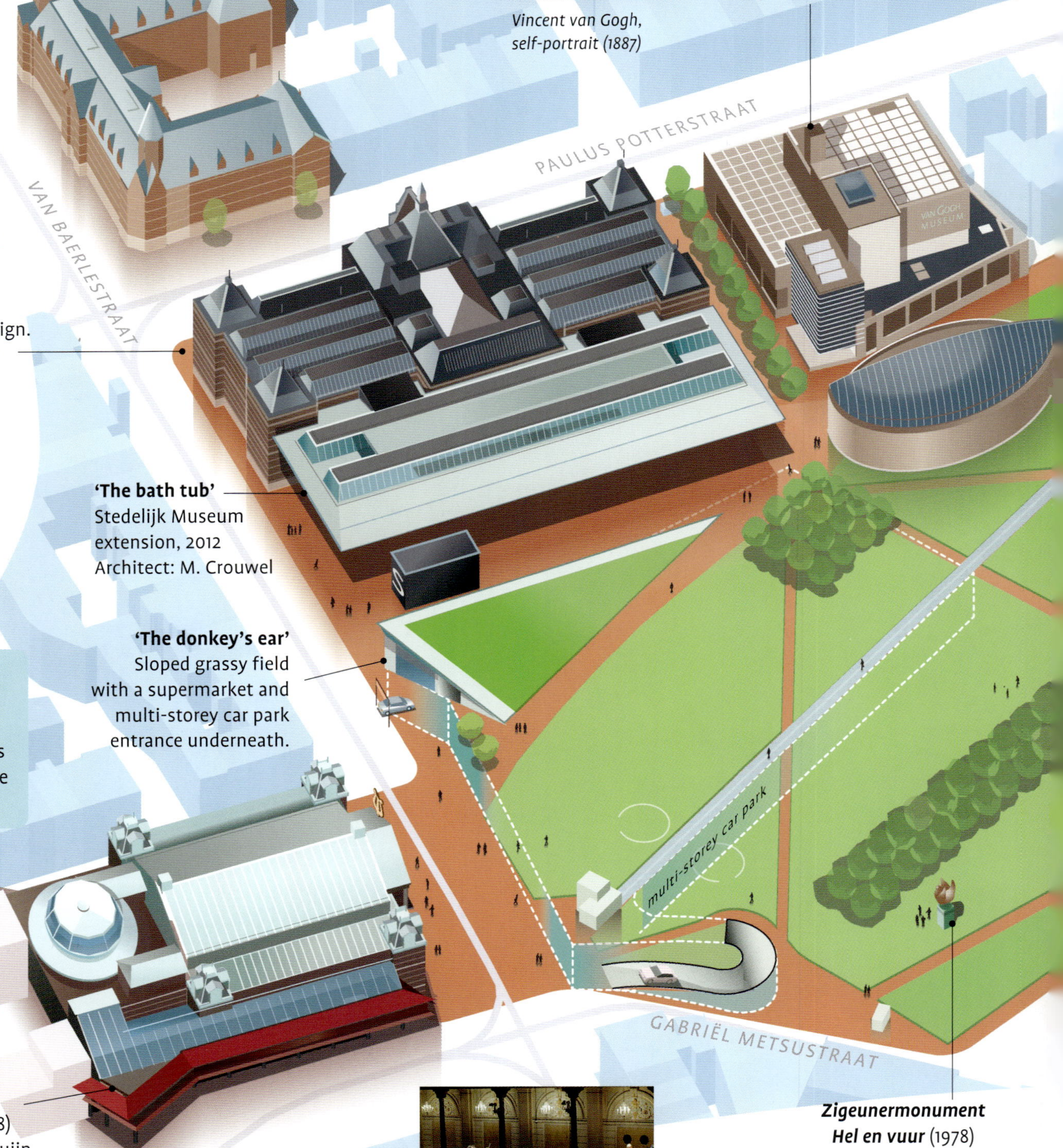

Former Sweelinck Conservatory
(1985-2008)
Previously Rijkspost-spaarbank (1901-1984).
Now a very luxurious hotel.

Stedelijk Museum Amsterdam (1895)
Museum of modern and contemporary art and design.
Architect: A. W. Weissman

Karel Appel, Dieren (1951)

'The bath tub'
Stedelijk Museum extension, 2012
Architect: M. Crouwel

'The donkey's ear'
Sloped grassy field with a supermarket and multi-storey car park entrance underneath.

Museum entrances
The museum entrances have been moved to the square side in recent years in order to further upgrade the square.

Royal Concertgebouw
(1888)
Architect: A. L. van Gendt

Side wing extension (1988)
Architect: P. de Bruijn

The Royal Concertgebouw Orchestra is one of the best in the world.

Zigeunermonument Hel en vuur (1978)
Bronze statue commemorating the millions of gypsies murdered during World War II.

Source: City of Amsterdam; Photos: © ANP Photo (Van Gogh, Royal Concertgebouw Orchestra) / © Corbis (Karel Appel) / © Rijksmuseum Amsterdam (Night Watch) / © Hollandse Hoogte (Uitmarkt)

Rembrandt, The Night Watch (1642)

Rijksmuseum (1885)

Museum providing an overview of Dutch art and history.
Architect: P. J. H. Cuypers

Refurbishment
Cruz y Ortis (2013)
2 large atriums with glass roofs

Diamond Museum Amsterdam

Unusual diamonds and information about the way in which they are mined and cut.

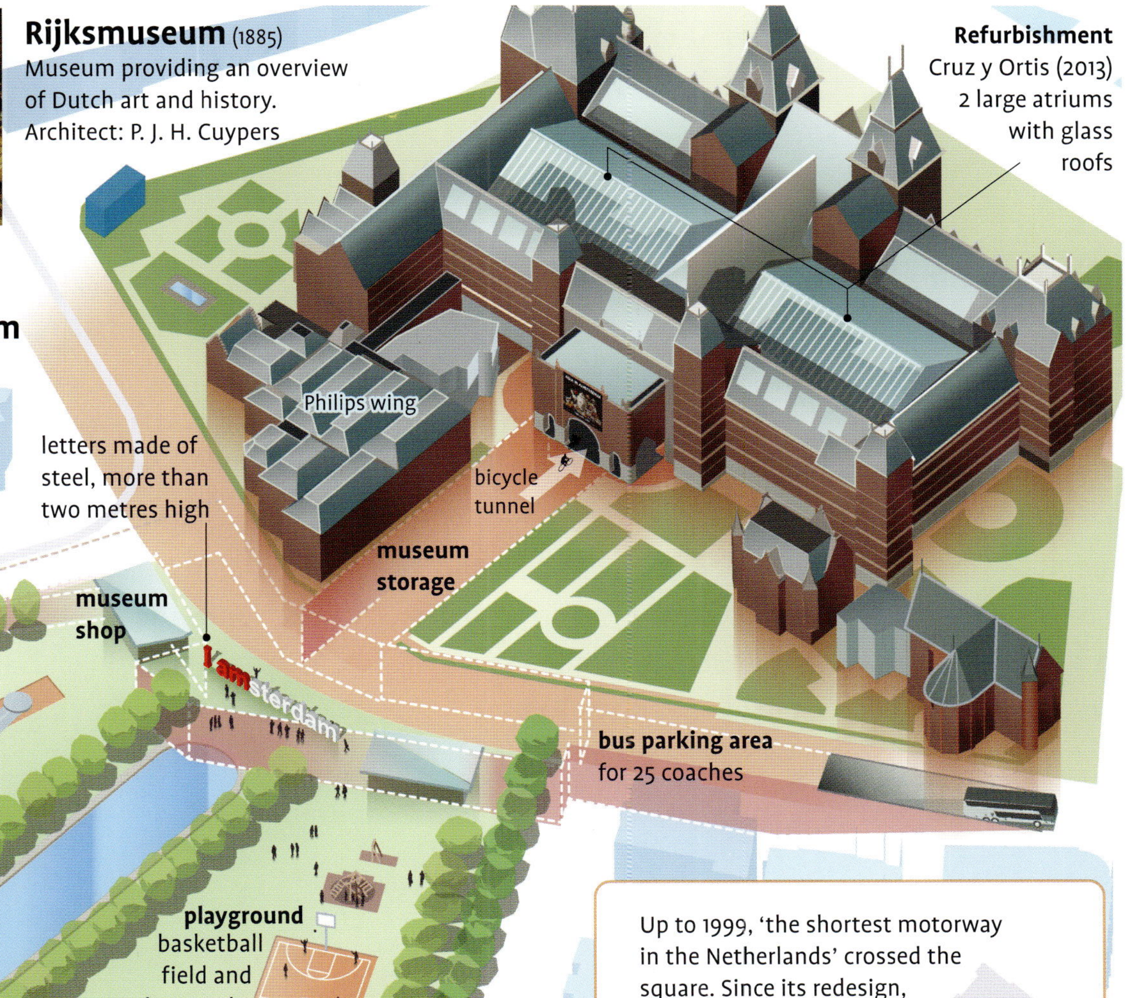

New Van Gogh Museum wing (1998/2015)
Used for exhibitions and as an entrance.
Architect: K. Kurokawa

- **Old name:**
  IJsclubterrein, Museumplein since 1903
- **Original layout:**
  P. J. H. Cuypers and the city council (1891)
- **Post-war modernisation:**
  C. van Eesteren and H. Warnau (1947)
- **Current layout:**
  S-I. Andersson and S. Gall (2001)

Up to 1999, 'the shortest motorway in the Netherlands' crossed the square. Since its redesign, the square has been car-free.

In order to further upgrade the square, the entrances to all museums have been moved to the square side in recent years.

Monument Vrouwen van Ravensbrück (1975)
In memory of the 90,000 women and children and 20,000 men who were murdered in the Ravensbrück concentration camp.

Events on Museumplein attract hundreds of thousands of people. There are dance festivals and political demonstrations, and football finals are displayed on big screens. One of the biggest events is the annual Uitmarkt.

Museum visitors per year

The number of visitors to the Van Gogh Museum remains stable. The number of visitors to the Rijksmuseum and Stedelijk Museum have increased significantly following the refurbishments.

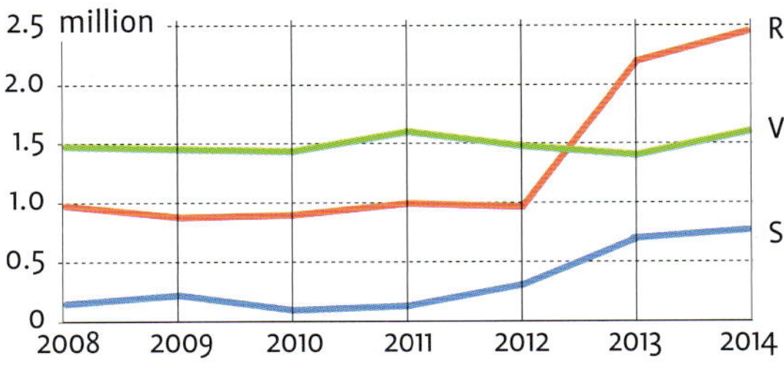

Consulate General of the United States

© Noordhoff Uitgevers

Rembrandt's city

Rembrandt went for a walk through Amsterdam at some point in 1644 and sketched the Montelbaanstoren in his sketchbook. Back home, he turned that sketch into a beautiful pen and ink drawing and he also immortalised numerous other locations in Amsterdam in the same way.

In 1631, Rembrandt moved from Leiden to Amsterdam and took up residence in the home of art dealer Hendrick van Uylenburgh on the, at that time, extremely fashionable Sint Antoniesbreestraat (now Jodenbreestraat). This is where he met Saskia, VanUylenburgh's niece, whom he married in Sint-Annaparochie in 1634. The relationship with Van Uylenburgh turned sour one year later and Rembrandt and Saskia moved first to Nieuwe Doelenstraat and then to Zwanenburgerstraat. In 1639, Rembrandt, who was by that time one of Amsterdam's most highly paid painters, purchased a spacious home at Jodenbreestraat 4, which is now the Rembrandt House Museum. However, he went bankrupt in 1658 and had to move to Rozengracht 184, where he died on 4 October 1669.

❶ Sites in Amsterdam associated with Rembrandt

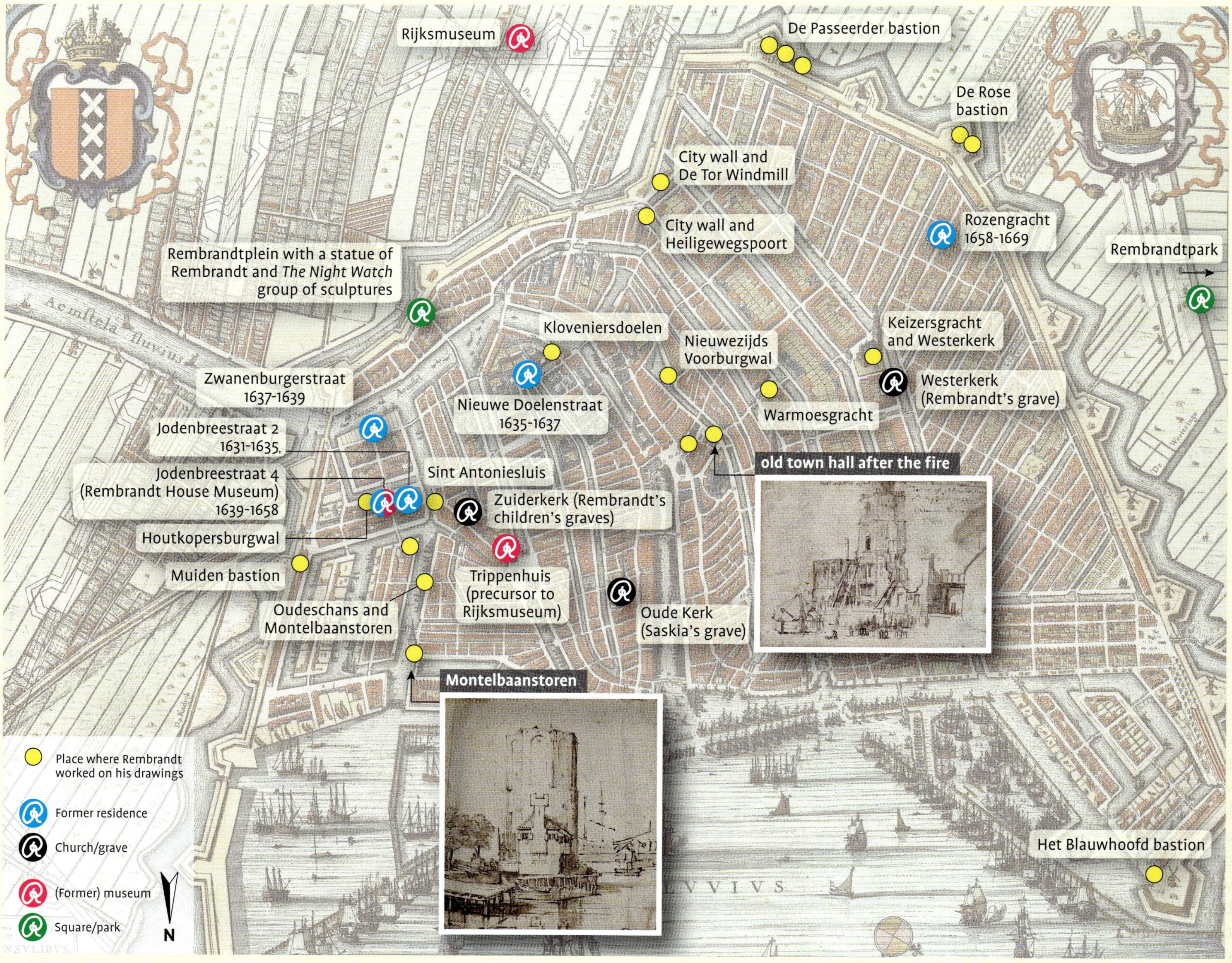

Sources: Special Collections of the University of Amsterdam: Map of Amsterdam by Joan Blaeu (1649) (background) / B. Bakker and others, Het landschap van Rembrandt, Wandelingen in en om Amsterdam / Photos: © Rembrandt House Museum

© Noordhoff Uitgevers

❷ Amstelland sites associated with Rembrandt

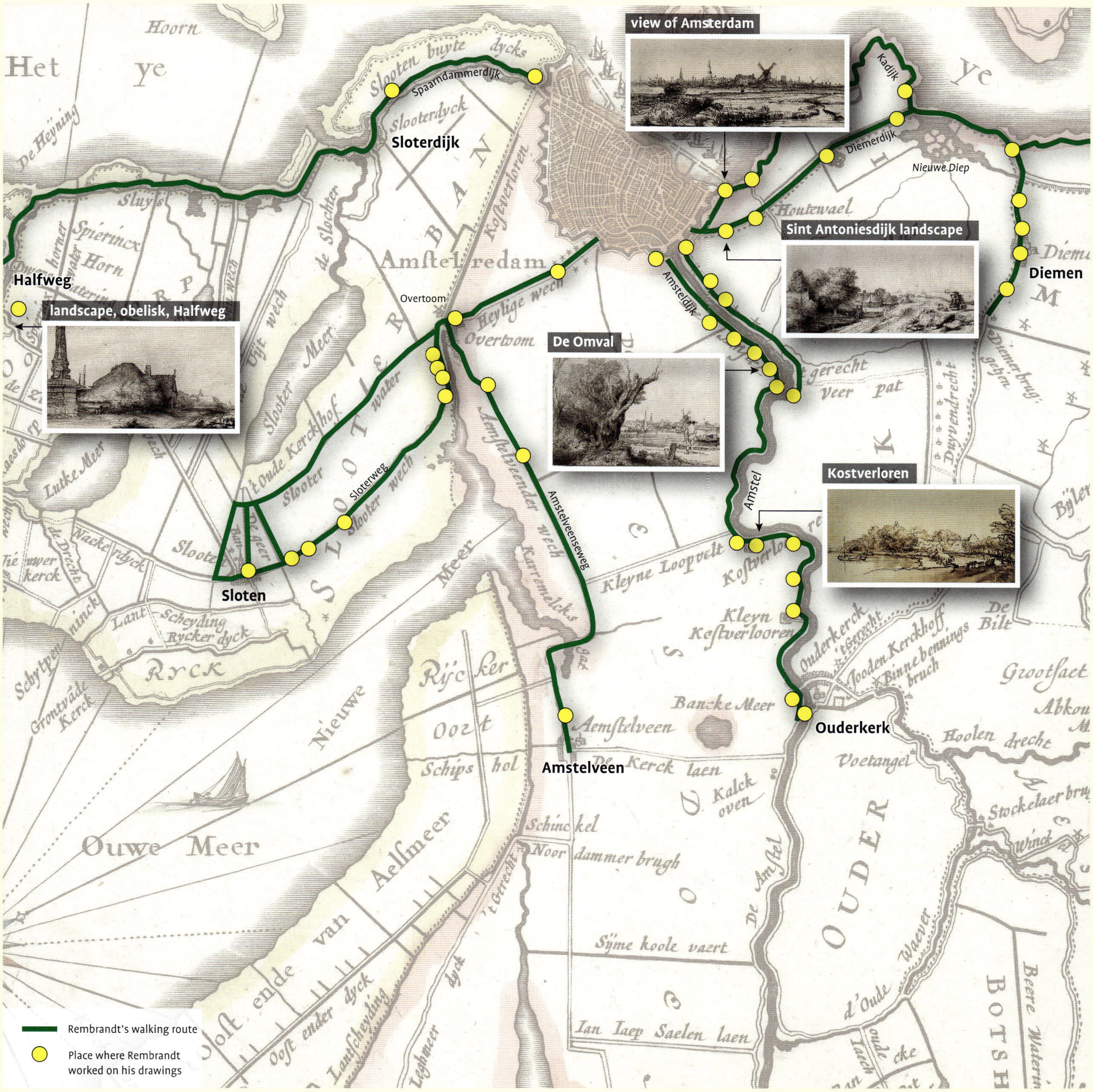

❶ History and disrepair

Rembrandt is mainly known for his paintings, but he also produced many hundreds of drawings and etchings, some 140 of which depict Amsterdam and the surrounding area. He preferred to draw buildings in the city that had a venerable history or that had fallen into disrepair, like the Kloveniersdoelen, the Montelbaanstoren and the town hall on the Dam, which burned down in 1652. Rembrandt must have often walked along the new city wall with his sketchbook. The footpath on this five kilometre long, twenty metre wide and five metre high wall gave him an unrestricted view of the city, the expansive polder landscape and the dozens of windmills, so he made a great many drawings from this vantage point.

❷ Real life in Amstelland

Rembrandt also took many walks outside the city, almost exclusively along the mediaeval dike roads that linked Amsterdam to the surrounding villages of Diemen, Ouderkerk, Amstelveen, Sloten and Sloterdijk. In Rembrandt's day, Amstelland was still sparsely populated, with the odd village here and there, a few summer residences and a number of farms where the farmer's family and livestock lived under the same roof. Rembrandt's drawings and etchings of Amstelland date back to the period from 1640 to 1652. Although he had drawn landscapes before that period, they were fanciful panoramas and imaginary mountain vistas. After 1640, he suddenly stopped producing imaginary works and started to draw what he saw in real life. His favourite walk was a route along the winding Amsteldijk to Ouderkerk. Around 34 illustrations of this route still exist, including four depicting the Omval with its inn, windmills and ship's beacon, five of the long bend in the river Amstel near Kostverloren and one of the dilapidated summer residence at Kostverloren.

Sources: Special Collections of the University of Amsterdam: Map of Rijnland by Willem Jansz Blaeu (1631) (background) / B. Bakker and others, Het landschap van Rembrandt, Wandelingen in en om Amsterdam / Photos: © Rembrandt House Museum

© Noordhoff Uitgevers

Music

With its wide range of venues, ensembles and bands, Amsterdam has a lot to offer music lovers. Two classical music ensembles are among the best at international level – the Royal Concertgebouw Orchestra, which is based in the Royal Concertgebouw, and the Dutch National Opera, which shares the Dutch National Opera & Ballet Theatre with the Dutch National Ballet. People come to Amsterdam from all over the country to see these ensembles perform.
There are many pop venues all over the Netherlands, but Amsterdam has the most. Paradiso, the 'temple of pop', is of particular significance, with many bands performing there before making a name for themselves. For example, Coldplay gave its first foreign concert in Paradiso in 2000, attracting an audience of just 145.

❶ Music venues

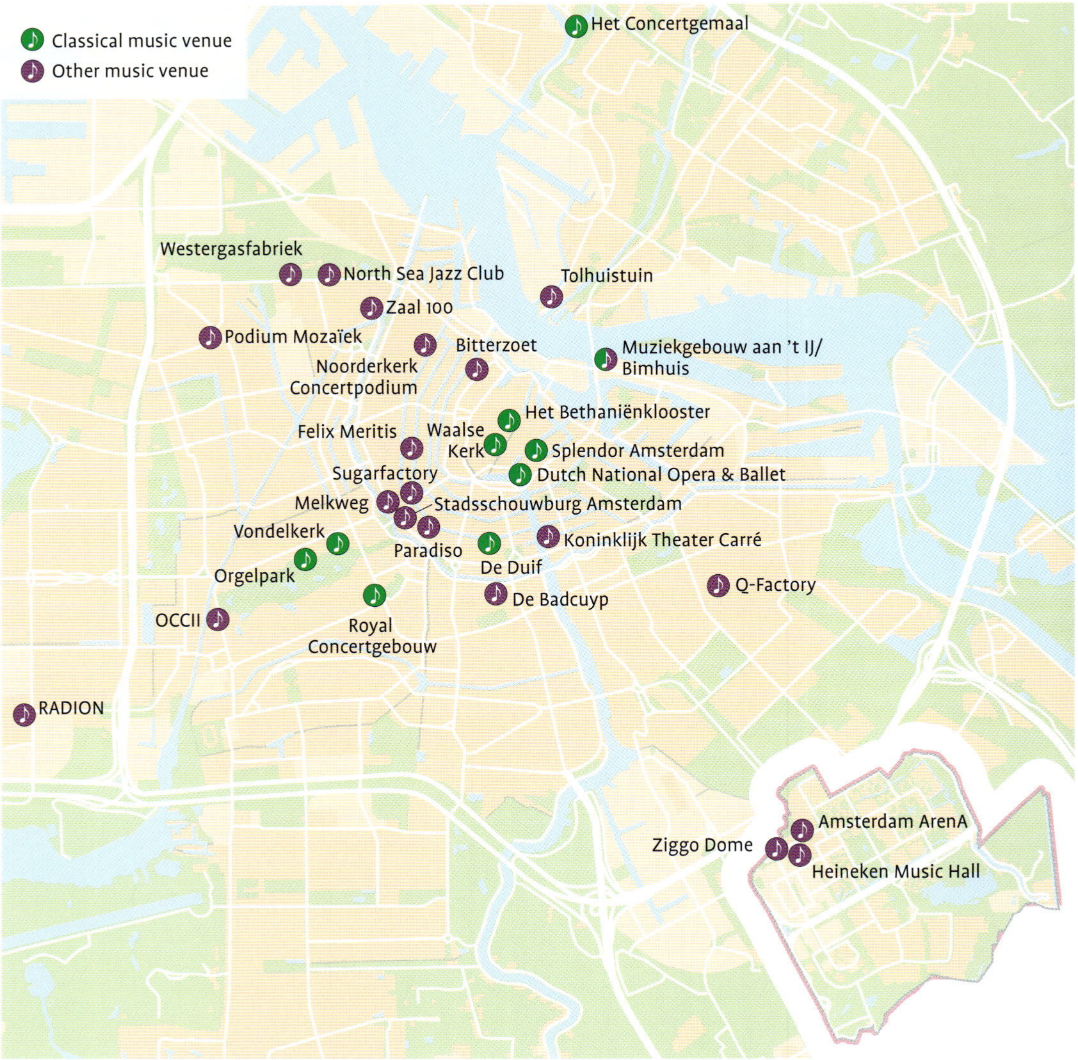

❷ Major classical music venues

Royal Concertgebouw
Building opened: **1888**
Architect: **A. L. van Gendt**
Capacity: **2000 seats** (Main Hall)
Performances/concerts: **832**
Visitors: **724,653**

Dutch National Opera & Ballet
Building opened: **1986**
Architect: **C. Dam/W. Holzbauer**
Capacity: **1600 seats**
Performances/concerts: **163**
Visitors: **214,355**

Muziekgebouw aan 't IJ
Building opened: **2005**
Architect: **K. H. Nielsen**
Capacity: **725 seats**
Performances/concerts: **302**
Visitors: **116,553**

2014 data

❸ Royal Concertgebouw Orchestra's world tour

Sources: OIS, Research, Information and Statistics, City of Amsterdam (1, 2); The Royal Concertgebouw (3)

© Noordhoff Uitgevers

❶ - ❷ Pop and classical music
The Zuidoost district is home to all the main commercial pop music venues – the Amsterdam ArenA (capacity 55,000), the Ziggo Dome (17,000) and the Heineken Music Hall (5500). In comparison, the capacity of the largest classical music auditoriums is rather modest.

❸ Over 125 years old
The Royal Concertgebouw Orchestra (1888) is considered to be one of world's best orchestras and it toured the entire globe in 2013 to mark the occasion of its 125th anniversary. Its members are also extremely international – the 120 musicians have 20 different nationalities.

❹ - ❺ Temples of pop
Paradiso and the Melkweg are long-standing pop music venues with a glorious history and have hosted many famous bands since they opened in the 1960s and 1970s. With origins in the squatting movement, OCCII (Onafhankelijk Cultureel Centrum In It, 1984) is a newer addition to the pop scene and is one of the key venues that receive government funding in support of the development of pop music.

❻ Young and old
Music audiences differ significantly depending on the genre. Pop concerts attract the largest audiences and certainly not just young people. Musicals and dance events attract a roughly equal balance of young and old, whereas jazz, classical music and opera appeal to the older generations.

❼ Amateur art
Many Amsterdammers sing, dance, act or play a musical instrument and the government tries to encourage this by awarding grants. Choirs and orchestras are by far the most subsidised amateur groups.

❻ Performance/concert attendees

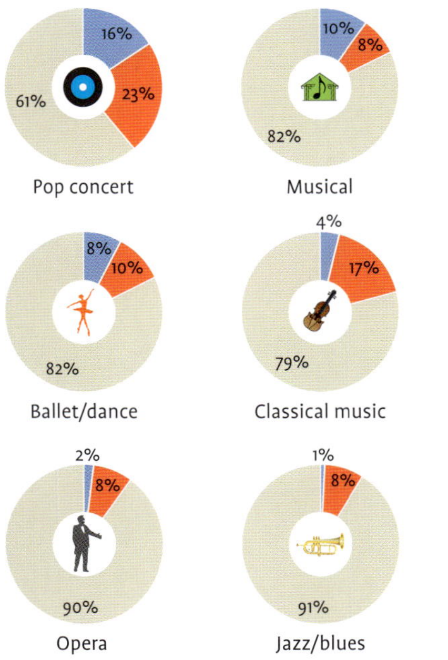

Do not visit music performances
Young people (aged 12 - 17)
Adults (aged 18 and above)

❹ Paradiso

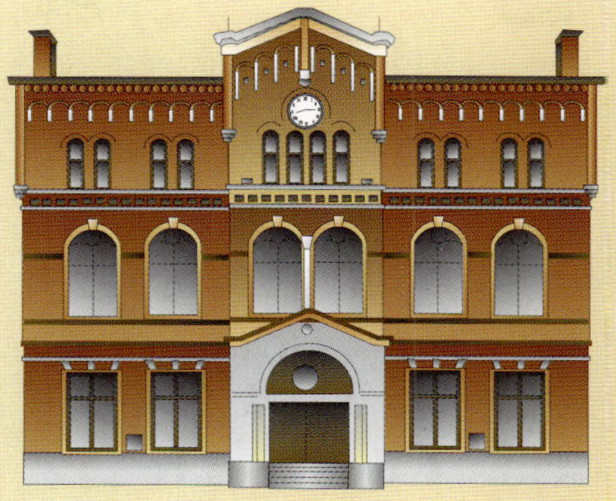

Paradiso (as a music venue) opened on 31 March **1968**.

Capacity
Large auditorium: **1500** people
Small auditorium: **250** people
Basement: **150** people

Staff: **250**
Turnover: **16 million** euros per year
Visitors: **500,000** per year
Programmes: **1000** per year

Artists who have performed in Paradiso

The Rolling Stones, De Dijk, Pink Floyd, U2, David Bowie, Lady Gaga, Velvet Underground, James Brown, The Police, Nirvana, Prince, Coldplay, Adele, Lenny Kravitz, Amy Winehouse

❺ Pop venues

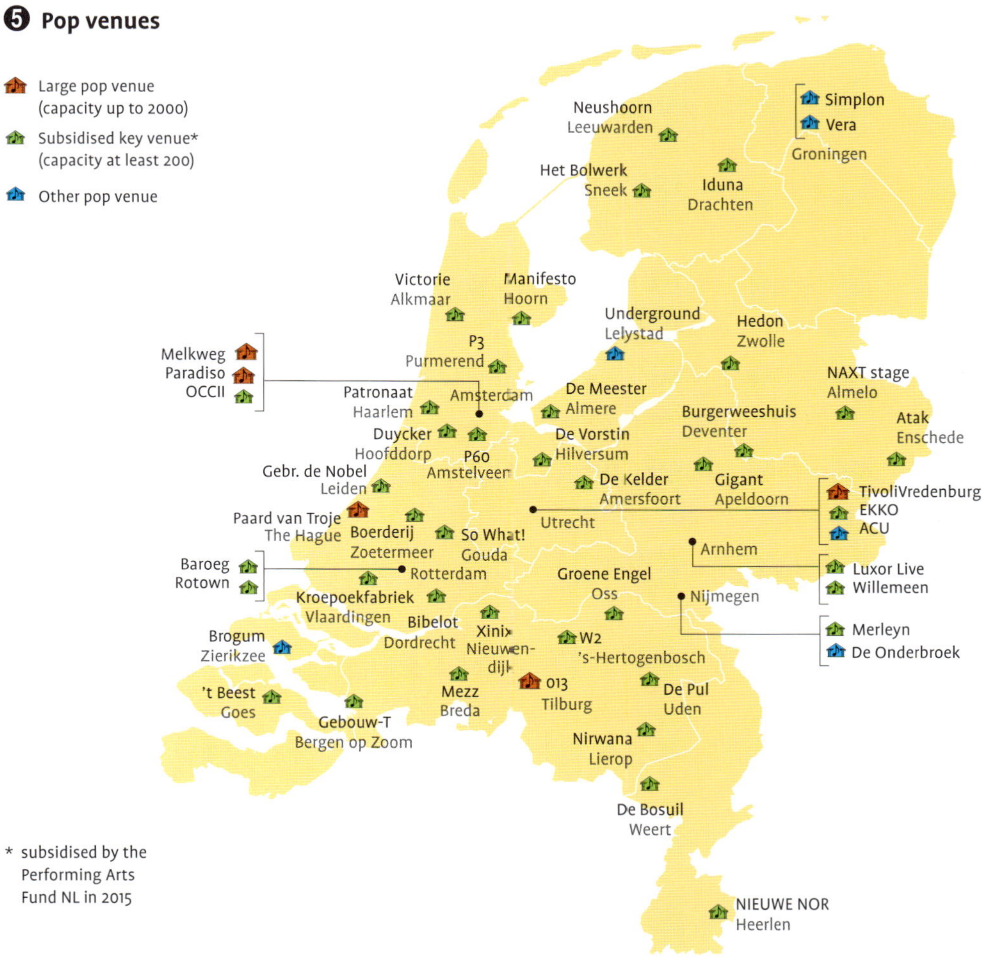

* subsidised by the Performing Arts Fund NL in 2015

❼ Number of subsidised amateur art organisations

Vocal music		Instrumental music		Dramatic expression		Other	
General choirs	83	Orchestras	50	Theatre companies	39	Visual arts	6
		Drum bands	15	Opera, operetta, musical	27		
Oratorio and opera choirs	9	Accordion orchestras	6	Dance companies	10	Umbrella organisations	3
		Mandolin orchestras	1	Majorette/twirling groups	2		

2015 data

© Noordhoff Uitgevers

Theatre

Amsterdam's theatre, cabaret and dance world generally shows few signs of the difficulties currently plaguing the cultural sector. Existing companies like Toneelgroep Amsterdam and the Dutch National Ballet have received nothing but praise at home and abroad, while Toomler's Comedytrain has delivered a seemingly endless succession of well-known stand-up comedians since it started in 1990. Theatre festivals are flourishing as never before. The new DeLaMar Theater (2010) – built with the financial support of Joop and Janine van den Ende – is a further sign of the sector's success and there is even enough demand for a brand-new huge facility, Theater Amsterdam, which was built especially for *Anne*, a play about the life of Anne Frank. The latter two theatres run without state funding, which is a sign of the times.

❶ Theatre venues

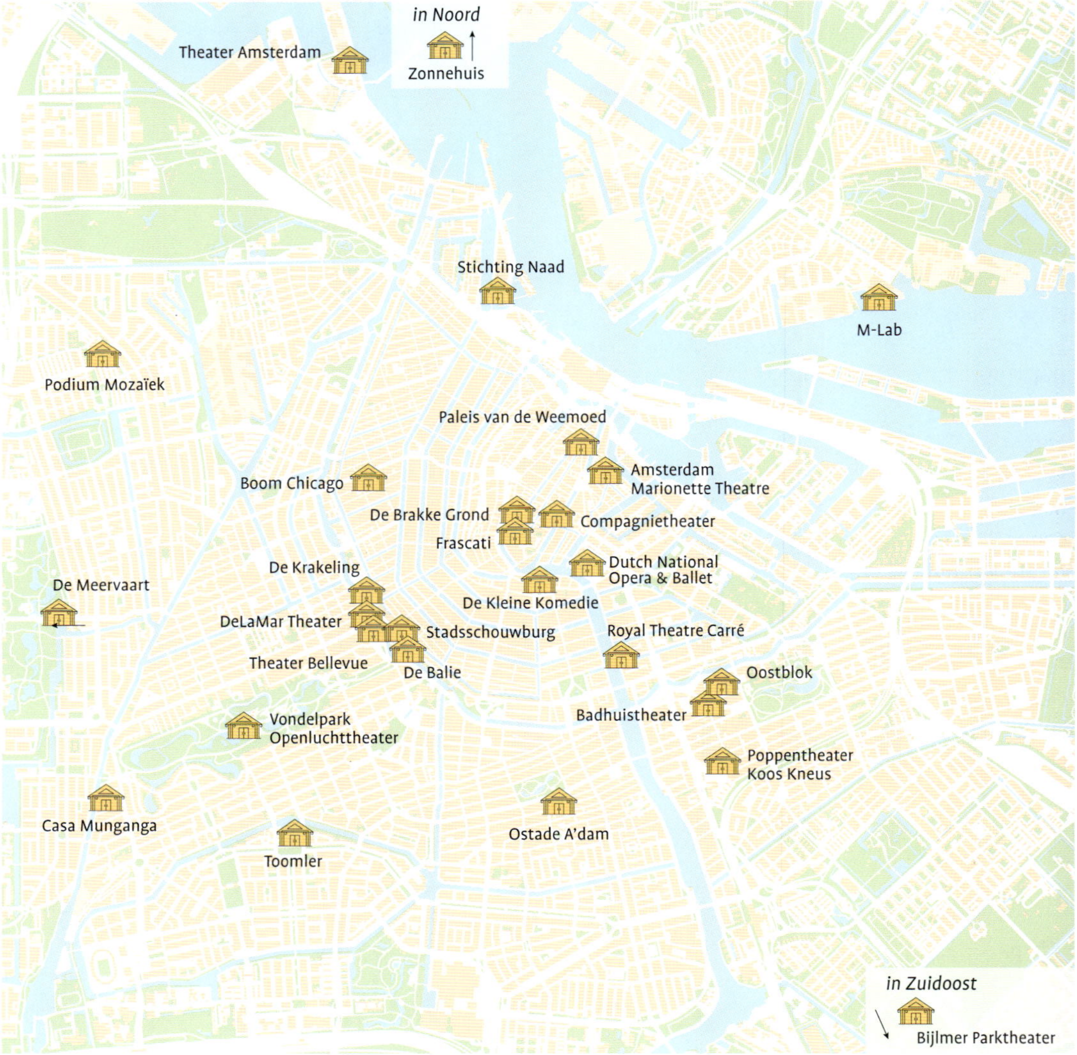

❷ Attendees for each company

❸ Attendees for each venue

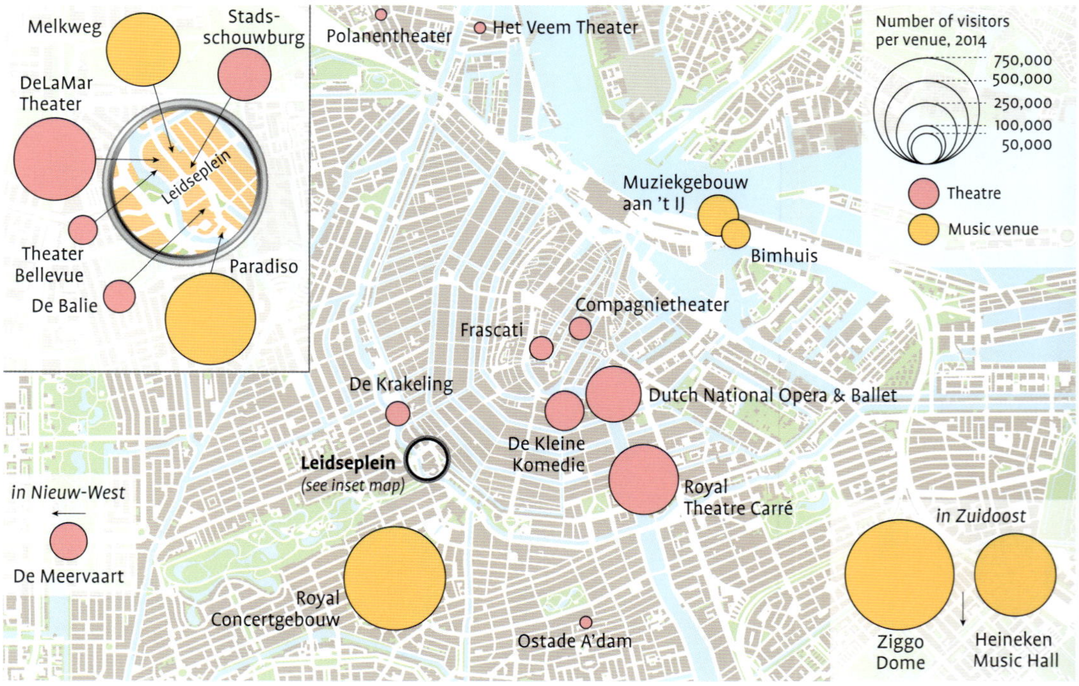

Sources: I amsterdam (1); OIS, Research, Information and Statistics, City of Amsterdam (2, 3)

© Noordhoff Uitgevers

❶, ❸ and ❺ Theatres and attendance

Theatres attract far fewer visitors than music venues. Some of Amsterdam's theatres also draw a public from outside Amsterdam – around half of attendees at the Stadsschouwburg come from outside the capital.

❷ and ❹ On tour

Toneelgroep Amsterdam gives more performances than any other theatre company in the city and also achieves the highest attendance figures, closely followed by Theater Het Amsterdamse Bos, which performs in an atmospheric open-air theatre. Toneelgroep Amsterdam has now also made a name for itself abroad.

❻ and ❼ Old and new theatres

Carré is the oldest circus theatre in the Netherlands and still holds an annual Christmas circus event. The steeply sloped tiers of seats are arranged in a semicircle around the performers' ring. One disadvantage, for 'ordinary' theatre performances, is that not all of the seats have a good view of the stage when there are also seats in the ring. The brand-new Theater Amsterdam has eliminated this problem and its computer-controlled system even enables the tiers to rotate around the stage.

❽ Getting a taster of productions

Festivals are a great way of getting to know Dutch and foreign theatre producers. The ITs Festival, for example, gives young and talented producers the opportunity to showcase their work.

❹ Toneelgroep Amsterdam's international performances

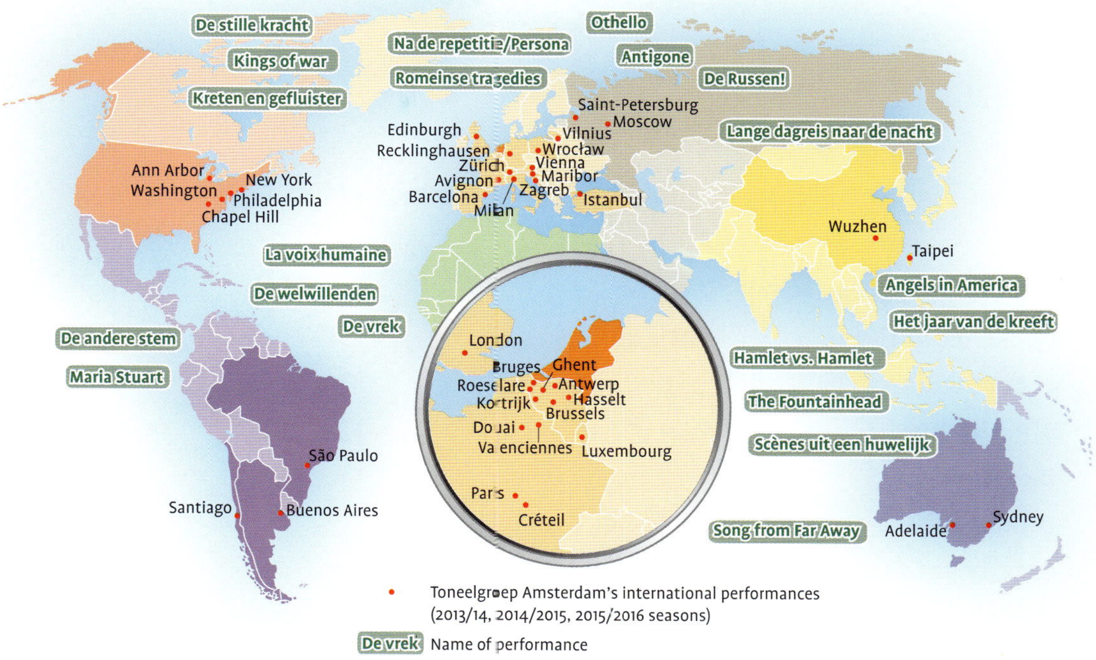

❺ Origin of Stadsschouwburg visitors

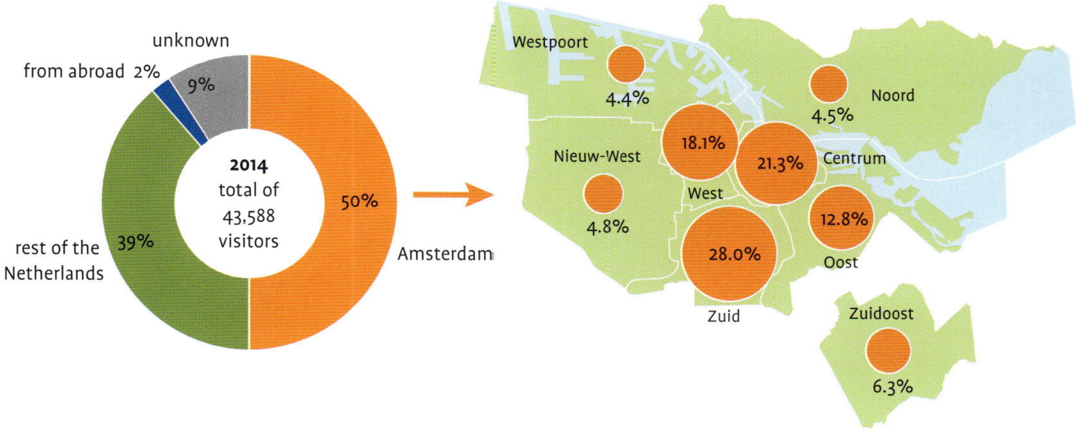

❽ A selection of 2015 theatrical festivals

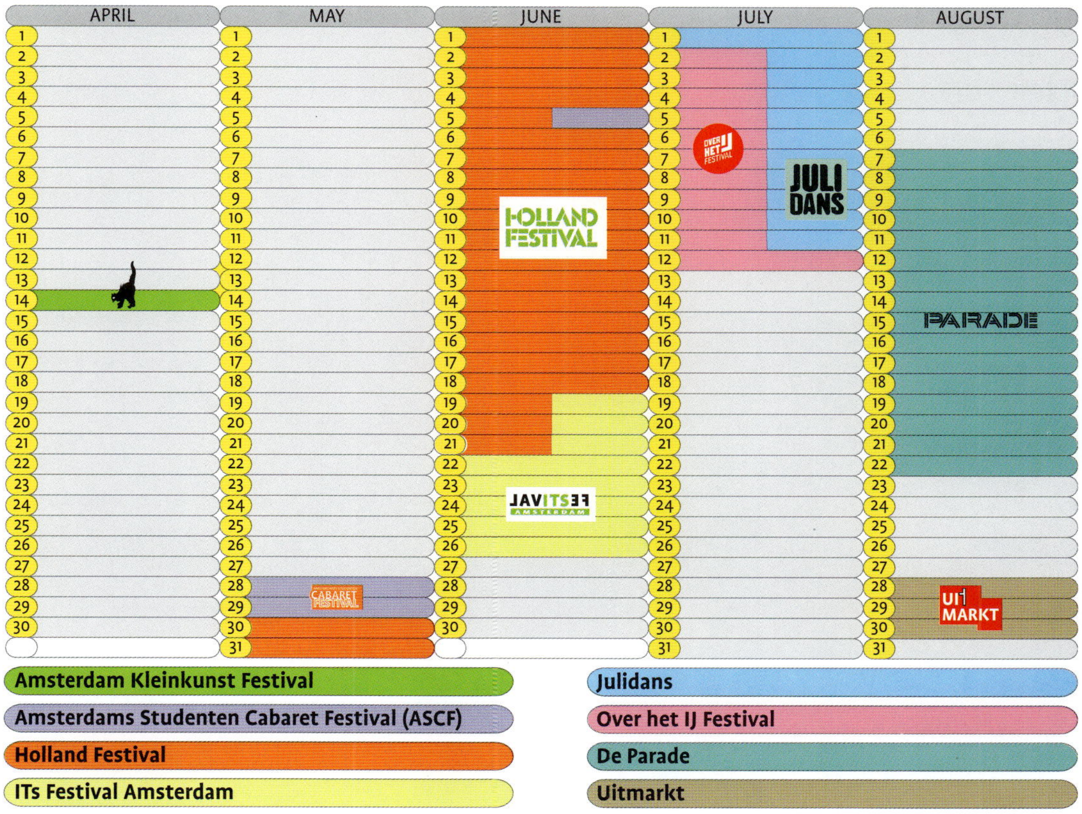

❻ Royal Theatre Carré

Year of construction: **1887**
Renovation completed: **2004**
Surface area: **3600**m²
Number of seats: **1750**

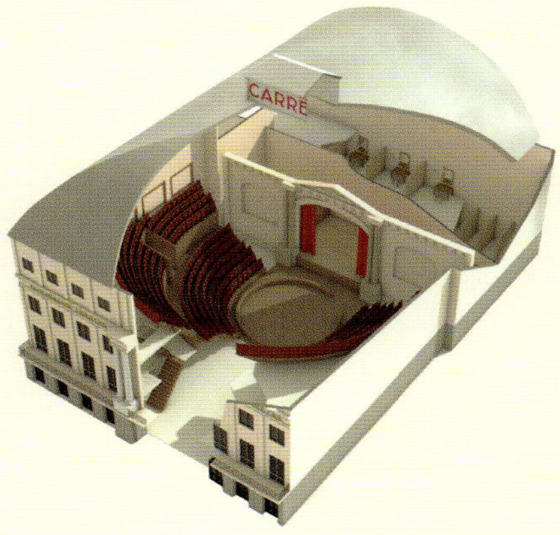

❼ Theater Amsterdam

Purpose-built for **Anne production**
Completed: **2014**
Surface area: **4200**m²
Number of seats: **1100**

Sources: Toneelgroep Amsterdam (4); Stadsschouwburg Amsterdam (5); Royal Theatre Carré (6); Theater Amsterdam (7); www.theaterfestivals.nl (8)

© Noordhoff Uitgevers

Literary city

Amsterdam is the literary capital of the Netherlands. Most major Dutch publishing houses are based in the city, either in the Canal Ring or Zuid, and the Amsterdam Stadsschouwburg hosts the Boekenbal, an annual event held since 1947 to mark the start of the Boekenweek or Book Week. Even those who want to protest against the strict invitation policy for the Boekenbal by attending the alternative Bal der Geweigerden or Ball of the Rejected (since 2002) also have to travel to the capital's Paradiso. The above average number of bookshops is indicative of the literary climate and the city also has an extensive network of public and academic libraries.

❶ Literary publishers and meeting places

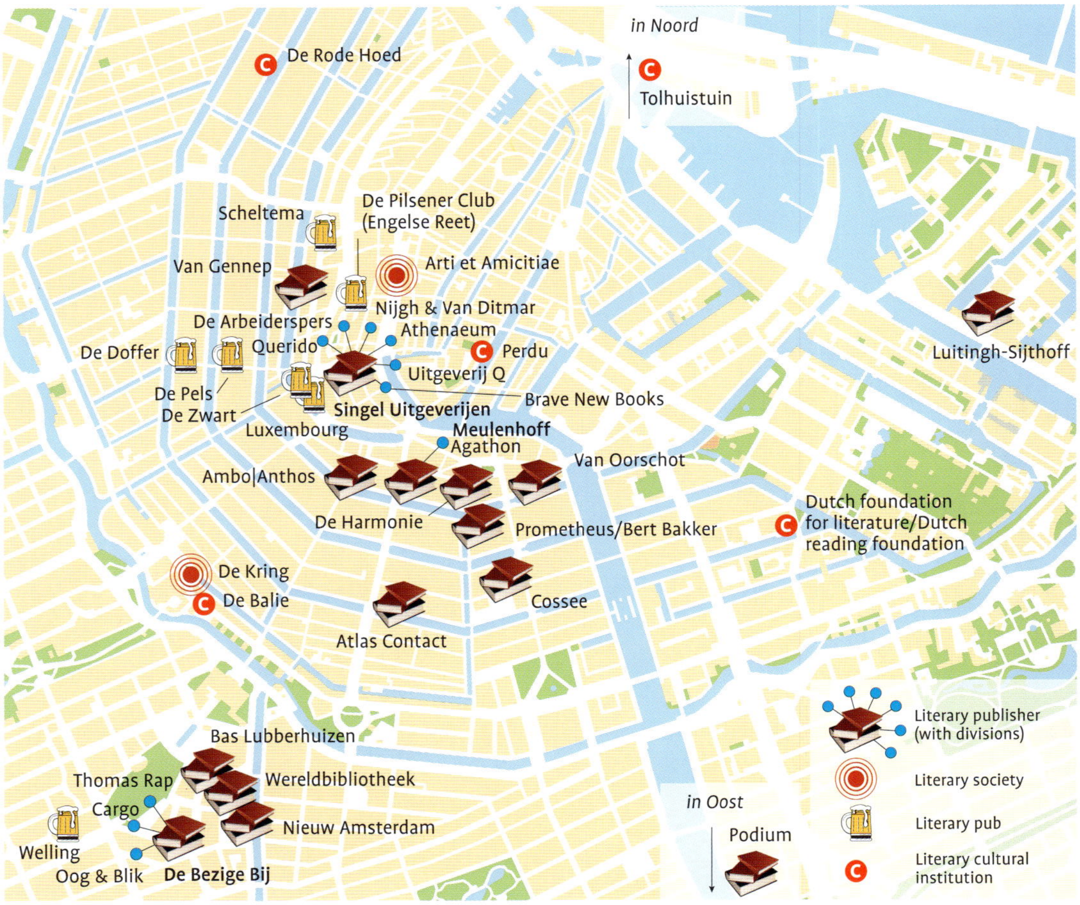

❷ Bookshop density

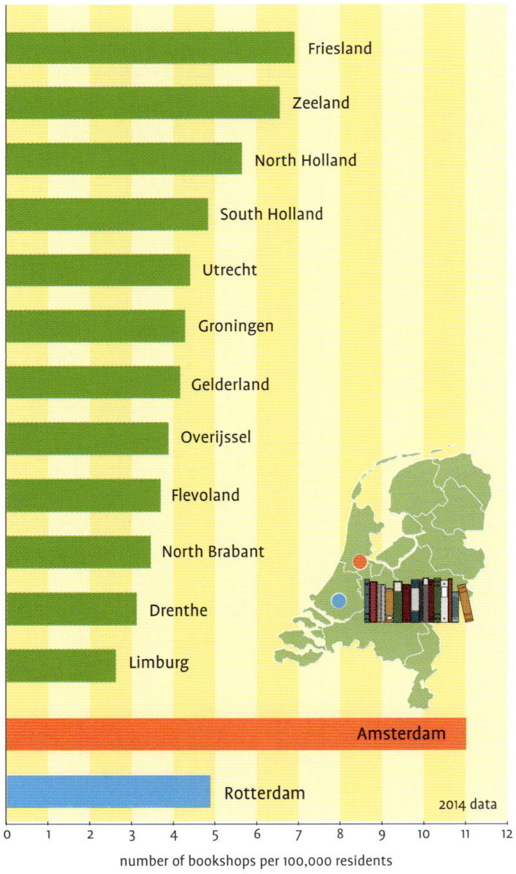

❸ Selection of general and specialist bookshops

© Noordhoff Uitgevers

❹ Openbare Bibliotheek Amsterdam (OBA)

1 Central Library
25 branches
1 digital library
30 loan stations, in places such as assisted living and health-care centres
collection of **1.5** million items
4 million users each year
171,000 members
1.2 million Internet users
3.5 million loans

Central Library
28,000m² surface area
300 workstations with Internet access
seating capacity of **1000**
1 library theatre with **250** seats
one warehouse with **25,000** metres of bookshelves
1 reading cafe, **1** lounge and **1** restaurant
1.8 million users each year

Central Library

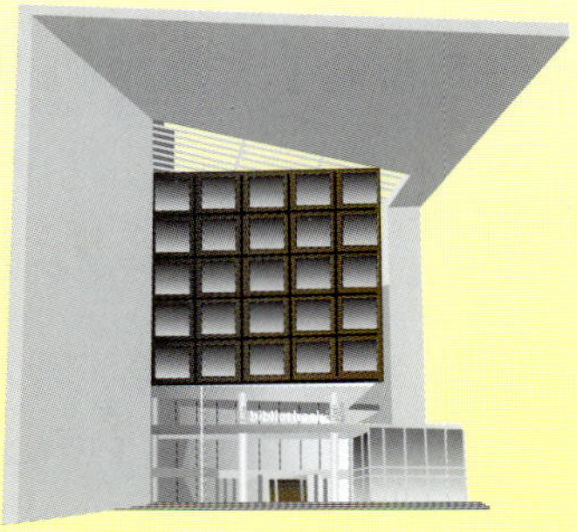

❺ Libraries

2015 data

❶ Pubs and societies

Dutch literary life largely centres on Amsterdam, where writers, publishers and journalists traditionally meet each other at a handful of pubs, societies and cultural institutions.

❷ and ❸ Fierce competition

Bookshops are struggling to survive, partly due to the rise of the Internet. Relatively speaking, Amsterdam's bookshops are still successful, which presumably reflects the presence of many highly educated people and the opportunities for specialisation. For example, Amsterdam has specialist bookshops for Italian and East European literature.

❹ and ❺ Wealth of information

Four million people go to the Openbare Bibliotheek Amsterdam – the public library – each year, making it the city's most frequently visited cultural institution. Amsterdam also has two university libraries (operating from various sites) and several specialist collections, including those of the International Institute of Social History, the Jewish Ets Haim library and the City Archives.

❻ Central Library

In 2007, the Central Library, the main site of the Openbare Bibliotheek Amsterdam opened in a new building near Centraal Station. After the opening, the number of users doubled in just one year. The library is not only popular as a place to borrow books, but also as a place to meet up and work. However, the number of book issues dropped sharply by 30% between 2003 and 2013.

❼ Literary statues

Some writers are so popular that a statue has been put up in their honour. The oldest statue of a writer is that of Joost van den Vondel in the Vondelpark. Not all of the memorials stand out. For example, Gerard Reve's memorial, near the house where he was born, requires some searching. It is a lamppost with three small doors that each conceal a photograph and text.

❻ Central Library users

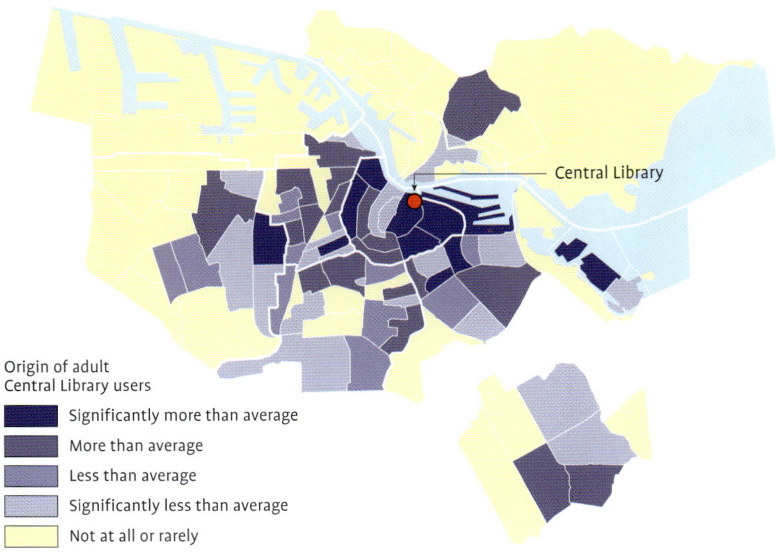

❼ Statues of writers and literary characters

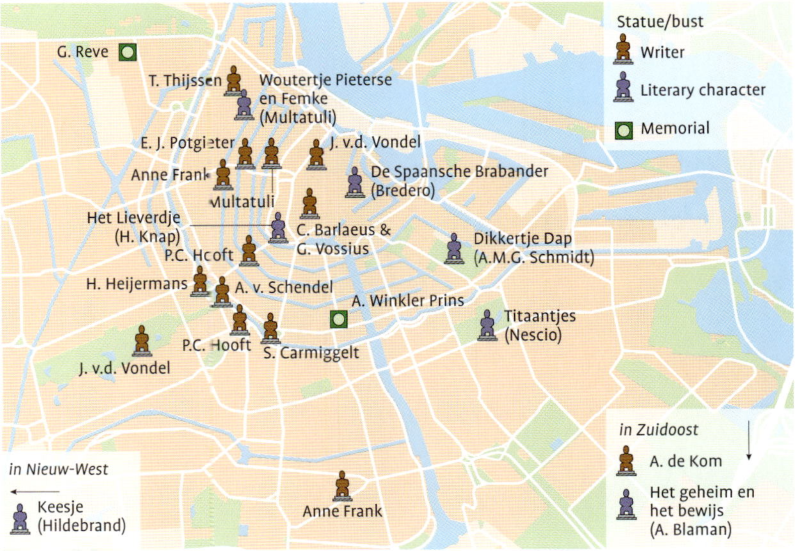

Sources: *Openbare Bibliotheek Amsterdam (4, 5); OIS, Research, Information and Statistics, City of Amsterdam (6); www.buitenbeeldinbeeld.nl / www.vanderkrogt.net (7)*

© Noordhoff Uitgevers

Film

Of all forms of culture, film is the most democratic – more than half of all Amsterdammers go to the cinema now and then. However, there is no 'typical' cinema as such, with the Pathé and arthouse cinemas each attracting different types of people. As well as scheduled films, there are all kinds of film festivals, such as IDFA, the world's biggest documentary film festival.
The Film Academy and many production companies are also based in Amsterdam, making it the centre of the Dutch film industry. Even so, the industry is relatively small and Amsterdam is primarily interesting as a set for film makers.

❶ Cinemas

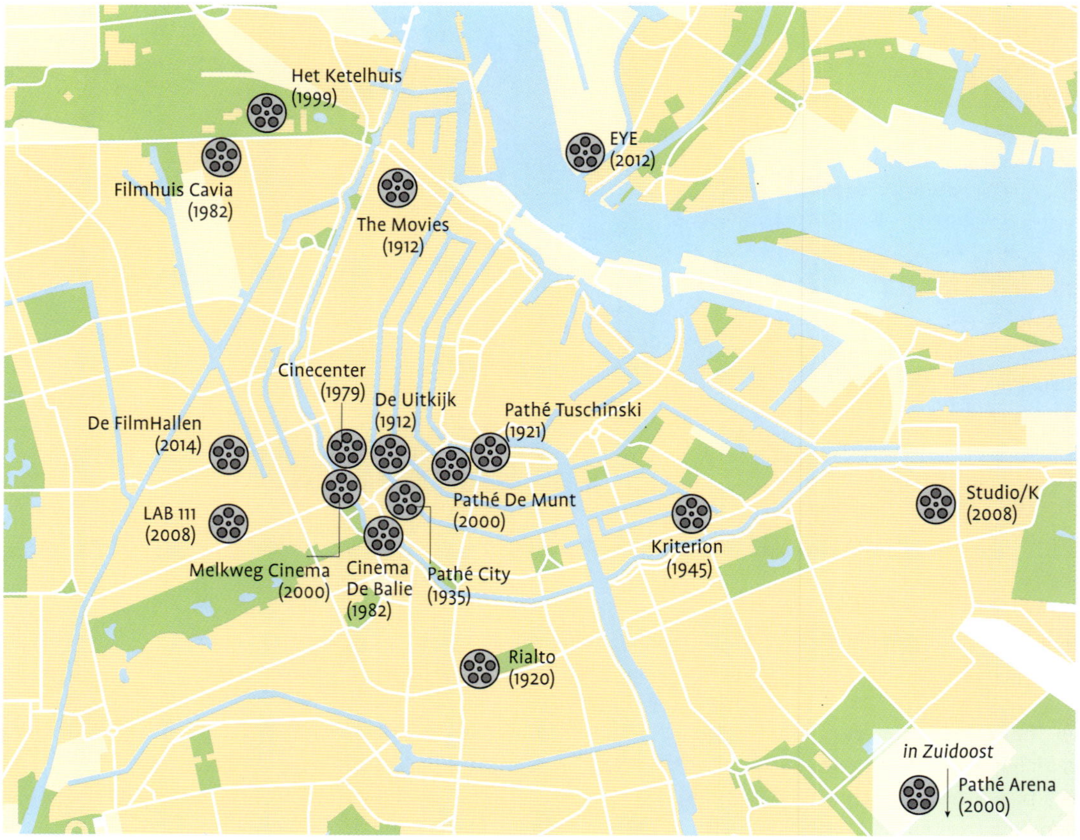

❷ Pathé Tuschinski

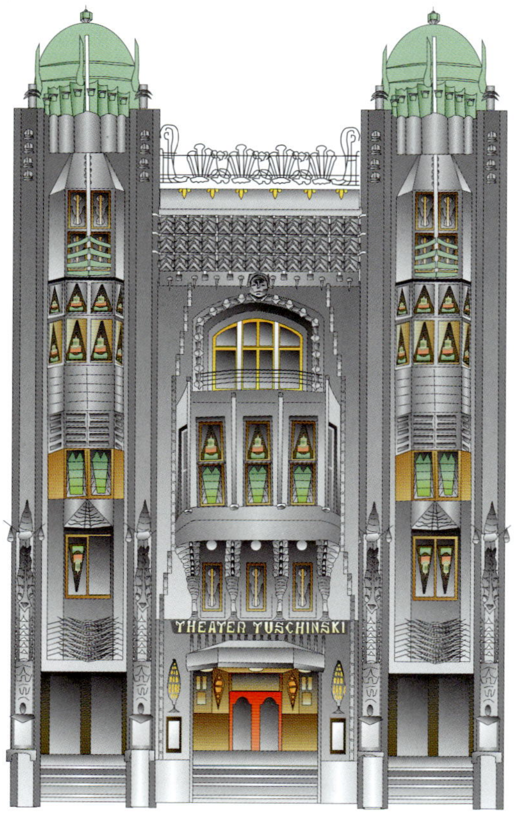

❸ Cinema visits

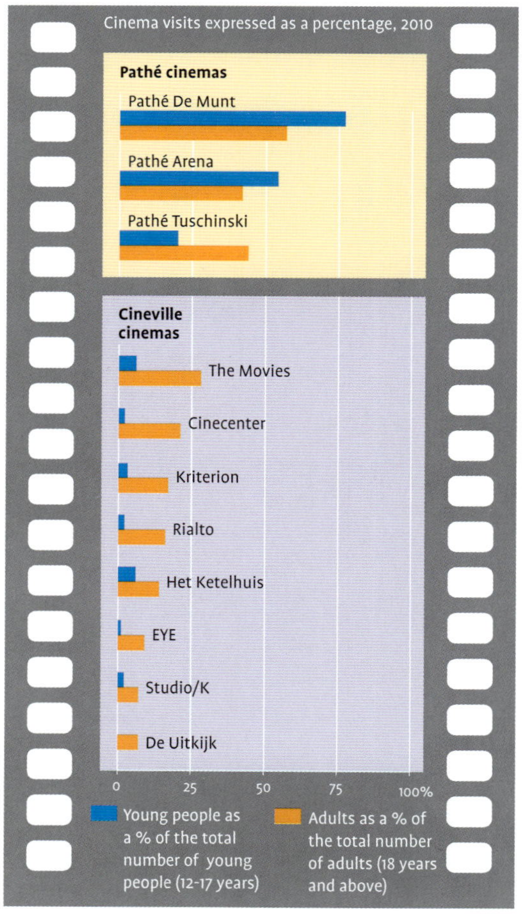

❹ Cultural outings

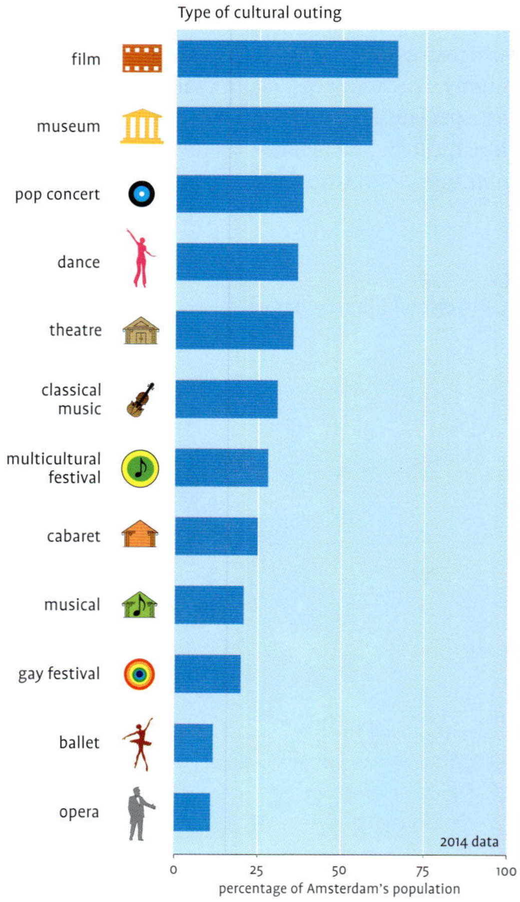

Sources: T. Bakker (1); OIS, Research, Information and Statistics, City of Amsterdam (3, 4)

© Noordhoff Uitgevers

❶ Large number of cinemas
Some cinemas, such as The Movies, Rialto, the Uitkijk and Tuschinski, have a long history. The largest cinema is Pathé Arena in Zuidoost, with fourteen screens and more than four million visitors each year.

❷ 'Enchantingly beautiful'
Visitors to the Tuschinski cinema are guaranteed a great night out. When it opened in 1921, the theatre with all its sumptuous decorative features was described as an 'enchantingly beautiful playhouse', so it is with good reason that many Dutch film premières are shown here.

❸ and ❹ Popular night out
Going to the cinema is the most popular night out among Amsterdammers and one that is enjoyed by both young and old. However, young people go relatively more often to one of the two Pathé multiplex cinemas. Visitors to Pathé Tuschinski and the smaller arthouse cinemas are generally somewhat older.

❺ Visitors' origin
The Pathé cinemas show major commercial films. Pathé De Munt attracts visitors from all over the city, with the exception of Zuidoost, which is home to another multiplex cinema. The Movies arthouse cinema largely depends on areas within cycling distance.

❻ Famous bench
In recent years, Amsterdam has become popular as a film set, particularly for Dutch films, but also for a few foreign films like *The Fault in Our Stars*. The bench on Leidsegracht where Hazel and Gus have a serious conversation and kiss attracted visitors en masse before the film was even released in the Netherlands.

❼ Festivals
Film festivals are held all over the country, but Amsterdam has more than its fair share, including some major ones like IDFA and Cinekid (kids' films). The biggest Dutch film festival is the International Film Festival Rotterdam.

❺ Who goes to which cinema?

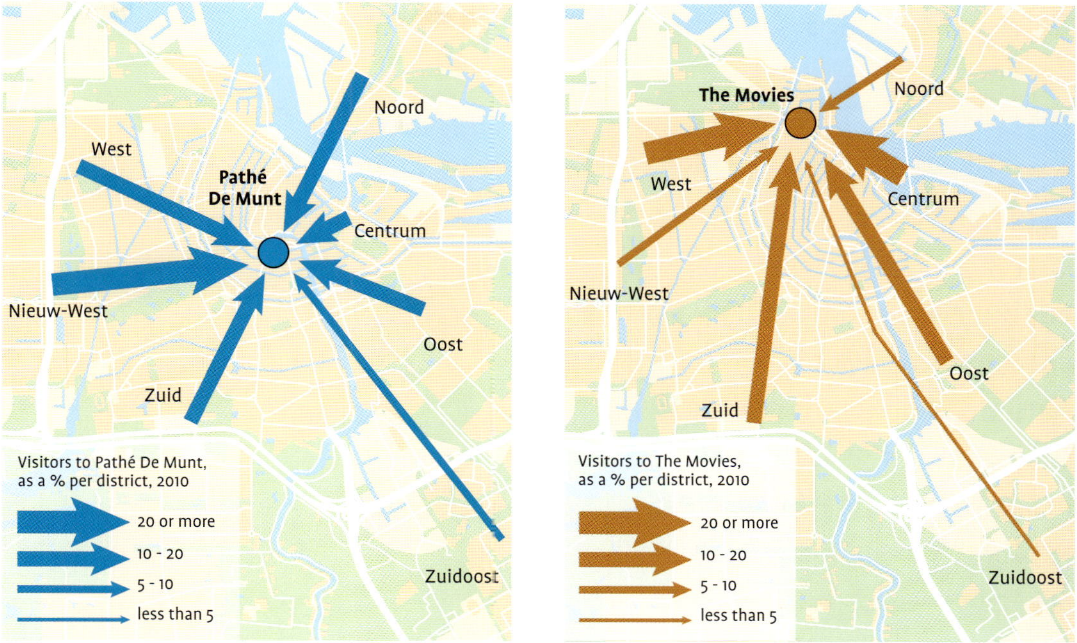

❻ Amsterdam in films

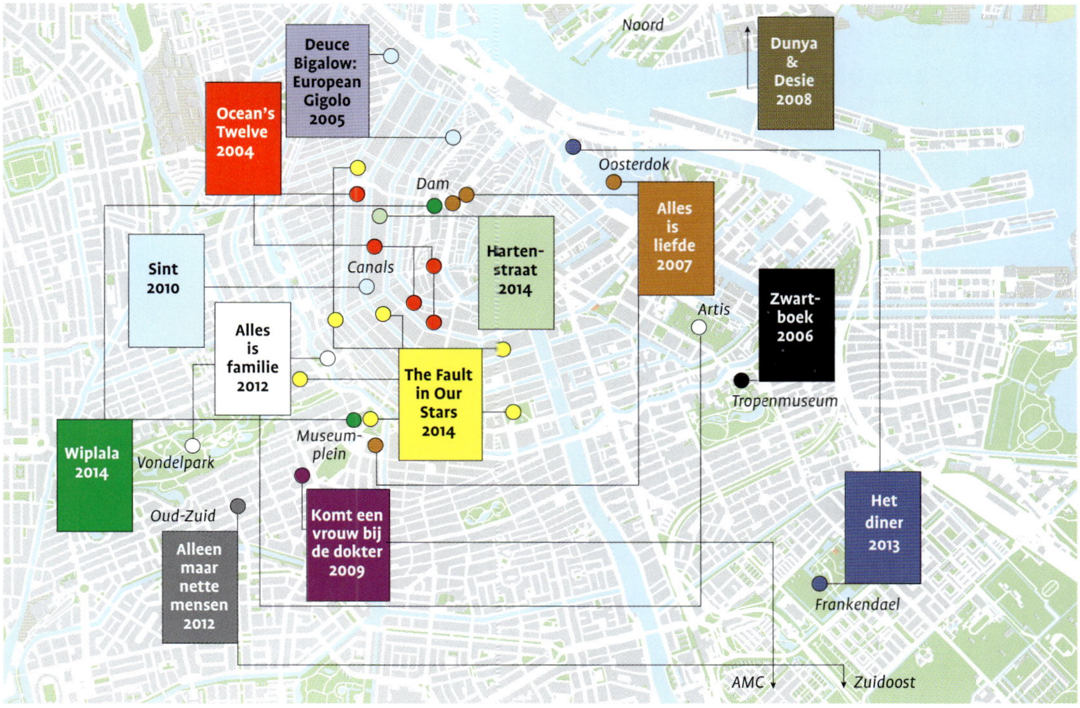

❼ Film festivals

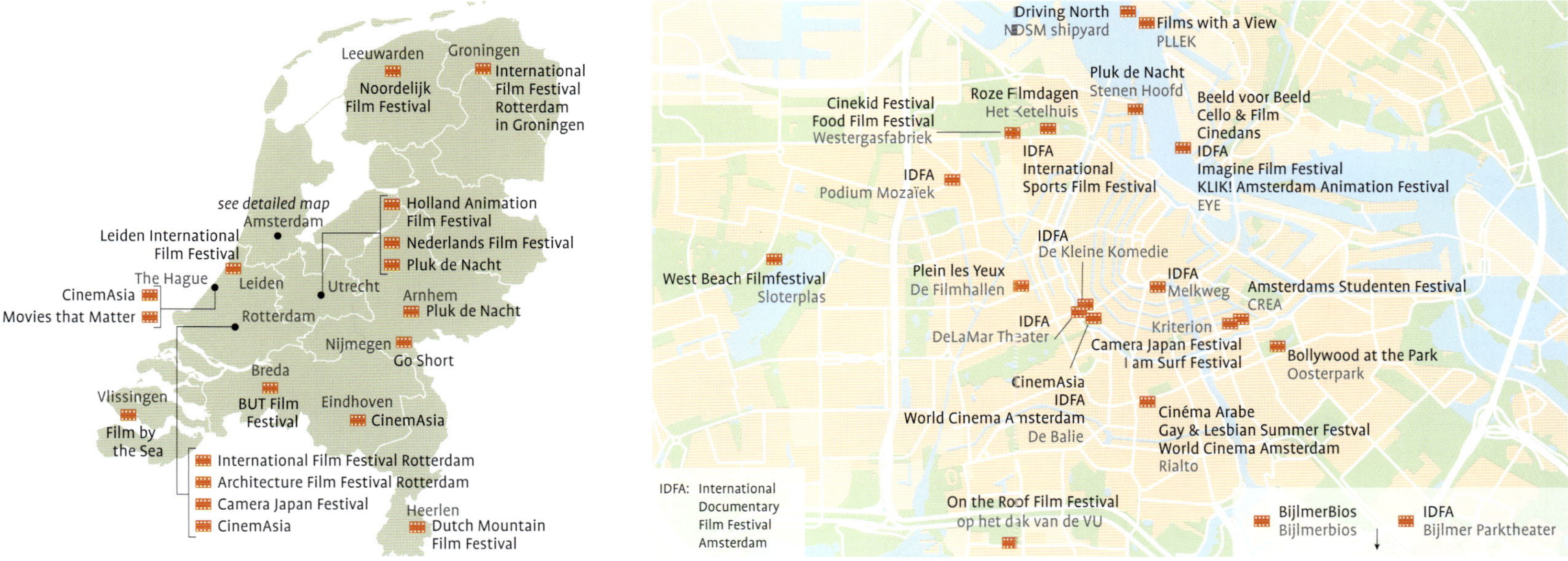

Sources: City of Amsterdam (5); I amsterdam (6, 7)

© Noordhoff Uitgevers

Media

National television and radio is largely broadcast from Hilversum, but more and more radio and TV programmes have been recorded in Amsterdam in recent years, e.g. the daily *De Wereld Draait Door* talk show in Studio Westergasfabriek and *RTL Late Night* in Brasserie NH Schiller. Several television and radio channels in Amsterdam like AT5, SALTO and StadsFM broadcast local news. Amsterdam is the undisputed centre of the printed media industry, as the editorial teams of most national daily and weekly newspapers are based in the city. In 2012, *NRC Handelsblad's* editorial staff even moved from Rotterdam to Amsterdam's Rokin and started to produce a weekly Amsterdam special shortly afterwards. For the time being, *Het Parool* is the main source of regional news. Incidentally, all daily newspapers are struggling to compete with the Internet, which has penetrated into almost every household.

❶ Daily and weekly newspapers

❷ Daily newspaper readership in Amsterdam

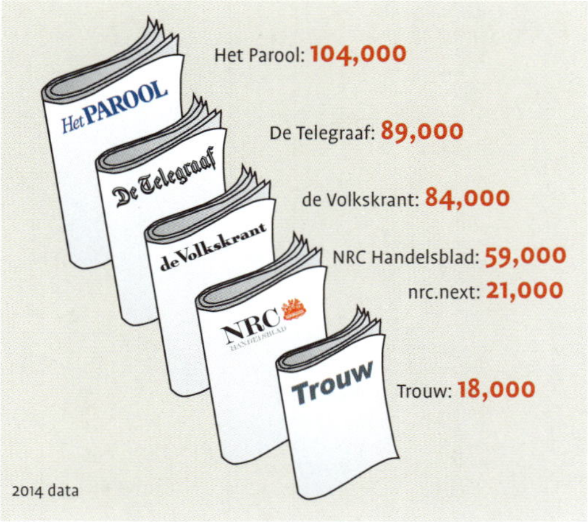

❸ Readers of Het Parool

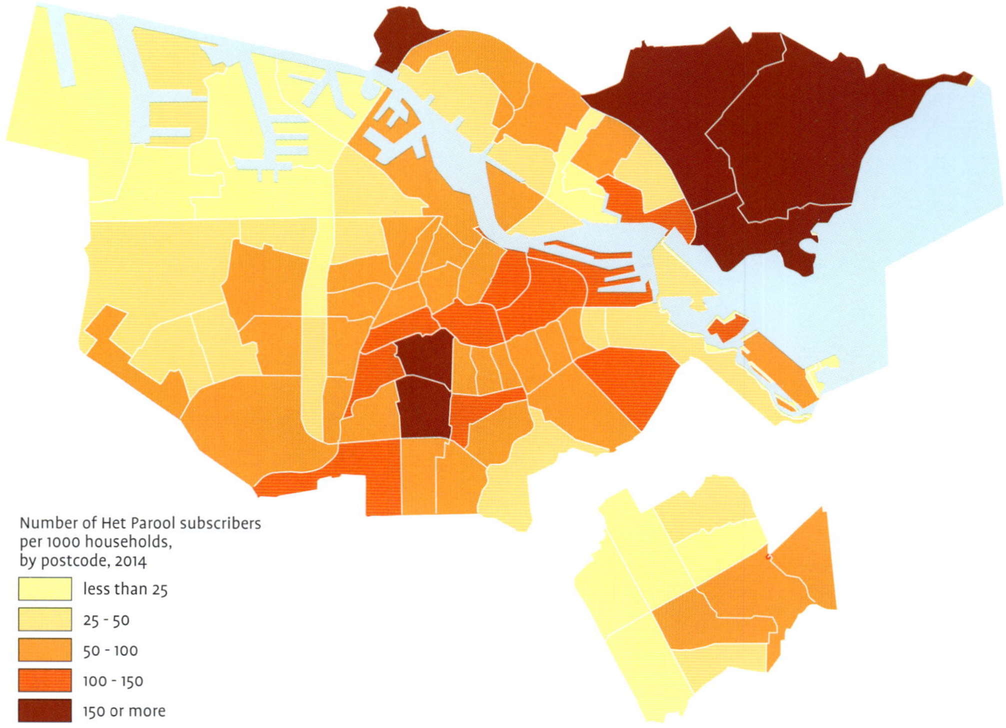

Sources: Nationaal Onderzoek Multimedia, Print Monitor 2014 (2); Het Parool (3)

© Noordhoff Uitgevers

❶ Editor's note
Het Parool, *Trouw* and *de Volkskrant* are subsidiaries of the same group and their editors work at the same address.

❷ and ❸ Amsterdam newspaper
Initially published by the Resistance, *Het Parool* is now the Amsterdam region's leading daily newspaper. Its readers largely come from the city of Amsterdam (57%), but also from the surrounding area. Just like other daily newspapers, *Het Parool* has seen its paid circulation fall dramatically – from 161,200 (1980) to 56,000 (2014).

❹ and ❺ Amsterdammers online
Just like other Dutch people, nearly all Amsterdammers have access to the Internet. Older people lagged behind the young at first, but that gap is continuing to close. Young people and the well educated use social media a lot more than older people and people with a lower level of education.

❻ and ❼ Amsterdam radio and TV
For local news, many Amsterdammers watch the daily broadcasts produced by AT5. People also follow the news online – the AT5 app has been downloaded by 100,000 people and 200,000 people follow AT5 on social media. Most channels are 'publicly accessible' – any organisation can purchase broadcasting time as long as the programme matches the broadcasting company's objectives. The intention is to create as diverse a schedule as possible for all ages, religions and political and social movements.

❽ Live from Amsterdam
Amsterdam has several professional radio and TV studios. Some of the AT5 editorial staff work from a location in Vondel CS, the former film museum where programmes like *Basta* (an educational programme for children) and *Het gesprek met de burgemeester* are made. Talk shows such as *De Wereld Draait Door* and *Pauw* are broadcast every day from the studio in the Zuiveringsgebouw, a listed building on the Westergasfabriek site.

❹ Internet access in Amsterdam

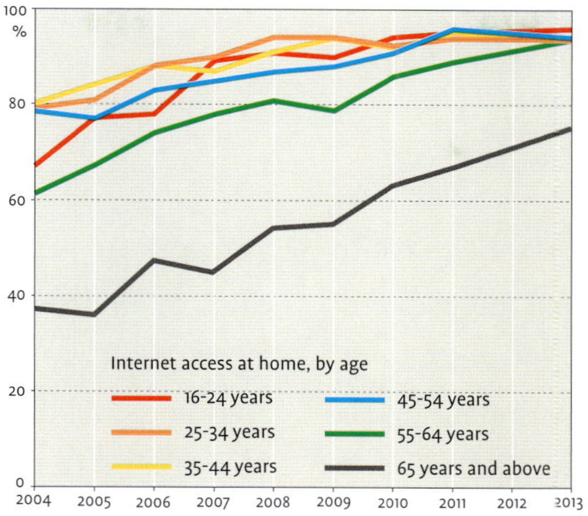

❺ Use of social media by Amsterdammers

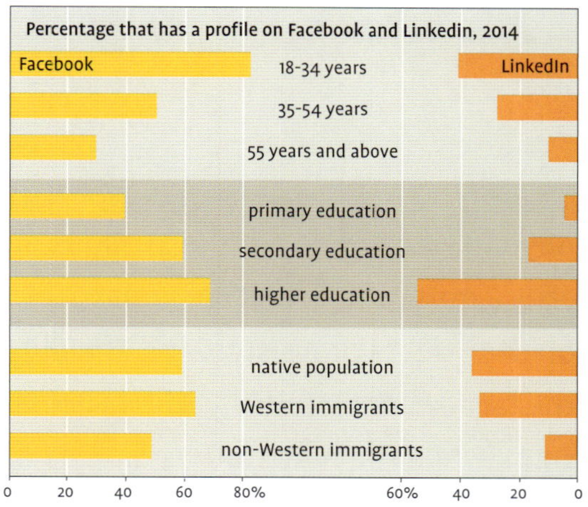

❻ Publieke Omroep Amsterdam

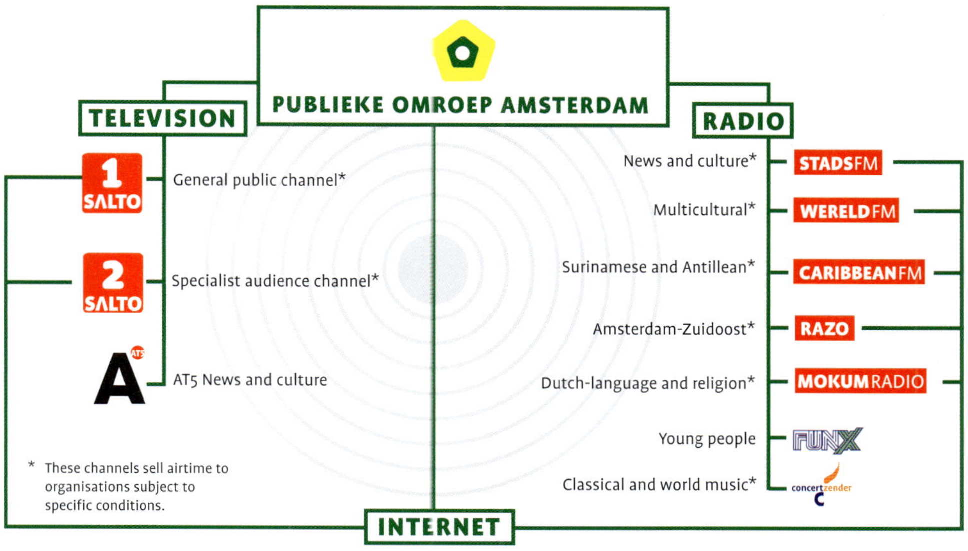

❼ Viewing trends for local television channels

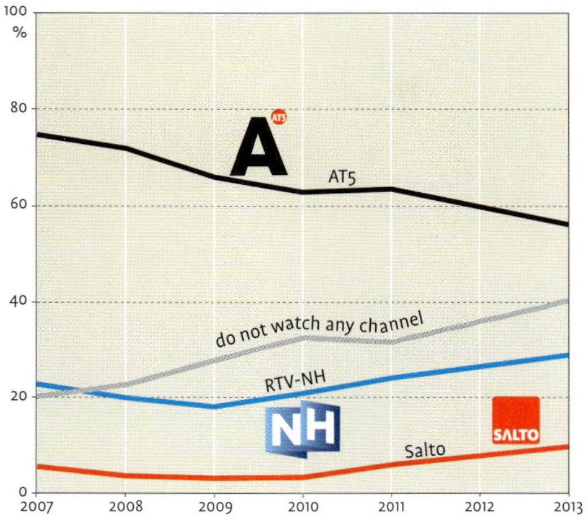

❽ National television broadcasts from Amsterdam

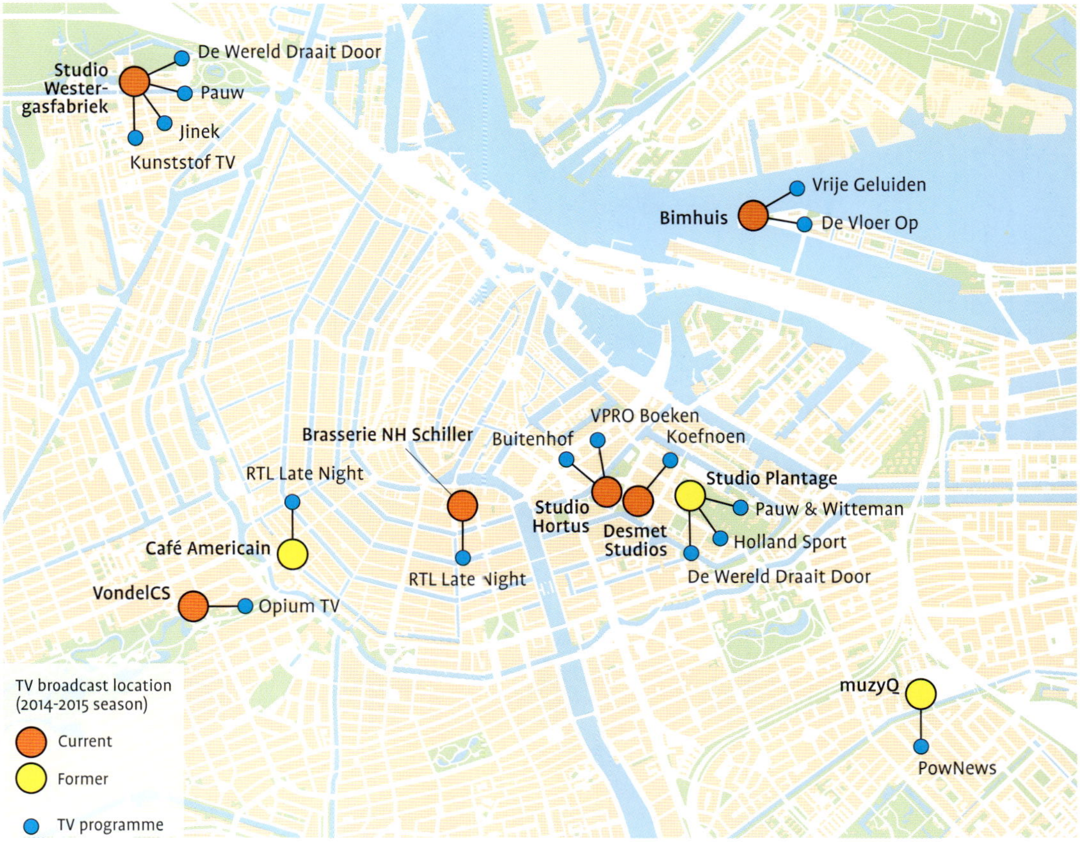

Sources: OIS, Research, Information and Statistics, City of Amsterdam (4, 5); Publieke Omroep Amsterdam (6); OIS, Research, Information and Statistics, City of Amsterdam (7)

© Noordhoff Uitgevers

Street art

Anyone wanting to admire art does not necessarily have to visit a museum. Sculpture in particular is well represented on the streets of Amsterdam. The oldest sculptures grace the facades of historic buildings like the Royal Palace on the Dam, while the first statues date back to the 1800s when Amsterdam's citizens took the initiative in commemorating national heroes like Rembrandt (1852) and Vondel (1867). Since then, architecture and sculpture have remained closely entwined. Cuypers, Berlage and the Amsterdam School architects used a lot of sculpture in their buildings. In 1922, the city council made an important decision – under the motto of 'art for the people', it set aside funds for works of art on public roads. Since then, sculptors such as Hildo Krop in particular have been given the opportunity to embellish countless bridges and public buildings. While architects were increasingly unwilling to decorate their facades, the number of free-standing sculptures, including several (war) monuments, grew strongly after 1945.
Organising temporary sculpture exhibitions outdoors is a more recent trend, one example in Amsterdam being ArtZuid. There are also regular open atelier routes for anyone wanting to visit the artists in their ateliers. This form of art experience is also free of charge.

❶ Unusual sculptures on public roads

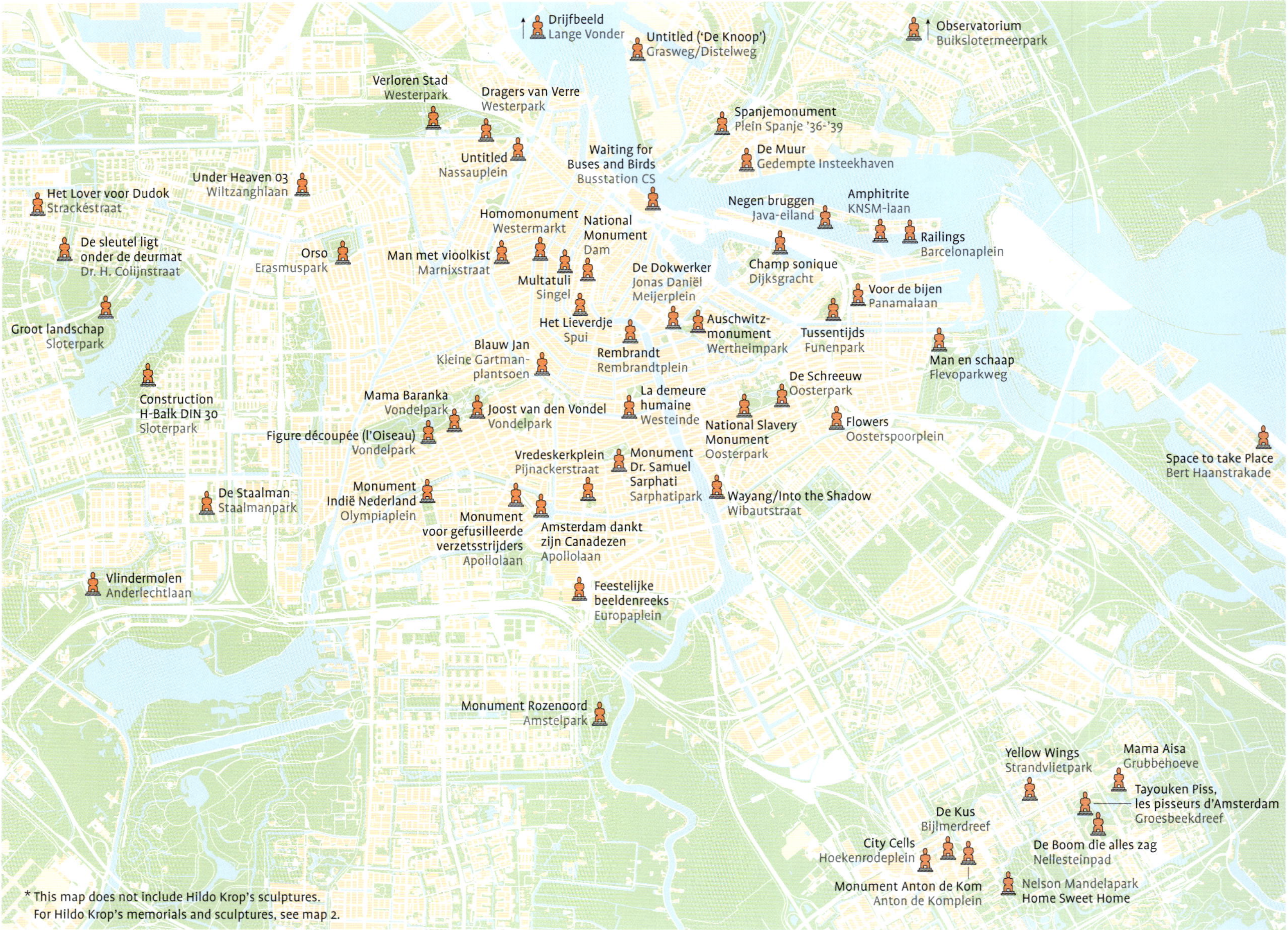

© Noordhoff Uitgevers

❶ From *De Dokwerker* to *De Schreeuw*

Making a selection from the over one thousand unusual sculptures in Amsterdam is impossible. The works on this map are scattered through both time and space and they remind us of the city's history. e.g. *De Dokwerker* (February Strike) and *De Schreeuw* (Theo van Gogh's murder). They also form a guide to all of the city's sculptural styles – from the expressionism of the Amsterdam School (Joseph Mendes da Costa and Lambertus Zijl) to the post-war abstract art of André Volten.

❷ Hildo Krop

From 1916 to his death in 1970, Hildo Krop was employed part-time by the Department of Public Works and his work gives an explicit identity to many of the public spaces in the city. His expressionist style can be seen on many buildings, bridges and viaducts.

❸ and ❹ Artistic routes

People have the opportunity of keeping up with international sculpture during ArtZuid, a sculpture event organised in Amsterdam-Zuid every two years. Anyone wishing to meet contemporary Amsterdam artists can follow one of the many atelier routes.

❷ Hildo Krop's works in Amsterdam (selection)

❸ Open Ateliers Westelijke Eilanden

❹ ArtZuid

Sources: E. J. Lagerweij-Polak, Hildo Krop: beeldhouwer (The Hague, 1992) (2); Open Ateliers Westelijke Eilanden (3); 12 Provinciën | The World of Maps / Foundation ArtZuid (4)

© Noordhoff Uitgevers

Festivals

❶ Cultural appetiser

The Uitmarkt attracts large numbers of people each year – around 500,000, spread over the three days that the event lasts. They come to enjoy everything that the new cultural season has to offer. Uniquely, artists perform for free and no entrance fee is charged. The Uitmarkt has existed since 1977 and is organised by Amsterdam's Uitburo. In recent years, the event has taken place on Museumplein and Leidseplein. As well as music, dance, theatre and musicals, the Uitmarkt also features a literary programme and a large book market. Dating back to 2006, the Uitmarkt's traditional closing event consists of a sing-along of fragments from the upcoming season's musicals and is broadcast live on television. Other cities like Rotterdam and The Hague also organise their own Uitmarkt, but the one in Amsterdam is the largest and is seen as the national opening of the new cultural season.

❷ Innovative theatre

In early July, the former NDSM shipyard in Amsterdam-Noord is transformed for ten days into Festivalstad or Festival City, the location for the Over het IJ Festival. This festival was held for the first time in 1993 and has become more and more elaborate each year. Cooperation with young theatre producers is typical of the festival, which gives them the opportunity to present their work. A further characteristic is the prominent role assigned to site-specific theatre. As well as theatre, the festival also features music and visual arts. A new element – *The city of tomorrow* – was added to the programme in 2015 and involves performances, workshops and debates focusing on future society and the role played by ordinary citizens and artists. The Over het IJ Festival attracts around 30,000 visitors each year, who are mostly aged between 20 and 40.

❸ In the spotlight

During the dark winter months, Amsterdam lights up brightly for fifty days as part of the Amsterdam Light Festival. The festival was first held in 2012 and has been organised every year since. Visitors can walk a route through the inner city, the *Illuminade*, which takes them past many illuminated works of art in the form of light sculptures and projections on historic buildings. There is also a sailing route, Water Colors, on the canals and the river Amstel, which not only passes various artistic and architectural works, but sometimes actually goes through them. Related events also take place in museums, theatres, shops and restaurants. For example, the Grachtenfestival organised a winter special with classical concerts by candlelight during the Amsterdam Light Festival of 2012/2013.

Photos: © Hollandse Hoogte (1); © Saris&DenEngelsman (2); © Hollandse Hoogte (3)

© Noordhoff Uitgevers

❹ Holland Festival
The first Holland Festival performance, Debussy's opera *Pelléas et Mélisande*, was given in the Amsterdam Stadsschouwburg on 15 June 1948. Since then, the festival has become an essential element of the Dutch cultural landscape, aiming to introduce the public to innovative art at the highest international level. Young and established artists from all over the world work together and inspire each other. The festival includes dance, music, theatre, opera and film and the performances are held exclusively in Amsterdam, at a variety of locations such as the Royal Concertgebouw, the Bimhuis and the Westergasfabriek.
On average, around 70,000 visitors have come to the performances in recent years and in 2014, the festival attracted a record number of visitors with the successful British theatre show, *War Horse*.

❺ Different view of the world
The International Documentary Film Festival Amsterdam (IDFA) focuses on artistic and innovative documentary films that reflect the film maker's identity. These films encourage the audience to look at the world differently. IDFA has existed since 1988 and has become the world's largest documentary film festival. A total of around 250 films are shown over twelve days. Unlike other film festivals, the number of visitors is increasing, from 180,000 in 2010 to 255,000 in 2014. The film entries compete for prizes in eight categories, including the VPRO IDFA Award, the main prize for the best long documentary. Most of the prize winners are selected by a panel of professional judges, but there is also an audience award. Activities for film makers, producers and distributors also take place during IDFA, which plays a major role in promoting documentaries.

❻ In conversation with your favourite author
A newcomer in the world of literary magazines, *Das Magazin* (2011) has organised a literary festival since 2013, which lets readers participate in a reading group. Thirty groups get together on a single evening at special locations, such as here in the Artis library, but also in the former study of Harry Mulisch. Up to 25 participants can take part in each reading group and there are two types of group – ones where a recent book is discussed in the presence of the author and host or hostess and ones where a prominent reader discusses a classic text. In 2015, Jelle Brandt Corstius talked about the first book in Karl Ove Knausgård's *My struggle* series. All participants are sent a copy of the book in advance and have the opportunity of discussing it online with each other before the event. The festival attracts some one thousand visitors and concludes with an after-party. Similar festivals are now organised in Antwerp, Berlin and London.

Photos: © Holland Festival, Janiek Dam (4); © Hollandse Hoogte (5); © Ewout Lowie, Amsterdam (6)

© Noordhoff Uitgevers

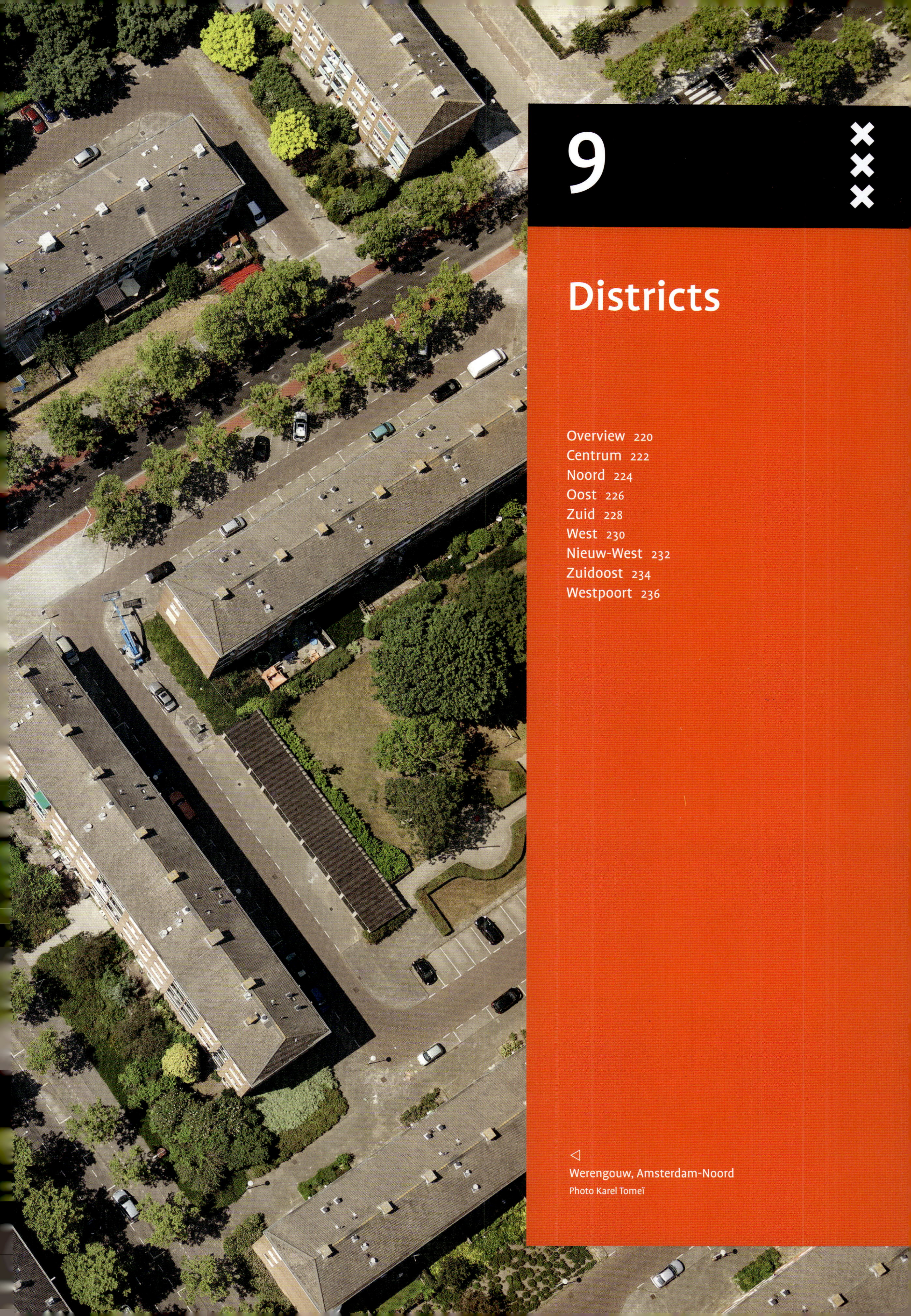

9

Districts

◁
Werengouw, Amsterdam-Noord
Photo Karel Tomeï

Overview

Amsterdam is subdivided into seven districts, plus the Westpoort docks area. All of the districts except Westpoort have a population equivalent to that of a medium-sized or large Dutch city – Zuidoost has 84,000 residents and Nieuw-West 144,000, for instance. The districts are very different, not only in terms of size and land use, but also socially, economically and culturally. The latter differences are illustrated by four indicators on the following pages – the WOZ value of the properties in the district (determined under the Dutch Valuation of Immovable Property Act), the composition of the households, the number of shops and the Cito school test results. Information on land use and the political composition of the governing committees is given in each case. Three of each district's typifying aspects are also discussed in detail, while a map shows the most characteristic buildings.

1 Districts since 2010

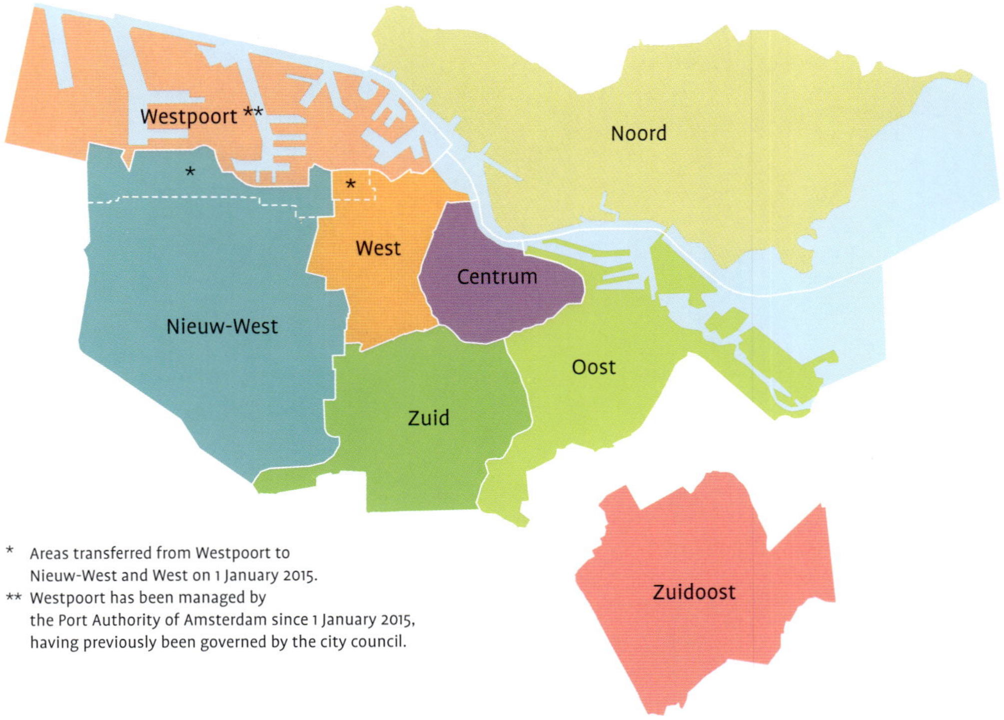

* Areas transferred from Westpoort to Nieuw-West and West on 1 January 2015.
** Westpoort has been managed by the Port Authority of Amsterdam since 1 January 2015, having previously been governed by the city council.

2 Surface area and population

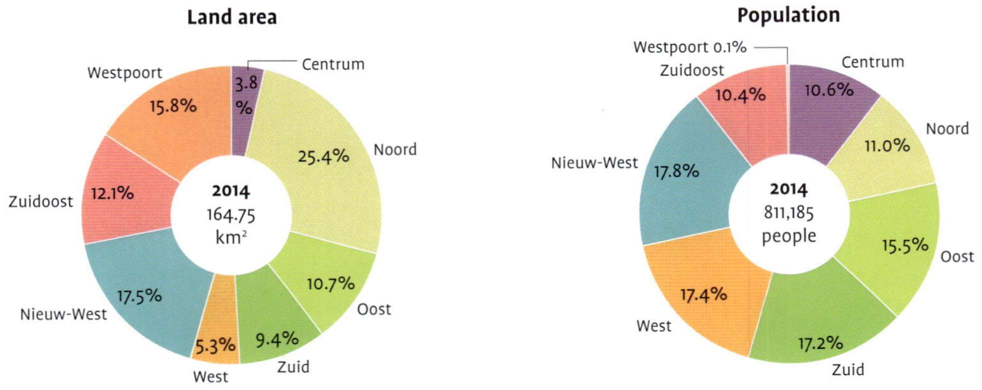

3 Districts 1986-1998

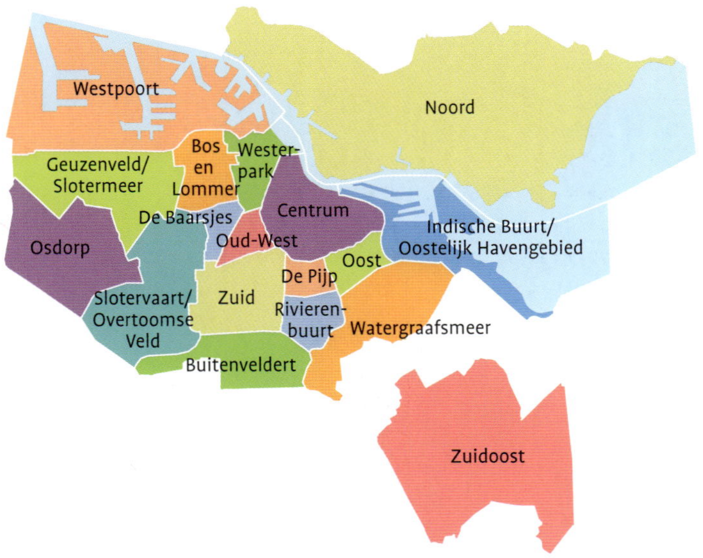

4 Districts 1998-2010

Source: OIS, Research, Information and Statistics, City of Amsterdam (1-4)

© Noordhoff Uitgevers

❺ WOZ value

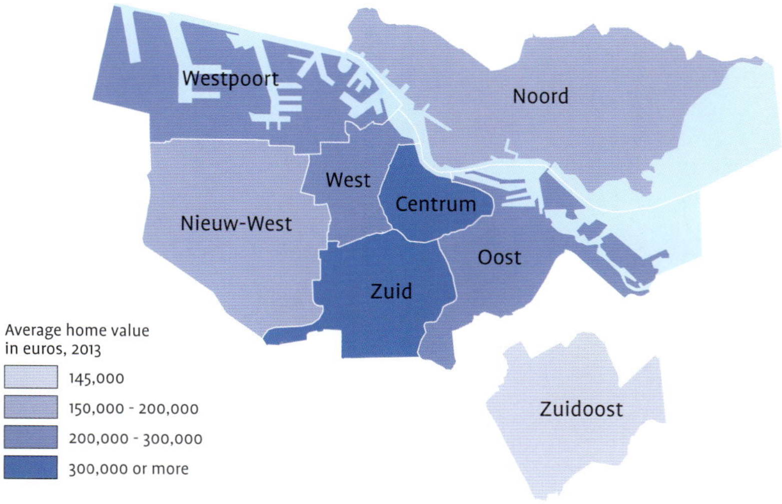

❻ Families

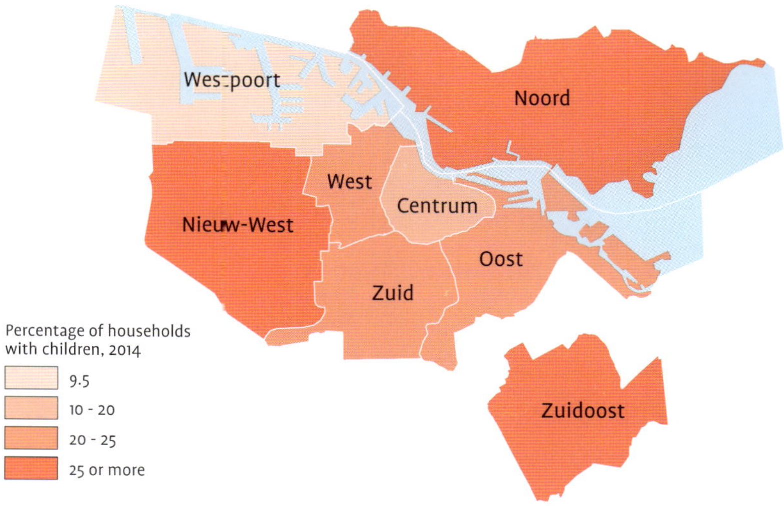

❼ Number of shops

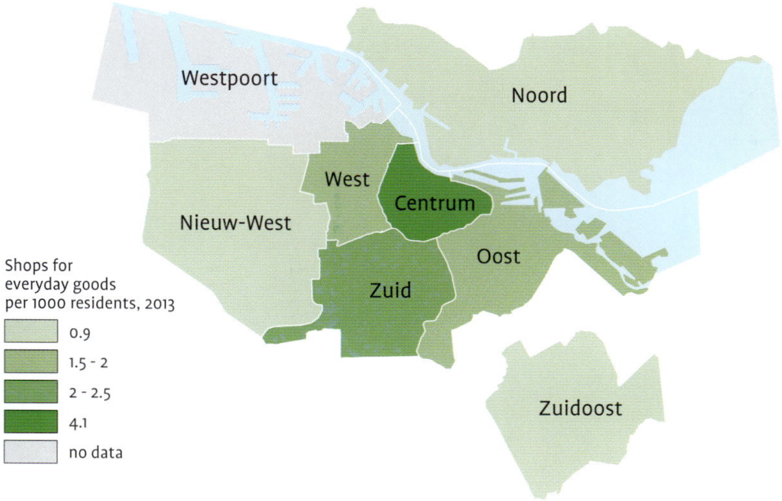

❽ Cito test

❾ Population, education, employment and income

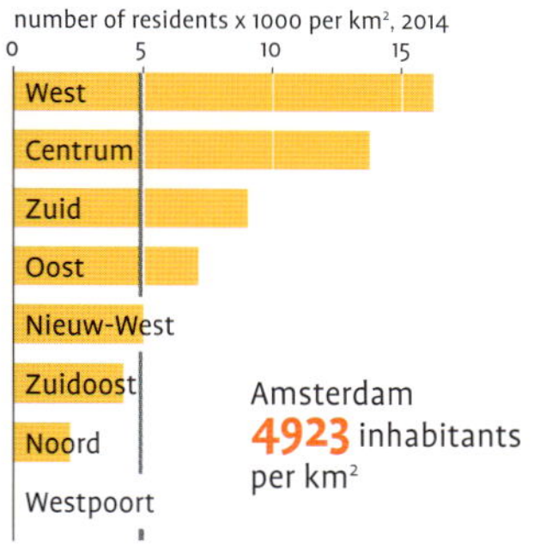

Population density

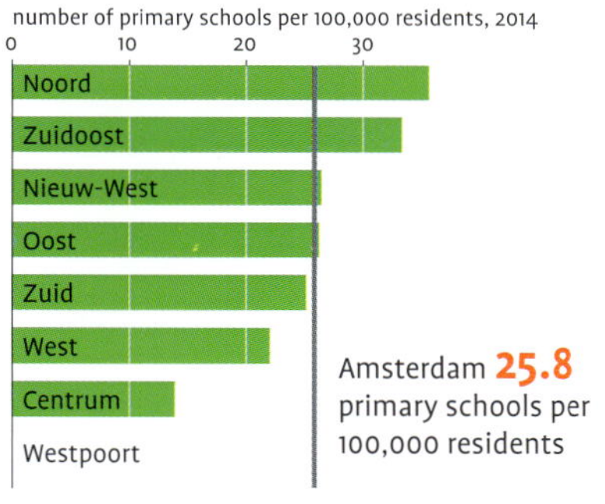

Primary schools

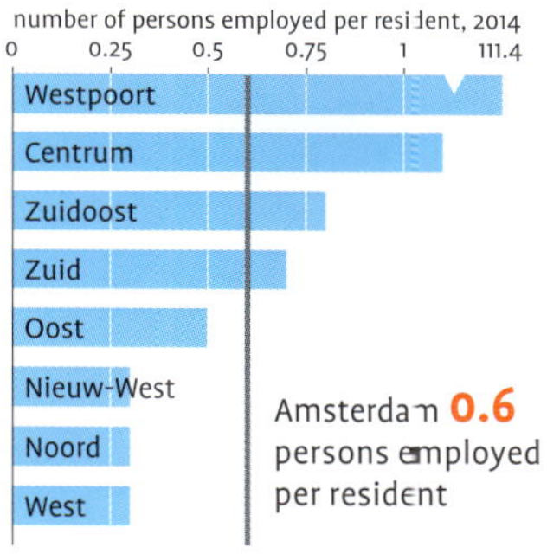

People in employment

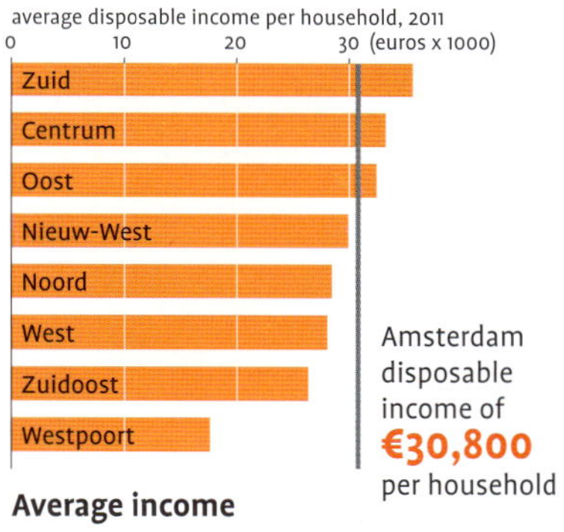

Average income

❶ - ❹ District council to governing committee

In the 1970s, an attempt was made to narrow the gap between politics and ordinary citizens by introducing districts governed by democratically elected district councils with extensive powers. Amsterdam-Noord and Osdorp were the first to implement this new system in 1981, and by 1986, there were eighteen councils. The government found this too many and reduced the number to 7 in 2010. These councils were then replaced by seven less powerful governing committees in 2014. The districts mainly focus on welfare, public spatial planning and waste collection. They are also the neighbourhood's eyes and ears and act as a link to the town hall.

❺ - ❽ Centrum and surrounding areas

The districts differ significantly in socio-economic terms. Centrum and Zuid are the wealthiest areas, with many successful single-person households and childless double-income families. The further away you go from this area the more households there are with children and the lower the general level of prosperity. This is not only reflected by the housing prices and number of shops, but also by the Cito test results.

The overview of the districts is therefore fairly clear-cut, but this is not so within the districts themselves. At neighbourhood level, the four indicators reveal more complex patterns.

❾ Each district totally different

Amsterdam's most exceptional area is Westpoort. It is home to just 423 people (as of 1 January 2014) and is almost purely industrial and commercial. In absolute numbers, employment is highest in Centrum and Zuid, while other districts also have specific traits. West, for example, is by far the most densely populated, but has relatively few primary schools. The opposite applies in Noord, which has numerous schools and a great deal of space (the meadows of 'rural Noord'). People in West and Zuidoost have less to spend than those in Zuid, but not much less than the amount the average Amsterdammer can afford to spend.

Source: OIS, Research, Information and Statistics, City of Amsterdam (5-9)

© Noordhoff Uitgevers

Centrum

With its mediaeval centre and the 17th-century canal ring, the Centrum district is still the beating heart of the city. For Amsterdammers, this is the number one area for shopping and going out. Millions of tourists visit Amsterdam each year, mainly to see the museums and experience the atmosphere, and their presence leads to crowding and nuisance. Even so, most residents feel privileged to live here.

❶ Neighbourhood boundaries

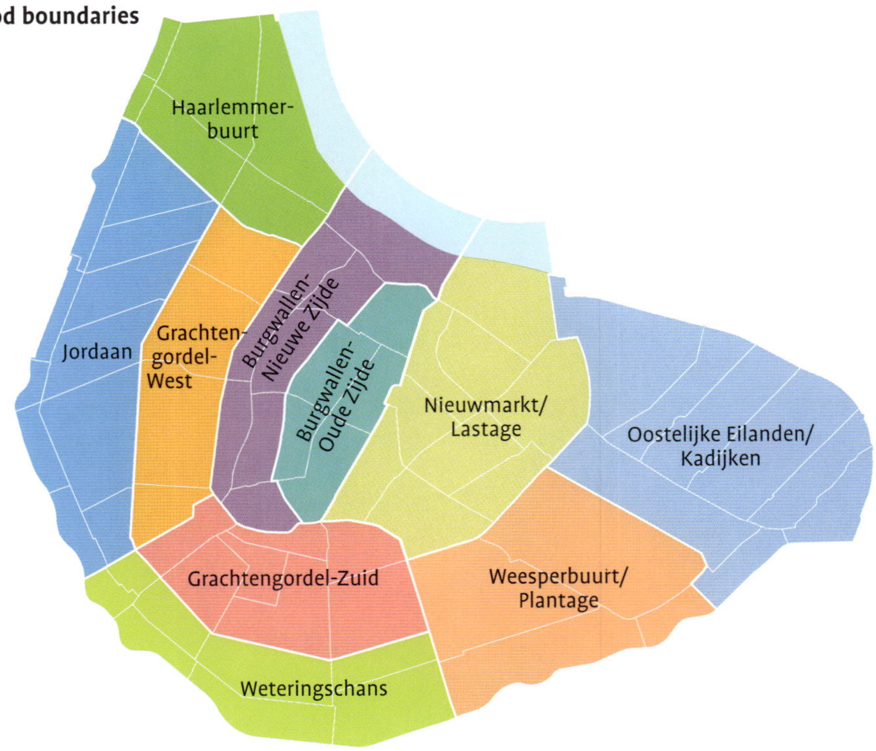

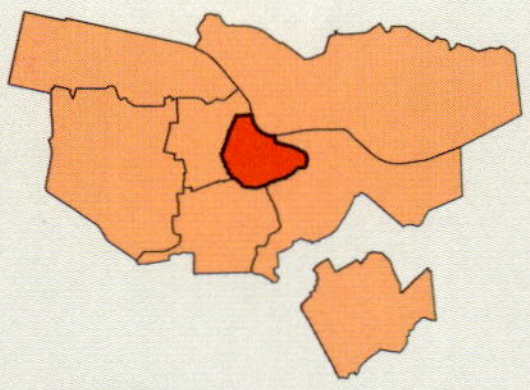

Population
86,098

Land area
6.29km²

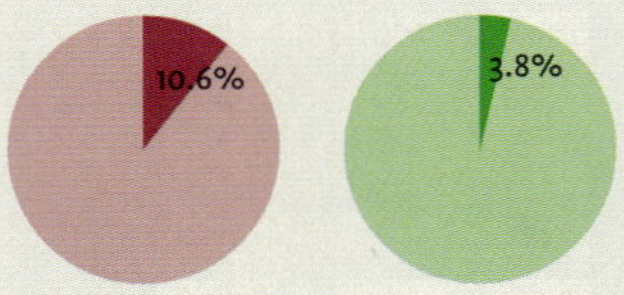

Land use

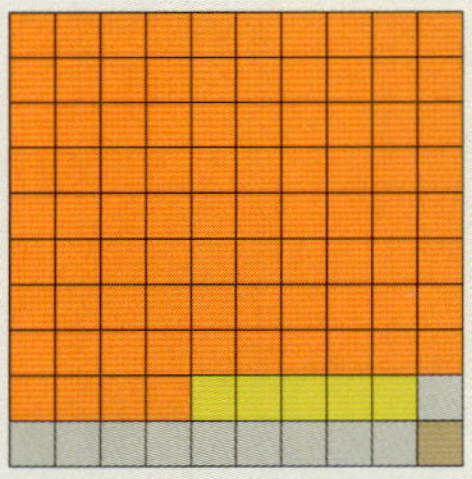

Land/water split

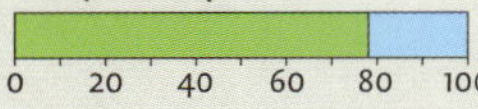

Land: 6.29km²
Water: 1.76km²

Politics

General governance

Governing committee (13 members)

- 5 D66
- 2 GroenLinks
- 2 PvdA
- 2 SP
- 2 VVD

Daily governance

Chairman
- D66

Members
- GL
- PvdA

❷ WOZ value

Average home value in euros, 2013

- 250,000 - 300,000
- 300,000 - 350,000
- 350,000 - 400,000
- 400,000 - 500,000

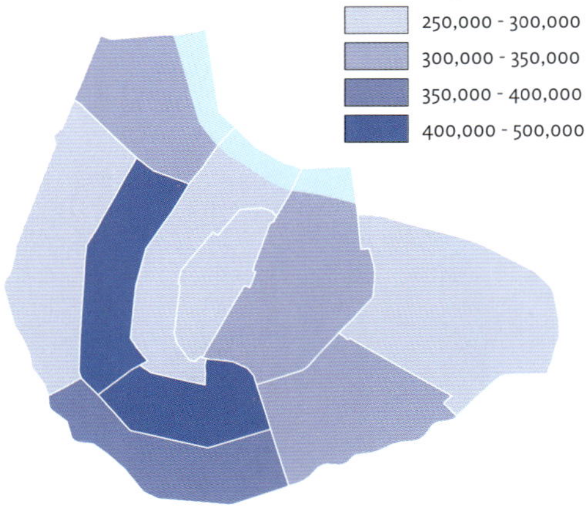

❸ Families

Percentage of households with children, 2014

- less than 10
- 10 - 14
- 14 - 18
- 18 or more

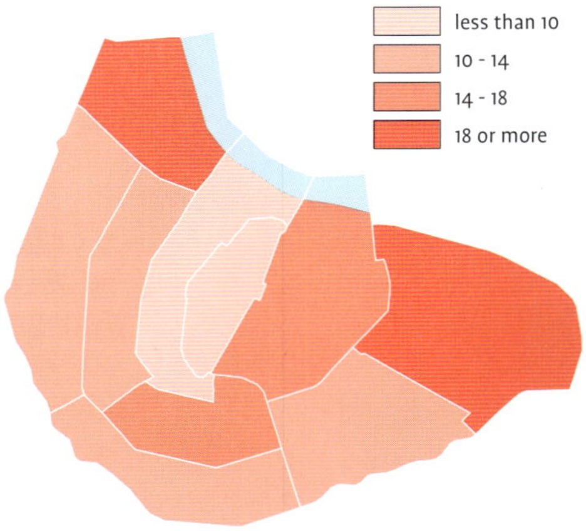

❹ Number of shops

Shops for everyday goods per 1000 residents, 2013

- less than 2
- 2 - 4
- 4 - 6
- 10 - 20

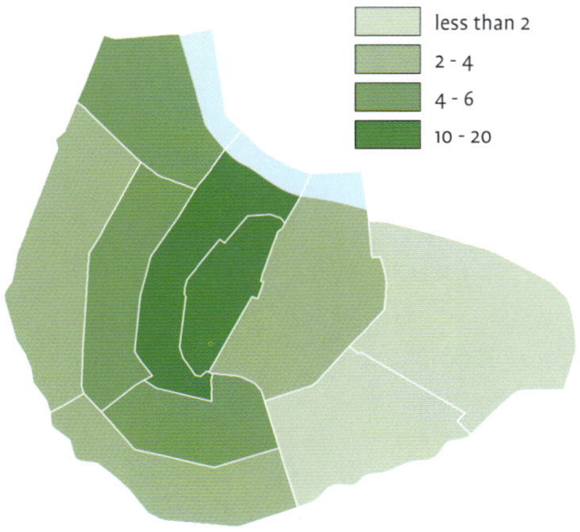

❺ Cito test

Average Cito test score by home address, 2014

- 537.4
- 538 - 540
- 540 - 542
- 542 or more

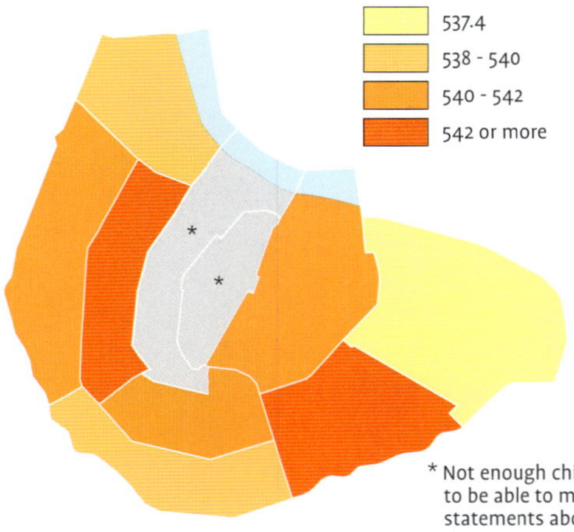

* Not enough children to be able to make statements about the Cito test score.

Source: OIS, Research, Information and Statistics, City of Amsterdam (1-5)

© Noordhoff Uitgevers

❻ Overview

❼ National heritage sites

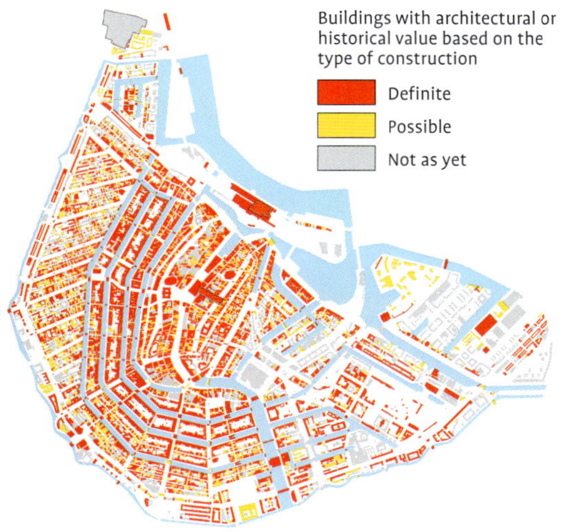

❽ Single-person households

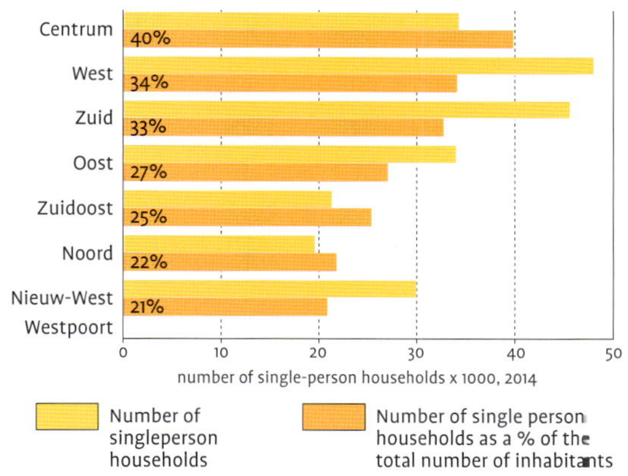

❾ Green roofs

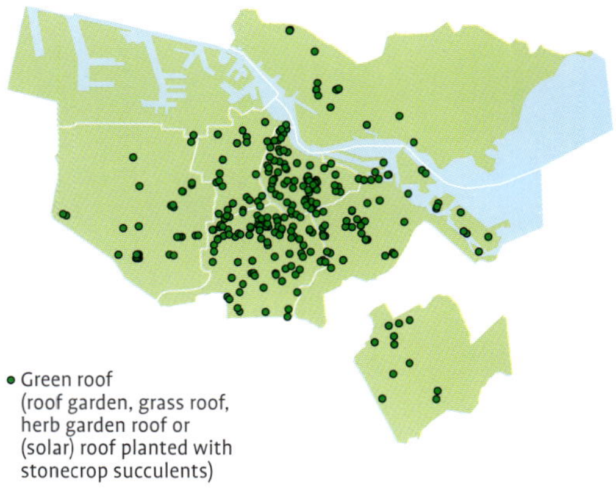

❼ City full of heritage

Amsterdam has around 7503 national heritage sites, 6280 of which are located in the Centrum district. Only 621 are located in all of the other districts together.

Centrum also has hundreds of city heritage sites. In 1999, the main city canal area was designated a protected cityscape, a status that was also assigned to part of Noord in 2014. The canal ring has been listed as a World Heritage Site since 2010.

❽ Out of balance

By national standards, the composition of Amsterdam's population is out of balance, with a relatively high number of single-person households and cohabiting couples without children. Expressed as a percentage, Centrum has the most single-person households in the entire city – almost 35,000 of the 86,098 residents live alone. The district also has the most single-room and two-room homes – nearly 40% of the housing stock (53,932) comes under this category.

❾ Succulents

Centrum does not have many green areas. In an attempt to brighten up the neighbourhood, many residents have flower boxes or planters on their window sills or outside on the pavement. The number of green roofs has also increased significantly in recent years, most of them planted with stonecrop succulents, which act as a sound barrier, offer good protection against heat and cold and improve air quality and biodiversity. Centrum has more green roofs than any other district.

Sources: City of Amsterdam, Civil Registry (6); City of Amsterdam, Bureau of Monuments and Archaeology (7); OIS, Research, Information and Statistics, City of Amsterdam (8-9)

© Noordhoff Uitgevers

Noord

People in Noord sometimes say that they are going into town, meaning the other part of Amsterdam, across the river IJ. Even though there are various easy ways to get to Noord, the IJ is still instinctively seen as a barrier. This has given Noord a unique character, especially in the pre-war working-class neighbourhoods.

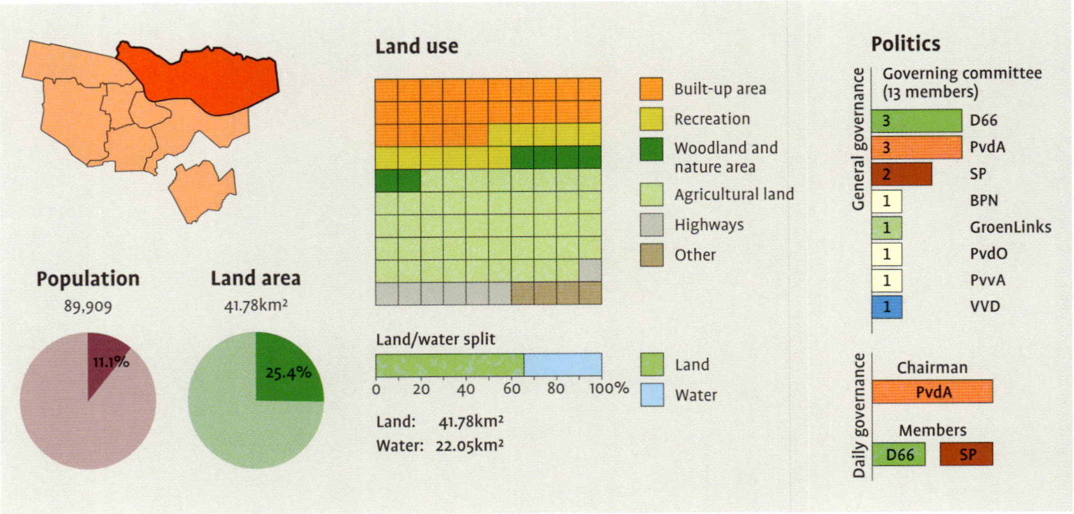

❶ Neighbourhood boundaries

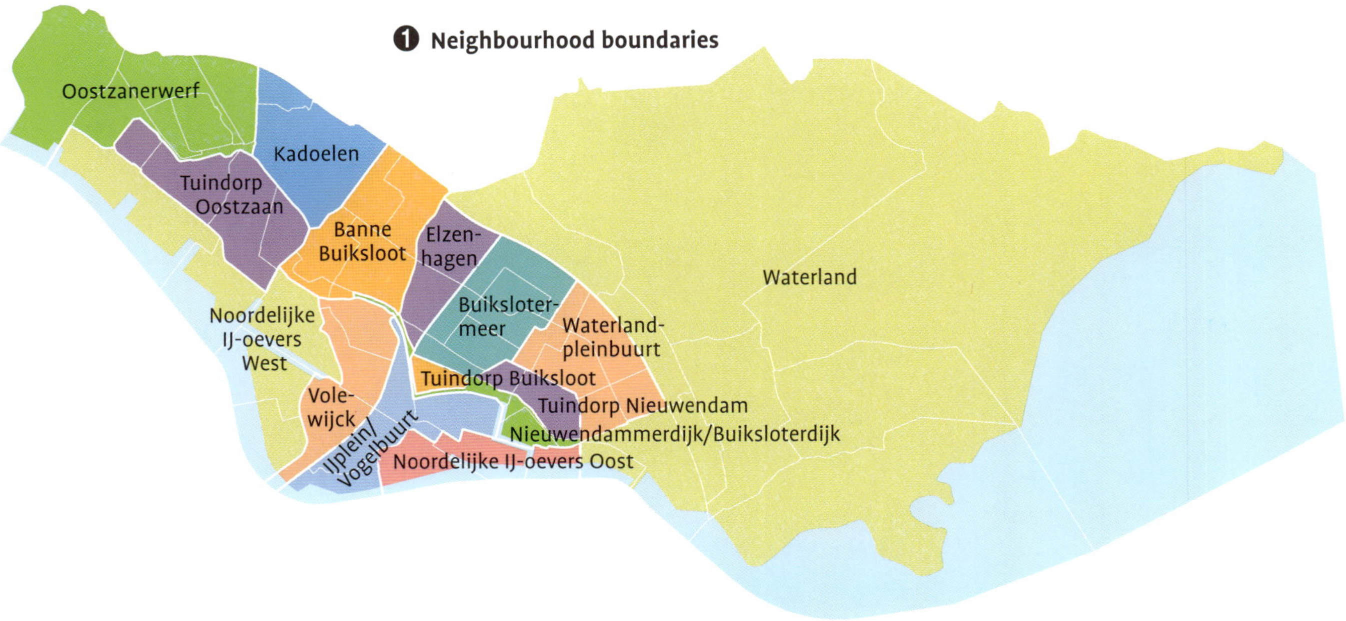

❷ WOZ value

Average home value in euros, 2013

- 150,000 - 200,000
- 200,000 - 250,000
- 250,000 - 300,000
- 350,000 - 450,000
- no data

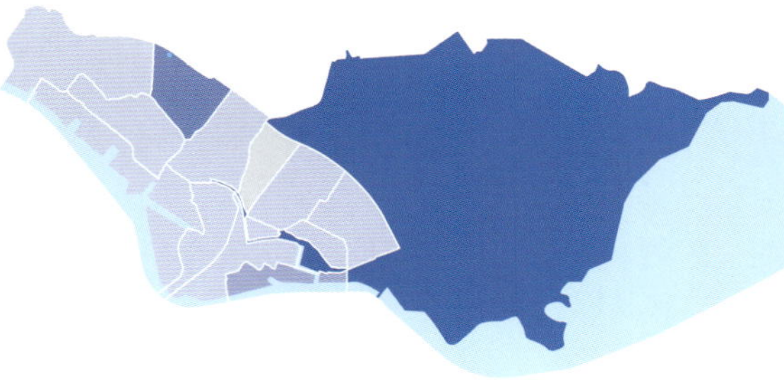

❸ Families

Percentage of households with children, 2014

- less than 20
- 20 - 30
- 30 - 40
- 47
- no data

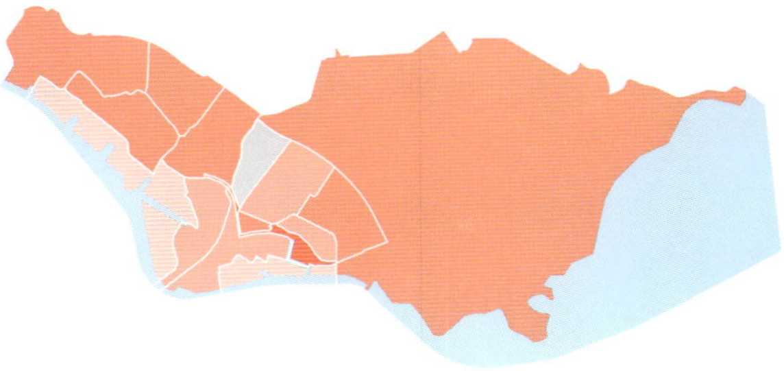

❹ Number of shops

Shops for everyday goods per 1000 residents, 2013

- less than 0.5
- 0.5 - 1
- 1 - 2
- 2 - 3
- no data

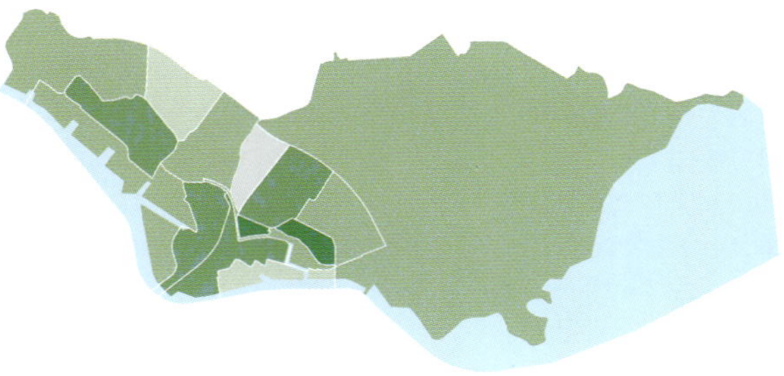

❺ Cito test

Average Cito test score by home address, 2014

- 529 - 533
- 533 - 537
- 537 - 540
- 540 - 543

* Not enough children to be able to make statements about the Cito test score.

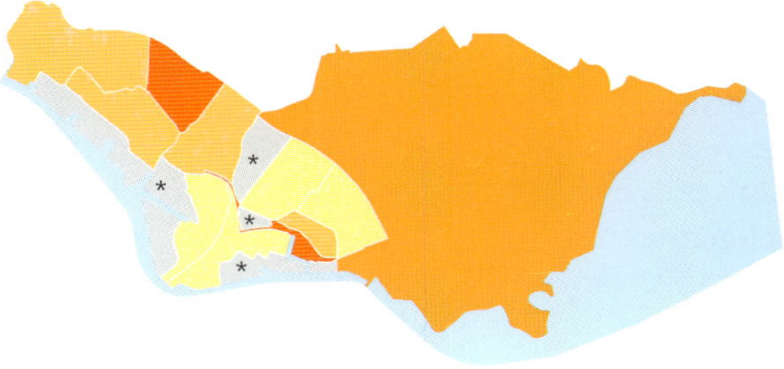

Source: OIS, Research, Information and Statistics, City of Amsterdam (1-5)

© Noordhoff Uitgevers

❻ Overview

❼ Obesity

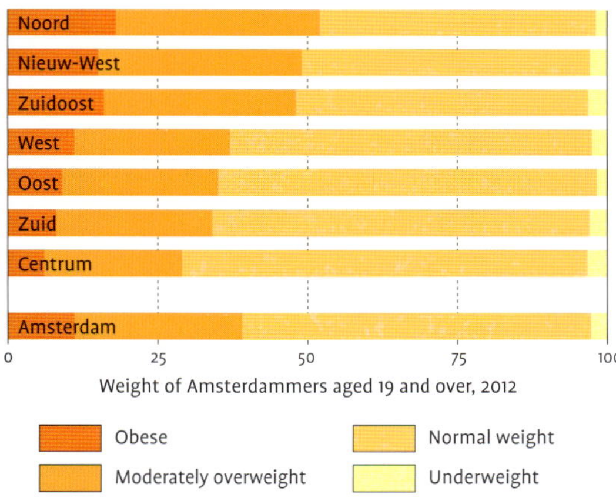

❽ Mopeds and scooters

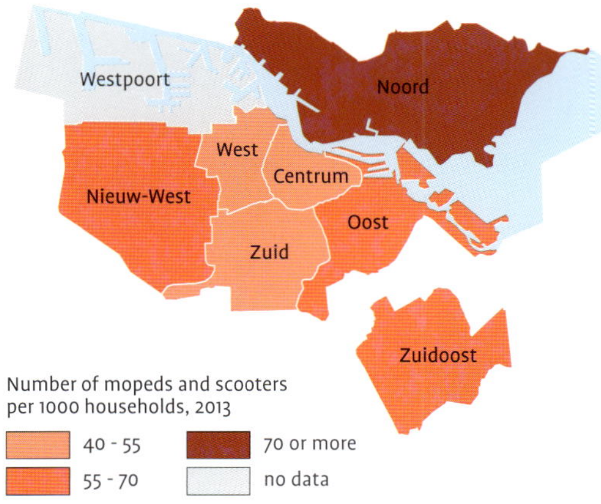

❾ Tuindorp Oostzaan

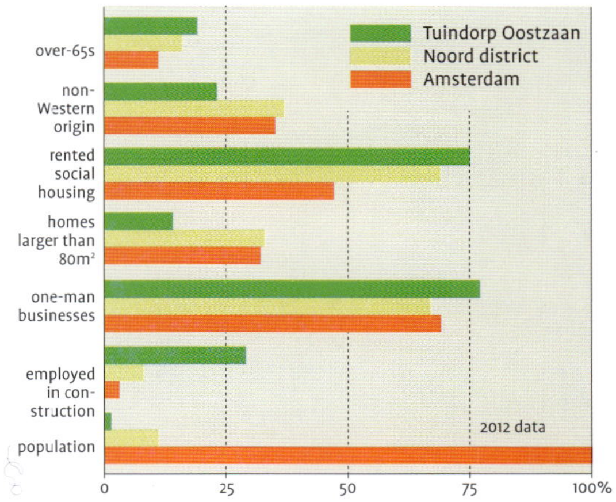

❼ Too fat

Public Health Service figures indicate that 40% of Amsterdammers are overweight. In Noord, more than half of the adults are heavier than they should be and 18% are obese, the highest percentage in Amsterdam. These statistics can partly be explained by lifestyle – the residents of Noord exercise less and eat fewer vegetables. However, there are significantly fewer excessive (8%) and heavy drinkers (10%) than in Centrum and Zuid.

❽ Many blue and yellow number plates

Residents of Noord exercise less, but have more motorcycles, mopeds and scooters than in other districts. Noord has 95 electric bicycles, scooters and mopeds with blue number plates per thousand residents, whereas Zuidoost has 36. Noord also has the most mopeds and scooters with yellow number plates – 83 per thousand residents – and the most powered invalid carriages and motorised cargo bikes with blue number plates.

❾ A unique district

Tuindorp Oostzaan (nearly 11,000 residents) is a unique district in many ways. The composition and occupations of the population differ significantly to the rest of Noord and Amsterdam and the residents also vote differently. During the 2014 city council elections, the turnout here was less than 40%, the lowest percentage in Noord. Tuindorp Oostzaan was the only neighbourhood in Amsterdam where there was a majority vote for the Socialist Party.

Sources: City of Amsterdam, Civil Registry (6); Public Health Service, Amsterdamse Gezondheidsmonitor, OIS, Research, Information and Statistics (7); City of Amsterdam (8-9)

© Noordhoff Uitgevers

Oost

Oost is a varied district and is often seen as Amsterdam's main multicultural district. Native Amsterdammers are in the majority, albeit only narrowly at 52%. There are significant differences between the neighbourhoods, which range from old, largely renovated areas around the Dappermarkt and the somewhat isolated Betondorp to IJburg, which is still being developed intensively.

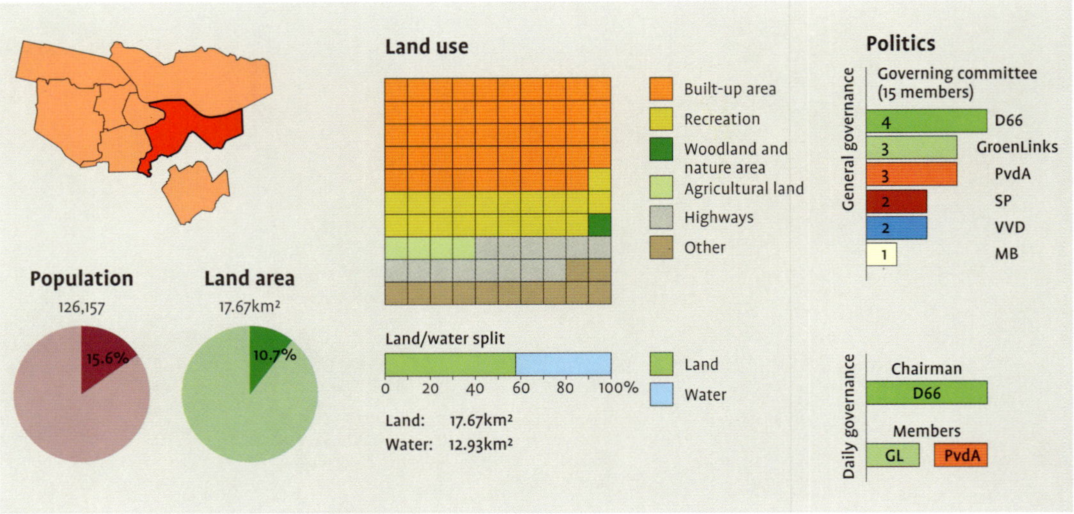

❶ Neighbourhood boundaries

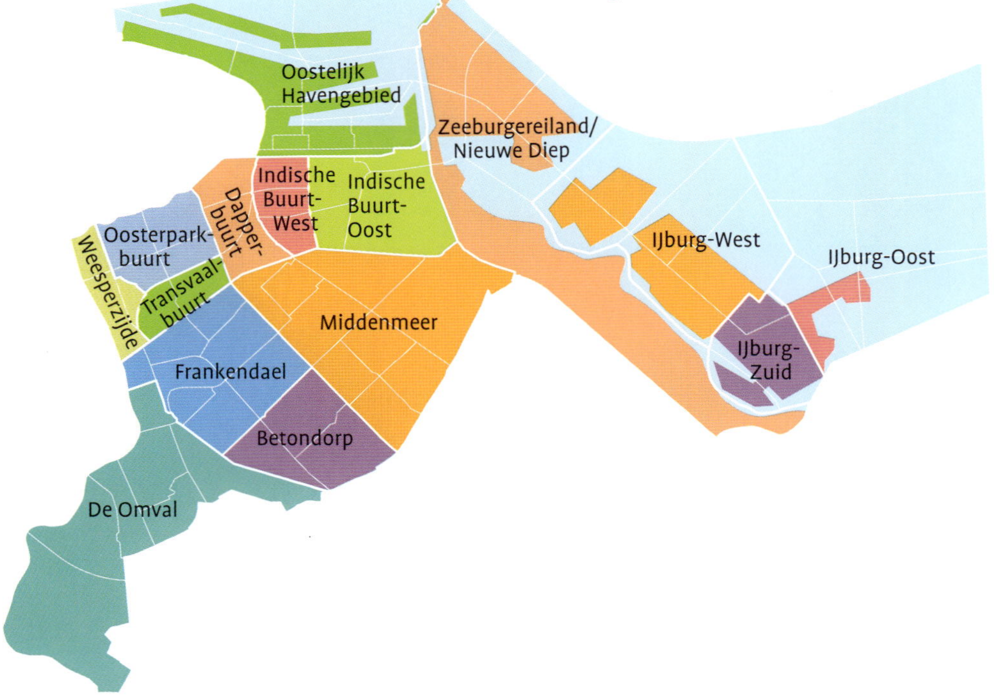

❷ WOZ value

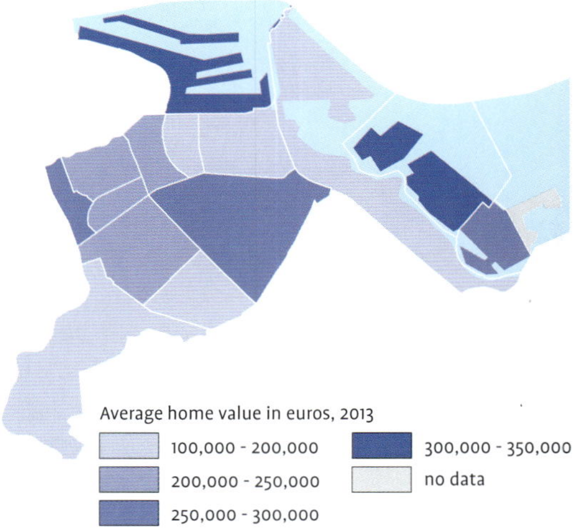

❸ Families

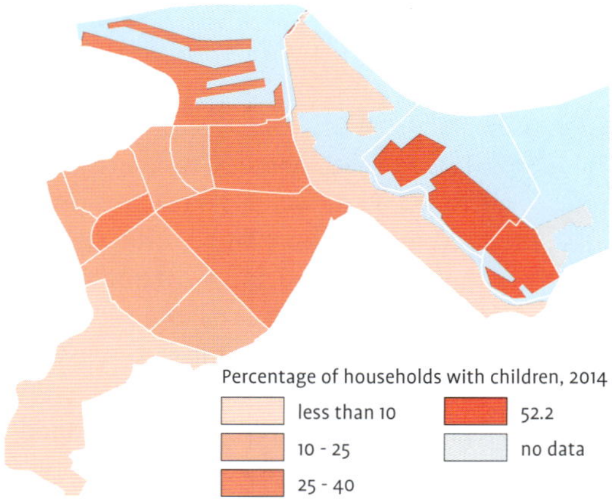

❹ Number of shops

❺ Cito test

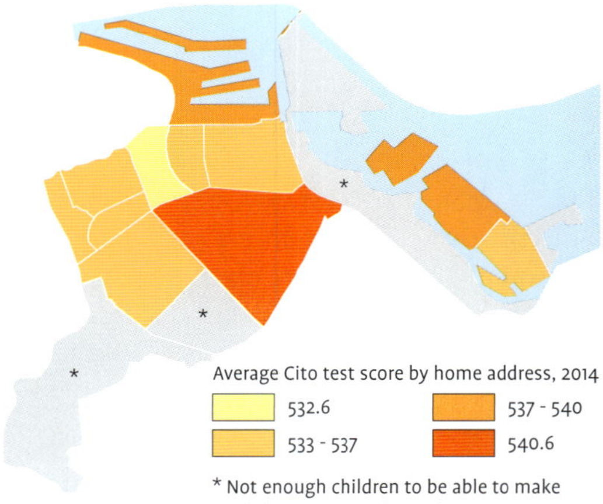

* Not enough children to be able to make valid statements about the Cito test score.

Source: OIS, Research, Information and Statistics, City of Amsterdam (1-5)

© Noordhoff Uitgevers

6 Overview

7 Health

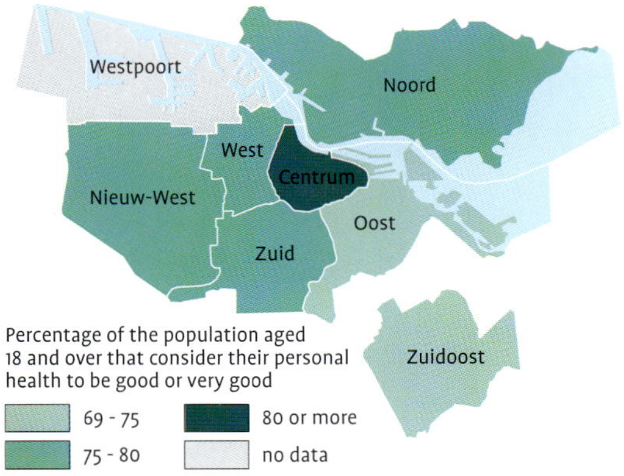

8 Neighbourhood differences

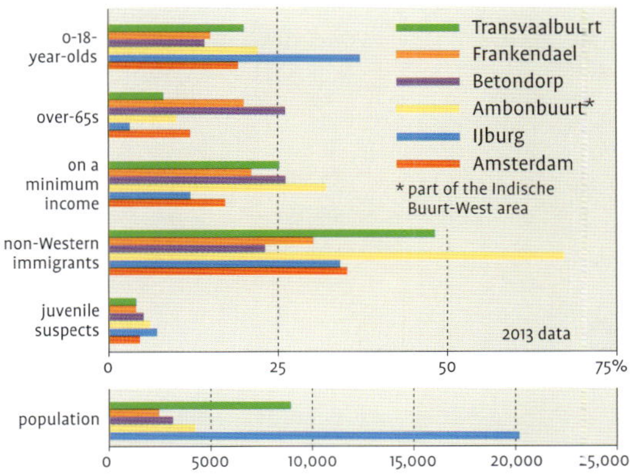

9 Complaints of neglect

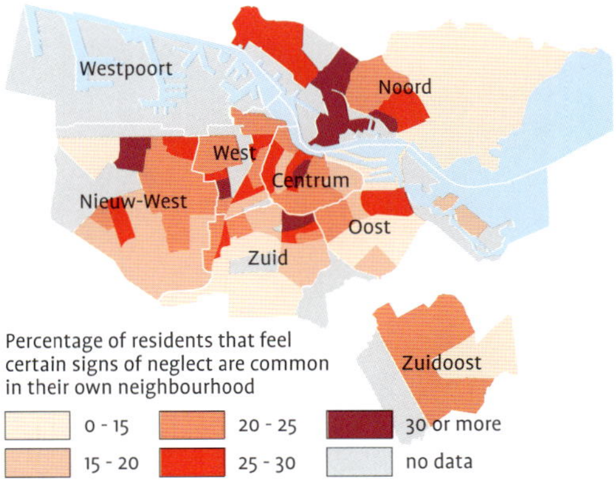

7 Healthier than expected

A quarter of Oost's residents do not feel all that healthy and this is the worst figure in Amsterdam. However, the facts tell a different story. Only 9% of the residents are obese, much fewer than elsewhere in Amsterdam, while the percentages for diabetics, people with cardiovascular disease, smokers, alcoholics and patients suffering from chronic diseases and psychological complaints are around the Amsterdam average.

8 Multifaceted

Oost is a multifaceted district. Its largest neighbourhood, IJburg, is relatively young in terms of both its development and its population. Despite IJburg's relative prosperity, juvenile crime is above average. The opposite applies in Betondorp and Frankendael, which have many older residents and lots of people on a minimum income. Residents of the Transvaalbuurt and Ambonbuurt are relatively young, but more likely to be of non-Western origin than in IJburg.

9 Rather satisfied

The Dutch complain a lot and Amsterdammers are no exception. Their complaints are often justified, but not always. The City of Amsterdam runs an annual survey to find out what its residents think of living conditions in their neighbourhood. With the exception of the Indische Buurt, Oost's residents rate their district very highly, as there is little rubbish and dog dirt on the streets. The residents of the red light district and De Pijp complain the most.

Sources: City of Amsterdam, Civil Registry (6); OIS, Research, Information and Statistics, City of Amsterdam (7-9)

© Noordhoff Uitgevers

Zuid

Zuid has the reputation of being the most fashionable area in Amsterdam. A relatively large number of wealthy people do indeed live here – and that shows. Shopping on P. C. Hooftstraat is an activity reserved for the 'happy few'. Anybody wanting to buy a house in the Apollobuurt or Willemsparkbuurt should expect to pay upward of one million euros and even a 30m² apartment in De Pijp, once an impoverished working class neighbourhood, costs at least 200,000 euros.

❶ Neighbourhood boundaries

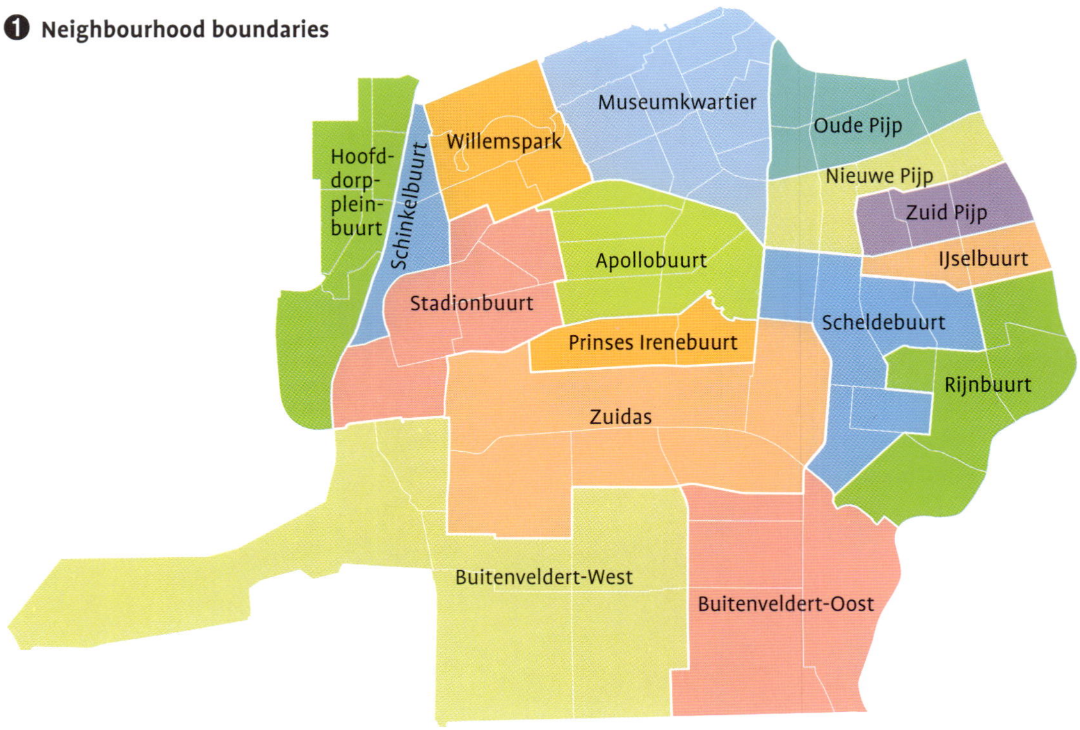

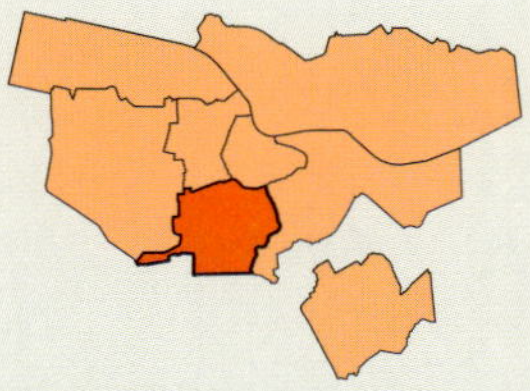

Population
139,524

Land area
15.45km²

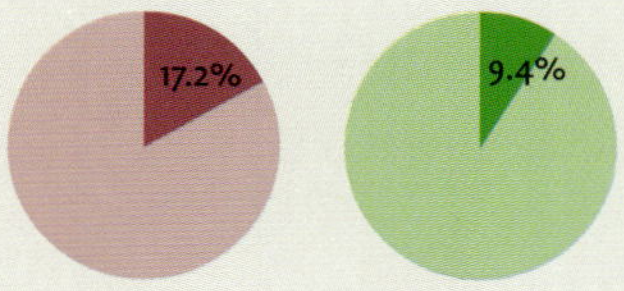

Land use

- Built-up area
- Recreation
- Woodland and nature area
- Agricultural land
- Highways
- Other

Land/water split

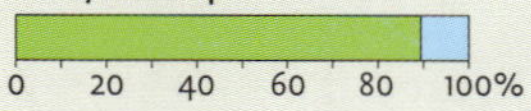

- Land
- Water

Land: 15.45km²
Water: 1.83km²

Politics

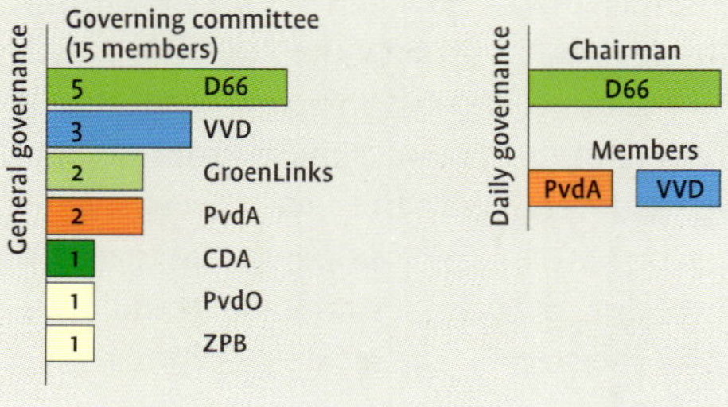

❷ WOZ value

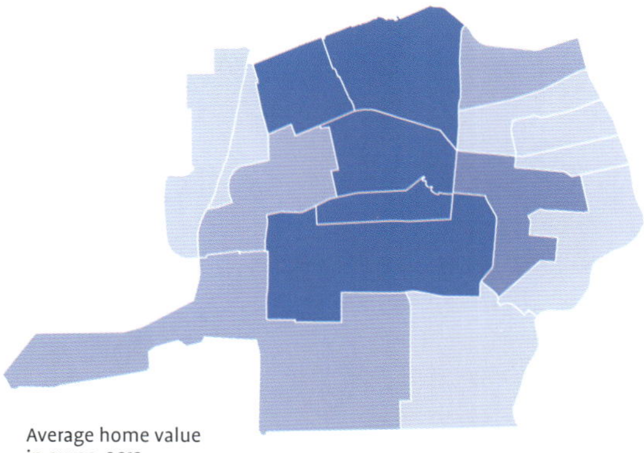

Average home value in euros, 2013

- 200,000 - 250,000
- 250,000 - 300,000
- 300,000 - 350,000
- 500,000 - 700,000

❸ Families

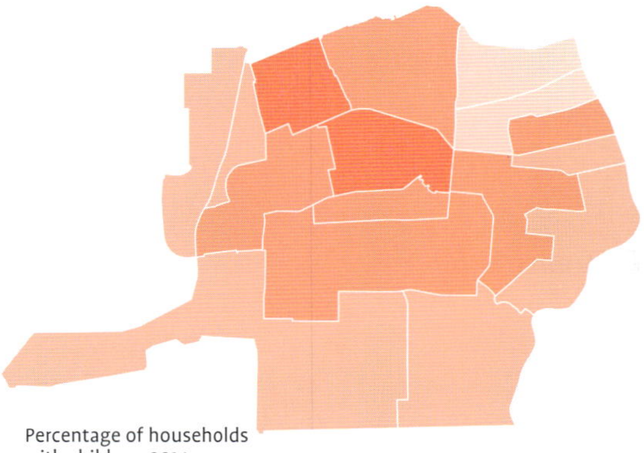

Percentage of households with children, 2014

- less than 15
- 15 - 20
- 20 - 25
- 25 or more

❹ Number of shops

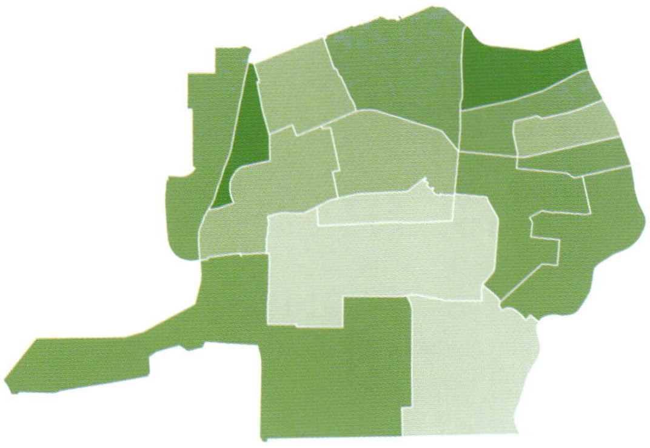

Shops for everyday goods per 1000 residents, 2013

- less than 1
- 1 - 2
- 2 - 4
- 4 - 5

❺ Cito test

* Not enough children to be able to make valid statements about the Cito test score.

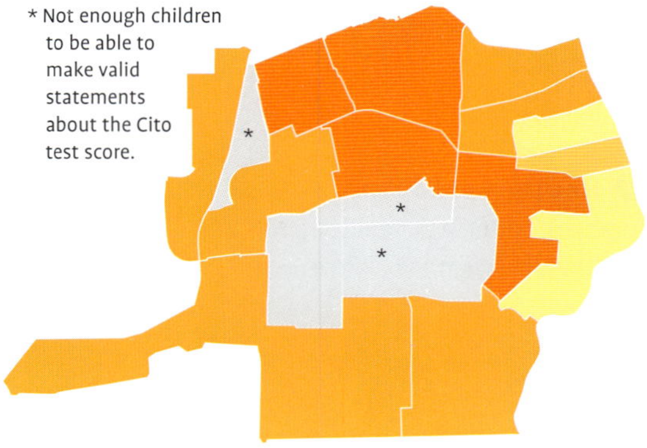

Average Cito test score by home address, 2014

- 533 - 535
- 535 - 537
- 537 - 540
- 540 - 545

Source: OIS, Research, Information and Statistics, City of Amsterdam (1-5)

© Noordhoff Uitgevers

❻ Overview

❼ Sports facilities

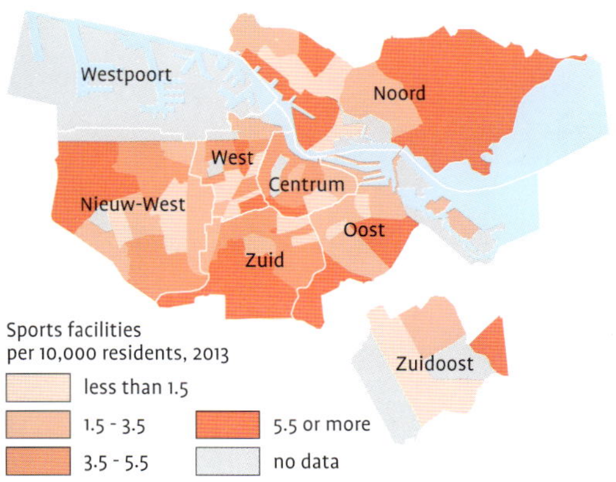

❽ Safety

❾ Highest asking prices in Amsterdam

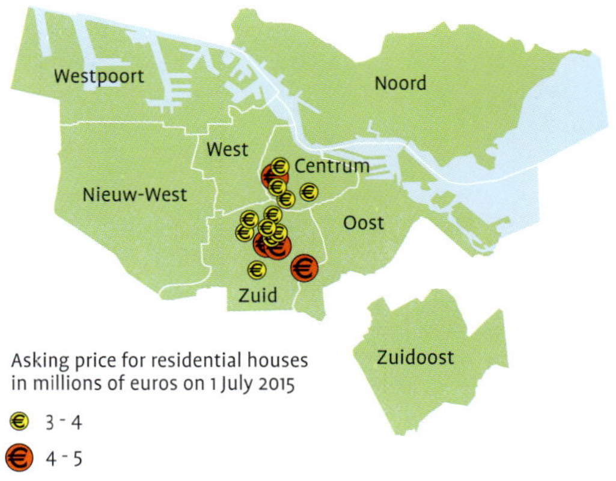

❼ Healthy in body and mind

In absolute terms, Zuid has the most sports facilities in Amsterdam. Zuid residents obviously use them intensively because Public Health Service statistics show that they are the most active Amsterdammers. Together with the residents of Centrum, they are also the most positive about their physical and mental health.

❽ Objective and subjective

Amsterdam has becoming increasingly safe in recent years, but this is sometimes perceived differently. In objective terms, Zuid is Amsterdam's safest district and its residents feel safer than any others in the city. Most other Amsterdammers perceive their neighbourhood as less safe than it actually is. Centrum is the exception and is in fact the least safe district in Amsterdam. Even so many of its residents are particularly positive about their neighbourhood.

❾ A few million

On 1 July 2015, the property websites Funda and Huizenzoeker listed fifteen houses in Amsterdam at an asking price of more than 3 million euros. Ten of them were located in Zuid. The most expensive house, with an asking price of 4,950,000 euros, was on Zuidelijke Wandelweg. The cheapest of the fifteen was a house on Apollolaan that was expected to sell for a 'mere' 3,250,000 euros.

Sources: City of Amsterdam, Civil Registry (6); OIS, Research, Information and Statistics, City of Amsterdam (7, 8); Funda (9)

© Noordhoff Uitgevers

West

Busy West is not a trendy district. In fact, it is rather working-class, which many people feel makes it much nicer than Zuid. Its appearance has improved noticeably over the last twenty years, with a major new attraction – the De Hallen complex. The 23 hectare Food Center Amsterdam ('the stomach of Amsterdam') in the middle of West will also be revamped over the next 25 years, and the imposing Central Market Hall will be given a new, consumer-friendly purpose, just like De Hallen.

❶ Neighbourhood boundaries

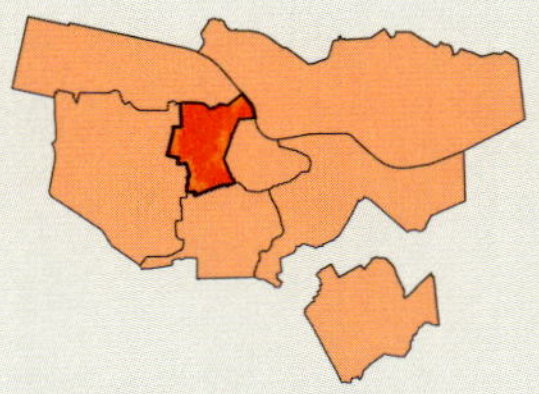

Population
141,095

Land area
9.39km²

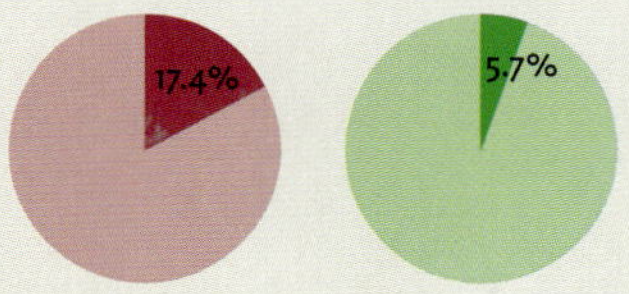

Land use

Land/water split

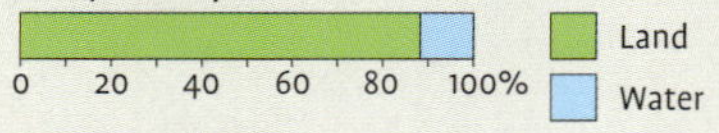

Land: 9.39km²
Water: 1.25km²

Politics

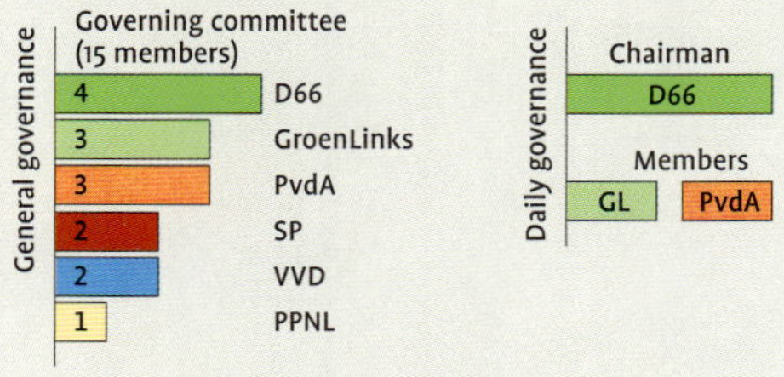

❷ WOZ value

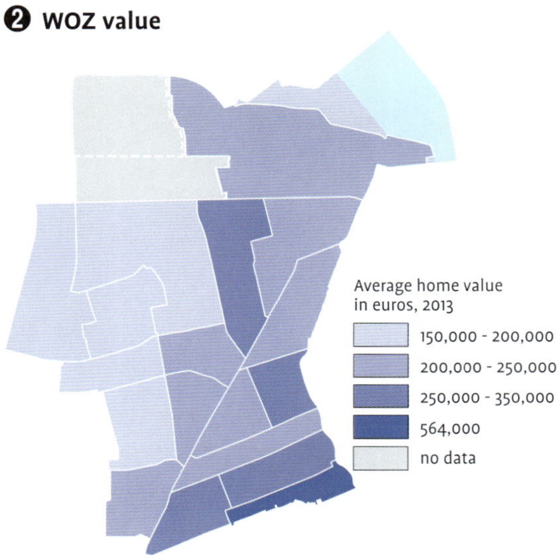

❸ Families

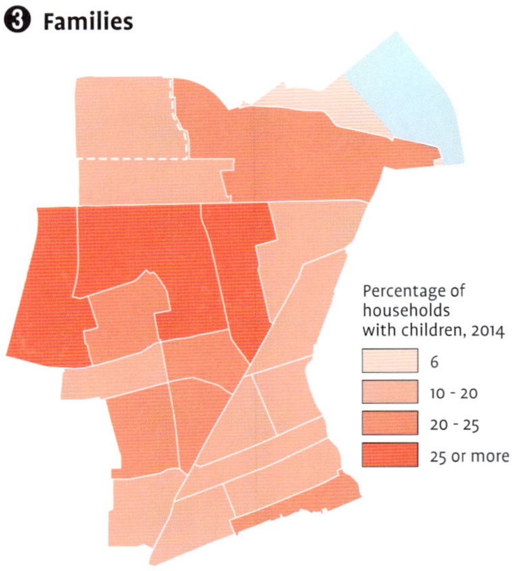

❹ Number of shops

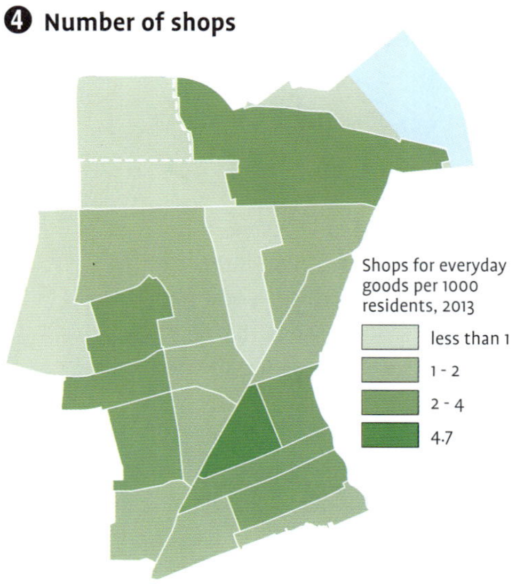

❺ Cito test

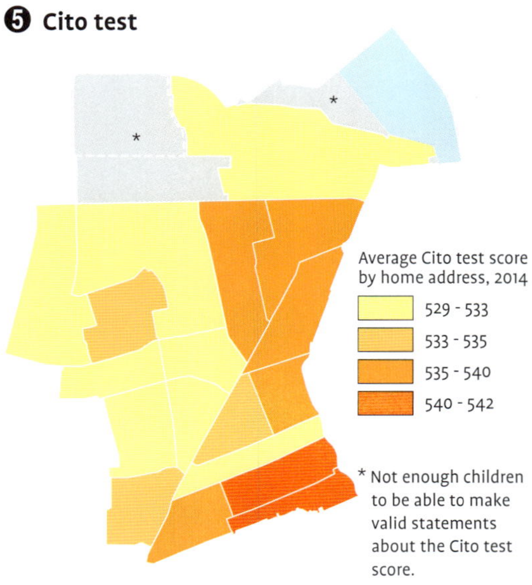

Source: OIS, Research, Information and Statistics, City of Amsterdam (1-5)

© Noordhoff Uitgevers

❻ Overview

❼ Housing density

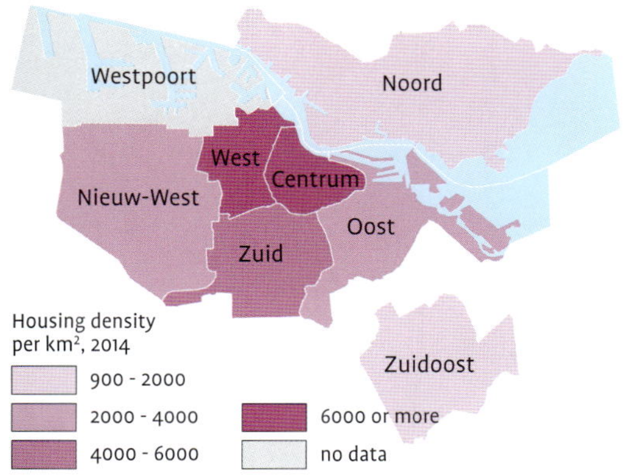

❽ Single-room and two-room apartments

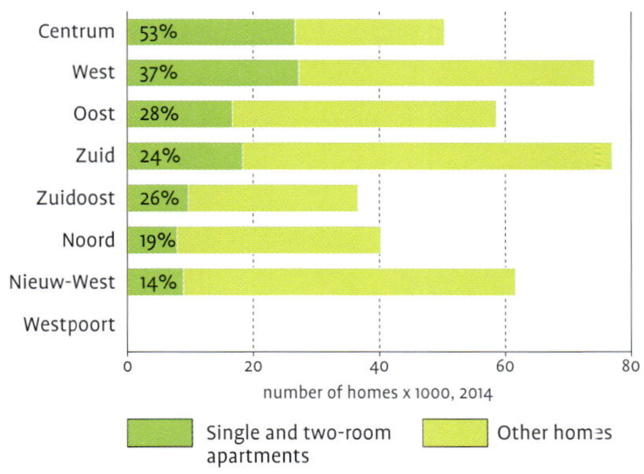

❾ Number of cafes

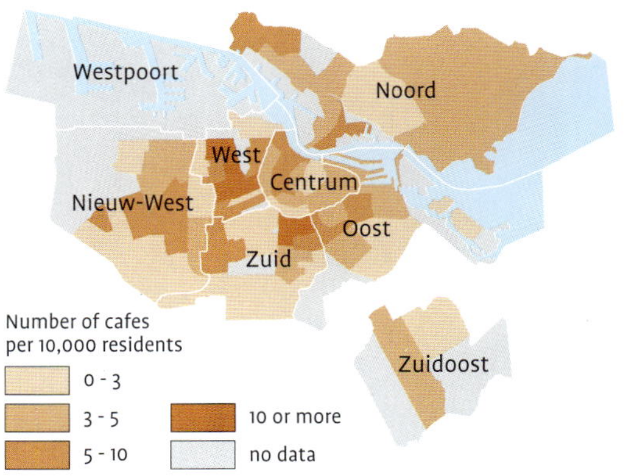

❼ Full and crowded

Centrum may seem full and crowded, but West definitely is too. At the beginning of 2014, the district had 16,206 residents per km², as opposed to 13,710 in Centrum. This makes West the most densely populated district. The housing density is also highest here – 8439 homes per km², as opposed to nearly 8000 in Centrum. The total housing stock in 2014 was 50,333 in Centrum and 74,100 in West. Nearly 60% of the homes in West date back to before the war.

❽ Cramped accommodation

Amsterdam-West has 2404 single-room apartments and 23,989 two-room apartments, which together account for around 37% of the total stock of 74,100 homes. Only Centrum shows a higher percentage, but West still has a higher proportion of people living in cramped accommodation. Around 60% of the homes there have less than 60m² of usable floor space, as opposed to only 40% in Centrum. These percentages are much lower in the other districts.

❾ Unhealthy eating habits

West's residents do not have to travel far for a snack such as a croquette or frikandel. This district has about 90 cafes, many more than the average per district, and even Centrum has fewer. However, the large number of cafes does not have a noticeably adverse effect on health. The residents of West are no fatter than the average Amsterdammer and no more likely to suffer from cardiovascular disease. However, they do smoke the most (together with people in Zuidoost).

Sources: City of Amsterdam, Civil Registry (6); OIS, Research, Information and Statistics, City of Amsterdam (7-9)

© Noordhoff Uitgevers

Nieuw-West

Once developed as a garden city where people could enjoy light, spaciousness and garden views in their typical suburban homes after a day at work, Nieuw-West currently has a negative image. While the district does indeed have to contend with typical city problems, living there is hardly intolerable. Nieuw-West also includes newer and more compactly structured neighbourhoods like De Aker and Nieuw Sloten.

❶ Neighbourhood boundaries

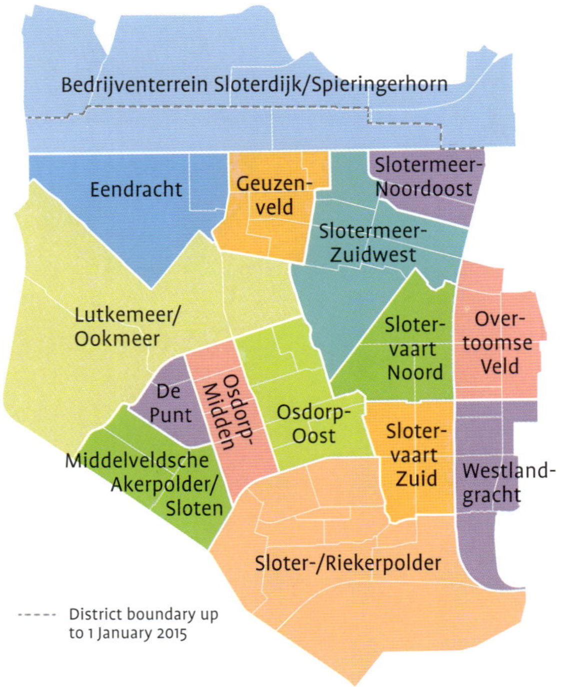

----- District boundary up to 1 January 2015

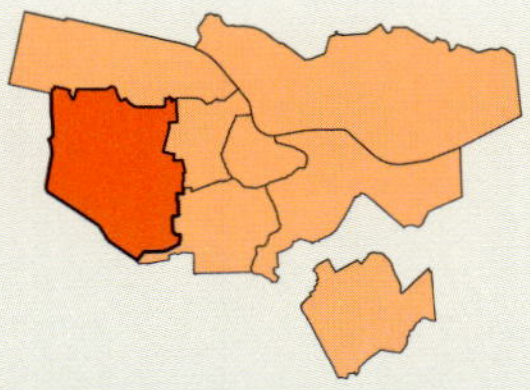

Population
144,091

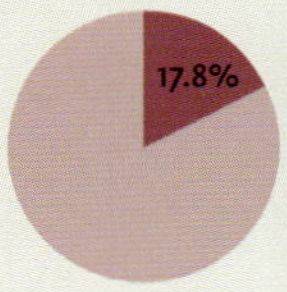

Land area
33.93km²

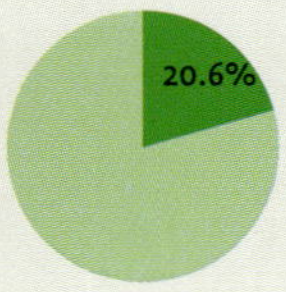

Land use

- Built-up area
- Recreation
- Woodland and nature area
- Agricultural land
- Highways
- Other

Land/water split

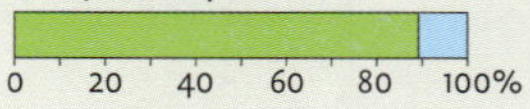

- Land
- Water

Land: 33.93km²
Water: 4.09km²

Politics

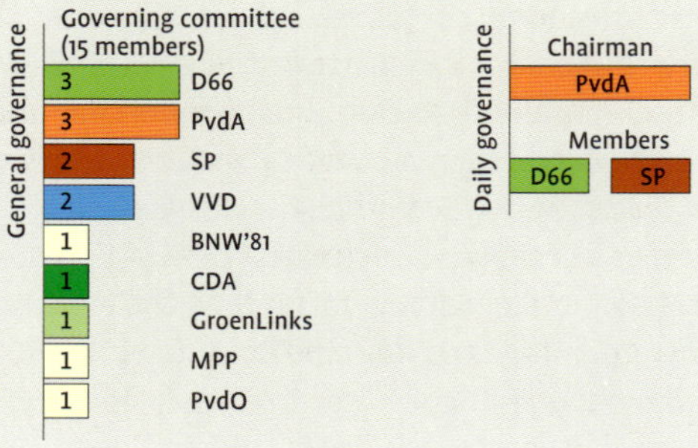

❷ WOZ value

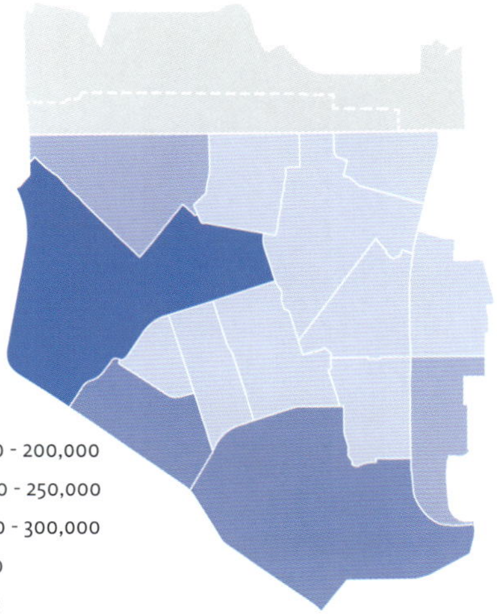

Average home value in euros, 2013

- 100,000 - 200,000
- 200.000 - 250,000
- 250,000 - 300,000
- 374,000
- no data

❸ Families

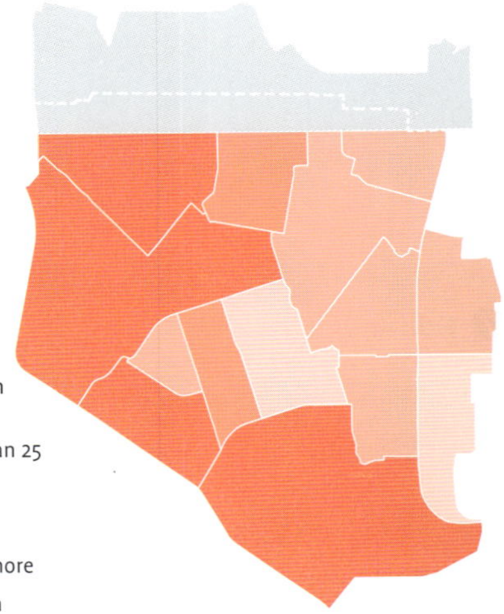

Percentage of households with children, 2014

- less than 25
- 25 - 35
- 35 - 40
- 40 or more
- no data

❹ Number of shops

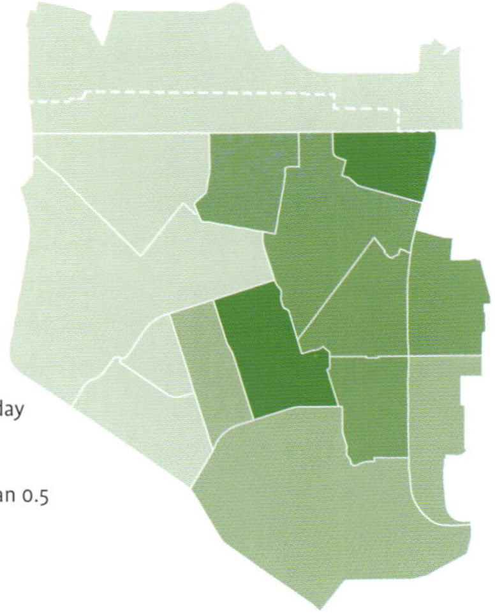

Shops for everyday goods per 1000 residents, 2013

- less than 0.5
- 0.5 - 1
- 1 - 2
- 2 - 3

❺ Cito test

* Not enough children to be able to make valid statements about the Cito test score.

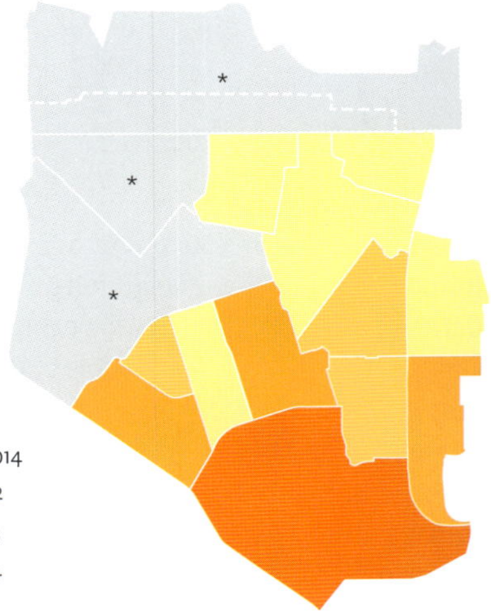

Average Cito test score by home address, 2014

- 530 - 532
- 532 - 533
- 533 - 534
- 534.1

Source: OIS, Research, Information and Statistics, City of Amsterdam (1-5)

© Noordhoff Uitgevers

6 Overview

- Railway station
- Metro station
- Public administration building
- Museum
- Theatre
- Hotel
- Church (still in use or converted)
- Mosque
- Hospital
- Windmill
- Cemetery
- Football pitch
- Indoor swimming pool
- Marina or yacht club
- Lock, sluice
- Other notable landmark or building

9 Old centre of Sloten

- Registered and candidate national or city heritage site
- Building worthy of being a heritage site, with added architectural or cultural-historical value
- Characteristic building with added architectural or urban development value
- Building characteristic of the construction period, but without specific added value
- Built-up after 1940
- National heritage site
- City heritage site

7 Young troublemakers

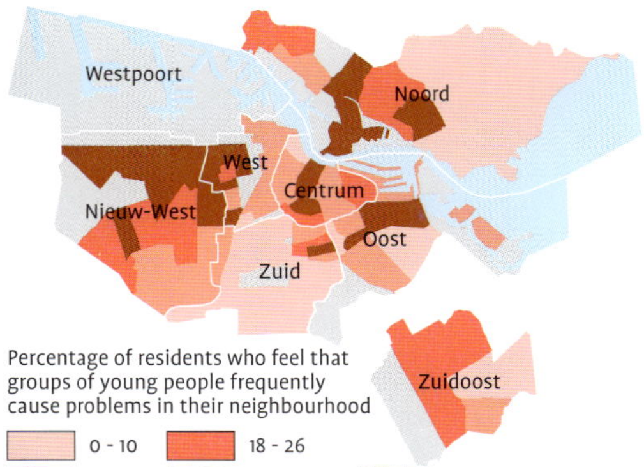

Percentage of residents who feel that groups of young people frequently cause problems in their neighbourhood

- 0 - 10
- 10 - 18
- 18 - 26
- 26 or more
- no data

8 Non-Dutch people

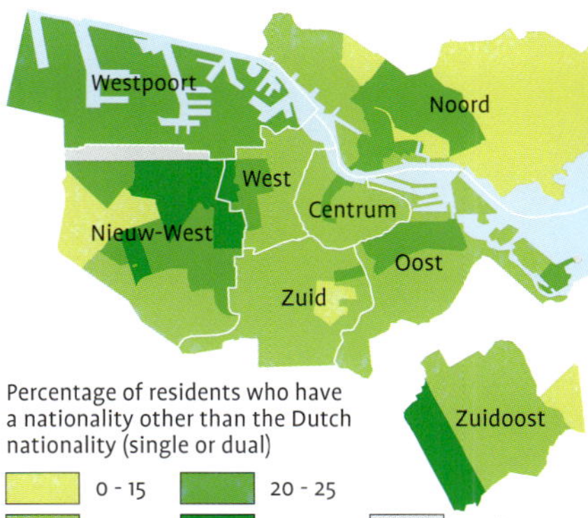

Percentage of residents who have a nationality other than the Dutch nationality (single or dual)

- 0 - 15
- 15 - 20
- 20 - 25
- 25 - 30
- no data

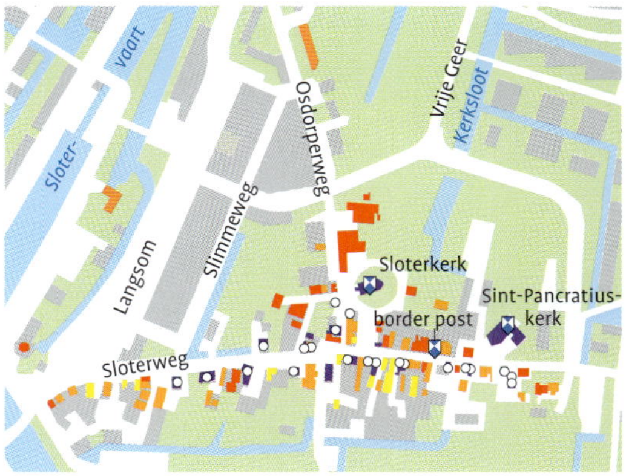

7 Young people loitering

Nieuw-West's residents claim to have the most problems with young people loitering and residents of Slotermeer and Geuzenveld even feel less safe than all other Amsterdammers. Nieuw-West does have a relatively high number of young people under the age of 24 – 33% in fact. However, the highest juvenile crime rates do not occur in Nieuw-West. The true problem areas are the Indische Buurt and some neighbourhoods in Zuidoost and Noord.

8 Non-western majority

At 64% and 51% respectively, Zuidoost and Nieuw-West are the districts with the highest proportion of residents of non-Western origin. Many Surinamese and African Amsterdammers in particular live in Zuidoost.
However, Nieuw-West's non-Western residents mainly come from the Mediterranean area. Of the 144,000 residents registered in Nieuw-West, some 18,000 are of Turkish origin and 30,000 Moroccan.

9 An enclave

The name Sloten first appeared in a written document in 1063, two centuries earlier than the first mention of Amsterdam. In the 12th century, the population of Sloten relocated the village from the Sloterplas to Sloterweg. In 1921, Amsterdam annexed the land belonging to Sloten, including the historic village centre and three national heritage sites – the Sloterkerk, Pancratiuskerk and one of the 'border posts', which marked Amsterdam's area of jurisdiction in days gone by.

Sources: *City of Amsterdam, Civil Registry (6); OIS, Research, Information and Statistics, City of Amsterdam (7-8); City of Amsterdam, Bureau of Monuments and Archaeology (9)*

© Noordhoff Uitgevers

Zuidoost

Originally called Bijlmermeer, Zuidoost started out as a utopian vision in the 1960s, but soon degenerated into an example of everything that could possibly go wrong with large-scale urban development projects. The district is now being subjected to a thorough facelift and is slowly losing its negative image.

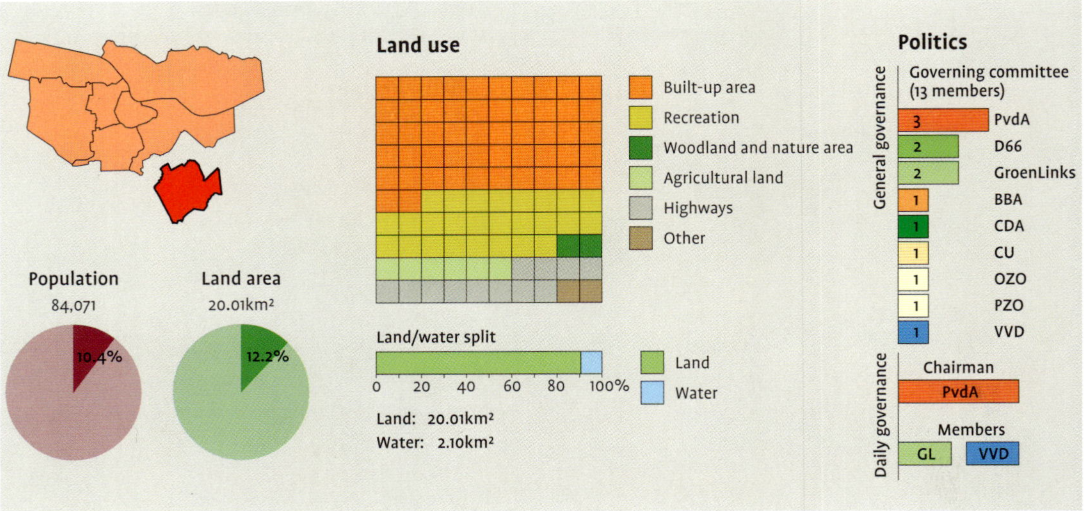

❶ Neighbourhood boundaries

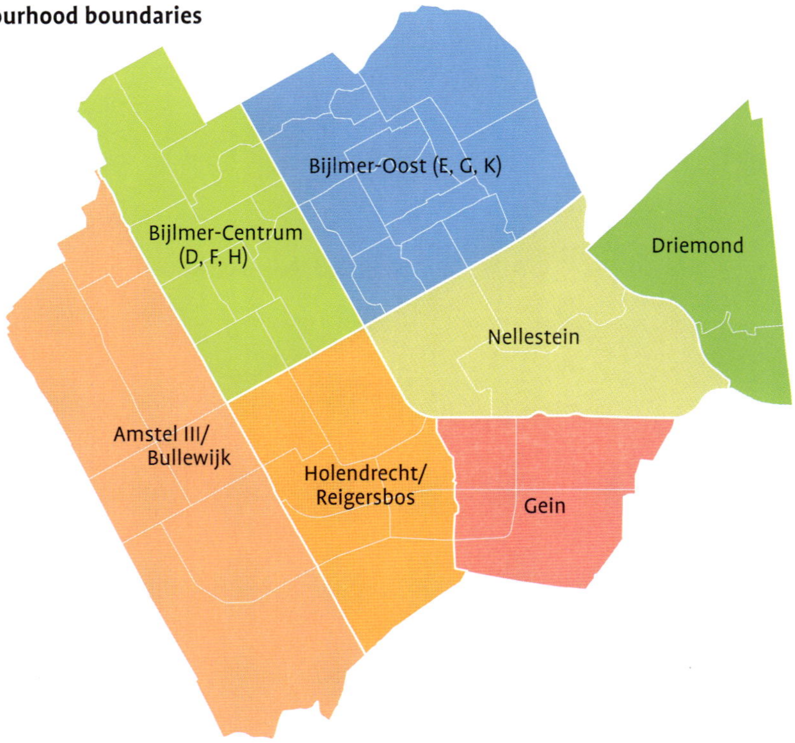

❷ WOZ value

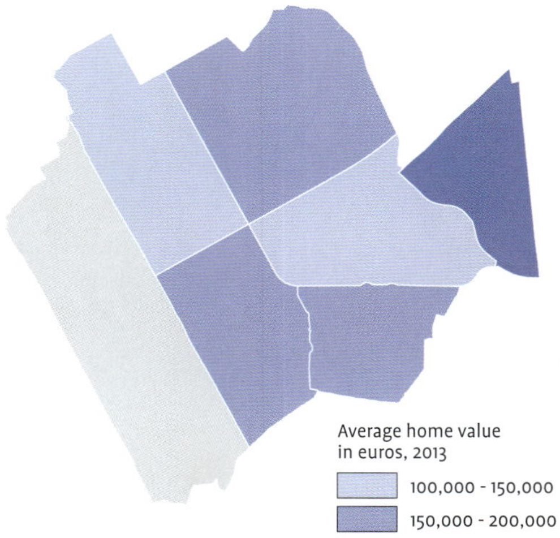

Average home value in euros, 2013

- 100,000 - 150,000
- 150,000 - 200,000
- 228,000
- no data

❸ Families

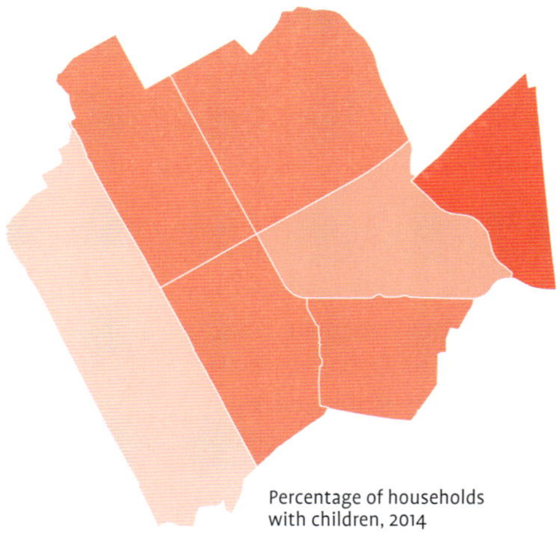

Percentage of households with children, 2014

- less than 10
- 10 - 25
- 25 - 40
- 40 or more

❹ Number of shops

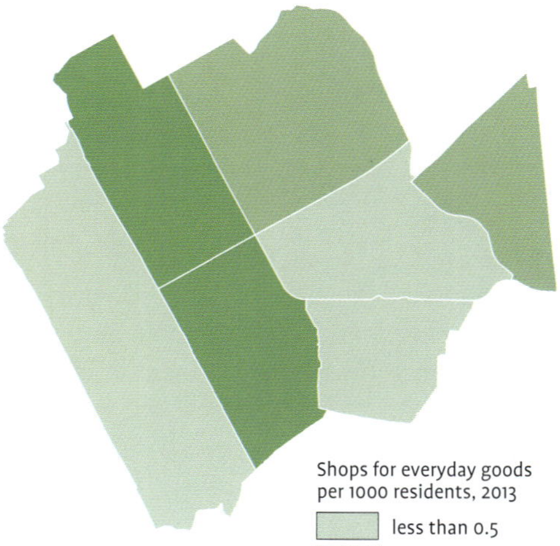

Shops for everyday goods per 1000 residents, 2013

- less than 0.5
- 0.5 - 1
- 1 - 2

❺ Cito test

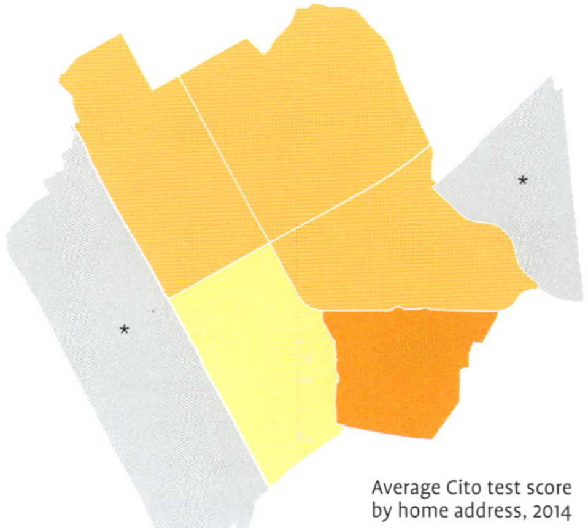

* Not enough children to be able to make valid statements about the Cito test score.

Average Cito test score by home address, 2014

- 528 - 529
- 529 - 531
- 531 - 533

Source: OIS, Research, Information and Statistics, City of Amsterdam (1-5)

© Noordhoff Uitgevers

❻ Overview

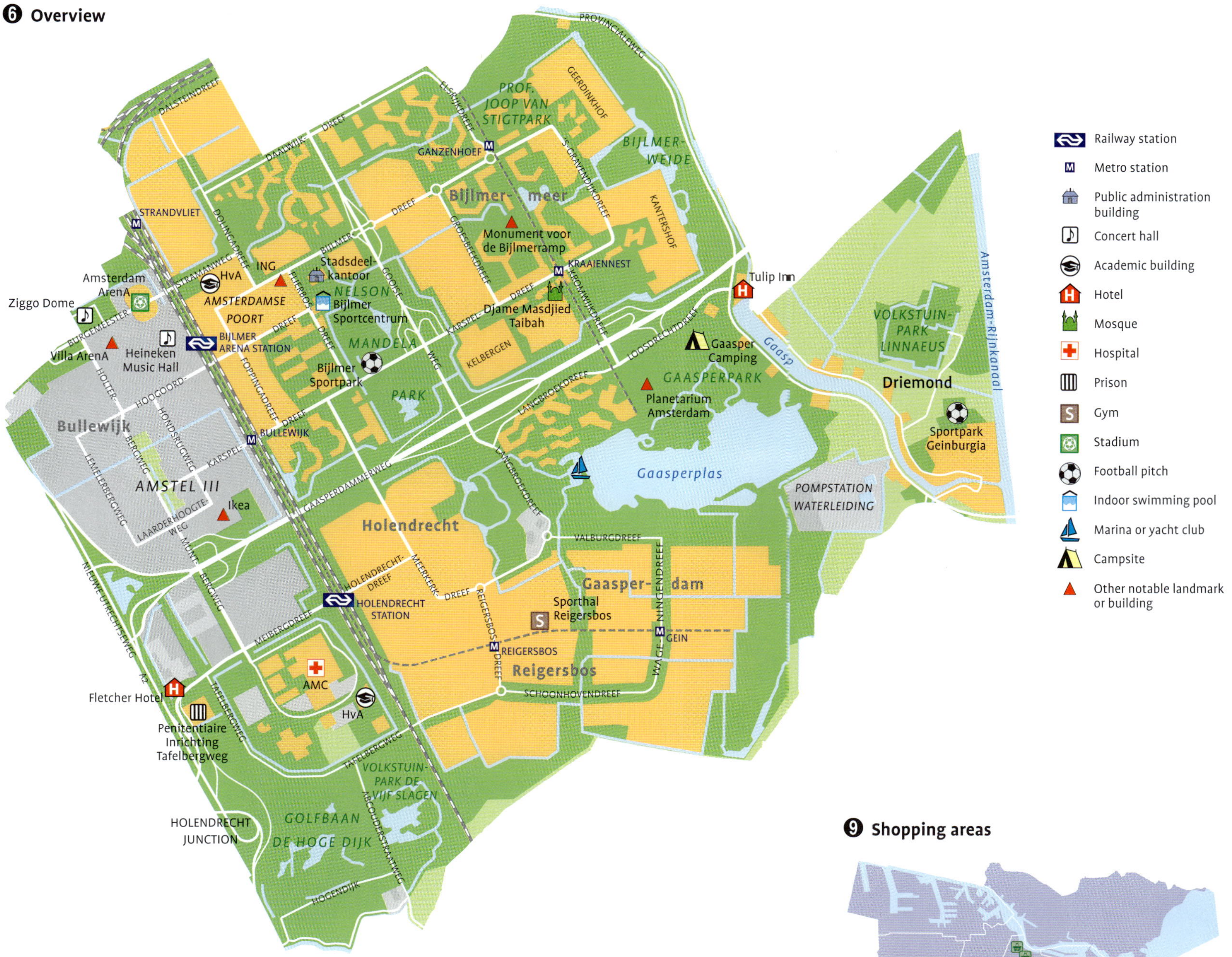

❾ Shopping areas

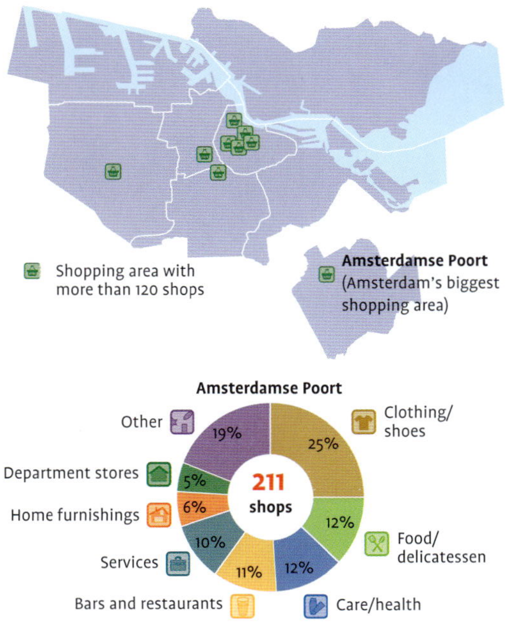

❼ Non-western immigrants

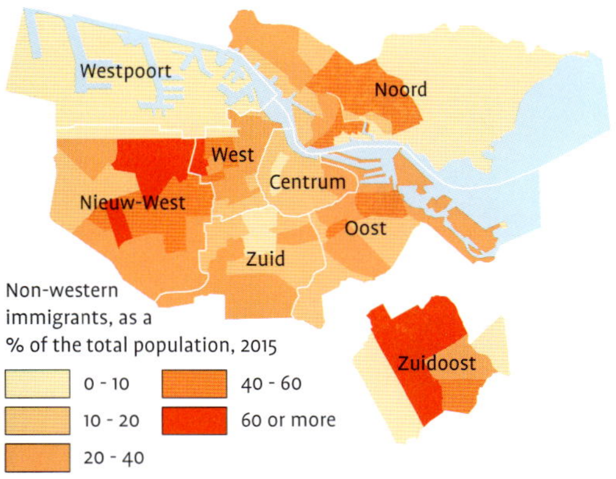

❽ Quality of life

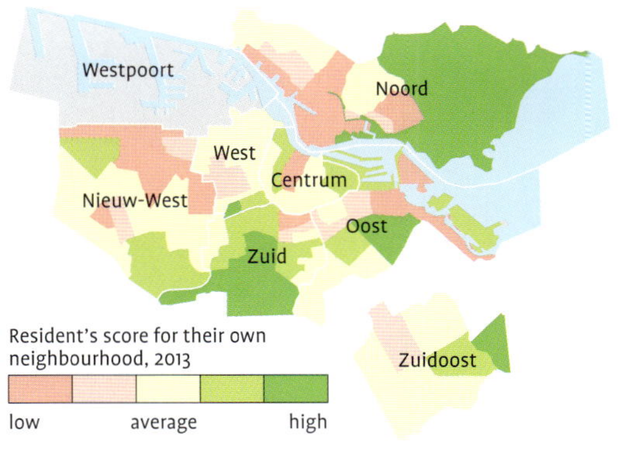

❼ Little Suriname

The demographics of Zuidoost are completely different to those of the other districts. Almost three quarters of the 84,000 residents are of non-Western origin and Amsterdammers of Surinamese (26,000) and African origin (20,000) form the majority. Immigrant Amsterdammers are only outnumbered by natives in Driemond and Nellestein. With over 130 nationalities, Zuidoost is Amsterdam's most multicultural district.

❽ Nice place to live

Every two years, a survey is run to investigate the quality of life in Amsterdam's neighbourhoods and the results are highly diverse in Zuidoost. The district is largely associated with the much maligned Bijlmer area. However, the more rural and village-like Nellestein and Driemond are given above average ratings. Not even one of the ten least appreciated neighbourhoods is located in Zuidoost; they are situated in Centrum (two), Noord (four), Nieuw-West (three) and Oost (one).

❾ Ample choice

With over 200 shops and a retail floor area of around 35,000m², the Amsterdamse Poort complex of offices and shops (built in 1986) is the largest single shopping area in Amsterdam. Zuidoost residents show more loyalty to the shops in their own district than any other Amsterdammers, even when it comes to non-everyday products. On average, they spend 76 euros a week on food, the least in the whole of Amsterdam.

Sources: City of Amsterdam, Civil Registry (6); OIS, Research, Information and Statistics, City of Amsterdam (7-8); City of Amsterdam (9)

© Noordhoff Uitgevers

Westpoort

Until 2015, the 37km² Westpoort docks area and industrial estate was not a district with its own governing organisation, but fell directly under the authority of the central city council. On 1 January 2015, the industrial estate east of Ringweg (Sloterdijk I) was added to the West district and the section to the west of Ringweg was added to Nieuw-West. The docks area now falls under the supervision of the privatised Port Authority of Amsterdam.

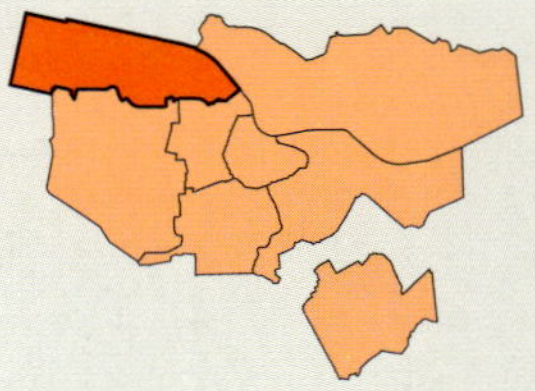

Population
242

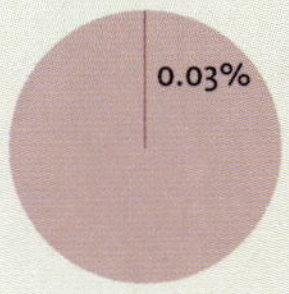

Land area
20.17km²

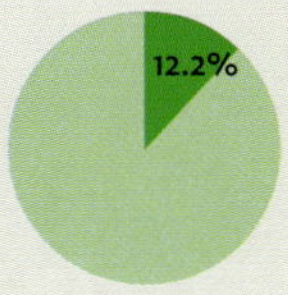

Land use

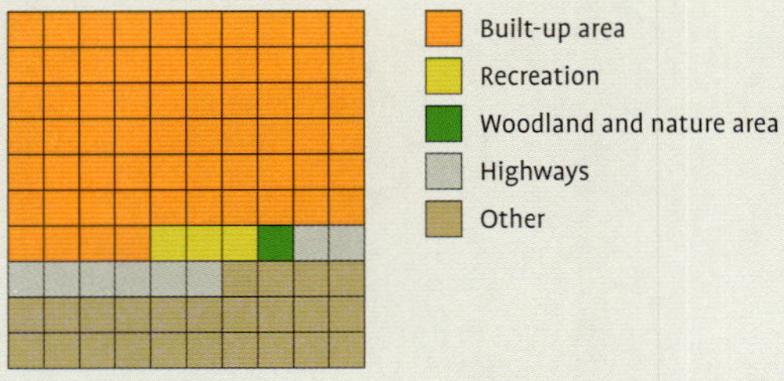

Land/water split

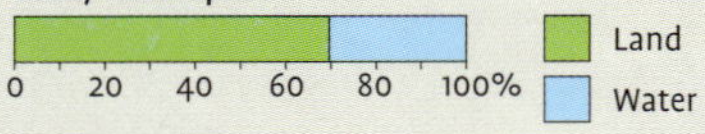

Land: 20.7km²
Water: 8.83km²

Politics

Westpoort has been managed by the Port Authority of Amsterdam since 1 January 2015, having previously been governed by the city council.

❶ Neighbourhood boundaries

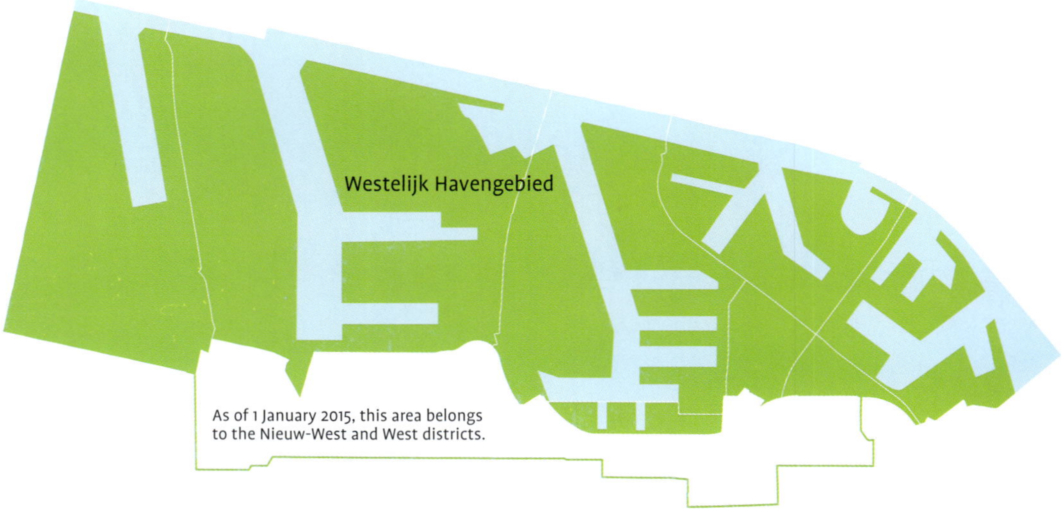

❷ WOZ value

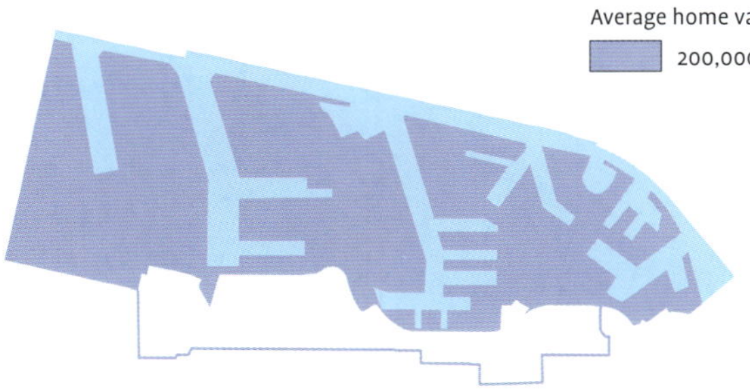

❸ Families

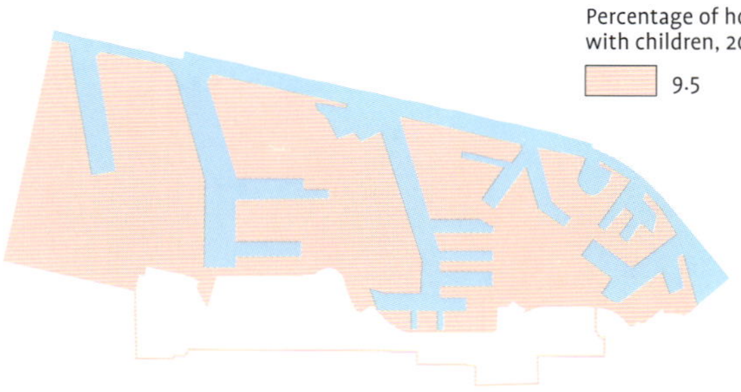

❹ Number of shops

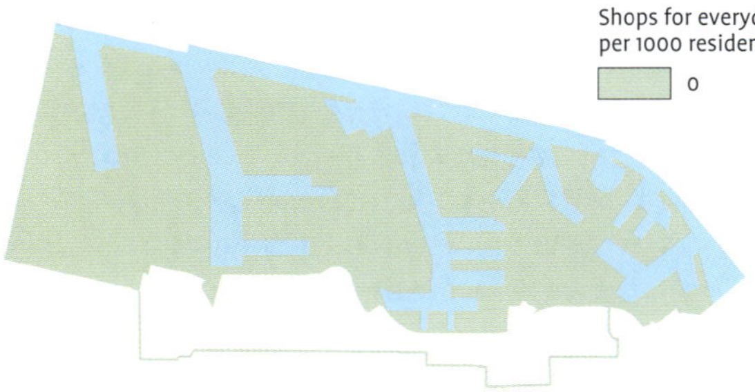

❺ Cito test

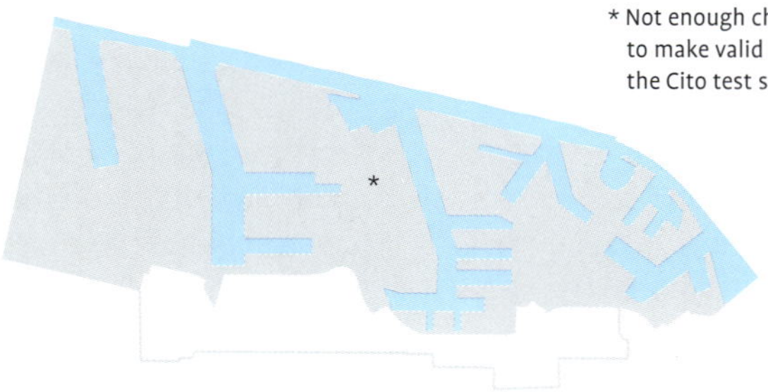

* Not enough children to be able to make valid statements about the Cito test score.

Source: OIS, Research, Information and Statistics, City of Amsterdam (1-5)

© Noordhoff Uitgevers

6 Overview

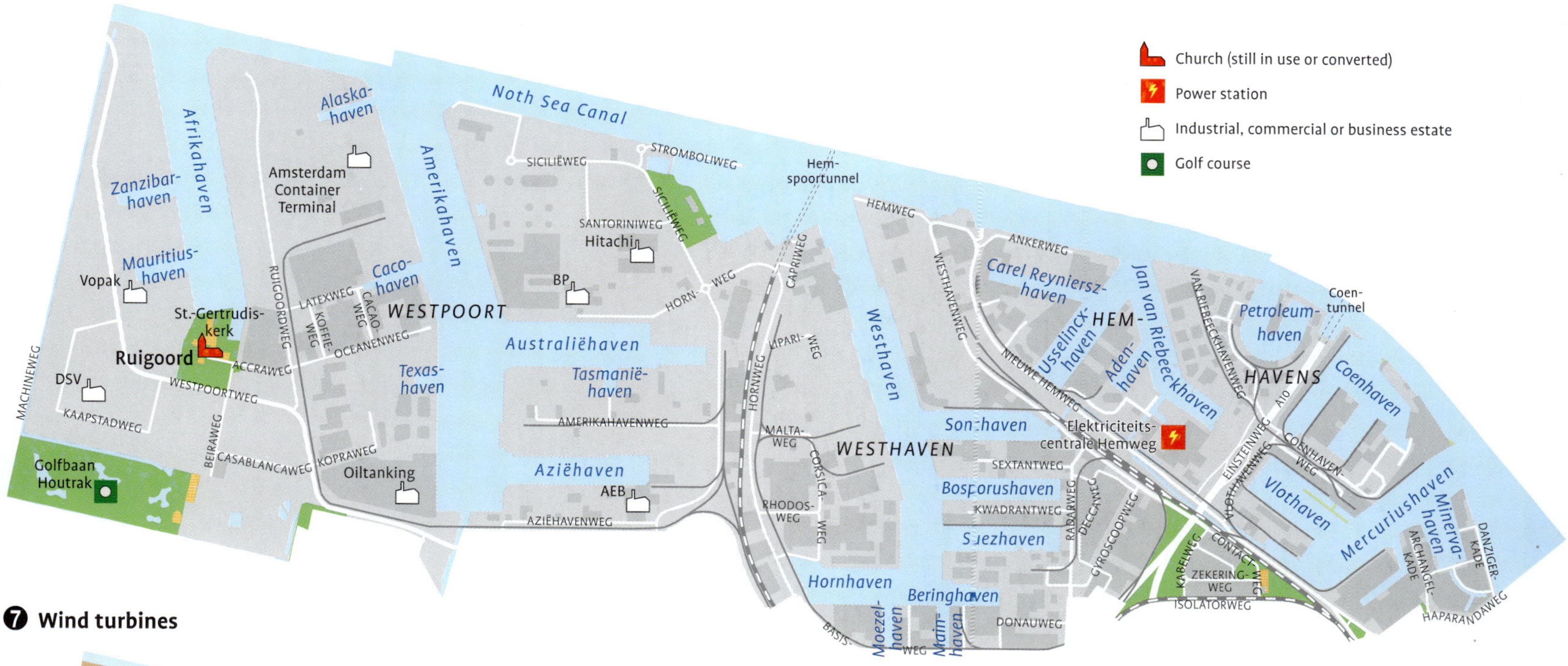

7 Wind turbines

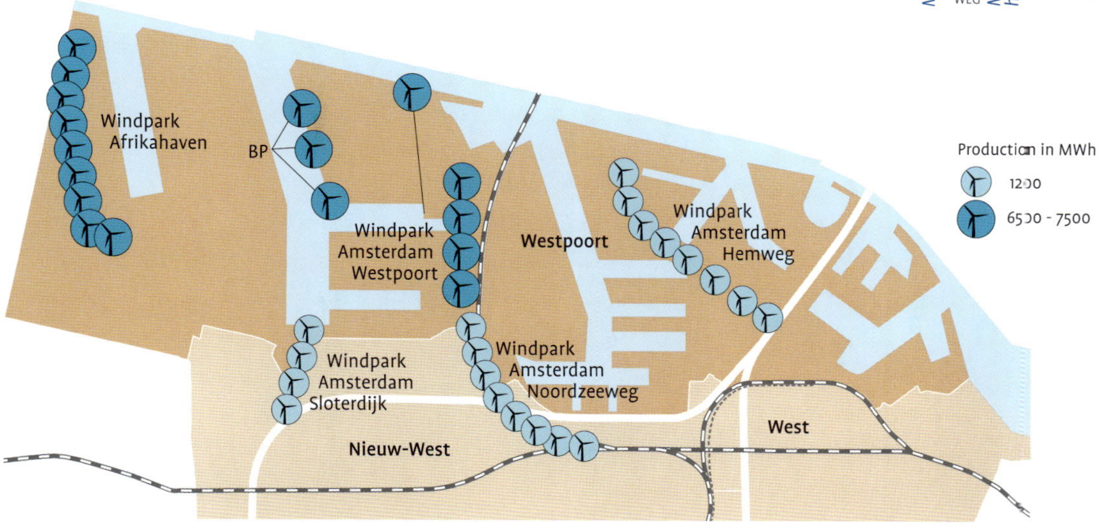

8 Cruise ships

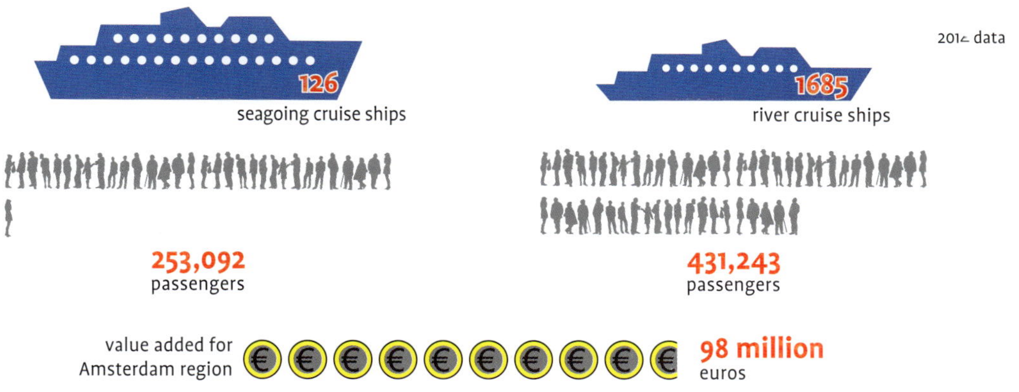

9 Employment in transport and logistics

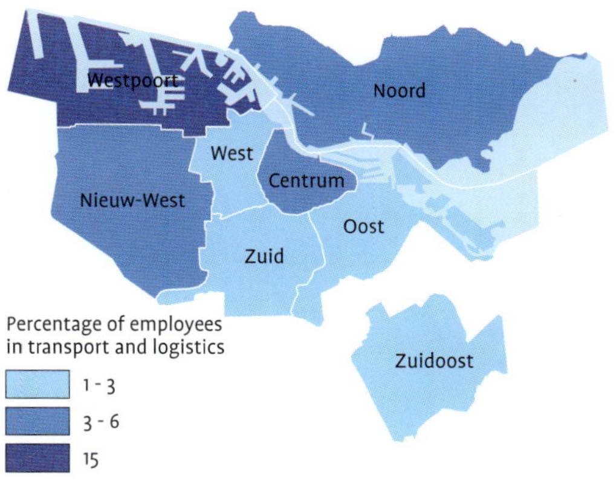

7 Revolving turbines

Until 2015, Amsterdam's only wind turbines were located in Westpoort, but due to the boundary changes, some are now located in Nieuw-West. A single large turbine can provide a few thousand households with electricity each year, so the city council wants to significantly increase the number of turbines. Possible locations include the northern banks of the IJ, the A10 North section of the ring road, Zeeburgereiland, the Nieuwe Diep, the Science Park, Gaasperplas and Amstel III.

8 Passengers in Amsterdam

Amsterdam is a popular destination for cruise ship operators. Even so, the number of seagoing cruise ships docking in the Oostelijk Havengebied reduced in 2014, mainly because the increasingly large ships struggle to negotiate the Noordersluis lock in IJmuiden. The largest cruise ship ever to visit the Port of Amsterdam is the 333-metre *MSC Splendida* (1 July 2015). The number of river cruises does continue to increase each year, with most going to Basel and Budapest.

9 Busy business area

Westpoort is the largest combined port, industrial and business area in the Netherlands. Nearly 1200 companies are based there, along with another 100 in the neighbouring Sloterdijk area (now allocated to a different district). More than 47,000 people work in Westpoort – around 10% of all jobs in the city area. The companies here account for about 15% of Amsterdam's income. With 7100 jobs, transport and logistics is the largest sector in Westpoort.

Sources: City of Amsterdam, Civil Registry (6); City of Amsterdam (7); Port of Amsterdam (8); OIS, Research, Information and Statistics, City of Amsterdam (9)

© Noordhoff Uitgevers

10

City map

◁ Prinsengracht-Keizersgracht
Photo Karel Tomeï

Westport, northern Nieuw-West

Source: City of Amsterdam, Civil Registry

D
E
F
1
2
3
4
Zaandammerpolder
ZAANDAM
ZUIDERHOUT
HAVEN-
BUURT
HEMBRUG
ZAANSTAD
VIJFHOEK-
PARK
SPORTPARK
SPOELENBURG
CREMATORIUM
ZAANSTAD
Achtersluispolder
Isaäc Baarthaven
Dirk Metselaarhaven
BRUYNZEEL
North Sea Canal
Hoofdtocht
Grote Tocht
Kanaalkade
Rijder
Cornelis Bruijnzeelweg
Gerrit Bolkade
Schiethavenkanaal
Stormhoek
Pieter
Provincialeweg
Archangelstr.
Symon Spiersweg
Ghijsen-
laan
G. Kiststr.
Havenstraat
Hemkade
Zijkanaal G
Zijkanaal H
Dr. J.M. den Uylweg
Wilbautstraat
Zuiddijk
Vredeweg
Noorder IJ- en Zeedijk
Barndegat
Stuispolderweg
Rijshoutweg
Kruisbaken
Bolbaken
Sluispolderweg
Stromboliweg
Nieuwe Zeehaven
Wim Thomassenhaven
Hemspoortunnel
Hempont
Ankerweg
Carel Reynierszhaven
Dukdalfweg
Westhavenweg
Kajuitweg
Octaanweg
Usselincxhaven
Benzolweg
Adenhaven
Jan Van Riebeeck-
haven
Petroleum-
haven
HEMHAVENS
Petroleumhavenweg
Jan van Riebeeckhavenweg
Butaanweg
Hexaanweg
Westerhoofd
Nieuwe Hemweg
GROOTE
IJPOLDER
Capriweg
Elbaweg
Liparíweg
Hornweg
Australiëhavenweg
Nieuw-Zeelandweg
Westhaven
Sonthaven
ELEKTRICITEITSCENTRALE
HEMWEG
A10
Coenhavenweg
Vlothaven
Einsteinweg
Maltaweg
WESTPOORT
Sextantweg
Bosporushaven
Kwadrantweg
Suezhaven
Marifoonweg
Radarweg
Deccaweg
Gyroscoopweg
Dynamostraat
Kabelweg
Neptunushaven
Zekeringstraat
Rhodosweg
Sardiniëweg
Corsicaweg
Kretaweg
Westpoortweg
Hornhaven
Beringhaven
Valreep
Plimsollweg
Donauweg
Basisweg
Westrandweg
A5
Moezelhaven
Moezelhavenweg
Mainhaven
Mainhavenweg
Isarweg
SLOTERDIJK II
Oderweg
Mekongweg
Kapoeasweg
Humberweg
Kastrupstr.
Rhôneweg
ISOLATORWEG
TAQWAH
Accumulatorweg
Generatorstr.
Elementenstr.
Elektronstr.
Contactweg
Isolatorweg
Transformatorweg
Schakelstr.
Turbinestr.
Magneetstr.
Condensatorweg
Contactweg
Baloner
Berchvliet
Diepen
Benit
Luwenes
Sierenborch
Bristou
Peterin
Accason
Stapels
Theemsweg
MEININGER
Piarcoplein
La Guardiaweg
Gatwickstr.
Hatostraat
SLOTERDIJK
Orlyplein
Changiweg
Sloterdijkerweg
SLOTERDIJK
VOLKSTUINENPARK
SLOTERDIJKERMEER
Naritaweg
Plesostraat
Teleportboulevard
ORLY PLAZA
(HOLIDAY INN)
Tempelhofstr.
Velserweg
PETRUSKERK
Australiëhavenweg
VOLKSTUINENPARK
DE BRETTEN
Seineweg
SPORTPARK SPIERINGHORN
Otoperweg
Barajasweg
Radarweg
Arlanda
Kimpoweg
Kingsfordweg
REGIS
GOLDEN TULIP
AMSTERDAM-WEST
Haarlemmervaart
Haarlemmerweg
DE BLOEM
Nieuwpoortstr.
Haarlemmervaart
1200 ROE
Anton Struikstraat
Coronelstr.
F. Cor Ijnst.
Antony Moddermanstr.
Vervoorenstr.
B. v. Grounstr.
Burgemeester Vening Meineszlaan
Ruys de Beerenbrouckstraat
W. Ripperdastr.
Kenau Simons
Hasselaarstr.
EENDRACHTS-
PARK
Tobias Asserstr.
Nico Snijdersstr.
Prof. Oranjestr.
Bernard Loderstr.
Burgemeester de Vlugtlaan
Burg. Eliasstr.
De Tourton Bruynsstr.
Burg. Fockstraat
Joh. Poststr.
BURGEMEESTER
DE VLUGTLAAN
Albardagracht
Kruisherenpad
J. de Greefstr.
Plein
40-'45
VAN EESTEREN-
MUSEUM
Theodorus Dobbestr.
Burg. van Leeuwenlaan
Jan de Louterstr.
DE VEREDOOS
Du Perronstraat
Van Moerkerkenstraat
J. v. Kuyckstr.
Dirk Sonoystr.
BLUE SQUARE
Slotermeerlaan
Burg. Eliasstr.
F. Huyckstr.
Wiltzangh-
Akbarstraat
Nannostr.
BLUE TOWER
Bos en
Lommer-
plein
Bos en Lommerweg
FRANCISCUS VAN
ASSISIKERK
Cibraltarstr.
Admiraal de Ruijterweg
Kilkdunstraat
Solebaystraat
Bos en Lommerweg
Den Brielstr.
Willem de Zwijgerlaan
Hofwijckstr.
Leeuwendalersweg
Egelantiersstraat
PODIUM
MOZAÏEK
Reinaert de Vosstraat
K. Doormanstraat
Bestevaerstr.
Granidastr.
Gulden Winckelstr.
Elephstr.
Stracké-
str.
J. van Houtenstr.
Albersestr.

Key, see page 257

© Noordhoff Uitgevers

Noord inside the ring road, the IJ

Source: City of Amsterdam, Civil Registry

Scale 1 : 20,000

0
250
500m
D
E
F
1
2
3
4
LANDSMEER
WATERLAND
De Broekermeer
HET SCHOUW
Grote Blauwe Polder
'T NOPEIND
ZUNDERDORP
BUIKSLOOT
NIEUWENDAM
Noord
SCHELLINGWOUDE
Het IJ
Meerkoet-straat
Lepelaar-straat
Taling-weg
Van Beekstraat
Stoutenburg
Burgweg
Rhijnestein
Dr. Martin Luther King-straat
Eerste Dors
Tweede Dors
Dorspad
Halfsloot
Loetsloot
Zuidsloot
Nieuwe Gouw
De Zuid
Het Amsterdamse Pad
IJdoornlaan
Ringweg Noord A10
Noord-Hollands Kanaal
Kanaaldijk
Veer
De Dollard
Broekervaart
Middenweg Broekermeer
Slochterweg
Termieterweg
Broekermeeringsloot
Termietergouw
't Nopeind
Het Voor werf
Torenven
Kerklaan
Nieuwe Gouw
Buikslotermeerdijk
GOLFBAAN WATERLAND
Zunderdorpergouw
SPORTPARK KADOELEN
Kadoelenweg
Vorticellaweg
Kadoeler-breek
Nieuwe Leeuwarderweg
NOORD
JEUGD-LAND
Scheurleeweg
Buikslotermeerdijk
DE NIEUWE NOORDER
BOVENIJ ZIEKENHUIS
Jan Thoméepad
D'ADMIRAAL
Gaudinstr.
Bep v. Klaveren-boulevard
Spyridon Louisweg
BUIKSLOTER-KERK
SPORTPARK BUIKSLOTER-BANNE
SPORTPARK ELZENHAGEN
STADSDEELHUIS AMSTERDAM-NOORD
Amerbos
H. Cleyndertweg
J.H. van Heekweg
Elpermeer
J. Drijverweg
Th. Weeversweg
Buikslotermeer-plein
BAANAKKERS-PARK
IJsperveldstraat
Beemsterstraat
Markengouw
Ganzenveldstraat
Dijkmanshuizen-straat
Wieringerwaard-straat
TUINPARK BUIKSLOTER-MEER
SPORTPARK DE WEEREN
Buitengouw
Ringweg Noord A10
Alkmaarstraat
Schoorlstraat
Vlierengouw
Groetstraat
Katrijpstraat
Waterland-plein
Volendammer-weg
Waalenburg-singel
Hilversumstraat
Zuiderzeeweg
WIJKERGOUW
SPORTPARK SCHELLINGWOUDE
Schellingwouder-breek
Monnikendammerweg
Edammerstr.
Wognummerstraat
Ilpendammer-straat
Purmer-plein
Watergangseweg
Molengouw
Purmerweg
KLEINSTE ZAALKERKJE VAN AMSTERDAM
ST. AUGUSTINUS
NIEUWENDAMMER KERK
Grote Haven
TWELLEGEA
Zwarte Pad
Nieuwendammerdijk
Pereboomsloot
W.H. VLIEGENBOS
CAMPING VLIEGENBOS
TUINPARK BUITENZORG
Zamenhofstraat
Zijkanaal K naar Nieuwendam
Nieuwen-dammer-ham
Johan van Hasseltkanaal-Oost
Johan van Hasseltweg
Pont-haven
Hoekschewaardweg
Waddenweg
Waddendijk
Rode Kruisstraat
Nieuwe Purmerweg
Het Laagt
Loenermark
Dotterbloem-straat
FLORADORP
Floraweg
NOORDERPARK-BAD
Reiger-vijver
NOORDER-PARK
Azaleastraat
Hortensiastr.
Ribesstr.
Berberisstr.
KOPTISCHE KERK
NH GALAXY
APOSTOLISCH GENOOTSCHAP
DE TANKER
Mos-plein
Mosveld
Distelweg
Distelkade
Lavendelstr.
Heimansweg
Meidoorn-plein
Van der Pek-straat
Hagedoornweg
NOORDERPARK
Pluvier-plein
Hasseltweg
Fazantenweg
Koekoeksstr.
Meeuwenlaan
Adelaarsweg
BETHLEHEM
Havikslaan
Spreeuwen-park
Gedempt Hamerkanaal
Hamerstr.
Schaafstraat
KROMHOUTHAL
Motorkanaal
Ketelmakerij
Bankwerkerij
Gedempte Insteekhaven
Meeuwenlaan
IJplein
Noordwal
WILLEM I-SLUIS
Sixhavenweg
IJpleinveer
IJtunnel
MÖVENPICK HOTEL
MUZIEKGEBOUW AAN 'T IJ
IJhaven
Javakade
Tosari-tuin
Sumatrakade
Imogiri-tuin
Java-eiland
Kompaseiland
ORANJESLUIZEN
PRINS WILLEM ALEXANDERSLUIS
Zuider IJdijk
Noorder IJdijk
Schellingwouderdijk
SCHELLINGWOUDER-KERK
Paterslaan
Liergouw
Zuiderzeeweg
Buiksloter-kanaal
Klaprozenweg
Papaverweg
Hulstweg
Kamperfoelieweg
Heggerankweg

© Noordhoff Uitgevers

Rural Noord

Source: City of Amsterdam, Civil Registry

D
E
F
ZUIDERWOUDE
Kerk Ae
Aandammergouw
Zwet
Bergsloot
Oosterpoel
CAMPING UITDAM
Bozen-meertje
Kleine Meer
Grote Meer
Alewijksloot
Zeedijk
Zwaksloot
Molensloot
Arken Ae
WATERLAND
Opperwoud
Aandammergouw
Rijperdwarsweg
Rijperweg
Rijperweg
Rijperweeren
UITDAM
Uitdammer Dorpsstraat
Uitdammer Die
Holysloter Die
Dorpsstraat Holysloot
WITTE KERK
HOLYSLOOT
Gerritsloot
Uitdammerdijk
Smeerketel
De Leek
Barnegat
Papesloot
Blijkmeer-polder
Bloemendalergouw
Wijhesloot
De Munt
Markermeer
Kinselmeer
Vaargeul Pampus
1
2
3
4

Key, see page 257
© Noordhoff Uitgevers

Nieuw-West, Badhoevedorp

Source: City of Amsterdam, Civil Registry

D
E
F
1
2
3
4
Nieuw-West
Sloterplas
Nieuwe Meer
Polder Meerzicht
NIEUWE MEER
De Nieuwe Meer Junction
Ringweg-Zuid A10
A10
A4
Erasmusgracht
Burg. van Tienhovengracht
Osdorpergracht
Slotervaart
Postjeswetering
Admiralengracht
Schinkel
Stadiongracht
Varkensbaai
SLOTERPARK
SPORTPARK OOKMEER
REMBRANDTPARK
VONDELPARK
ERASMUSPARK
GERBRANDYPARK
KASTERLEE PARK
PIET WIEDIJK PARK
SPORTPARK RIEKERHAVEN
SPORTPARK DE SCHINKEL
SPORTPARK ZUID
SPORTPARK SLOTEN
VOLKSTUINENPARK ONS BUITEN
DE OEVERLANDEN
TUINPARK LISSABON
SIEGERPARK
TUINGROEP EIGEN HOF
TUINPARK VAT
SCHINKEL
BEDRIJVENTERREIN
Parkeiland
Wetlands
Bosbaan
Bosbaanweg
Cornelis Lelylaan
Postjesweg
Einsteinweg
Jan van Galenstraat
Burgemeester Roëllstr.
Plesmanlaan
Sloterweg
Oude Haagseweg
Nieuwe Haagseweg
Amstelveenseweg
Henk Sneevlietweg
Johan Huizingalaan
Jan Tooropstraat
Delflandlaan
Hemsterhuisstraat
Robert Fruinlaan
Meer en Vaart
Slotervaart
Lelylaan
Heemstedestraat
Amstelveenseweg
OLYMPIC STADIUM
Stadionplein
AMSTERDAM UNIVERSITY OF APPLIED SCIENCES
HOTELSCHOOL THE HAGUE
GERRIT RIETVELD ACADEMIE
TEAM ACADEMY
SINT LUCAS ANDREAS ZIEKENHUIS
SLOTERVAART ZIEKENHUIS
NETHERLANDS CANCER INSTITUTE (ANTONI VAN LEEUWENHOEK)
VUMC
MERCURE AMSTERDAM AIRPORT
AIR TRAFFIC CONTROL THE NETHERLANDS
WORLD FASHION CENTRE
DE MEERVAART
STADSDEEL NIEUW-WEST
STADSDEEL WEST
SLOTERPARKBAD
SPORTPLAZA MERCATOR
DE DUIKELAAR
WV SLOTERPLAS
DE BOEKANIER
DE KOENEN
MEERZICHT
DE SCHINKEL
SLOTERKERK
PANCRATIUSKERK
PAULUSKERK
AGNESKERK
AUGUSTANAKERK
OPSTANDINGSKERK
ST.-JOSEPHKERK
JERUZALEMKERK
MARANATHA
WESTERMOSKEE
HET SIERAAD
TITUSKAPEL
HERDENKINGSKERK
CALVARIEKERK
IMMANUELKERK
DE ARK
VERRIJZENISKERK
BLAUWE MOSKEE
MOSKEE SULEYMANIYE
SCHUTTERSTOREN
SLOTERTOREN
BLUE TOWER
BLUE SQUARE
RAMADA APOLLO
BASTION
WEST SIDE INN
DE ONTMOETING
DE OLIJFTAK
DE VERFDOOS
SLOTERMEER-SCHUTSLUIS
JAN VAN GALENSTRAAT
GVB BUSDEPOT
AMSTELVEENSEWEG
HAARLEMMERMEERSTATION
APOSTOLISCH GENOOTSCHAP
STADSTUIN OVERTOOM
NLR
IPABO

© Noordhoff Uitgevers

Centrum, Zuid, Oost

Source: City of Amsterdam, Civil Registry

D
E
F
1
2
3
4
Het IJ
IJhaven
Java-eiland
KNSM-eiland
Kompaseiland
Ertshaven
Eiland Zeeburg
Oosterdok
Spoorwegbassin
Entrepothaven
Nieuwe Diep (Benedendiep)
FLEVOPARK
OOSTERPARK
ARTIS
Oost
PARK FRANKENDAEL
SPORTPARK MIDDENMEER
SPORTPARK VOORLAND
VOLKSTUINPARK NIEUWE LEVENSKRACHT
SPORTPARK DRIEBURG
PARK SOMERLUST
AMSTEL BUSINESS PARK
DE OMVAL
DUIVENDRECHT
DIEMEN
DIEMEN-ZUID
HOLLAND PARK
Watergraafsmeer junction
Amstel junction
Ringweg Oost
Ringweg Zuid A10
Amstel
Weespertrekvaart
NEMO
NATIONAL MARITIME MUSEUM
MÖVENPICK HOTEL
PASSENGER TERMINAL AMSTERDAM
MUZIEKGEBOUW AAN 'T IJ
TROPEN-MUSEUM
NIEUWE OOSTERBEGRAAFPLAATS (DE NIEUWE OOSTER)
AMSTERDAM MUIDERPOORT
AMSTERDAM SCIENCE PARK
AMSTERDAM AMSTEL
DIEMEN-ZUID
SCIENCE PARK AMSTERDAM (UvA)
CAMPING ZEEBURG
HOLLAND SPORT BOAT CENTRE
FLEVOPARKBAD
JAAP EDEN IJSBAAN
AMSTERDAM UNIVERSITY OF APPLIED SCIENCES
MEERTENS INSTITUTE
MERCURE

© Noordhoff Uitgevers

Zeeburg, IJburg, Diemen

Source: City of Amsterdam, Civil Registry

D
E
F
1
2
3
4
Hoeckelingsdam
Vaargeul Pampus
Vuurtoren-
eiland
Buiteneiland
Middeneiland
entrumeiland
Strandeiland
FORT PAMPUS
Pampus
IJmeer
Diemer-
vijfhoek
ELEKTRICITEITSCENTRALE
DIEMEN
Overdiemerweg
Diemerzeedijk
Jan Kerstenpad
Pampusweg
Muidertrekvaart
Diemerpolderweg
A1
Maxisweg
Kruitpad
Noorder- of
Rietpolder
FORT MUIDEN
MUIDERSLOT
P.C. Hooft-
laan
C. Huygens-
laan
Herengracht
Kazernestr.
MUIDEN
Gemeenschaps-
polder
MUIDEN
Papelaan
MUIDERBOS
Singelgracht
Singelstr.
Zeestr.
Weesper-
str.
Hellingstr.
ST. NICOLAAS
WEESPER-
POORTSLUIS
GROTE- OF
NICOLAASKERK
MUIZENFORT
Zuidpolderweg
Naardertrekvaart
Noordpolderweg

Key, see page 257
© Noordhoff Uitgevers

Schiphol, Amsterdam Forest, Bovenkerk

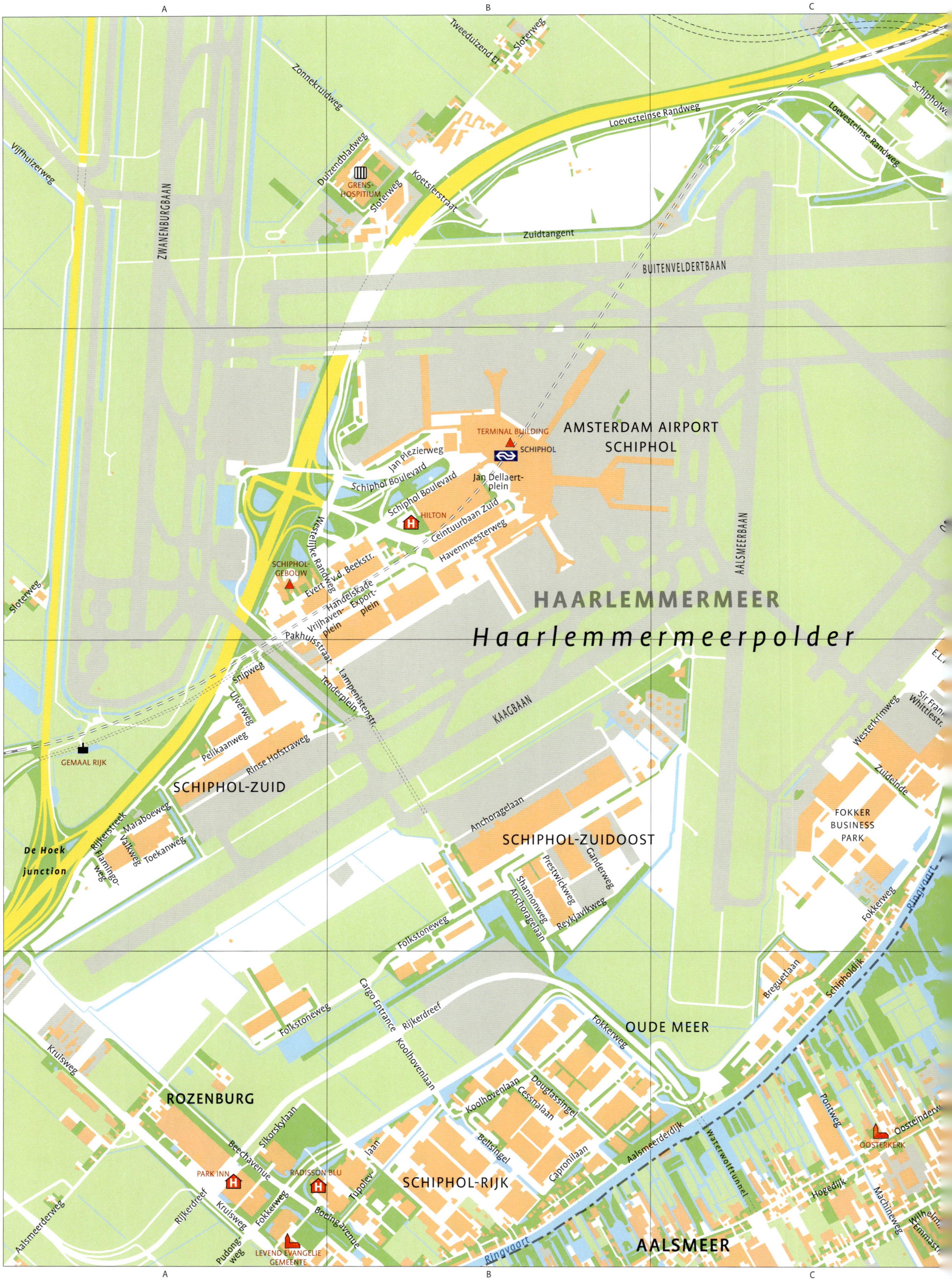

Source: City of Amsterdam, Civil Registry

D
E
F
1
2
3
4
Polder Meerzicht
NIEUWE MEER
GOLFTERREIN NIEUWE MEER
KLM
PHOL-NOORD
Cateringweg
Loevesteinse Randweg
Nieuwe Meerdijk
Eosbaan
Bosbaanweg
Van Nijenrodeweg
Bolestein
Gunterstein
De Cuserstr.
AUGUSTINUSKERK
Kalfjeslaan
Nieuwe Kalfjeslaan
SPORTPARK NIEUWE KALFJESLAAN
Jan Tooropiaan
Amsterdamseweg
C. v. Clevelaan
Willem van Beierenlaan
H. v. Borsselenkade
Gr. Florislaan
Grote Vijver
GROTE SPEELWEIDE
AMSTERDAM FOREST
JAC P. THIJSSE-PARK
Emmakade
Pr. Beatrixlaan
Amsterdamse Weg
Pr. Marijkelaan
De Braak
BRAAKPARK
PAULUSKERK
Dijkgravenlaan
Laan Walcheren
Walaardt Sacréstraat
Thermiekstraat
Nieuwe Meerlaan
BIZONWEIDE
Kleine Vijver
SPORTPARK OVERBURG
V.d. Hoochlaan
De Ruwiellaan
Oude Karselaan
Nwe. Karselaan
Charlotte van Montpensierlaan
KRUISKERK
SCHIPHOL-OOST
Burgemeester van Sonweg
SPEELWEIDE
Da Costalaan
Talmastraat
Patrimoniumlaan
Vijverlaan
Spoorlaan
Bors van Waverenstr.
Keizer Karelweg
Van der Veerelaan
De Ruyschlaan
Navigatorstraat
Behoudenvaartweg
Stationsplein
Schipholdijk
Ringvaart
STEIGENBERGER AIRPORT HOTEL
Burgemeester A. Colijnweg
ZONNEWEIDE
Bleekerskade
Katerstraat
Smeenklaan
Molenweg
DE DIKKERT
BROERSEPARK
Graaf Aelbrechtlaan
Heemraadschaplaan
IMMANUELKERK
AIR TRAFFIC CONTROL THE NETHERLANDS
Haliin P.K. straat
Voltweg
Kemajoranstr.
Nieuwe Meerlaan
Mr. Troelstralaan
De Savornin Lohmanlaan
Thorbeckelaan
COBRA MUSEUM
Sandbergplein
Mr. Jac. Takkade
KERSENBLOESEMPARK
Burg. A. Colijnweg
Doorweg
Badlaan
DORPSKERK
Dorpsstr.
Stadsplein
SCHOUWBURG AMSTELVEEN
A9
RAADHUIS
De Poel
Bovenkerkerkade
Fokkerlaan
Soerlaan
Gr. Zeppelinlaan
Ouderkerkerlaan
Parmentierlaan
OAKPARK
AMSTELVEEN
Huesplein
Van der Leeklaan
SCHINKELBOS
Bosrandweg
CAMPING HET AMSTERDAMSE BOS
Grote Tocht
Schinkelpolder
Dr. Plesmansingel
Handweg
Lindenlaan
Haagbeuklaan
Populierenlaan
Abelenlaan
Pruimenlaan
Appellaan
Benderslaan
PAASKERK
Boothlaan
BOVENKERK
Noorddammerlaan
Kleine Poel
Legmeerdijk
Bosboom Toussaintlaan
Mgr. Dr. H. Poelslaan
Betje Wolfflaan
St. Urbanusstr.
Vierlingsbeeklaan
Salamander
Ringslang
Specht
RTE RUITER
Rietwijkeroordweg
Oosteinderweg
Sportlaan
Van der Hooplaan
Wimbledonpark
Zetterij
Binderij
Walderij
SPORTPARK NOORDDAMMERWEG
SPORTPARK SPORTLAAN
DE MEERKAMP
SPORTPARK STARTBAAN
Startbaan
MARNE
AALSMEER
Aalsmeerderweg
Beeckestijn
Ockenburgh
Eyckenstein
C. van Renneslaan
Hammarskjöldsingel
AMSTELVEEN
Beneluxbaan
PETRUS EN PAULUS
STEINDE
Kerkweg
Legmeerdijk
Luttickduin
Kennemerduinen
Rosa Spierlaan
Betsy Perklaan
Aletta Jacobslaan
Spinnerij
SPINNERIJ
Smederij
BEDRIJVENTERREIN LEGMEER
Bouwmeester
Chirurgijn
Troubadour
Poortwachter
Mars
Kramer
Boogschutter
Weegschaal
GONDEL
osteinderpoelpolder
Schweitzerlaan
Sparrendaal
Boschplaat
Birkhoven
Gasterland
Assering
Noorddammerweg
Slingeduin
Sacharovlaan
SACHAROVLAAN
Poortwachter
Veldlust
De Uitvlucht
WIJKPARK MIDDENHOVEN
Grote Beer
Noorderkroon
Orion
Logger
Gondel
Jol
Zwanenwater
Marshallsingel
De Grote Wielen
A. v. Dalsumlaan
Fie Carelsenlaan
Jan Teulingslaan
Spinnerij
Langs de Werf
Klipper
Bouwerij
Zanderij
Bovenkerkerweg
Dr. Willem Dreesweg
De Parel
De Nessermolen
De Wateringsbrugmolen
De Eendracht
Brink
BRINK
Dr. W. Dreesweg
Melkweg
MEENT
Praam
Mercurius
Jupiter
Saturnus
Juno
Vlinderweg
Koolwitjestraat
Atalantalaan
Karperstraat
Koningsstraat
Brasemstr.
Snoekbaarsstr.
Middentocht
WESTWIJK
Westhove
Duivenvoorde
Heemstede
Westhove
Hillenraad
Sterkenburg
Middachten
Wedderborg
Adamshoek
Cannenburgh
Noorddammerweg
Loevestein
Jane Addamslaan
Weerdesteyn
Loethoollaan
Bertha von Suttnerlaan
Jan Nelissenlaan
Boudier-Bakkerlaan
SPORTPARK DE KEGEL
GRAND HOTEL AMSTELVEEN
Nesserlaan
De Zon
Pallas
Schoener
Bakboord
Klipper
Stuurboord
VOLKSTUINPARK NESSERLAAN
Citroenvlinderstr.
Cath.-Amaliaalaan
Jac. Takkade

© Noordhoff Uitgevers

Amstelveen, Ouderkerk aan de Amstel

Source: City of Amsterdam, Civil Registry

D
E
F
1
2
3
4
DUIVEN- DRECHT
Amstel junction
HOLLAND PARK
SPORTPARK DE HOOP
ST. URBANUS-KERK
Stationsplein
DUIVENDRECHT
TUINPARK DIJKZICHT
TUINPARK DE FEDERATIE
TUINPARK ONS LUSTOORD
TUINPARK NIEUW VREDELUST
AMSTERDAM OLD COURSE
SPORTPARK STRANDVLIET
STRANDVLIET
BERGWIJK-PARK
INHOLLAND DIEMEN UNIVERSITY OF APPLIED SCIENCES
EMERALD
CAMPUS DIEMEN-ZUID
GVB
DE NIEUWE STAD
BIJLMER-MEER
STADSDEEL ZUIDOOST
AMSTERDAM UNIVERSITY OF APPLIED SCIENCES
ING FINANCIAL PLAZA
AMSTERDAMSE POORT
BIJLMER SPORTCENTRUM
BIJLMERPARK-THEATER
Zuidoost
NELSON MANDELA-PARK
BIJLMER SPORTPARK
AMSTERDAM ARENA
ZIGGO DOME
Arena Boulevard
HEINEKEN MUSIC HALL
BIJLMER ARENA
VILLA ARENA
ABN AMRO
HOLIDAY INN ARENA TOWERS
ATLAS ARENA
BULLEWIJK
GOLFBAAN AMSTELBORGH
SPORTPARK DE TOEKOMST
Groot Duivendrechtsche-polder
Polder de Nieuwe Bullewijk
AMSTELBAD
AMSTEL III
HOLENDRECHT
A9
A2
Gaasperdammerweg
Holendrecht junction
HOLENDRECHT
DE BASCULE (JEUGD-GGZ)
AMC
MUSEUM VROLIK
NIN
UvA
AMSTERDAM UNIVERSITY OF APPLIED SCIENCES
FLETCHER HOTEL
P+R AMSTERDAM (TAFELBERGWEG)
Ouderkerkerplas
VOLKSTUINPARK DE VIJF SLAGEN
GOLFBAAN DE HOGE DIJK
Burgemeester van Sonweg
Amstelweg
Holendrechter en Bullewijkerpolder
Voetangelweg
Hogendijk
Abcouder-meer
HET MEERBAD
ABCOUDE
OUDERKERK AAN DE AMSTEL
AMSTEL
Bullewijk
Rondehoep

© Noordhoff Uitgevers

Zuidoost, Weesp

Source: City of Amsterdam, Civil Registry

Scale 1 : 20,000 0 250 500m

Gemeenschaps-
polder
MUIDEN
Bloemendalerpolder
Molenwatering
MUIDERBOS
MUIDEN
NICOLAAS
GROTE- OF NICOLAASKERK
WEESPERPOORT-SLUIS
Vestinggracht
Naardertrekvaart
Zuidpolderweg
Nooit Gedacht
Marlahoeveweg
Uitwatering van het Naardermeer
Muiderweg
Weesperweg
Vecht
Korte Muiderweg
WEESP
Papelaan
Bloemendalerweg
Zuiderzeelaan
IJsselmeerlaan
Eemmeerlaan
Gouwzeestr.
Flevolaan
Kanaalpad
SPORTPARK PAPELAAN
Leeuwenveldseweg
Sportparklaan
Lobbrich
Boudgerslaan
Frederica
Zeijdelaarweg
Lijsbet Eelantsplein
Goolmeer-str.
Gemeen-schaps-polder-weg
Ambachtstraat
Pampuslaan
Keurstraat
Hoogeweyselaan
Waarschapsstraat
Lageweyselaan
Kostverlorenstr.
E. du Perronstraat
Martinus Nijhoffstraat
Rembrandt van Rijnstr.
J. Vermeerstr.
Papelaan
WEESP Stationsplein
Stationsweg
Nijverheidslaan
Lange Muiderweg
Reaalspolderweg
Amsterdam-Rhine Canal
Kanaaldijk West
Amstellandlaan
Aquamarin
Heren-singel
ST. LAURENTIUSKERK
LAURENSKERK
FORT AAN DE OSSENMARKT
JACHTHAVEN DE ZEEMEERMIN
Zeeburgstr.
Diemerdijk str.
Korte Stammerdijk
Buitenveer
'T HAANTJE
Smal Weesp
Prinses Irenelaan
Achtergracht
Oudegracht
Nieuwstr.
Hoogstr.
Middenstr.
M. LUTHERKERK
Singel
VAN HOUTENKERK
SPORTPARK GEINBURGIA
Rijnkade
VAN HOUTEN INDUSTRIEPARK
Driemond
Burg. Bletzstr.
C.J. van Houtenlaan
Aetsveldse Laan
DE VRIENDSCHAP
S. de Vliegerlaan
DE EENDRACHT
's-Gravelandseweg
J.A. Fijnvandraatlaan
M. Dotingalaan
Goollandse Weg
Bastionweg
De Schans
Blokland
De Vennen
Kruisland
Begijnepolderweg
G.J. Wiefferingdreef
AETSVELD
Schoolpad
Reigersweide
Kievitshof
Meeuwenveld
Blauwschildershof
Gildemeesterweg
GOLFCENTRUM WEESP
VICTORIABAD
Bijlwaterpad
Basisweg
Kanaaldijk Oost
Kanaaldijk West
Vecht
Utrechtseweg
CARSPELHOF
Goollandse Weg
Aetsveldse Weg
WEESP
Aets- veldsche Polder
Nigtevechtse Pad
Kanaaldijk Oost
Aetsveldse Weg
Klompweg
FORT HINDERDAM
HINDERDAM
Hinderdam
ZWAANWIJCK
STICHTSE VECHT (PROVINCE OF UTRECHT)
NIGTEVECHT
Vecht
Spiegel- polder
Spiegelweg
KEY
Attractions and landmarks
Concert hall
Theatre
Museum
Castle, fortress, (former) fortification
Windmill
Infrastructure
Railway station
Bus station
Railway
Metro line and station
Metro station under construction
Tram line and stop
Ferry connection
Public amenities and public administration
Hotel
Campsite
Marina or yacht club
Stadium
Swimming pool
Town hall, district council building
Academic building
Hospital, medical or psychiatric care centre
Water management and utilities
Pumping station
Lock, sluice
Water treatment plant
Power station
Other special buildings and locations
Church (still in use or converted)
Mosque
Synagogue
Cemetery
Prison or jail
Other notable landmark or building
Administrative boundaries
Municipal boundary
District boundary

© Noordhoff Uitgevers

Index

◁
Entrepotdok
Photo Karel Tomeï

A

B

© Noordhoff Uitgevers

© Noordhoff Uitgevers

© Noordhoff Uitgevers

© Noordhoff Uitgevers

M

N

O

© Noordhoff Uitgevers

P

Q

R

S

© Noordhoff Uitgevers

T

U

V

© Noordhoff Uitgevers

© Noordhoff Uitgevers

© Noordhoff Uitgevers

© Noordhoff Uitgevers

© Noordhoff Uitgevers

© Noordhoff Uitgevers

The *Atlas of Amsterdam* could not have been written without the enthusiastic cooperation and input of a large number of professional specialists, who provided sources, data and copy, and also critically reviewed the chapters. We are deeply grateful for their cooperation. The editorial team of the atlas remains responsible for the final selection, interpretation and presentation of the material.

City of Amsterdam
We owe special thanks to the City of Amsterdam, particularly OIS, Research, Information and Statistics. The collection of information and data analyses provided by OIS have been invaluable in compiling the atlas. We wish to explicitly acknowledge the contribution made by Jeroen Slot, Head of Research and Statistics, Sara de Wilde and Peter van Hinte. They edited and supplied sources, wrote accompanying texts and contributed their ideas on the cartographic sections. OIS staff also critically reviewed atlas pages in their final draft form.
We would also like to thank Aad Vuyk and Jeroen Riemens of the City of Amsterdam's Civil Registry for supplying various basic data sets.

Atlas design and accompanying texts
Noordhoff Atlas Productions is responsible for the design of the atlas.
Advice on the content of the chapters was provided by drs. E. Beukers, drs. L. Coffeng, drs. J. Slot and drs. B. M. J. Speet.
The accompanying texts were written by:

- drs. E. Beukers (introductions to the chapters)
- drs. B. M. J. Speet (chapters 1, 3 to 7 inclusive, and 9)
- drs. J. Slot (chapter 2)
- drs. L. Coffeng (chapter 8)

Final editing
Drs. E. Beukers

Cartography
Noordhoff Atlas Productions provided the cartographic material for the atlas.
Publisher: Peter Vroege
Atlas editorial team manager: Amanda Possel
Atlas editorial team: Annemieke Altena, Mathie Hoenjet, Willeke Baumgartner, Menno Bolder, Douwe de Jong, Jelle-Jan Schouwstra, Tjeerd Tichelaar

The infographics are the work of Michel van Elk (*A-Select*), *vof Unger-Kisman*, Max Unger, Chantal van Wessel (*Het Parool*), Jorris Verboon (*Het Parool*), René van Asselt (*René van Asselt ontwerp & illustratie*) and Manon den Hartog (*Omdat Ontwerp*).

Cartographic input was also provided by Ernst van Oort (*Van Oort redactie en kartografie*), Maarten Slooves (*Slooves Grafische Vormgeving*), Menno Faber (*Schaal 10*), Marijn Bosma (*Bosma Grafiek*), Jim Handstede (*12 Provinciën | The World of Maps*) and Merlijn Hoenekamp (*Donkergroen Ontwerp & Advies*).

Photography
Karel Tomeï (*Flying Camera*) took almost all of the aerial photos. We are greatly indebted to him for the many hours he spent flying above Amsterdam in order to photograph the city as clearly and attractively as possible.
We would also like to thank Martin Stevens (*Wolverlei*) for his photographic input to this atlas.
Roel Kooister (*roelkooisterbeeldredactie*) was responsible for photo editing and research.

Noordhoff Uitgevers has endeavoured to identify all copyright holders with regard to use of the photographic material and ask their permission for publication. However, if you feel that publication of specific material infringes any rights you may have, please contact us and provide substantiation.

We wish to thank the following for their contributions...
AEB Amsterdam
AFC Ajax
Alliander
Ambulance Amsterdam
Ambulancezorg Nederland
Amsterdam ArenA
Amsterdam Dance Event
Amsterdam University of Applied Sciences
Brandweer Amsterdam-Amstelland
Cemeteries: Beth Haim, Buitenveldert, De Nieuwe Noorder, De Nieuwe Ooster, PC Hooft Groep, Sint Barbara, Zorgvlied
City of Almere, Research & Statistics
City of Amsterdam

- *Art and Culture*
- *Bureau of Monuments and Archaeology*
- *City Archives*
- *Civil Registry*
- *OIS, Research, Information and Statistics*
- *Urban Planning*
- *Zuidoost District/Projectbureau Vernieuwing Bijlmermeer*

Cyclists' Union of Amsterdam
Duke Faunabeheer
Dutch National Opera & Ballet
Elsevier
Explanation Design
Faunabeheereenheid Noord-Holland
Foundation ArtZuid
Foundation for International Education in the Netherlands
Guerrilla Games
GVB Amsterdam
Het Parool
I amsterdam
Joods Maatschappelijk Werk
Koninklijk Instituut voor de Tropen
Mauritshuis
National Archives of the Netherlands
National Library of the Netherlands
Natura Artis Magistra
Nederlandse Spoorwegen
*NOC*NSF*
NRC Handelsblad
Oostelijk Havengebied Amsterdam
Openbare Bibliotheek Amsterdam
Oude Kerk
Paradiso
PBL Netherlands Environmental Assessment Agency
Port of Amsterdam
Protestant Church in Amsterdam
Public Health Service of Amsterdam
Rembrandt House Museum
Rijksmuseum Amsterdam
Rijkswaterstaat
Royal Concertgebouw
Royal Palace Amsterdam
Royal Theatre Carré
Schiphol Group
Sociale Verzekeringsbank
Stadsschouwburg Amsterdam
Statistics Netherlands
Theater Amsterdam
Toneelgroep Amsterdam
University of Amsterdam

- *Communications Office*
- *Special Collections, Map Room*

Van Gogh Museum
Villa ArenA
VU University Amsterdam
Waternet

E. Duivenvoorden
T. Dejonghe
S. van Hoof
P. Nijssen
A. P. Scholten
E. Slot
E. van Wageningen

MIX
Paper from responsible sources
FSC® C118189

Editing and cartographic design: Noordhoff Atlas Productions, Groningen
Translation: *HHCE*, Nijmegen
Cover design: *Bloemvis*, Groningen

Cover photo: Centrum, © Cor Harteloh, *www.harteloh.nl*, The Hague
Front flyleaf photo: Centraal Station, © Karel Tomeï, *Flying Camera*, Eindhoven
Photo on pages 4-5: Schinkelsluis, © Peter Elenbaas, *Elenbaas Visuals*, Amsterdam
Back flyleaf photo: IJburg beach, © Karel Tomeï, *Flying Camera*, Eindhoven

© 2016 Noordhoff Uitgevers bv, Groningen

0 / 16
ISBN 978 9001 85423 2

Even though the compilers of this atlas have taken the greatest care to ensure its accuracy, its content is purely informative and not suitable for professional use. The publisher and compilers of this atlas assume no liability whatsoever for any errors and omissions, and any consequential losses.

All rights are reserved. No part of this publication may be reproduced, stored in a retrieval system, or transmitted, in any form or by any means, electronic, mechanical, photocopying, recording, or otherwise, without the prior written permission of the publisher.